Health Design in New Zealand

Health Design in New Zealand

Te Whaihanga o Ngā Whare Hauora o Aotearoa

Chris Thom

MASSEY UNIVERSITY PRESS

Foreword

Designing a hospital is one of the biggest challenges any designer will face. The blend of ever-changing briefs, evolving clinical services, high political and community expectations, deeply technical engineering requirements and constant time and cost pressures can make designing and delivering environments that support healing and enrich the human experience overwhelming.

Health design has increasingly become a highly specialised discipline, which seeks to integrate complex clinical functions and engineering and building design to create human-centred spaces. In hospitals, we are at our most vulnerable and our most joyful – they are literally places where life changes. In such existential extremes, the design of health environments takes a supporting role and often becomes invisible. Like roads and drains, we expect it to be present and to work – we only notice it when it fails.

The designers of essential social infrastructure like hospitals play a crucial nation-building role but are often anonymous, or not well known. In New Zealand, our focus continues to be on today's challenges – funding, designing and delivering health infrastructure – rather than dwelling on what has gone before. So now, for the first time, this book captures and celebrates the health design stories, settings and people unique to this place. It sheds light on some of our unsung champions, explains much of our built hospital environments, and records many of our untold tales. And it traces the threads of current health design trends, people and places back through time.

The history of health design in New Zealand echoes our short history as a nation. Through pre-European, colonial and post-colonial periods, New Zealand's built environment has been shaped by remoteness, a challenging geography and a low population density by international standards. These characteristics have fostered both 'cherry-picking' health design trends and themes from the rest of the world and rapidly prototyping and adapting home-grown solutions.

The development of international design guidelines and standards such as the Australasian Health Facility Guidelines (AHFG) replaced earlier, local iterations like the so-called 'Blue Book' (Accommodation in Hospitals, Code of Practice, Department of Health, Wellington 1991), allowing local health designers to benchmark work against international best practice. As technology advanced and the global exchange of knowledge and personnel accelerated through the twentieth century, so New Zealand hospital design evolved in parallel with design and construction trends in other sectors and other countries.

As designers' confidence and resources have grown, developing, trialling and refining local variants has become more common. Both Australian and New Zealand hospital projects now feature regularly in international conferences and awards. The story of health design in New Zealand continues to evolve from the rich and detailed narrative in this book.

++

New Zealand's small health design community makes a high level of collaboration between designers possible across regions and projects. The New Zealand Health Design Council (NZHDC), established in 2011, has supported an open environment in which the health design community regularly shares lessons, research, projects and successes. NZHDC has successfully built up a strong network of professionals working in health design, and continues to support skill and knowledge development and to champion higher quality in health design and delivery. International collaboration with health design organisations such as the Australian Health Design Council, the UIA (International Union of Architects) Public Health Group and others allows local designers to continue to connect with current trends, global research and best-practice delivery.

New Zealand's remoteness and small size is a challenge for health infrastructure. Recent reviews of our hospitals and health facilities have identified the same problem: buildings and infrastructure are ageing and deteriorating, and are not properly planned, sized nor located. Even more concerning, health services are constrained and are beginning to be compromised by our buildings as clinical staff are required to 'make do' in challenging environments.

Remedying New Zealand's major health infrastructure deficit will require at least four to five times the current rate of recent capital investment, and affordability issues become more acute every year. Health designers recognise the responsibility to creatively respond with new ideas, efficient design and project-delivery strategies and standardised design elements. Balancing creativity and constraint will continue to shape New Zealand's health design work for the foreseeable future.

Globally, indigenous voices are increasingly heard in the design and delivery of social infrastructure. In New Zealand, Te Tiriti o Waitangi, our founding document, calls for a partnership between Māori and the Crown. Hospitals and health services have recently been shaped more strongly by greater inclusion of indigenous knowledge and perspectives in briefing and design processes. Health designers are becoming increasingly familiar with working alongside tangata whenua and others to meaningfully weave cultural themes and concepts appropriate to local communities into the design of hospitals.

++

It is a truism to say that each of us either is, has been or will be a patient and so will experience a health environment at some time in our lives. Most health designers have some personal experience in a hospital, and this shapes perceptions and drives a personal commitment to improve the experience and environment for others.

New Zealand health designers, like others around the world, are increasingly understanding that providing a functional design solution is no longer sufficient to meet human needs. There is a growing awareness that design itself can be an agent of care, and that the built environment itself can enhance human experience and facilitate healing. In his recent book *Constructing Health*, the Canadian architect Tye Farrow draws connections between mind health and the built environment and advocates that designers need to be 'designing and constructing environments to actively cause health and enrich human experience'. Balancing all these influences will occupy health designers in New Zealand as we continue to shape our story and our environment.

Darryl Carey
Architect, health designer, founder NZHDC

Kia whakatōmuri te haere whakamua
I walk backwards into the future with my eyes fixed on my past

Introduction

Hospitals are among the largest public buildings in our communities and require a significant investment of society's resources in their creation and operation. Most people will use them at some point in their lives, often at a time of personal crisis. Yet healthcare facilities tend not to be well represented in architectural histories or awards. This is perhaps because their form follows their function far more than with most other building types, or because the time taken to complete them can result in them being outdated by the time they open. This book attempts to provide a greater recognition of the buildings erected to provide healthcare in Aotearoa New Zealand throughout its history.

It also looks at some of the designers who created these facilities, setting their work in health design in the context of their lives. Some are well known, and their other buildings well publicised; others have left little record. Sometimes, the designer is identified on the opening plaque or foundation stone. They may also appear in photographs, but the captions may identify only the individual, not the firm, and the connection is not necessarily obvious. Occasionally, references attribute different designers to the same building, perhaps due to an assumption based on style or because credit has been given to only one member of a team when the greater scale and complexity of buildings in recent years has made collaboration between firms increasingly common.

One term that recurs in histories of hospitals in New Zealand is 'Architect to the Board'. In some cases, hospital boards did employ their own architects, some of whom had a department of supporting staff. Over time, some practices, both private and public, developed a specialty in health design and were engaged by boards across the country. Often, however, the Architect to the Board was a local practitioner who had built up a detailed institutional knowledge and goodwill and was engaged on a project-by-project basis, sometimes over several decades.

The aim of this book throughout has been to set the commissioning, erection and eventual removal of these buildings, and the lives of their designers, in the wider historical context and in chronological order. The buildings covered in the main chapters are generally those associated with public hospitals, while specific health facility types such as mental health, elderly care, maternity and infant care, private hospitals and primary healthcare are covered in separate sections. Nurses' homes feature because although not healthcare facilities in themselves they were often some of the largest buildings on hospital campuses when staff were expected to live onsite. Several have been successfully repurposed for outpatient or administration uses.

Of all the areas of building design, that for healthcare possibly requires the greatest amount of collaboration between the architect, other members of the design team, clinicians, users and others. For reasons of space only, this history focuses mainly on the architects, with a separate section on the engineers and specialist consultants who have been increasingly relied on for specialist support as technology has advanced.

Surprisingly little has been written about the buildings of some larger existing facilities, while some smaller, often long-gone hospitals have been extensively documented. In fact, the imminent threat of closure has often generated the most interest among historians. Facilities throughout the country are included, with some greater emphasis on the larger tertiary hospitals and those that have been operating the longest.

Opening dates have been somewhat problematic to establish and records are sometimes contradictory. Sometimes the opportunity was taken for a visiting dignitary to open a barely completed shell, well before patients were admitted. In other cases, the building was operational for some time before it was officially opened. A particular difficulty arises where larger facilities were completed in stages over several years. Where possible, the dates stated are those inscribed on plaques, either still in existence or visible in photographs.

The book is broken up into roughly quarter-century eras, based on what was happening in wider society at the time. Of course, not all the buildings and practices considered fall neatly into a particular period. Many practices operated in only one era, possibly two, but a small number of practices continued their existence across multiple periods. They are grouped in the era that seemed most appropriate, but where possible their work is also mentioned where it occurs elsewhere.

Within each era, hospitals are generally considered from the north of Aotearoa New Zealand to the south, with allowances made for the country's complex geography. This is relatively straightforward in the earlier eras, when settlement and development tended to move roughly in that direction anyway. In more recent times, specialist practices have carried out work throughout the country, so the grouping is more by practice and time.

As with any history, some sources for one hospital, building or designer contain conflicting narratives. In these cases, reliance has been placed on press articles of the time or records held at the relevant facility or at Archives New Zealand. While every attempt has been made to correct existing errors, it is inevitable that some will have carried through into this text. Readers interested in further exploration of places and people in this book are encouraged to use the references provided as a starting point for their own research, and to draw their own conclusions.

1

Hauora Māori

AFTER THEIR MIGRATION TO AOTEAROA from central Polynesia – a gradual process generally thought to have occurred between 1200 and 1300 CE – Māori modified building forms and techniques brought from their homelands to suit the different materials available for construction and the greater need for warmth in a cooler climate. They generally lived in whānau-based kāinga near food sources such as rivers, beaches and forests, though they would also occupy temporary camps as they moved between seasonal resources. More permanent villages included a variety of building types such as pātaka (food store), kāuta (kitchen) and sometimes a wharenui (meeting house).[1]

The most common type of building, providing shelter while sleeping, was the wharepuni, which tended to be rectangular, with low side walls, resulting in a small air space that was easier to heat, but in which people were unable to stand. It was constructed of a variety of materials such as timber, raupō, ponga and kiri, and generally had thatch-clad walls and roof, with rush linings. During the warmer months, it is thought that the whakamahau (porch), attached as an extension of the roof or as a lean-to, was the preferred location for sleeping. It was also used for work and social activities, as a place to receive visitors and to engage in activities that were tapu inside, such as eating. The whakamahau could also be used as a place for the sick to sleep, separating them from the rest of the occupants.[2]

The concept of tapu is complex, but eminent Māori psychiatrist Sir Mason Durie has noted that its conferment 'was essentially a safety measure designed to invoke a sense of caution and to warn of threatened danger'. It was believed that illness arose when people offended the gods or violated tapu. By contrast, ordinary or common things, or those free from the restrictions of tapu, were considered noa.[3] As in the rest of the world at that time, an understanding of the scientific principles of hygiene and infection was limited, but religious practices and restrictions had some empirical basis. For example, tapu played an important role in guiding practices for sanitation and water supply, and in Māori villages the turuma (toilet) was generally well separated from living areas.[4]

Tapu also affected childbirth, and whare kōhanga were built for use by women and attendants before and after labour and delivery.[5] Separate temporary shelters were generally built outside the village for other conditions considered tapu, such as whare rāhui for the sick, thus helping to prevent the spread of disease, and whare mate for the dying and their immediate families. In contrast to hospitals in other parts of the world, which remained in use despite many patients dying in them, to Māori death was highly tapu and could render a dwelling house uninhabitable.[6]

Māori led active lives, usually had a diverse diet and were generally healthy. Their geographical isolation also protected them from many of the infectious diseases common in other parts of the world. They were, however, 'probably affected by pneumonia, tetanus, gastroenteritis, arthritis, rheumatism and various skin diseases', and it is now known that the root of the bracken fern, eaten by a number of iwi, can lead to cancer. 'The fibrous Māori diet meant people tended to wear their teeth out, which over time led to malnutrition, disease and death.'[7]

Tohunga were central to the healing process, focusing on body, mind and spirit. As well as protecting the tribal memory and possessing knowledge and expertise in many fields, they were able to confer and remove the restrictions of tapu. Their diagnostic practice concentrated on uncovering any breaches of tapu and on restoring balances between tapu and noa. They were the professional experts in various fields, and through extensive training developed a deep understanding of physiological principles and the healing properties of plants. Because tohunga themselves could be tapu, at times they could not touch other people or food.[8]

2

The first hospitals

1830–1851

Māori treated illness with karakia (prayers), ritenga (rituals), rongoā rākau (medicinal plants) and wai tapu (immersion in sacred water), with an emphasis on finding the cause of the illness, and hence eliminating the spirit or dealing with the transgression causing it. As Durie has pointed out, like Western medicine at the time, Māori rongoā was limited in dealing with acute conditions. Some ailments were regarded as mate atua, supernatural afflictions, but more pragmatic treatments were adopted for those known to be mate tangata, human illnesses. For example, cuts were sewn up with muka (flax fibre), splints were used to bind broken bones and boils were incised and drained.[9]

Durie has used the analogy of a house to describe the holistic approach of Māori to health, likening its four key components to the four walls or sides. These consist of taha tinana (physical health), taha wairua (spiritual health), taha whānau (family health) and taha hinengaro (mental health). Should one or more of these supports be missing or damaged, then, just as with a building, a person or group may become unbalanced, unwell and potentially die.[10]

++

In comparison with European medical practice of the late eighteenth and early nineteenth centuries, Māori traditional healing relied less on surgery, used herbal rather than chemically manufactured medicines, and adopted a communal and holistic rather than an individual and specific diagnostic approach. Neither culture, however, understood the biological causation of disease. In pre-European times, the average life expectancy of Māori was approximately 30 years. Although this may seem low, it should be noted that in the early nineteenth century the life expectancy in Britain was only marginally higher, at around 35 years.[11]

At the time of James Cook's landing in 1769, the Māori population of Aotearoa is estimated to have been around 100,000. By 1840 it had declined by 10–30 per cent, mainly due to introduced diseases such as measles and influenza 'and the effects, direct and indirect, of the [1830s] musket wars, including dislocation from lands that were important for agriculture and provided access to mahinga kai'.[12] Their geographical isolation meant that Māori had little or no immunity to illnesses that were not fatal in Europe. Sexually transmitted diseases spread wherever there was contact between coastal Māori and foreign seafarers, and acute intestinal infections such as dysentery and typhoid were also probably present before 1840.[13]

Because most Māori lived some distance from the ports and the new European settlements and were dispersed, they avoided the complete devastation that affected indigenous people elsewhere. Also, as demographer Ian Pool has noted, because New Zealand was so far away, the most virulent diseases had often killed the vulnerable on ships en route to New Zealand, leaving the survivors immunised and not infectious before they arrived.[14]

↑

A sketch of a wharepuni by W. A. Taylor.

↩ ↗

The residence of a New Zealand chief, by Augustus Earle, who spent eight months in Northland in 1827, is a detailed depiction of a wharepuni.

THE MISSIONARIES WHO CAME TO AOTEAROA seeking to convert Māori to Christianity established the first schools, and subsequently the first hospitals. In 1814 the Reverend Samuel Marsden founded the first Church Missionary Society station at Rangihoua in the Bay of Islands. After the second mission station was established in 1819 at Kerikeri, site of Kemp House and the Stone Store, and now one of the country's most revered historic places, Henry Williams set up a third at Paihia in 1823. He was joined by his brother William, who had trained as a surgeon in Britain, and when they established the first inland mission station, 20 kilometres away at Te Waimate in 1834, they incorporated a rudimentary hospital building.[1]

Hospitals were an integral part of other mission stations such as at Kaitāia, where the Reverend Joseph Matthews opened one in 1837 after completing three months of basic medical training in Auckland that year. When the Reverend Richard Taylor moved from Te Waimate in 1844 to establish a station at Pūtiki, on the banks of the Whanganui River opposite the new settlement of Petre (later Whanganui), he, too, set up a hospital.[2]

In the South Island, after 57 French settlers arrived in Akaroa on the *Comte de Paris* in 1840, the crew of the accompanying naval corvette *L'Aube* erected in Rue Lavaud 'a small hospital, big enough to house a doctor and his medicines and at least eight patients. . . . The hospital was in the same building as the store, and together they formed a substantial one-and-a-half-storey weatherboard building.' This was for years the town's only public building, before falling into disrepair in the 1850s. Until 1846 French naval doctors worked at the hospital and provided free visits, hospital treatment and prescriptions for everyone on Banks Peninsula.[3]

The New Zealand Company, established by Edward Gibbon Wakefield to promote British settlement, sent its first emigrants to Aotearoa in 1840: they landed at the future Wellington in January. Further north, the company also, that year, began to settle Petre.

When New Zealand Company subsidiary the Plymouth Company established New Plymouth in Taranaki the following year, it sent with the first settlers on the *William Bryan* a prefabricated hospital building that was erected at the base of the Kawau pā, on the north side of what is now Huatoki Lane between Currie Street and James Lane.[4] Although this has been referred to as the town's first hospital, it was barely large enough to house a dispensary and soon proved inadequate. It was relocated to the corner of Devon and Brougham streets, now the site of the Kings Building, where it remained until around 1880.[5]

As the company's first South Island settlement began at Nelson in 1842, a small facility was built in Trafalgar Street, again mainly for use as a dispensary. Later in the decade this was moved to a lean-to attached to the immigration barracks on Church Hill.[6] Such barracks were erected in new settlements throughout the country to provide temporary accommodation for migrants once they had disembarked and before they found work. Though basic and sometimes barn-like, they were a step up from tents or huts. Once they were not required to house migrants, their large open dormitory spaces were often repurposed for hospital use.[7]

++

After the signing of the Treaty of Waitangi/Te Tiriti ō Waitangi in 1840, Lieutenant Governor William Hobson established his first capital on a property purchased at Okiato in the Bay of Islands, near the township at Kororāreka, renamed Russell. Surveyor-General Felton Mathew intended to adapt the several existing Okiato buildings for a variety of uses, including a hospital.[8] There is, however, no mention of this being built before Ngāti Whātua offered 1400 hectares of land on the shores of the Waitematā Harbour, which became the site of the new capital of Auckland in 1841. The first hospital there was a small military facility, set up that year

↗

The Church Missionary Society mission station at Te Waimate, 1836.

→

Te Waimate Mission, c.1850. The hospital is at far right.

↩

New Plymouth Colonial Hospital.

The Waimate New Zealand
The Bishops House
Carpenters Shop
Native Teachers School
Hospital

↖

Early New Plymouth, with the prefabricated dispensary often referred to as the town's first hospital on the left.

↖

St John's College Hospital in Auckland, c.1902.

in the barracks built on the ridge overlooking the new settlement, now the site of parts of the University of Auckland and Albert Park.[9]

At Taurarua (Judges Bay) Mary Martin, wife of first Chief Justice William Martin, and Elizabeth Smith, who appears to have done much of the nursing, set up a hospital and dispensary service for Māori patients in 1842. 'The hospital first consisted of two or three rough huts and a tent made from blankets. Eventually a three-roomed raupō hut was built,

financed by friends in England.' As her biographer has noted, 'Although Mary Martin had brought a good stock of quinine and other medicines from England, the remedies were usually simple – good food, rest, herbal poultices, fresh air and prayers.'[10]

Some of the first fighting in what are now known as the New Zealand Wars was between Ngāpuhi and government soldiers at Kororāreka in the Bay of Islands in 1845. 'The major causes were the concern of some Ngāpuhi that the moving of the capital from the Bay to Auckland had hurt them economically, and that the Crown was exceeding its authority in the area.'[11] As large numbers of imperial troops arrived to protect the capital, it is thought that the single-storey stone hospital building at the barracks expanded to 50 beds in six wards, which would have made it large for its time, certainly for the new colony.[12]

↑

A panorama of St John's College in Auckland painted by Caroline Harriet Abraham, c.1844–62. The hospital is the third building from left, with a brown roof.

↗

The Frederick Thatcher-designed Auckland Colonial Hospital, c.1850s.

++

After petitioning by Māori leaders, Sir George Grey, New Zealand's third governor from 1845 to 1853, proposed in his first year in office to construct hospitals that would enable Māori to have access to European medical treatment. In 1846 he allocated funding for four facilities, later known as the 'colonial' or 'native' hospitals. As part of his policy for integrating Māori and Pākehā, Grey wished to provide hospitals that would be available to both, with their services

free for Māori. The hospital in Wellington provided treatment to Pākehā at 1 shilling per day plus rations, and the others seem to have had similar arrangements. The patients at the first Napier hospital paid 7 shillings a day two decades later.[13]

Grey commissioned architect Frederick Thatcher to design the hospitals in Auckland and New Plymouth. Two years after arriving in New Zealand in 1842, the country's first Anglican bishop, George Augustus Selwyn, had established St John's Theological College at Te Waimate. Later that year he relocated it to land purchased by the Anglican church in east Auckland, where the original buildings have been variously attributed to William Mason, considered to be the first architect to work in New Zealand, and Sampson Kempthorne. Because Mason was in increasing demand elsewhere, and Selwyn was becoming dissatisfied with Kempthorne's work, he asked Thatcher, who had emigrated to New Zealand in 1843, to complete the bishop's house and the kitchen and dining hall.[14]

In 1846 Selwyn commissioned Thatcher to design Auckland's first purpose-built civilian hospital at the college. This had seven rooms, including separate male and female wards and a doctor's quarters, with a spacious loft. Its occupancy fluctuated: it was overloaded during outbreaks of disease, but at other times its beds were not required and instead it housed the college's Māori Adult School and the weaving department. It was demolished in 1922 to make way for the red-brick Selwyn Block, itself removed in the late 1980s. In 1847 Thatcher also designed the chapel at the college, which still stands and is now a Category 1 Historic Place.[15]

↖

The Frederick Thatcher-designed New Plymouth Colonial Hospital.

↑

Frederick Thatcher.

Thatcher, who had been appointed superintendent of public works in 1845, designed Auckland's 1847 colonial hospital, on land allocated for the purpose on the western side of the Auckland Domain and occupied by Auckland Hospital to this day. Not the central-city location it is now, the selection of this site followed the principle of keeping hospitals away from populated areas to limit the transmission of disease. The building itself stood close to the main entrance of the current hospital. It was H-shaped in plan, like the one at St John's, but substantially larger, with four wards, each holding eight to 10 patients, two five-bed wards, a surgery, a kitchen and three small staffrooms. The steeply pitched roof created a loft for staff accommodation and there was a detached dead house, or morgue.[16]

In 1846 Grey split the duties of superintendent of works between engineer Charles Whybrow Ligar in the north, and Thomas Henry Fitzgerald, designer of the Wellington colonial hospital, in the south.[17] This allowed Thatcher to focus on the design of the hospitals in Auckland and later New Plymouth. Tenders for the Auckland building closed on 4 January 1847, and because Thatcher was often out of Auckland, having been appointed the governor's assistant private secretary in 1846, architect Reader Gillson Wood supervised the building's construction. It was completed on 11 September 1847 and, although it was not officially opened until November, the wards were used from August because of a typhus outbreak in the town.[18]

++

The 1848 colonial hospital that Thatcher designed for New Plymouth stood on an elevated 2-hectare property between Mangorei Road and the Henui River, now part of the site of New Plymouth Girls' High School.[19] Surveyor Frederic Alonzo Carrington's town plan had allocated a hospital reserve in the south-western section of the town, but the topography there seems to have proved less amenable to the imposition of his grid.[20] Built of heart rimu on a brick foundation, the building took some time to complete due to a shortage of workers, and bricks and mortar had to be brought from Nelson.[21] Rather than the H-shaped plan of Thatcher's two earlier hospitals, the New Plymouth design was a cross form, with offset wings and a polygonal dispensary nestled into one of the junctions. It has been suggested that this was based on his 1841 design for the parsonage of St Clement's in Hastings, Sussex, one of only two buildings in England that have been attributed to Thatcher. It is unclear, however, why he would have used a familiar design for his last hospital, rather than his first.[22]

Arthur Guyon Purchas, a qualified surgeon and physician who had trained at Guy's Hospital in London and emigrated to New Zealand in 1846, was given charge of the new hospital at St John's College. This would probably have been too late for him to have influenced the design of Auckland's colonial hospital but would have provided ample opportunity to discuss the New Plymouth design. Both Thatcher and Purchas were ordained as priests in 1853, and both designed churches around the North Island; for some time, some of Purchas's work was misattributed to Thatcher.[23]

Like Selwyn, Thatcher was a follower of the Camden Society, founded in Cambridge in 1839, and its 1846 successor, the Ecclesiological Society, both of which aimed to return churches to the supposed religious splendour and piety of the Middle Ages. The architectural manifestation of this was the growth of the Gothic Revival style in the Victorian era. This was to prove challenging in New Zealand, where early stone buildings, such as Kempthorne's St Thomas' in Kohimarama and the first St Stephen's Chapel in Parnell, built in 1847 and 1848, soon proved structurally unsound and were demolished. In the early colony good-quality stone, and qualified stonemasons who understood how to use the local materials, were difficult and expensive to obtain. By 1846 masonry construction had been abandoned at St John's College, and Thatcher instead used timber on a stone foundation for the hospital there, with walls clad in vertical planks on exposed structural timber framing.[24]

He also considered stone for the Auckland Hospital building, but again this was ruled out because of cost. Instead it had a whitewashed rough scoria base and external walls of battened 30-centimetre vertical 'ploughed and tongued' (tongue-and-groove) kauri planks fixed to a frame of exposed timber plates and braces, with leadlight windows. The shingled roof sloped down to cover a verandah supported on four sets of double posts. Aiming for an honest expression of the nature of materials, Thatcher specified that the exterior timber be rendered in linseed oil, rather than painted. Apart from a brick foundation, the hospital building at New Plymouth had a similar timber Gothic construction to the two in Auckland, including the projection of the upper rooms out over the ground floor.[25]

Thatcher managed to adapt the Gothic Revival style to timber construction with remarkable success in his 'Selwyn' churches such as All Saints in Howick, St Stephen's Chapel in Parnell and his acknowledged masterpiece, Old St Paul's in Wellington. He applied the same design principles to all three of his hospital buildings, including their distinctive 60-degree pitch roofs influenced by the Ecclesiologists' association of the equilateral triangle with the Trinity. Thatcher's hospitals and churches were a unique architectural response to New Zealand conditions.[26]

New Plymouth's second medical superintendent, Dr Peter Wilson, described the hospital as 'one of the most prominently picturesque ornaments of the settlement', but it was also criticised for being 'cold and cheerless inside in winter, even with a fire', poorly ventilated and lacking ceilings. The single layer of timber boards, providing both external cladding and internal lining, may have been economical, and adequate for intermittently used buildings such as churches, but it provided little insulation. Additional layers of boards were later applied to some of Thatcher's buildings to cover the exposed bracing, which explains their changing appearance in photographs. Others complained about the lack of treatment facilities. There were no bath houses for hot, cold or vapour baths, which some practitioners considered important for treatment, promoting cleanliness and removing disease. The water closets, of necessity external, were too far away from the buildings for some.[27]

Auckland's colonial hospital was well used by Māori, who came from as far afield as the Bay of Islands and Taupō, but after Te Āti Awa leader Rāwiri Waiaua died in the New Plymouth hospital in 1854 and a tapu was placed on it, inpatients' use decreased significantly.[28] In fact, Māori preferred to be treated as outpatients at all the colonial hospitals, returning to their own homes or staying with friendly locals while recovering. The New Plymouth hospital was also too distant from the settlement for most Pākehā, resulting in a later push for a more centrally located facility.[29]

++

Wellington's colonial hospital was the outcome of a collaboration between two Irish brothers from Carrickmacross, County Monaghan, architect Thomas Henry Fitzgerald and Dr John Patrick Fitzgerald, who arrived at Port Nicholson with the earliest New Zealand Company settlers on the *Oriental* in 1840 and was appointed colonial surgeon by Hobson.[30] Following the relocation of the settlement to Wellington, John Fitzgerald operated from a raupō hut, until the New Zealand Company established a small dispensary, known as the Medical Hall, just to the

↑
Thomas Henry Fitzgerald.
John Patrick Fitzgerald.

↗
The first Wellington Hospital in Thorndon, c.1840s.

north of Barrett's Hotel on Thorndon Quay. When Wellington's first colonial hospital, designed by Thomas Fitzgerald, opened on 15 September 1847, John Fitzgerald was its first medical superintendent, a role he held until 1854. A proponent of good ventilation and bathing, he insisted on a more functional approach to its design.[31]

The 10-bed hospital was built opposite the Pipitea pā, at the corner of Murphy, Pipitea and Moturoa streets in Thorndon, on land gifted for the purpose by local iwi Te Āti Awa, and now occupied by Wellington Girls' College. It was a two-storey brick-and-plaster structure with a gabled roof, and the front elevation had a central bay window with symmetrically arranged sash windows for ventilation. On the ground floor was a large surgery, where Dr Fitzgerald performed the country's first operation under general anaesthetic when he removed a large tumour from the back of a rangatira.

Opposite this was another room used as a two-bed ward for patients in a critical condition or with an infectious disease, and offices. The first floor held a large ward that ran the length of the building and could house eight to 10 patients. If well enough, each patient, when admitted, was taken to the bathrooms, which had steam baths and showers.[32]

At 1.40 a.m. on 16 October 1848 Wellington experienced a severe earthquake. Four people died, and the hospital was among the many buildings to suffer significant damage.

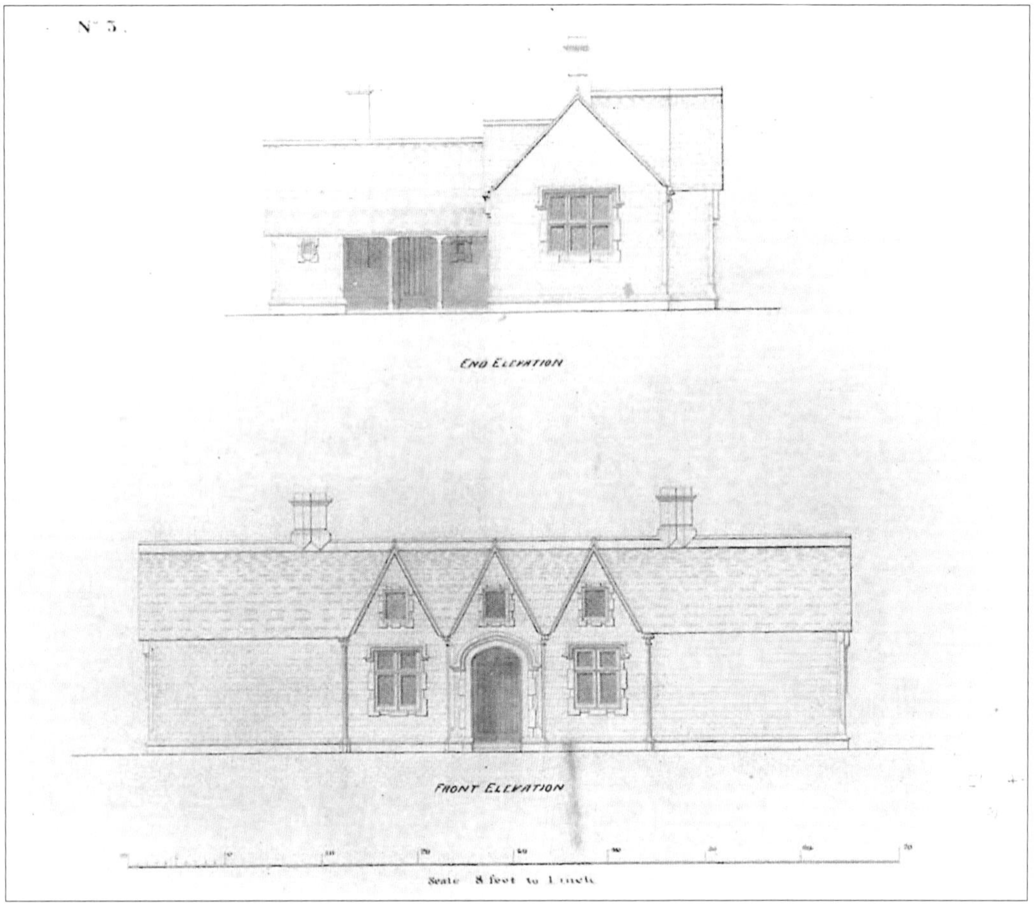

↑

Elevations for Wanganui Hospital, c.1849–50.

←

Wanganui Hospital.

Patients were evacuated to the former home of New Zealand Company agent Colonel William Wakefield, which served as the town's first Government House and stood where the Beehive is today. Later a hotel that had just been finished became a temporary hospital.[33]

++

By 1846 the fighting in the New Zealand Wars had reached Whanganui and imperial troops were based at the town's Rutland Stockade, where a military hospital was built the following year; it was replaced by a larger one in nearby Ridgway Street in 1849. Whanganui's colonial hospital opened in 1851, on a site of 0.4 hectares at St George's Gate – in Church Place, running down to the riverfront, now Somme Parade – which had been selected by the Reverend Richard Taylor.

Also designed by Thomas Fitzgerald, it was constructed by Thomas Higgie under the supervision of the Royal Engineers. After the experience of the 1848 Wellington earthquake, the building's construction was changed from brick to timber, with a shingle roof. Although the hospital had three steeply pitched gables, the detailing deviated from the honest expression of materials adopted by Thatcher, incorporating elements such as rusticated window and door surrounds to imitate brickwork.[34]

As at Wellington, the original 12-bed building had a steam bathroom. It was extended in 1876 and by 1883 had two 12-patient wards, plus a room for two to three beds. The wards were 5.2 metres wide, and the width of each bed space was just 1.5 metres. A government inspector's report in 1883 criticised the poor lavatory facilities – there was only one outdoor privy – the lack of heating and the dumping of waste in a pit beside the building. It remained the town's hospital until a new facility was built on the current site in Gonville, then was deliberately destroyed by fire in 1897.[35]

++

Grey's plans for 'native' hospitals did not extend to the South Island, where the Māori population was smaller and more widely dispersed. Its early settlements had to rely on their own resources for the development of the first rudimentary facilities.

Dunedin was founded in 1848 by settlers associated with the Free Church of Scotland. Not long afterwards, a group of prominent citizens held a competition for the design of a hospital, which was won by local builders Henry Clark and Alexander Garvie. This opened in 1851 on the 1.6-hectare site at the Octagon now occupied by the municipal chambers and the town hall. Timber-framed, with brick nogging and weatherboard cladding and a steeply pitched gable over the entrance, it had a plan similar to those of Thatcher and Fitzgerald, though its external form was more utilitarian, with decoration provided by finials and shaped bargeboards. In its first years it was underutilised and for a time it doubled as the town's asylum. A collection of stone and timber buildings grew around it and increasing demand meant that the former immigration barracks in Princes Street were also used as temporary hospital accommodation.[36]

In December 1850 the first four ships of the Canterbury Association reached Lyttelton, bringing the 'pilgrims' who would populate a settlement founded on Church of England principles. Because the Port Hills were a significant barrier between the port and the new town of Christchurch, initially most development was centred in Lyttelton. In 1851 John Robert Godley, resident chief agent for the association, called for a hospital similar to those in the other settlements, and a member of Thomas Fitzgerald's southern district staff, John Henry Cridland,

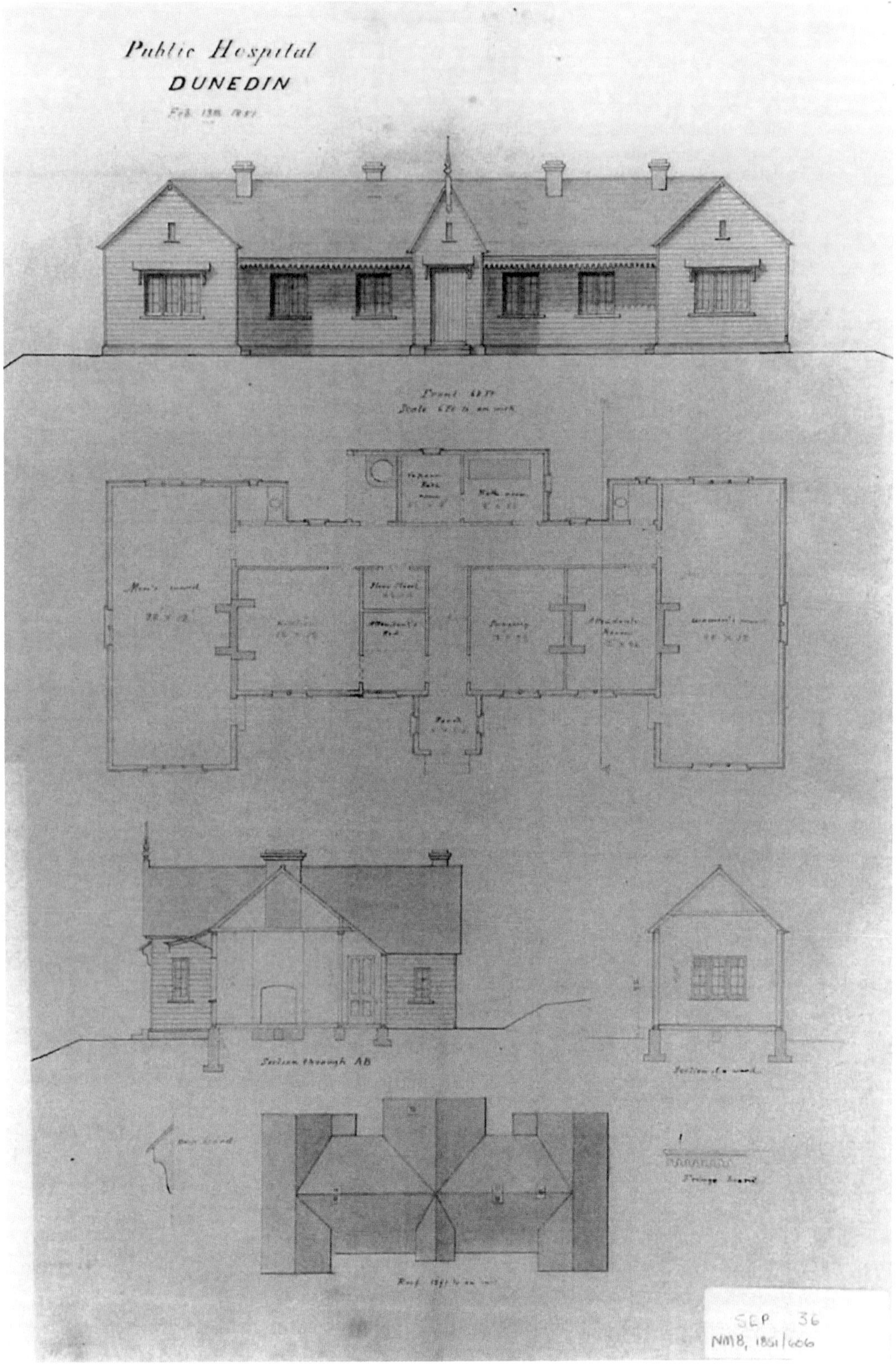

↖

Plans for the Dunedin Hospital in the Octagon, 1851.

↗

John Henry Cridland's plans for a hospital in Lyttelton, 1851.

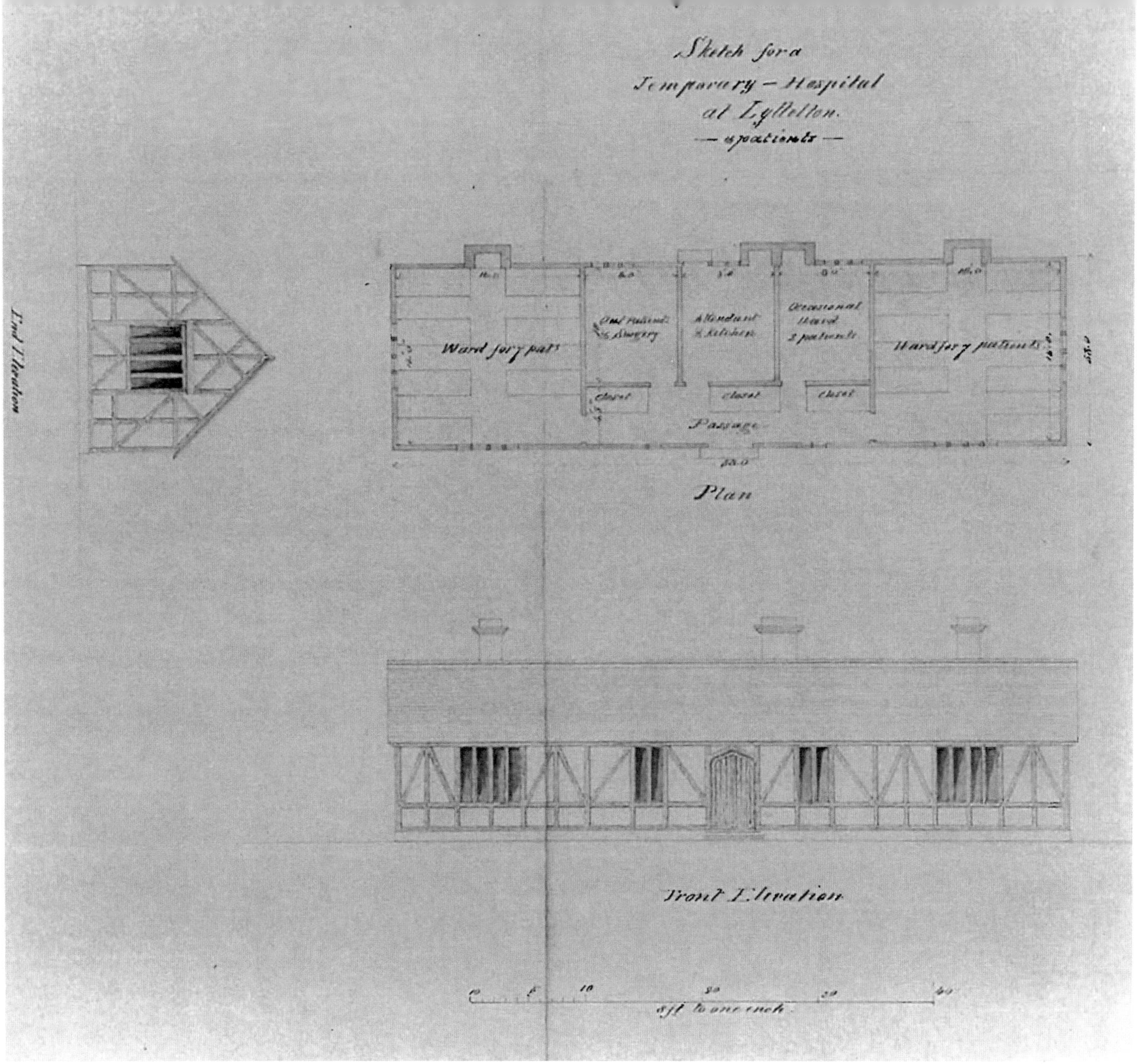

drew up a design. This building would have accommodated 16 patients in two seven-bed wards, plus two patients in a smaller one. Cridland proposed a half-timber construction filled in with moulded cob that would then be plastered and the joints covered by timber fillets.[37]

Despite Cridland's assurance that this was the cheapest form of construction then available in Canterbury, his hospital was not built.[38] Instead, Lyttelton's first hospital was opened in the rented house of the Reverend Octavius Mathias in 1851, containing six beds and furnished with equipment brought out on the *Charlotte Jane*, the first of the Canterbury Association ships to arrive. In 1854 the hospital was moved into a converted customs house building in the port. A similar situation occurred in Nelson, where the hospital was relocated to former New Zealand Company agent Francis Dillon Bell's two-storey house on the corner of Rutherford and Examiner streets in 1852.[39]

3

Colonisation and conflict 1852–1870

AS FIGHTING CONTINUED IN THE NORTH ISLAND, a lack of conflict and the discovery of gold in Otago in 1861 and on the West Coast in 1864 meant that the South Island grew more rapidly in this period. Wellington received a boost when the capital was transferred there in 1865. In 1852 New Zealand had been divided into six provinces, each with its own government; there was also, from 1854, a central representative government, the General Assembly, in Auckland. Although this arrangement recognised that some decentralisation of administration made sense in a country with a widely scattered population and limited infrastructure, the smaller provincial governments were often financially constrained, and there was ongoing tension between them and the General Assembly. The provinces were abolished in 1876.[1]

Through most of the nineteenth century, hospitals in New Zealand were charitable institutions intended for the indigent, those unable to pay and those without family support. Early European settlers were typically young and fit, and, if not affluent, aspired to be. Hospitals were considered to offer little in the way of effective treatment, were often too far away from those living in rural areas and were regarded as a place of last resort by the self-respecting. Most preferred to be cared for at home, where there was less risk of infection.[2] The 1846 Ordinance for the Support of Destitute Families and Illegitimate Children reinforced this focus: the first responsibility lay with the family.[3]

Finances for public institutions could be severely constrained. In his history of Christchurch Hospital, F. O. Bennett notes that in 1864 the governors issued a decree denying admission to those with a wide range of conditions: 'no woman in an advanced state of pregnancy, or child under six years (except in cases of sudden accident), no person disordered in their senses or subject to epileptic fits . . . or those apprehended to be in a dying condition'.[4]

Because many parts of New Zealand were sparsely populated, and geography hindered movement and communication, hospital services were generally the result of the efforts of isolated groups acting on their own initiative, sometimes more as a demonstration of a district's progress and status than from need. The colonial government had taken responsibility for public health services from 1840 to 1854, but then devolved much of this to the provinces until their abolition, and although central government provided some financial support, hospitals were initially largely funded from local contributions. As a result, and as settler numbers increased from the 1860s, an increasing number of hospitals and hospital districts were managed by small local bodies and community groups. Some served very small populations, or large geographical areas, or both.[5]

In the Far North there was an attempt to set up a public hospital at Mangōnui in 1859, but this was short-lived due to the inability to retain suitably qualified staff.[6] For more than half a century after it was established, Auckland's was the only hospital of any significance serving Northland and much of the Waikato, as well as Auckland city itself. A second building at the hospital was erected further down the hill in 1851, to serve as what was then known as a lunatic asylum. It was repurposed as an obstetrics ward for destitute women when a new asylum opened in Avondale in 1867, and later became a home for the aged and infirm poor.[7]

Thatcher's original 1847 building was extended in 1860 with a plainer weatherboard wing that housed a new ward and a day room; further additions in 1865 added male and female wards, a larger kitchen and a new dead house. This much-modified building was eventually burned down deliberately in 1890 to make way for the Costley wards.[8] Between the original building and the asylum, several single-storey cottages were added for patients with infectious diseases, including a wooden building erected beside the original Thatcher building in just 14 days to deal with a typhoid epidemic in 1887.[9]

↑ Charles Heaphy's sketch of Auckland Hospital viewed from the Domain, 1855.

↩ Seaview Asylum, Hokitika, c.1904.

++

As fighting intensified and spread to New Plymouth by 1860, to Waikato after an 1863 invasion by government troops, and to the Bay of Plenty, British soldiers were stationed in these areas and the first hospitals were generally military facilities. Hamilton's, established around 1855, was relocated in 1864 to the site of today's central police station, then closed in 1867 as troops were withdrawn.[10] Tauranga's hospital opened in 1864 on the site of the old government building in Willow Street. The execution of the missionary Carl Völkner in Ōpōtiki in 1865 led to the establishment of a garrison there, and a small corrugated-iron hospital followed in 1868. In 1865 a military hospital was set up on the beach at Pātea, between New Plymouth and Whanganui, and a more permanent facility opened in 1869.[11]

By 1860 the military had taken over New Plymouth's colonial hospital as a defence outpost and the ousted medical services occupied a variety of sites for short periods. In 1864 what was then known as the Provincial Military Hospital moved into the Militia Office building, a relocated and extended farmhouse on the corner of Gill and Kawau streets. The hospital returned briefly to the old Thatcher building in Te Henui, which also served as an old men's home from 1890 to 1903.[12]

In Hawke's Bay, also a site of tension and fighting, the port of Napier had been established in 1855 at Ahuriri, on the north side of Mataruahou, or Scinde Island, now known as Napier Hill, which was then connected to the mainland by only a narrow strip of land. Its two highest points were later distinguished as Bluff Hill and Hospital Hill.[13]

In 1858 the 65th Regiment set up an army field hospital in the Barrack Reserve in the Onepoto Gully, on what was later the Hospital Hill side, and shortly afterwards a house in Emerson Street was rented for military and civilian patients. The 1855 plan for the town had designated a hospital reserve on an elevated site on the Bluff Hill side, and the new single-storey, weatherboard Hawke's Bay Provincial Hospital was built there on what is now the corner of Harvey and Sealy roads in 1860. Designed by Thomas Shepherd, this 12- by 9-metre single-storey weatherboard building had a male ward and a female ward, each with five beds,

↑

Napier Hospital on Sealy Road.

↖

The second Wellington Hospital on Pipitea Street in Thorndon, c.1866–83.

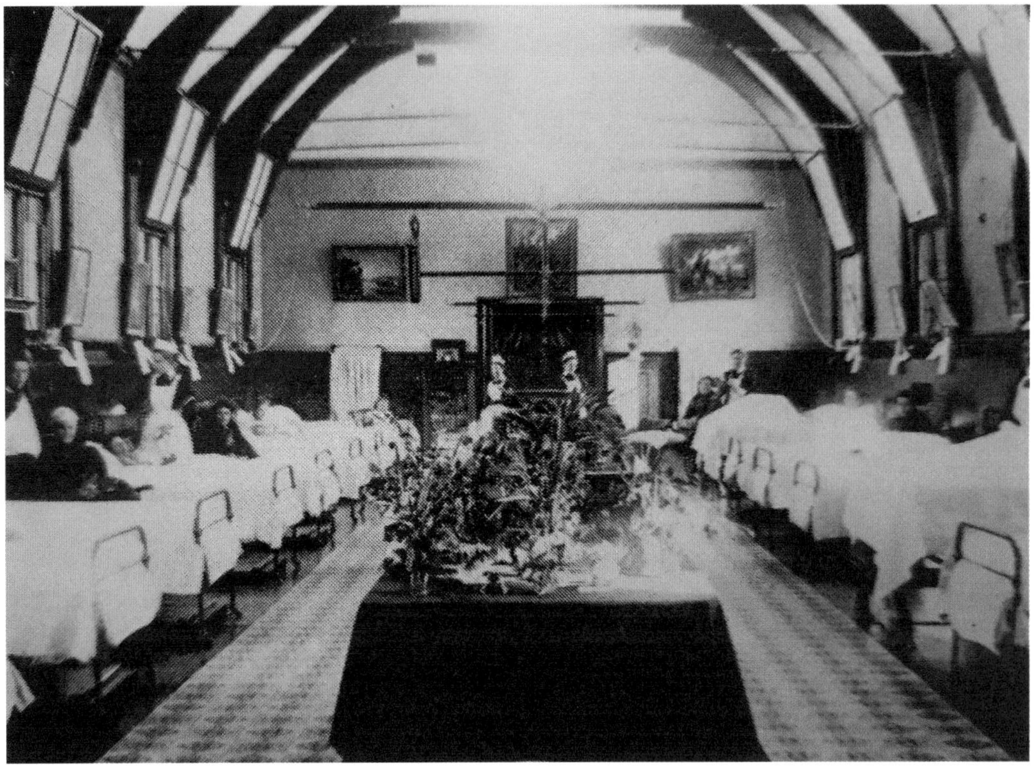

↗

Christchurch Hospital ward.

→

Christchurch Hospital, 1862.

a surgery, and a kitchen and sleeping apartment for the master and matron. There was also a detached washhouse and dead house.[14]

By the 1850s it was clear that Wellington needed a larger hospital. Thomas Fitzgerald is said to have been involved with designing the replacement for the earthquake-damaged original building, but he appears to have been superseded as its architect by Edward Roberts in 1851,[15] when plans for the building were drawn up. Built on the same site as its predecessor, the 40-bed single-storey Elizabethan domestic-style hospital opened in 1852. The central portion accommodated a female ward, plus surgery, dining room, ablutions and vapour bath rooms. There were four male wards in the two wings, with a kitchen and a morgue in separate buildings at the rear, connected by a covered walkway. Built of wood, as so many buildings in the town were after the 1848 earthquake, this building served Wellington for the next three decades.[16]

++

As Christchurch grew, it took some time to settle on a site for a hospital, let alone build one. The provincial government had allocated land on the corner of Durham and Armagh streets for this purpose, and set aside £1500 for construction, but in 1858 political expediency led to the Provincial Council Chambers being built there instead. Eventually, the current site in Riccarton Avenue was carved off the eastern edge of Hagley Park, despite vocal protests by some citizens.[17]

When Canterbury Provincial Council member John Ollivier introduced the Public Hospital Bill in October 1859, he noted that he was asking to use only what was an 'isolated and otherwise nearly useless corner' and pointed out that a hospital 'should be so placed as to have sufficient ground to allow of free air and some exercise within its precincts for convalescents'. He argued, too, that 'the only hospital in the settlement now was that wretched building so designated in Lyttelton, which he had felt to be a cause for shame to the Province'.[18]

For the design of the new building, the Christchurch Hospital governors engaged provincial government architects and Gothic Revival advocates, Birmingham-born Benjamin Woolfield Mountfort and his brother-in-law, Isaac Luck, and the hospital finally opened in

↑
Lyttelton Hospital, c.1853.

↗
The first Frankton Hospital, near Queenstown, c.1863.

1862. Constructed with timber weatherboards on a stone base, the two-storey building was Tudor in manner with projecting gables, an ornate porch and dormer windows. F. O. Bennett considered it 'an ugly building in a barren setting': Hagley Park, created in 1855, was then still quite a desolate place. The *Lyttelton Times* described it as 'a strange-looking building, with excrescences like feelers stretching towards the road'.[19] (Nothing of this original building has survived; the last component was removed in 1917.) In 1867 a wing with an operating theatre and consulting rooms on the lower floor and a male ward above was added to the eastern end. By the time a wing for 20 patients was built two years later, Christchurch Hospital had grown, by a series of small extensions, to house a total of 67 beds.[20]

When the hospital in Lyttelton was moved into the customs house building in 1854, those classed as lunatics were relocated into the older hospital, but because of the damage they caused they were moved to the Lyttelton Gaol, where they remained until Sunnyside Lunatic Asylum in Christchurch opened in 1864.[21] After land for a new hospital was purchased in Governors Bay, at the head of Lyttelton Harbour, Mountfort & Luck was commissioned to design a purpose-built facility that opened in 1863. By 1865, after being extended, it housed 24 male and two female patients. With Christchurch's public hospital completed, the Governors Bay facility was closed in 1869, apart from its casualty ward, and repurposed as the Canterbury Orphanage.[22]

From the 1860s settlers moved rapidly to develop the flat hinterland south of Christchurch, and the port of Timaru was established at the southern end of the Canterbury Bight. In 1862 a four-room cob house became the town's temporary public hospital until it was replaced by a six-bed wooden building two years later. But the swampy gully site at the corner

of North Street and West Belt (now Craigie Avenue) proved unsuitable for a hospital, and in 1868, on land that had been reserved for a park, the building of a new facility began where today's hospital stands, in the north-eastern corner of what is now the Botanic Gardens. The architect was William Williamson.[23]

++

Following the discovery of gold in Otago and later on the West Coast, new towns sprang up in both districts and a number of small hospitals were built to deal with mining accidents and illnesses spawned by the often harsh environments, poor sanitation and inadequate water supply. Fourteen hospitals, mostly very modest in size, were set up on the South Island fields during the gold rushes.[24] In the Wakatipu district, local businesses raised funds for a hospital, but because land in Queenstown was scarce the building was erected in nearby Frankton and opened in 1863. The hospital on this site has been variously known over the years as Frankton, Wakatipu, Queenstown or Lakes District.[25]

Dunstan District Hospital, a 50-bed wooden building in Clyde, also began taking patients in 1863. It had three wards, for males, females and Chinese – miners from China faced a good deal of prejudice and would have been kept separate from others. In 1878 it was threatened by floods and had to be moved to higher ground. The first hospital in the remote Māniatoto district to the east was a 12-bed single-storey building in Naseby dating from 1863.[26]

On the West Coast, where the gold rush led to a population boom, an emergency hospital constructed of timber slabs with a canvas roof opened in Hokitika's North Revell Street in 1865. The following year it was replaced by a new hospital designed by James Rochfort. Sitting beside the Māhinapua Creek, this could be accessed only by boat. Also in 1866, the Grey River Hospital in Greymouth opened on a site in Guinness Street, then known as Hospital Street, which would later be occupied by the town's post office. Conditions were so poor that patients often had to sleep on the floor.[27]

The new Buller District Hospital opened in Westport in 1868, replacing a temporary facility in a disused government store. A timber and iron building with four rooms and a long verandah, it faced the sea at the beach end of Cobden Street. The 40-bed Gladstone Memorial Ward for female patients was added around 1898. Ross's 20-bed Totara Hospital opened in 1868 and Charleston had a hospital from 1867 to 1910. Kumara's hospital, which opened some time before 1881, grew to have 15 beds plus a detached fever ward and an old men's home; a new wing was added in 1907.[28]

++

Thanks to the Otago gold rush, Dunedin developed rapidly, and from 1874 to 1882 overtook Auckland as the country's largest city. It was an expression of its confidence when a group of citizens decided to hold the nation's first exhibition in 1865. Although a much-reduced version of Britain's famous Great Exhibition of 1851, the event attracted displays from around the world and thousands of visitors. Because the grand Italianate building erected especially for the occasion – on the current Dunedin Hospital site between Great King and Cumberland streets – was intended to serve as a general market after the exhibition, architect William Mason designed it with narrow wings surrounding a large covered central court.

Then the largest masonry building in New Zealand – its overall dimensions were 43 metres by 33 metres – it had a primarily brick exterior with a stucco finish on a rusticated base. Each of the two frontages had a central tower rising to 37 metres. The one on Great King

↖

Grey River Hospital, c.1890s.

←

Dunstan Hospital at Clyde, 1907.

Street was a clock tower that defined the main entrance; smaller campanile-style towers in each corner provided for water storage. The 8-metre-wide gallery on the upper floor enclosed a large central space with a lantern-light roof.[29] Projects such as this propelled William Mason into greater prominence and surely vindicated his decision to move to Otago in 1852.[30]

A site on the Arthur Street Reserve had been allocated for a new hospital and local architect David Ross, who had left a brief partnership with Mason formed only the year before, won an 1863 design competition for the building.[31] When this did not proceed for financial reasons, the Otago Provincial Council proposed reusing the exhibition building after its closure. To achieve this, they commissioned the provincial engineer, Northumberland-born John Turnbull Thompson, who had designed Tan Tock Seng Hospital in Singapore in 1844, while he was superintendent of roads and public works there. When the new Dunedin Hospital opened in 1866, its eight wards provided accommodation for 104 male and 26 female patients.[32]

++

The first hospital in the Southland town of Invercargill, established as an offshoot of Dunedin in 1853, was a collection of small huts, constructed of ponga and sod, which opened on The

↑

The former South Seas International Exhibition building that was converted to house Dunedin Hospital, 1865.

↗

The porter's lodge at Dee Street Hospital, Invercargill, with the later central block behind.

Crescent in 1861. This soon proved inadequate, and in 1862 a hospital reserve was established in Dee Street, at the junction of the north and proposed west town belts. The first building, the two-storey brick north wing, opened in 1864, and had a 10-bed ward on each level, with males on the ground floor and females above. A cement render on the brickwork and the addition of a verandah later improved its original plain and sombre appearance. It was extended with a six-bed annex in 1874, and a porter's lodge, in a more picturesque style, was added at the hospital entrance in 1866. The designer of these buildings is unknown, but it may have been early Invercargill architect Angus Kerr.[33]

A lunatic asylum, constructed of iron, was also built on the site in 1866. Later a canvas ceiling was suspended 30 centimetres below the iron, with the air flow in between adjusted to control the temperature. The asylum was converted into a fever ward in 1876 to provide accommodation during disease outbreaks. This was pulled down in 1885 and replaced by a new fever hospital at the rear of the site, with two small wards constructed with cement floors and walls plastered with Keene's cement, a hard plaster mainly used for ornamental work.[34]

Victorian asylums

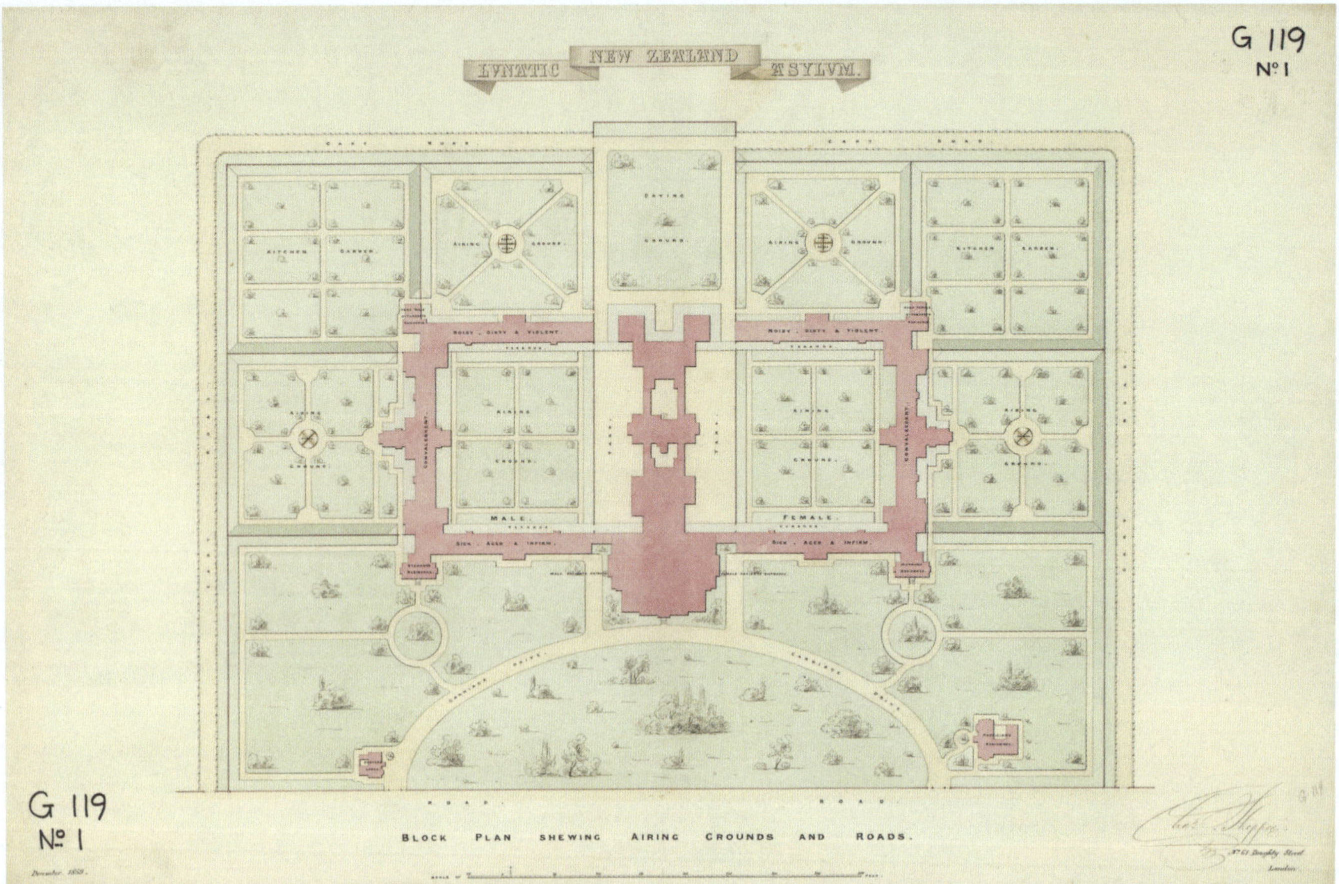

Most early European immigrants may have not needed or desired hospital care, but the rigours of settler life could take a heavy mental toll, often compounded by the effects of poor-quality liquor. Isolation and distance from family and friends led to depression and more serious psychiatric conditions, and suicides were not uncommon. Wealthier people with mental illness could be shielded within their own families, but those with limited means had little support.[1]

The country's first homes for lunatics were buildings attached to the Wellington and Auckland gaols in 1844. In Wellington the immigration barracks were relocated to that site. 'Inmates received no treatment but were confined and watched to stop them harming themselves or others.' In other towns the mentally ill were also sent to gaols. They proved difficult to manage 'but the only alternative was the overcrowded wards of public hospitals'.[2]

Mainly because of the attitudes of society and the medical profession, like most Western countries New Zealand developed parallel and largely independent services for the mentally and physically ill. Under the 1846 Lunatics Ordinance, once certified, a mentally ill person could be sent to a gaol, a public hospital or a specialist asylum, though the latter did not yet exist. Hospitals and prisons remained the only choice until the provinces began to provide purpose-built asylums in the 1850s.[3]

↑
Plans for the New Zealand Lunatic Asylum, 1859.

Modelled on those in Victorian Britain, New Zealand's asylums grew to become some of the largest buildings in the country, and certainly far bigger than any public hospital buildings of the time. Each province typically provided only one asylum to serve its entire population. Because New Zealand had the advantage of large areas of land, most of the asylums were set on extensive estates, allowing space for them to have their own farms and gardens. With most staff living onsite, they became virtually self-contained townships. They were, however, generally some distance from the main urban populations they served, separating them from the mainstream of social, professional and political life and reinforcing the stigmatisation of the inmates.[4]

In 1876 the Lunatic Asylums Department, which became the Mental Hospitals Department in 1906, took direct control of all the country's asylums. In this way, although most health services were provided at a district level through hospital boards, mental health services generally became the responsibility of central government, a situation that continued for the next century. Known from 1920 as the Mental Health Division (or for a time the Mental Hygiene Division) of the newly established Department of Health, it continued to administer all of the country's mental health facilities until late in the twentieth century.[5]

++

In 1858 the government considered building a national lunatic asylum in Nelson, which was chosen from a long list of possible sites. London architect Charles John Shoppee, who was commissioned to prepare designs, had been resident architect at the Middlesex County Lunatic Asylum at Colney Hatch, a paupers' asylum then considered the most modern facility of its type in Europe.

↑
Mount View Asylum in Wellington, 1906.

Colney Hatch was built for 1250 patients; the New Zealand facility was intended to accommodate only 112. Set within pleasant kitchen gardens, the building was to enclose 1.2 hectares of land, with central landscaped airing courts that had walking paths with summer houses at their junctions. There would be individual bedrooms rather than dormitories, in wings branching off a central administrative and service spine, males and females on opposite sides. It was to be built in timber for earthquake resistance – there had been a huge earthquake in the Wellington area in January 1855 – with English half-timbered and plastered walls and Staffordshire tile roofs. The project did not proceed, however, as the government decided instead to make the provinces responsible for the care of the mentally ill.[6]

++

Karori Lunatic Asylum, which operated from 1854 until 1873 on the site now occupied by Karori Normal School, was New Zealand's first true asylum on its own dedicated site. It is thought that the first building was a house already on the 2-hectare site, which accommodated 10 patients and an attendant. It was enlarged to also take patients from Nelson and Canterbury, but by the late 1860s it was overcrowded and its structure was decaying, so a replacement facility was planned.[7]

Mount View Asylum, opened in 1873, occupied a 20-hectare site in the town belt in Newtown and was designed by Christian Julius Toxward, who would later be responsible for Wellington's new public hospital, also in Newtown. The cottage-style building, based on the new Albert Hospital in Melbourne, had a two-storey central block with separate male and female wings and quarters for the aged and infirm, and could accommodate 100 patients. Its facilities included a large dining room, library and workshops. It closed in 1910 when the current Government House was built on the site.[8]

Porirua Lunatic Asylum was established in 1887, on what was then a 56-hectare rural site purchased in 1884. By 1925 this had increased to 460 hectares stretching from the Porirua Harbour to the top of Colonial Knob. The first building was a 24-bed wooden

↖

Porirua Lunatic Asylum, c.1891–1900.

↑

Christian Julius Toxward. Government Architect John Campbell.

↗

Plans for the Porirua Lunatic Asylum, 1891.

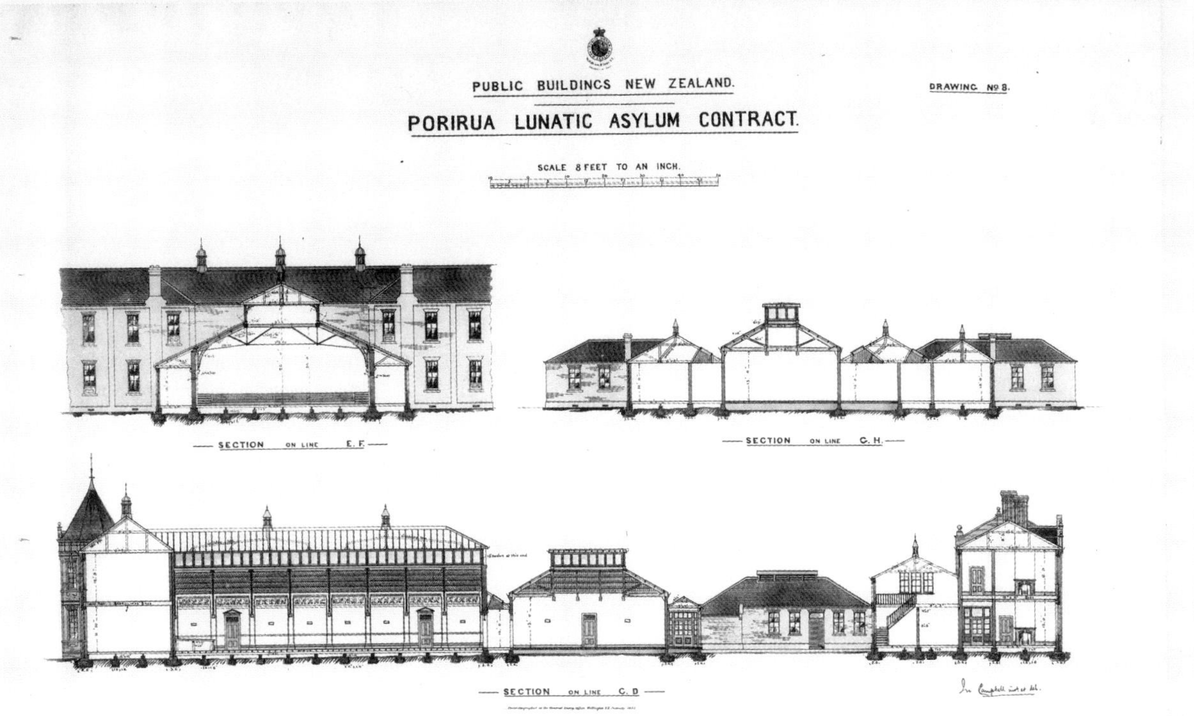
PUBLIC BUILDINGS NEW ZEALAND.
DRAWING No 8.
PORIRUA LUNATIC ASYLUM CONTRACT.
SCALE 8 FEET TO AN INCH.
SECTION ON LINE E.F.
SECTION ON LINE G.H.
SECTION ON LINE C.D.

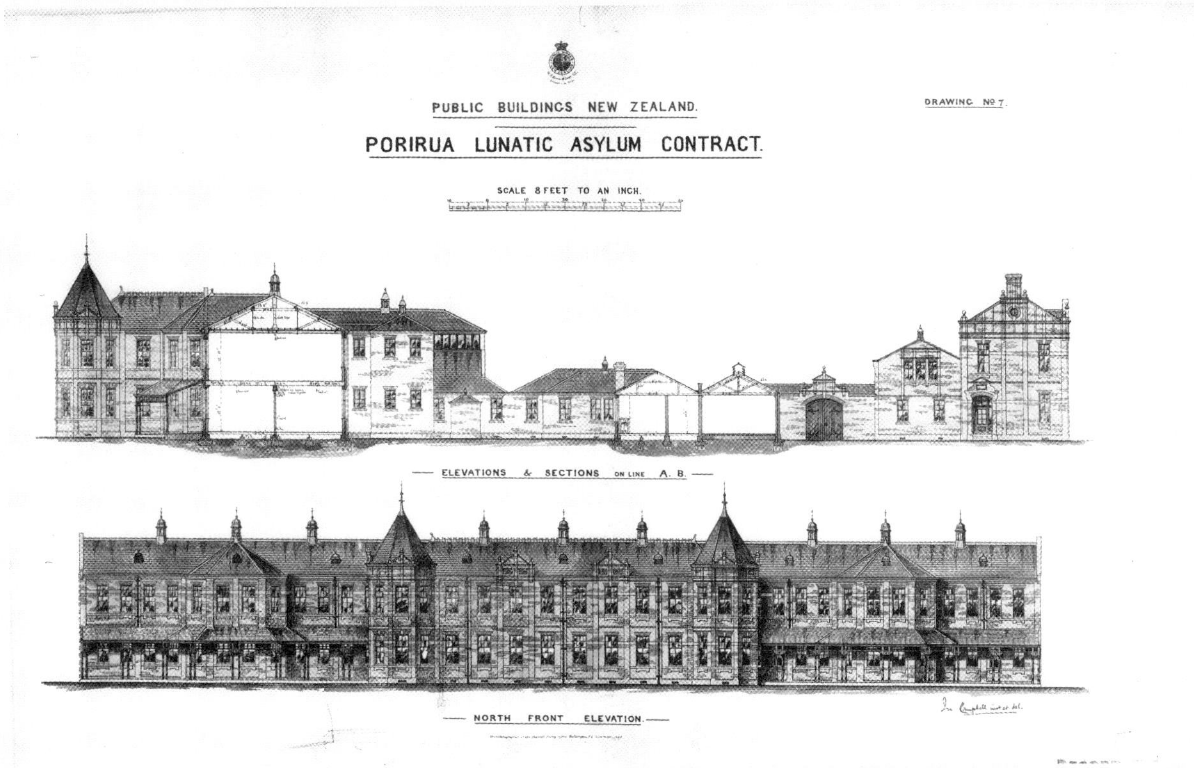
PUBLIC BUILDINGS NEW ZEALAND.
DRAWING No 7.
PORIRUA LUNATIC ASYLUM CONTRACT.
SCALE 8 FEET TO AN INCH.
ELEVATIONS & SECTIONS ON LINE A.B.
NORTH FRONT ELEVATION.

cottage, later known as H Ward, which was demolished in 1969. But this was soon too small and John Campbell, of the Public Buildings Department and later the country's first Government Architect, has been credited with designing the 500-patient main Porirua building, which opened in 1895.[9]

It grew in a piecemeal fashion. The first portion, completed in 1894, generally followed a cruciform plan, with a central spine of dining room, kitchen and stores, dormitories feeding off the northern end, and the administration building at the south.

Until the opening of a new two-storey, 100-room brick nurses' home in 1928, staff had to sleep in the main building.[10] The northern dormitories incorporated bay windows and verandahs, providing space in the open air for convalescence. A male wing of similar style was added in 1896, as was a clock tower with an ogee cap. The female wing was completed in 1899 and there were further additions to the male wing in 1900. These wings angled back towards the central spine, with day rooms forming the pivots.[11] In 1906 came a new initiative: reception houses established as self-contained communities to assess and provide early treatment of patients. The aim was to cure and discharge them without their having to be committed.

The main brick hospital building, which was by then housing 700 people, was badly damaged in the 7.2 magnitude Wairarapa earthquake of June 1942 and was demolished a year later. A single-storey timber extension built in 1910, known as F Ward, remained in use until 1977. Ten years later it was converted into the Porirua Hospital Museum, which is now a Category 1 Historic Place. Designed by the Public Works Department, and constructed of weatherboards with a corrugated-steel roof, its walls are insulated with pumice fill.[12]

++

↑

Auckland Lunatic Asylum, later Oakley Hospital, c.1890s.

↗

Auxiliary Asylum, Oakley Hospital, Auckland, 1898.

Auckland's first real asylum opened on the hospital site in Grafton in 1851, but by the 1860s had become overcrowded and the search began for a new site. In 1862 81 hectares were endowed for a lunatic asylum in Avondale, a then remote location considered ideal for isolating inmates from the general population. Opened in 1867 as the Auckland Lunatic Asylum at Whau, this facility has operated under several names: Avondale Hospital, Auckland Mental Hospital, Oakley Hospital and finally Carrington Psychiatric Hospital.[13]

Modifying the plans of a Mr Barrett in England, Auckland architect James Wrigley, known for the Northern Club in Princes Street, designed the initial stage, the central entrance wing and the east wing, one of two planned for patient accommodation. Mostly of yellow brick, bands of red brick carried across the façade and formed pointed arches over the semicircular-headed windows. The roof was clad in slate tiles.[14] The main entrance was finished with encaustic floor tiles and a grand staircase led to the first floor. The central wing behind housed administration on the ground floor, with a dining room and kitchen behind, and a chapel on the floor above. The east wing housed patient dormitories, bathrooms and day rooms, behind which sat a single-storey workshop building.

At this point work was halted due to cost, and in 1867 the first inmates moved in, with males housed on the ground floor and females above. Initially designed for 60 patients, by 1875 it held 105 males and 57 females and was grossly overcrowded. In 1877 a fire broke out in a wooden female annex: one patient died and most of the first floor of the east wing was destroyed.[15]

Auckland architect Philip Herapath was given the task of overseeing the rebuilding of the damaged area and creating a new west wing.[16] This housed the male patients in 1881, while the east wing was repaired and used for female accommodation. Herapath emulated many of Wrigley's original details. Innovations for the time included under-bed ventilation and roof ventilators.[17]

There were more additions in the 1880s: a new laundry and boiler house in 1881 and, in 1883, an auxiliary asylum for 60 male patients that included workshops for carpenters, tailors and shoemakers. A female dining room, visiting rooms, a reception hall and a superintendent's residence were added to the main buildings. Extensions to the female wing, kitchen and boiler house, as well as new farm buildings and a mortuary, were completed in 1886, and in the following year the women's wing was further extended and a new kitchen built. A new brick building for females opened in 1888. From 1886 the design was carried out by the Public Works Department.[18]

Architect Charles Edward Beatson was responsible for a substantial extension of the central block in 1890, with a new dining room and the spaces between the wings developed as 'airing' or exercise courts. A new kitchen and storeroom were also added. In 1891 there was an urgent extension of the male wards, with the upgrading of sanitation facilities, and further internal modifications took place in 1892. New swimming baths opened in 1893.[19] Additional single rooms were developed in the male wing in 1895, but severe overcrowding meant that the day rooms were converted into dormitories the following year. A further auxiliary asylum at Avondale opened in 1896. A symmetrical building with verandahs and a central bow window, it has been credited to Government Architect John Campbell.[20]

In 1900, a two-storey wing was added to the west of the men's wing and 20 extra beds went into the female wing in 1901. Auckland architect Robert Wladislas de Montalk was responsible for the work from 1895 to 1901.[21] By 1900 there were 494 patients – 306 male and 188 female – at the asylum. In 1903 there were further modifications to the central block, with new dormitories and dining rooms, and the kitchen was altered. Both the male and female wings were further extended from 1903 to 1905.[22]

Despite the various designers involved, the extensions generally respected the original architecture. There are subtle differences between the various architects' work, but a general coherency of style. The main building, consisting of approximately 9000 square metres of floor space, which still stands, is a mixture of Georgian, Italian Renaissance and Victorian styles.[23]

By 1950 the hospital housed 1200 patients, and the alterations during the following decade were not as sympathetic. Many of the original windows were replaced with glass louvres to allow for more fresh air, and the original ceilings were destroyed to allow for the installation of a sprinkler system. A new chapel was dedicated in 1962.[24] Renamed Oakley Hospital in 1960, it was transferred from the Crown to the Auckland Hospital Board in 1972, becoming Carrington Psychiatric Hospital. However, as most people with mental illness were by then being cared for in the community, it was decided that treatment at the facility should cease. An area of land in the north-western part of the property was set aside to house the Mason Clinic forensic mental health unit, which opened in 1992, the year that Carrington finally closed.[25]

++

Christchurch's Sunnyside Asylum opened with 17 patients in 1863, in a building designed by Mountfort & Luck on the corner of Lincoln and Annex roads. The main hospital buildings, the work of Mountfort after he ended his partnership with Luck in 1864, took many years to complete. The original plans date from 1871 and one block was opened in 1880, by which time the asylum held 191 patients.[26] Thomas Cane, who was appointed provincial architect in 1875,

↑

Benjamin Mountfort.

↗

Sunnyside Asylum, Christchurch, c.1880.

was commissioned for new work at Sunnyside around this time.[27] The central block was completed in 1884; a contract was not let for the southern, main entrance block until 1891.

The first warden of Sunnyside Asylum, Edward William Seager, who had earlier been superintendent of the Lyttelton gaol, was a campaigner for the more humane treatment of those with mental illness.[28] The hospital's administration and entrance building, designed by John Campbell for the Public Buildings Department, opened in 1892. It featured a symmetrical central block with a steep hipped roof, and minor Gothic details to link it in style to the older buildings.[29]

++

Dunedin's first asylum, established in 1862 on the Cemetery Reserve, now the home of Otago Boys' High School, rapidly outgrew its site. The following year, Edward Rumsey, the architect of Auckland's High Court, won a design competition for an asylum for the Otago

province, but this was not built. Instead, because outdoor exercise and employment were considered 'powerful curative influences' on insanity,[30] the government established Seacliff Asylum on 364 hectares of land, 28 kilometres north of Dunedin, which had extensive views of the sea. A pioneer wooden asylum was established there in 1879. As the *Otago Daily Times* noted, 'These patients, after clearing the ground, fenced it in, and planted it with potatoes and other vegetables.'[31]

Seacliff Asylum was designed by architect Robert Arthur Lawson in a Scottish

↑

Seacliff Asylum, Dunedin, 1890.

↖

Architect R. A. Lawson's drawing of Seacliff Asylum, 1883.

Baronial style, with steep stepped gables, turrets and a central tower. The construction was of brick finished with cement and Ōamaru stone facings, and the roof was of Welsh slate. Land instability caused problems during its construction, and a slip in 1887 undermined the foundations, leaving the north wing uninhabitable. The resulting commission of inquiry held Lawson responsible for many of the failings, and he returned to Melbourne in 1890. John Campbell attempted to stabilise the land in the 1890s.[32]

At its peak, Seacliff housed 1500 patients and was the largest building in New Zealand: its main hall could accommodate 900 people. A fire in 1942 destroyed one ward, killing 37 of its female patients, who could not escape from their locked and barred rooms.[33] In 1945 parts of the building, including the tower, were removed. The unstable ground conditions continued to be difficult, and several wards were deemed unsafe and removed. From the 1950s patients were gradually moved to the new Cherry Farm Hospital. Seacliff finally closed in 1970, and almost all of the buildings were removed. The site is now a Category 1 Historic Place.[34]

++

Nelson citizens with mental illness were initially sent to the local gaol or across Cook Strait to the Karori Lunatic Asylum. The town's first lunatic asylum, opened on Shelbourne Street in 1861, was intended for three people, but was often required to accommodate more. In 1864 female residents were moved to a building that had been built to hold refugees from Taranaki during the New Zealand Wars. Nelson's immigration barracks in Waimea Road

↑

Robert Arthur Lawson.

↗

Braemar Hospital, Nelson.

were also used for the care of people with mental illness; by 1872 there were 43 patients, many of them from the West Coast.[35]

Local architect Charles Beatson designed the new purpose-built Nelson Lunatic Asylum, opened in 1876, opposite Nelson Hospital in Waimea Road. It accommodated 30 males and 30 females, living in 30 small cells or in eight larger dormitories, but its 3.2-hectare site was considered too small. Conditions were basic: the beds were straw mattresses on wires. By 1896 the asylum housed 128 people, far more than it was designed for.[36] A brick building housing 54 male patients was added in 1898. Credited to John Campbell, this had an H-plan with Flemish gables at each end and a verandah between.

By the time an old school building was relocated to the site in 1901 to provide more accommodation, the patient population had reached almost 140.[37] The Mental Hygiene Division purchased a property at Stoke in 1920 for a new mental hospital, with the intention of closing the 1876 asylum. It continued to operate, however, and was renamed

↑

Nelson Mental Hospital, c.1878–94.

↗

Seaview Asylum, Hokitika, c.1904.

Nelson Mental Hospital in 1912. There was another name change, to Braemar Hospital, in 1961, when it became a psychopaedic hospital for children with intellectual disabilities. By 1969 it housed 223 patients.[38]

++

On the West Coast, Seaview Asylum was established in 1872, just north of Hokitika, where it was joined later that decade by the town's new public hospital. Although more modest than its counterparts in the larger centres, by 1876 it had 57 patients. John Campbell worked on extensions and alterations there in the 1890s.[39]

New Plymouth had a four-person asylum as part of the general hospital, but this ceased to provide mental healthcare in 1879. Napier's asylum, a one-storey wooden house built as an extension to the local gaol, accommodated up to 15 people but closed in 1886. Patients from both facilities were transferred primarily to Porirua.[40]

4

Progress and pain

1870–1890

NEW ZEALAND'S POPULATION BOOMED in the 1870s, thanks to the ambitious policies of Colonial Treasurer Julius Vogel, whose 'Grand Go-Ahead' programme of public works and immigration brought 100,000 assisted migrants to New Zealand and led to rapid construction of roads, telegraph lines and a railway network. The new arrivals also settled in new towns and cities and in rural areas that became more accessible. But then Vogel's overseas borrowing was halted by an international financial crisis and New Zealand slipped into what is known as the Long Depression of the 1880s, 'in which borrowing and an associated debt burden (especially on land) became a weight on the economy'.[1]

In 1876, the year in which the provincial governments were abolished, New Zealand had 24 public hospitals and a total of 942 hospital beds. In that year, 4346 patients (3373 males and 973 females) were treated, a relatively low number for a population of around 420,000.[2] By 1884, the number of public hospitals had risen to 38, with half of their funding coming from central government, approximately 20 per cent each from local bodies and donations, and the remainder from patient fees. Government attempts to rationalise the public hospital system and place hospitals under districts, supported by contributions from local authorities, met some resistance.[3]

There were medical advances in this period. In Britain, John Snow demonstrated the importance of good sanitation when he traced the start of the 1854 cholera outbreak in London back to broken sewers contaminating the water supply, and in the second half of the century the development of germ theory by Louis Pasteur and others began to replace the previously held beliefs that disease was the result of miasmas, or clouds of bad air.[4] Nevertheless, outbreaks of infectious diseases were common in colonial New Zealand with its often inadequate sewerage systems. There were outbreaks of scarlet fever in 1876 and 1881, which caused 834 and 257 deaths respectively; and measles outbreaks in 1874 and 1881, with 834 and 257 lives lost. Typhoid was endemic from 1874; outbreaks occurred around the country, resulting in an average of 143 deaths per year. From 1890 to 1894, influenza claimed 1393 lives. Other significant epidemics included diphtheria in 1872 and 1881, pertussis (whooping cough) in 1873 and 1883, and smallpox in 1872. The response, in a time before effective vaccinations and antibiotics, was to rapidly build (often temporary) fever hospitals, more to separate the afflicted from the healthy than to provide any effective treatment.[5]

Joseph Lister had promoted the concept of sterile surgery in his *Principles and Practice of Surgery* in 1855. Ether began to be used in the 1840s, and the first operations under general anaesthetic were performed. From the 1860s, antiseptic techniques began to enter hospital practice generally and surgical procedures became safer.[6] Treatment relied heavily on nursing, and hospital stays could be lengthy (months or even years). Historian of Wellington Hospital Donald Macdonald Wilson notes that until around 1890, except for accident cases, it was mainly 'an old people's home, as surgery as known today was not practised'.[7]

In the latter half of the nineteenth century, hospitals in Britain, Europe and the United States began to be designed following the pavilion plan principles popularised and encouraged by Florence Nightingale and others. (Nightingale's development of professional nursing and infection control resulted from her experience in the Crimean War of 1853–56. Her groundbreaking *Notes on Nursing* was published in 1859.) These hospitals had open wards of limited length and width, with patients' beds facing inwards in rows along the outside walls and a central aisle with tables for nurses.

The ward 'pavilions' were separated, but connected by a circulation spine, and naturally ventilated by windows along the long walls and typically also by wall and roof vents. They often

allowed for patients to be outdoors on verandahs, or in pergolas or sunrooms. Nightingale also pushed for hospitals to be built in the countryside, to provide 'pure air', although medical staff and the public generally wanted them located closer to the centre of population for better access.[8]

New Zealand architects, most of whom had emigrated from Britain, drew on the eclecticism of the Victorian era, selecting from a variety of historical styles to suit the circumstances and client preference, and modified as required by the availability of materials and construction skills. These ranged from neo-Gothic and neo-Tudor to neo-Classical and, in the latter part of the century, the developing Arts and Crafts movement. In New Zealand, size and cost often dictated a plain, domestic aesthetic, but there would be an increasing spectrum of design opportunities in these decades as the population continued to grow and more hospitals were built.[9]

++

In 1872 Philip Herapath won a design competition for a new three-storey main building at Auckland Hospital, which was opened five years later. In the Italianate style, it was built of scoria stone on a dressed bluestone base and said to be modelled on St Thomas' Hospital in London.[10] The central porticoed entrance block was capped with an octagonal tower, and the four corner towers contained lavatories and bathrooms. Ventilation was by air entering through a narrow upper strip in the large casement windows, which was then ducted and expelled through the campanile on top of the building. It also had linen and waste chutes, and there was provision for a lift, though this was not installed until 1909. In 1908 new ablutions towers were added on the south side, and the northern ones were converted to bedrooms. The building was demolished in 1964 to make way for the new main block.[11]

In the Coromandel the discovery of gold in 1852 had led to a rush, but this was short-lived and the Thames goldfield only got under way in 1867. Still, the discovery of rich reefs

↑
The Herapath Building at Auckland Hospital, c.1880.

↩
Reefton Hospital, c.1904.

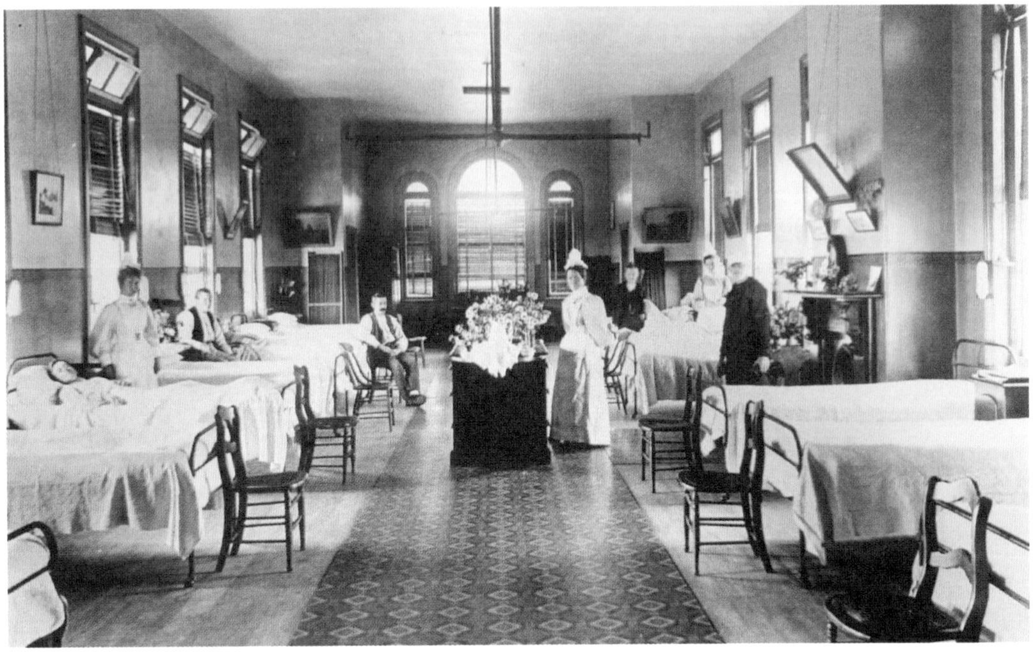

accelerated interest and the population of the area burgeoned.[12] Local iwi Ngāti Maru donated land beside the Karaka Stream, and Thames Hospital, designed by local architect George A. Beere, opened there, on the corner of Mary and Baillie streets, in 1868. A new wing was added on Mary Street in 1885 and a fever ward built next to the hospital in 1890.[13] The temporary hospital established in Coromandel township in 1871 moved to a former government office building on Rings Road two years later. Badly underfunded, the hospital closed in 1879 but was reopened after a mining accident in 1881.[14]

Under the Hospitals and Charitable Institutions Act passed in 1885, Waikato, Waipa and Raglan were made part of the Auckland hospital district. Following public pressure, and representations from Hamilton mayor William Graham, the government agreed to the establishment of a separate Waikato Hospital Board, which met for the first time in 1887. After considerable public debate as to whether there should be one central hospital in Hamilton, or smaller cottage hospitals throughout the Waikato region, the former option won the day. On 50 acres (20 hectares) leased by Graham at Ōhaupō, just south of the township, and overlooking Lake Rotoroa, a six-room kauri farmhouse already on the land was converted into the first seven-bed cottage hospital building. Despite criticism that access from the town was through swampland, the land was purchased in 1888, and a building with two eight-bed wards, bathrooms, an operating room, a dispensary and a kitchen, a 12-bed old men's refuge and a six-bed fever hospital were added in 1889, designed by Thomas White. Built of kahikatea timber, the wards were demolished in 1907 after excessive warping led to leaks.[15] Today's hospital stands on the same site.

In Taranaki, in the 1860s it was decided to move New Plymouth's hospital closer to the location proposed in Carrington's original plan for the town. Later known as the Barrett Street site, after the road built on its southern boundary, this consisted of an area of elevated land between Fulford Street and a continuation of Downe Street. Initially it was intended to relocate Thatcher's colonial hospital building there, but instead several houses erected hurriedly in St Germain's Square in 1862–63, to house settlers displaced in the New Zealand Wars,

↑ Auckland Hospital ward.

↗ Waikato Hospital, late 1890s.

were moved to form the nucleus of the hospital. When this opened in 1867, the design of the assembled buildings was attributed to Provincial Secretary Thomas Kelly.[16] A women's ward was added in 1871, and a small lunatic asylum the following year. The 1867 building operated as an old persons' home from 1887 to 1893, when it was demolished by burning.[17]

Gisborne's old men's home, known as the Poverty Bay Hospital, opened in Aberdeen Road in 1876. Cook Hospital, which had 18 beds for males and seven for females, was designed by local architect William Peter Finneran and built next to this. It opened in 1880; an isolation ward was added in 1883.[18]

In 1880 Napier's hospital was relocated further west to part of the Barrack Reserve on Napier Terrace, on the west side of the Botanical Gardens, where it was to remain for the next century. Following an 1877 competition, Napier architect Walter A. Dugleby was commissioned to design a new single-storey, 35-bed building, with three wards, a kitchen and a dispensary. It had views of the spit and harbour, and its four wings surrounded an open square, around which ran a verandah. The main entrance led into a 3-metre-wide passage, off which opened the resident surgeon's quarters and a surgery. There was a wing each for male and female wards; the latter had a day room and a separate room for private patients. The rear wing had a private ward for males, a day room and an operating theatre. A passage led to the kitchen and scullery, and bathrooms with lavatories were attached to each ward. A new wing and children's ward added in 1884 increased the hospital's capacity to 54 beds. Despite objections from the recently founded New Zealand Medical Association, which considered that such facilities should be kept well separated, a fever ward was added as a wing of the hospital in 1887.[19]

++

As the pastoral lands of the Wairarapa were developed, several towns grew up and it was not clear for some time which would become the main centre. When the district's first hospital, designed by Richard Wakelin, founder of the *Wairarapa Standard*, opened in Greytown in 1875, it consisted of a two-ward cottage with a scullery. The Victoria Ward was added in 1889 and

an operating theatre extension designed by Varnham & Roe around 1900.[20] Greytown Hospital finally closed in 1997, but the original building still exists as part of the Cobblestones Museum and is a Category 2 Historic Place.[21]

In 1877 Selina Sutherland, who was later briefly the matron of Wellington Hospital, proposed a new hospital in Masterton and led a community fundraising effort for a 14-bed wooden building, located opposite the current hospital in Te Ore Ore Road. Designed by local architect George Fannin, it opened in 1879.[22]

By 1870 Wellington's original Thorndon colonial hospital was too small for the town, which was growing to the south across the flatter land in Te Aro. Planning began for a new hospital in Newtown in 1875, and in 1878 the government granted a site of 3.2 hectares, later

↑

Cook Hospital, Gisborne, c.1900.

↖

Napier Hospital. Later photographs show the roof in the central portion raised to create a two-storey section.

↑

Greytown Hospital.

↗

Masterton Hospital, 1879.

increased to four, on Riddiford Street, where the capital's current hospital stands. A new 100-bed hospital opened there in 1881, designed by Danish architect Christian Julius Toxward, who, as noted, had also designed the nearby Mount View Asylum in 1873.[23]

When an *Evening Post* reporter visited the new hospital on 5 May 1881, just before it opened, he gave a very detailed description. He was not impressed by the exterior, which he thought 'squat' and whose architecture he considered 'exceedingly plain', but otherwise could find 'little fault'. He considered the interior 'lofty, convenient, commodious and well ventilated. The wards and rooms are 20 feet [6 metres] high, have plastered walls and ceilings, and are well lighted.'[24] There were indoor lavatories, plunge and steam baths, and pleasure grounds for the promenading of patients.

↑

The Toxward Building at Wellington Hospital, on its new site in Newtown, 1880s.

↖

Wellington Hospital, 1890.

Built by prisoners from the Terrace Gaol, the hospital was constructed largely of bricks made from clay excavated on the site, which were then plastered over. Overall, it was 85 metres long and 49 metres deep. The front entrance was in a two-storey block that also housed offices, consulting rooms, a casualty department and a dispensary, with accommodation for the resident medical officer above.[25]

Behind this, a corridor 3.6 metres wide and 5.5 metres high ran east to west, off which four single-storey, 24-bed Nightingale pavilion-style wards extended to the south. There were two smaller private wards, each with two beds, off the north side of the corridor, giving 100

beds in total. A smaller corridor ran parallel to the wards at the south end, creating courtyards between them, and on the other side of this, at the end of each ward, was a toilet block with lavatories. A separate fever ward, built at the same time but remote from the main building, held another eight patients.[26] As the *Post* concluded, it was a 'fine new institution' and 'it would puzzle anyone to find a flaw in its equipment'.[27]

The original hospital was located roughly where the clinical services building now stands, with the main entrance facing north and accessed by a long driveway from Hospital Road. The original wards were demolished between 1968 and 1973.[28]

++

Marlborough's first hospital was a cottage-style facility, designed and built by local contractors Avery Brothers, that opened in the port town of Picton in 1865. It was soon noted that most of its patients were coming from the Wairau area, so the Blenheim Borough Council rented a five-room cottage on Maxwell Road and converted it into the first four-bed Wairau Hospital in 1878. The hospital was partly relocated to the former immigration barracks in Blenheim's Park Terrace in 1879, but conditions were poor in both facilities.

↑
Clockwise from top left:
Picton Hospital.
Nelson Hospital.
Wairau Hospital, c.1887.
The first Blenheim Hospital.

After considerable debate as to whether two hospitals were needed to serve the district, the borough council bought the current hospital site on the Amersfoote estate on Maxwell Road in 1884. Three years later the Wairau Hospital moved into a new 25-bed building, designed by the architect to the council's hospital committee, William Douslin, who also designed extensions six years later. The building soon proved less than ideally planned.[29]

The first purpose-built hospital in Nelson opened in 1869 on the current site in Waimea Road.[30] Designed by John Blackett, engineer and architect to Nelson province, and built at a cost of £2500, it was situated on 2.8 hectares of land. The wooden building contained two large wards, one for men, one for women, accommodating a total of 45 patients, an overflow ward, two isolation rooms, an operating room and various other rooms and facilities for staff and patients. The hospital also had several shelters, open to the air, for tuberculosis patients.[31]

↑

Westland Hospital, Hokitika, c.1904.

↖

Reefton Hospital, c.1904.

↗

Christchurch Hospital, c.1880.

On the West Coast, Reefton Hospital was established in 1872, on the site that it still occupies on Broadway. An accident ward was added in 1896, and by 1906 it had four wards, including one for women and one for contagious diseases, and an operating theatre.[32] In 1875 the hospital in Greymouth was shifted to a new building designed by local architect John Adam Eissenhardt on the current site on Waterwalk Road, beside Karoro Lake, otherwise known as the lagoon.[33] In 1877 Hokitika's original hospital was replaced with a 50-bed wood-and-iron building, also designed by Eissenhardt, containing two male and one female wards, on the hill adjacent to the recently opened Seaview Asylum. An old men's home was later added to the building. Kumara Hospital was also extended around 1873 to a design by A. C. Campbell.[34]

++

In Canterbury, the establishment of a medical school in Dunedin in 1875 galvanised the Christchurch board into action to make its hospital suitable for another possible school. After a series of smallpox and typhoid outbreaks, two 24-bed fever wards (Numbers 4 and 5, later known as Maunsell) were built in 1876, designed by the hospital's original architect, Benjamin Mountfort. Ward 6, later known as Rolleston, added in 1878, was probably also by him. These were shed-like buildings with half-timber walls, incorporating corrugate-iron cladding and sharp dormer lights, and connected to the hospital with a long, covered walkway.[35] Mountfort also designed the 1875 administration building and house surgeons' premises in a similar style.[36]

This work at Christchurch Hospital was considered the start of a next phase of development on the site; all earlier buildings were regarded as obsolete and slated for

replacement. In 1880 Inspector General of Hospitals Frederick Skae described the new Ward 6 as 'the model ward of the colony' and made a special note of its 'noble and imposing corridor'.[37] Nevertheless, the hospital's contaminated water supply, drawn from shallow bores not far from where its waste was released directly into the Avon River, often made its patients more ill. After a long-running battle between the hospital board and the drainage board, the hospital was finally connected to the city's sewerage system in 1884.[38]

A new Ward 3 and a second operating theatre opened in 1886, the same year a long verandah and balcony were added, followed by a new kitchen in 1887 and a boiler house in 1889. A further 12-bed infectious ward built in 1887, bringing the bed count to 116, was demolished in 1914. Some of these buildings may have been designed by Thomas Cane,[39] who was also responsible for a more permanent Lyttelton hospital, opened in 1876 near the mouth of the railway tunnel, which had been completed in 1867. Intended initially to provide only emergency care, the hospital was extended in 1886 to consist of two four-bed wards and remained a hospital in its own right despite continuing plans to close it.[40]

As towns sprang up across the Canterbury Plains and in Otago to service the burgeoning number of farms, hospitals soon followed. Ashburton, some 85 kilometres south of Christchurch, began to grow in the 1860s but did not really develop until the railway reached it in 1873. Its county council pushed for a hospital to signify the community's independence and importance, and the funding was shared equally between the council and the government. Ashburton (County) Hospital opened in 1880, on its current site at the west end of the domain.

Designed by Ashburton architect James (Stanley) Bruce, it was a two-storey building, with a single-storey annex, and had two six-bed wards, six private rooms and an operating

↖

Clockwise from top left:
Oamaru Hospital, 1908.
The second Timaru Hospital, c.1870.
Timaru Hospital.
The third Timaru Hospital, 1908.

↗

Arrow District Hospital in Arrowtown, c.1855.

room. The ornate exterior façade, of tuck-pointed brickwork and Ōamaru stone, was intended to be a statement of the wealth of the town and its surroundings. Part of this original building was demolished in 1989, the rest around 2015.[41]

After a fire destroyed several of the existing buildings, Timaru Hospital was rebuilt on its current site and a 32-bed facility opened in 1872. To this two-storey central portion, the Luxmoore Ward was added to the west in 1875, the Belfield Ward to the east in 1877 and in 1880 the Selfield and Hall wards were built, one at each end, as well as an extension to the south to form the Le Cren Ward, providing a total of 72 beds. Designed in a 'Plain Italian' style by architect Thomas Roberts, the building had pavilion wards with brick walls, cemented on both sides, on a bluestone base.

A concrete floor slab with a suspended kauri floor above provided good subfloor ventilation to prevent moisture. The original hospital structures were of Timaru bluestone, with the distinctive patterning seen in remaining older city buildings, but most of the later additions used Timaru red brick, made from the local seam of hard-packed loess.

In 1891 a plan to use Middlesex windows to improve ward ventilation proved too expensive, so Tobin tubes were used instead. These were rectangular metal ducts set into the walls with the lower end 15 centimetres above the floor and the upper end venting outside below roof level. They proved so successful that they were still in use when the buildings were demolished almost a century later.[42]

The first hospital in Waimate, inland from the main route between Timaru and Ōamaru, was a cottage for the isolation of fever cases, built in 1875. It was replaced four years later by the purpose-built Waimate District Hospital, plus a separate smaller building for typhoid patients.[43] Oamaru Hospital's original building was a modest single-storey building erected by local builder Thomas Glass in 1872, with four wards of two beds each, a day room and a surgery, to which a separate fever ward was added in 1876.[44] The new 16-bed wing opened in 1878 was designed by the local architectural partnership Forrester & Lemon.[45]

++

At Dunedin Hospital, the layout of the converted exhibition building proved to be unsuitable and was considered gloomy and uncomfortable. William Mason and his partner Nathaniel Young Armstrong Wales were commissioned to design improvements to it, and probably also designed the operating theatre annex that was added in 1887.[46] Mason had formed the

partnership with Wales in 1871, after employing him as clerk of works on the Bank of New Zealand project in Dunedin in 1863. Mason & Wales would carry out a great deal of work for the Otago Hospital Board over the next century; it is now the oldest architectural practice still operating in New Zealand.[47]

Apart from this, little work seems to have been done during this period at the hospital.[48] But in 1875 New Zealand's first medical school opened at the University of Otago in William Mason's 1865 Exchange Building on Princes Street. Three years later it moved to the new Anatomy and Chemistry (now Geology) building near the River Leith, designed in a mixture of Gothic and Scottish Baronial styles using bluestone and Ōamaru stone facings. The architect, Maxwell (Max) Bury, also designed the university's famous 1879 clocktower building on the opposite side of the river.[49]

++

Despite their proximity to Queenstown, Arrowtown residents raised money for their own Arrow Hospital, which opened in 1880. Five years later both the Queenstown and Arrowtown hospitals came under the control of the new Southland Hospital Board.[50] Further south, Invercargill's Dee Street hospital was extended when the more decorative central block and the plainer south wing were built, in 1876 and 1879, to Victorian Classical designs by Scottish-born Frederick William Burwell, who was responsible for several Invercargill buildings after moving there from Queenstown in 1874. As Heritage New Zealand Pouhere Taonga notes, because the south wing mimicked the style of the north wing, it completed a '(largely) symmetrical trio of buildings. The central and south wings have survived, and in 1984, along with the earlier porter's lodge, were designated a Category 1 Historic Place. By 1881 the hospital had 30 beds. Burwell also designed the hospital established in Cromwell in 1877.[51]

↑
Dee Street Hospital, Invercargill, c.1890.

Caring for the elderly

↗

The Home for the Aged Needy, Wellington, c.1888.

Towards the end of the nineteenth century, many of New Zealand's early settlers were ageing and in need of increasing care – and there was no old age pension until the Liberal government introduced one in 1898. Society expected that families would take in elderly family members and care for them, but because most of the first Pākehā arrivals had been male, and it took some time for the gender imbalance in the population to even out, many when elderly were single and childless.[1]

Those who were unlucky had few options available. Public hospitals would provide care only for the sickest, and many found themselves in lunatic asylums for want of anywhere more suitable. Early elderly care was offered by charities, benevolent institutions and churches, and such facilities often also accommodated orphaned or destitute children. Most had dormitory wards, separated by gender, with a refractory ward for those patients who proved particularly difficult to manage.[2]

In Auckland the Old Men's Refuge originally occupied the former lunatics' asylum, and the Old Women's Refuge the former colonial hospital, both on the public hospital grounds. The former was established after the asylum moved to Avondale in 1867, and the latter followed the opening of the new main hospital building in 1877. Both were replaced by the Costley Home in 1890.

Other refuges, such as those opened in the 1870s in Gisborne, Napier, Whanganui, Nelson, Christchurch, Ashburton and Timaru, occupied buildings that had served as either immigration or military barracks, sometimes both. Napier's was described as a refuge for the 'incurably sick, feeble minded, orphan children, pauper maternity cases, the destitute and the homeless'.[3]

Before homes for the elderly appeared in the capital, private boarding houses tended to provide accommodation. Wellington's Home for the Aged Needy opened in 1889, in a new building of brick with Ōamaru stone facings on Adelaide Road, behind the public hospital. It was designed by Yorkshire-born Joshua Charlesworth, who won the 1887 design competition, and would later repeat this success for the Wellington Town Hall. The home evolved into Te Hopai Home and Hospital, which still occupies the original site.[4]

In January 1893, the Wellington Benevolent Institution (previously Society) opened a new home built between Ohiro Road and Epuni Street. The architect was William Charles Chatfield, who had worked for the Public Works Department before setting up his own practice in Wellington in 1876. As the *Evening Post* noted when reporting on the opening,

the home would 'replace the system of "boarding out" which has hitherto been in vogue'.[5] A new central wing was added in 1904. The building became Central Park Hospital in the 1930s. This closed in 1975 and was demolished in 1977.[6]

The first Alexandra Home in Nelson opened in the house of a T. Hodson in 1895, and incorporated the Nelson Refuge after the latter was destroyed by fire in 1909. A new building opened on the corner of Queen and Hill streets in Richmond in 1917. The Alexandra Hospital still operates, but on a different site.[7]

↑

Wellington Benevolent Institution in Brooklyn, c.1976.

↖

Queen's Jubilee Home in Woolston, Christchurch, c.1921.

↗

The Otago Benevolent Institution in Caversham, Dunedin, c.1890s.

In Christchurch, and designed by renowned architect Samuel Hurst Seager, the Queen's Jubilee Home for the Aged Poor was built in the suburb of Woolston in 1889 to meet the needs of the destitute and infirm. (Queen Victoria's 1887 jubilee, marking 50 years on the throne, was responsible for a plethora of street and building names across the country.) The main block was brick, with single-storey row cottages arranged in an octagon around a central enclosure. The Jubilee home was extended in both 1897 and 1921. An infirmary ward was added in 1908 and a chapel dedicated in 1948. The hospital, which closed in 1989 and had been designated a Category 1 Historic Place, was demolished in 2011 after being severely damaged in the 2010–11 Canterbury earthquakes.[8]

When the Otago Benevolent Institution in Caversham, designed by John Lowe Shaw, opened in 1866 with 102 beds, it was probably the country's largest charitable institution. By 1887 it accommodated 119 adults and 40 children, and from 1888 25 women passed through its lying-in, or maternity, ward each year. After 1896 it was predominantly a facility for the aged. In 1929 it became the Talboys Home, and was renamed Parkside in 1948. Mason & Wales designed extensions in 1949 and 1954.

From the 1890s the Department of Public Health encouraged the development of old persons' homes on the outskirts of towns so that residents could help to help grow their own food, and in order to reduce their access to alcohol and other negative influences. Even when the old age pension was instituted, many elderly people continued to rely on such homes.[9]

In Napier the 100-bed Parke Island Old People's Home, designed by Walter Philip Finch in brick with a Marseilles tile roof, opened in 1907 on the site of a former quarantine facility built in 1874. Fifteen of its residents were killed when the building was destroyed in the 1931 Hawke's Bay earthquake.[10]

Ashburton's facility was moved into a new brick building, designed by Richard Bird, architect and for a time mayor, in 1902. Renamed the Tuarangi Home, it sat in large grounds on the outskirts of the town. A new infirmary ward was added in 1908. The home eventually moved to a more central location in the town.[11]

In 1886 a home for the aged, infirm and orphaned children was constructed on a 0.8-hectare site in Bowmont Street in central Invercargill. C. H. Roberts designed its replacement, the 40-bed Lorne Farm, which opened in 1899 on the northern outskirts of the town. A children's wing added three years later closed in 1937. A chapel was dedicated at the Lorne Home in 1962 and a 46-bed extension added in 1966.[12]

These early elderly care facilities were often not pleasant places, and so several hospital and charitable aid boards established their own old persons' institutions. There were at least 20 of these around the country by 1920.[13] Gisborne's refuge on Aberdeen Road relocated to a group of old cottages in 1891 to allow for expansion of the Cook Hospital, and a new home was built in 1903. This was replaced by the Memorial Home at Mangapapa in 1926.[14] The Jubilee Home in Aramoho, Whanganui, had been built in 1880 as a Māori girls' school, but in 1892 the local hospital board purchased it and converted it to the Jubilee Home for Elderly Men. It was expanded to a design by Clifford Newton Hood in 1942.[15]

Various church groups developed care facilities, including Catholic orders such as the Little Sisters of the Poor in Auckland, Christchurch and Dunedin, Presbyterian Social Services, which opened the Ross Home in Dunedin in 1918, and the Salvation Army, which established Eventide Homes around the country from the 1920s.[16]

Later facilities had improved conditions, and included the Ranfurly Home built in Auckland in 1903 on a 223-hectare farm owned by wealthy businessman Alfred Buckland. Its establishment was suggested by the then governor, Lord Ranfurly, for veterans returning from the South African War, and also those who had served in the Crimean and New Zealand Wars.[17]

After the 1930s Depression, people began to live longer and the number of females increased. In the mid-twentieth century, New Zealand's per capita provision of care facilities for the elderly was high by international standards, and government policy moved towards encouraging 'ageing in place', providing services to help people remain in their own homes for as long as possible.[18]

By 1969 30 public facilities for the care of older people, with an average of 60 beds each, were operating throughout New Zealand. According to the 1966 census, however, only 4 per cent of people 65 or older were institutionalised; most continued to live in the wider community. Central government also provided rental accommodation for the elderly in state housing developments, as did several local councils.[19]

Following the Second World War, the retirement village concept of a purpose-built complex of residential units, with access to ancillary facilities and emergency call, was introduced from the United States. The Selwyn Village, established by the Anglican Church in Point Chevalier, Auckland, is thought to have been the first of these.[20] Another early example was the Roskill Masonic Village, established by the Freemasons in Auckland in 1960 and bought by the Selwyn Foundation in 2005.[21]

By the 1960s, most elderly care facilities were operated by church-based social agencies or other charitable organisations. Most of these have now been privatised or taken over by community trusts, and many formed the basis of retirement villages which developed rapidly towards the end of the twentieth century to cater for the retiring post-war baby boomer generation. From the 1980s people were increasingly encouraged to age in their own homes and rest homes also became more home-like. Institutions set up by churches (for example, Presbyterian Support Services, now Enliven) or charities began to be corporatised or sold. Many of the villages

↑
Clockwise from top left:
Lorne Farm, Invercargill, c.1920s.
Tuarangi Home, Ashburton, 1909.
Jubilee Home, Whanganui, c.1880.
Parke Island Home, Napier, 1907–08.

developed by commercial bodies at the turn of the century did not provide the full continuum of care, instead marketing a resort lifestyle. A number have done so since, however, including dementia and higher acuity care.[22]

Ryman Healthcare, established in 1984, opened its first village, Woodcote, in Christchurch, in 1986. Rowena Jackson Village in Invercargill, opened in 1996, was their first to offer a full continuum of care; Ryman now has 45 villages throughout the country.[23] Summerset Group was founded in 1994 and opened small hospital facilities in Levin and Waikanae. Its first comprehensive retirement village with hospital and rest-home care opened in Whanganui in 1997; it now has 23 villages.[24] Ryman and Summerset manage most of their design and construction in-house.

Others with significant portfolios of villages include Metlifecare, established in 1994 and which now has 43, British-based Bupa, Arvida and Oceania.[25] Several other providers, such as Northbridge, established by a charitable trust in Auckland's Northcote in 1976, have only one village. Although the design of retirement facilities is beyond the scope of this book, the involvement of several designers in this area is mentioned in later chapters.

5

Liberal treatment

1890–1914

DURING THEIR 21 YEARS IN POWER, from 1891 to 1912, much of that time under the leadership of Richard John 'King Dick' Seddon, the Liberals laid the foundations for the welfare state in New Zealand. Underpinned by a strong belief that central government had a key role in solving economic and social issues, their reforms included women gaining the right to vote in 1893, setting a minimum wage and establishing compulsory arbitration in 1894, and the introduction of old age pensions in 1898.[1]

Infectious diseases in the community became increasingly common after the turn of the twentieth century, with outbreaks of measles, smallpox and typhoid. There was an almost continuous risk of tuberculosis. Such diseases required specialist facilities, initially simply to isolate the contagious, but later also to provide treatment. Some of these were built on public hospital grounds, others in remote locations. A variety of locally managed institutions developed: base hospitals, fever hospitals, sanatoria, cottage hospitals and specialist maternity, children's and convalescent hospitals. All of these were in addition to the mental health institutions already operated by the central government.

Advances in medical knowledge in the late nineteenth and early twentieth centuries meant that many treatments could be provided only in hospital conditions. In 1895 German scientist Wilhelm Roentgen created the first anatomical image using x-rays, and by the 1910s they were being widely used for imaging and in cancer treatment. William Hosking, medical superintendent of Masterton Hospital, imported a 15-centimetre coil for generating x-rays in 1896, installing it in his own home. Auckland, Wellington and Christchurch hospitals installed their own x-ray equipment in 1898, followed by Dunedin in 1904. Hosking also pioneered radiotherapy in New Zealand, using radium to treat a carcinoma of the lip early in the twentieth century.[2]

Thanks to dramatically improved infection control, a hospital admission was no longer seen as more dangerous than being treated at home. Existing public hospitals expanded and there was greater demand for new ones as towns grew to service the ever-expanding rural hinterland.[3]

The Hospitals and Charitable Institutions Act of 1885 had attempted to impose some order on the provision of hospital and other social services in New Zealand. This legislation established a national system of hospitals and poor relief by setting up local hospital and charitable aid boards in order to remove inequalities in relief practices and spread funding equitably between central government and local communities. But the Act was only partially successful. Originally there were to be only 12 boards across the country, but 28 were formed in 1885, and the number grew to 35 by 1908. Some districts had combined hospital and charitable aid boards, but in others the two functions were managed by separate organisations, although this situation was later rectified.[4]

Following an amending Act in 1920, all hospital and charitable aid boards became known simply as hospital boards. Funding was initially a joint local and central government responsibility, but increasingly fell to the latter. This national system of locally elected district boards would own and manage public hospitals for the next century.[5]

The 1885 Act had also set up a Department of Hospitals and Charitable Institutions. A separate Department of Public Health was established in 1901 as a result of a bubonic plague scare. The two organisations amalgamated in 1909, absorbing the Mental Hospitals Department to form the Department of Health in 1920.[6]

Hospitals continued to be designed on the pavilion principle. New Zealand architects followed the latest trends in Britain, where Victorian eclecticism reached its peak towards the end of the century, being gradually replaced by a Queen Anne revival and then Edwardian, or Imperial Baroque.[7] Architects gradually formed professional bodies, initially locally, such as the

Canterbury Association of Architects in 1871, and then nationally with the establishment of the New Zealand Institute of Architects (NZIA) in 1905.[8]

++

By the turn of the century, a purpose-built hospital was urgently needed in the Far North, but the question was whether it should be in Mangōnui or move west to the growing township of Kaitāia. Eventually, after much debate, a 20-bed facility with an operating theatre, an x-ray room and a maternity unit opened on a new site in Mangōnui in 1907.[9]

As several villages along the Pouto Peninsula and the Wairoa River vied to become the district's main centre, there was disagreement in the northern Kaipara, too, about where a hospital should be built. After land was donated at Te Kōpuru, 14 kilometres south of Dargaville, the Northern Wairoa Hospital was built in 1903 to a design by Horace Hammond, the engineer to the Hobson County Council.[10] An isolation ward was added in 1919, a further annex in 1927.

The general ward closed in 1956, when the new Dargaville Hospital opened, but Te Kōpuru continued to serve maternity and elderly patients. Following a fire in 1959, patients were moved into the old disused isolation block, which was rebuilt to provide 26 beds in 1961. Further north, the Mount Pleasant Hospital in Dargaville was built around 1905.[11]

++

↑
Mangonui Hospital, Northland, c.1920.

↩
Wanganui Hospital, 1910.

Also in the north, in 1900 a cottage home for old men opened in Whangārei, but it took in other patients while planning proceeded for a general hospital. Edward Bartley designed the new Whangarei Hospital with two five-bed pavilion-style wards branching off a central entrance that was flanked by offices and a casualty department. At the rear was an operating room lit by skylights; there was a separate cottage for nurses' accommodation. At the opening in 1901, it was noted that Bartley had designed the building without charge. A separate isolation ward, later used by Te Roopu Whitiora Kaupapa Māori mental health service, opened in 1911, as did a medical superintendent's house.[12]

During his long career Bartley also designed Auckland's Costley Home for the Aged Poor in 1890 and its church eight years later. The home was named for Irish-born philanthropist Edward Costley, who had emigrated to New Zealand in 1840 and gradually amassed a large portfolio of property around Auckland. Costley, who never married and who chose to board in lodgings rather than owning his own house, left a large estate which was to be divided among several Auckland charities, including Auckland Hospital, to provide for the aged poor.

↑

Northern Wairoa Hospital, Te Kopuru, 1903.

↖

Whangarei Hospital, 1901.

↑

Auckland Hospital main building and Costley Nurses' Home, 1900.

↗

Waihi Hospital, c.1910s.

In 1887 his bequest allowed for the purchase of 6.8 hectares of land next to Cornwall Park in Epsom and the construction of the 156-bed home.[13] The original two-storey brick building, fronted by a portico with Corinthian columns and featuring a verandah with ornamental balustrading and a gable bearing an inscribed panel of Ōamaru stone, was later incorporated into Green Lane Hospital.[14]

Bartley was also responsible for several buildings at Auckland Hospital financed by Costley's generosity. The first section of the nurses' home was opened in 1890 and later added to in 1891, 1896 and 1900. The two-storey Costley Block opened in 1898, with four 12-bed wards on two floors and wide verandahs on two sides. The operating theatre block, built in 1905, and a two-storey surgical wing with two wards of 22 beds each, were attached. Other additions included the kitchen in 1896 and the medical superintendent's residence in 1904. A 14-bed fever ward, also designed by Bartley, opened in 1906. The original nurses' home was expanded to 97 beds in 1912, and a military annex was added further down the hill in 1915. The Islington wing, added in 1927, increased the capacity to 300 beds.[15]

Bartley also designed the 20-bed Waihi Hospital, opened in 1903, and the extensions and a nurses' home there three years later. An operating theatre was added in 1909. Auckland architect G. W. Allsop designed a new ward extension in 1911 and a maternity annex was added in 1940, then expanded and altered in 1953. The following year came a new kitchen and alterations to the men's ward; a chapel was dedicated in 1958. When the hospital closed in 1994, the building became a private old persons' home. Now a retirement village, it is a Category 2 Historic Place.[16]

When the Royal New Zealand Foundation for the Blind, which Dr Arthur Purchas had been instrumental in founding in 1890, moved to its Parnell site in 1892, Bartley designed the 1892 workshops, the 1894 main institute building and the Jubilee Building in 1909. In Gothic Revival style in red brick with Ōamaru stone dressed arches, it is now a Category 1 Historic Place.[17] Bartley knew Purchas well, as both were original members of the Auckland Choral Society, and in 1875 he designed a three-storey building for Purchas at 444–472 Karangahape Road, which at the time of writing still stands.[18] Bartley also designed the Knox Home for Incurables (now the Elizabeth Knox Home and Hospital), which opened in 1914 on 200 hectares of land in Panmure, Auckland. It relocated to a new campus on Ranfurly Road in Epsom in 1974.[19]

++

↑
Clockwise from top left:
Thames Hospital, 1873.
Thames Hospital, c.1900.
Coromandel Hospital, c.1900–30.
Mercury Bay Hospital, Whitianga.

The 1898 Mercury Bay Hospital in Whitianga was the work of William Henry Skinner, who also designed two well-known Auckland buildings: the Grand Hotel in Princes Street in 1889 and St Paul's Anglican Church in Symonds Street in 1895. A female ward and a morgue were added to the hospital in 1900. By the 1980s it was mainly providing geriatric care; it closed in 1995. Now a private residence, it is a Category 2 Historic Place.[20]

In 1900 Thames Hospital moved to a new building in Baillie Street, consisting of a main block plus an operating theatre and four ward wings. An infectious ward was added in 1907 and two isolation shelters around 1909. A delirium tremens ward and a new operating theatre opened in 1913.[21] In 1896 the Sisters of Mercy, who had established a convent and school in the area in 1882, took over the running of Coromandel Hospital.[22] The main hospital building was constructed in 1898, in a vernacular interpretation of Queen Anne style. It is surrounded by Victorian bay villa cottages. Heritage New Zealand Pouhere Taonga credits Thomas Mahoney of Edward Mahoney & Sons as the architect. Coromandel Hospital closed in 1994 but is now a designated historic area and the remaining buildings are a Category 2 Historic Place.[23]

++

Māori had long recognised the curative properties of the waters in the thermal areas around Lake Rotorua, and the colonial government was keen to develop their tourist potential. In 1881 the government acquired 1295 hectares of land from Ngāti Whakaue in order to develop the new township of Rotorua. Two years later, when the iwi gifted the Pukeroa Reserve in trust for a recreational reserve, one condition was that their sick would receive free treatment at the future government hospital. It took some time, however, for this to be honoured.[24]

In 1881 tenders were called for the construction of the first sanatorium in Rotorua's Government Gardens. Designed by Mr Mahoney, probably Thomas, it was intended primarily to serve tourists, though there was a small 'native' hospital within its grounds. The 12-bed sanatorium opened in December 1885, in time to treat victims of the Tarawera eruption in June the following year. On the corner of Hinemoa and Hinemaru streets, it was a single-

↗
The Costley Home, Green Lane West, Epsom, 1918.

storey building with a shingle roof and a long verandah.[25] The building was destroyed by fire in November 1888 and replaced in 1890 by a larger building with a 12-bed male ward and a nine-bed female ward. A small isolation hospital was built in its grounds in 1912. The facility closed as a sanatorium in 1948 but continued to be used as a home for old men until it was demolished in the 1970s.[26]

In 1908 the new Bath House, now the Rotorua Museum, opened in the Government Gardens to provide medical and therapeutic treatments; its south wing was added in 1911. Under the supervision of Government Architect John Campbell, three men prepared the design of this building for the Department of Tourist and Health Resorts, created in 1901. They were B. S. Corlett, nominally a draughtsman but possibly an architect in Campbell's office; former builder, then inspector of works W. J. Trigg; and Rotorua architect J. W. Wrigley.[27]

++

At the Barrett Street Hospital in New Plymouth, a new building designed by local architect James Sanderson was erected higher up the hill fronting Dawson Street in 1887. The single-storey wood-and-iron 19-bed main block had five large steeply pitched gables and a verandah stretching along its frontage. It was used as an infectious diseases facility after the new hospital building opened in 1916. A fire in 1965 resulted in the demolition of the western section, and the remainder was gradually removed; the last portion went in 2017. Sanderson's firm was to be responsible for several other hospital buildings in Taranaki in subsequent decades (see pages 125 and 353). A 40-bed old persons' home opened in 1901 and a separate building for consumptives was built four years later. In 1908 a second floor was added to the nurses' home.[28]

A private hospital opened in Hāwera by Sarah Hughes in 1880 was taken over by the Hospitals and Charitable Aid Board and continued as the Hawera Cottage Hospital until 1894. That year a new single-storey hospital, a small timber building with a verandah, designed by James Sanderson, opened on Gladstone Street.[29] A new men's ward, designed by local architect Charles Clarson, opened in 1904, its most distinctive feature being the ornate fountain at its entrance erected in memory of local worthy Lawrence Milmoe, who had left a large sum of money to the hospital.[30] A brick children's ward designed by James Higgins was added in 1914. In 1930, after the hospital was relocated to its new site in Hunter Street, it became the Ngahuru Home for the elderly.[31]

↖

Government Sanatorium, Rotorua, c.1901.

↑

Napier Hospital operating theatre, 1902.

↗

New Plymouth Hospital, c.1887.

++

Architect Richard Septimus Rounthwaite was responsible for two hospitals on the East Coast: a small maternity hospital built at Waipiro Bay in 1904 – isolation and the distance to Gisborne made this necessary – and the area's general hospital, opened at the nearby Te Puia hot springs in 1907. In 1926 a nurses' home was built at Te Puia, the wards were expanded to 10 beds and plant was installed to harness the steam from the springs for heating. The nurses' home, destroyed by fire in 1928, was replaced in 1929, along with a new men's ward and an operating theatre. A new 21-bed maternity ward opened in 1938.[32]

++

The first hospital in Wairoa, then known as Clyde, opened in the old courthouse on Lucknow Street, near Lambton Square, in 1888.[33] Designed by Napier architect Robert Lamb, it had separate male and female wards, each containing three beds. These were added to the original building,

which was converted to hold an operating theatre, a dispensary and nurses' accommodation.[34] Lamb also designed, at Napier Hospital, a two-storey six-bed nurses' home, which was built in 1895 and expanded to 15 beds in 1897.[35] An operating theatre was added in 1902; by 1907 Napier Hospital had 38 beds in three main wards (12 male medical, 12 male surgical, 14 women) plus three fever wards, for diphtheria, scarlet fever and typhoid fever. A 30-bed nurses' home was added in 1909, along with a chronic ward and shelters for tuberculosis patients.[36]

Waipawa County Hospital in Waipukurau opened in 1879, with two wings for males and females and staff accommodation between. A fever ward was added some time before 1886, an additional ward in 1890 and a nurses' cottage in 1898. The name of the architect is not certain, but Robert Lamb is known to have worked on buildings there in the early 1890s.[37] After the local community resisted a 1905 proposal to build a large hospital at Dannevirke and downgrade Waipukurau's Waipawa County Hospital to a small cottage hospital, it was renamed Waipukurau Hospital in 1907. Two years later a brick inpatient ward was added; a two-storey building with offices and staff accommodation above followed in 1915.[38]

++

Alfred Atkins, responsible for the design of several hospitals across the country during this era, was at the centre of a wider circle of health designers. In 1880 he purchased the Whanganui practice of Arthur Cole, and three years later was joined in partnership by Frederick de Jersey Clere. Clere moved to Wellington in 1886, and the partnership dissolved in 1888.[39]

↖

Clockwise from top left:
Waipawa Hospital, Waipukurau, c.1910s.
Waipiro Bay maternity annex, Tairāwhiti, 1964.
Wairoa Hospital, c.1905.
Hawera Hospital, 1901.

↗

The nurses' home at Napier Hospital, 1917.

Clere established a series of partnerships, including one with Gerald Fitzgerald and E. T. Richmond in the second half of the 1890s. This trio was appointed architects to the Wellington Hospital Board, for whom they carried out several projects, including the two-storey 1888 matron's wing, which housed a 22-bed children's ward, staff facilities, teaching rooms and accommodation for 21 nurses above, at the western end of the hospital's northern main corridor. Clere and Richmond also designed a new two-storey ward block (Ward 5, Fraser, and Ward 6, Allen), built in 1894 at the eastern end of the main corridor.[40]

Other architects who carried out work at Wellington Hospital around this time included Crichton & McKay (see page 144), but it is unclear who designed some of the buildings erected there.[41] The separate 23-bed corrugated-iron 'Hill' ward was built hastily for fever patients during an 1892 typhoid outbreak. The hospital's first x-ray tube was set up in a toolshed in 1899.[42] At the main hospital building, the Victoria operating theatre was added in front of the private wards to the west of the main entrance in 1901, when a new kitchen and laundry also opened. An outline of the former appears on a plan of the hospital buildings done by John Sydney Swan while working with Clere, Fitzgerald & Richmond, though it is not clear whether they were its designers.[43]

Also, while with the partnership, Swan designed the fever ward built at Wairau Hospital in 1898, which was planned to maximise fresh air and light.[44] By 1900, when they were in partnership, Clere & Swan designed the outpatient building at Wellington Hospital, which had separate male and female entrances and waiting rooms.[45]

Meanwhile, Alfred Atkins was appointed architect to the Wanganui Hospital Board and the new hospital he designed there opened in 1897, on the Gonville site that it still occupies today.[46] It was the first large brick building to be erected on the west coast of the North Island, and its construction was vindicated later that year when it survived an earthquake that damaged much of the town. Two wards, Reid and Bakewell, sat on each side of a two-storey administration building; the Simpson Ward added later that year increased the hospital's capacity to 68 beds. The wards were in connected pavilions, each with an open verandah at one end.

Despite the ending of their partnership, Clere and Atkins remained close and Clere provided support during the design of the new Wanganui Hospital. The design was so well regarded that Atkins was subsequently commissioned to design other hospitals, following the same principle.[47]

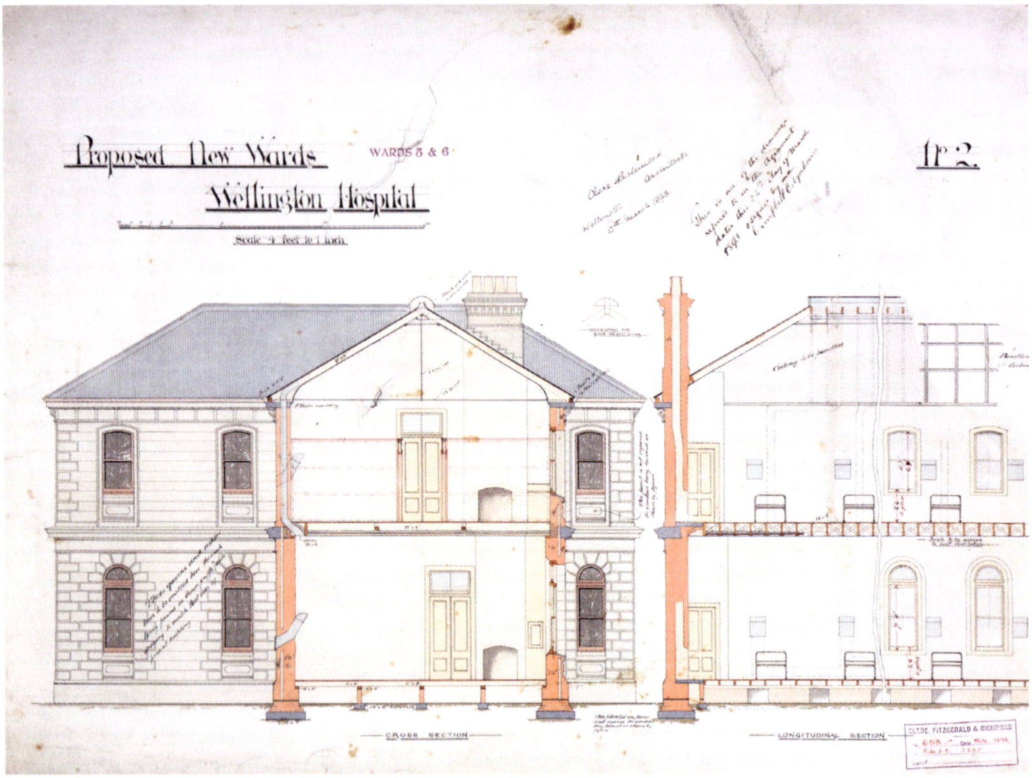

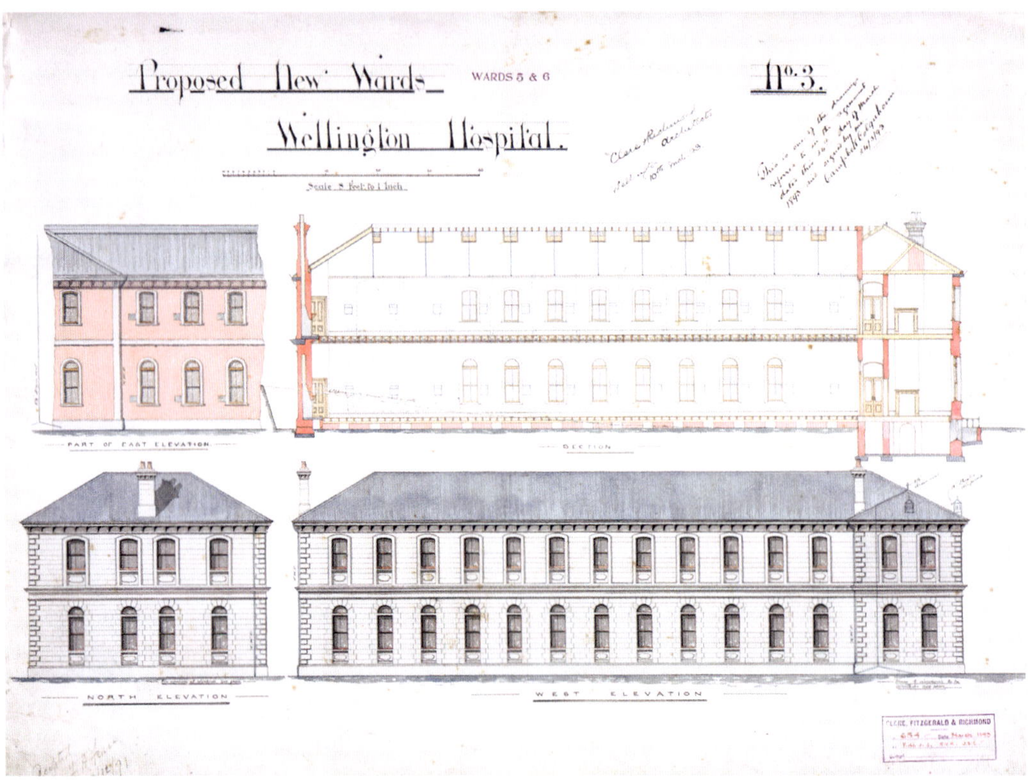

↖

Frederick de Jersey Clere's plans for new wards at Wellington Hospital, drawn in 1893.

↗

John Sydney Swan's plan for Wellington Hospital, 1891.

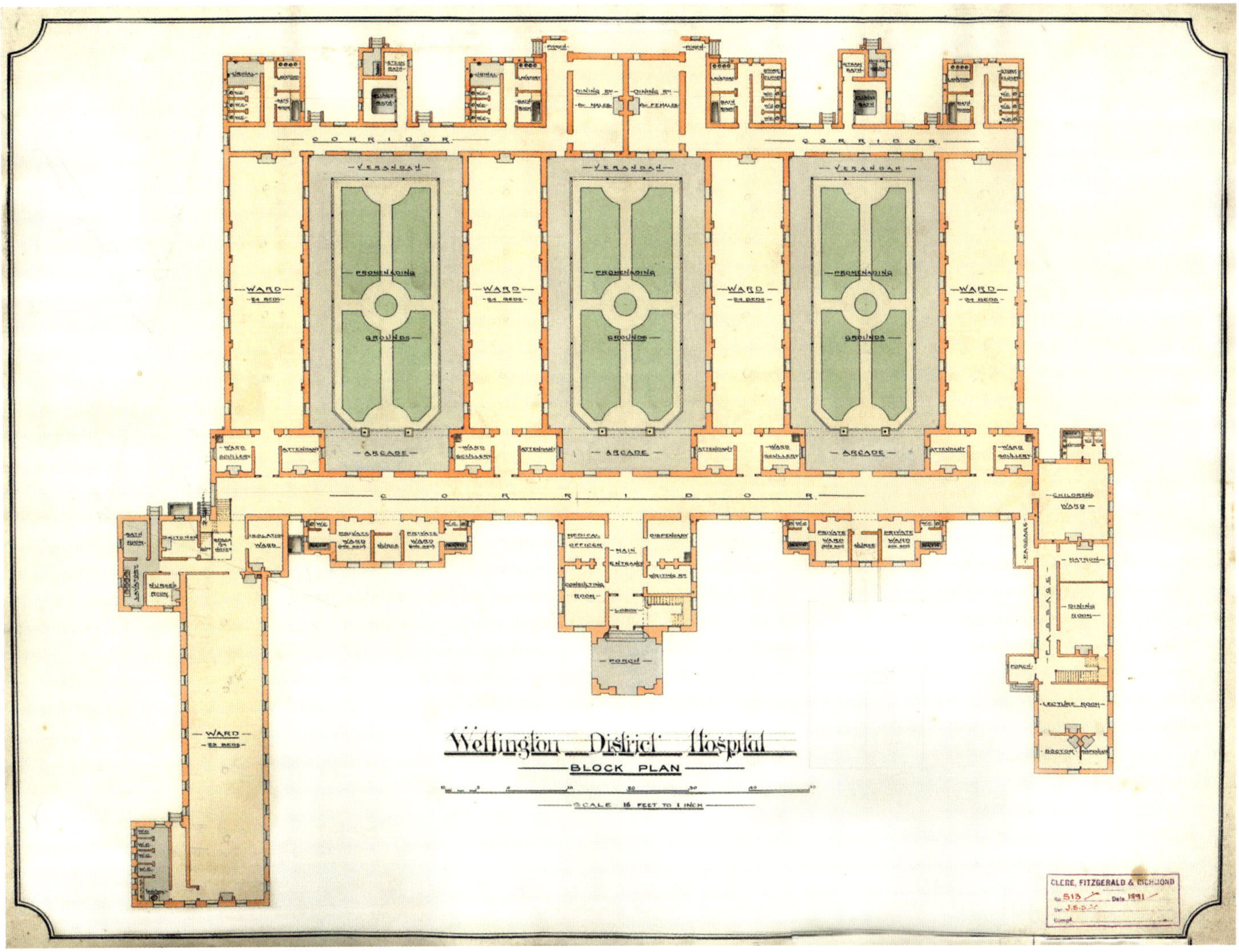

As the MP for Westland, Premier Richard Seddon was keen to establish a new hospital at Greymouth and, impressed by what he saw when opening the facility at Whanganui, recommended that Atkins design it.[48] It is unclear whether Atkins undertook this alone or, given the logistics of travel between Whanganui and the West Coast, he collaborated with other South Island architects. Greymouth Hospital opened in stages. The first three wards were the 12-bed Victoria, or Jubilee, for men's medical in 1900 – this honoured the Queen's Diamond Jubilee in 1897, the 10-bed Petrie for women in 1907 and the 12-bed Hannan for surgical cases. A two-storey central block with an operating theatre and nurses' accommodation, and a nine-bed home for old men, also opened in 1907.[49]

In 1906 the original building at Waikato Hospital was replaced by a new 24-bed brick and roughcast plaster Nightingale-style ward block, designed by Atkins. Two further 24-bed wards, with overflow spaces on the verandahs and linked to the original with a central corridor, were added in 1908, as was the first operating theatre. The 20-bed Rothwell Nurses' Home, built in the same year, was extended in 1912 and 1916. An x-ray machine was installed in 1911, and the Bailey Ward built in 1913 for tuberculosis patients later became a ward for geriatric patients.[50]

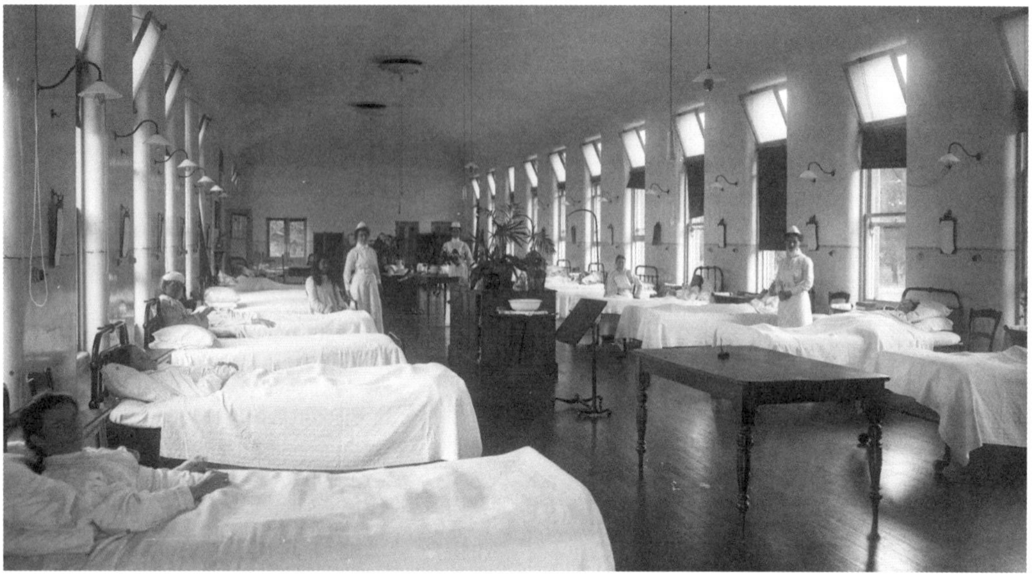

After moving to Wellington in 1907, Alfred Atkins formed a partnership with Roger Francis Bacon while maintaining a branch in Whanganui.[51] Their new practice won the 1908 Wellington Hospital Board competition for a new main hospital building, but lack of funds meant it was not built. Nevertheless, Atkins & Bacon became the country's most prolific hospital designers of the early twentieth century. The practice's first commission appears to have been preparing plans for Reefton Hospital in 1907, after the Government Architect declined due to pressure of work.[52]

Their two-storey 72-bed King Edward VII Memorial Hospital for Children, which opened at Wellington Hospital in 1912, consisted of two wings with a play court between. It was of faced brick construction with a white roughcast upper floor. The interior featured a series of Royal Doulton panels depicting nursery rhymes. It was only in 1929 that this building was connected to the main hospital, with a lift to replace the primitive windlass-operated hoist.[53]

↑

The Victoria Ward at Wanganui Hospital, 1907.

↖

Wanganui Hospital, 1910.

↗

Greymouth Hospital, 1908–09.

At Greytown, Atkins & Bacon designed the 20-bed ward for incurable patients, donated by Walter Buchanan, which opened in 1912.[54] In Hawke's Bay, on the current site in Kitchener Street, a second Wairoa Hospital opened in 1903: a large single-storey wooden building housing four 20-bed wards and an operating theatre. The architect is unknown, but Atkins & Bacon designed a new building for the hospital, which opened in 1912, and the following year they added a new operating theatre.[55] They were also appointed as architects to the Waipukurau Hospital Board in 1908 and designed a new administration block there in 1914.

After 9.3 hectares were acquired for a new hospital in Gisborne, at the end of what is now Hospital Road, some of the original hospital buildings were moved there in 1911 and a new 138-bed hospital, designed by Atkins & Bacon, opened three years later.[56] This had four 24-bed wards, a 12-bed children's ward, several private wards, an isolation block, a superintendent's residence and a 60-bed nurses' home. In New Plymouth, Atkins & Bacon designed the new 100-bed hospital building on the Barrett Street site, opened in 1916.[57]

++

In 1909 Atkins & Bacon employed Lucy Adelaide Greenish (later Symes) as a trainee draughtswoman. (*Making Space: A History of New Zealand Women in Architecture*, edited by Elizabeth Cox and published in 2022, is dedicated to Greenish.) While there, she became the only woman out of 315 architects to be registered under the Institute of Architects Act of 1913 and the first to be elected an associate of the institute. It is unknown which of the firm's hospitals she worked on, but she was commissioned to design the large ceremonial keys to mark the opening of some of their hospitals. Atkins & Bacon was clearly a progressive practice. Other women employed there include Rima Willcocks, who joined in 1916, possibly replacing Lucy Greenish, A. M. McIntyre, and a Miss Ahern, who was their sole employee from 1919 to 1922.[58]

++

Thomas Harvey James, who succeeded Alfred Atkins as architect to the Wanganui Hospital Board, held the position for 30 years. His name appears on the drawings for the 20-bed brick Queen Victoria Ward of 1902, but given its similarity to Atkins' buildings it is unclear what role each of them might have played in its design. He is, however, credited with the design of the 1904 nurses' home, a two-storey building of wood and Marseilles tiles, and possibly a 1915 office building for the Wanganui Hospital Board on the corner of Campbell and Guyton streets.[59] A new hospital laundry opened in 1902 and the Easson Ward for mothers and children was added in 1910. From around 1912 to 1918, he appears to have been in a partnership with W. T. Higgins.

James designed several buildings at Wanganui Hospital in the 1920s and 1930s: the Alexander and Bruce wards for children in 1922, the mortuary in 1924, a second nurses' home of brick construction in 1925 and an x-ray and physiotherapy block in 1927.[60] He was also responsible in 1922 for additions at Taihape Hospital, which had originally opened in 1911.[61]

The Patea County Hospital opened in two immigration cottages in 1876; three years later a two-storey building was built on Pembroke Street. By the turn of the century, Patea Hospital had become overcrowded, and a bequest made a new hospital possible. Thomas James designed the ward on Dorset Street, just south of the existing hospital on Pembroke Street, which opened in 1909. This was constructed in brick with a hipped corrugated-iron roof. The old building became the nurses' home until a new one was built in 1925.[62]

++

↖

King Edward VII Hospital for Children, Wellington, c.1920–30.

↑

Thomas Harvey James.
Lucy Greenish, New Zealand's first women registered architect.

↗

Patea Hospital staff and patients, late 1800s.

Palmerston North's first hospital, converted from a timber immigration barracks building in 1878, was a one-bed temporary holding centre for patients being transported to Bulls, where a hospital had opened in 1876, or Whanganui, which had the region's only significant hospital. By the end of the nineteenth century, however, Palmerston North was establishing itself as the major centre serving the developing farmlands on the Manawatū Plains. Considerable local lobbying led to the 1890 purchase of 4 hectares of land in Terrace Street (now Ruahine Street), which became the nucleus of the current hospital site.[63] Although James, then in practice in Palmerston North, and Frederick Clere won the 1892 design competition for the new hospital, the commission was instead awarded to local architect Ernest Larcomb. This may have been because his success as an inventor and businessman enabled him to help fund the construction of the new building.[64]

Palmerston North Hospital opened in 1893 in a building constructed of wood and iron, containing four wards providing a total of 27 beds (17 male, eight female and two isolation rooms) and an operating theatre. It was generally single storey but an upper floor over part of the building provided nurses' accommodation. A five-bed private ward was added soon after.[65]

++

Clere continued to be involved in the design of several hospital buildings, either in his own right or with one of his many architectural partners. A cottage hospital in Ōtaki designed by Clere, Fitzgerald & Richmond opened in 1899. A new wing was added in 1904, but the facility closed in 1929.[66] The 1907 Otaki Sanatorium, also designed by Clere and built on an adjoining

piece of land, housed male and female tuberculosis patients until 1919. In 1917 both the hospital and the sanatorium came under central government control to provide treatment for sick and wounded soldiers returning from the First World War. From 1919 to 1956, however, it accepted only female patients, being the only such facility in the North Island. It was renovated in 1927 and extended in 1951.[67]

F. de J. Clere & Son – Frederick de Clere was now in business with his son, Herbert – won the 1912 competition for the old persons' home on Maxwells Line at Awapuni, opened in

1915 and later known as Awapuni Hospital. As it was some distance from the main Palmerston North hospital, falling patient numbers and earthquake risk resulted in its closure in 1989.[68]

++

At Wellington Hospital, the 1904 three-storey nurses' home to the north-east of the main hospital building, which was extended in 1907 and 1910 and gained a new wing in 1925, was designed by Francis Penty.[69] Buller Hospital (Westport District Hospital) was relocated to a site further up Cobden Street, where a two-storey brick and tile building was erected to a design by Francis Penty and Edward McCallum Blake in 1908. A brick nurses' home was added in 1913, and the nearby O'Connor Home for the elderly, run by the Sisters of Mercy, opened in 1917. Blake left the partnership in 1909 to establish his own practice, and became architect to the Wellington Hospital Board, although other firms continued to carry out work there.[70]

++

A 28-bed hospital opened in Picton in 1902 was designed by Sir Arthur Penrose Seymour, later chairman of the Picton Hospital Board, who had visited the new Ōtaki hospital and proposed improvements there. A separate ward for infectious diseases was added in 1911 and a maternity annex in 1913. William Chatfield carried out work for the Blenheim Hospital Board in 1904, but apart from the fever ward it seems that little, if anything, was built at Wairau Hospital, because the board could not agree on finance.[71]

Development at Nelson Hospital also appears to have been limited in these years, possibly because the town itself was beginning to stall, as other centres with larger agricultural hinterlands became more accessible. A Mr Bethwaite designed a doctor's residence there in 1900. A cottage hospital at Havelock, designed by architect W. K. Matthews, opened in 1903 and closed 60 years later.[72]

↖

Palmerston North Hospital, c.1894.

←

The Princess Mary and Prince of Wales wards at Palmerston North Hospital, 1945.

↑

Buller Hospital, Westport.

↑ Wairau fever ward.

↖ Otaki Sanatorium, c.1950–59.

↗ The second Picton Hospital.

++

In his history of Christchurch Hospital, F. O. Bennett relates that in 1892 the government questioned why it was being asked to fund new buildings there when two original wards were vacant, but the staff maintained that these were unfit for use, being 'impregnated with disease'. Eventually the government inspector agreed that, though not wonderful, they could be used if better ventilation was installed, a decision Bennett described as 'the most economical method of increasing the bed state that the hospital has ever known'. When new hopper ventilators were installed, it was found that the old ones were stuffed with dead birds. In fact, after statistics were reviewed, the old wards were found to have less sepsis than the more modern ones.[73]

In 1891 prominent Christchurch architect Joseph Clarkson Maddison was asked to draw up plans for a new nurses' home, based on the one recently opened in Dunedin. With two floors, and built in brick with a slate roof, it was completed in 1895 and accommodated 36 nurses.[74]

After Polish-born local businessman Hyman Marks left £5000 to build a new ward at Christchurch Public Hospital, local architect Frederick Strouts, perhaps best known for designing houses for the Canterbury elite and the Jacobean Ivey Hall at Lincoln College, was commissioned to design it, assisted by his partner Robert Anderson Ballantyne. Replacing an earlier Tudoresque-Colonial style ward, the new block was set away from the other buildings at the west end of the site and connected to them by a long corridor on the southern side.

The large two-storey building (51 x 17 metres) housed 50 patients, in two wards, and took the hospital's capacity to 160 beds. The front facing the river had a high-pitched gable and was surmounted by carved stonework, with two octagonal towers at the sides housing the lavatories. The east and west sides were plainer, with gables and segmented headed windows. Local two-tone red and orange brickwork with white stone inserts and terracotta decorative elements formed the external walls; the roof was of grey slate.[75]

The building had a variety of defects, including falling plaster, and despite opening in 1897 was not occupied until 1900. Maddison was asked to review the project, as were Christchurch architects John Collins and John Whitelaw, who took over the works to resolve the problems. The building required major repairs after being damaged by fire in 1908 and was finally demolished in the 1980s.[76] Strouts also designed the 1887 Rhodes Convalescent Home in Cashmere, with half-hipped gables and mullioned windows.

The 1896 water tower, which sat incongruously in front of the hospital until it was replaced in 1911, was an early example of the potential pitfalls of value management. Four tenders were received for its construction, but an expert review rejected all of these on cost and technical grounds. Instead, a design-build contract was called for, but with punitive terms for performance. Only one tender was received, but the contractor had covered his potential risk with a significantly increased price, and then pulled out when technical issues with his proposal were pointed out. Various other options were considered, before Whitelaw was asked to design a simple utilitarian tank stand, the cost of which was dwarfed by the abortive fees spent.

Other elements of the hospital's expansion proved less fraught. The first x-ray equipment was installed in 1898 and electric lighting the following year, when two female wards and a children's ward were also added. A second laundry was built in 1900, a third operating theatre in 1902, a medical superintendent's house in 1904 and the old nurses' home was extended in 1907.[77]

++

The six-bed Diamond Jubilee Convalescent Ward at Ashburton Hospital, designed by Richard Bird, later designer of the Tuarangi Home, opened in 1898 and was extended south in 1903,

↖

Wellington Hospital nurses' home, c.1910s.

↑

Christchurch Hospital nurses' home, 1895.

↗

The Hyman Marks Building at Christchurch Hospital, 1900. After surviving a fire in 1908 it was used until the 1980s.

with a corridor to connect it to the rest of the hospital. A two-storey nurses' home was added some time in the 1900s, and the hospital was extended and renovated in 1911 and 1912, when a surgical ward and an x-ray room were added.[78]

Further south, at Timaru Hospital, new nurses' quarters and a ward for infectious cases opened in 1902. A fever ward was built above two of the original wards in 1903, a new operating theatre opened in 1906 and a laundry in 1907. When the eight-bed Seddon Memorial Children's Ward opened in 1908, 10 separate shelters were erected for consumptive patients, as tuberculosis sufferers were then known. By 1910 Timaru Hospital had 74 beds. Nearby Waimate Hospital had four wards, an operating theatre and a separate fever ward by 1907,

and could accommodate 33 patients. Herbert Hall, Timaru architect and later designer of the Chateau Tongariro, carried out work at Waimate Hospital at around this time.[79]

++

In Dunedin, several purpose-built hospital buildings were gradually added on to the 2-hectare block surrounding what was known as the 'Old Building', which continued to serve as the main entrance and administration block until it was demolished in 1934. The first of these was the 1893 Campbell Pavilion, a two-storey block of brick on an arched Port Chalmers stone base, built to the north and housing the Houghton and Miller wards, each with 24 beds. In 1897 an operating theatre block was added to the east of the pavilion. The first nurses' home, a two-storey brick building, was built on the corner of Cumberland and Frederick streets in 1892, and thanks to demand was extended twice, in 1903 and 1908–09.

All of these additions were designed by Mason & Wales. A laundry and boiler house opened on Cumberland Street in 1894 and a new kitchen opened in 1897. The Campbell Pavilion, operating theatre block and nurses' home were all demolished in 1974 to make way for the 1980 ward block.[80]

Mason & Wales also designed the 1899 two-storey Victoria Pavilion, next to the theatre block, housing the children's wards. Accommodating 16 patients on each floor, it was built in a similar style to the Campbell Pavilion and based on the latest in international children's health practice. It was demolished in 1962 to make way for the 1969 clinical services building. To

complement the Campbell and Victoria pavilions, Mason & Wales also designed the 1908 Ward Pavilion, on the corner of Great King and Hanover streets, which housed the Dominion and Plunket wards. This was demolished in the early 1980s. Buildings for outpatients, a laboratory and x-ray equipment opened in 1910.[81]

The Dunedin City Council had set up a fever hospital in the town belt in the 1870s, but this was closed within a year because of public concern about the risk of infection spreading. Instead a facility was opened on Quarantine Island/Kamau Taurua in Otago Harbour. It was not until 1908, five years after the government had placed the responsibility for infectious diseases cases with local hospital boards, that a purpose-built infectious diseases hospital was erected in what was then an isolated spot at Pelichet Bay, on the shores of Lake Logan (now Logan Park). After some wrangling with the Defence Department, which was using the site as a rifle range, a portion was leased to the Health Department.[82]

Designed by Dunedin architect Patrick Young Wales, working with his father Nathaniel Wales at Mason & Wales, the fever hospital was pavilion in style, with a central block and narrow wings to maximise ventilation. Placing the wards apart provided more protection against the spread of disease, and the plan took account of the need for fresh air, good drainage and clean water. There was space, too, for patients to exercise outside. Constructed of wood and plaster, the building had tall windows and iron air vents in the bedrooms. A disinfectant room and a morgue were placed in an outbuilding.

↖

Ashburton Hospital, 1916: part of the original hospital to left, later extension to right.

↑

The third Timaru Hospital, c.1910s.

Never large, the bed numbers reached a maximum of 20. Only a few years after its doors opened, Dunedin doctors were concerned about the conditions at the hospital and it closed in 1924, while the New Zealand and South Seas Exhibition was on in the park next door. It reopened in 1926 and kept going until its final closure in 1952. The building is a Category 1 Historic Place.[83]

++

In Central Otago, Dunstan Hospital was moved to higher ground after floods in 1878 and in 1900 a new wooden building went up, almost certainly designed by Mason & Wales, who were also responsible for a temporary infectious diseases ward in 1909 and a doctor's residence in 1921. A new nurses' home was built in 1937 and a maternity unit opened in 1946; the latter was possibly also designed by Mason & Wales.[84]

After the Frankton hospital in Queenstown burned down in 1894, the hospital board considered centralising services at the 16-bed Arrow Hospital, but the inspector general of hospitals recommended closing Arrow and rebuilding at Frankton because it was more central

↖

Dunedin Hospital, c.1910.

↑

Pelichet Bay Infectious Diseases Hospital, north Dunedin. The bay, near Albany Street, has since been reclaimed.

↗

The second Frankton Hospital, Queenstown.

for the various Wakatipu townships. The new Frankton Hospital, designed by Mason & Wales, was operational by 1898 and by 1915 consisted of two wards and a dispensary. The Arrow Hospital finally closed in 1915.[85]

++

At Invercargill's Dee Street hospital, three female wards were added in 1896, and the North Wing was demolished to make way for the 1898 Victoria Wing. Designed by local architects

McKenzie & Wilson, its two male wards accommodated 36 patients. The main entrance was flanked by two octagonal towers and a cast-iron verandah ran along one side. An outpatient building opened in 1902 and the fever ward was adapted for tuberculosis patients in 1908. Edmund Wilson designed a surgical wing of brick and concrete, consisting of an operating theatre and supporting rooms, which opened in 1910, as did a new children's ward.[86]

The adjacent 1907 nurses' home in Leven Street was designed by Invercargill architect Cuthbert John Brodrick in an Arts and Crafts style, then enlarged to a design by Edmund Wilson in 1916. Converted to a social services centre by the Salvation Army in 1977, the building is now a Category 2 Historic Place.[87]

↑

Victoria Ward at Dee Street Hospital, Invercargill, c.1942–50.

↗

The nurses' home at Dee Street Hospital, Invercargill.

When the new hospital was completed on the current site at Kew in 1937, Dee Street continued primarily as a maternity facility and was upgraded and renamed the Queen Victoria Hospital in 1942. It became maternity only in 1957 when the new West Wing opened at Kew. By the 1960s it was simply known as the Dee Street Maternity Hospital and was expanded with a 20-bed annex and a 20-bed staff extension. A new office building for the hospital board opened nearby on the corner of Dee Street and Victoria Avenue in 1952. With the transfer of maternity services to Kew, the Dee Street hospital finally closed in 1979. Most of the buildings were demolished from 1985, though the 1870s Central Block and South Wing (now Burwell House) and the porter's lodge, were retained. Heritage New Zealand Pouhere Taonga notes that Dee Street, which is now a Category 1 Historic Place, is the only surviving collection of nineteenth-century hospital buildings in the country.[88]

In Riverton, the Wallace and Fiord Hospital, established in the old immigration barracks in 1875, was replaced in 1888 by a new four-ward building designed on the pavilion principle by architects G. Latham and H. W. Potter. An operating theatre was added in 1902 and a maternity unit in 1929.[89]

Maternity and infant care

Many early settlers lived in remote areas, and a woman giving birth was fortunate if she had another woman with her to provide support. As more families arrived, however, certain women gained a reputation for their skills in assisting with deliveries. Government provision of maternity services was limited, and there was considerable doubt as to whether they were required. Birthing in hospitals was considered dangerous, as the risk of sepsis was so much greater there, and most 'respectable' women gave birth in their own homes.[1] Puerperal fever, caused by bacteria, was the major reason for death in childbirth. Maternity cases were, in fact, excluded from many public hospitals. Only two public hospitals set up dedicated lying-in wards, as they were known: Dunedin from 1863 and Ōamaru from 1874.[2]

As the twentieth century began there was increasing concern over the number of deaths of mothers and babies in childbirth – 81 per 1000 births in 1903 – and the wildly varying standard of midwifery. Driven by Grace Neill, assistant inspector of hospitals for the Department of Health, in 1904 the Liberal government passed the Midwives Registration Act, which formalised their training and certification.[3]

From this grew Neill's establishment of the world's first state-run maternity hospital, which also trained midwives, and also the next three of what would be a group of seven maternity homes around the country. In order to stroke Premier Richard Seddon's 'considerable ego', she suggested that these be named St Helen's after the premier's Lancashire birthplace.[4] Neill's successor, Hester McLean, was responsible for setting up the other four, and to keep costs down while providing a homely environment, they initially purchased and refurbished existing residential buildings.[5]

Despite being public institutions, the St Helen's hospitals were intended to provide care for the wives of working men, did not take single mothers and charged a fee for their services. Another driver for their establishment was the improving maternity care being provided by mainly church-run facilities, leading to a concern that 'indigent' mothers were receiving better care than the women with employed husbands.[6]

The first St Helen's Hospital opened on 29 May 1905 in a rented 24-room building in Wellington's Rintoul Street, but this soon proved unsuitable, and there was a move to a larger building in Colombo Street, Newtown, in 1908. High demand led to the purchase of a property in nearby Coromandel Street, where a new hospital with 30 beds, designed by the Public Works Department, opened in 1912.[7]

Seddon opened Dunedin's St Helen's Hospital in a house in Regent Road at the end of September 1905. The inaugural superintendent was Dr Emily Siedeberg, New Zealand's first female medical graduate. The Otago Medical School lobbied to use the hospital for obstetrics training, but it was considered inappropriate for female trainee midwives and male medical students to use the same facility. Dr Ferdinand Batchelor, who taught and championed obstetrics and gynaecology at the Otago Medical School, therefore established the Forth Street Maternity Hospital (later renamed the Batchelor Maternity Hospital) in 1907, which provided practical training and served mainly single girls, who were excluded from St Helen's. In 1918 the Health Department allowed medical students to train at St Helen's with patient consent. The two Dunedin facilities were later replaced by the Queen Mary Maternity Hospital.[8]

The first Auckland St Helen's Hospital opened in 1906 at Challinor, the former family home of Dr Arthur Guyon Purchas, built on Pitt Street in 1880. When it moved into an adjacent purpose-built facility in 1922, designed by the Public Works Department, the house became a nurses' home.[9]

The former Sydenham Hotel, on the corner of Durham and Battersea streets, was converted to become Christchurch's first St Helen's Hospital in 1907. A simple wooden two-storey building, with a projecting corner balcony, it held 16 beds. This soon proved unsuitable, but plans for a replacement were put on hold during the war, and continued to be for decades.[10] Gisborne's St Helen's opened in 1915 in the former Townley Maternity

↖

Nurses at St Helen's Hospital, Colombo Street, Newtown, Wellington, 1962.

↑

Grace Neill, c.1910.

↗

St Helen's Hospital, Wellington.

Home, established in 1909. Demand reduced in 1935 after the maternity annex opened at Cook Hospital and it closed in 1961. In Invercargill a St Helen's opened in 1917 in a property bought on Nelson Street, Georgetown. This shut its doors in 1952.[11]

The Jessie Hope Gibbons Maternity Hospital, next to Wanganui Hospital on Heads Road, started life as a home built in 1906 by A. G. Bignell, who loaned it to the government in 1918 as a convalescent home for returned servicemen. In 1921 Hopeful (Hope) Gibbons, a successful businessman and for a time mayor of Whanganui, bought the building and gave free use of it as a St Helen's maternity hospital. When he donated it to the hospital board in 1933, it was renamed in memory of his wife. Local architects Don A. Wilson and Eddie E. Belchambers later designed alterations to the building.[12]

++

From the 1920s hospital boards took a much greater responsibility for maternity care. By 1918 there were maternity wards in the hospitals at Mangōnui, Rāwene, Picton and Cromwell, and separate maternity hospitals had been established in Kawakawa, Te Puke, Napier, Blenheim and Naseby. By 1926 there were 41 hospital board maternity annexes or separate maternity homes, as well as the seven St Helen's hospitals and others run by voluntary institutions. In 1932 providing maternity services for the 'indigent' became the responsibility of local hospital boards. By 1933 almost 60 per cent of infants were born in a hospital, rising to over 99 per cent in the 1960s, but by the end of that decade it had dropped to 85 per cent as home births regained popularity. Several private facilities opened during the 1950s baby boom, supported by increased government subsidies.[13]

↖

St Helen's Hospital, Dunedin, 1952.

↑

The nurses' home at St Helen's Hospital, Auckland.

↗

St Helen's Hospital, Auckland, 1922.

++

Improved maternity care was not sufficient on its own, however, and concerns remained about the care and nutrition of infants and young children. In Victorian New Zealand, infectious diseases, especially childhood illnesses such as diphtheria and scarlet fever, were rife. Children were often viewed as 'incomplete human beings, with a fragile hold on life, on whom it was wasteful to devote too much care and attention'. But in the last decades of the nineteenth century a new nationalism shifted opinions, and children were regarded as the 'source of future progress and survival'. This led to the foundation of the Plunket Society and the associated Karitane Hospitals, in part by doctor and health reformer Sir Frederic Truby King.[14]

In 1898 King, who was superintendent of Seacliff Mental Hospital from 1889 to 1920, bought land at Karitane, where he built a seaside home, and infants, mainly neglected or illegitimate, were cared for there. The success of this led to the foundation, in 1907, of the Society for the Promotion of the Health of Women and Children, soon named the Plunket Society after the wife of the then governor-general. The Plunket philosophy emphasised routine, hygiene, fresh air and diet. The society also trained specialist community nurses and opened clinics throughout the country. From 1910 Plunket established six hospitals as training institutions for Karitane nurses, while caring for babies with malnutrition and other dietetic complaints and those born prematurely. They also offered mother-care training and assistance.[15]

The first Karitane Baby Home opened at Andersons Bay in Dunedin in 1910, in a homestead gifted by businessman Woolf Harris. In 1934 the name changed to the Truby King Harris Hospital; five years later it was replaced by a two-storey early modernist concrete building designed by local architect Arthur Louis Salmond with a flat roof and large sunny balconies. The hospital closed in 1978 but the building remains as a Category 1 Historic Place.[16] The Lady King Karitane Hospital in Christchurch opened in 1917, in the

↑
Forth Street Maternity Hospital, Dunedin, 1913.

↑

Architect William Gray Young. Plunket Society and Karitane founder Frederic Truby King, 1938.

↗

The opening of St Helen's Maternity Home in Christchurch, 1907.

former 10-room brick home of Sir Heaton Rhodes in Cashmere, which was purchased through community fundraising. This was replaced by a new building, designed by Warren and Mahoney, built next to it in 1963.[17]

Whanganui's Stewart Karitane Hospital opened in 1919, after John Stewart donated his large two-storey house on Campbell Street. A nurses' home was built in 1930 and a new block added to the hospital in 1966. In Auckland businessman Andrew Caughey gifted his home, built of kauri in the 1880s, for a Karitane hospital. After a substantial extension by local architect Arthur White, it opened in 1924. When a new hospital designed by Haughey & Fox was opened next door in 1962, the old Caughey house became a nurses' home. The Truby King Hunt Karitane Hospital in Invercargill opened in 1926 in a wooden building on a large site donated by Sir William Hunt. Most of the hospital was demolished in 1948 and a new facility opened seven years later.[18]

After King was appointed the first director of child welfare in 1921, he moved to Wellington, where he commissioned a house in Melrose, designed by William Gray Young and completed in 1924.[19] Next door, in the same year, Gray Young also designed the Karitane Products Society factory to manufacture the infant feeding products that King had developed.[20] Although breastfeeding was encouraged, King recognised that this was not always possible, and developed 'humanised' milk products for infant nutrition.

Gray Young was responsible, too, for the Truby King and Lady King Karitane Hospital, a purpose-built facility in a two-storey brick building, which opened on an adjacent site in 1927. Fresh air and sunlight were available to every room, all the wards had french doors opening onto the garden and babies were put out on a sunporch every day.[21]

In 1963 the 40-bed Cobham House Nurses' Home, a two-level white concrete slab on pilotis that is still a landmark on the skyline above Wellington airport, was opened beside the hospital. The fair-faced concrete frame, finished with Gunac sprayed concrete,

↑

Karitane Hospital, Christchurch, c.1920.

↖

Jessie Hope Gibbons Maternity Hospital, Whanganui.

←

Townley Street St Helen's Maternity Hospital, Gisborne, 1963.

↑

St Helen's Hospital, Invercargill.

↗

Truby King Harris Hospital, Dunedin, c.1938–45.

is infilled with an aluminium curtain wall with baked enamel panels. The *New Zealand Institute of Architects Journal* credits the design of this to John Standish, although it is unclear whether he was employed by Gray Young, Morton, Young, Calder & Fowler at the time, or working in collaboration with them.

As the public system began to provide many of the functions of the Karitane hospitals, they were closed from 1978 onwards; Invercargill's was the last to go, in 1980. The factory ceased production in 1986.[22]

++

A new Wellington St Helen's Hospital, designed by Calder, Fowler, Styles & Turner, the firm that had evolved from Gray Young's practice, opened in Coromandel Street in 1965. The practice also designed the 1975 nurses' home and kitchen there.[23]

In 1964 the three remaining St Helen's hospitals in Auckland, Wellington and Christchurch were transferred from the Health Department to their respective local

↖

John Stewart's house in Whanganui, photographed in 1911, before it became Stewart Karitane Hospital in 1919.

↑

Karitane Hospital, Invercargill.

←

Karitane Hospital, Mount Albert, Auckland.

↑

The Melrose, Wellington, premises of the Karitane Products Society, 1940.

↗

Truby King and Lady King Hospital, Wellington.

→

St Helen's Hospital, Wellington, 1965.

hospital boards. Excluding these, and hospitals such as North Shore and Waitākere, which started as maternity hospitals but were intended to grow into larger general hospitals, by 1969 there were 82 separate public maternity hospitals, that is, not sited on main hospital campuses. With an average of 11 beds – some had as few as three – these were very small facilities, typically found in smaller rural townships from Kaikohe in the north to Bluff in the south.[24]

6 →

War, Depression and the welfare state

1914–1945

LIKE THE REST OF THE WORLD, New Zealand became embroiled in the First World War, suffered in the influenza pandemic that killed millions in 1918 and endured the Great Depression that struck in the late 1920s. The first Labour government, elected under Michael Joseph Savage in 1935, expanded the welfare state, including the development of state housing and the passing of the 1938 Social Security Act, which gave all New Zealanders the right to free hospital healthcare, putting increased pressure on the public hospital system.

By the early years of the twentieth century the increasing provision of clean water and better sanitation was having a marked impact on public health, but New Zealand continued to remain subject to such diseases as tuberculosis. Greater urbanisation caused more rapid spread of infection through the community – typhoid, measles and, from 1914, poliomyelitis. Devastating outbreaks of polio, as it was known, continued until the development of a vaccine by Jonas Salk in 1956.[1]

The discovery of blood types in 1901 allowed for safe transfusions. Both the latter, and the pioneering plastic surgery techniques developed by New Zealander Harold Gillies, owed their development to the First World War. Although Scottish physician and microbiologist Alexander Fleming had discovered penicillin in 1928, it took some years for it to be generally available and antibiotics were used in the Second World War. Thanks to the work of New Zealand plastic surgeon Archibald McIndoe, who pioneered life-changing treatments for severely burned wartime air crew, burns treatment also advanced in the 1940s.[2]

The implications of some innovations took some time to be understood, however. In 1914 Arthur Wohlmann, balneologist at the Rotorua Bath House, began adding radon to the waters to create an early form of radiation therapy. Radium institutes were established at Dunedin Hospital in 1917, Wellington in 1923 and Christchurch in 1924. However, the hazards for inadequately protected staff were only realised years, sometimes decades, later.[3]

Innovations in sanitary practices and the development of medical technology increasingly drew middle- and upper-class patients to public hospitals for the first time, rather than relying on treatment at home or in small private facilities. Public hospitals continued to be operated by the various district hospital boards, and the Department of Health controlled the psychiatric (or mental, as they were called) hospitals, the St Helen's maternity hospitals and two special hospitals, Queen Mary at Hanmer Springs and Queen Elizabeth at Rotorua.[4]

Overseas, the pavilion principle for hospital planning evolved into what historian Michael Murphy has referred to as the 'bar' concept, which allowed for a mixture of open wards and wards with private rooms, which in turn allowed for the control of infection and noise. More complex planning aimed to maximise efficiency and allowed for the accommodation of new technical apparatus and medical specialisation, and the emphasis on the efficient planning of factories began to cross over into hospital design.[5]

From Arts and Crafts to Edwardian Baroque, early twentieth-century architects in New Zealand followed the styles being developed internationally: Art Deco, Spanish Mission and early modernism. Until the School of Architecture at the University of Auckland was established in 1918, the country had no formal tertiary training in architecture. Instead, aspiring architects served articles of apprenticeship with established practitioners or went overseas.

Even once the Auckland school opened, it could be difficult for those from other parts of the country to attend full-time. As a result, the Architectural Students Association formed an atelier in Wellington in 1918 – another opened later in Christchurch – in which students undertook graded exercises in design while in employment. The 1931 Hawke's Bay earthquake led to a major upgrading of New Zealand's building standards, particularly for seismic design.[6]

++

In Northland, Rawene (later Hokianga) Hospital opened with 12 beds in 1904, in the converted Wharf Hotel (now a Category 2 Historic Place) and moved to a new site in 1909.[7] When, in 1914, Scottish-trained George Marshall McCall Smith became medical superintendent of Rawene Hospital, which served a mainly Māori population, he found that the hospital's water supply and other amenities were substandard and the Hokianga Hospital and Charitable Aid Board would not upgrade them. Through his efforts, by 1920 the hospital had 39 beds, with an operating theatre and an x-ray room. Next, after organising fundraising that included the proceeds from an illegal casino, he managed to get a new 40-bed hospital built. He was also very much responsible for the planning; Auckland architects Chilwell & Trevithick committed his ideas to paper. Smith acted as clerk of works during the construction of the new facility, which was 'reported to be the most up-to-date in the country when it opened in 1928'. Its features included greater subdivision of spaces to prevent cross-infection and exposed services to facilitate maintenance.[8]

Vernon Brown, lecturer at the Auckland School of Architecture and mentor to the Group Architects, and his business partner Robin Simpson designed buildings at Rāwene in the 1940s, including a nurses' home. Several other architects also worked on the hospital: Charles Corne of Whangārei designed the 1954 x-ray wing, and J. M. Stiffe worked on a rest home a year later. Later developments included a two-storey nurses' home in 1956 and a children's ward in 1962. A health centre opened in 1987, with six consulting rooms and two treatment rooms, and in 1993 a community trust took over the running of the hospital.[9]

↑

The opening of Rawene Hospital in Hokianga, 1909.

↩

Napier Hospital nurses' home after the earthquake of 1931.

Bay of Islands Hospital opened with 12 beds in Kawakawa in 1913; the architect credited was A. M. McLeod of Whangārei. An isolation ward was added in 1922, a female tuberculosis shelter in 1926 and a maternity annex in 1927. A larger tuberculosis block added further up the hill in 1943 was expanded later in the war to a design by the Public Works Department to provide 10 beds for tuberculosis patients and 20 beds for military patients.[10]

A new men's ward was added to Whangarei Hospital in 1914, a women's ward and maternity annex in 1918 and a children's ward in 1919; the foundation stone for this last building records McLeod as the architect. In 1913 a second floor was added to the nurses' home. After purchasing the Mann estate in 1929, the hospital converted the house on it into the Kowhai Cottage for old men.[11]

The 1927 nurses' home at Whangarei Hospital was by Horace Massey and Alfred Morgan (see page 261). The latter was appointed architect to the board, but thanks to the Depression little work was carried out in the 1930s. A new women's ward opened in 1937, a maternity annex in 1948.[12]

Pressure to establish a hospital in the Northland town of Kaitāia continued for decades. Eventually Kaitaia Memorial Hospital opened in 1927, with three maternity and three emergency beds. Despite considerable public protest, the hospital at Mangōnui closed in 1934 and most of its buildings were moved to Kaitāia to create a 54-bed facility.[13]

++

↖

Bay of Islands Hospital, Kawakawa, 1958.

↑

Whangarei Hospital, c.1910s.

↗

Whangarei Hospital nurses' home, 1924.

When Auckland's Costley Home in Epsom became seriously overcrowded at around the turn of the century, Edward Bartley was asked to prepare preliminary plans for its extension. The hospital board did not, however, seem satisfied with these and called for applications from other architects. George Wilfred (G. W.) Allsop was eventually selected and appointed architect to the Auckland Hospital Board, replacing Bartley.

A new male infirmary ward for 33 patients was built in 1906. In 1917 Allsop added another floor, enabled by raising the roof 4 metres, and extra female wards, providing total accommodation for 178 males and 58 females.[14] The building, which still stands, is generally Edwardian in style, with a symmetrical front elevation, central entrance, roof cupola and tall sash windows. The exposed half-timbering on the gables and in the towers at each end is

Elizabethan, and the brickwork, terracotta roof tiles and finials impart a Queen Anne touch. The verandahs, a response to local climatic conditions, allowed patients to enjoy the fresh air while being protected from the sun.

Twelve tuberculosis annexes were added in 1919, and in 1924 the institution was renamed the Auckland Infirmary. A separate female facility, since demolished, opened west of the main block in 1923. The first wing of a new two-storey brick nurses' home opened in 1925; the original 1912 nurses' home was demolished in 1964.[15]

At Auckland Hospital, Allsop also designed the 1918 two-storey Princess Mary Hospital for Children, with four wards providing accommodation for 100 patients and, about 1922, the 146-bed extension to the nurses' home. He also designed the four-storey 140-bed G.U. (probably genitourinary, later Wallace) block erected in 1925 beside the domain gates at Auckland Hospital. A three-storey infectious diseases block was added at the hospital in 1931.[16]

Allsop also worked south of Auckland and had designed extensions and alterations made in 1911 to Bartley's Waihi Hospital. After being appointed architect to the local hospital board in 1915, Allsop was commissioned to design the expansion of Taumarunui's first six-bed cottage hospital on Ward Street, designed by the Public Works Department in 1909, to 20 beds, and in 1916 added a new nurses' home. He designed the new 52-bed (for 34 men and 18 women) single-storey brick-and-tile hospital when it was relocated to the current riverside site on Kururau Road in 1925. Also credited to Allsop, in 1919, are a two-storey 25-bed brick-and-tile nurses' home, plus a water tower and a 1923 laundry block and mortuary. The nurses' home was extended several times. Plans for this, by F. L. and B. E. O'Reilly, are dated 1937 and, by the Architectural Branch of the Health Department, 1941.[17]

At Thames Hospital, Allsop designed a new nurses' home in 1920 and a new ward wing the following year. A maternity annex was developed in the old Thames High School building north of the nurses' home in 1924, and by 1938 the hospital's bed capacity had reached 100.[18] Allsop also designed the 1923 brick Franklin Memorial Hospital in Waiuku. Initially a nine-bed general and maternity hospital, it was converted to a geriatric hospital in 1977.[19]

↖

Wallace Block, Auckland Hospital, 1960s.

↑

Auckland Infirmary, Green Lane.

↗

Princess Mary Hospital for Children, Auckland, 1918.

Recognising that early intervention could prevent more serious illness in future, the Auckland Hospital Board opened a separate dental hospital in 1909, then built a new one in Kitchener Street in 1917. It is possible this was also designed by Allsop, given the date and style.[20] After a dispute with the Auckland Hospital Board over the specification of AC rather than DC motors for the hospital's laundry, which he considered a 'small technical matter, capable of adjustment', Allsop retired in 1926.[21]

++

After moving from Stratford to Hamilton in 1906, John Willing Warren was appointed architect to the Waikato Hospital Board, having held a similar position when he was in Taranaki. He appears,

↑

Taumarunui Hospital, 1909.

↖

Taumarunui Hospital, 1925.

←

Franklin Memorial Hospital, Pukekohe, 1923.

↗

Dental Hospital, Auckland, 1917.

however, to have carried out earlier work at Waikato Hospital: he is credited with the design of the 1893 superintendent's house, later known as Hockin House and now the headquarters of the Waikato Historical Society. Warren formed several partnerships in Hamilton, including one with engineer John Blechynden in the 1910s and a later one with Gordon S. Reid.[22]

A second staff residence opened at Waikato Hospital in 1914, and a three-bedroom staff residence, Kowhai House, was added in 1920. A second operating theatre also opened in 1920. Waikato Museum holds drawings by Warren & Blechynden for a 1916 nurses' home, the 1918 26-bed old persons' home, the 20-bed infectious diseases ward of 1919, and for a ward labelled 'Russell' in 1922. Electricity, with power provided by a steam generator, was reticulated through the hospital in 1916.[23]

In 1903 the Department of Public Health established Te Waikato, near Cambridge, as a sanatorium for the treatment of tuberculosis. Around 1906 the local hospital board bought the Thornton homestead, which was extended to form the Cambridge Sanatorium. When it closed in 1922, the building was relocated to Waikato Hospital, as part of the expansion of the infectious diseases ward, and to provide a new paediatrics ward. This first 60-bed children's ward, later known as the Sunshine Ward, opened in 1923. By the following year Waikato Hospital had 250 beds.[24]

In 1927 the 36-bed Ward 4 (Douglas), 36-bed Ward 5 (Rothwell) and a two-storey 50-bed brick nurses' home were added to the hospital campus. (The nurses' home was probably the one for which Waikato Museum holds drawings dated 1924 by both Warren & Blechynden and Warren & Reid, implying a change in the partnership around that time.) A new upper level added to the infectious diseases ward in 1931 provided 34 beds. The 18-bed Campbell Johnstone maternity ward, opened that year, was expanded in 1944 and 1954 to give a total of 54 beds and a delivery suite. The south end of this was removed in 1992 and replaced with a new kitchen and cafeteria. The remaining structure is one of the last remnants of the earlier hospital buildings.[25]

The former Waikato Hospital Board office building on Hamilton's Hood Street was built to a design by Thomas Mahoney in 1903. Following a fire in 1911, Warren renovated this in a Stripped Classical style.[26] He also designed the 12-bed 1926 Huntly Hospital for the Waikato board, using the creamy honey-coloured brick for which the district is renowned.

Te Puea Hērangi

↘

The great-granddaughter of Pōtatau Te Wherowhero, the first Māori king, Te Puea Hērangi (Waikato) was a prominent figure in the Kīngitanga movement. Determined to give her people a new home after the devasting effects of the 1860s land confiscations and the 1918 influenza epidemic, in the 1920s Te Puea set up a new community at Ngāruawāhia, the original home of the Kīngitanga. This would be Tūrangawaewae, the place to stand, promised by her grandfather, the second Māori King, Tāwhiao Te Wherowhero.[1]

The first building was Tūrangawaewae House, erected as a kauhanganui, or parliament building, for the Kīngitanga, with John Willing Warren of Warren & Blechynden credited as the architect.[2] Te Puea then led the building of the meeting house Māhinārangi, completed in 1929, which was also intended to serve as a hospital, offering the benefits of European healthcare in a traditional setting. Ngāti Porou leader Āpirana Ngata provided many of the carvers and craftspeople, and arranged for the plans to be drawn by Richard Wills, who had built the School of Māori Arts and Crafts in Rotorua for him.[3]

To encourage her people to seek treatment there, Te Puea wanted the facility to be staffed by Māori doctors and nurses, and to have a familiar and hence comforting form. The traditional wharenui design was modified to allow for a free central aisle: there are no poles running along the ridgeline. On the side walls windows allow for ventilation and natural light and there is a second covered entrance. However, health authorities turned down Te Puea's application to use the building as a hospital, and instead it is used as a reception hall. It can only be speculated whether the outcome would have been different if Te Puea had engaged Warren, given his considerable hospital experience by then.[4]

↖

Māhinārangi, Ngāruawāhia.

↑

Te Puia Hērangi, 1937.

↗

Māhinārangi interior.

In 1910 the people of Te Kūiti decided to build a hospital as a memorial to King Edward VII, who had died in May of that year. After considerable fundraising and campaigning, the town's first public hospital, designed by Warren & Reid in red brick with a tiled roof, eventually opened in 1926 with 21 beds, plus an eight-bed isolation unit and accommodation for nine nurses. A nine-bed maternity unit was added in 1938.[27]

++

In the Bay of Plenty, Tauranga's current hospital site, between Cameron Road and Clarke Street, had been gazetted as far back as 1879, but the first hospital did not open there until 1914. A house on the corner of Cameron Road and Sixth Avenue, known as the Victoria Hospital, served as a fever facility for various epidemics in the town until 1913.

The first building on the current site, designed by Tauranga architect Herbert Henry Clemson, consisted of a 250-square-metre E-shaped building with a four-bed male ward and a two-bed female ward – both opening onto a verandah – an accident room, a surgery, a kitchen and a matron's room. An attached surgery was lined with asbestos cement, 'rendering it germ-proof'. An isolation ward, also by Clemson, was added two years later.[28] These buildings soon proved inadequate, and a larger, more modern facility was proposed. Despite Allsop offering his services, the Tauranga Hospital and Charitable Aid Board decided to appoint Clemson as their architect and commissioned him to proceed with the design. When the new 46-bed hospital building was opened in 1925, the existing building was converted into a nurses' home.[29]

Clemson also designed the Te Puke Maternity Hospital, which opened in 1925, to replace a small cottage hospital established in 1918 and eventually closed in 1989. A modest maternity hospital was also opened in Katikati in 1942. Once the buildings at Tauranga and Te Puke were completed, the board saw no need to retain an architect and Clemson's part-time appointment was terminated.[30]

↖

The opening of the Cambridge Sanatorium, 1903.

↑

Huntly Hospital, now a hotel.

↗

Te Kuiti Hospital, 1926.

The Anglicans opened a small mission hospital in Whakatāne in 1913, and four years later the Bay of Plenty Hospital and Charitable Aid Board finalised an agreement with the church to use part of this as a temporary public hospital. Over the next decade, several buildings were moved onto the site. After several locations had been considered, the current public hospital, on the corner of Garaway and Stewart streets, was completed in 1923. Constructed in concrete, with 24 beds, an operating room and an x-ray room, it was surrounded by other buildings that had been relocated from the mission hospital. The designer, Harold (Harry) L. D. West, was architect to the Bay of Plenty Hospital Board.

A maternity unit was opened in 1927 and in 1928 the first nurses' home, also by West, was built and a doctor's residence added. In 1931 West recommended strengthening the hospital buildings in the wake of the Hawke's Bay earthquake. A laundry and a boiler house were added in 1937, and the hospital was modified further in 1940 with an expanded women's ward, which was later converted into the psychiatric unit. By 1948 Whakatane Hospital had 100 beds.[31]

A new cottage hospital opened in Ōpōtiki in 1914, on Woodlands Road on the western side of the Waioeka River. Tender notices for this list the addresses of both Clemson and local architect Thomas H. White, so it is unclear which of them was the designer. The hospital burned down in 1946, and a new maternity hospital in the township was used as a temporary replacement until a new facility was opened in 1952. It is also unclear for which hospital in the town the 1943 drawings by Edgecumbe, White & Leigh apply.[32]

++

In Taranaki, there had been attempts to establish a hospital at Stratford since 1894, but the Department of Health resisted these as there were already hospitals at New Plymouth and Hāwera. Stratford Hospital eventually opened with 14 beds in 1907. The main building had a nine-bed male ward and a five-bed female ward, with a services block attached to the end of each and connected by a dining room that was later converted into a six-bed children's ward. There was also a theatre block with a matron's flat, a kitchen and a nurses' dining room. The buildings were of brick with tiled roofs.[33]

The designer of the original hospital is thought to have been John Willing Warren, then the Stratford Hospital Board's architect, but after the opening he resigned and left the district. His replacement, John D. Healy, continued to work for the board for more than 25 years. In 1919 the wards were expanded with a further 15 beds and a nurses' home was added and then extended in 1925. A 10-bed maternity block opened in 1923. In 1930 part of Portia Street, between Romeo Street and Opunake Road, was purchased and added to the hospital site, and in 1939 a section of Romeo Street was added. The main building was extended with two additional 12-bed wards and an antenatal block added in 1931 to a design by Healy.[34]

↖

Tauranga Hospital, 1914.

↑

The opening of Whakatane Hospital, 1923.

↗

Te Puke Hospital.

In many regional centres, the buildings at their hospitals were the work of one architect or practice over a long period. New Plymouth was no exception. In 1903 local architect Frank Messenger prepared a plan for the Barrett Street Hospital and designed the early timber nurses' homes of 1902 and 1905. Another home, built in 1908, was replaced in 1922 by a roughcast concrete building designed by Messenger and Horace (Victor) Samuel Griffiths, with whom he formed a partnership in 1917 after the latter ended his partnership with James Sanderson.

Extended in 1928, 1936, 1945 and 1950, it is now the last remaining building on the site. Messenger also designed the old persons' home at Barrett Street, dating from about 1905.[35]

Messenger, Griffiths & Taylor – they were joined by W. Norman Taylor in about 1920 – designed other buildings on the site, including the x-ray annex, about 1924, the 1927 board offices, the 1932 two-storey George Tabor building for children and a laundry and a store. A medical superintendent's house was built on the corner of Barrett and West streets in 1926. Messenger & Taylor designed an isolation block and a laundry in 1931, plus additions and alterations to the outpatient block in 1933 and the kitchen in 1934.

Later buildings on the site by Messenger, Taylor & Wolfe, as the firm was by then, included a 1938 chest block or tuberculosis ward, a maternity unit in 1940 and an outpatient building in 1945, along with additions and alterations to the x-ray annex, laundry and kitchen through the early 1940s. In 1950 a tutorial block was also added above the chest block.[36]

Griffiths appears to have left the partnership in the 1930s but continued to carry out work at the hospital. Griffiths & Stephenson are credited with additions to the operating theatre and kitchen block in 1936, and Griffiths & Syme also carried out work in 1944 in association with Duffill & Gibson.[37]

As architect to the Opunake Hospital Board, Victor Griffiths designed the 1922 Opunake Cottage Hospital. Since it had only three maternity and two emergency beds, the Department of Health considered it too small to be a general hospital and would only permit it to handle maternity cases. In 1990 it became a rest home operated by a community trust.[38]

++

In Tairāwhiti a hospital was built at Te Araroa in 1928–29, although there appears to have been a small facility there before then. The architect of this transitional Californian bungalow-style building is unknown. The hospital was short-lived, closing in 1932. In Gisborne, the nurses' home at Cook Hospital was extended in 1923 to a design by local architects Burr & Mirfield. The Cook

↖

Stratford Hospital.

↑

Frank Messenger.
H. Victor S. Griffiths.

↗

Opunake Cottage Hospital, 1922.

Maternity Home, designed by Frederick Howard Forge, opened in 1935 on the hospital site. Forge worked in Wellington before moving, in about 1910, to Gisborne, where he maintained a practice until at least 1940. Along with a new nurses' home in 1941, a chest, or tuberculosis, block and a polyclinic block in 1945, all designed by Natusch & Sons, other additions at Cook Hospital in the later 1940s included a new maternity home and a boiler house.[39]

++

Both the 1908 Margaret Williams Ward for women and the 1910 children's ward at Napier Hospital were designed by Wellington firm Crichton & McKay (see page 144). An x-ray room was added in 1913 and both the 16-bed Shrimpton Ward for children and the Jellicoe Ward for convalescent soldiers opened in 1918. In 1915, in response to community fundraising for a maternity home, farmer Leslie Harding McHardy donated the town house built in 1908 for his family in Bracken Street, near Napier Hospital. Used in its first year for convalescing soldiers, it was extended in 1917. The brick portion was severely damaged in the 1931 earthquake. After the Arohaina maternity unit opened at Napier Hospital in 1977, McHardy became a home for elderly women and is now used as boutique accommodation.[40]

Other developments at Napier included further tuberculosis shelters in 1923, the Midgely Ward in 1927 and the Coleman Ward the following year.[41] The four-storey 80-bed nurses' home at Napier Hospital, opened in 1926, was designed by Horace Massey and Alfred Morgan.[42]

The Hawke's Bay earthquake of the morning of 3 February 1931, which caused catastrophic damage to both Napier and Hastings and the surrounding area, killed 256 people, and almost completely destroyed Napier Hospital; 21 perished there, both staff and patients. Eight nurses and three office staff were also killed when the nurses' home collapsed,[43] and the McHardy Maternity Home was seriously damaged. The recently opened, and relatively undamaged, cottage hospital in Hastings (see page 138) became a dressing station, preparing patients for evacuation to hospitals outside the region. It was far too small, however, to cope with the number of casualties, and with Napier Hospital out of action, temporary hospitals were set up at the racecourses in both towns.[44]

++

At Wanganui Hospital, the McKenny Ward for tuberculosis patients opened in 1935. In 1938, based on the similar building they had completed in New Plymouth, Messenger, Taylor & Wolfe were commissioned to design the Newcombe Ward specialist infectious diseases block. This 33-bed unit replaced a predecessor that had been hurriedly built for the 1918 influenza epidemic and was pulled down in 1937.[45] It became a polio ward in the 1940s and later a day hospital with physiotherapy and occupational therapy services. An ambulance building also opened in 1938.[46] Clifford Newton Hood designed the 1937 laboratory and additions to the kitchen in 1943. He was also responsible for alterations to the Jubilee Home in Whanganui in the 1940s.[47]

Raetihi Hospital opened in 1922, changing its name to Waimarino Hospital in 1935. Newton Hood designed several buildings there, including the 1941 nurses' home, a maternity block two years later, a boiler house and a laundry. By the time it closed in the 1990s and was replaced by the Waimarino Health Centre, it had 11 general and four maternity beds. The Whare Ora Hospital in Hunterville opened as the Bethel Home for the Elderly in 1925 and became the Whare Ora private hospital in 1934. In 1946, after it was bought by the hospital board, it became a general and maternity hospital. It closed in 1976 but continued as a community-run home for the elderly until 1989. Newton Hood also designed the 12-bed, single-storey Puanui maternity block, which opened at Taihape Hospital in 1951.[48]

↑

Te Araroa Hospital, Tairāwhiti, 1966.

↖

Cook Hospital, Gisborne, c.1920–29.

↗

Napier Hospital nurses' home, 1929.

→

Napier Hospital nurses' home after the earthquake of 1931.

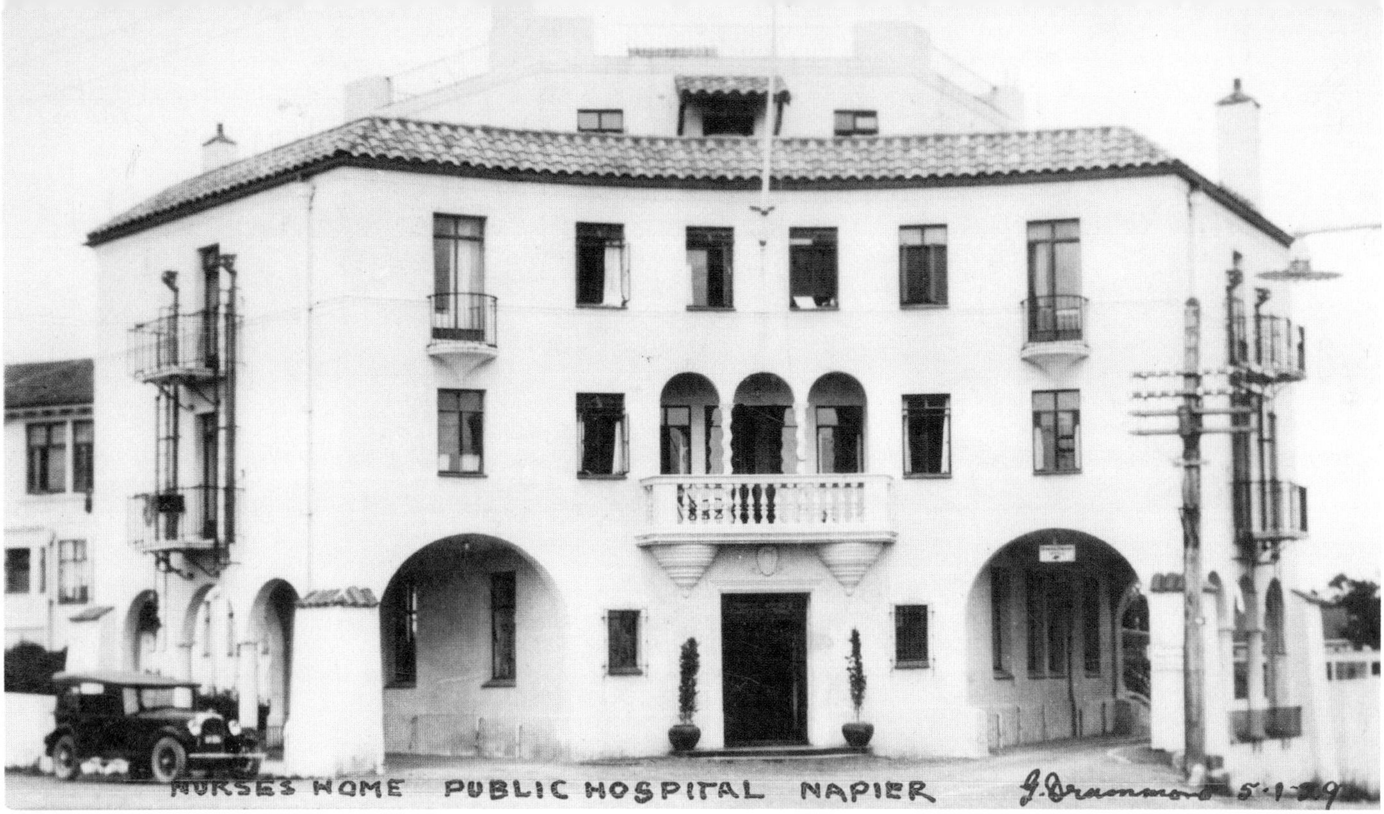

++

The Pukeora Sanatorium opened in 1918 on a hillside between Waipukurau and Takapau to provide care for soldiers returning from the First World War with respiratory illnesses, particularly mustard-gas injuries. When the Featherston Military Training Camp closed in the 1920s, several of its buildings were relocated to Pukeora, including one that became an isolation ward. As the demand for military rehabilitation decreased, the hospital was gradually repurposed for the treatment of tuberculosis patients, with the addition of verandahs and open-air sheds.

Davies & Phillips designed the 1942 ward block, which provided 64 beds. In 1957 the sanatorium was converted to a home for physically disabled young people, modelled on the Wilson Home in Auckland's Takapuna. The occupational therapy block and school opened in 1966. In 1998, as care was devolved to the community, the facility was closed and now operates as a vineyard and function centre.[49] As a result of the influenza pandemic, Danish-born architect O. A. (Oscar) Jorgensen designed an infectious diseases annex at Waipukurau Hospital, which began welcoming patients in 1919.[50]

Dannevirke Hospital, designed by Norwegian-born local architect Ragnar Jenssen, opened in 1906, and Oscar Jorgensen designed the 1917 isolation wards. The 1925 children's ward and nurses' home were designed by the Public Works Department, while local architect C. J. Kirk designed alterations to the administration building in 1937, and the Health Department altered the boiler house in 1939. The hospital continued to expand into the 1940s; at one point the bed numbers reached 180. Reginald Thorrold-Jaggard designed most of the work there up to 1960, including the 1944 kitchen, the 1950 nurses' home and a new clinical services building, commissioned in 1961.

George W. Callander designed further alterations in the 1960s and Brogden & Davidson were responsible for the 1974 administration building. A purpose-built psychopaedic facility also opened in the early 1970s. The hospital closed in 1997 when the new nine-bed Dannevirke Community Hospital opened.[51]

++

In the early years of the twentieth century Danish-born and -trained local architect Ludolf Georg (later Ludolph George) West was responsible for many of the new buildings at Palmerston North's hospital: an eight-bed women's ward block in 1903, an isolation unit known as the infectious diseases hospital in 1906, the two-storey Royal Alexandra female ward block in

1907, an operating theatre and a laundry in 1908, a 'padded cell' in 1909, a tuberculosis ward for women added in 1910 and, in 1912, a consumption annex. His firm, L. G. West & Son, was also responsible for the 1913 children's ward and the 1915 50-bed brick nurses' home, which replaced the original built in 1906 and was enlarged in the 1930s.[52]

In the 1920s, however, the Palmerston North Hospital Board decided to engage architects from outside the district to design the next wave of expansion, with the 1920 Princess Mary and Prince of Wales wards by Wellington architects Crichton & McKay. The Technical Inspector's branch of the Department of Health designed the District Maternity Home opened on Heretaunga Street in 1926, which later became a nurses' home before being turned into offices, the 1930 two-ward Wilson Block, with Wards 11 and 12, and a new operating theatre in 1931.[53]

Keen not to lose further work to outside practices, local architects lobbied hard to be engaged for the next major hospital projects, including the proposed administration building, through a body known as the Palmerston North Guild of Registered Architects and Structural

↖

Raetihi Hospital, 1923.

↑

Pukeora Sanatorium, Waipukurau.

↗

Dannevirke Hospital, 1909.

Engineers, formed in 1926 'for the mutual edification and fostering of good fellowship amongst architects'. The chair at the first meeting was Robert Edwards, who had designed a private hospital in Palmerston North in 1902; Ernest West succeeded him in 1927. The original secretary, Robin Hood, appears to have remained in that role for most of the guild's existence. Other members included Oscar Jorgensen, Reginald W. Thorrold-Jaggard and Arthur Robert Allen.[54]

By 1934 the guild seems to have become more commercially oriented. A set of articles, most likely from that year, stated that Allen, Hood, Jaggard and West (now of L. G. West, Son & Hornibrook) had agreed to be 'participants in the preparation of plans and such other works connected with the erection of an administrative block for the Palmerston North Hospital Board'. West's practice would be entitled to two-fifths of the remuneration, with Allen, Hood and Jaggard receiving a fifth each. The articles reinforced the maintenance of a united front, and that all decisions were to be made by the guild as a whole.[55]

In 1935 tender notices under Hood's name were made for the administration building at Palmerston North Hospital, as well as the additions and alterations to the old persons' home at Awapuni, which were added to the guild's scope. No individual architect seems to have been responsible for the design: at the opening in 1936, the design was credited to the Palmerston North Guild of Architects. On the ground floor of this brick building, which formed the entrance to the hospital from Heretaunga Street, was an admissions office and an automatic telephone exchange on one side, with accommodation for reception, admission and the medical examination of patients on the other. The first floor had house surgeons' quarters, a laboratory, a boardroom and offices.[56]

The administration building was the last for which guild members were responsible,

however, as the board raised concerns about overcharging. Despite a submission by West, Thorrold-Jaggard and Allen, the board decided to employ its own architect; in 1936 Victor Robert John Hean accepted the position of resident architect to the board, a position that he held until 1942.[57] The guild held its penultimate meeting in 1936 and was wound up a decade later.

It is unclear who designed the accident and emergency block, built next to the administration building later in the decade. Drawings for it are on the title block of the Palmerston North Hospital Board, but unlike other buildings there around that time, they do not carry Hean's name. Graeme Laurenson, who worked at the Department of Health in the 1930s, and would become chief architect to the Health Department before leaving to establish his own practice in 1947, recalled preparing plans for buildings at Palmerston North Hospital while working there, so it was possibly a collaborative effort.[58]

Hean designed the two-storey 1939 children's ward, the 1942 Centennial Block and a 48-bed isolation unit the same year, as well as carrying out work at the Awapuni Home. Hean was succeeded by George W. Callander, who designed the 1942 tutorial block for nurse training and operating theatre alterations in 1947. A military block, which was intended to be temporary but lasted for more than 50 years after being converted to four general wards, was designed by the Public Works Department, as was a new outpatient block, housing pharmacy, physiotherapy and x-ray facilities, opened in 1944. Callander later joined the Wests' practice, and the Levin Maternity Hospital, dating from 1952, was designed by L. G. West, Son & Callander.

↖

Palmerston North Hospital entrance and administration building.

↑

Palmerston North Hospital accident and emergency block.

Public works

From 1852 responsibility for most public works was given to the provincial governments, whose architects designed the asylums in their areas. Design of general hospitals was primarily done by the private sector, as hospital boards had a vested interest in supporting businesses in their districts and hence tended to employ local architects. As part of his 'grand go-ahead' improvement programme, in 1870 Julius Vogel established the Public Works Department, which became responsible for government infrastructure throughout the country when the provinces were abolished in 1876.

William Henry Clayton, the first and only colonial architect, from 1869 to his death in 1877, was initially independent, before his office, then known as Public Domains and Buildings, was incorporated into the Public Works Department in 1873. As the programme wound down and the Long Depression took hold the government proposed to close the department but retained it temporarily to oversee relief works.[1]

After Clayton's death, his role in the North Island was unofficially taken over by Pierre Finch Martineau Burrows, rather than Clayton's assistant, Charles Edward Beatson.[2] Burrows had a staff of two, Beatson and the cadet William Crichton. Private architects were to be commissioned for public work in the South Island, and from 1884, when Burrows was dismissed, for the entire country. The Public Buildings branch was transferred to the Defence Department in 1889 to complete buildings still in progress before its proposed closure. When the Public Works Department was eventually retained, the Public Buildings office was merged back into it in 1890 while maintaining a degree of autonomy. The emergence of a well-organised architectural department in the public service would become a source of significant concern to architects in private practice.[3]

++

The first designated Government Architect, John Campbell, who was appointed at the end of the nineteenth century, designed extensions and alterations to six of the major mental asylums: Avondale, Porirua, Nelson, Seaview, Sunnyside and Seacliff. He also worked on some general hospital buildings; his work at Westland Hospital in Hokitika was probably due to its connection to Seaview. As well, Campbell designed the 1902 buildings at the Sumner Deaf and Mute Institute (now Van Asch College) in Christchurch, which consisted of a director's house and separate boys' and girls' blocks, and anticipated the construction of villa-style accommodation such as that later developed for Tokanui.[4]

John Thomas Mair, who succeeded Campbell as Government Architect in 1923, appears to have been much more active in procuring work from hospital boards around the country, as during his tenure the number of general hospital projects taken on by the Public Works Department increased significantly. Mair designed the 1927 nurses' home at Gore Hospital and possibly other work there around that time.[5] At Wairoa Hospital, the Public Works Department designed a kitchen block and alterations to the women's ward in 1926, and an administration block in 1927.

As well as checking and approving other architects' designs, the Technical Inspector's branch of the Department of Health, led by Charles Scott Allan, took on design commissions during this era. They designed additions to the wards and kitchen at Wairoa Hospital in 1929, and a tuberculosis ward at Waipawa Hospital in Waipukurau around the same time. No doubt some boards saw this as a way of ensuring that their proposals were approved, but several began to express their frustration at the lack of availability of Allan and his staff, as they were

↖

Sunnyside Hospital administration building, c.1980s.

↑

Hawke's Bay Fallen Soldiers' Memorial Hospital, Hastings.

working on hospitals across the country, including several on the West Coast. Architects were brought in from the Public Works Department to assist, but boards complained that they were not being provided with the level of expertise that they had been promised, and several went back to engaging private architects. Additions in 1940 to the women's ward at Wairoa were designed by local architect Harry Ratcliffe. At Waipukurau Hospital a two-storey brick nurses' home opened in 1926, an administration block in 1927 and the former office area was transformed into a children's ward, all designed by the Public Works Department, but subsequent work there was designed by local private practices.

John Mair also designed the 1928 Hawke's Bay Fallen Soldiers' Memorial Hospital.[6] By the beginning of the twentieth century, Hastings had grown rapidly to become the principal service centre for the surrounding rural area. The idea of a hospital for the town was first raised in 1898, and proposals continued as, although only 20 kilometres away, Napier's hospital was considered too distant for emergency cases and to allow regular visits from Hastings. Napier's site was constrained by its topography, whereas Hastings had ample flat land for development. Nevertheless, the Napier Hospital Board continued to resist the idea of a second hospital in its district.

The establishment of an emergency hospital at the racecourse during the 1918 influenza pandemic revived calls for a hospital, and in 1919 the board finally agreed to establish a small hospital in Hastings with a maternity ward and a casualty ward. In 1920 the Hawke's Bay Fallen Soldiers' Memorial Committee, formed the year before, bought The Ridge, a 17.2-hectare property a mile from town. They commissioned local architects Hyland & Phillips to prepare sketch plans, but these were well over budget, and the Depression hindered further progress.

The Department of Health approved a reduced plan for a cottage hospital with a 10-bed maternity ward and a 10-bed accident and children's ward, but the Napier community remained concerned that the hospital could grow to rival their own. In the face of continued cost concerns, the Department of Health submitted its own alternative, and supposedly cheaper, design prepared by the Government Architect. After further complications, in 1926 the Napier Hospital Board gave approval for Mair to prepare full documentation. The plans were approved, tenders were called and construction at last began in 1927.

The Hawke's Bay Fallen Soldiers' Memorial Hospital opened on Anzac Day 1928. The *Hawke's Bay Herald* of 11 April that year described the completed hospital as a 'low, widespread building of red brick, cream facings, and of glazed plaster, rimu and blue and white silvered tiles between'. From the central memorial entrance hall extended two wings, where 'sun porches and pergolas give an airy and lightsome touch'. The roof was of Marseilles tiles.

Entry to the single-storey Spanish Mission-style building of painted brick was through the memorial hall, with bronze tablets displaying the names of local soldiers who had died.[7] The central administration block also contained a dispensary, an office and doctors' and matron's living quarters. Wings on either side housed single- and four-bed wards with glass-enclosed sunporches. The southern wing had a general ward, an operating theatre, a sterilising plant and an emergency entrance. The northern wing housed a general ward, plus wards for maternity and children. In total the building housed 20 patients, including seven maternity beds, with room for a further 10 on the sunporches. The two-storey 12-room nurses' home of similar design, the architect of which is unclear, sat to the south. Plans for an addition to house outpatients were approved in 1930.[8]

++

There were some criticisms of the loss of commissions by private practitioners and the monotony of the Government Architect's designs, but this was also a period of rapid growth, and the department was in no position to dominate the market. Similar criticisms arose in the early 1930s, when the government's initial response to the Great Depression was a 75 per cent cut in the public works budget.[9] The department was, however, again retained to manage relief works and Mair supported architects in private practice by giving them work. The expanded public works programme of the first Labour government, elected in 1935, resulted in such Government Architect-designed buildings as the 1940 Children's Dental Clinic in Wellington. The 1931 Hawke's Bay earthquake had also created significant rebuilding work and led to a greater integration of engineers and architects in the design of public buildings.[10]

++

To deliver the large number of buildings required during the Second World War, Robert Adams Patterson, who became Government Architect in 1942, worked closely with Sir James Fletcher, the founder of Fletcher Construction, who had been appointed commissioner of defence construction.[11] Patterson's work in delivering hundreds of buildings for military bases, barracks and hospitals was recognised with the Imperial Service Award.[12]

The Ministry of Works was established in 1945, absorbing both the Public Works Department and the separate Housing Construction Department.[13] Only the Ministry of Works had the necessary size and experience to deal with the backlog of public works delayed by the war and to meet the post-war demands. Both the Depression and the Second World War had, however, restricted training opportunities, leading to a serious skills shortage; staff had to be recruited from overseas. Turnover in the following years was high as staff left the public service to join private enterprise or start their own firms, but some private contractors produced poor work compared with the ministry.[14]

When Patterson's successor in 1952, Francis Gordon Wilson, died suddenly in 1959, Fergus George Frederick Sheppard became acting Government Architect before

↑

John Thomas Mair.
Robert Adams Patterson.

↗

Children's Dental Clinic, Wellington.

being appointed permanently to the role, in which he continued until 1971.[15] From the mid-1960s, the ministry appears to have done little healthcare design work, apart from that on the mental health facilities operated by central government, and buildings such as the Artificial Limb Centre in Auckland. Because hospital boards often objected to the conditions that accompanied the government funding on which they relied, relationships with the bureaucracy in Wellington could be strained.

This may partly explain why the Public Works Department (later the Ministry of Works, then the Ministry of Works and Development from 1973), which was for many years New Zealand's largest multi-disciplinary consultancy, did not design many hospital buildings after the war.[16] Those it did work on tended to be associated with other ministry projects such as hospitals for workers' villages at hydro-electric power schemes. The ministry did, though, cooperate with the Department of Health regarding guidelines on health planning and hospital design. These were produced by the department in 1977 and 1991, the latter with an associated Code of Practice, colloquially known as the 'Blue Books'.[17] One covered demographic projections for regions across the country and recommended numbers of different bed types based on population size. Another gave recommendations for the sizes of different room types and their fitout.

Throughout the twentieth century, Ministry of Works architects were seconded to other departments, including the Department of Health, which also employed architects in its Hospital Technical Branch during the 1940s, and there was movement of staff between them as demand required.

Robert (Bob) H. Barton was appointed chief architect with the Hospitals Division of the Department of Health in 1953. He had joined the Housing Department in 1939 and became a sectional architect at the Ministry of Works in 1950, before being seconded to the Department of Health. His work at Cromwell Hospital in 1960 is described on page 222. Barton, who influenced hospital boards in the careful selection of architects for their projects, retired in 1972 and was succeeded by D. C. Shaw, who had joined the ministry as an architect in 1943 and went to the Health Department in 1964.[18] To improve the efficiency of hospital design, from 1972 a Hospital Design and Evaluation Unit, with the input of clinical staff, made detailed studies of the operation of wards and the movement of staff within them.

++

The public service limited the number of women it employed in the early twentieth century, and banned them from sitting its entry exams until 1913. Nurse Grace Neill, inspector of factories and later assistant inspector of lunatic asylums, and New Zealand's first senior woman public servant, recalled being asked to enter the office at different times to her male colleagues, 'so that the men's feelings would not be hurt'.[19] The labour shortages during the two world wars created more opportunities for women, but often only on a temporary basis. Despite this, five of the first six women to graduate with a Bachelor of Architecture degree in New Zealand worked in the public service, with at least four involved in health design, and government employment offered increasing opportunities for women entering the architectural profession.

In 1933 Alice (Merle) Greenwood was the first New Zealand woman to graduate with a Bachelor of Architecture from the Auckland University College Architecture School. She was also the first woman to work as an architect in the New Zealand public service. With few employment opportunities during the Depression, she worked without pay for Gummer

↖

Francis Gordon Wilson.
Merle Greenwood.
Mary Edwards.

↗

Christchurch Women's Hospital, 1989.

↑

Fergus Sheppard.

& Ford, and later Horace Massey, before joining the Department of Housing Construction in Wellington in 1937. Greenwood was seconded to the Department of Health in 1943, presumably to work on hospital design. She moved to Melbourne in 1944.[20]

In 1935 Dorothy (D. M.) Wills became the second woman in the country to graduate with a Bachelor of Architecture and the second to register as an architect, in 1936. Her fifth-year project at the Auckland Architecture School was for a private hospital and her drawings for this were used in the university's 1935 prospectus. Wills worked for architect H. L. D. West in Tauranga from 1933 to 1936, when she left for Britain, where she spent time with the intelligence service during the war. After her return to New Zealand in 1949, she joined the Housing Division of the Ministry of Works, before being seconded to the Health Department. There she was responsible for the oversight of several hospital projects being undertaken by private consultants.[21]

Marjorie Penty graduated with a Diploma in Architecture in 1937 and worked for Horace Massey from 1938 to 1942. During the war she served in the Women's Auxiliary Air Force before joining the Ministry of Works in 1945. In 1962 Penty was seconded to the Department of Health and in 1972 joined the newly established Hospital Design and Evaluation Unit, where she carried out studies of the services provided at Hāwera, Wellington and Hutt hospitals.[22]

Mary Edwards worked with Eric Miller in Dunedin in 1928 before going to university in Auckland. After graduating in 1938, she joined the Public Works Department, where she worked on a variety of projects, including hospitals. Edwards gained her registration in 1940. She joined Gummer & Ford in 1954, then worked for the Auckland Education Board from 1961 to 1964 before rejoining the Ministry of Works, where she designed the 1971 Whangarei Health Camp.[23]

7

Designing from the heart

IN THE FIRST DECADES of the twentieth century the Wellington-based practice established in 1891 by William Crichton became prominent in health design, responsible for projects from Taranaki to Nelson. While employed by the Public Works Department in the 1880s, Crichton also took on private commissions, including some for work at Wellington Hospital, beginning a long relationship with the local hospital board.

James Hector McKay joined Crichton in practice in 1901. One of their first commissions was the head office building for the Bank of New South Wales on Wellington's Lambton Quay, in which they established their office on the top floor. Although the building was gutted by fire in 1906, it was reinstated in 1907, and the practice remained there until 1958.[1]

Crichton & McKay designed the two-storey, 40-bed Victoria Hospital for the Chronically Incurable, which opened to the south-east of the capital's public hospital near Mein Street in 1905. They probably also designed the 1906 Seddon Ward for tuberculosis patients, with separate one-person timber shelters, on the hill to the east of the hospital. There are references to other work by the firm at Wellington Hospital around this time, and drawings of buildings by other practices are held in the archive that was passed down from Crichton & McKay. It is possible that Crichton collaborated on some projects or acted as the hospital board's representative on them.[2]

A new two-storey block with x-ray and outpatient departments on the ground floor, and a laboratory above, was added at the west end of the main corridor, close to Riddiford Street, in 1913. Ward 7, a specialist centre for eye, ear, nose and throat patients built above Ward 4, opened in 1917, and an outpatient department for those specialties was added in front of Wards 3, 4 and 7. Another building, erected over the private suite between the main entrance and Wards 5 and 6, accommodated a nurses' sick bay, accommodation for resident medical staff and a diphtheria ward.[3]

The current hospital site in Masterton, then known as Landsdowne and opposite the original hospital on Te Ore Ore Road, was purchased in 1903 and the 24-bed brick Masterton Hospital, designed by Crichton & McKay, opened there in 1907. A fever hospital was also built in Hope Street but abandoned in 1909. An isolation ward opened in 1917, and an isolation block built in 1920 was extended in 1938. There were extensions in 1918 and 1930 to the eight-bed nurses' home added in 1912. Other additions included a new laundry in 1915, along with repairs due to fire damage to some of the buildings, a women's ward and a maternity ward (later to become the children's ward) in 1921 and a new operating theatre in 1937.[4]

The earlier isolation wards at Wellington Hospital, which had developed since 1881 and had been extended in 1906, were soon over capacity, and Crichton & McKay were commissioned to design a new fever hospital on Coromandel Street. This 60-bed facility, later named the Ewart Hospital, and an associated 15-bed nurses' home were opened in 1910. In an English Queen Anne-revival Arts and Crafts style, with flared stuccoed brick walls, small-paned windows, steeply pitched tiled roofs and half-timbered gables, the buildings had a more domestic feel than those of the main hospital. A second storey was added in 1919. The 1910 hospital was later demolished to make way for the Ewart Geriatric Hospital, now an outpatient facility, but the original nurses' home was retained, and in 1930 another 15-bed wing was added. In 1980 the building was converted into the Parkview Clinic, Wellington's abortion service, but this use ceased in 2009.[5]

A new brick-and-stucco fever hospital, also by Crichton & McKay in a similar Arts and Crafts style, opened in 1920 further up the hill on Alexandra Road. The V-shaped plan provided two long wings for wards with verandahs facing north and sunporches at the ends.

↑

Masterton Hospital, 1904.

↗

Wairau Hospital, Blenheim.

↩

The Seddon Wing, Wellington Hospital, 1975.

The facility closed in 1953 but reopened as a chest hospital in 1970, with a third ward block added between the original two. The building, now the home of the Wellington SPCA, is a Category 2 Historic Place.[6]

In Marlborough a 52-bed three-ward brick hospital, designed by Crichton & McKay, opened on the current Wairau Hospital site in 1915. It also included an operating theatre, a kitchen and staff quarters. Extensions to one of the general wards in 1924 allowed for one of the other wards to be converted into a children's ward.[7] At Nelson Hospital the firm

collaborated with local architect Arthur Reynolds Griffin on the 1916 Dalton House Nurses' Home, but there appears to be no reference to Crichton & McKay working with him when he designed the 1926 main hospital building there (see page 164).[8] At Palmerston North Hospital, Crichton & McKay designed the 1920 brick Princess Mary and Prince of Wales wards, which added 54 surgical beds, and, in 1921, a new laundry and boiler house on Ruahine Street.[9]

Wellington-born Vivian Palmer Haughton joined the practice in 1907 as a draughtsman. After serving in the war, where he sustained a serious gunshot wound to the head at the Battle of the Somme, Haughton returned to work with his former employers. Although the firm was known on some projects as Crichton, McKay & Haughton from 1923, Haughton did not actually become a partner until 1926.[10]

The main entrance and ward blocks at Wellington Hospital, designed by Crichton, McKay & Haughton, opened in 1927. The three-storey administration building (the front block) on Riddiford Street also included casualty and outpatient departments and was the main entrance to the hospital for many years. Designed in a restrained neo-Georgian style, it was built in reinforced concrete with brick facings and coloured cement trimmings. Behind this sat a three-storey block, containing Wards 8, 9, 10 and 10A, from which the toilet towers projected at angles to maximise ventilation. When the front and ward blocks were demolished to make way for the new Wellington Regional Hospital in 2008, the front portico was carefully relocated to a courtyard behind the new building.[11]

Crichton was injured while visiting this site in 1926 and the subsequent illness contributed to his relatively early death in 1928. When McKay retired in 1926, Haughton became the sole partner. The firm was also responsible, in the 1920s, for the Huddart Parker and Dominion buildings in Wellington, and the Art Deco Bank of New Zealand in Napier, with its distinctive Māori motifs in the column capitals and frieze. Their Levy Building of 1928 was the tallest in Wellington at the time.[12]

↖

The main entrance and ward block of Wellington Hospital.

↑

Vivian Palmer Haughton.
William (Bill) John McKeon.

↗

Hawera Hospital.

++

Crichton, McKay & Haughton continued to win projects beyond Wellington. In association with local hospital board architects Duffill & Gibson, the firm designed the neo-Classical Hawera Hospital that opened on a new site in Hunter Street in 1930. A brick-and-concrete structure with jarrah floors, the building included two operating theatres and an x-ray room. The Milmoe fountain was relocated there in 1930 and a three-storey nurses' home constructed.[13]

During the Depression, the government cut expenditure on hospitals, and for a time Crichton, McKay & Haughton was a skeleton crew of Haughton and two draughtsmen, with Crichton's close friend William (Bill) John McKeon assisting them as required.[14] The Hawke's Bay earthquake stimulated work in that part of the country, but elsewhere construction stalled. Both Haughton and McKeon were members of the Allied Building Industry, a group of builders, architects and merchants set up to lobby the government for more opportunities; McKeon was its secretary. Haughton also formed a partnership with other building tradespeople in 1932 to create work by erecting the 1933 Featherston Chambers office building in the capital. In 1935 McKeon joined Haughton in partnership, but it was some time before the firm changed its name to Haughton & McKeon.[15]

By 1931 Wellington Hospital was chronically overcrowded and plans were made to extend the Victoria Hospital, but these did not proceed. In 1935, however, after Labour initiated its large public works programme, the Wellington Hospital Board proposed to erect a new four-storey, 100-bed building ward block and administrative centre, to be known as the Centenary

Block, on a site north of the front block. In 1936 it was decided to move the site to the north of the pathology block and add two floors, and initial concept plans showed a central block from which four wings radiated, later reduced to three.[16]

Haughton had continued to be architect to the Wellington Hospital Board and Australian firm Stephenson & Turner, well regarded for its emphasis on efficiency and its speedy construction of hospital buildings, was engaged as associate architect. Particularly modern for the period, the Y-shaped plan maximised sunlight and outlook and reduced corridor lengths. In 1937 McKeon returned to his hometown of Melbourne to work on the design alongside Stephenson & Turner.[17]

By then the scope of the build had increased to six operating theatres and 350 beds, and further increased to 500 by the end of the year. Costs ballooned, but approaches to the government for more funding were unsuccessful. A royal commission appointed in April 1938 to investigate the Wellington Hospital Board's care and treatment of patients recommended a new hospital for the Hutt Valley and the reduction of the new Wellington building by one wing. In the interim, a temporary 50-patient ward would go up between the children's hospital and the Victoria wards. It was calculated that these temporary beds would be insufficient by 1939, and plans were made for a 150-bed, three-ward emergency hospital on the Kilbirnie recreation ground, but this did not eventuate.[18]

Construction on the Centenary Block did eventually start in 1939 and the site was excavated before government funding was again withdrawn. Drawings from 1939, bearing the names of both Stephenson & Turner and Crichton, McKay & Haughton, show a six-storey, 500-bed main block, with four wings radiating from a central core. But cost pressures and the demand for a new Hutt hospital led to gradual decreases in scope. Agreement was finally reached on a three-storey, 210-bed building and construction began again in 1941. The Centenary name was dropped and the building became known as the Emergency or 210 Block.[19]

It had three narrow wings and was innovative in setting beds in cubicles and parallel to external walls rather than perpendicular, as in the older Nightingale-style wards. Walkways ran along the façades, terminating at north-facing sunrooms, and the exterior was free of decoration. Because wartime restrictions had led to an increasing scarcity of reinforcing steel and other materials, the building above the lower floor of load-bearing brick was built in diagonally sarked timber framing sheathed in asbestos cement boards with timber battens.

The wooden structure contravened local building by-laws, and a permit was granted only after a promise to provide multiple fire-exit ramps on the upper levels. The building finally opened in 1944. By this stage, Stephenson & Turner was no longer involved, and none of its work with Haughton at Wellington Hospital seems to have come to fruition.[20]

As the war intensified, accommodation for wounded servicemen soon became urgently needed and in 1941 the Defence Department hastily added a separate two-storey Soldiers' Block in front of the Toxward Building's main entrance. This was later redeveloped as a maternity annex, which opened in 1947 and was finally demolished in 1984.[21]

The Crichton, McKay & Haughton name seems to have been retained for work at Wellington Hospital: it still appears on drawings for the emergency block and the new nurses' home, opened in 1945. Hospital design became a mainstay for the firm during the war years, increased by the need to accommodate ill and wounded returning soldiers. High workloads led to the sharing of work with other practices. Bernard Johns assisted with the female domestic staff block at Hutt Hospital and Dawson & King worked on both Hutt and Wellington Hospital projects. At least two women were manpowered to help: Patricia Leahy (later Bell), who joined

↑
The Clocktower Block at Hutt Hospital.

Crichton, McKay & Haughton in 1940, and Elizabeth Taylor (later Brown), who worked on hospital design with Haughton & McKeon as a university student.[22]

In 1946 there were commissions at Wellington Hospital for sanitary block additions, additions to the Ewart Hospital and ward block alterations. Haughton & McKeon worked on the laundry block, staff facilities and clinical services, and alterations to the pathology block, nurses' home and several wards.[23]

++

Much of the growth in the Wellington region during this era was in the Hutt Valley, where the larger area of flat land available was attractive to industry and allowed for cheaper construction of housing and other infrastructure. The Wellington Hospital Board purchased a site on Penrose Street, Lower Hutt, for a future cottage hospital, but this did not eventuate, and in 1937 the property was sold to the Education Board and later became Hutt Intermediate School.[24]

After a massive state housing scheme was launched in the Hutt Valley in 1937, and following the recommendations of the 1938 royal commission, the hospital board bought the current site on High Street in 1939. The existing Pearce House became the High Street Maternity Hospital, opening the same year; this building was relocated to Ōtaki in 1994. Two emergency blocks were rapidly erected in 1941 to accommodate wounded servicemen. The demand for public hospital services led to the erection of an emergency hospital with four 50-bed wards of timber and asbestos cladding. Hutt Hospital officially opened in 1944.[25]

Haughton & McKeon were commissioned to design the new hospital, and since Haughton was committed on the new Wellington block, McKeon took over the Hutt project. Although he had little experience in hospital design before joining the firm, he rapidly caught up. Hutt Hospital eventually took precedence over the Centenary Block project. It included new wards, operating theatres, a nurses' home and kitchen and laundry facilities. Thanks to the war, the required ward capacity almost doubled from 210 to 410 beds, with the addition of two 100-bed emergency wards when much of the building was already under construction. The new entrance, or Clocktower building, designed by Haughton & McKeon, which would eventually have 350 general and 40 maternity beds, opened in 1945.[26]

The buildings were undecorated, due to the need for economy during the war years, and possibly under the modernist influence of Stephenson & Turner. The pitched tiled roof gave a domestic feel, and generously glazed solariums, or sunrooms, were placed at the ends of the north-facing wings. The lowest floor was raised to provide subfloor ventilation and safety when the Hutt River flooded. Because of the steel shortage, several buildings at both Hutt and Wellington were intended to be temporary. The government gave special dispensation for the main block and nurses' home at Hutt to be built in reinforced concrete.[27]

Haughton & McKeon also worked on the military hospital that opened at Silverstream in 1942. It was initially intended to serve the New Zealand troops based at the nearby Trentham Military Camp, and to treat returning war wounded, but before its completion it was decided to increase its size and hand it over to the US Navy to treat malaria victims and those injured in the Pacific. At its peak it could accommodate 1600 patients. After the war, Silverstream was taken over by the Wellington Hospital Board and reduced to 168 continuing care beds, 14 for rehabilitation and four for intermittent care. A new day rehabilitation centre opened in 1977; the hospital was closed in 1989.[28]

When McKeon left the partnership in 1951, Haughton's son, Robert Besant Haughton, became a partner in his place, the firm becoming V. P. Haughton & Son in 1952. Robert had joined the firm as a junior straight from school in 1936. As a Territorial, he was one of the first to depart for overseas war service. Other men also left and more women were taken on to assist with draughting.[29]

V. P. Haughton & Son is the name on the drawings for Wellington Hospital's women's psychiatric ward and alterations to the men's psychiatric ward, completed in 1953. The firm designed the first of two nurses' homes at Wellington Hospital in 1943, though it was not built until some time after the war. In line with modern design trends, the windows were cut cleanly into flat walls and there were north-facing solariums and a large rooftop recreation and activity area. At Paraparaumu the firm was responsible for a new maternity hospital and associated nurses' home, a rambling single-storey building in a domestic style. This was designed in 1951, but working drawings did not begin until 1955. V. P. Haughton & Son also designed the Elderslie Private Hospital in Upper Hutt around this time.[30]

John (Lindsay) Mair, son of Government Architect John T. Mair, joined Crichton, McKay & Haughton in 1938 as a draughtsman, and left the following year to work in the Sydney office of Stephenson & Turner, probably after receiving an employment offer from Arthur Stephenson during the latter's visit to Wellington. Mair rejoined the firm in 1954 and became a partner. Haughton, Son & Mair is the name on drawings for the 1954 occupational therapy building and

↑

Lindsay Mair.
Robert Haughton.

↗

The Seddon Wing, Wellington Hospital, 1975.

the 1955 210-bed Block A, both at Wellington Hospital. On Vivian Haughton's death in 1956, the name was simplified to Haughton & Mair.[31]

The firm designed the five-storey nurses' home opened at the north end of the Wellington Hospital site in 1949, an eight-storey 235-bed block built to its east in 1958, and the Nurses' Memorial Chapel between them, added in 1965, as well as a cafeteria and recreation hall in 1967.[32] A 'temporary' timber operating theatre block was inserted between the 210-block and the maternity annex in 1958 and the next year work started on an extension to the north of the front block. This housed medical records on the ground floor, a fracture clinic on the first floor and administrative services on the top floor. A thick concrete bunker was built in 1961 to house a cobalt unit for radiotherapy and a new laundry in 1966.[33]

Land was purchased in Paekākāriki to build a new tuberculosis hospital to replace the ageing facilities at Ewart Hospital and the Otaki Sanatorium. Staff, however, objected to this isolated location and plans were developed for a 120-bed chest facility on the site of the old Seddon shelters at Wellington Hospital. The seven-storey, 167-bed Seddon Wing, designed by Haughton & Mair and opened in 1966, was originally intended for this purpose, but the decline in tuberculosis meant that it was repurposed to house medical wards, the hospital's first dedicated coronary care unit, renal dialysis and two cardiothoracic theatres. It was demolished in 1999.[34]

Haughton & Mair also designed the 1968 Kenepuru Maternity Hospital, the first development on the site that had been carved off Porirua Asylum land to create a new general hospital. The building had a reinforced-concrete frame with aluminium windows and blue Belgian

glass spandrels. With two 20-bed wards, it opened when maternity hospitals were transitioning from the nursery system, where babies were kept separate from their mothers, to rooming in, so there was flexibility in the plan to add a nursery if required.[35] Staff accommodation was provided by a block of doctors' flats in 1965 and a 37-bed nurses' home the following year. Most of these buildings were demolished to provide space for the later mental health facility, but one, repurposed as the community health service building, remains.[36]

Aged care facilities by Haughton & Mair include the c. 1972 Presbyterian Feilding Home for the Aged. They also designed the Central Institute of Technology in Lower Hutt, which opened in stages from 1973 to 1978.[37]

++

A master plan developed in the 1960s for a new 1200-bed hospital on the Wellington Hospital site consisted of six interconnected 10-storey tower blocks, a lower accident and emergency and outpatient block and an attached academic building for a proposed third medical school. All buildings on the site would be demolished, apart from the Seddon Wing and the nurses' home to the north. The planning was originally done by Haughton & Mair in conjunction with Stephenson & Turner, but the latter's involvement ceased at some point, and eventually both were superseded by Thorpe Cutter Pickmere Douglas (see page 244).[38]

Haughton & Mair designed the psychiatric unit for 30 inpatients and 40 day-stay patients that opened on Mein Street, as part of the Wellington Hospital campus, in 1973. Two years later a three-storey staff accommodation block, now used as offices, opened on Mein Street and a two-storey artificial limb centre was built on the other side of the road. The now-demolished laundry at the corner of Adelaide Road and Mein Street opened in 1970.[39] The firm designed the first of the new multi-storey buildings at Wellington, the 1978 11-storey clinical services block, and the 1981 Total Energy Centre, which included a gas-fired power station to improve the hospital's energy resilience, further up Mein Street.[40] Also in 1981 a staff sports complex was built next to the nurses' home.

After becoming the Wanganui Hospital Board's architectural consultants in 1946, Haughton & McKeon was commissioned to carry out master planning for Wanganui Hospital in 1949. Up to the 1980s the firm and its successors designed all the clinical buildings at the hospital, along with the Lambie Nurses' Home and the staff dining room.[41]

By the 1950s most of the buildings at Wanganui Hospital were overcrowded and very run-down. In 1955 the two-level 44-bed maternity services building, designed by Haughton & McKeon (Haughton & Son by the time the work was completed), replaced the three existing maternity hospitals in the area: Jessie Hope Gibbons, Cairnbrae and Picardy.[42] This building was refurbished in 1998, but demolished in 2008. A recreation hall for nurses opened in 1952, a swimming pool five years later. The five-level 142-bed Lambie Nurses' Home by Haughton & Son opened in 1960 and the single-level dining room and kitchen annex in 1962. The home has since been converted to office accommodation.[43]

The five-storey surgical block designed by Haughton & Mair, with operating theatres, a sterilising department, two 60-bed surgical wards, offices and a cafeteria, opened in 1963. It was extended by the same firm in 1977, but because of earthquake risk was reduced to two floors for records and office use and reclad in 2009. The clinical services block, designed by Haughton & Mair, with emergency, radiology, laboratory, allied health and outpatients, opened in 1970, as did the chapel. The latter was extended in 1987. Dalgleish Architects designed later modifications in the early 2000s.

A new ambulance station, designed by the Haughton Partnership, opened in 1984. The 1987 four-storey ward and administration block was also their work.[44] An alcohol and drug assessment centre opened in 1979, and a 20-bed acute psychiatric unit in 1982, were also the partnership's work. In 2013 the unit was reopened as the 12-bed Te Āwhina unit, following reconstruction to a design by Worley Consultants.[45] Further works were carried out there by Dalgleish Architects, who also designed refurbishments for the 2013 Stanford House forensic mental health unit. The Food Services building at Whanganui, by Bulleyment Fortune, the successor to the Haughton Partnership, opened in 1988.[46]

↖

Kenepuru Maternity Hospital, Porirua.

↗

The Clinical Services Building, Wellington Hospital.

++

The various Haughton partnerships also designed most of the buildings at Hutt Hospital in the second half of the twentieth century. A new 60-bed maternity wing and a six-storey 100-bed extension to the nurses' home (now the YMCA) on Pilmuir Street opened in 1966, both designed by Haughton & Mair.[47] The Chapel of St Luke, built in 1980 and dedicated a decade later, the 1982 seven-storey Heretaunga Wing and the 1989 two-storey rehabilitation block were all designed by the Haughton Partnership.[48]

After Lindsay Mair retired in 1972, earlier partners R. B. Haughton, John O. Creagh and Arthur E. J. Williment were joined by Chris J. Brooke-White, Alan L. Bulleyment and John G. Duurloo in 1973. Haughton and Brooke-White had left by 1979, the year that the practice was renamed the Haughton Partnership.[49] In the 1980s, in another iteration of its long history, the firm became Bulleyment Fortune Architects, who designed the extension and redevelopment of the acute psychiatric unit at Wellington as Te Whare o Matairangi, and extensions to the Stephenson & Turner-designed Haumietiketike and Pūrehurehu mental health units at Porirua.[50]

Following the 'Save Our Hutt Hospital' campaign of 1991, opposing the closure of the hospital and the centralisation of services at Wellington, Hutt was retained and a new block with the emergency department and four operating theatres, designed by Bulleyment Fortune, was completed in 1997.[51] The firm also designed the 2014 dialysis unit at Kenepuru Hospital.

After the death of Denis Fortune in 2018, staff from the firm joined McKenzie Higham Architects, which holds the Bulleyment Fortune archive with significant records from its predecessor firms.[52]

↖

Wanganui Hospital's Lambie Nurses' Home.

↗

Surgical block, Wanganui Hospital.

→

The Heretaunga Block at Hutt Hospital.

King George V and Queen Mary hospitals ↘

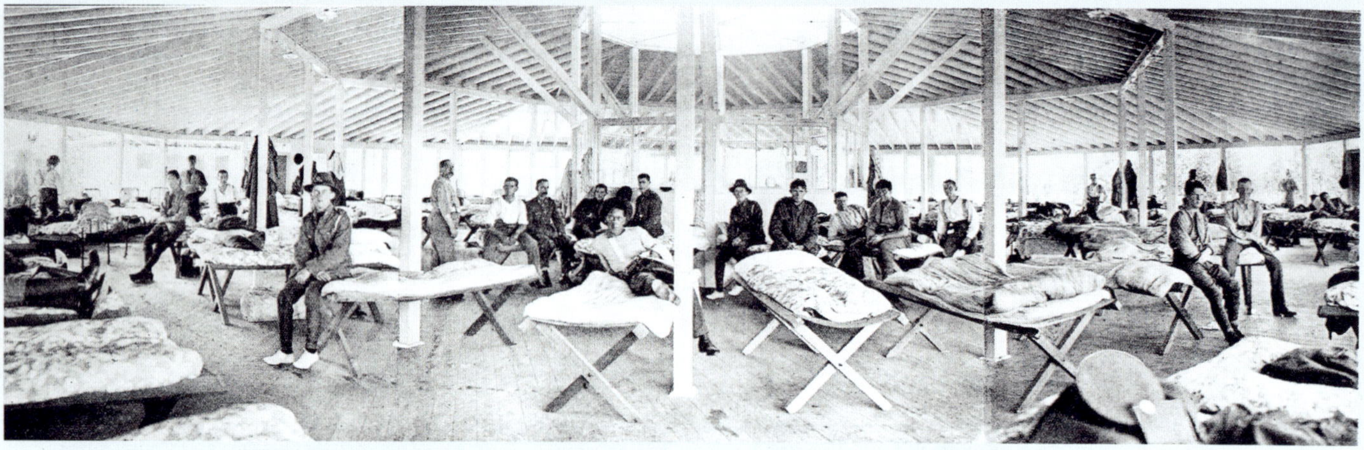

Both during and after the First World War, convalescent homes and hospitals were needed for returning soldiers who had been wounded, both physically and psychologically. Four locations were chosen: Hanmer Springs in North Canterbury, Rotorua in the central North Island, Trentham in the Hutt Valley and Featherston in Wairarapa, both of the latter home to military training camps. A site at Trentham was developed first, in 1915, to provide an initial processing facility. In the same year a distinctive, octagonal-shaped rotunda ward was built at the medical precinct in Featherston; a second was added in 1916. This seems to have formed the template for those later built in Rotorua and at Hanmer Springs.[1]

According to Heritage New Zealand Pouhere Taonga, no international precedent has been found for these wards. It has been suggested that the inspiration for the design may have been an octagonal kiosk at Trentham Racecourse, possibly repurposed for medical use in 1914, or a totalisator building of similar shape at Featherston's satellite camp at Tauherenikau Racecourse. Each ward had a large octagonal room with a rectangular annex. The rotunda wards at Queen Mary have a diameter of approximately 24 metres and an overall area of around 450 square metres, as does the remaining Rotorua one, now relocated to Ōtaki.

If there had been 200 occupants, as has been suggested, this would have meant just over 2 square metres per bed. In accordance with the 'open-air' treatment of the day, the windows were originally unglazed and had hessian or canvas screens to maximise natural ventilation. They let in plenty of fresh air and sunlight, but glass was later added to provide some relief from colder winter temperatures.[2]

During the 1918 influenza pandemic, which killed 177 in the Featherston camp, two of them nurses,[3] its larger buildings were converted into temporary hospital wards with the worst cases being treated in the rotundas. The buildings were removed between 1920 and 1926, and the site was returned to pasture. Barracks were built again in 1943 to house Japanese prisoners-of-war.[4]

Most of the buildings at the military camps were designed by the Public Works Department, under John Campbell's direction. Heritage New Zealand Pouhere Taonga, however, credits the design of the rotunda wards to a partnership between the department and private firm Hoggard, Prouse & Gummer, formed in Wellington in 1907 by Jack Hoggard and William Prouse, who were joined by William Gummer in 1913. This

combination was also responsible for the rotunda wards at Hanmer Springs and Rotorua. It is probable that the volume of new buildings needed urgently during the war led the department to share the workload with outside practices.[5]

++

In Rotorua the Defence Department erected a small cottage hospital on the Pukeroa Reserve in 1915, but since Ngāti Whakaue had donated the land for recreational use, this building was only intended to be temporary. It was expanded in 1916 and named the King George V Military Hospital for Convalescent Patients. As the *Dominion* reported, 'The main features of the buildings are two octagon-shaped wards at either end, in each of which from 150 to 200 men may sleep, and in the centre, a dining hall, large enough to accommodate this number of men. At the back is the administrative section, consisting of the commandant's quarters, the non-commissioned officers' quarters, and the other administrative buildings.' The Public Health Department was proud that the buildings were erected in just five and a half weeks. The design allowed for the addition of a third rotunda ward, but this was never built.[6]

In 1918 capacity at the Rotorua hospital was increased from 238 to 560 beds with the addition of more traditional dormitory blocks, but the war ended before this was needed. The newer buildings appear to be those repurposed for the Lowry Ward orthopaedic surgery wing, with operating theatres and 136 beds, as the hospital became an orthopaedic specialist centre after the war.[7]

Although the King George V Military Hospital was intended to be temporary, and at times it appeared that it would be closed, thanks to the 1918 influenza pandemic and poliomyelitis outbreaks it continued to be used as a public hospital throughout the 1920s.

↖

The rotunda ward, King George V Hospital, Rotorua, 1916.

↑

William Gummer.
William Prouse.

↗

King George V Hospital, Rotorua, after 1916.

A maternity wing was erected in 1918. In 1921 the hospital was transferred to the Health Department and renamed the King George V Orthopaedic Hospital.[8]

By the 1930s the buildings were in a poor state, and the government considered three options: redeveloping the hospital on its current site, merging it with a small infectious diseases hospital that had been built on the old sanatorium site or combining it with the sanatorium and bath house. Following negotiations with Ngāti Whakaue, the King George V Hospital in Rotorua was transferred from the Ministry of Health to the Waikato Hospital Board in 1934 and renamed Rotorua Hospital. Some older ward blocks were removed and the bed capacity was reduced to 73. In 1940 the government approved a 999-year lease of the Pukeroa Reserve site to the Waikato Hospital Board and planning began for new buildings on the site.[9]

++

↑
Otaki Children's Health Camp.

In an effort to reduce malnutrition and the prevalence of diseases such as tuberculosis in children, high-profile medical practitioners such as Sir Frederic Truby King advocated for the establishment of children's health camps. In 1919 Dr Elizabeth Gunn, a pioneer in this field, established an initial temporary camp at Turakina, between Whanganui and Marton. Then, in 1923, came a camp at Ōtaki Beach, and after the two Rotorua rotunda ward buildings were relocated there in 1931 the new facility opened in 1932. Dismantling the buildings was no easy task as the various nuts and bolts used in their construction had been fused together by the Rotorua sulphur.[10] The eastern rotunda was later demolished to make way for an administration block, but the other one survives. A timber kitchen, dining hall and ancillary buildings were added in 1941. From 1942 to 1945 the camp served as a temporary wartime emergency hospital.[11]

After the Labour government decided to expand the model across the country, several government-operated health camps were opened, including Gisborne and Roxburgh in Otago in 1941, Glenelg in Christchurch in 1945 and Pakuranga in Auckland in 1949. There were also shorter-lived camps at Whanganui in 1937 and Nelson in 1941. The Princess of Wales Health Camp opened in Rotorua in 1983.[12]

++

A government spa had been established at the thermal pools in Hanmer Springs in 1883 and in 1897 a sanatorium was built to offer Swiss-style spa treatment. Once the war started, the therapeutic properties of the thermal springs were considered ideal for treating veterans, but the sanatorium was destroyed by fire in 1914. The following year, local sheep farmer Duncan Rutherford offered the use of the nearby Lodge Hotel while the Queen Mary Hospital for Sick and Wounded Soldiers, which accommodated 200 soldiers, was built on the sanatorium site. It opened in June 1916. The grounds were laid out by Canterbury landscape designer Alfred Buxton. The Queen Mary was intended especially for men suffering from what was then often called shell shock.[13]

The first new building, known as the Soldiers' Block, consisted of two octagonal rotunda wards, joined by a recreation room and staff quarters. The wards were oriented to maximise sunlight and outlook and, as at Featherston, the windows had no glass to provide natural ventilation. The annex to the northern Ward 1 contained a treatment room, bathroom, kitchen and a series of smaller wards; the annex to the southern Ward 2 had an operating theatre and three smaller wards. The two were connected by a corridor and a large central hall for meals, recreation and socialising. The wards were named after the French and British military leaders Joseph Joffre and Herbert Kitchener, and the dining hall after British nurse Edith Cavell, who had been shot by the Germans in 1915 for helping 200 Allied soldiers to escape from Belgium.

A verandah was added to the front in 1917. The Soldiers' Block provided male accommodation until 1940, after which it was used for therapy programmes. In 1922 the Queen Mary Hospital was transferred from the military to the Health Department and became the national centre for the treatment of functional nervous disorders and neurasthenia.[14]

The 1926 single-storey 55-bed Chisholm Ward for women, in an Arts and Crafts bungalow style, was designed by the Public Works Department under John T. Mair. It consisted of wings of single rooms branching off a central block containing a dormitory, lounge, dining room and kitchen. A 56-room nurses' home, also designed by Mair, was

added in 1929. The 65-bed Art Deco-style Rutherford Ward, opened in 1940 for the rehabilitation of Second World War troops, was designed to take a second level, but this was never built.

All these Hanmer buildings faced north with views of the mountains and were built with plenty of windows and verandahs to maximise sunlight and fresh air. Other buildings include the 1916 site maintenance engineer's office, a hospital administration block and central kitchen in 1929 and a medical centre and operating theatre.[15]

After the war, the hospital was used for the treatment of patients with tuberculosis. In the 1960s Queen Mary became the national specialist centre for the treatment of drug and alcohol dependency. The hospital was transferred to the North Canterbury Hospital Board in 1990 and its capacity reduced from 117 to 55 beds. In 1997 it was purchased by a private group aiming to continue its services, but it finally closed in 2003. In 2004 it was designated as a Historic Site and the Soldiers' Block, nurses' home and Chisholm Block were designated Category 1 Historic Places in 2005.[16]

↖

Rutherford Ward, Queen Mary Hospital, Hanmer Springs.

↗

Chisholm Ward, Queen Mary Hospital, Hanmer Springs.

8

Hospitals of the south

1914–1945

THE YEARS OF DEPRESSION AND WAR also brought changes to hospital architecture in the South Island Te Waipounamu. In the north of the island, at Wairau Hospital, a two-storey brick nurses' home, designed by H. S. Clarkson, was added in 1926. The 1887 building became the Amersfoote Home, much of which was destroyed by fire in 1953. Architect Alexander Stewart carried out further work at Wairau in 1938. The large number of troops in the area during the Second World War at Woodbourne air force base and a nearby army camp resulted in the opening, in 1943, of a two-storey, three-ward, 90-bed wood-and-fibrolite building, plus a concrete mortuary. A 19-bed children's ward was built in 1959, and a recreation hall in 1968.[1]

To provide maternity care in the district, in 1916 a private residence on Blenheim's Maxwell Road was bought and converted into an eight-bed maternity home. Two years later, it moved to a larger home, known as Holmdale, on the corner of Weld and Litchfield streets. Despite being some distance from the hospital, this was used for several decades and even extended in 1946.[2]

On the current Nelson Hospital site, a store building was erected in Waimea Road in 1915 to serve the hospital and the Braemar Mental Hospital on the other side of the road, and a community clinic building opened in Kawai Street in 1920. The first dedicated nurses' home, the two-storey Dalton House, opened on Franklyn Street in 1916, was of roughcast ferro-concrete with a tiled roof. It was designed by local architect Arthur Reynolds Griffin, grandson of the founder of biscuit makers Griffin & Sons, working with Crichton & McKay. A two-storey timber and roughcast-plaster annex was added to it in 1935, though this burned down in 1938. The original hospital building on the site was replaced by a new building, also by Griffin, in 1926.[3]

++

On the West Coast, a maternity ward opened at Reefton Hospital only weeks before the building was badly damaged in the massive Murchison earthquake of 17 June 1929 that killed 17 people and caused widespread destruction. The Department of Health recommended closure, but public pressure led to the hospital being demolished and replaced with a new 39-bed weatherboard building designed by the department's architects.[4] A new nurses' home, laundry and boiler house designed by Christchurch architect W. H. Trengrove opened in 1949. A hospital building, also designed by Trengrove, opened in two stages in 1952 and 1953, with operating theatres, and emergency and maternity facilities. In 1957 it was extended to create a children's ward.[5] The Inangahua Hospital Board, which operated Reefton, also opened a small hospital designed by architect R. Tudehope at the gold-mining town of Waiuta in 1914. After it closed, it was destroyed by arson in 1980, but rebuilt as a lodge by the Department of Conservation.[6]

At Greymouth Hospital a children's ward designed by Department of Health architect Charles Scott Allan was added in 1928, a two-storey building accommodating the O'Brien women's and McBrearty maternity wards in 1938 and, in 1940, the Samuel Saltzman Tuberculosis Annexe Block, all designed by the Public Works Department. The Tasman Home opened in 1925 for the care of the elderly.[7]

By the beginning of the twentieth century, the old wooden buildings at Hokitika's Westland Hospital were reaching the end of their lives and were replaced by the Manson and Ellis wards in 1907. The Mandl Ward and a two-storey administration building of brick and roughcast concrete, designed by the Health Department under Allan, were added in 1922. An x-ray room was added by the Public Works Department in 1934.[8]

The two-storey Butler Nurses' Home opened in 1937 and the Williams Ward for children the following year. Both were designed by Trengrove. In 1963 the Ellis Ward was rebuilt as an

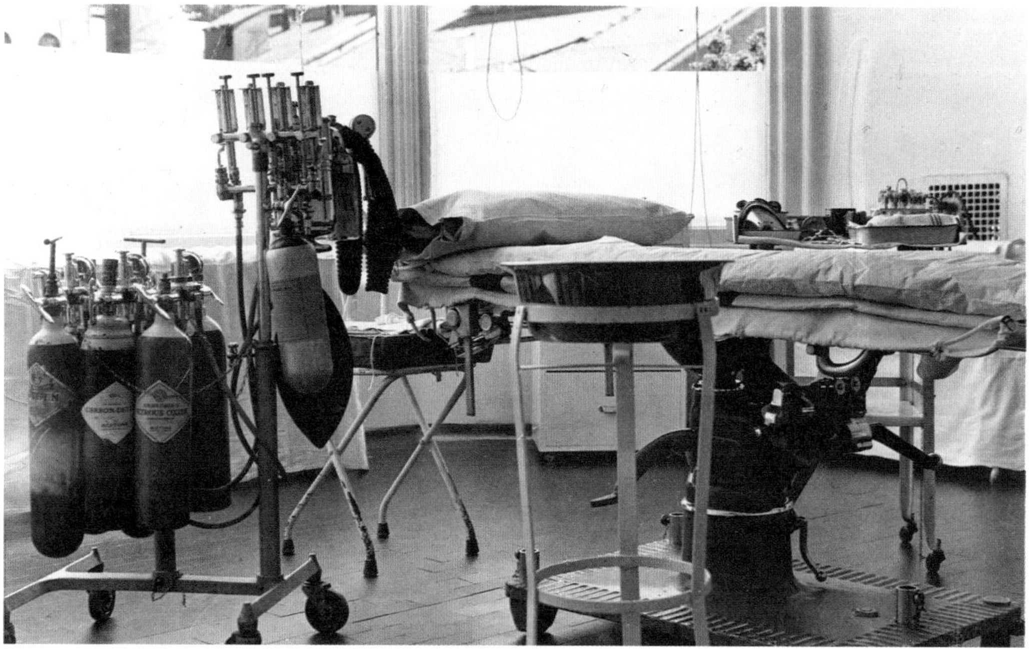

↑
Wairau Hospital nurses' home, Blenheim, c.1925.

→
Wairau Hospital operating theatre.

↩
Seddon Memorial Hospital, Gore.

11-bed maternity unit and an x-ray unit was added, but despite developing an orthopaedics specialty in the 1950s the hospital gradually lost services to Greymouth. The last patients moved out in 1989 and large public protests could not prevent its closure in 1992.[9]

++

Tuberculosis, often simply called TB, was a major scourge in early New Zealand, especially for Māori, and persisted well into the twentieth century, peaking during the Second World War. A disease caused by bacteria that attack the lungs, it was subdued by vaccination from the 1930s and can now be treated with antibiotics, but up to the 1950s the main treatment was rest and exposure to sunlight and fresh air.[10]

In Christchurch in 1904, Nurse Sibylla Maude, who had resigned from her role as matron of the public hospital in order to establish district nursing in the city, raised money to set up a tent-based sanatorium for men at New Brighton. As her biographer Beryl Hughes has recorded, 'Although conditions were rough and uncomfortable, the improvement to the patients' health was so great that in 1905 Nurse Maude established a camp for women at Burwood, appealing to the women of Christchurch for money.'[11] When the Cracroft-Wilson family donated a site for a more permanent facility on a spur of the Port Hills on the edge of their Cashmere estate, the two camps were closed.[12]

In 1910 the first patients were admitted to Cashmere, which was designed by Samuel Hurst Seager of Hurst Seager, Wood & Munnings, and supervised during construction by Collins & Harman. The single-storey administration building was brick with a tiled roof, and its verandahs led to separate wings. Patients were housed in shelters open to the elements. Near these were the porter's hostel and morgue; the medical superintendent occupied a substantial

↖

Holmdale maternity annex, Wairau Hospital, Blenheim.

←

Nelson Hospital nurses' home, 1916.

↑

Nelson Hospital, 1933.

brick house further down the hill. More shelters were added in 1912, 1913 and 1916, and a children's pavilion in 1916. Although the elevated site had been chosen to escape the pollution of the city, it was very exposed to the wind and had poor drainage.[13]

The next building on the site was the 43-bed King George V Coronation Memorial Hospital, of brick with a tiled roof and designed by Collins & Harman, which opened further down the hill in 1914. This section became known as the lower sanatorium, and the original building and shelters the middle sanatorium. In order to treat soldiers returning from the First World War with tuberculosis, the building was extended in 1917. A further extension in 1920 added 24 beds; another floor in 1929 added another 37.

←

Cashmere Sanatorium and Coronation Hospital, Christchurch, 1940s.

↑

Samuel Hurst Seager.

↗

Sanatorium Hospital, Cashmere Sanatorium.

→

Cashmere Sanatorium TB shelters, 1913.

In 1917 a nurses' home was built above the middle sanatorium. A military tuberculosis hospital opened on the summit of the hill in 1919; it became the men's sanatorium in 1925. Later known as the upper sanatorium, it closed in 1931. To the east of the men's sanatorium, another 32-bed facility opened for the children of patients in 1923, with a school added three years later. This tall wooden gabled building with high brick chimneys and deep verandahs,

known as the Children's Fresh Air Home, was later the Huntsbury Children's Home and closed in 1971. Further up the hill from this, a new 32-bed sanatorium, designed by the Public Works Department, opened in 1942 for soldiers returning from the Second World War.[14]

The North Canterbury Hospital Board architect's department worked on the hospital in the 1940s: in 1942 under S. Minson and in 1946 under S. T. Townsend. Manson, Seward & Stanton also carried out work there in the 1950s.[15]

The last patient left the main sanatorium in 1960, and it became a hospital for geriatrics, which closed in 1991. The buildings and shelters were removed, the latter finding new uses as garden sheds or sleepouts in Christchurch backyards, and the site was redeveloped as the Broad Oaks subdivision.[16]

++

The North Canterbury Hospital and Charitable Aid Board, which was responsible for healthcare in Christchurch as well as the large area of rapidly developing farmlands on the plains, was established in 1910. For the next half century, most of its buildings were designed by the one firm, founded in Christchurch in 1869 by William Barnett Armson. After Armson's death, John

↑

King George V Coronation Memorial Hospital, Cashmere, 1910s.

↗

Christchurch Hospital nurses' home, c.1925–30.

James Collins, who had been articled to him in 1871, bought the firm with his partner George Lloyd. In 1884 Richard Dacre Harman bought Lloyd's interest in Armson, Collins & Lloyd and the practice became Armson, Collins & Harman. It was renamed Collins & Harman in 1886, although Armson's name was retained for some commissions up to 1928. John Goddard Collins, who had been taught by Samuel Hurst Seager, joined his father's staff in 1903.

At some point, the firm was officially appointed as architects to the North Canterbury board. After a Wellington office was established, Joseph Fearis Munnings joined to run this and the firm was renamed Collins, Harman & Munnings until he left in 1922. After Harman's death the firm became Collins & West, a name that seems to have been retained for some time after Edgar West left in 1928.[17]

At Christchurch Hospital, in 1911, a new building with a children's ward and a women's surgical ward, designed by Collins & Harman, was added to the west of the Hyman Marks building and a new two-storey wing was added to the nurses' home on the corner of Oxford Terrace and Riccarton Avenue. The administration building, including outpatients, a dispensary and pathology, the main hospital corridor and the porters' lodge were all completed in 1914, as were further ward extensions.[18]

A significant donation by Jane Chalmers, who had inherited a large Canterbury rural landholding, allowed for further development. The second Ward 3 was removed in 1914, and the last of the original buildings demolished in 1917 to make way for a new building for chronic cases. The Chalmers Block, designed by Collins & Harman, opened in July 1917, but from 1918 to 1921 it was taken over as a military hospital. Although simpler in form than the earlier Hyman Marks building, it had a tall brick tower set at an angle to the rest of the building. It was demolished in the 1980s.[19]

A military orthopaedic unit was added at Christchurch Hospital in 1917. Cheaply built and intended to be temporary, the two wards that it provided remained in use for some time. New premises for x-ray and physiotherapy opened in 1918, a new morgue the following year.

Collins & Harman also designed the 1920 boiler house and chimney. A two-theatre annex was built in 1922 and 1926 brought a new Ward 11 for women and an extra floor for the administration building.[20]

The 1927 Nurses' Memorial Chapel, designed by John Goddard Collins of Collins & Harman, who is said to have waived his fee, is in a style typical of Arts and Crafts churches, with detailed brickwork and a finely crafted timber interior. It was erected as a memorial to three nurses from Christchurch Hospital who died when the troopship *Marquette* was torpedoed in the Aegean Sea in 1915, and two who had died in the 1918 influenza epidemic, but now remembers Christchurch nurses who have served overseas in all wars. Threatened with

demolition or relocation several times, the chapel is now protected in its original location as a Category 1 Historic Place.[21]

The new three-storey steel-framed Hagley Hostel Nurses' Home opened in 1931, designed by Collins & Harman to accommodate additional floors; another three storeys were added in 1941. In 1938 the old military premises became Wards 14 and 15. Wards 12 and 13 were extended in 1942, a third laundry built in 1945 and the theatre block doubled and modernised in 1948.[22]

There was little development on the Christchurch site after the Second World War, in anticipation of a major redevelopment and the possible establishment of a satellite hospital campus elsewhere in the city. However, the theatre block was expanded in 1948 and workshops were erected in St Asaph Street in 1951, followed by a bulk store, a recovery ward and a cobalt unit for radiotherapy in 1957 and, in 1958, new premises for records plus a tutorial block and nurses' recreation hall. The medical superintendent's house was converted to offices in 1956 and a new boiler house built in 1967.[23]

++

An outbreak of plague in Noumea in 1899, which then spread to Sydney, sparked panic in New Zealand and calls for precautions and appropriate treatments in such eventualities. In 1903 reserve land was set aside at Bottle Lake, near Burwood, north of New Brighton, for a permanent infectious diseases hospital. Collins & Harman prepared plans for a new building, and the first patients, suffering from scarlet fever and smallpox, were transferred there from Christchurch Hospital in 1904. By the end of the year, the hospital was caring for all of Christchurch's scarlet fever cases, as well as soldiers returning from the South African War with tuberculosis. A series of detached buildings was added in 1909; these included

↖

Christchurch Hospital looking west: the old nurses' home, administration block and Chalmers' ward at bottom; main corridor, early wards, Hyman Marks and children's and women's wards in centre; and the new nurses' home at top.

↗

The interior of the Christchurch Hospital Nurses' Memorial Chapel, c.1950s.

a doctor's house and a cottage for smallpox cases, colloquially named 'Tipperary', for its distance from the other buildings. A nurses' cottage was opened in 1913 and a new nurses' home completed the next year.[24]

When a new facility consisting of two three-ward buildings was built in 1917, the name was changed from Bottle Lake Hospital to the North Canterbury Infectious Diseases Hospital, Burwood. In the 1920s and 1930s, visitors were not permitted, and gifts for patients had to be thrown over the barbed-wire fence surrounding the site. A boiler house was erected in 1923 and a diphtheria ward in 1938. There was another name change, to Burwood Hospital, in 1941, and two new wards (5 and 6), a matron's cottage and nurses' accommodation were added. A plastic surgery unit opened there in 1942 to cater for servicemen returning from the war; two further wards (7 and 8) opened in 1946.[25]

On the other side of the Port Hills, a maternity annex was added at Lyttelton Hospital in 1919, possibly also designed by Collins & Harman. The former home for the caretaker to the Lyttelton orphanage, between Brittan and Cressy terraces, was renovated and extended, and opened as the Lyttelton Maternity Hospital in 1931. This closed in 1960.[26]

In Akaroa a new seven-bed cottage hospital designed by Collins & Harman opened on a new site in Ōnuku Road in 1924. This replaced the town's first dedicated hospital, which had begun in a small cottage-like building in 1880 on the Bruce Terrace frontage of what is now the site of Akaroa Area School. The 1924 building was severely damaged in the 2010 Canterbury earthquake and demolished. The original intention was to replace it with a health centre, but successful public fundraising allowed a new 12-bed hospital to open in 2019.[27]

++

In the early decades of the twentieth century, a wave of cottage hospitals appeared throughout Canterbury to serve the scattered rural population. A private hospital opened in Kaiapoi in 1900, subsidised by the North Canterbury Hospital Board, and after coming under

the board's control the existing building was extended and opened as a maternity hospital in 1939. Kaikoura Hospital opened in 1912 and a new maternity block designed by Collins & Harman opened five years later. This was renovated by Collins & West in 1937 and a new nurses' home designed by J. G. Collins was added in 1941.[28]

The combined 1920 cottage and maternity hospital for the village of Waikari, north of Waipara on the way to Hanmer Springs, was designed by Collins & Harman, as was Amuri Hospital near Culverden, which opened two years later. At Little River, east of Lake Ellesmere, an existing house was extended to form a cottage maternity hospital in 1920; Collins & Harman designed a 1927 hospital building. Rangiora's new hospital opened its doors in 1924, replacing a house that had been rented in 1921 as a temporary maternity home. Collins & West designed the 1940 extension to the hospital.[29]

Cottage hospitals were also opened in Oxford in 1920, Malvern in 1921, Methven and Rakaia in 1923, Ellesmere in 1926 and, in 1927, Darfield, Cheviot and Lincoln. Most were underutilised as access to better facilities in Christchurch became easier, and gradually they were either closed or their services were considerably reduced. A hospital also opened on the Chatham Islands in 1927, under the umbrella of the North Canterbury Hospital Board. A simple timber building with an iron roof, it was designed by Collins & Harman.[30]

On the West Coast, the firm designed the children's ward that was added to Westport's Buller Hospital in the early 1920s. Joseph Munnings carried out further additions and alterations in 1922, after he had left the practice but still in association with it. These probably included the Forman Ward. The Department of Health's architects did work there around 1931, and the 1944 laundry block was designed by Archibald MacDonald, architect of the moderne-style 1941 Westport Municipal Chambers. At Greymouth, J. G. Collins designed additions to the Victoria Ward in 1949.[31]

++

↖

Burwood Hospital surgical block, 1966.

↗

Kaikoura Hospital.

In mid-Canterbury, at Ashburton Hospital Collins designed a new surgical ward and nurses' home in 1913 and group of TB shelters around 1914. William (Billy) Thomas, designed an infectious diseases ward there while working with local contractors Tuckers. In future years he would design many of the hospital's buildings (see page 219), but Ashburton architect Ernest Mitchell Gabites was responsible for most of the work at the hospital for the next decade. In 1919 a new fever ward and medical superintendent's residence were built, along with a second floor on the nurses' home. A floor was added over the Jubilee Ward in 1923 to

↑

Chatham Islands Hospital.

↖

Outpatient building, Ashburton Hospital.

↗

Timaru Hospital, c.1963.

provide outpatient accommodation. The Malvern Private Nursing Home was converted to a public maternity hospital in 1923.

As she had at Christchurch, Jane Chalmers made another generous donation towards a new women's ward and operating theatre, which opened in 1925. In 1929 a single-storey extension of brick with a slate roof was added for administration, x-ray, outpatients, a laboratory, massage and a dispensary. Gabites also designed the Methven Maternity Home, which opened in 1922. In 1944 two two-storey ward blocks of stucco on timber framing, designed by Thomas, tripled Ashburton Hospital's bed capacity to 125.[32]

A new nurses' home opened on Queen Street in Timaru in 1921, and three years later the six-bed Jean Todd Maternity Annexe was built above one of the original wards. Local architects Turnbull & Rule, who were appointed architects to the South Canterbury Hospital Board, designed the superintendent's residence, later known as Kowhai House, in 1924 and a brick administration building on High Street in 1931, which formed the main entrance to the hospital and housed casualty and outpatients. Both these buildings were demolished in 2017.[33]

The firm was responsible, too, for the surgical wards in 1935, additions to the nurses' home in 1936 and, in 1939, the surgical block, a three-storey building with operating theatres, an x-ray room and a delivery suite, and nurses' quarters on the top floor. This block won Turnbull & Rule a gold medal that year from the New Zealand Institute of Architects, the first to be awarded for a hospital building. A new boiler house opened in 1938, a replacement 24-bed Jean Todd Maternity Annexe in 1939 and a kitchen and an extension to the nurses' home in 1941.[34]

The Talbot Fever Hospital in Timaru was opened on a separate site in Otipua Road in 1906. An old men's hospital was built next door in 1913. Many years later, in 1943, Turnbull & Rule designed the 15-bed chest block at what was by then known as Talbot Hospital. After serving as a convalescent home for returning soldiers, it later became solely an aged care facility. This closed in 2021 and is now used as a hub for community outpatient services.[35]

The Second World War also affected Waimate Hospital, where buildings were added by Turnbull & Rule in 1945 to help cope with the influx of sick and wounded soldiers. They also designed the laundry and powerhouse in 1943 and general extensions to the hospital through the 1940s. When Waimate Hospital closed in 1997 it was gifted to Waimate Health Developments. The separate Waimate Maternity Hospital opened in 1874 and closed in 1980.[36]

Turnbull & Rule were also behind the 1930 six-bed Temuka Maternity Home, which closed in 1973. In 1924 the South Canterbury Hospital Board purchased the six-bed Fairlie Hospital, built in 1916 by Dr S. G. Trail primarily for maternity cases but with two beds occasionally used for general patients. This closed in 1977 and was converted into a home for the aged. The maternity home that opened in Geraldine in 1924 was replaced in 1960 by the eight-bed Geraldine Maternity Home. This, too, became an aged care provider after maternity services ceased in 1988.[37]

++

Oamaru Hospital's original building was demolished, and a new 40-bed hospital opened, in 1907. This was probably designed by Forrester & Lemon, as the firm seems to have had a remarkably continuous involvement with the hospital through its history. John Meggett

↑

Timaru Hospital surgical block, 1939.

↖

Talbot Hospital, Timaru.

↗

Fairlie Maternity Hospital.

→

Geraldine Maternity Hospital.

Forrester, only son of Thomas, took over Lemon's share of the practice in 1890, and of his father on his death. W. I. C. (Ivan) Steenson joined the firm in 1904, became a partner in 1921, and took over the firm from Forrester on the latter's retirement in 1931. Ivan was later joined by his son H. K. (Harry) Steenson, who continued the practice until 1993.[38]

John Forrester designed the TB shelters added in 1912, and the 1920 nurses' home, 14-bed isolation block and eight-bed children's ward; two more tuberculosis shelters were added later. A two-storey ward building opened in 1930 gave the hospital a total bed capacity

of 92. Ivan Steenson designed extensions to the nurses' home in 1942, the Rodman and Forrester wards in 1943, new wards, an x-ray room and operating theatres in 1941 and a new maternity annex in 1949. He was responsible for further alterations through the 1950s. The Adelaide Jones Maternity Annex opened in 1952. A 46-bed nurses' home followed in 1958, a boiler house in 1962 and a 23-bed ward in 1964. The 1925 Kurow Maternity Hospital was also designed by Forrester & Steenson.[39]

++

In Otago the 1930 Maniototo Hospital in Ranfurly, by Dunedin architect Henry McDowell Smith, shows the transition from interwar Stripped Classical style to the modern. A 14-bed building, with a central two-storey block and single-storey wings, it is constructed of brick with a Marseilles tile roof. In the words of Heritage New Zealand Pouhere Taonga, this is 'a notable example of a rural twentieth century hospital built in the modern style', and remarkably advanced when compared with other hospital buildings of the time. It was built to replace the deteriorating hospital in Naseby, which was closed and demolished in 1934, and extended around 1950 in a similar style. No longer functioning as a hospital, it is a Category 2 Historic Place but has been threatened with demolition.[40]

At Dunedin Hospital, the King Edward Pavilion, designed by Mason & Wales, was erected in 1914 on the corner of Cumberland and Hanover streets, where the oncology building now stands. This held the 24-bed Florence Nightingale and Batchelor wards, one on each floor, as well as three two-bed wards. A third storey, housing the Queen Alexandra Ward, was added in 1919. Intended for women's services, it was subsequently used for soldiers returning from the

↑

Oamaru Hospital, 1936.

↗

Maniototo Hospital, Ranfurly.

Second World War. It was demolished in the early 1980s.[41] In 1917 a nurses' home designed by Mason & Wales was built on the opposite side of Cumberland Street. A wing was added to the home in 1926 and a six-storey extension fronting Castle Street in 1941. All three are now occupied by the University of Otago's Cumberland College for student accommodation.

A small x-ray building opened in 1925. The 1930 boiler house, designed by Mason & Wales, and a nearby outpatient building were built on Cumberland Street. These were demolished in 1962 to make way for the clinical services building. In 1935 a new three-storey reinforced-concrete administration building, designed by Mason & Wales, was built on the site of the original exhibition building. It also housed the casualty department and is now the home of psychiatric services.[42]

Queen Mary Maternity Hospital, designed by Mason & Wales, opened on Castle Street next to Dunedin Hospital in 1937. The financial constraints of the Depression meant that its original 44 beds had to be reduced to one wing of 26 beds. To cater for the post-war baby boom, a second wing was added in 1953. Mason & Wales also designed, in 1961, a 50-bed extension that opened on Frederick Street.[43]

In 1946 the Fraser Building and adjacent therapeutic pool, designed by Mason & Wales, were built as part of the New Zealand School of Physiotherapy on the block opposite the hospital on the corner of Cumberland and Hanover streets. The exterior is of horizontal bands of brick and concrete, with some limited Art Deco detailing, and reinforced-concrete portal frames span the main pool area. The building is now used for health support and hospital services. Also opened in 1946, the Neurosurgical Pavilion on Hanover Street, another Mason & Wales design, incorporated the smaller 1925 x-ray block. It still stands today as the Children's Pavilion. The chapel, behind the medical school in George Street, was dedicated in 1964.[44]

The Otago Medical School soon outgrew its original premises, and after much debate as to whether it should be separated from the university campus, the wishes of the school's dean, Lindo Ferguson, prevailed, and it moved to the site opposite Dunedin Hospital on Great King Street. The first building to open in 1917 was that housing the bacteriology and pathology department, a three-storey brick building with Ōamaru stone facings and steel-framed windows designed in a neo-Classical style by Mason & Wales. Now known as the Scott

Building, and a Category 2 Historic Place, it has Classical pilasters with stone capitals, a coat-of-arms adorned pediment and a central entrance with a low arch.[45]

Ten years later this was joined by the four-storey brick-and-stone Anatomy and Physiology (later Lindo Ferguson) Building designed by Edmund Anscombe, who by that stage had established himself as the university's primary architect. Its greater height and length, and larger pedimented façade give it dignity but somewhat dominate its older neighbour. Anscombe also designed the 1924 Dental School on Great King Street.[46]

In Cromwell, architect E. M. Walden designed a maternity ward in 1912, and Mason & Wales designed a new 20-bed hospital in 1937.[47] In the early twentieth century, the Otago Hospital Board used the former Rock and Pillar Hotel in the Central Otago town of Middlemarch as a sanatorium along with, from 1910, some shelters in Palmerston. Eventually seven South Island boards combined to develop the 12-bed Waipiata Sanatorium for tuberculosis patients in Central Otago, which opened in 1924 and incorporated an earlier private facility run by Dr George Byres. Edmund Wilson has been credited with its design, possibly with assistance from A. C. Ford. The facility closed in 1961 when the 'white scourge' of tuberculosis was finally under control.[48]

Middlemarch's other health facility, the Louisa Roberts Hospital, opened in 1922. Originally a Salvation Army Home for Girls, it was purchased through funds provided by the Roberts family and converted. Essentially a large house with two wings, it had two maternity wards, an emergency ward, an operating theatre, a sterilising room, a dispensary, staff accommodation and a kitchen.[49]

++

↖

King Edward Pavilion, Dunedin Hospital, 1914.

↑

Queen Mary Maternity Hospital, Dunedin.

↗

From left: The Hercus, Scott and Lindo Ferguson buildings at the University of Otago, 1950s.

The original hospital in the Southland town of Gore, named Seddon Memorial in honour of the recently deceased premier, opened in 1909. A two-storey building of red brick with white facings, its architect was Charles Roberts of Invercargill. A 16-bed men's wing was added in 1923, followed by a nurses' home, designed by Government Architect John Mair, in 1928, which was extended in 1942.[50]

In 1907 the Southland Hospital Board bought a block of land at Kew, 3 kilometres south of central Invercargill, and a six-bed fever ward opened there the following year. It soon proved too small, but rather than expand it, the Bowmont Street home for the elderly was converted to a fever hospital. By 1915 a mainly tented fever hospital had been erected at Kew to cope with a diphtheria outbreak. A 20-bed tuberculosis ward was added two years later and, following another diphtheria crisis in 1918, the tents were replaced by wooden shelters for 50 patients. A convalescent hospital for children also opened on the Kew site in 1920.[51]

Once the decision was made in 1918 to relocate Invercargill's public hospital to Kew, a larger block of land was purchased, but despite several proposals, economic constraints meant that construction did not begin until 1935. The first stage of the new 124-bed hospital was opened in 1937, but it was seriously damaged by fire in 1939 and the Lorne Farm elderly care facility was reopened to house the displaced patients. After major repairs, the hospital reopened in 1940.[52]

Local architect Edmund Richardson Fitz Wilson, who had worked for both William Crichton and Frederick de Jersey Clere, designed the 1937 central administration building, flanked by the inpatient building on its west side and nurses' home on the east. The 1939 fire meant that the roof of the inpatient block had to be replaced and the administration building was extended to the rear in 1944. Although each of the buildings has a distinctly different design, they are all loosely neo-Georgian in style, with red brick walls and 45-degree hipped slate roofs.[53]

The original ward buildings have been demolished, but the administration building and nurses' home remain. The original buildings at Kew are now a Category 1 Historic Place. As Heritage New Zealand Pouhere Taonga notes, 'No other collection of hospital buildings in New Zealand from the first half of the twentieth century has survived to nearly the same extent.'[54]

↑

Seddon Memorial Hospital, Gore.

↗

Southland Hospital, Kew.

→

Waipiata Sanatorium, Central Otago, 1924.

A new approach to mental health

↘

By the start of the twentieth century, it was recognised that the Victorian asylum was not a suitable model for the treatment of mental illness. New Zealand also faced a problem in that most of its asylums were in the South Island, with only two in the North. Nevertheless, demand for spaces grew, partly due to population growth, but also because of a decreasing societal tolerance for the 'abnormal'. Pavilion (villa) style mental hospitals had begun to be built in Britain as early as the 1860s.

The new facilities were based on villas of a more domestic scale, laid out along garden-city principles. (Originating in Britain, garden cities were planned communities that combined the advantages of rural and urban living and emphasised a healthy existence in nature.)[1] Separate psychopaedic facilities were also built for the care and training of children and adolescents with mental illness and intellectual disability.

The 1904 redevelopment of Seaview Asylum in Hokitika could be considered the forerunner of the use of villas in mental health facilities in New Zealand, but its buildings were only 'villas' by virtue of the small size of the facility. Seaview's patient population peaked at 549 in 1955, and a chapel was dedicated there in 1963. By the time it closed in 2009, it had only 22 patients.[2]

Intended to be an experiment in asylum design and operation, Tokanui Hospital opened near Te Awamutu in Waikato in July 1912. Although the originally intended garden-city concept did not eventuate, the finished buildings did pioneer the new villa style. Most of the buildings on the site were designed by the Public Works Department. Additional villas were added in 1915 and 1921, before a major expansion between 1928 and 1930. Further villas were added from 1958 to 1960. St Barnabas Chapel was dedicated in 1963. By 1969 Tokanui housed 880 patients, and there was further significant expansion in the 1970s, with more villa-style accommodation. When Tokanui finally closed in 1998, the last patients were transferred to the new Henry Rongomau Bennett Centre at Waikato Hospital.[3]

↑

Tokanui Hospital nurses' home, 1930.

↗

Tokanui Hospital.

At Porirua, construction started in 1943 on 11 new villas, designed in a 'modern Scandinavian style' to replace the demolished main building. Further villas were built from the 1960s and a new 110-bed male admissions unit, on the site of the original building, opened in 1962, followed a year later by a female disturbed unit. Male staff quarters, which later became the clinical services building, opened in 1964. There was a new chapel in 1966, and by 1969 the institution had 1119 beds. New villas continued to be added in the 1970s and a swimming pool in 1971. The Puketiro Centre opened in 1980 as a regional base for multi-disciplinary services for children with developmental problems.[4]

From the 1950s much of the property was subdivided off to became part of the growing satellite city of Porirua; only the area around the main building, to the south of the city centre, was retained. Today's mental health facility, now known as Rātonga Rua-o-Porirua, occupies the northern section of the remaining site and Kenepuru general hospital the southern portion. A new housing area is being developed between them.[5]

The Stoke Orphanage that opened in the Ngawhatu Valley, south of Nelson, in 1886 became the St Mary's Industrial School for Boys, run by the local Catholic parishes, the Franciscan Brothers and then the Marists. After the original building was destroyed in a fire in 1903, a new Romanesque-style building, designed by John Sydney Swan and constructed of brick with plaster facings and a Marseilles tile roof, opened in 1905. It included a chapel and a belltower, with a separate hospital building behind.

When the Education Department took over in 1917, the school became the Stoke Training Farm for Delinquent Boys. In 1920 it was transferred to the Department of Health, and the main building was redeveloped to create a new asylum, which opened in 1922. Patients then began to be transferred from the Nelson Mental Hospital. In 1925, to relieve pressure on the original building, the Viewmont villa was built in the property's Highland Valley. Three more villas, Dunoon and Clovelly for females, and Airdrie for males, were opened in 1929, and Kinross, Lanark and Stirling in 1939.

A new laundry and boiler house began operating in 1935. Eventually 13 villas, each housing 40–60 people, were erected on the site. A new sports pavilion opened in 1968, and by 1970, when the new chapel was dedicated, there were 641 patients. The original

orphanage building was demolished in 1967, Dunoon was removed as an earthquake risk in 1988 and by 1991 all the villas had gone. Ngawhatu closed in 1999.[6]

In Christchurch, Sunnyside was renamed Hillmorton Hospital in 1950; by 1969 the facility had 995 beds. Because several villas had been erected, the original buildings were no longer used from 1999, and demolition of the last Sunnyside building, Campbell's administration/entrance, began in April 2007. The current mental health facility occupies the remaining northern section of the site; most of the remainder has been redeveloped for housing.[7]

↑

Ngawhatu Hospital, Nelson, 1961.

↖

A villa at Ngawhatu Hospital, 1961.

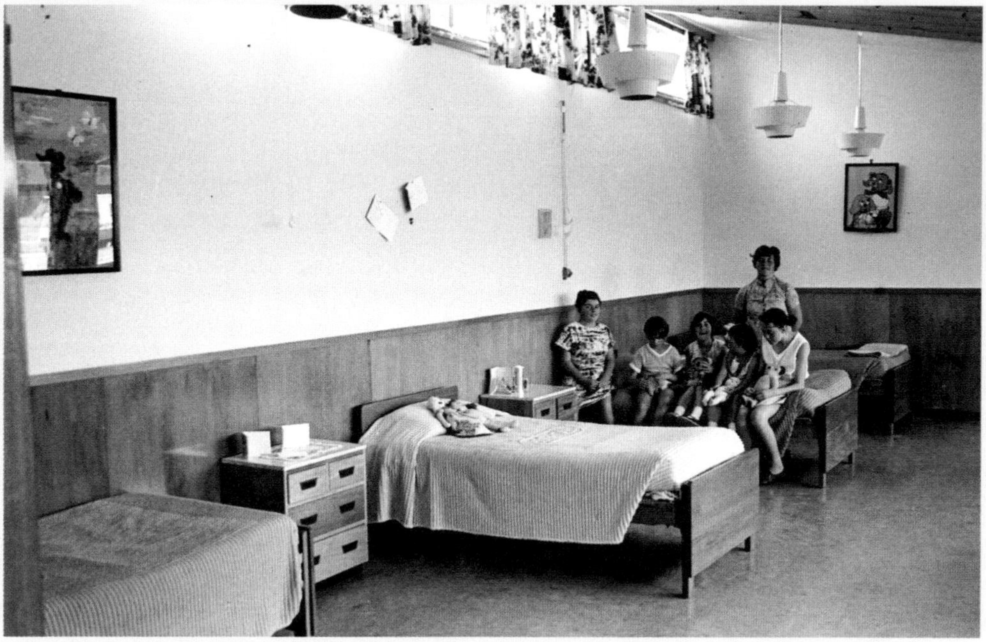

↗

A dormitory at Templeton Hospital, Christchurch, 1970.

The North Canterbury Hospital Board centralised its linen services on the site around 1982, in a building designed by Cowey Mills & Co.[8] A 15-bed medium-secure forensic unit, Te Whare Manaaki, opened in 1991 and was later extended with the 15-bed Te Whare Hohou Rongo unit. Other buildings include the Te Awakura and Te Whare Mauri Ora units, for which four of the earlier villa units were repurposed. Trengrove, Trengrove & Marshall, now Totem Architects, was responsible for the master planning and several of the later buildings.[9]

Christchurch's Templeton Hospital opened in 1928, initially intended as a replacement for Sunnyside. A year later the Templeton Farm Colony (later School) was set aside for the care and control of boys with intellectual disabilities and eight large dormitory-style villas were built between 1930 and 1937. In 1947 the villas were separated into male and female units. A nurses' home opened in 1955, male staff quarters in 1959. The interdenominational Chapel of the Holy Family, designed by George W. Lucking of Lucking & Vial, was dedicated in 1966. A new administration building opened in 1968, and six new villas were built in the 1970s. By 1969 Templeton had 530 beds. A gymnasium and indoor pool were added in 1975; the Industrial Training Complex opened in 1977. From 1989, however, villas were closed as residents were moved into the community, and the Templeton Centre, as it was known from 1988, closed in 1999.[10]

South of Auckland, Kingseat, which opened in 1932, followed the villa concept for its wards, of which there were initially two. Originally to be called Puhitahi, it was instead named after a pioneering villa-style institution in Aberdeen, Scotland, which had impressed Dr Theodore Gray, the head of the Mental Hospitals Department.[11] Like Tokanui, it was designed by the Public Works Department. By the end of the 1930s, Kingseat had a total of 12 villas, each housing around 50 patients, a nurses' home and an administration building. There were 868 patients in 1946; by 1969 the figure had grown to 936. A chapel was dedicated in 1966, an industrial and occupational therapy building opened in 1969, a tutorial block in 1970 and a swimming pool in 1977. When Kingseat finally closed in 1999, its last patients were transferred to the new secure mental health unit in Bairds Road, Ōtara.[12]

↑

Main building, Kingseat Hospital, south Auckland.

↖

Mangere Hospital and Training School, Auckland.

←

A villa at Cherry Farm Hospital, near Dunedin, c.1958.

Also in South Auckland, Raventhorpe Hospital was built in Drury in 1941 as a convalescent facility for returning soldiers.[13] After the Health Department took it over in 1946, the facility was repurposed as a hospital for the intellectually disabled and relocated to Papakura. It became an annex of Kingseat in 1972, at which point it housed 347 patients. It closed in 1988.[14]

In 1963 the Division of Mental Health purchased St Mary's Anglican Orphanage in Wyllie Road, Papatoetoe, originally built in 1909 to a design by Auckland architect George Selwyn Goldsbro', for use as a hospital for the intellectually handicapped, renaming it St John's Home. On land bought in Robertson Road, Māngere, the first building at Mangere Hospital opened in 1966, designed by the Government Architect, housing 13 females and 10 males. It was fully commissioned by 1971 and is now operated by Spectrum Care.[15]

When government funding for mental hospitals increased in the 1940s, it gave New Zealand the opportunity to create new architectural responses to changing approaches to patient care. In 1945 Cherry Farm, north of Seacliff near Waikouaiti and 35 kilometres from Dunedin, was chosen as the site for Dunedin's new mental hospital. The Cherry Farm villa design, developed by the Ministry of Works from 1949, was replicated across six other psychiatric hospital from 1953. It was a radical departure from the Victorian asylum but, as architect Rebecca McLaughlan has suggested, the villa design was not the innovative architectural solution that the Division of Mental Hygiene claimed. Rather 'a retrograde architectural design was given a post-rationalised explanation, aimed to counteract longstanding prejudices towards mental hospitals'.[16]

While some single bedrooms were provided, most patients continued to be housed in dormitories. However, at a maximum of 16 beds, these were significantly smaller than in the Victorian asylums, where dormitories accommodated 40 patients or more, and with only minimal partitions between them.

Once Cherry Farm opened in 1952, patients were gradually moved there from Seacliff. From then it became the region's main psychiatric hospital for acutely disturbed and long-term psychiatric patients, and at its peak it had 1060 beds. Facilities were added such as a chapel dedicated in 1964 to to cater for the growth. A satellite unit established at Orokonui near Waitati in 1969 accommodated another 302 people. By 1976 Cherry Farm was housing 850, a figure that decreased to fewer than 400 by 1991. Cherry Farm closed in 1992 as patients were encouraged to live and be treated in the community, and core mental health services were relocated to a 35-bed unit at Wakari Hospital.[17]

In the 1930s it was felt that the North Island needed a home for 'sub-normal or mentally defective' children, similar to that at Templeton. This opened in Levin in 1945, using repurposed barracks from a wartime air force camp. Gradually this accommodation was replaced by villas similar to those designed for Cherry Farm. The age range of those living at the facility expanded and it was renamed the Levin Hospital and Training School, later the Kimberley Centre. Not far away, at Ōtaki, the Wellington Hospital Board had operated a sanatorium for tuberculosis sufferers since 1907. When this closed in 1963 and the Health Department took over its control, it became the Otaki Annex to Levin Hospital. By 1969 Levin had 671 beds, and the Otaki Annex 100. The facility closed in 2006.[18]

In 1937 the government purchased 218 hectares of land 8 kilometres from Marton. Of this, 34 hectares was allocated for a 1000-bed psychiatric hospital; the remainder was to be used as a farm and gardens to provide food for the facility. A 1945 plan provided for separate male and female precincts, each with 20 two-storey, 11-bed villas,

four two-storey, 50-bed villas, one single-storey, 60-bed villa and three occupational therapy buildings. Lake Alice Hospital opened in mid-1950; by the beginning of October 50 patients were in residence.[19] Villas were added throughout the 1950s, and in 1965, because the relatively isolated setting was considered a suitable and safe location, an adult maximum-security unit for those regarded as criminally insane. A 100-bed villa for disturbed patients was added in 1972, as was what became a notorious child and adolescent unit. At its peak, Lake Alice had 960 beds, but by 1969 that had reduced to 295, plus 57 in the maximum-security unit.[20]

When control of New Zealand's other mental hospitals was passed to local hospital boards in 1972, Lake Alice remained under the Health Department. It was transferred to the Wanganui Area Health Board in 1986, and by the following year patient numbers had decreased to 272. It was gradually disestablished through the 1990s as mental health facilities, including forensic units, were opened closer to the populations they served.[21] Lake Alice finally closed in 1999, and as with many institutions investigated by the Royal Commission into Abuse in State and Faith-Based Care and documented in its 2024 report, left an appalling legacy of trauma for many of its former residents.[22]

++

↑

Kimberley Centre, Levin, 1913.

↗

Lake Alice Hospital, near Marton.

By 1969 New Zealand had 11 psychiatric hospitals with a total of approximately 8000 beds, as well as four psychopaedic institutions with approximately 2000 beds. During the 1980s several incidents, including a violent attack and a number of suicides, led to public concerns over the treatment of the mentally ill and the government set up a committee of inquiry, under Judge Ken Mason. What became known as the Mason Report of 1988 found that many facilities were not fit for purpose, and that many people had been unnecessarily institutionalised. It called for integrated bicultural services to better meet the needs of Māori, who were, and continue to be, disproportionately represented in mental health statistics.

After further failures Mason conducted a more wide-ranging inquiry in 1995–96. As a result, care for most patients was devolved to the community, and acute mental health units were established at general hospitals.

Around the turn of the century, specialist forensic mental health facilities were developed at Wakari in Dunedin, Stanford House at Wanganui Hospital, Porirua in Wellington, Hillmorton in Christchurch and the Mason Clinic in Auckland. The last three were built on remnants of the original asylum properties.[23]

9

Local growth

1945–1970

FOLLOWING THE SECOND WORLD WAR, New Zealand entered a sustained period of growth. Thanks to a post-war baby boom, the country's population grew from 2 million in 1952 to 3 million by 1973.[1] It also became more diverse, as people from the Pacific were encouraged to immigrate. The Māori population also began to recover, and became increasingly urbanised. New Zealand's expansion in infrastructure, as dams and power stations, an oil refinery, a steel mill and an aluminium smelter were built, was paralleled by advances in medical care here and overseas.

The first linear accelerator for radiotherapy began operation in 1953, and medical imaging was greatly improved by the introduction of computer-assisted tomography (CT scanning) and magnetic resonance imaging (MRI) in the 1970s. New Zealand was quick to adopt these and other technologies. After being recruited back to New Zealand by medical reformer Sir Douglas Robb, cardiac surgeon Sir Brian Barratt-Boyes performed the country's first open-heart surgery at Green Lane Hospital in 1958.

Green Lane was also the site of the world's second heart-valve replacement in 1962 and New Zealand's first heart transplant in 1987. Sir Graham (Mont) Liggins pioneered life-saving treatments for premature babies in the 1960s and Sir William Liley developed techniques to improve the health of foetuses in utero. Interestingly, Robb received an honorary fellowship of the NZIA in 1969 in recognition of his efforts to improve the design of New Zealand's health facilities.[2]

During and after the Second World War, the range of conditions that could be treated effectively with drugs expanded vastly. Diseases such as tuberculosis and poliomyelitis, which had been the scourge of previous generations, could now be prevented by vaccination and cured by medication. Nevertheless, the reduction in tuberculosis cases among Māori lagged behind that of the general population, and rates also increased among the growing number of Pasifika immigrants.[3]

Hospital districts began to amalgamate, reducing from 47 in 1947 to 31 by 1969. After the passing of the 1957 Hospitals Act, expenditure on public hospitals became entirely the responsibility of central government and the legislation reinforced the responsibilities of the minister of health for ensuring adequate and efficient nationwide hospital services.[4]

Concerned that most hospital boards were seeking approval to proceed with major new building projects without considering longer-term planning requirements or the need to replace or upgrade older building stock, the Health Department made the preparation of a proper development plan and report a mandatory requirement for all boards. Further changes resulted from the Hospitals Amendment Acts of 1970, 1971 and 1977, and the psychiatric institutions and remaining St Helen's hospitals were transferred from central government to local hospital board control.

Advances in building technologies and a drive for the efficient use of land led to the development, in the 1950s, of what Michael Murphy has termed the 'block' concept of hospital planning, with large floor plates and many levels. (The Stephenson & Turner acute block at Auckland Hospital is probably the best New Zealand example of this.) The hospital began to be considered as a medical machine and developed a monolithic form in a minimalist modernist style.

The plates housed specialised zones for different services, resulting in large amounts of space without natural light or outlook, and with windows sealed for mechanical control. International examples include the 1973 building referred to as 'the Cube' at New York's Bellevue Hospital and the 13-storey North Wing at St Thomas' Hospital in London, opened in 1975. Louis Kahn introduced the concept of an interstitial floor dedicated to services in the

1965 Salk Institute in California; however, with a few exceptions, this proved too expensive to be adopted in New Zealand. Medical gases such as oxygen, medical air and suction began to be piped around hospital buildings, with outlets provided at ward bedheads.[5]

An alternative to the block approach was what Murphy has referred to as the 'mat' plan, in which a hospital was assembled from a horizontal series of less formal low-rise buildings and courtyards, possibly punctuated by a single high-rise element housing offices or wards. Examples of this are the 1959 Northwest Community Hospital in Arlington Heights, Illinois, and the 1965 Wexham Park Hospital in Slough, England. Such plans gave greater connection to outlook, light and nature, but meant significantly longer walking distances for staff.[6] Gisborne Hospital is a good New Zealand example of this approach.

In 1951 the Health Department outlined its expectations for public hospitals: a maximum of 600 beds in most general hospitals; ward blocks oriented east–west to avoid significant temperature changes, ideally with patients on the north side and support on the south; and a separate clinical services block with facilities for outpatients, casualty, x-ray, physiotherapy, occupational therapy and laboratories. General wards were to contain 30 beds, with six four-bed and six single rooms; maternity wards were to have 20 beds, with four-bed and single rooms in the same ratio.[7]

There were problems to be addressed, too, regarding the services architects provided to public hospitals. According to the Consultative Committee on Hospital Reform, which reported in 1954, these were often inadequate, resulting in unnecessary and wasteful

↑

Cornwall Park Hospital, Auckland, 1957.

↩

Middlemore Hospital, 1967.

expenditure. Because hospital design was becoming increasingly complex, the architects employed by the hospital boards needed adequate experience. In the public service, because secondment periods of architects to the Department of Health were too short, boards and their architects were not receiving adequate quality advice and assistance. The Department of Health was to focus more on strategic advice and the development of design standards.

Because only some hospital boards had been able to commission or recruit architects with considerable healthcare work experience, plans submitted to the department required onerous levels of checking and, often, amendment. The report proposed the formation of a panel of architects with skill and experience in hospital design. It also proposed that the department facilitate greater standardisation of hospital building components.[8]

Modernism was the dominant architectural style in this period. For hospitals, the economics of construction and operation tended to favour buildings with strips of windows between deep spandrels, rather than full-height curtain walls. The 1932 Paimio Sanatorium in Finland, designed by Alvar Aalto to maximise cross-ventilation and increase exposure to air by using verandahs and terraces, had a significant influence on hospital designers in the mid-twentieth century. The Brutalist style, with its large areas of exposed concrete structure, also became popular for public buildings from the 1960s.[9]

++

During the later stages of the Second World War, large numbers of casualties were expected from battles in the Pacific. From June 1942 to mid-1944, thousands of American servicemen were in camp in New Zealand, and because Auckland already housed several military bases for them, and for Kiwi troops, it made sense to locate most of the large military hospital facilities there.

In 1942 the United States requested the use of 926 hectares of Cornwall Park, near the Auckland Infirmary, to house the 39th General US Army Hospital. Completed in 1943, this 34,095-square-metre complex of 122 light timber-frame buildings had 48 wards and could take 1500 patients. After 1945 the Auckland Hospital Board continued to use the buildings as a temporary public hospital. Half the facility was allocated to geriatric patients, and the remainder, for obstetrics and gynaecology, became the first National Women's Hospital in 1955. Removal of the buildings began in 1961. The final elderly patients were transferred to Waitakere Hospital in 1974 and the following year the site was returned to the Cornwall Park Trust Board.[10]

A military annex designed by the Public Works Department was built on the grounds of Auckland Hospital and the adjacent domain, and in 1942 the US No. 4 Mobile Hospital was erected on the site now occupied by Dilworth School in Market Road.[11] The US No. 6 Navy Hospital in Avondale was designed by Tibor Donner, later Auckland's city architect, while he was employed by the Public Works Department. The brief called for the building to be readily converted to a secondary school after the war. By the time it was completed in 1944 it was no longer needed and Avondale College opened there in 1945.[12]

The Auckland Infirmary was renamed Green Lane Hospital in 1942, and its six-storey, 264-bed main building, opened the next year, is an early example of functionalist design in New Zealand hospitals. Built in concrete, it incorporated wards with a maximum of six beds in any room and had cantilevered balconies. It was designed by Raymond Leslie (Ray) Farrell, who had been appointed architect to the Auckland Hospital Board in 1938.[13] After qualifying from Auckland University, Farrell went into partnership with his father, John Farrell, to form J. Farrell & Son, later Farrell Son & Glover. Their firm was associated with work for the Auckland Hospital Board from 1926, the year that G. W. Allsop retired.[14]

Also at Green Lane, the old Costley building was modified to accommodate a casualty department on the ground floor and operating theatres that were moved to the ground floor of the main block in 1950. The brick nurses' home was enlarged in 1946, and in 1953 the 12 tuberculosis shelters erected in 1919 were amalgamated to form a chest annex.[15]

By the mid-twentieth century, the Auckland Hospital Board was facing a dilemma. Its existing buildings were ageing and unable to cope with advances in medical technology and models of care just as the growing city was demanding more capacity. The military facilities had only been a temporary measure.

The board developed in-house expertise by employing their own architects from the early 1950s. The head of the architect's department at that time was Louis (Neil) Orchard, who worked on the 1954 maternity hospital at Helensville. R. A. Wilkie led the team from 1956 into the 1970s, James Garrett in the early 1980s. Commissions were also awarded to a few small Auckland firms willing to develop a specialty in health design. Bruce Henderson designed alterations to Princess Mary and the Costley blocks in 1967 and 1972, and Gillam Morton Graham carried out work at Auckland Hospital around the same time.

Board architects designed the 1200-square-metre, steel-framed central stores building, built in 1960, which was relocated to the Carrington site in 1988 to make way for construction of the Starship Children's Hospital. Other work included the Auckland Blood Transfusion Centre in Park Avenue near Auckland Hospital.[16]

The board also accepted that, because of the limited number of experienced hospital designers in New Zealand, overseas specialists would be needed to design their higher-acuity buildings – those for patients with severe illnesses or injuries that need continued treatment and monitoring – but required these firms to establish offices in this country and, where possible, to work alongside local practices and share their knowledge.

++

↗
Middlemore Hospital nurses' home.

Middlemore Hospital in Ōtāhuhu also developed from a military facility for which the government had requisitioned 24 hectares of land from the Auckland Golf Club during the Second World War. Although road access was poor, the site did sit beside the main trunk railway line. Named Middlemore after the homestead of the original farm, it was of more permanent construction to

allow it to continue to provide treatment and rehabilitation for military patients, and eventually civilians, after the end of the war. The 10-ward, 300-bed facility, designed by Government Architect Robert Patterson, was well built with heart rimu timber framing, matai floors, stucco walls and orange clay tile roofs. Its main corridor, later known as the Rainbow corridor, was so wide and strong that an army Jeep could be driven along it.

After buying Middlemore in 1946, the Auckland Hospital Board reopened it as a public hospital the following year. As well as providing a general hospital for the growing South Auckland community, it retained the orthopaedic specialty developed during the war.[17] After the conversion to civilian use, the first new building constructed, in 1961, was a 123-bed nurses' home, which received a 214-bed, four-storey extension in 1965 by Orchard & Allison, the practice formed in the early 1950s by Neil Orchard, after leaving his position with the board, and David Charles Allison.[18]

The 60-bed maternity block (now the Bray Building), also designed by Orchard & Allison with Stephenson & Turner as consultants, opened in 1961. Orchard had probably won the Middlemore commission before joining Allison, as some of the maternity block drawings carry only his name. Its distinctive vertical fins slope outwards to support a concrete hood at the top, and its curved-glass-clad stairwell is reminiscent of the one in the model factory designed by Walter Gropius and Adolf Meyer for the 1914 Deutscher Werkbund exhibition. Designed to connect to Stephenson & Turner's later Acute (Galbraith) Block, this four-storey building had three 20-bed wards above the ground-floor delivery and theatre suites. There were, however, a series of problems, from a leaking flat roof to the exterior's blue-green decorative panels shattering when knocked, resulting in their later replacement with baked enamel aluminium panels.[19]

Other buildings by Orchard & Allison at Middlemore include the 1965 household staff quarters on the Ōrākau Road site on the other side of the railway line, and the 1968 resident doctors' quarters.[20] In 1966 three old ward blocks were relocated from Cornwall Park Hospital and refurbished to create a geriatric unit. They were replaced 12 years later with a new building behind the four-storey nurses' home extension, which was later repurposed as the Esme Green office building.[21]

Orchard & Allison also designed the 1958 remodelling of the Wallace Block at Auckland Hospital, adding a floor and staircases, the modernist style of which resulted in a somewhat unusual hybrid.[22] Allison continued to undertake projects for the Auckland Hospital Board after ending his partnership with Orchard, including the laundry on the Carrington campus, which won an NZIA Award in 1980.

++

↖

Middlemore Hospital, maternity wing at left and Galbraith Block at right, 1967.

↗

Middlemore Hospital maternity wing, 1963.

Following the opening of the Auckland Harbour Bridge in 1959, the North Shore began to grow rapidly, and the Auckland Hospital Board purchased 18 hectares of land beside Lake Pupuke in Takapuna from the Sisters of Mercy for a new public hospital. North Shore Maternity Hospital, designed by the Auckland Hospital Board architect's department, opened in 1958, with 44 beds and a small emergency department.[23] Waitakere Obstetric (later Maternity) Hospital, also designed by the Auckland Hospital Board architect's department, opened in 1964 in Lincoln Road, Henderson, after relocation from nearby Te Atatū, where it had been established in 1945. This was extended to 135 beds with accommodation for geriatric patients and eventually became a general hospital.[24]

EXISTING HOSPITAL
NEW NURSES HOME
KITCHEN & DINING ROOM
NEW RECREATION HALL
PRESENT NURSES HOME

↖

Main block, Green Lane Hospital, Auckland.

←

Middlemore Hospital looking west: nurses' home at top, geriatric wards below, 1953.

↑

Otara Civilian Rehabilitation Centre, Auckland.

↗

Otara Spinal Unit, c.1979.

South of Auckland, the town of Pukekohe had developed to service the horticultural industry on the rich volcanic soils of the area, and its growth was later boosted by the opening of the nearby Glenbrook steel mill in 1969. Pukekohe Hospital opened in 1953 as a maternity unit; a geriatric ward was added in 1979.[25]

Newman, Smith & Associates, established in 1957 by Geoffrey Newman and Gordon Smith, won the 1959 competition for Auckland's new St Helen's Hospital, which opened on Linwood Avenue, Mount Albert, in 1968.[26] This 6300-square-metre complex consisted of a four-storey 52-bed ward block connected to a circular delivery suite, with a separate nurses'

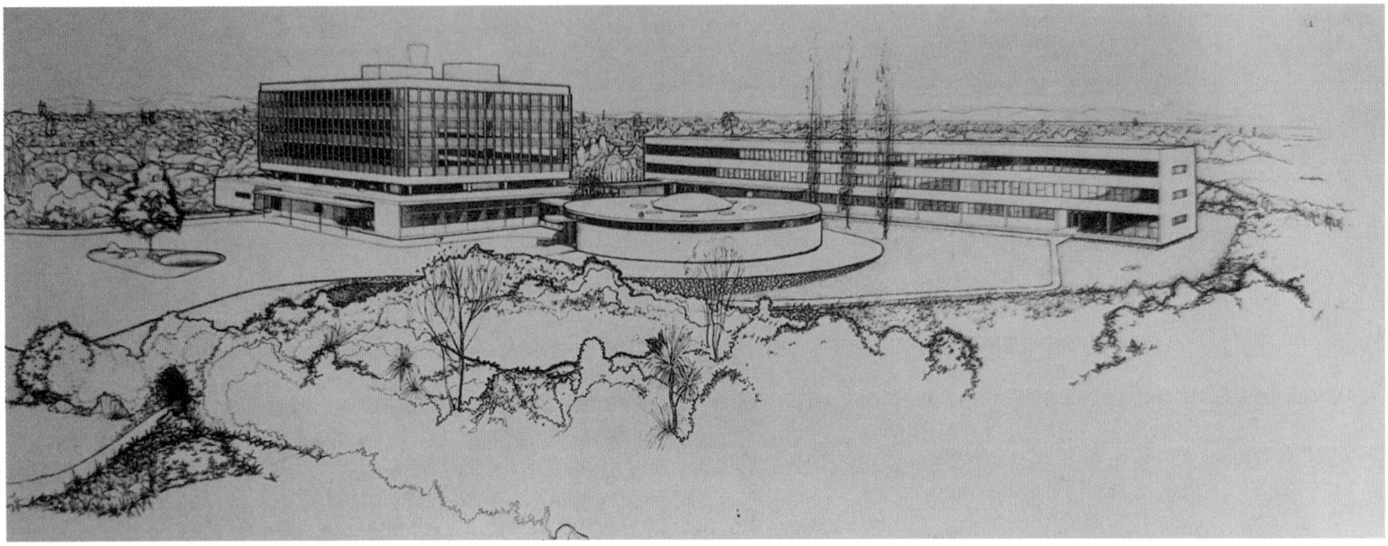

home, and was documented in association with Orchard & Allison. The hospital closed in 1990, when maternity services were amalgamated at National Women's Hospital, and the building is now the Auckland Institute of Studies.[27]

The 30-bed Otara Civilian Rehabilitation Centre, which opened in Bairds Road in 1958, had incorporated the former home of Morton Coutts, head of Dominion Breweries, which still operates on the opposite side of the road. Newman, Smith & Associates designed the Paraplegic Rehabilitation Centre there, which opened in about 1965, and Newman's later firm, Gillespie, Newman, West & Pearce, designed the 1977 Otara Spinal Rehabilitation Unit.[28] Newman, Smith & Associates also designed the 1969 Ngāti Whakaue Acute Medical Block at Rotorua Hospital.

++

In the Bay of Plenty, Tauranga Hospital's Macmillan Ward, a 12-bed unit for tuberculosis sufferers, opened in 1941, followed by a new children's ward and a two-wing extension to the nurses' home. The building added in 1944 for military patients, designed by board architect C. H. D. (Harold) Porter in association with the Public Works Department, was converted for use as a 13-bed maternity annex later that year. Both the 1925 building and the annex were demolished in 2010.[29]

Health Department chief architect Graeme Laurenson had recommended closing the road on the southern side of the Tauranga Hospital site and buying farmland beyond it to allow for further development. The first building on the newly acquired land was the 1948 laundry, designed by Harold Porter, working with engineer Lloyd Mandeno of Auckland firm Mandeno, Lee & Brown (later Worley Mandeno). This was completed after some delays, and although most of these were outside Porter's control, his appointment was terminated. The laundry building was later converted into the hospital's laboratory.[30]

++

In the Coromandel district Auckland architect Lewis Maitland Howey Walker was appointed architect to the Thames Hospital Board in 1945. That year Baillie Street between Mary and

Bella streets was closed in preparation for major redevelopment of the hospital in the 1950s and early 1960s. A new ambulance station opened opposite the hospital in Mackay Street in 1953. The next year a three-storey nurses' home and kitchen, designed by Walker, was built on the corner of Mary and Rolleston streets, followed in 1958 by a three-storey, 88-bed ward block designed by his later firm, Lewis Walker & Hillary, with two 30-bed general wards, a 28-bed ground-floor maternity annex and theatre and a kitchen. A boiler house, workshop and laundry were added in 1959. The main five-storey ward and theatre block on McKay Street, opened in 1963, provided a further 112 beds, with an operating theatre suite on the top floor and a children's ward at ground level. Both were designed by Walker, Hillary & Swan. Walker also worked on the nurses' home at Taumarunui with Ronald Muston.[31]

++

By the end of the Second World War the Waikato Hospital Board was responsible for the 544-bed base hospital in Hamilton, as well as the public hospitals at Rotorua, Te Kūiti, Matamata, Huntly, Kāwhia, Taupō, Te Aroha and Ōtorohanga. When board architect John Willing Warren retired, his role appears to have passed on to the practice of Edgecumbe & White, formed by John Harold Edgecumbe and Harold L. White in 1919. Despite a series of mergers and splits over the years, this longstanding Hamilton firm endured well beyond Edgecumbe's retirement in 1948.

It designed the 1939 Hamilton Post Office in association with the Government Architect, and a successor firm – White, Leigh, De Lisle & Fraser – designed the 1962 Founders' Memorial Theatre. The Hiwa Maternity Home in Hamilton East, which in 1930 replaced the house in which Wilhelmina Olsen set up her facility in 1918, was designed by Edgecumbe & White and is now part of Metlifecare's Wilson Carlile Village.[32]

The firm was also responsible for the 1937 expansion of the nurses' home at Waikato Hospital. A new kitchen, dining room and a third storey were added, and the building was renamed the Ryburn Nurses' Home. A new Art Deco administration block opened in 1938,

↖

Artist's impression of St Helen's Hospital, Auckland, c.1959.

↗

Tauranga Hospital, 1948–49.

↖

Waikato Hospital administration block, c.1948.

←

Artist's rendering of the Smith Ward at Waikato Hospital.

↗

Waikato Hospital looking north: Smith ward block top right, Menzies ward block top centre, Elizabeth Rothwell building top left, Hilda Ross Nurses' Home lower centre.

to which a third storey was added in 1968, and a new infectious diseases building opened in 1942. The two-level Hockin Block was built in 1943, with four 46-bed wards, as temporary accommodation for military patients. In 1944 a temporary building, known for its appearance as the 'Woolshed', was erected for outpatient clinics, and the two-storey 84-bed Douglas Nurses' Home, designed by Edgecumbe, White & Leigh, became the first reinforced-concrete building at the hospital.

A block relocated from the Narrows Air Force camp in 1946 added more nurses' accommodation, as did the Findlay Nurses' Home completed in 1947.[33] Edgecumbe also designed a 200-bed extension at Rotorua Hospital in 1939, and Edgecumbe, White & Leigh carried out extensions at Te Kuiti Hospital in 1939.

The Waikato Hospital Board then decided to establish its own in-house architect's department, appointing Alfred Smith, who had emigrated from England in 1946 to take on the position.[34] During his tenure, an additional floor was added to the administration block to accommodate five operating theatres, the Campbell Johnstone maternity ward was extended in 1953, and a 32-bed ward, plus an extension to the 'Woolshed', were added in 1954. The three-storey 155-bed Hockin Nurses' Home opened in 1956; in the mid-1970s this was converted to office accommodation and in 1991 a third floor was added. Four new operating theatres were commissioned in 1957. The Nurses' Memorial Chapel dedicated in 1958 was demolished in 1997 to make way for the Henry Rongomau Bennett Centre.

In 1960 a large portion of the Rothwell Nurses Home was moved and connected to the Hockin Nurses' Home. A temporary building was added to the Hockin ward block in 1961, a new laundry block opened in 1959, and in 1963 the Infectious Diseases Nurses' Home was converted

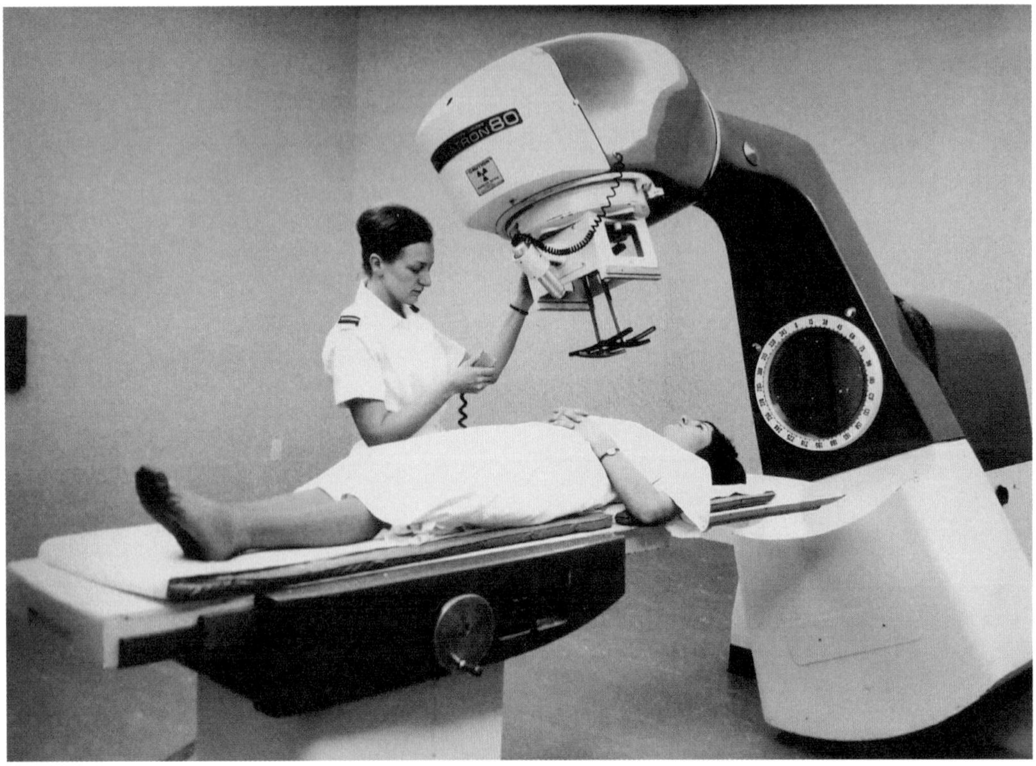

to an outpatient unit. A new cafeteria and kitchen block were opened in 1965. In 1968 a 32-bed ward was added to the Campbell Johnstone building and a 32-bed geriatric ward built.[35]

The major work at Waikato Hospital by Smith and his staff, however, consisted of the three multi-storey ward blocks on the north side of the site, facing the lake. The first was the 1964 six-storey, 200-bed Smith Block, named for board chairman George Smith, which had one ward per floor. The adjacent oncology building for radiotherapy, which opened in 1966 and was renamed Lomas in 1993, was where the hospital's first linear accelerator was installed in 1980. The nine-level Menzies (or East–West) ward block, with 439 beds in 18 wards, opened in 1973, on the site of the three original wards that had been demolished in 1969.[36] The 12-storey Waikato Women's Hospital (later renamed the Elizabeth Rothwell Building) opened in 1979. Two older ward buildings were relocated in 1976, becoming the Ryburn Buildings in 1993.[37]

Te Kuiti Hospital was extended to a design by Smith and his team in 1952, increasing the hospital's capacity to 27 general and 17 maternity beds. In 1964 a boiler house, kitchen, stores and laboratory were added. They also designed a cottage hospital at Benneydale, but this closed and the building was relocated to Te Kūiti six years later, where they also carried out extensions to the nurses' home and staff facilities in 1949 and 1973. His department also designed, in about 1962, the new Te Aroha Maternity Hospital, which boasted 20 bedrooms, a delivery suite and a 15-bed nurses' home.[38]

++

↖ **The Betatron x-ray machine at Waikato Hospital.**

By the 1960s, the workload on the Waikato Hospital site was too much for the board's in-house team to handle, and local firm T. F. Gillman & Co. (later Gillman Garry Clapp & Sayers) was commissioned to collaborate on the design of the eight-storey, 136-bed Hilda Ross Nurses' Home, opened in 1963. Gillman Garry Clapp & Sayers went on to design the 1971 Clinical Services (Waiora Waikato) Building and the 1978 operating theatre block (see page 291).[39]

A new laundry was built in 1960, a new kitchen in 1967 and the NICU (neonatal intensive care unit) in 1967. A cancer hostel opened in 1971 was eventually relocated to the Lion Lodge on the former Braemar Hospital site in 2011. The Hockin Nurses' Home was redeveloped as the hospital's corporate centre around 1990 and the new main kitchen completed in 1992. Part of the Hilda Ross Nurses' Home was redeveloped as the Bryant Education Centre in 1994, with the establishment of the Waikato academic division of the Auckland School of Medicine, and this was extended in 2002 as the Peter Rothwell Academic Centre and Gudex Library.[40]

As architect and politician Michael Fowler wrote in 1984, 'The Waikato Hospital is really a large medical centre, dominant in the Hamilton townscape. Certainly, from the south of the city it is the main building feature atop its hill site – a parthenon on its acropolis – and even from the north it rivals the few office towers of the central city. If there is one lesson to learn from the Waikato Hospital, as with most others in New Zealand, it is this: medical practitioners should stick to medicine, the Department of Health to administration and leave the architects to design.' And Fowler did not restrict his opinions to Waikato: 'I know of no country in the world that is as over-hospitalised as this one. An imbalance in our welfare conscious state has caused us as a nation, or did, to expend enormous resources over the last four decades in creating vast permanent structures for the treatment and caring of our ill, and maybe far too little in addressing the causes of those illnesses. This is not unusual in relatively new societies where the effect is often addressed before the cause, and it is writ large to the eye, at least in the North Island where most principal towns and cities have placed their hospital atop the highest hill, where it stands like an acropolis – large, symbolic, ominous, but inevitably of pedestrian design epitomising years of unordered priorities, yet nevertheless, a caring community. I cannot help recalling Samuel Butler's *Erewhon* where the sick were imprisoned, and the criminals hospitalised.'[41]

++

In 1957, two years after a fire destroyed the kitchen and outpatient buildings at Rotorua Hospital, the 90-bed Bridgeman Building, the first of the new buildings on the site, was opened. This was followed by the 1962 clinical services block designed by Gillman Garry Clapp & Sayers. In 1965, a new boiler house opened, as did the 40-bed Edward Guy Maternity Annex, designed by Alfred Smith. A three-storey building, on a floating foundation due to the ground conditions, it utilises geothermal heat to boost that from the boiler house.[42]

The 90-bed Ngāti Whakaue Acute Medical Block, designed by Newman, Smith & Associates, was added to the Bridgeman Wing in 1969. Also on a raft foundation, it consisted of a series of pavilions with white concrete walls and contrasting cedar facings. It housed the children's ward on the ground floor with an external play area, and two floors of wards above, and adopted a double-corridor arrangement with central service rooms to reduce staff movement.[43] White, Leigh & De Lisle also carried out work at Rotorua Hospital around this time.

During the 1930s plans were drawn up for a new sanatorium in Rotorua, between the existing one and the Bath House. The foundations were laid, but work stopped during the war and eventually the project was abandoned and the foundations buried. In 1941 the council agreed to the building of a temporary services convalescent hospital – it had to be

removed within 10 years – next to the Government Gardens on borough council land between Whakaue and Hinemaru streets.

The King George V Hospital site had been considered, but its hillside location was too expensive for the foundations required and the sanatorium site close to the lake offered ample flat land for recreation. Designed by the Public Works Department, under Robert Patterson, it was a plain, serviceable building with fibrolite walls and a malthoid bituminous felt roof. Opened in 1942, it housed 75 patients, later increasing to 160, and had four 40-bed wards, an operating theatre and a therapy pool. Arawa House, built on the corner of Arawa and Amohau streets as a parsonage in 1889, was later used as the nurses' home for the convalescent hospital.[44]

Most military patients had left the hospital by 1948, but it was kept open to deal with the 1947–48 polio epidemic. By this time, rheumatic and arthritic conditions had become a significant problem, and it was decided to use the building as a specialist treatment centre. This was transferred to the Department of Health in 1948 and renamed the Queen Elizabeth Hospital for Physical Disorders. The old sanatorium was transferred to the Waikato Hospital Board and became an old persons' home.[45]

In 1950 a laboratory and x-ray unit were added and in 1954 a nurses' home was built near the abandoned foundations of the proposed sanatorium. The old home became the Whare Aroha elderly care facility. By 1955 the council wanted to take over the iconic Bath House from the government and, in return, agreed to an extension of the lease of the Queen Elizabeth site. A hydrotherapy wing was added in 1965, but construction was delayed as water from the nearby Priest Spring was too hot and needed to be cooled by lake water, which was found to be too polluted to use. Instead water had to be piped from the more distant Rachel Spring.[46]

↑
Ngati Whakaue Acute Medical Block, Rotorua Hospital.

↗
Rotorua Hospital looking south-east: the Bridgeman Building lower centre, c.1960.

Queen Elizabeth Hospital was managed by the Department of Health until 1968, when it was transferred to the Waikato Hospital Board, and then in 1989 to the Bay of Plenty Area Health Board. A new rehabilitation block opened in 1968 and in 1974 the Gardenholme Residential Home and the Roberts Day Care Centre were built between the hospital and the nurses' home. Never a large facility, by 1969 Queen Elizabeth had 135 beds. In 1993 it became a private institution governed by a community trust.[47]

A unit opened at Queen Elizabeth in 1951 became the national specialist centre for children with cerebral palsy and childhood rheumatic complaints. It was replaced by the 1972 Child Potential Unit at the hospital, designed by Smith Grant Architects, a practice formed by Waikato board architect Alfred Smith's son, Rod Smith, and Kelvin Grant in 1969. This provided accommodation and outpatient care for the assessment of up to 20 children with developmental and neurological conditions. Of concrete-block construction, it also had asbestos cement walls and roof cladding due to the corrosive geothermal atmosphere. The unit consisted of four main areas – living, school, treatment and administration – all grouped around a central courtyard and geothermally heated pool, and was located between the hospital and the nurses' home. In 1988 it came under the joint management of Rotorua Hospital and the Department of Education, but was eventually closed in 1996 and later demolished.[48]

++

The 1965 Matariki Geriatric Hospital in Te Awamutu, designed by Rod Smith, was built on the site of the old Matariki Private Hospital. The new domestic-style building provided 40 beds, arranged around central service rooms, with day spaces and occupational therapy at the northern end. Sunscreens on metal frames allowed soft natural light into the interior. The older buildings on the site were retained for staff accommodation and storage.[49] Smith Grant Architects also designed the 1973 administration building at Tokanui Hospital.

↑

Government Sanatorium, Rotorua, c.1943.

↖

Child Potential Unit, Rotorua.

↗

Palmerston North Hospital, Nash Memorial Wing centre right, c.1960.

In 1982 Robert B. Finch's Whangārei practice joined Smith Grant, the firm becoming Smith Grant Finch & Associates. Finch had designed several significant Northland buildings, among them the Settlers Motor Inn in Whangārei, and the 1952 theatre, ward and administration block at Bay of Islands Hospital, plus later additions that included a staff amenities building in 1962 and a physiotherapy annex in 1963. A whānau house was added in 1972.[50]

++

During the 1950s and 1960s the Hawke's Bay firm of father and son Ernest Arthur Williams and Lawrence Garbutt Williams, worked on both Napier and Hastings hospitals. In 1954 the partnership designed Napier's four-storey Hinepare Nurses' Home on the corner of Napier Terrace and Spencer Road in the International Style. It was intended to provide 88 beds in an E-shaped complex, but the eastern wing was never built.[51] E. A. & L. G. Williams also carried out a significant amount of work on the Hastings site in the 1950s. Around 1955 they designed the orderlies' quarters and the resident medical officers' flats, about 1957 the two-storey store, linen and mortuary building and additions to the tutorial block, and in 1959 the new boiler house.

They were also the architects for the 15-bed West Wing psychiatric unit, opened in 1967, and in 1968 refurbished Ward 1, which was later incorporated into the Health Villa complex.[52] Other work in Hawke's Bay during this period by Davies, Phillips & Chaplin, and the various Natusch partnerships, is described in Chapters 10 and 11 respectively.

++

The Palmerston North Hospital Board continued its own architect's department under Jack Bennett Reynolds, who was appointed in 1948.[53] The four-storey J. A. Nash Memorial Wing, containing laboratories and three wards, opened in 1956. A new maternity suite, with delivery suite and antenatal clinics, was added in 1957 and extended in 1962 with a further 40 beds. A new chapel designed by Reynolds opened in 1957, replacing the one dedicated in 1948, and a super-voltage facility for radiotherapy opened in 1959.

Reynolds was also responsible for the two-storey maternity unit, with two 20-bed wards and a delivery suite, that opened in 1962 when the theatre block was also altered. In 1964 a three-storey block was added beside the Nash Block for medical records and a library.[54] A new boiler house was built around 1953, designed by the Public Works Department, and the 1970 40-bed Manawatu Psychiatric Unit, also known as the Manawaroa Centre for Psychological Medicine, was designed by the Ministry of Works.[55]

Reynolds also designed the chapel at Awapuni Geriatric Home in Palmerston North, which was dedicated in 1963,[56] and a 46-bed extension added in 1959. The 1967 Horowhenua Geriatric Hospital, with two 25-bed wards, a 23-bed nurses' home, a kitchen and a boiler house, was also his work. This site had been purchased in 1945 for a tuberculosis sanatorium, and a small building erected in 1948, but was not developed further as tuberculosis declined thanks to vaccination. After Reynolds' sudden death in 1969, Gillman Garry Clapp & Sayers took over the work of the architect's department and looked after all its facilities and building records.[57]

++

Several small hospitals were developed in the Whanganui–Manawatū region during this time. The Marton and District Hospital, which opened in 1954 with 10 maternity and two emergency beds, was replaced in 1997 by the Rangitikei Health Centre. The Abbotsford Maternity Hospital in Waverley was a private hospital until 1945, when it was taken over by the hospital board. It closed in 1986 and is now used for a variety of health services. Waiouru Army Camp had a small maternity hospital created by connecting three state houses in the 1950s. This closed in 1962 before being taken over as a private facility. It reopened in 1981 but finally shut its doors in the 1990s.[58]

Belchambers, Low & Associates designed additions and alterations at Taihape Hospital in the 1960s, and the new main building there in 1982.[59] The hospital closed in 2011, becoming the Taihape Health Centre. The firm also designed the 1972 central laundry at Wanganui Hospital, and alterations to the Jubilee Home in Whanganui, but the latter was eventually demolished in 1978.[60]

++

In 1935 local architect Fred Daniell was appointed architect to the Wairarapa Hospital Board, His extensions to the Buchanan Ward at Greytown opened three years later. The hospital was redeveloped after damage from the 1942 earthquake, and in 1947 a new maternity ward, men's ward and operating theatre were built there, all to his design. A new five-bed maternity ward was added at Greytown in 1958 and a kitchen in 1960.[61]

Pahiatua Hospital opened in 1902. There, Daniell designed a new maternity ward in 1947 and a general ward and staff accommodation two years later.[62] Wards were added in the 1940s and 1960s, and among other buildings Daniell designed a kitchen and an operating theatre. The nurses' home, from about 1924, was by Watson, Gooder & Lee of Masterton. Pahiatua Hospital closed in 1998 and was converted into the Masters Hall conference venue. Daniell's practice also designed a maternity hospital at Martinborough. In 1948, Daniell designed a building for the Eketahuna Maternity Home, which became a rest home in 1979 and closed in 2001.[63]

At Masterton Hospital, Daniell designed the 56-bed, three-storey, brick Art Deco-style nurses' home, with Joseph MacClatchie Dawson and Jack Ian King, later of King & Dawson, which opened in 1938, as did his new ward block, built in 48 hours to cope with a poliomyelitis outbreak. After the 1942 Wairarapa earthquake, several hospital buildings at Masterton,

↑

Frederick Charles (Fred) Daniell.
Trevor Hamilton Daniell.

↗

Pahiatua Hospital.

including the nurses' home, were rebuilt. In 1943 construction started on a ward block intended for soldiers, but the war ended before it was complete and it became the maternity annex instead. They also designed an x-ray block and a new kitchen in 1948. Daniell & Wevers collaborated with Wellington practice Porter & Martin on the 1963 three-storey ward and specialist services block at Masterton Hospital (see page 269) and also worked with Haughton & Mair on a proposed second three-storey block there, though this did not eventuate.[64] The firm also designed a 24-bed staff accommodation block in 1969, a two-storey theatre and central sterile supply department (CSSD) block, a new boiler house, a laundry and a workshop.[65]

++

Further south, at Nelson Hospital, the Public Works Department designed a ward block in 1942 and a new nurses' home, built in 1946. The latter was expanded several times during the 1950s. Local architect Alexander (Alex) Bowman also designed work at Nelson Hospital, including a temporary ward block and staff quarters in 1956. He also worked with board architect R. Duke on Reefton Hospital in the 1950s, including a new boiler house.[66]

In 1952 Christchurch's St Helen's Hospital moved into a brand-new purpose-built maternity hospital between Colombo and Durham streets, north of Salisbury Street, designed by then Government Architect Robert Patterson. This was transferred to the North Canterbury Hospital Board in 1964 and after a 60-bed wing opened in 1968, gynaecological patients were transferred there from Princess Margaret Hospital the following year. A pilot scheme for a women's hospital providing full obstetrics and gynaecology care, its success led to the

↖

St Helen's Hospital, Christchurch.

↑

Princess Margaret Hospital, Christchurch, c.1957–58.

other St Helen's hospitals being transferred to local hospital boards. Renamed Christchurch Women's Hospital, in recognition that it provided a full range of obstetrics and gynaecology services, it was relocated to the Christchurch Hospital campus in 2005.[67]

Before the Second World War, the North Canterbury Hospital Board began planning a subsidiary hospital on Cashmere Road and had bought 6.8 hectares of land for this purpose. Gummer & Ford won a 1938 competition for the design of a '200-bed, eight-ward hospital, capable of being doubled in size, with associated nurses' home and boiler house'. (Massey, Morgan & Beatson came second and Helmore, Cotterill & Harman third.) War stalled the Cashmere project, however, and when it was revived in 1946, A. H. Manson of Manson, Seward & Stanton, a successor firm to the practice established by the Luttrell brothers in 1902, was engaged to design a large general hospital for the site.

The six-storey 256-bed Princess Margaret Hospital, opened in 1959, was one of the first large new hospital developments undertaken in the country after the war. Architectural historian Terence Hodgson referred to it as 'a project in which the design is both practical and possesses poise. Its axial planning allows good access to natural light, ventilation and views, and for the possibility of future extensions. And in the generally rectangular shape, the incorporation of the curve in the stairwells and entrance ingoings suggests an approach to design which veers away from the totally minimal.'[68]

It has been suggested that the design is a clear demonstration of the influence of Scandinavian and Dutch modernism on New Zealand architecture, through its plan, form and detailing, and that it was probably influenced by Stephenson & Turner's New Zealand hospital projects of the 1930s. Built in reinforced-concrete construction, with red-brick facings, the ward wings are at angles, opening out from the central block, which housed circulation and services. The wards had glazed balconies, and each wing ended with a curved-glass stairwell. However, only about two-thirds of Manson's design was built, and when the blocks east of the main entrance were eventually constructed after 1961, they were single storey. The 222-bed nurses' home of 1956 was also designed by Manson, Seward & Stanton and the chapel was dedicated in 1972.[69]

The first Presbyterian church to be built in Christchurch, St Andrew's Church, stood on a triangular site at the intersection of Oxford Terrace, Tuam Street and Antigua Street until it was relocated in 1986. Its manse, Sunday school and a kindergarten were on a larger piece of land on the other side of Riccarton Avenue, which the government purchased as the site

↖

Ashburton Hospital, 1987.

←

Timaru Hospital looking south: J. C. McKenzie clinical services block centre, Jean Todd Building at top, new nurses' home to right.

↗

Jean Todd Building, Timaru Hospital, completed in 1961.

for a new St Helen's Hospital. This was never built, and the land was sold in 1942 to the North Canterbury Hospital Board. The St Andrew's specialist outpatient building opened there in 1944 and was replaced by a new facility, designed by Manson, Seward & Stanton, in 1952. The Lodge at 36 Hereford Street, bought in 1950, provided accommodation for out-of-town visitors and was the first of several such facilities to the east of the hospital.[70]

++

In Canterbury, at Ashburton Hospital, William (Billy) Thomas, who had designed the 1916 infectious diseases ward, was responsible for most of the buildings there throughout the 1940s. Work by Thomas includes an addition to the nurses' home in 1942, the new ward block in 1944, a new maternity ward and nurses' home in 1948 and a workshop and boiler house in

1950. Three years later Christchurch architect Clifford Burnard Wells designed alterations to the wards, followed by an extension to the outpatient building in 1956 and a laundry in 1957. Thomas then entered a partnership with Garner Hannaford (Hank) Ward and together they designed most of the hospital buildings until 1969, when Thomas retired and Ward continued the practice on his own, before forming Ward & Flatman for a short time in the mid-1970s.[71]

A verandah was added on the north and the east sides in 1950, a bulk store in 1952, an extension to the outpatient building in a similar style to the original in 1954, a 16-bed nurses' home extension in 1958, a tutorial block in 1960, theatre additions in 1962, additions to the Chalmers Ward in 1964 and a new boiler house in 1967. Ward designed a maternity ward in 1970 and a new chapel, laboratory and laundry in 1973, Ward & Flatman a tutorial and seminar block in 1976. The men's ward was converted to a cafeteria in the 1970s.[72]

In Tīmaru, Owen Wiles MacDonald, initially in the partnership of Heaney, Beaven & MacDonald, designed most of the work at the hospital in this period. A strip of the adjacent Botanic Gardens purchased in 1947 allowed for expansion of the hospital. The 52-bed six-storey Lindsay Wing, or southern section of the nurses' home (now Gardens Block), was built there in 1966; the northern portion was added in 1988.[73] The 58-bed Jean Todd Building, designed by MacDonald, opened in 1961. This four-level building had operating and labour rooms on the ground floor, two maternity wards above and a geriatric ward on the top floor. A store and tutorial block opened in 1958, the laundry in 1962.

MacDonald also designed the 1969 chapel, with angled walls and a high skylight to direct light towards the sanctuary. The five-level J. C. McKenzie clinical services block, also by MacDonald, opened in 1976. The single-storey annex for accident and emergency opened in 1978, the new mortuary and boiler house the following year. MacDonald was also responsible for converting the old outpatient building to administration offices in 1980, and for the Kensington Centre psychiatric unit, with 30 beds and outpatient facilities, built opposite the hospital in Queen Street in 1985. A block of flats for medical staff had also been erected in the same street in 1971. MacDonald also did work at Talbot Hospital in the 1960s, including a nurses' home.[74]

↖

Timaru Hospital nurses' home, now Gardens Block, c.1975.

↗

J. C. McKenzie Block, Timaru Hospital.

++

In Otago, the construction of hydro-electric power stations and dams by the Ministry of Works on the Clutha and Waitaki rivers required temporary villages for the workers, and each had a hospital of some kind. As many of the workers were young, often with families, these tended to be maternity facilities with an accident and emergency component. The hospital that opened in Kurow, the village for the first Waitaki dam, in 1929 had a four-bed maternity unit, with an x-ray room and a laboratory; a 12-bed tuberculosis unit was later added.[75]

The first major dam on the Clutha was at Roxburgh, where the existing township was expanded in 1947. A hospital designed by the Ministry of Works opened there in 1951, as an annex to the small 1923 public hospital; Mason & Wales possibly designed this, having been responsible for work there as far back as 1930. The buildings were designed to be relocatable and when the project was completed most were moved to the new village of Otematata, built in 1958 to service construction of the Aviemore and Benmore dams on the Waitaki River. Roxburgh Hospital closed in 1997, but a medical centre was retained and a rest home opened in an adjacent building in 2004.[76]

Twizel, the new town established in 1968 to provide accommodation for workers on the Waitaki power scheme, also inherited used buildings for its 12-bed Ministry of Works-designed maternity hospital, which opened in 1970 and closed in 1984. The town was intended to be removed, but after pressure by residents it was retained as a service centre for the Mackenzie Basin and a new Twizel Medical Centre opened in 2016.[77]

Cromwell Hospital's 10-bed maternity block, which opened in 1960, was designed by Health Department architects under Bob Barton. The maternity ward, built with a steel structural frame and metal windows, featured bedrooms around the perimeter and a central block of service rooms, which was a new approach at the time. The floors were mostly linoleum, with terrazzo in the delivery suite. A 14-bed nurses' home opened in 1967. Cromwell Hospital closed in 1990.[78]

At Oamaru Hospital, the chapel, designed by Ted McCoy, was dedicated in 1963. Mason & Wales took over work at the hospital from Ivan Steenson in the mid-1960s, possibly including the 1963 three-storey building to house emergency and radiology facilities and a children's ward opened the next year. New geriatric wards and an administration block opened in 1984. When the hospital was threatened with closure in 1991, public protests led to its retention, but surgery ceased and the maternity annex was closed in 1997. After the new, more centrally located, facility opened, the old 'hospital on the hill' was demolished in 2016.[79]

Dunedin's Wakari Hospital opened in 1915 as an infectious diseases centre and later became a sanatorium. In the 1950s the decision was made to build a general hospital there to provide service while the main Dunedin Hospital site was redeveloped. The new four-level, 8454-square-metre main building at Wakari Hospital, by Mandeno & Fraser, opened in 1957. Successor practice Fraser, Oakley & Pinfold designed the radiotherapy unit in 1969. Other buildings at Wakari were designed by various Dunedin architects during the 1950s. These include Helensburgh House (originally the nurses' home), designed by Miller, White & Dunn, and staff accommodation units by Salmond & Burt.

The three-level Te Oranga Tonu Tanga secure forensic mental health unit, an outpatient building, the 1964 chapel and the workshop and boiler house were by Mason & Wales.[80] The Ministry of Works designed a psychiatric unit in 1963 and further staff housing in 1969. Later buildings include Padget House and the Rehabilitation Flats, added in the 1970s, the 1980 Isis Psychiatric Centre, the secure and acute mental health units of 1993 and Helensburgh Cottage, built in 2011.[81]

Further developments at the Otago Medical School included the 1948 Preventive Medicine, Pathology and Bacteriology (later Hercus) Building, built to the south of the Scott Building in brick and in Art Deco style by Miller & White. A single-storey brick building was erected to the north of the Lindo Ferguson Building for Surgery and Obstetrics and

↑

Main block, Wakari Hospital, Dunedin, c.2022.

↗

Wakari Hospital, Dunedin, looking west: main building top left, Helensburgh House top right, mental health unit bottom centre.

Gynaecology in 1956. This was replaced in 1972 by the fair-faced concrete Sayers Building, housing the Medical Library, and designed in the Brutalist style by Alan Neil of Fraser, Oakley & Pinfold, later Oakley, Pinfold, Turvey & Neil.

The Wellcome Medical Research Institute, designed in the International Style by Neil Wales of Mason & Wales, opened in 1963 on the corner of Great King and Frederick streets. This has strip windows, brise-soleil shades and off-form pebble-dashed concrete. The multi-storey Adams Building for the school's administration offices, designed by Miller, White & Dunn, was added behind the Sayers Building in 1973. The lower microbiology block in Cumberland

Street was built in a similar style in 1974.[82] Allingham, Harrison & Partners designed the Otago Hospital Board offices in nearby Hanover Street and were also responsible for alterations at Maniototo Hospital in Ranfurly in 1983.[83]

Also at the University of Otago, the 1961 School of Dentistry, now the Walsh Building, was designed by Ian Brampton Reynolds, later of KRTA, under Government Architect Francis Gordon Wilson. This five-storey block has an aluminium-and-glass curtain wall framed by concrete walls and a projecting lift tower.[84]

++

Milton Hospital in South Otago opened in 1920; a maternity annex designed by Mandeno & Fraser was added in 1942. It eventually became a facility for geriatric patients only.[85] Further south, Balclutha Hospital opened in 1926. There, Mandeno & Fraser designed an eight-bed TB block in 1937 and a 38-bed nurses' home extension in 1959. Operating theatre and maternity block extensions in 1962 and an outpatient block in 1967 were designed by Fraser, Oakley & Pinfold. Its replacement, the 17-bed Clutha Health First Hospital, providing general medical, inpatient and maternity care, opened in 1998.[86]

Allan Charles (A. C.) Ford established a practice in Invercargill in 1920. Although this was independent of the practice run by Edmund Wilson, they are understood to have collaborated on some projects, such as work at the Waipiata Sanatorium.

At Southland's Gore Hospital, Ford designed the 1941 children's ward and, in 1955, a new ward block, with a 30-bed women's ward on the ground floor and a 23-bed maternity unit above. The chapel was dedicated in 1963. Successor firms Ford, Gray & Derbie and Ford, Gray, Derbie & Hurd carried out work there in the 1960s and 1970s respectively.[87]

↖

Wellcome Institute, University of Otago School of Medicine.

←

Adams and Sayers buildings, University of Otago School of Medicine, 1974.

↗

University of Otago Faculty of Dentistry building.

Ford, Gray & Derbie also designed the 1946 Southland Hospital Board office building in central Invercargill. At the hospital in Kew, the firm designed the 1946 and 1954 extensions to the nurses' home, two concrete three-storey wings added to the inpatient block in 1950 and, after more land was purchased to the south of the site in 1953, the four-storey west wing, with accommodation for 30 patients on each floor in 1957. The chapel was dedicated in 1963 and four years later the occupational therapy building was inserted between the nurses' home and administration buildings. A laundry and boiler house, designed by Ford, Gray & Derbie, opened in 1967.[88] The Howard Hunter clinical services block, since demolished, opened in 1970 and the nurses' home was extended again in 1972, with a dining room and a kitchen. The nurses' home was redeveloped in 1992 to create the Southland Hospice.[89]

At Lakes District Hospital in Queenstown, Ford carried out work from 1941. A small addition at Frankton in the 1940s added a sluice room, a sitting room for patients and a staff toilet. There were further small additions and alterations by Ford, Gray & Derbie in 1956 and 1971, but by the time the new Lakes District Hospital opened the original building remained substantially as it had been 90 years earlier. Gray, Hesselin & Baxter, the successor firm to Ford's practice, designed the new 1989 Lakes District Hospital at Frankton, with 10 inpatient beds, plus five for maternity and six for the elderly.[90]

Its opening resulted in the closure of the 1947 Queenstown Maternity Hospital, also by Ford, on the corner of Melbourne and Sydney streets, close to the town's centre. Lakes

District Hospital was redeveloped in 2019, with a new nine-bed emergency department and two resuscitation spaces, a CT scanner and outpatient facilities.[91]

At Riverton Hospital, the Wallace Maternity facility opened in 1939. Ford designed the Dyer Memorial Wing, built in 1949 for tuberculosis patients. A chapel was dedicated in 1963. Three years later the maternity hospital and operating theatre were closed and the hospital became a geriatric facility before taking on its next identity as a private rest home in 1997.[92]

Ford's daughter, Monica F. Barham, worked with her father for a time before setting up her own practice, Barham & Barham Architects, with her husband, Cecil V. Barham. They designed the 1956 Don Street Medical Centre in Invercargill, which won the Southern Region NZIA Award for Enduring Architecture in 2023.

↖

Clockwise from top left:
Milton Hospital, South Otago, 1960s.
Milton Hospital, showing the extension added in 1942, c.1960s.
Balclutha Hospital, c.1970–80.
Balclutha Hospital, early 2000s.

↑

Kew Hospital, later Southland Hospital, c.1940s.

++

During these years, too, New Zealand practices were starting to become involved in the design of hospitals overseas. Everest conqueror Sir Edmund Hillary had already built five schools in the region around Kumjung, 270 kilometres east of Kathmandu, when he established a hospital there, which opened in 1966. Its simple design was developed by Mark-Brown, Fairhead & Associates to suit local skills. The walls were of dry-stone construction; other materials were flown in from New Zealand. The main 11-bed building has a linear layout of intensive care ward, surgery, kitchen and staff quarters, linked by a roofed external walkway.[93]

↑

Queenstown Maternity Hospital, 1956.

↖

Lakes District Hospital, Queenstown.

←

Khunde Hospital, Nepal, 1967.

Private hospitals

Private hospitals played a valuable role in reducing the demand on the public system, but until the Second World War most were very small, usually little more than large houses. Many of the bigger private institutions were established and supported by churches or religious orders. Although they were some of the earliest health facilities in the country, the first private hospital licence was only issued in 1903. By 1942 there were 321 private hospitals in New Zealand, with an average of fewer than 10 beds. Rising costs forced many to close and by 1969 there were only 151. These did, however, tend to be larger, as the average size had increased to 23 beds.[1]

++

The original building at Auckland's Mater Misericordiae (later Mercy) Hospital in Mount Eden was the home of Thomas Macfarlane, built around 1865 and purchased in 1900 by the Sisters of Mercy. To this was added Kiwi, the home of the Dignan estate, which was converted into a convent building in 1925.[2]

Over the next 50 years Auckland architect Daniel Boys Patterson designed almost all of the buildings on the site. He was responsible for the two-storey Stella Maris Wing, a purpose-built hospital and surgical facility opened in 1918, and for the main block of the hospital in 1936. This had three operating theatres, x-ray and laboratory facilities, as well as a mixture of private rooms and public beds. The opening of this building made the Mater New Zealand's largest private hospital. In 1952 a 13-bed hospice opened in a Gilgit Road property that had been bought the previous year. A new 39-bed hospice, designed by Patterson. opened in 1959. The single-storey timber Mary Agnes Maternity Annex added in 1952 was replaced a decade later by a four-storey maternity block on Mountain Road, again designed by

↗
Stella Maris Wing, Mercy Hospital, Auckland.

↖

Main building, Mercy Hospital, Auckland, 1930s.

←

Mercy Hospital, Auckland, looking east: main building top centre, Stella Maris centre left, 1950s.

Patterson.[3] In 1969 a cardiothoracic unit under Brian Barratt-Boyes opened at the Mater, set up with funding from businessman Sir William Stevenson. The original house was demolished in 1982 to make way for the angiography and laboratory departments.[4]

By 1993 there were five Mercy hospitals in New Zealand: St Mary's Mercy Hospital in Whangarei, Mercy Hospital and Mercy Parklands Hospital and Retirement Home in Auckland, Mercy Hospital in Palmerston North and Mercy Hospital in Dunedin. The Mater in Auckland survived a financial crisis in 1979, but the maternity unit was closed. In 1988 the Mater became the Mercy Hospital Outreach and in 1993 this was incorporated as a separate company. In 2002 it was sold to become part of the Mercy Ascot group.[5]

++

Seven members of the Sisters of Mercy arrived in Dunedin in 1897. In 1935 the order bought a property on Royal Terrace, known as Marli, the former home of businessman Percy Hallenstein, to be the site of their new Mater Misericordiae hospital, which opened in 1936. The sisters also staffed the Port Chalmers Maternity Hospital from 1958 to 1966.[6] In 1969 they relocated the hospital to Marinoto, the grand former home of businessman Percy Sargood and his family in Newington Avenue, Māori Hill, built between 1878 and 1883 in the Scots Baronial style, with Port Chalmers bluestone and Ōamaru stone facings. The order's second Mater Misericordiae hospital, built in Marinoto's extensive grounds, was designed by Stephenson & Turner and had 64 beds and two operating theatres.[7] The Sisters used the Marinoto residence, now a Category 2 Historic Place, as their convent for over 40 years. The hospital changed its name to Mercy Hospital in 1989 and a new Marinoto building for consultant clinics, designed by Mason & Wales, opened in 1992. The top floor of Marinoto was fully restored in 2020.

Mercy Hospital Dunedin Ltd, established in 1994, was transferred in 2009 to Tiaki Manatū Mercy Ministries New Zealand Trust. The theatre suite was extended, an ICU was added in 1999 and in 2008 the Coolock Ward and day surgery unit opened. The Mercy Heart Centre was established in 2004, the Mercy Cancer Centre in 2011.[8] Dunedin architects McCoy & Wixon designed the 2015 Mercy Care East Building and the Manaaki by Mercy day surgery unit, with two operating theatres, a CSSD and a cancer centre, which opened in 2017.[9]

++

The first hospital established in New Zealand by the Sisters of the Little Company of Mary was Lewisham Hospital in Christchurch in 1914. This later became the Calvary Hospital and was sold to Southern Cross Hospitals in 1979. A Calvary Hospital opened in Invercargill in 1968 still operates there as an aged care facility. In Wellington in 1929 the order established Lewisham Hospital, on the site in Newtown's Florence Street where its successor, Wakefield Hospital, now stands. The original building was designed by Luttrell Brothers of Christchurch, whose Wellington representative, Ernest Charles Rhind Anderson, oversaw the construction.

A new west wing was added in 1932 and the open verandahs were glazed to give better protection from the Wellington weather. It was renamed the Calvary Hospital in 1953, and in 1958 a new convent and chapel, linked to the existing hospital by a bridge and designed by McKeon & Patience, was opened. McKeon also designed the 1968 cobalt therapy unit and 12-bed ward block there. The treatment room contained a Theratron 60

↑

First Mater Misericordiae Hospital, Dunedin.

↖

Second Mater Misericordiae Hospital, Dunedin.

↗

Calvary, now Wakefield, Hospital, Wellington.

cobalt machine and had concrete walls that were almost a metre thick.[10] By 1989 the hospital had become Wakefield and has since been expanded and upgraded. It is now part of the Evolution Healthcare Group.

French religious sister Suzanne Aubert came to New Zealand in 1860, where she formed the Daughters of Our Lady of Compassion in 1892. As well as an orphanage at Jerusalem on the Whanganui River, she established two hospitals in Wellington, St Joseph's Home for Incurables in 1900, and Our Lady's Home of Compassion at Island Bay in 1907. The latter was designed by James O'Dea, but structural issues led to strengthening work being carried out by John Sidney Swan. The hospital closed and was demolished in 2002.

++

In Christchurch in the 1920s, Anglican Canon John Russell Wilford was the driving force behind the establishment of a Church of England private hospital. St George's Hospital opened in 1928 on land bought in Milford Street, off Papanui Road. It was designed by brothers John Steele Guthrie and Maurice James Guthrie, who were also responsible for buildings at Christchurch Boys' High School and the famous Edmonds factory.[11] Another local architect, R. S. D. Harman, designed a new wing, added in 1931, and was also responsible for two 1941 projects: a nurses' home, which was extended in 1943, and a 17-bed maternity hospital on the top floor of the main building. He also designed the 1948 Wilford House, with accommodation for junior nurses, and the conversion of the east wing into a children's ward in 1949.

A house on the corner of Milford Street and Papanui Road, donated in 1957, became the first Milford Chambers. A further two blocks were later built on adjoining land in Milford

Street; a new boiler house was commissioned in 1959. A surgical block with two operating theatres and sterilisation facilities, designed by Stewart Minson, former architect to the North Canterbury Hospital Board, and Holger Henning-Hansen, opened in 1968.[12]

The original St George's buildings were demolished in 2012 following earthquake damage. A day surgery unit opened in 1991, and the Canon Wilford Wing, with four operating theatres and two surgical wards, in 2002. Separate buildings housing consulting rooms include Milford Chambers in 1995, Hiatt Chambers in 2000 and Leinster Chambers in 2008. The St George's Cancer Care Centre opened in 2010; the radiation treatment suite six year later. The 2017 Randolph Wing and the 2020 Cressy Wing added more operating theatres and a maternity centre. Many of the post-1980s buildings were designed by Trengrove, Trengrove & Marshall, later Trengrove & Blunt, and now Totem Studio.[13]

Trengrove and Totem were also involved in projects at the Nurse Maude Home in Christchurch, named for district nursing pioneer Sibylla Maude. In 1918 Sir Heaton and Lady Rhodes donated a two-storey brick building in Madras Street, which was the home of the Nurse Maude District Nursing Association until 1973. This building was demolished after being damaged in the September 2010 Christchurch earthquake. McDougall House in Merivale, gifted to the Nurse Maude Association in 1949, also suffered earthquake damage but was retained and restored by Totem Studio Architects.

The Nurse Maude Hospital and Hospice was developed on the surrounding land. Stephen Matthews Architect, in conjunction with Trengrove Architects, designed the two-storey aged care building that accommodates 75 residents and replaced an existing smaller facility irreparably damaged in the earthquakes. The two firms also designed the utilities building as the first stage of the site redevelopment.

++

In Timaru, in 1912, Sister M. S. McArthur established a hospital in a two-storey brick building designed and built by Lust & Moriarty, in what was then Chester Street. In 1935 a group of local businessmen bought what they renamed the Timaru Private Hospital, and a new two-storey building, designed by P. W. Rule of the Timaru firm Turnbull & Rule, opened in 1936. It had 26 beds on the lower floor, with an operating theatre, an x-ray room and 12 beds for nurses above. In 1961 Owen MacDonald was commissioned to design an extension. When the Bidwill Trust took over in 1977, MacDonald was appointed to design further upgrades. A major redevelopment in the 1980s included the addition of the Halstead Wing. In 1986 architect D. J. Wilson designed upgrades that included a new entrance, which opened in 1988.[14]

A single-storey facility with 14 beds and two operating theatres opened on the corner of Elizabeth and York streets in 2001, and extensions designed by Trengrove & Blunt around 2010 added a day surgery unit and a third operating theatre. The 2018 consulting room expansion was by NB Architects. Trengrove & Blunt designed the 2020 radiology extension, with MRI suite, offices and support.[15]

++

Ashburn Hall – established at Halfway Bush beyond Wakari, near Dunedin, in 1882 as a humane alternative to the state hospital mental healthcare of the day – operates as a not-for-profit therapeutic community and psychiatric hospital. It originally occupied a stone homestead designed by former colonial architect William Henry Clayton. John Arthur Burnside, who was indentured to Mason & Wales and is said to have been the first New Zealand-born qualified architect, designed a wing to accommodate 40 patients in individual bedrooms. A new wing, designed by McCoy & Wixon, opened in 2021.[16]

++

As a result of private sector concern about the inadequacy of government contributions to private hospital costs, the Southern Cross Healthcare Society was formed in 1961 to allow New Zealanders access to health insurance. In 1977 the society formed what became

↖

St George's Hospital, Christchurch.

↗

Bidwill Hospital, Timaru.

the Southern Cross Hospital Trust to manage and operate private hospitals that might approach them for finance and management expertise.[17]

The trust bought its first hospital, the Lavington in Auckland, in 1979. The building was demolished and replaced by a new building with two 30-bed wards, designed by Carter Leuschke, around 1983.[18] This is now part of a cluster of hospitals in Epsom. Brightside Hospital was also purchased in 1979 and refurbished in 2000, and following the formation of a partnership with the Gillies Hospital in 2001, this became a fully owned facility in 2014.[19]

Calvary Hospital on Bealey Avenue, Christchurch, was purchased in 1981 and has developed to become Southern Cross's largest campus. In 1983 Southern Cross bought St Andrew's Hospital on Otonga Road, Rotorua, which had opened with 24 beds in 1965 and was extended to 33 beds in 1973. It merged with QE Hospital in 2007 and there were significant redevelopments in 2009 and 2012, designed by Chow:Hill. The facility is now wholly owned by Southern Cross. After Iona Hospital in New Plymouth, established in 1947, was purchased in 1984, a major redevelopment began. Local architects Asplin James West designed the first stage – replacing the north ward wing, constructing a separate services block and upgrading the theatre suite, kitchen and laundry.[20]

In 1982 Southern Cross Hospitals bought the Northcote Private Surgical and Geriatric Hospital, which had opened on Grey Street, Palmerston North, in 1897 and had been remodelled in 1944 by local architect Reginald Thorrold-Jaggard. A purpose-built hospital opened in Carroll Street in 1987. The Aorangi Private Hospital, also designed by Thorrold-Jaggard, opened on Grey Street in 1935. The Sisters of Mercy bought the building in 1950 and operated it as the Mater Misericordiae Hospital; the name was changed to Mercy Hospital in 1969. The chapel, dating from about 1971, was the work of Callander & Brogden. When a group of medical specialists bought the hospital in 2000, the name was changed again to Aorangi, but after the Southern Cross Aorangi partnership was formed in 2012, the two hospitals were combined and renamed Crest Hospital the following year.[21]

Southern Cross North Harbour, designed by Peddle Thorp, was developed in 1986. Archimedia was responsible for an extension in 2018. Southern Cross Wellington was designed by Devine Erby Mazlin on land purchased in 1988. The same firm designed Southern Cross Brightside in Auckland in 2000. In 2005 Southern Cross bought the Auckland Surgical Centre, which had been worked on by several architects since it was built in 1986 to a design by Haughey Woolford Gillespie Architects.[22]

↑

Reginald Thorrold-Jaggard.

↗

Northcote Hospital, Palmerston North.

→

Southern Cross Central Lakes Hospital, Queenstown.

10

Nationwide expansion 1945–1970

IN 1950 THE AUCKLAND HOSPITAL BOARD took an initiative that was possibly the most active involvement of any New Zealand public body in the establishment of an independent private architectural practice. Following years of debate, the board resolved to proceed with a new National Women's obstetrics and gynaecological hospital at Green Lane. Deciding to use this project as an opportunity to develop local skills, they canvassed the local architectural community and drew up a list of suitable candidates.

From this, Raymond Armstrong Thorpe, George Clayton (Mick) Cutter, Ralph Arnold Pickmere and Kenneth Walter Douglas, all of whom had served as officers in the Second World War, were selected to design the hospital, on the condition they formed a single practice, and thus Thorpe Cutter Pickmere Douglas was born. The new firm was awarded £15,000 towards developing sketch plans. As architectural historian Gregory Smith notes, 'Thus the foundations of one of the country's major architectural firms of the late modern period were laid.'[1]

The firm's first completed hospital seems to have been the 1956 brick and tile Dargaville Hospital on Awakino Road, for the Northland Hospital Board. Early drawings for this have only Thorpe's name on them, so this was probably a commission he had won before entering the partnership. It comprised two 30-bed wards (male and female), a 15-bed children's ward, two operating theatres and x-ray, physiotherapy and a pharmacy. The firm also designed a laboratory wing extension in 1965.[2] The two-storey nurses' home built at Rawene Hospital in 1956 was also their design and they possibly carried out other work there. They also came third in the 1959 competition for Auckland's new St Helen's Hospital.[3]

National Women's Hospital opened in 1964 on 4.4 hectares of land next to Green Lane Hospital that had been annexed from Cornwall Park in 1947. The 11-storey main block, with a three-storey annex, had 282 beds in four 33-bed post-natal wards, a 38-bed antenatal ward and two 34-bed gynaecology wards, with a nursery for 54 premature and sick babies. There was a delivery suite, four operating rooms and a large outpatient department. A connected 28-bed isolation block included research facilities on the upper levels.[4]

The firm's first completed hospital seems to have been the 1956 brick and tile Dargaville Hospital on Awakino Road, for the Northland Hospital Board. Early drawings for this have only Thorpe's name on them, so this was probably a commission he had won before entering the partnership. It comprised two 30-bed wards (male and female), a 15-bed children's ward, two operating theatres and x-ray, physiotherapy and a pharmacy. The firm also designed a laboratory wing extension in 1965.[5] The two-storey nurses' home built at Rawene Hospital in 1956 was also their design and they possibly carried out other work there. They also came third in the 1959 competition for Auckland's new St Helen's Hospital.[6]

Thorpe Cutter Pickmere Douglas was engaged for two Christchurch Hospital projects: the redevelopment approved in 1963 and the subsidiary clinical school that the University of Otago decided in 1969 to establish there. Buildings designed by the firm include the 277-bed Riverside ward block, opened in 1977, the 1978 Clinical Services Building to the north-east of the site, the 1973 Christchurch School of Medicine and the 259-bed Parkside ward block of 1977 to the south and the laboratory building and services complex, opened in stages diagonally opposite on Hagley Avenue.[7] The practice also designed the centrally located oncology building, where Christchurch's first linear accelerator began operation in 1969. New Zealand's first CT scanner was installed at Christchurch in 1973, an MRI two decades later.[8]

Although these buildings were built around the same time, they mark a clear transition in the firm's style. Riverside has a horizontal spandrel and window form similar to the buildings at Green Lane. Architect Michael Fowler commented on its design: 'Surrounded by Hagley

↗

National Women's Hospital, Auckland.

→

Dargaville Hospital.

↩

Grace Neill Block, Wellington Hospital, 1979.

17

Park and overlooking the River Avon, the Christchurch Public Hospital enjoys an incomparable site. The seven-floored ward block on the east of the site, while hardly an Alvar Aalto design, is nevertheless a modest circumspect building, maybe even purposefully neutral in form and proportion to minimise detraction from the beautiful trees and gardens adjoining the river.'[9]

The remaining buildings were designed in the more finely detailed Brutalist style popularised by Le Corbusier and refined further by Kenzo Tange in Japan and Denys Lasdun in Britain, reflected in the deep projecting floors and slender pre-cast concrete screens. A further feature was the form of the high-pitched mansard-style roofs. Delays due to significant replanning of the ward blocks, as open wards gave way to more subdivided spaces, may explain the more dated external design of Riverside compared with the other buildings built at the same time.[10]

↑

Green Lane Hospital, Auckland, looking south: from left, Infirmary and Costley blocks, main block with new ward block behind, National Women's and nurses' home.

↖

Administration building, Green Lane Hospital, Auckland.

↑

Green Lane Hospital nurses' home, Auckland.

↗

Riverside ward block, Christchurch Hospital.

Around 1979 Thorpe left to form his own practice, Raymond A. Thorpe & Associates. As Cutter Pickmere Douglas, the firm designed most of the next wave of major buildings at Wellington Hospital, which further refined the distinctive Brutalist style introduced at Christchurch.[11]

Cutter Pickmere Douglas continued as a separate practice in Christchurch, and was engaged for the redevelopment of Ashburton Hospital, designing the 1979 alteration to the Chalmers Ward, a 1980 recovery ward and further alterations in 1983. The 1987 admissions unit was designed by what was now the Cutter Douglas Partnership, and the former men's ward was converted to a therapy facility when the hospital was extensively altered in 1989. Cutter Pickmere Douglas also designed a laboratory extension and 1980 extramural unit

at Middlemore Hospital. Whether these were by the Christchurch practice, or a remnant in Auckland, is unclear. Cutter Douglas was wound up in 1994.[12]

Thorpe Cutter Pickmere Douglas, hailed by Gregory Smith as 'a pivotal and influential practice in New Zealand's modern architectural history', nurtured many talented architects who left to form their own practices.[13]

++

By the late 1960s plans had been made for Wellington to have its own medical school and a new 1200-bed hospital. A master plan was prepared showing two pairs of 10-storey ward buildings, each pair having its own support block, plus a two-storey building with accident and emergency and outpatient departments, as well as an academic building for the medical school. It was eventually decided that, as at Christchurch, Wellington's clinical school would be operated by the University of Otago; the firm's Christchurch involvement may have helped it to win the commission. By 1964 revised demand projections resulted in the hospital being scaled back to 800 beds.[14]

Most of the existing buildings, apart from the nurses' home, had to be removed, and the Toxward buildings were demolished in 1968–69. The first building completed, in 1977, was the Medical School, which connected through the Link Block to the nine-storey Ward Support Block, both opened in 1980. The latter abutted the Haughton & Mair-designed Clinical Services Building and was intended to form the vertical circulation spine for two ward blocks radiating from it. It was therefore designed with several external walls having sacrificial long-run steel cladding, and a large core with only a narrow floor space between its concrete walls and the external windows.[15]

During construction, however, the master plan seems to have been abandoned. Concrete panels replaced the temporary cladding, and the lift and stairwells were filled in to form office space. By this point, the 10-storey Grace Neill obstetrics and gynaecology block had already been completed, in 1978, and it now sits somewhat isolated at the north end of the

↖

Parkside ward block and medical school building, Christchurch Hospital.

↑

Ward Support Block, Wellington Hospital.

↗

Wellington Children's Hospital.

site. The change in programme also meant that both the Ward Support and Grace Neill blocks were only fully commissioned in 1982.[16]

Rather than the multi-storey ward block between these two buildings, a two-storey two-ward 40-bed children's hospital was built in 1988. The architects noted on the drawings for this were Cutter Pickmere Climie, the Wellington-based successor to Thorpe Cutter Pickmere Douglas, after William (Bill) Y. Climie had become a partner. Photos of the site board during construction also show, as collaborating architects, Booth, Sweetman & Wolfe, who later designed the Waitangirua Health Centre in Porirua and the Ewart geriatric unit in Wellington, both opened about 1976,[17] and the 1977 cafeteria and kitchen at Middlemore Hospital. After the new children's building opened, the King Edward VII Children's Hospital and the Seddon Wing were demolished.

++

Several hospitals across the North Island were the work of Thomas (Tom) Fitzroy Haughey, who had set up in practice on returning from the war in 1945. His first health project was Opotiki Hospital, built in 1952 on Hukutaia Road on the other side of the Waioeka River from the township. This was extended with a 22-bed children's ward in 1959, and 15-bed domestic staff quarters in 1962. It closed in 1997 to be replaced, in 1999, by a new health centre in the town's commercial area; the hospital was then demolished. In 1952 Haughey was joined by

Graham F. Fox, who had been assistant architect to the Palmerston North Hospital Board, and in 1961 the practice became Haughey & Fox.[18]

Some of the work at Opotiki Hospital in the late 1950s, including a new staff quarters, was by Rotorua practice Alleman, Land & Verrall. As Alleman, Newnham & Verrall, they were responsible for the 1961 laundry extension at Ōpōtiki, and they modified the existing operating theatres in 1963.

At North Shore Hospital, a four-ward single-storey geriatric unit with 140 beds, designed by Haughey & Fox, opened in 1972. The firm was then engaged for the 1984 stage 2 building, consisting of a 10-storey, 300-bed ward tower on a three-storey podium with emergency, radiology, nine operating theatres, an ICU, an outpatient department and non-clinical support. The podium was designed to allow for the construction of a further 300-bed ward tower, but this never eventuated.[19] After maternity moved into the main building in 1988, the original maternity hospital was converted into a mental health facility.[20] Haughey & Fox also designed the staff accommodation building at Waitakere Hospital, which opened in 1973, and the 1974 general hospital building.[21]

The Wilson Home for Crippled Children opened in 1937, when Mr and Mrs W. R. Wilson gave their home and 5.2 hectares of land in Takapuna for the benefit of children with disabilities. The Chapel of St Leonard, designed by Denis Hewson and Robert Drake of Haughey & Fox, who had won the competition for it, was dedicated there in 1966, and won the NZIA Enduring Architecture Award in 2008.[22] A new nurses' accommodation building was also completed in 1966 and the Ronald Caughey Assessment and Treatment Centre opened in 1977. Six villas were added in 1983 and 1984.[23]

++

In the 1950s Haughey & Fox was engaged to design the redevelopment of Whangarei Hospital, needed to serve the flourishing town. The central and west wings of the new nurses' home were ready in 1950, with an east wing added later to bring the accommodation up to 140 rooms; a swimming pool was opened in 1955. In the 1980s this second nurses' home was

↖

Grace Neill Block, Wellington Hospital, 1979.

↑

Thomas Haughey.

↗

Opotiki Hospital, 1958.

Below Right: Axonometric plan of Waitakere Obstetric.
Below: Axonometric showing the total development at Waitakere.

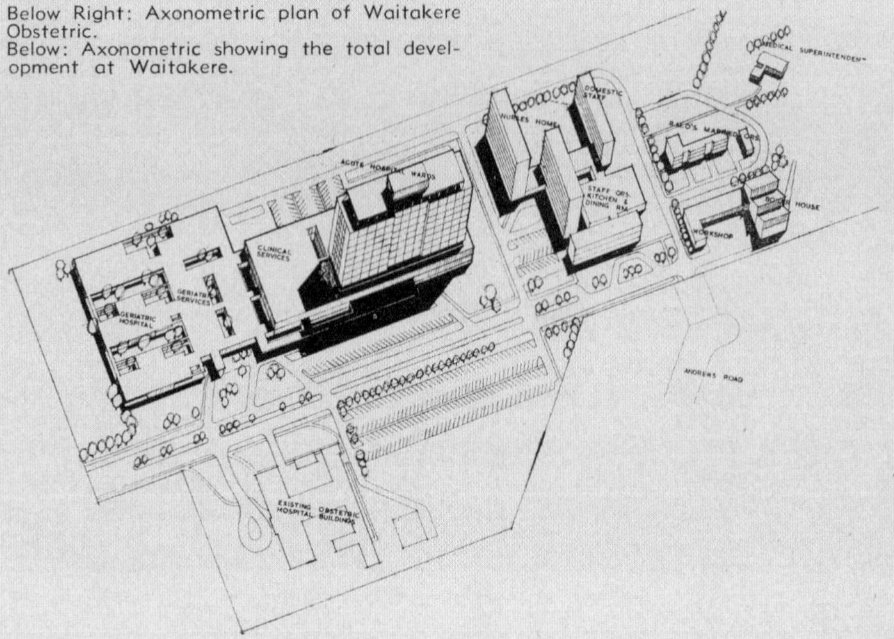

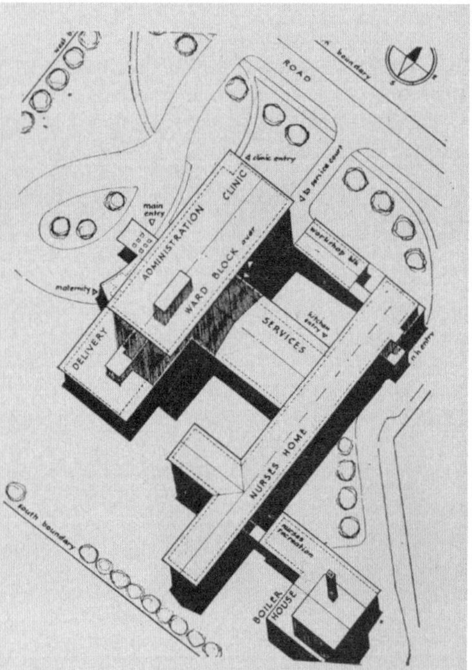

↖

The original concept for Waitakere Hospital, Auckland, 1965.

↖

North Shore Hospital, Auckland.

↑

Maternity, now Snelgar, Building, Waitakere Hospital, Auckland.

converted into offices for the area health board and renamed Maunu House. A laundry and boiler house were built in 1959.

The first phase of the new hospital building opened in 1962, with a 160-bed main ward block and a wing containing operating theatres, radiology, a laboratory and physiotherapy. The Chapel of St Luke was dedicated the same year. A central stores building opened in 1968, a new delivery suite was added in 1970, with the former maternity annex becoming a day care facility for the elderly, and in 1974 the old Kowhai Cottage was converted into a child health centre.[24]

At Kaitaia Hospital, the chest block became an outpatient facility in 1952, and apart from extensions to the operating theatres, laboratory and x-ray facilities, and a new ambulance station in 1959, there was little further development until public pressure led to a major redevelopment. The new hospital, designed by Haughey Fox & Partners, which opened in 1966, included a three-storey 93-bed ward block, a 27-bed maternity ward, a 52-bed nurses' home and a new boiler house. The firm also designed the new theatre suite, kitchen, administration block and chapel, which opened in 1970. In the 1990s, after public protests over closure threats, the hospital was retained with fewer services. Haughey & Fox also designed alterations at Rawene Hospital in 1954 and 1973, and at Dargaville in 1969 and 1977.[25]

The ward block at Bay of Islands Hospital was expanded to 22 beds in 1977, to a design by Fox, Blewett, Waite, Jeffs, the name adopted by the firm after Tom Haughey retired in 1976. A new boiler house was added in 1978 and a stores block in 1980.[26]

++

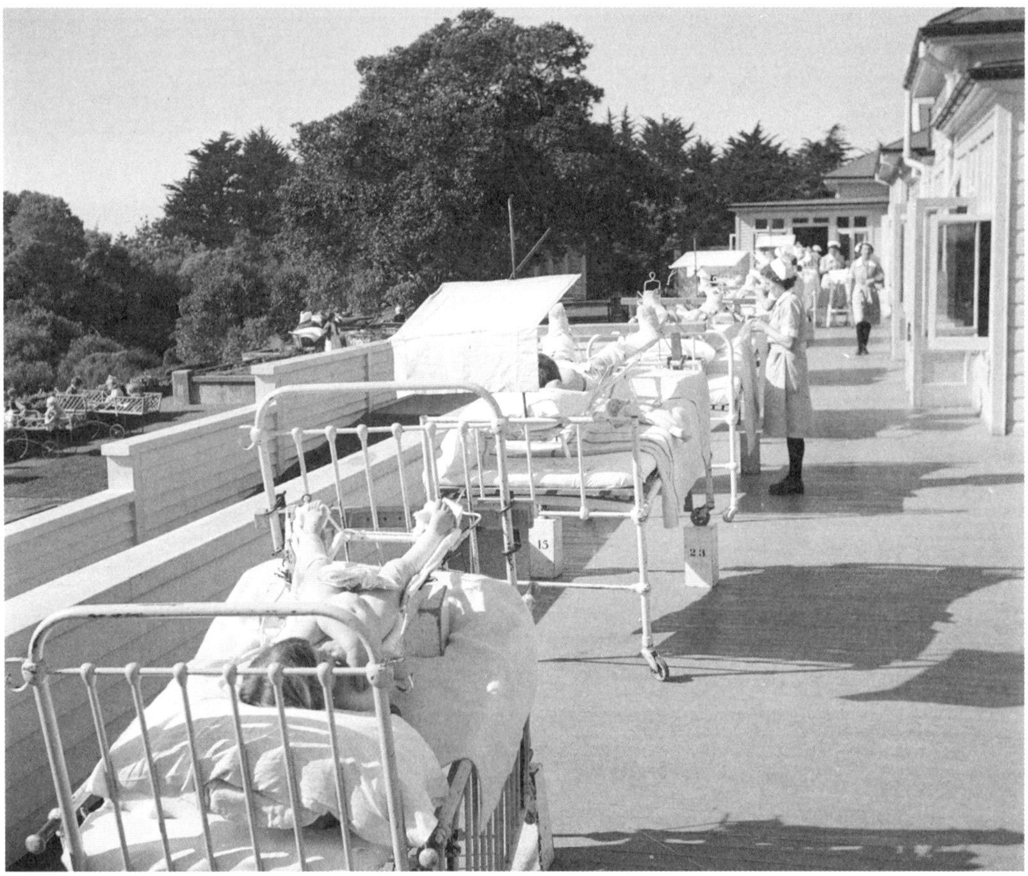

↖

An artist's impression of St Leonard's Chapel at the Wilson Home, Takapuna, 1965.

←

Children at the Wilson Home, Takapuna, 1943.

↗

Kaitaia Hospital, 1967.

Among the facilities built to process the timber from the maturing exotic forests on the Central Plateau was the Tasman Pulp and Paper Mill. With it came the new town of Kawerau, established in 1953. Because this was only 35 kilometres from Whakatāne, it made sense to expand the hospital there to serve the growing population of the surrounding district, rather than build one in the new town.

Domestic staff accommodation was built in 1950; this was converted into a geriatric unit in 1960, became a psychiatric unit in 1975 and was upgraded in 1982 to become the Te Toki Maurere mental health ward. The second nurses' home, built in 1941 and expanded in 1949, was added to again in 1954. The maternity ward was extended in 1955 and a 23-bed children's ward was added the following year; this was extended in 2007 and in 2008 became the Eastern Bay Energy Cancer Centre (Project Hope Building). A two-storey 37-bed ward building was erected in 1957, and a new boiler house and workshop in 1958.[27]

Haughey & Fox was appointed to prepare a master plan for the hospital and went on to design the next wave of buildings. In 1963 a 44-bed five-storey nurses' home was built and the two-storey 60-bed Dawson Block opened. A chapel was dedicated four years later and the five-storey Godfrey Santon Block (with main entrance, emergency, ICU, operating theatres and offices) opened in 1974. A kitchen opened in 1960, a laboratory building in 1969 and a mortuary in 1976. The destructive March 1987 Edgecumbe earthquake led to considerable strengthening and refurbishment in 1989. The Ko Matariki maternity unit opened with 14 beds in 2000, and a clinical school/library/Māori health block developed in 2011 used an assemblage of existing buildings.[28]

++

There had been a small farming community at Tokoroa in the 1900s, but NZ Forest Products developed the town from 1947 to attract and house the workers for its Kinleith mill, which began operating in 1953. After years of lobbying, a 60-bed general hospital, designed by Haughey & Fox with a series of single-storey wards projecting from a central corridor into the landscaped grounds, opened to serve the town in 1970.[29]

The firm was responsible, too, for the new Taupo Hospital opened in 1971, with 25 general and geriatric beds, on the current Kōtare Street site, in the Hilltop area a few kilometres from the town centre. This replaced the town's first wooden cottage maternity hospital, which had opened in 1944 at the corner of Spa Road and Kaimanawa Street and was extended in 1965.[30]

Haughey & Fox also designed later developments at Thames Hospital in the 1970s, including the 1972 physical medicine block, built between the two ward blocks and housing a laboratory, physiotherapy, and occupational therapy facilities, a pharmacy and administration

↑

Chapel of St Luke, Whangarei Hospital.

↖

Stage 1 ward block, Whangarei Hospital.

space, with extensions for allied health and offices in 1976. The firm also designed an outpatient department, a mortuary and a store, and the conversion of the newer nurses' home into what later became the Manaaki Family and Child Mental Health facility. A pharmacy and a laboratory were added in 1986; the old nurses' home was removed in 2000. Most of the 1958 ward block was demolished in 2005 and replaced, in 2009, by a clinical wing, kitchen and ward; a new birthing unit opened in 2011. The Thames Health Centre was built on the other side of Rolleston Street in 1979 to provide facilities for local general practitioners close to the hospital.[31]

↑
Artist's impression, Whangarei Hospital.

↗
Whangarei Hospital nurses' home, extension to left.

++

Haughey & Fox and their successor firms had a long relationship with the Cook Hospital Board, having designed buildings at both Gisborne's Hospital Road campus and its current site. At Hospital Road they designed the 1956 maternity block and the 1958 five-storey 68-bed nurses'

home extension.[32] The site, however, had significant land stability problems – there was a major slip beside the nurses' home in 1957 – and in 1960 the government decided that a new hospital should be built on the relatively flat hospital farm site, a kilometre further west on Ormond Road, which already housed the Memorial Home. The existing hospital had to be kept operational until the new one was available, and local practice Glengarry, Glengarry & Corson designed extensions and alterations there in the early 1960s. Other additions by Haughey & Fox included a 24-bed isolation block in 1962, a kitchen in 1965, and a chapel in 1968.[33]

The first building on the current site was the 1966 boiler house and laundry, followed by the four-storey 60-bed maternity building, designed by Haughey & Fox and opened in 1969. The top two floors initially provided nurses' accommodation and were later converted to geriatric wards.[34] In 1998 the maternity unit moved into the Puawai Aroha unit and in 2003 the original building, renamed Morris Adair, was converted into offices and a community health hub. The new Gisborne Hospital opened in 1985, designed by Blewett, Waite, Jeffs, Carter & Partners, the company's name from 1980, Graham Fox having retired in 1977.[35] This has a three-storey ward block, surrounded by a series of connected single-storey pavilions with landscaped courtyards.[36]

Other healthcare work by Haughey & Fox included Auckland's 1962 Karitane Hospital, the Dadley Foundation building for the Crippled Children's Society and the since demolished Plunket Society building on Symonds Street in Auckland.[37]

The firm designed a significant number of geriatric homes in the 1960s, including,

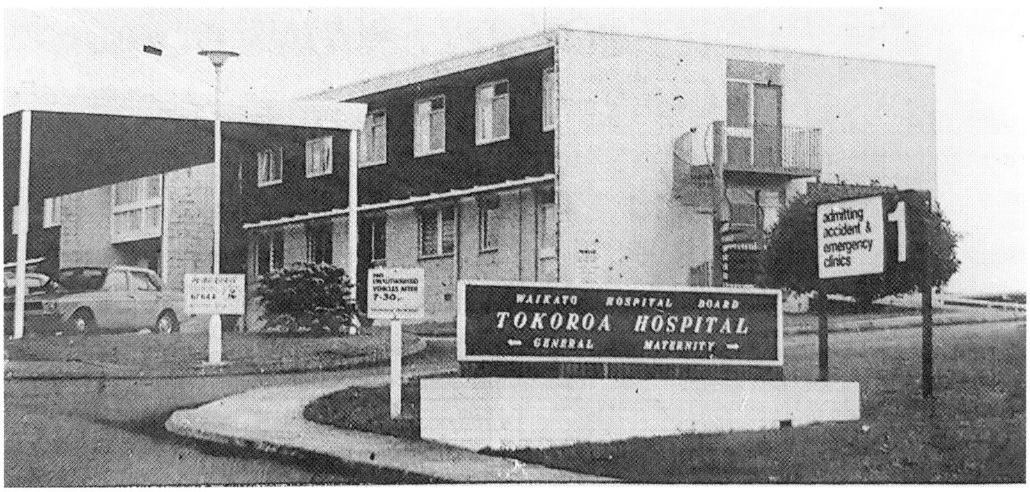

↖

Concept for Whakatane Hospital.

↗

Whakatane Hospital nurses' home.

→

Tokoroa Hospital.

in Auckland, the Lady Allum Home on the North Shore, the Eventide Home and the Wesley Hospital in Mount Eden,[38] the hospital at the Caughey Preston Home in Remuera and the Old People's Welfare Centre, as well as the Tamahere Eventide Home in Hamilton and the Fergusson Home in Rotorua. They also designed the Methodist Mission's Everill Orr Old People's Home in Mount Albert, which included the 1967 Enoch & Edith Bond Memorial Chapel, and the 1975 hospital at the St Andrew's Retirement Home, which had opened in Glendowie, Auckland, in 1957 as the result of a bequest from Sir George Elliot.[39]

In 1966 Tom Haughey was invited by George Warden of the Ministry of Works, who had spent two years in Afghanistan under the Colombo Plan, to visit pioneering New Zealand medical missionary Dr Howard Harper in Kabul. As a result, he was invited to design a school for the blind and an ophthalmic hospital for the International Afghan Mission in Kabul, which opened in 1969. Haughey & Fox prepared working drawings and some of the buildings were prefabricated in New Zealand.[40] Addressing 'problems of access to buildings by physically handicapped persons' was a focus of Haughey's research, and he worked to improve standards and educate the design profession.[41]

In the early 1970s the practice was offered the commission to design new buildings for Christchurch Hospital, but this required senior staff moving to the city, which none of the partners was prepared to do. The firm appears to have ceased operation some time during the 1980s.[42]

++

In 1910 another partnership was established that would make a lasting mark on hospital architecture in New Zealand. John Alfred (Jack) Duffill joined the Eltham practice of J. W. Rough that year, but the partnership ended in 1912 when Rough moved to Invercargill.[43] Duffill relocated to Hawera, where he practised on his own until he was joined by Stephen Gibson in 1916. Gibson did the firm's residential work, allowing Duffill to concentrate on the design of such technically challenging buildings as dairy factories and hospitals.[44]

Puke Ariki holds a 1916 drawing by Duffill for an operating theatre and a night nurse's cottage at Hawera Hospital and a 1920 drawing for additions to the laundry by Duffill & Gibson. These were presumably for the original hospital site. Drawings by Duffill & Gibson from 1924 and 1925 for an administration block, children's ward, operating theatre, nurses' home and kitchen may

↖

Taupo Hospital.

↑

Morris Adair building, Gisborne Hospital, 2022.

↗

Gisborne Hospital.

have been for either the original or new hospital site. As has been mentioned, the firm, as hospital board architects, collaborated with Crichton, McKay & Haughton on the new 1930 Hāwera Hospital. There are several drawings by the firm for buildings that were erected on the new site at the end of the 1940s, including a tuberculosis ward, a maternity ward, domestic quarters and a nurses' home, a tutorial block and additions to the maternity ward and nurses' home.[45]

At Patea Hospital, a two-storey nurses' home opened in 1925, at the south end of the site. A second home was built and connected to it in 1938. Plans held at Puke Ariki indicate that most of the buildings on the site between 1929 and 1940 were designed by Duffill & Gibson, including the 1930 children's ward, a men's ward and an operating theatre. These later buildings had concrete frames with red-brick infills and apart from a later two-storey entrance and administration building, were single storey. The hospital was modernised in the 1950s and 1960s by Graeme Laurenson & Associates, with the addition of a ward and eight-bed maternity annex, and in 1972 the ground floor of the nurses' home became the Te Mahana home for the elderly. Patea Hospital closed in 1990.[46]

The Duffill & Gibson partnership lasted until Stephen Gibson's death in 1945, after which Duffill carried on alone for two years, before being joined by Graeme Laurenson, who had left the Department of Health, and S. Townsend, as Duffill, Laurenson & Townsend. At some point in the next five years, Townsend left the practice. While engaged in general architectural work, the firm developed a specialty in hospital design under Laurenson, and was renamed Graeme Laurenson & Associates around 1960.[47]

At Stratford Hospital Duffill & Gibson collaborated with Griffiths & Syme on the operating theatre and kitchen block, dating from about 1944. After this, Duffill & Gibson appears to have been responsible for further work there in its own right. Other surviving drawings for Stratford Hospital include a nurses' home by Duffill & Gibson, dated 1946, a maternity unit and a new entrance block by Duffill, Laurenson & Townsend, extensions by Duffill & Laurenson, both dated 1947, and a nurses' home by Graeme Laurenson, dated 1953. The 1950 14-bed Avon Maternity Home was extended in 1953, and the old maternity ward was converted into a children's ward.[48]

A 12-bed extension was made to the nurses' home in 1962 and a two-bed domestic block and a boiler house were added in 1967. A 14-bed maternity ward opened in 1950, the 30-bed Hutchen Ward was added in 1968 and an operating theatre was built in 1978.[49] The old wards were converted into an outpatient facility in 1971, a services block with kitchen and dispensary was added in 1974 and an operating theatre block in 1978.[50]

Stratford Hospital's first medical superintendent, Dr T. L. Paget, also established his own private hospital in the town in 1907 in an iron-roofed timber building that contained a modern operating theatre. (It still stands as a private home at 24 Juliet Street.) A year after graduating from Otago Medical School in 1916, Dr Doris Clifton Jolly married fellow graduate William Gordon two weeks before he left to serve in the First World War. In 1918 she went into partnership with Dr Paget, and when William returned from the war in 1919, they bought the practice, renaming the facility Marire. However, she regarded the old hospital as a 'hotchpotch of architecture' and decided to build a new 14-bed facility beside their Portia Street home. The new private hospital and maternity unit was on Page Street, facing the Pātea River, between Portia and Hamlet streets, a block north of the public hospital. Opened in 1942, the new Marire hospital was designed by Duffill & Gibson.[51]

++

The hospital in New Plymouth had outgrown its Barrett Street site, which also had some geotechnical issues, so in 1950 the decision was made to relocate it to the current Westown site. This had been a farm supplying the hospital, as well as having the old persons' home that was moved there in 1911. Graeme Laurenson, appointed architect to the New Plymouth Hospital Board in 1949, was responsible for the new buildings at Westown for the next 20 years. Laurenson took on David W. Robinson and Jim Boon as partners, and the firm became Laurenson, Robinson & Jim Boon.

The initial stage was the four-storey, 104-bed nurses' home (now the Barrett Building), completed around 1955. The first of the main hospital buildings opened in 1957, containing a 60-bed chronic patients' block, 42-bed maternity ward, outpatient department, administration block, kitchen, laundry and boiler house.[52] The Chapel of the Good Shepherd was dedicated in 1965. Stage 2, which started in 1965, included the 1967 clinical services block and the five-storey Stainton Ward building (the latter demolished in 2013).

These buildings, designed by Laurenson, Robinson & Jim Boon, were officially opened in 1972,[53] by which point the hospital had 256 beds. The 1970 four-storey special departments

↑ Graeme Laurenson.

↗ Plans for Marire Hospital, Stratford, drawn by Duffill & Gibson for Doris Gordon, c.1939–41.

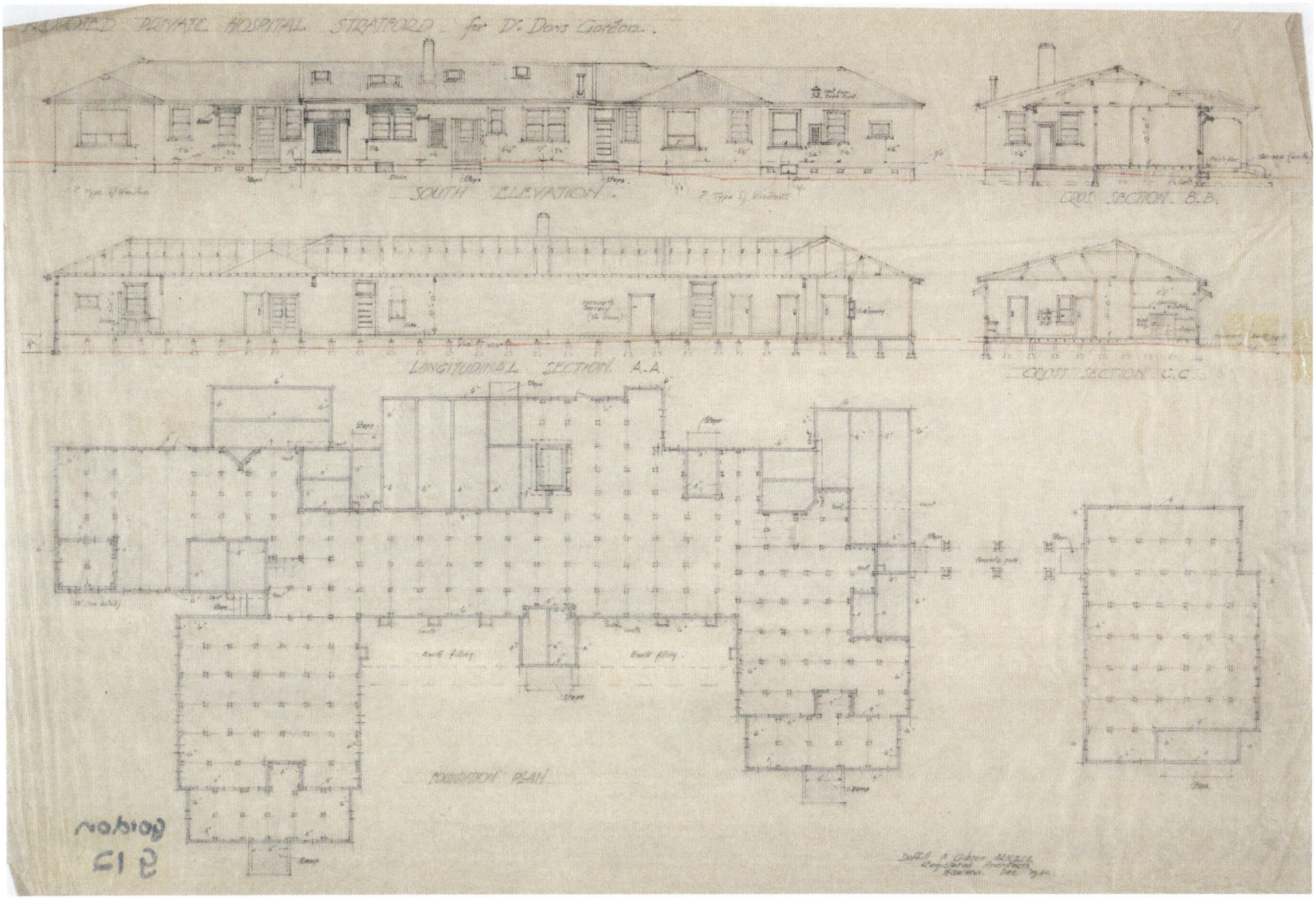

block and five-storey Block C, dating from 1975, were built behind the clinical services block.[54]

Further buildings included a new recreation hall in 1977, designed by Laurenson, Robinson & Jim Boon, an ICU block in 1980 and a new psychiatric unit with two 28-bed wards in 1985. A three-storey building housing medical records and rehabilitation was built in 1982, a mortuary in 1985 and an ambulance station in 1989. The Te Puna Waiora mental health unit opened in 1990 was expanded and redeveloped in 2001. The oncology building, along with a recreation centre and stores/orthotics buildings, opened in 1993, a neo-natal unit in 1995.[55]

In Hāwera the 20-bed Hawera Maternity Hospital, designed by Duffill, Laurenson & Townsend, opened in 1951. An engineering workshop and orthopaedic block was added three years later and Ward 1 was converted to use by outpatients and physiotherapy in 1957. The operating theatres were extended by Graeme Laurenson & Associates in 1959 and a new boiler house added in 1960. The two-storey Te Ramanui Ward building, and a laboratory block, designed by Laurenson, Robinson & Jim Boon, opened in 1969. Meanwhile, the Ngahuru old persons' home was redeveloped in two stages in 1966 and 1968.[56] The hospital buildings at Hāwera were closed in 2001 when the new Stephenson & Turner-designed building opened on the adjacent site. The 1930 building was demolished in 2011, the remainder by 2017.[57]

At Taumarunui, a 27-bed maternity annex designed by Graeme Laurenson of Duffill, Laurenson & Townsend, opened in 1952 as the first stage of the hospital's redevelopment. The 50-bed nurses' home, built by Boon Brothers, opened in 1954. Undated plans for the home by both Duffill, Laurenson & Townsend and Lewis Walker with Ronald Muston have survived. Whether these were competition entries, or one was for an extension of the other's, is unclear. Walker was, however, designing the nurses' home at Thames Hospital around the same time.[58]

The 22-bed Goodsir Ward for tuberculosis cases opened 1958, and a second 30-bed ward in 1959, also designed by Laurenson. A new boiler house by Laurenson was built in 1960 and a mortuary the following year. Two new 30-bed wards and a 25-bed extension to the nurses' home were added in 1965, a new administration block in 1967. A two-theatre operating suite opened in 1972. As the architects to the Taumarunui Hospital Board, Laurenson, Robinson & Jim Boon designed the laundry that began operating in 1975 and a workshop built in 1983. In 1997 the hospital was given a new entrance and outpatients and allied health facilities, before reopening as the Taumarunui Community Hospital and Healthcare Centre.[59]

++

A Hawke's Bay practice formed the core of a partnership that expanded across the North Island in the 1920s, and despite the latter being short-lived, the practice itself continued to design hospitals in the region and up into the East Coast for the next half-century. As noted previously, in 1920 the Hawke's Bay Fallen Soldiers' Memorial Committee commissioned local architects Hyland & Phillips to prepare sketch plans for a new hospital on a property they had purchased in the rapidly growing town. However, these were well over budget, the Napier Hospital Board was resistant to a second hospital in the district, and the Depression hindered further progress. Eventually the Government Architect, John T. Mair, was commissioned to design the main section of the 1928 Hawke's Bay Fallen Soldiers' Memorial Hospital, though it is possible that Eric Phillips' designs were used for some buildings such as the nurses' home. And the succession of firms he established after going into partnership with Hastings architect

Henry Hyland in 1920 was to be responsible for most of the subsequent buildings at the hospital for the next 50 years.[60]

In 1922 Hyland & Phillips were joined in partnership by Horace Massey and Alfred Percy Morgan, forming Massey, Morgan, Hyland & Phillips. The firm initially operated from offices in Auckland and Hastings; and in Whangārei when Morgan moved there in 1923. However, the partnership ended the same year, causing Phillips serious financial issues. When board approval to proceed with the Hastings hospital was finally obtained in 1923 a dispute arose over the fees claimed for the work done to date. Phillips pointed out that the firm had been dissolved, and the retiring partners, quoted as Massey and Hyland (implying that Morgan had left by then), had already been paid their share of the amount claimed, leaving him alone to carry the costs of the additional work.

There was also some debate over the legitimacy of the commission, as it was by the Hastings committee, not the Napier Hospital Board. An arrangement was finally agreed whereby Phillips would be paid some of the outstanding costs in return for being engaged for architectural supervision of the construction, but this seems to have lapsed as the Public Works Department both designed and supervised construction of the new hospital. Tenders were called for the Hawke's Bay Fallen Soldiers' Memorial Hospital in 1925, by Massey Hyland & Phillips, so they clearly still held the commission at that date, even though Massey had already left. The tender included the nurses' home and administration building, and it is possible that the former at least was built to the firm's design.

Massey and Morgan then formed their own practice, later Massey, Morgan & Beatson. Morgan left to practise separately, but did continue to collaborate on some projects. Their hospital work included the nurses' homes at Napier and Whangārei, in 1926 and 1927 respectively.[61]

↖

Taranaki Base Hospital, New Plymouth.

↑

Eric Phillips.
Alfred Percy Morgan.

↗

Boiler house, Hawera Hospital.

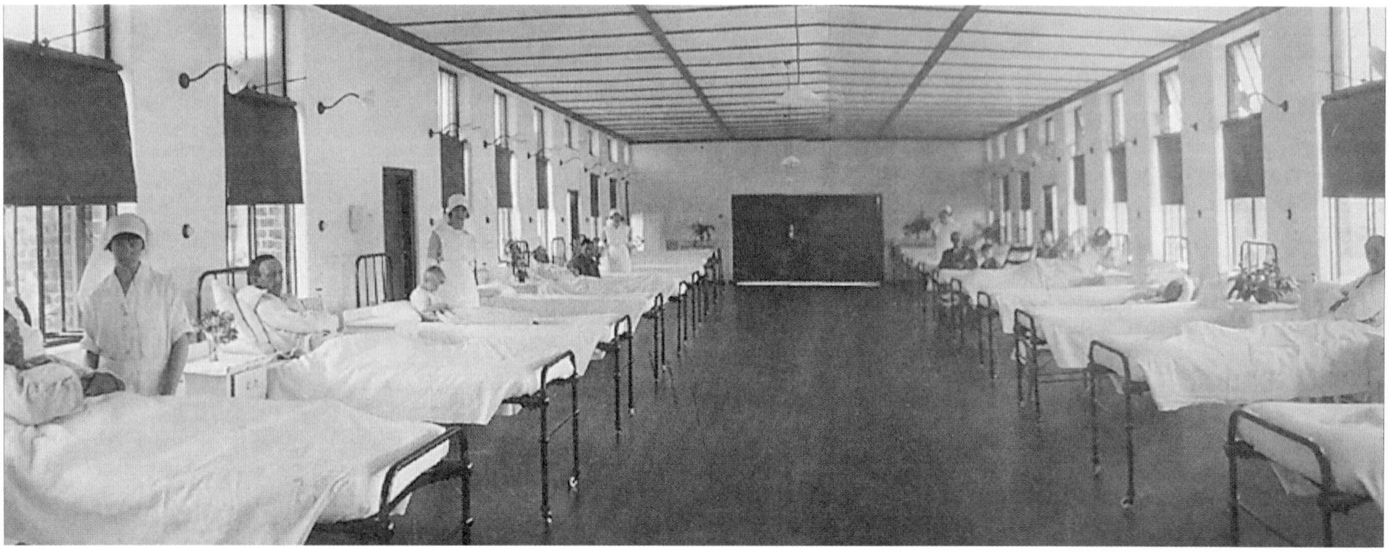

Morgan, who became architect to the Northland Hospital Board in the 1930s, designed hospital buildings at Whangārei, including a female ward, an administration block and a laundry in 1938, and a new nurses' home in 1948. He also designed buildings at Bay of Islands, Rawene and Kaitāia hospitals, including the 1949 nurses' home at the latter.[62] Because this allowed for more staff, the 14-bed chest block built as an emergency hospital during the war but not used could at last be opened. Morgan also designed the laundry and boiler house in 1939, maternity ward in 1950 and a new ward and kitchen in 1951.[63]

++

After the 1931 Hawke's Bay earthquake, Eric Phillips formed a partnership with Harold George (Pop) Davies and Albert Garnett, though the latter left in 1933. Davies & Phillips designed many of the post-1931 buildings at Hawke's Bay Fallen Soldiers' Memorial Hospital, as well as some at Gisborne Hospital. After the Second World War they were joined by Sidney (Sid) George Chaplin, who became a partner in Davies, Phillips & Chaplin in 1947.

In response to the devastating earthquake, several local architects formed an alliance known as Associated Architects, under the leadership of Napier's Rene Natusch, to facilitate the rapid repair and replacement of the many damaged buildings in the district, particularly public infrastructure. Documentation and supervision were divided between Natusch & Sons and other Napier architects such as E. A. Williams, D. B. Frame, Walter Philip Finch, H. A. Westerholm and Louis Hay. The agreement that Natusch & Sons would carry out the work at Napier Hospital, and Hastings firm Davies, Phillips & Garnett would do the same in their town, appears to have endured long after the post-earthquake reinstatement was completed.[64]

Henrietta L. Kelly, who had died in the earthquake, left a significant sum towards providing new hospital accommodation in Hastings. With the addition of a donation from Robert Harding, a new maternity block and a new nurses' home were completed in 1935. The Cecil Duff men's block, a new outpatient block and an operating theatre block opened in 1938, and a new children's ward, boiler house and further nurses' accommodation the following year, bringing the total number of beds to 49.[65]

The hospital in Hastings was gradually expanded in the 1940s, with a new clinic building in 1941 and a larger children's ward in 1942. At the time of writing, several of these

buildings remain as part of the Health Villas outpatient complex. The Wilson Nurses' Home and Community Health were added in the same period. The Art Deco nurses' home on Omahu Road, now housing Māori Health, was completed in 1941.[66]

In 1948 the hospital board called on a group of Hawke's Bay architects to develop plans for the redevelopment of Napier and Hastings hospitals. Architects represented included Rene Natusch, Harold Davies, Eric Phillips, S. G. Chaplin, E. A. Williams, L. G. (Lawrence) Williams and F. Kingwell Malcolm. The following year the board approved work at Hastings including the building of a new ward above the children's ward, conversion of the maternity ward to provide 70–80 general beds and a new maternity hospital on a site to be purchased next to the existing hospital.[67]

++

After plans for redeveloping the memorial hospital were prepared in 1943, additional land was purchased in 1949 and 1952. Meanwhile an annex was added to the maternity ward and a domestic services block opened in 1949. By 1950 the hospital had 86 beds and Napier 240, and the former especially was proving too small for the demand. Debate again broke out, however, as to where the main hospital for Hawke's Bay should be when the two towns were so close. Napier was chosen to have the base hospital for the district, and plans were made to expand it to 350 beds and Hastings to 250. Plans prepared and adopted in 1950–51 were deferred at the request of the minister of health, but in 1952 Sid Chaplin, referred to as 'architect to the board', submitted a design for a five-storey, 150-bed ward block, later reduced to four storeys and 120 beds. To meet what was now an acute demand, a 32-bed temporary ward opened in 1952, a 31-bed female ward and an orthopaedic block in 1953 and a 16-bed medical ward in 1959. Davies, Phillips & Chaplin designed a new wing to the 1941 nurses'

↖

Ward interior, Taumarunui Hospital, 1950s.

↑

Ward block, Hawke's Bay Fallen Soldiers' Memorial Hospital, Hastings.

home on Omahu Road, which was completed in 1951; this was converted into a Māori health unit to a design by Peter Holland around 1996. The firm also designed the 1954 Harding Hall recreation building for nurses, funded by another donation from Robert Harding, the building for hydrotherapy and a gymnasium, completed about 1952, and the tutorial block.[68]

Due to concern that the plans for the new hospital would result in three ward blocks eventually running longitudinally along Omahu Road, in 1955 Patience & Gabites, specialising in master planning, was asked to prepare a building development scheme for the Hastings site. This was amended to a T-shaped hospital of two five-storey ward blocks (with a total of 300 beds) joining a wing housing operating theatres, a laboratory, physiotherapy and administration.[69]

The five-storey stage 1 ward block, designed by Davies, Phillips & Chaplin, opened in 1961, with 122 beds. The ground floor had a 32-bed orthopaedic ward, 30-bed men's, women's and children's wards on the first, second and third floors respectively, three operating theatres on the fourth floor and staff accommodation on the top floor. A fourth theatre was added later.

↑
The Bates Block with the clinical services block behind, Napier Hospital.

Davies, Phillips & Chaplin extended the stage 1 building to the west with a four-storey ward block and a single-storey maternity annex in 1971.[70] Successor firm Kingsford, Sands, Norwell & Reilly upgraded the stage 1 ward block around 1979.

Davies, Phillips & Chaplin also designed the 1961 three-storey 85-bed Cashmore Nurses' Home, as well as the dining hall and kitchen. The chapel was then formed to their design from the original war memorial entrance hall and dedicated in 1964.[71] The firm converted the Wilson Home, an earlier nurses' home, into a psychiatric unit about 1974. Successor firm Norwell Reilly altered this around 1991 to create accommodation for community health services.[72]

About 1974 Davies, Phillips & Chaplin altered the orderlies' quarters (now Ballantyne House) to accommodate a psychiatric unit; 20 years later this was modified by Rex Design and extended for dialysis treatment in 2017 to a design by Architecture HDT. A new 25-bed psychiatric unit with a 15-bed rehabilitation unit, designed by Davies, Phillips & Chaplin, and now known as Puawānanga, opened on Orchard Road in 1979.[73]

The clinical services block, which was actually a complex of one- and two-storey buildings, was designed by Davies, Phillips & Chaplin and constructed during the 1980s. The first stage, a single-storey building with an ICU and a coronary care unit (CCU), opened in 1981, and the remainder – housing emergency, radiology, physiotherapy, occupational therapy, a laboratory and a pharmacy – opened in 1984, as did the building now containing the special care baby unit. Kingsford, Sands, Norwell & Partners also designed alterations to Ward 2, about 1981, and upgraded the boiler house in 1983.[74] Five years later the same practice converted and extended the 1965 West Wing to form part of the new 36-bed building for the assessment and rehabilitation of the elderly.

++

Also in the Hawke's Bay, the tuberculosis annex designed by Davies & Phillips and built at Wairoa Hospital in the 1940s was single storey, timber framed, clad in stucco and had concrete roof tiles. The boiler house and laundry were built around the same time to a design by Davies & Phillips. Davies, Phillips & Chaplin designed all the major buildings at Wairoa over the next three decades. A three-storey block (now known as C Block), with a 34-bed women's ward on the first floor and a 22-bed maternity ward on the second floor, and a connected annex containing x-ray and an operating theatre, opened in 1961. The block had reinforced-concrete walls and frames, with plaster walls and an iron roof.

To this was added, in about 1965, a single-storey kitchen and stores building. The firm also designed the 1965 timber-framed, weatherboard two-storey, 44-bed extension to the nurses' home, now known as Frances Kimble; the building had a concrete tiled roof. What is now known as D Block, the 1974 three-storey building housing a 33-bed ward on the first floor and administration above, was their work too.[75] Although Wairoa Hospital at one point boasted 120 beds, by 2000 it had only 14.

At Waipukurau Hospital, a medical administration, operating theatre and outpatient wing opened in 1935, followed in 1942 by the two-storey Fisher Ward and clinical services block (containing x-ray, laboratory and physiotherapy), designed by Davies & Phillips, and a concrete wing added to the nurses' home. The 10-bed Raymond Maternity Annex, also by Davies & Phillips, opened in 1948. A major redevelopment brought an administration block in 1961, a 62-bed ward block in 1963 and, in 1964, an operating theatre, all designed by the firm. A boiler house and laundry added in 1957 was expanded in 1964. The infectious

diseases annex became a geriatric unit in 1962 and four years later the maternity annex was enlarged. Waipukurau Hospital closed in 1999 and in 2000 was replaced by the Central Hawke's Bay Health Centre.[76]

By then operated by the Waiapu Hospital Board, Te Puia Springs Hospital was modernised in the 1940s. Davies, Phillips & Chaplin designed the main two-storey ward block, as well as the 1949 x-ray block and kitchen and the 23-bed nurses' home in 1951. Also added in 1945 was a 24-bed tuberculosis block that was later converted to a maternity annex before being replaced by a new maternity facility in 1959, at which point the Waipiro Bay hospital was closed.[77]

Probably based on their work on the new buildings at Hastings, Davies, Phillips & Chaplin were commissioned to design the major buildings in the redevelopment of Napier Hospital. The 137-bed Bates medical ward block and the connected clinical services building opened in 1970. The Bates Block had outpatients on the ground floor, a 30-bed women's

↑
Arohaina Block, Napier Hospital.

and geriatrics ward on the first floor and a 17-bed medical ward with an ICU and CCU on the second. A 30-bed medical ward, an infectious diseases ward and a children's ward occupied the third, fourth and fifth floors respectively, central sterile supplies the sixth. In the clinical services building, admissions and casualty were on the ground floor, x-ray and administration on the first, cardiology and a radio-isotope facility on the second, pathology on the third and staff quarters on the fourth floors.[78]

Davies, Phillips & Chaplin were also responsible for the three-storey chest block, which opened in 1971 and was converted into the Arohaina maternity block in 1977. A new kitchen and a boiler house (the latter by Rene Natusch's son, Guy) were added in 1986. The Napier site was, however, always restricted by its hillside location and access was difficult. Following proposals through the 1970s and despite significant public protest, the decision was eventually made to consolidate Hawke's Bay's hospital services on the Hastings site. Napier Hospital finally closed in 1998 and was demolished.[79]

++

After leaving his partnership with Vivian Haughton in 1951, Bill McKeon set up his own practice, specialising in hospital design.[80] He was responsible for the third Picton Hospital of 1953, with seven maternity and four general beds. Built with a concealed concrete frame with brick cavity walls, and linoleum-finished timber floors, its core was designed to allow for future expansion.[81] The old brick fever ward further up the hill was converted into a nurses' home. Picton Hospital closed in 1989.[82] McKeon designed several buildings at Wairau Hospital, including the chapel, dedicated in 1957. An operating theatre block that opened in 1954 was incorporated into a new 1969 clinical services building, with the main entrance, casualty, a laboratory, allied health and outpatient clinics also designed by McKeon. [83]

In the mid-1950s, McKeon partnered with Maurice Balfour Patience on the design of such buildings as the 1958 convent and chapel at Wellington's Calvary Hospital (see page 231). The pair dissolved their partnership in 1963. McKeon was also appointed architect to the Buller Hospital Board, where he designed the new 1964 Karamea Maternity Hospital, which replaced a converted house that had served the district since the 1920s.[84] The new building provided a delivery room, three bedrooms and staff accommodation, and was timber framed with Durock sidings, on concrete foundations.[85]

A two-storey timber nurses' home was built at Buller Hospital in 1954, with another 20-bed block added in 1962, and the Kawatiri Maternity Annex opened in 1960. The May 1962 earthquakes near Westport rendered most of the buildings unsafe and two new 30-bed wards, Dunsford and Foote, were completed in 1964. The adjacent 27-bed Kynnersley Home for the elderly was opened in the refurbished original hospital building in 1966. The far more severe 1968 Inangahua earthquake caused so much damage that all the old hospital buildings had to be demolished. A new theatre block opened in 1972, a wing for laboratory and physiotherapy in 1973. Bill McKeon remained the Buller Hospital Board's architect until his retirement in 1971, so he probably designed at least some of these buildings.[86]

While in partnership with Bill McKeon, Maurice Patience was also in another with Allott Gabites, which seems to have formed around 1949. The relationship between the two practices is unclear. Patience's partnership with Gabites appears to have ended in the early 1960s, around the same time as the one with McKeon, after which he set up on his own. Patience's name alone, however, is also on a 1952 master plan for Grey Base Hospital, implying that his partnerships were quite informal and possibly formed for specific projects.[87]

In 1965 Gabites formed another partnership in Wellington with James Albert Beard. William Hildebrand (Bill) Alington joined them around the same time, but the firm's name remained Gabites & Beard. The practice came second in the 1959 competition for Auckland's new St Helen's Hospital. In 1971 Gabites & Beard merged with the practice of Toomath & Wilson, designers of the 1964 concrete-block and redwood-clad library, administration and accommodation block at the Otaki Health Camp.[88] This partnership, though, lasted less than a year.

++

↑

Clinical services building, Wairau Hospital, Blenheim, 1969.

↖

Cobalt therapy building, Calvary Hospital, Wellington, 1969.

David George (George) Porter and Lewis (Lew) Edouard Martin, who formed their Wellington partnership in 1954, also made their mark on hospital design during this period. At Masterton Hospital, the ground floor of their ward and specialist services block, designed with Daniell & Wevers, housed the entrance, casualty, outpatient and physiotherapy departments. The first and second floors each accommodated a 31-bed ward with single and four-bed rooms in a racetrack arrangement. The ICU was on the top floor, next to proposed operating theatres in an extension that did not eventuate. Instead, a single-storey operating theatre and CSSD block was added in 1970. Large windows were installed to give patients good natural light and outlook, although the north–south alignment of the wards resulted in problems with glare and overheating, leading to the Department of Health banning such orientations in future ward blocks. The ward block, nurses' home, older ward buildings and the boiler house were demolished in 2021.[89]

At Greymouth Hospital, a boiler house and laundry were added in 1963 and a kitchen and trades block three years later. But significant damage caused by the 7.1 Inangahua earthquake in May 1968 meant that the existing hospital buildings had to be replaced in stages from 1971, with the 60-bed, three-storey Grey Base Hospital designed by Porter & Martin.[90] Michael Fowler later described this as a 'modest structure of reinforced concrete frame and brick panel which provides a good answer to the brief', although he noted that 'often, however, a hospital brief is a confusion of instructions, attempting to encapsulate in concrete a system of medical care which can be outdated by the time it is completed'.[91]

Porter & Martin's Clinical Services Centre opened at Gore Hospital in 1973. This contained emergency services, an intensive and coronary care unit, allied health and a laboratory. The hospital was closed in 1999 and demolished, and, given its relatively short life, the flexibility with which it was designed was 'ironic'.[92] At the time of writing, a vacant ward block remains isolated in the south-west corner of the Southland Hospital site in Invercargill. Its designer and date of construction are unclear, but it has some of the design hallmarks of

↑

David George (George) Porter. Lewis (Lew) Edouard Martin.

↗

Masterton Hospital ward block.

Porter & Martin's Greymouth and Masterton ward buildings and could possibly have been done by the firm while working at Gore. Their other healthcare work included the Petone Industrial Health Centre, dating from about 1962.[93]

++

At Nelson Hospital, the nurses' home was replaced in 1958 by the 155-bed Franklyn Hall, on the north side of Franklyn Street, a building designed by James Herbert Hall-Kenney in the International Modern style. Hall-Kenney also designed the hospital's six-storey 146-bed George Manson Ward building, opened in 1960.[94] A new boiler house was added in 1963, the chapel was dedicated in 1964 and the staff pool was ready for use in 1965. The six-level 90-bed Percy Brunette Building, designed by successor practice Rotman, White & Hay, opened in

↑

Grey Base Hospital, Greymouth.

↖

Dunstan Hospital and nurses' home under construction in Clyde, 1960.

↑

Franklyn Hall nurses' home, Nelson Hospital.

↗

Nelson Hospital: George Manson ward block to left, Percy Brunette to right.

1978. Hall-Kenney also designed the Motueka Maternity Hospital in 1969, which replaced the cottage hospital opened there in 1923.[95]

In Central Otago, ideas during the 1940s of closing the Cromwell and Clyde hospitals and replacing them with a new facility in Alexandra came to nothing. Instead, Dunstan Hospital was redeveloped to a design by Hall-Kenney, with a new nurses' home in 1957 and a 30-bed ward and 11-bed maternity unit in 1959. Hall-Kenney also designed a new nurses' home at Cromwell around 1949.

Primary health

General practitioners have always played a critical role in the delivery of New Zealand's healthcare. Originally most worked from their own homes, perhaps using a spare room for consultation and making house calls to patients. Gradually, however, the benefits of collaboration prompted many in urban areas to form joint practices, operating from rooms in repurposed houses or attached to suburban shopping centres. Some commissioned specifically designed facilities.

At the start of the twenty-first century, the government encouraged the development of integrated family health centres, where general practices are co-located with other health services such as pharmacy, radiology and laboratory sample collection, and other health professionals such as dentists, physiotherapists, optometrists and midwives.[1] Some examples follow of architecturally designed primary health facilities throughout New Zealand.

Orewa Medical Centre, 2012. Fat Parrot Architecture designed this refurbishment of 600 square metres of office and retail space containing eight consulting rooms, a facility for minor surgery and a nurse treatment area.[2]

Pakuranga Medical Centre, 2018. Medispace designed this two-storey 2500-square-metre building with 15 consulting rooms for GPs and other medical professionals. Specialist health property development company Medispace, established in 2010, has its own in-house architectural team, but also engages external architects as required.[4]

Vernon Brown designed this home for Dr M. Rosten in Sandringham Road, Auckland, where the consulting room is accessed via a separate patients' entrance; the client insisted on a much steeper roof pitch than is typical in Brown's work.[3]

Whitianga Medical Centre, 2023. Pacific Environments designed this new medical centre built by Hopper Developments, the developer of several beachside communities such as Pauanui.[5]

Hutt Valley Health Hub, 2020. Next to Hutt Hospital, and designed by Arthouse Architects, this is the first health hub in New Zealand of structural timber construction. Developed by Medispace, it provides a new home for Ropata Health, which had outgrown its previous 1988 Roger Walker-designed premises, as well as a community dialysis unit.[6]

Onslow Medical Centre, Wellington. This general practice facility by Tennant Brown Architects incorporates natural materials and an internal planted green wall lit from the skylight above.[7]

Riddiford Medical Centre, Wellington, 2015. In a heritage area next to Wellington Hospital, this design by Melling Morse Architects works with the existing street texture to provide retail tenancies on the ground floor, with two floors of consulting and procedure rooms above.[8]

Tahunanui Medical Centre, 1980, Nelson. GP clinics occupy this building, which was designed by local architect Ian Jack and has angled walls and cedar cladding to reflect its beachside setting.

Longhurst Health, Christchurch, 2013. David Childs was the architect for this 2020-square-metre building in Halswell, with GP clinics, a dentist, ultrasound, allied health, a pharmacy and a café.[9]

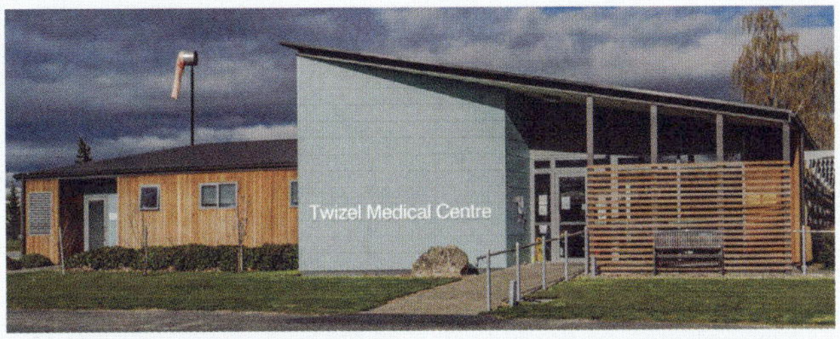

Twizel Medical Centre, 2016. Containing seven consulting rooms, x-ray and physiotherapy, this building also has, because of its remote location, an ambulance turnaround that doubles as a helipad. Designed by Parker Warburton Team Architects, it opened in 2016.

Heaton Street Medical Centre, Timaru, 2016. This 2350-square-metre building in a semi-industrial area was designed by NB Architects.

11

Economic shock and surgery 1970–2000

NEW ZEALAND'S POST-WAR BOOM YEARS ended in the 1970s, with Britain joining the European Union in 1973, and oil price shocks that year and in 1979. The economically interventionist National government under Robert Muldoon had experimented with the introduction of area health boards in 1983. This was accelerated after David Lange led Labour to power in 1984 and Roger Douglas oversaw a major restructuring of the public service: by 1989 all the former hospital boards had been replaced with 14 area health boards. These took on many of the public health functions of the former Department of Health, which became the Ministry of Health, with a greater focus on policy.

The 1988 Mason Report led to significant changes in the provision of mental health services. The Māori renaissance that began in the 1970s, and the formation of the Waitangi Tribunal in 1975, meant that greater consideration was given to the incorporation of Māori design principles in health architecture.[1]

To improve efficiency, wards began to move away from a single corridor model to a racetrack concept, with staff bases and service rooms in the centre, surrounded by a ring of bedrooms, which cut down walking distances and improved observation. Ensuites attached to bedrooms began to replace central ablutions blocks, reducing patient travel and improving safety and dignity. Architects began to react against the rigours of modernism by adopting a variety of styles, such as neo-classicism, deconstructivism and high-tech architecture, grouped under the umbrella of post-modernism. In skilled hands, this enabled the creation of more humane healthcare environments, but also came to be seen as a symbol of extravagance and excess.[2]

Although the government and hospital boards were encouraging the development of health design capability in New Zealand, some, particularly the Auckland and Otago boards, recognised that, for the large volume of new hospital building required, engaging overseas designers would reduce risk by giving access to resources and expertise. Australian firm Stephenson & Turner, established in Melbourne early in the 1920s, seized the opportunity, and for a time seemed to be synonymous with health design, at least in Auckland and Dunedin.

Sir Arthur George Stephenson was largely responsible for the firm's direction, particularly its specialisation in hospital and industrial architecture. Trips to the United States in 1926–27 and Europe in 1932–33 had a significant impact on the firm's design approach. Inspired by Bijvoet & Duiker's 1928 Zonnestraal Sanatorium in the Netherlands and Alvar Aalto's 1933 Paimio Sanatorium in Finland, Stephenson began to include deep balconies in his designs for access to fresh air and shade from the sun.

Under his leadership, the practice became Australia's leading hospital designers in the 1930s. Stephenson & Turner became a multi-disciplinary practice, employing services engineers to work alongside their architects, and adopted a modernist doctrine, not just in style but also in their systems-based approach. They implemented standard specifications, details and contract administration methods.[3]

Partner Geoffrey Moline, and then Arthur Stephenson himself, visited New Zealand in 1936, developing relationships with hospital boards around the country. Several schemes were developed for Auckland Hospital, and, in collaboration with Crichton, McKay & Haughton, for Wellington Hospital and the proposed facility at Hutt, but these did not come to fruition. The firm's early forays into New Zealand were not greeted enthusiastically by some hospital boards and local architects, and the only Stephenson & Turner building completed here before the end of the Second World War was the modernist Australian Pavilion at the 1940 Centennial Exhibition in Wellington, which was a stark departure from the general Art Deco theme of Edmund Anscombe's master plan.[4]

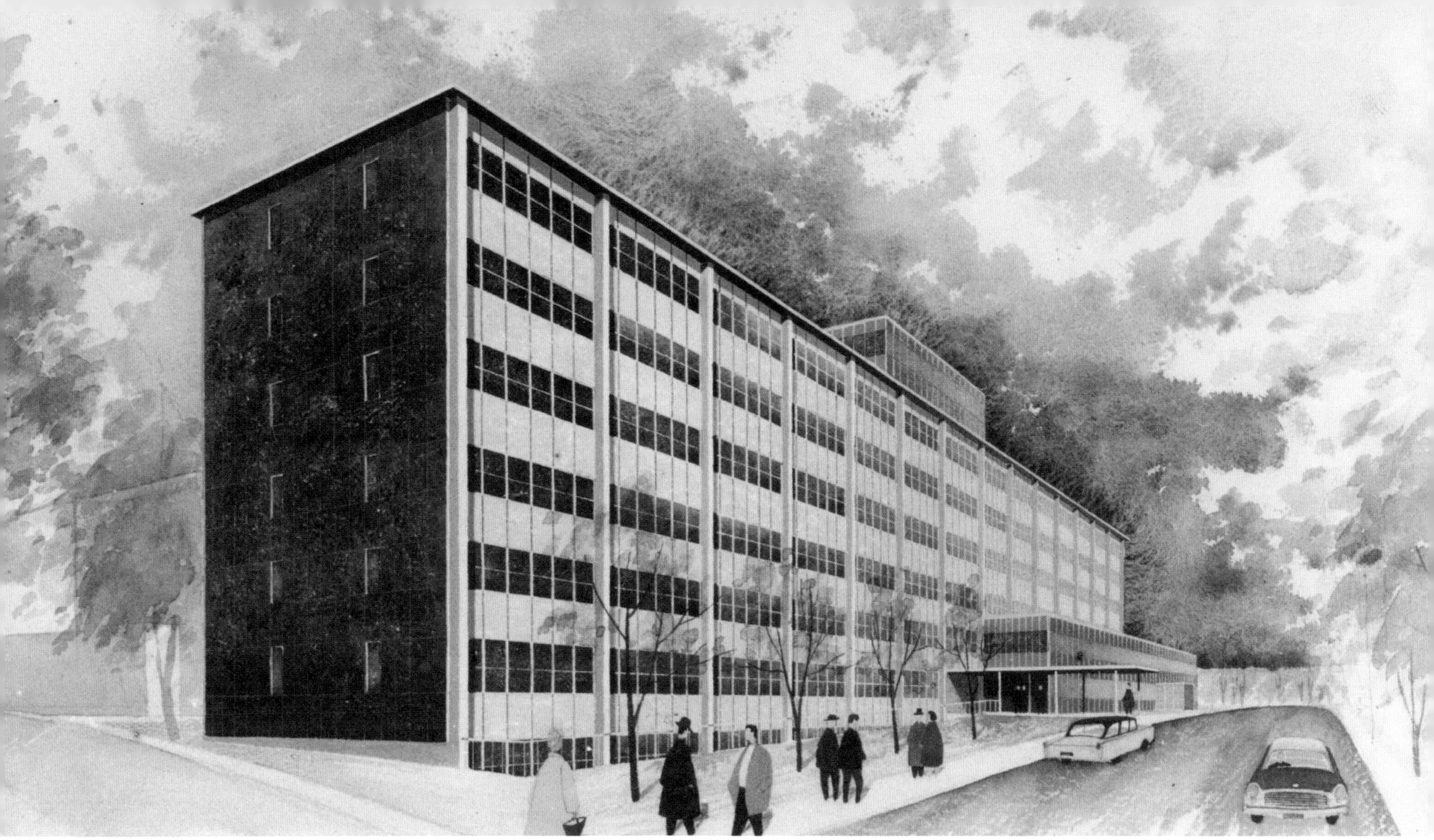

In the early 1950s the firm returned to New Zealand at the request of the Otago Hospital Board to review designs prepared by local firms for several hospitals, including Wakari. By 1955 Stephenson & Turner had enough projects to justify opening an office in Wellington, under Melbourne-based associate David Dunn, and a team arrived from Australia in 1956. A second office was opened in Dunedin in 1957.[5]

Stephenson had envisaged a core of two Australian offices providing advice to a ring of satellite offices, rather than seeking to develop expertise in every branch. (Its wealth of knowledge set the firm apart from most New Zealand firms at the time.) There was, however, a tension between this approach and the desire of the government and hospital boards to avoid relying on overseas experts and instead develop local skills. As Stephenson noted, '"foreign consultants" were not appreciated, whereas every encouragement would be given to the firm if it established an office on New Zealand soil.'[6]

Following an invitation from the Otago board in 1947, the firm's first building at a New Zealand hospital was humble, though essential in purpose: the boiler house and laundry in Dunedin in 1959, designed in collaboration with local architect Jim White, with whom Stephenson had studied at the Architectural Association.[7] In 1958 the Auckland Hospital Board approached Stephenson & Turner to extend Middlemore Hospital and undertake significant work at Auckland Hospital.

The firm's first clinical building in New Zealand was the six-level, 306-bed acute block at Middlemore, opened in 1964. Now known as the Galbraith Building, it consists of a ward block with two 34-bed wards per floor, on a two-storey podium housing six operating theatres, radiology and clinics.[8] T-shaped, it has a circulation core at the rear of the main ward block

↑

Artist's impression of Galbraith Block, Middlemore Hospital.

↩

Starship Children's Hospital, Auckland.

that connects to the Orchard & Allison-designed maternity building, maximising access to natural light and outlook. It had stronger articulation than many of the firm's Australian buildings, with exposed structural columns projecting beyond the spandrels.[9]

Stephenson & Turner developed a strong relationship with the Otago Hospital Board, resulting in further commissions at Dunedin Hospital, where they next designed the 1968 nine-storey, 12,773-square-metre clinical services building, housing operating theatres, a CSSD, x-ray, laboratories and a pharmacy.[10] The Melbourne office provided multiple designs, but the local knowledge of the New Zealand office prevailed in shaping the final outcome. In fact, a divergence in practice and style from the Australian base soon became apparent in the work at both Dunedin and Auckland hospitals.[11]

↑

Dunedin Hospital ward block.

↖

Dunedin Hospital, looking west: clinical services building in centre.

↗

Arthur George Stephenson.

The Australians were used to designing with fewer constraints; many Australian hospitals were on relatively flat greenfield or brownfield sites, but the New Zealand projects were generally additions and rebuilding in relatively restricted existing campuses. Budgets were tighter and the Health Department was wary of significant innovation. Seismic requirements added further complexity. As a result, the firm's New Zealand hospital designs developed their own specific characteristics.[12]

In 1980 came the 11-storey, 39,579-square-metre ward block at Dunedin, for which local partner-in-charge Maurice Tebbs was sent to Melbourne in the early stages of design to 'learn about hospitals'.[13] There he studied the work being done at Canberra and Royal North Shore hospitals. The Dunedin floor plan was again T-shaped, but in this case the stem of the T was to provide academic office space for the staff of the adjacent medical school. Designed for flexibility, it has a double-corridor system with standard bedroom modules. Some ducted services were run up the exterior walls, creating an articulating device that breaks up the building's bulk. Care was also taken at the ground level to soften the building's presence so that it did not dominate its more domestic-scaled neighbours. The adjacent 1975 lecture block for the medical school made a bold use of textured concrete and robust detailing, as at the University of Auckland School of Medicine, designed by the firm at the same time.[14]

++

Thanks to the relationship built with the Auckland Hospital Board through the Middlemore project, Stephenson & Turner were engaged to design almost all the major new buildings at Auckland Hospital for the next three decades, as well as the new University of Auckland School of Medicine on the opposite side of Park Road. In 1960 Ken Gold came from Adelaide to establish an office in Auckland and John Wilcox became the first New Zealand partner there in 1965.[15]

Stephenson & Turner had been working on designs for the main acute block at Auckland Hospital since 1936; Donald Turner had prepared the preliminary sketches. In 1960 Bruce McDonald and Warwick Smith from the Sydney office were selected to create a programme for the redevelopment of the hospital. As the Auckland office had not yet been opened, they began working from an old post-mortem room onsite at the hospital.[16]

The site for the new acute block at Auckland Hospital was constrained by roads and other buildings and the accommodation requirements far exceeded what could be achieved. Because it was designed to the maximum possible building envelope, the ward tower was only marginally smaller than the podium on which it sat. An H-shaped corridor system carved the interior into useable spaces, with multi-bed rooms on the north and south sides, and single rooms on the other two, reflected in the external design.[17]

Warwick Smith, who became the project architect, had intended to be in Auckland only short term. He had joined the firm in 1948, but left two years later to travel widely around Europe and the United States, working for several firms. The book he wrote on the planning of surgical suites brought him into contact with many experts in hospital practice and design, so that he gave a fresh perspective to the firm on his return in 1960; he became a partner in 1970.[18]

The expected procedure was for the Melbourne office to take the brief and design the project, but the hospital board rejected their sketch plans for Auckland. When board secretary Ray Galbraith requested that Smith be made available for the replanning, he relocated to Auckland permanently in 1961. The bedrooms had ensuites, then a novelty in hospitals, and the outpatient clinics were based on those at the Mayo Clinic, with patients entering on one side and staff and supplies from the rear. Construction started in 1964, and

the 670-bed building opened in stages from 1969 to 1975, with significant delays incurred by design changes and replanning.[19]

Stephenson & Turner also designed the new boiler house with its landmark tapering concrete chimney on the east side of the new building, bordering the Domain, and new trade workshops, followed in 1974 by the nurses' home and junior medical officers' residence on the western, Grafton Road, side of the site.[20] The firm also designed the two-level central stores building, also opened that year further down the sloping site to the north, as the existing one was removed to create the site for the proposed children's hospital.

++

A growing emphasis on patient experience is evident in the practice's 1987 oncology centre at Auckland Hospital, which consists of two buff-coloured brick blocks linked by a glazed barrel-roof atrium containing a fernery. Three radiotherapy bunkers replaced the 1958 super-voltage facility. The waiting area for these has large windows looking out on a large pōhutukawa tree and landscaped lightwells ease the transition for patients into the massive concrete bunkers, which are well below ground level.[21]

The 30,000-square-metre, 200-bed Starship Children's Hospital, opened in 1991, has a three-storey podium for diagnostic and treatment services, with four levels of wards above. The podium uses the steep site to provide vehicle and pedestrian access to each level and the narrow wards have good access to natural ventilation and light. Briefing on the building, which replaced the ageing Princess Mary Block, started in 1976.[22]

Two curved blocks, one accommodating the wards, the other support spaces, are set around a glass-covered atrium, providing an enclosed playground with glass-fronted lift cars, developed by Smith and project architect Geoff Land to form the heart of the building.

↖

Auckland City Hospital, 2025: acute block and oncology to left, Starship Children's Hospital centre.

↗

Starship Children's Hospital atrium, Auckland.

It has an exposed concrete structural frame with circular columns, post-modern decorative elements such as spherical capitals and individual windows with perforated metal sunscreens to reduce the scale and create a non-threatening environment. The use of bright vibrant colour and the inclusion of symbols representative of children's depictions of houses, such as gable-shaped pediments over doorways and multi-pane windows, were all used to make the building welcoming and sympathetic to younger patients. The curved floor plans soften the external form and avoid long, straight institutional corridors, but have created some planning challenges as the building has been adapted.[23]

The University of Auckland School of Medicine was officially opened in 1970, although the first students had arrived in 1968. This was the culmination of years of lobbying by Sir Douglas Robb, among others. The four principal blocks are the pre-clinical building, the link building with lecture theatres, both from 1970, the clinical building in 1974 and the pathology building in 1978. Overall, the building area was 3700 square metres on a 2.8-hectare site. The buildings have a 3.35-metre module, which suits both laboratories and offices, and were designed for expansion.[24]

Stephenson & Turner designed the pre-clinical and clinical buildings around a central core of highly serviced laboratories with staff offices on the perimeter. The Brutalist structure is face-finished concrete, with ribbed and hammered shear walls for the link building and, on the others, board-finished column and beam frames infilled with pre-cast concrete panels that have crushed bluestone aggregate facing. Sheet copper was used for the facias and canopies, and the windows are PVC-sheathed steel or polyurethane-coated aluminium. The clinical and pathology buildings had temporary long-run steel walls to allow for expansion.[25]

In her review of Stephenson & Turner's New Zealand healthcare work, Julie Willis wrote, 'Meticulously planned, and with significant innovations in servicing, efficiency and flexibility, the new blocks at the Auckland and Dunedin hospitals set new standards for hospital design in New Zealand. They also brought new ideas to Stephenson & Turner's collective expertise in hospital design, although at the time they were not yet fully appreciated.'

She also noted that, because of budget and programme constraints, 'exterior treatment lacked the elegance of the pre-World War II hospitals and the assuredness of the firm's New Zealand commercial work'. Nevertheless, they were proof that the Australian head office could not 'simply provide its expertise through a shopfront office' and that the New Zealand arm would 'come of age and emerge as important contributors to the development of hospital architecture in the region in their own right'.[26]

++

↑
University of Auckland School of Medicine.

Stephenson & Turner's New Zealand work also included several private hospitals, whose smaller scale and comparatively generous sites allowed for a more human scale and better engagement with the landscape. These include Dunedin's 1969 Mater Misericordiae, now Mercy Hospital, built for the Sisters of Mercy in the garden of the old homestead which became their convent, Wellington's 1971 Bowen Hospital and Auckland's 2001 Bledisloe Medical Centre (now Birthcare).[27] These buildings drew on an emerging New Zealand design spirit, exemplified in some of the early work by Warren and Mahoney, Peter Beaven and others, which emphasised strong geometrical forms and materiality. Brick was used often to soften the buildings and to bring a more domestic scale, and the curved forms at Bowen took advantage of the views of its bush-covered valley site.[28]

For the Seventh Day Adventist Church, the firm designed the 56-bed Auckland Adventist Hospital in St Heliers, opened in 1976, and the 1995 30-bed Bethesda Geriatric Hospital as part of the church's New Zealand headquarters development in Wiri.[29] At St Heliers, the 2.4 hectares of grounds allowed for future expansion, and the sloping site was used creatively to disguise the building's bulk. The adjacent medical centre, also developed by the church and designed by Stephenson & Turner, opened in 1993.[30]

++

From the late 1970s, New Zealand staff also consulted on several of Stephenson & Turner's large hospitals in Asia. Overseas health projects designed by the New Zealand arm include Ba Hospital and parts of Suva's Colonial War Memorial Hospital in Fiji and, in Sāmoa, Tupua Tamasese Meaole Hospital in Apia and Malietoa Tanumafili II Hospital in Savaii.[31]

The firm's mental health projects include the 1992 15-bed Pūrehurehu acute adult forensic unit and the 2003 Haumietiketike unit, both at Porirua Hospital,[32] the 1993 Fraser McDonald acute psychiatric unit of the same size in Auckland, the 1995 acute psychiatric unit at Kenepuru and the 25-bed Te Whare Ahuru mental health unit at Hutt Hospital in 1996. Other public health projects include a new building at the Otahuhu Rehabilitation Centre around 1965, the Botany Maternity Unit in 1991, and Hawera Hospital and the Kapiti Health Centre in Paraparaumu, both in 2002.[33]

++

Stephenson & Turner also designed one of the country's first curtain-wall office buildings, Shell House in Wellington, dating from 1960, which followed Ernst Plischke and Cedric Firth's nearby 1954 Massey House. The firm went on to design several high-rise office buildings, including the country's tallest at the time, the Bank of New Zealand building (now the Aon Tower) in Wellington. This was finally completed in 1986 after years of disputes with the Boilermakers' Union, leading to a nationwide move away from steel construction for some time.[34]

In 2022 the four New Zealand offices were set up as separate firms, which in turn own the central company of Stephenson & Turner NZ Ltd. Stephenson & Turner Auckland Ltd and Stephenson & Turner Wellington Ltd include engineering and architecture teams, Co-Studio Stephenson & Turner operates in Christchurch and the Waikato branch has become Shelter Architects in Taupō.[35] In 1961 Stephenson wrote, 'It is grand to be able to tell you what a vigorous and progressive section of the firm is developing in New Zealand. I am beginning to think that this office will teach us a thing or two before we are much older.' Given that it is the New Zealand arm that has kept the name alive, as the Australian offices have closed, this was a much truer statement than he could have envisaged at the time.[36]

++

A Hawke's Bay practice still operating today can trace its history back for more than a century to a firm established by one family's three generations of architects, and which was responsible for much of the health design in the eastern North Island. After a proposed partnership with Atkins & Clere did not eventuate, Lewis (Charles) Tilleard Natusch purchased the Napier practice of Robert Lamb, who had died in 1895. He was joined by his sons Charles A. (Aleck) in 1898, Rene in 1904 and Stanley in 1906. Offices were opened in Gisborne in 1900, Wellington in 1906 and Palmerston North in 1908. Charles Natusch moved to Wellington to run the office there, the Palmerston North office was operated by Aleck, and Rene took responsibility for Napier and Gisborne.[37]

All three sons served in the First World War, during which all the offices were closed, except for Napier and Wellington, both run by C. T. Natusch. Another office opened in the developing town of Hastings in the 1920s, but the Depression led to a significant reduction in work. The 1931 earthquake therefore came as a mixed blessing. The building housing the Hastings branch was badly damaged and condemned and the office closed, but Aleck and Stanley joined Rene in Napier, where the need for repairs and rebuilding resulted in numerous projects, and architects from elsewhere in New Zealand offered to work for the firm at low rates rather than go on the dole. During an inspection of the partly collapsed Upoko Poito Private Hospital in Napier, possibly designed by Crichton, McKay & Haughton for Dr Walter Moore, Rene became trapped under a beam during an aftershock. He later joked that it gave him the opportunity to study the formation of cracking in concrete.[38]

As noted earlier, Rene Natusch led the Associated Architects alliance to facilitate reconstruction after the 1931 Hawke's Bay earthquake; Natusch & Sons were responsible for the work at Napier Hospital. This was on a restricted 2.4-hectare hillside site, with limited room to expand and poor road access; the recently opened hospital in Hastings had a flat, easily accessible 7.2-hectare site. For a time, there was a proposal to close Napier and make Hastings the regional hospital for Hawke's Bay, but Napier was rebuilt after a bitter battle, and for the next 50 years the two grew as independent base hospitals. Thanks to some innovative repair techniques, the firm was able to bring the badly damaged Midgely and Coleman wards at Napier Hospital back into operation rapidly, using overlaid reinforced-concrete cages. The two-storey, 54-bed wooden Tuakana Nurses' Home opened in 1932.[39]

As the post-earthquake work wound down, Aleck and Stanley Natusch relocated to Wellington to run the office there. On being awarded the commission by the Marlborough Hospital Board to design a new nurses' home in Blenheim to replace one damaged in an earthquake, the firm instead proposed strengthening the old one using the same methods they had employed in Napier.[40] After the Napier Hospital Board's decision to redevelop the hospitals in Napier and Hastings, they initiated a building programme at Napier in 1949 that included a 70-bed chest block, an additional ward above the Coleman Ward, a laundry block and a new nurses' home.[41] The latter was designed in association with Ernest Arthur Williams and Lawrence Garbutt Williams.

As mentioned earlier, Natusch & Sons was responsible for much of the redevelopment of Cook Hospital in Gisborne during the 1940s, including the nurses' home in 1941 and the polyclinic block in 1945. They also designed the private Duart Hospital in Havelock North, dating from about 1964.[42]

↖

Lewis (Charles) Tilleard Natusch.
Rene Natusch.
Guy Kingdon Natusch.

↑

Dr Moore's Hospital on Marine Parade following the 1931 Napier earthquake.

↗

Boiler house, Napier Hospital.

Rene's son, Guy Kingdon Natusch, joined the firm in 1946 after serving in the navy during the Second World War. Despite the 1960s redevelopment of Napier Hospital having gone to Hastings firm Davies, Phillips & Chaplin, Natusch did design some ancillary buildings there such as the boiler house, from about 1986, which, at the time of writing, was the only building remaining on the main Napier Hospital site.[43] Davies, Phillips & Chaplin and their

successor firms in Hastings had ceased operating, so somewhat ironically Natusch was commissioned for much of the work associated with the major redevelopment of the Hawke's Bay Fallen Soldiers' Memorial Hospital campus in the 1990s. Further buildings were added in 1997 to create the Health Villa complex for outpatients.

About that time, successor firm Judd Fenwick Natusch converted the two-storey store and linen building to Villa 2, housing clinics and offices, and four new Villa buildings (1, 3, 4 and 5) were added. Two earlier 1940s-era wards were adapted to form Villas 6 and 8, and Villa 7 was created from an earlier building. Around 1999 Judd Fenwick, as the practice had become, converted the resident medical officer flats into the diabetes service and in about 2003 they converted the 1950s hydrotherapy pool and gym to Villa 9 for the child development unit.[44]

Between 1996 and 1997 Judd Fenwick Natusch/Judd Fenwick also refurbished the ward blocks and the 1980s clinical services building complex as part of the redevelopment, including radiology, a laboratory and an ICU and the addition of the services entry. About 1996 Judd Fenwick Natusch also extended the assessment, treatment and rehabilitation building to the west. The emergency department was redeveloped and an ICU/high-dependency unit block added; a pharmacy and acute assessment unit followed in 2004. Unfortunately, much of the original space between buildings in the complex was filled in, resulting in a deep plan building with poor coherence. Around 1999 Judd Fenwick also extended the chapel, formerly the main entrance. The upgraded hospital was officially opened in 1999.[45]

↑
Arthur Wicks Building, Wairau Hospital, Blenheim.

The six-theatre operating theatre block by Judd Fenwick Natusch, later Dougan Larkworthy Team Architects, in conjunction with Australian firm Woods Bagot, opened in 2000. The adjacent kitchen and café, from about 1997 and 1999 respectively, were also by Judd Fenwick Natusch, the former in conjunction with Hoogerbrug Architects and the latter with Bell Wright Architects.

Since it was extended in 1987, the boiler house and the adjacent chiller and maintenance blocks have undergone significant strengthening and redevelopment from the 2010s to the present. Other buildings include the kitchen and services entry in 1998, the maintenance facility in 2012 and the mortuary in 2014. The helicopter facility of about 2000 was designed by Pacific Projects and the single-storey Waioha primary birthing centre at the north end of the ward blocks opened in 2017.[46]

The Waipukurau Community Health Centre, designed by Judd Fenwick Natusch, was built around 1999. Judd Fenwick Team Architecture also designed the 2000 Napier Health Centre, built in the city centre as part of the redevelopment so that outpatient services could continue to be provided there, and several upgrades at Gisborne Hospital, including the accident and emergency department.[47]

++

At Wairau Hospital, the 1976 two-level, two-ward, 71-bed Arthur Wicks Building was designed by the Marlborough Hospital Board's architects, McArthur & Reeve, replacing many of the 1920s hospital buildings. Arthur Wicks, which now houses the emergency department and high-dependency unit, was seismically strengthened with external buttress bracing in 2016.[48]

On the West Coast, Greymouth architect Gary Hopkinson carried out alterations at Buller and Reefton hospitals in the 1980s. At Grey Base Hospital, the Parfitt paediatric ward and administration block, designed by Hopkinson, opened in 1996, and his later firm Hopkinson Kelsall Team Architects has been responsible for other work around the hospital since.[49]

++

By the end of the 1950s Christchurch's Burwood Hospital had become a permanent facility with acute general medical and surgical wards, and the older buildings were gradually replaced by more permanent two-storey structures. A swimming pool and a 62-bed extension were added to the nurses' home in 1957. In the 1960s came a visitors' entrance and office block, an operating theatre block and a chapel, a new surgical block and a boiler house and maintenance building. As the emphasis changed to rehabilitation, the Milner units for spinal patients were built in 1963 and the spinal injury unit opened 1979, followed by a hostel and self-care units in 1981. A hospice opened in 1982 and further self-care hostels for spinal patients in 1985. The 1986 physical medicine building housed physiotherapy, occupational therapy, hydrotherapy and speech and language specialties.[50]

There was a rationalisation of services at Burwood in the 1990s. Plastic surgery was transferred to Christchurch Hospital in 1995 and two years later the decision was made to retain Burwood as a centre for spinal and older persons' care. This resulted in a two-stage redevelopment. The first consisted of the 2001 Alan Bean Centre for orthopaedic rehabilitation, a 2003 orthopaedic rehabilitation ward and a new main entrance and administration building, designed by Christchurch practice Sheppard & Rout. The second stage, in 2006, added a block of four orthopaedic theatres, a ward and a special care unit.[51]

At Dunedin Hospital, more recent work by the long-lived firm Mason & Wales includes the 4524-square-metre Oncology Centre, from 1993, on the corner of Hanover and Cumberland streets. According to architect Peter Beaven, in his introduction to Peter Shaw's 1991 history of New Zealand architecture, the building designed by Mason & Wales director Ashley Muir 'has splendid Classical weight and mass with delicate, almost [R. A.] Lawson-like mouldings and a floating, tiled roof-light'.[52]

++

During this period, one practice was involved in the design of more healthcare buildings throughout the country, from as far north as Kaitāia to Timaru in the south, than any other. Several firms operating today trace their origins to it.

Edgar (Ernest) Gillman formally began his architectural practice in Paeroa in 1913, though he appears to have been working in his own right some time before then, developing an expertise in the design of dairy factories, but also a growing interest in hospital work. The Waikato Museum holds a 1912 drawing by him for a new six-bed children's ward at Thames Hospital, and other work of his there includes the delirium tremens ward.[53] He also designed the 1930 Paeroa Hospital, with six beds and a two-bed emergency unit; new nursing quarters were added to this in 1954. For many years primarily a maternity hospital, it closed in 1994.[54]

Gillman's business developed, and around the outbreak of the Second World War he was appointed architect to the New Zealand Co-operative Dairy Company, which meant relocating his family and business to Hamilton.[55] After completing a Bachelor of Architecture course at the University of Auckland, which had been interrupted by service in the air force, his son, T. F. (Frank) Gillman, joined him to form Gillman & Gillman Architects in 1947. As well as designing several dairy factories, Frank Gillman also developed a specialty in hospital architecture.

On Ernest Gillman's death in 1951, the firm became T. F. Gillman & Co. It then merged with that of architect Doug Angus and engineer Paul Marks to become Gillman, Angus & Marks, Architects and Engineers, but this partnership was dissolved in 1954 and the firm

reverted to its former name. By mutual agreement, the three partners divided the clients between them and Angus went on to form Angus, Flood & Griffiths.[56]

Ernest Gillman had been appointed architect to the Tauranga Hospital Board in 1949, beginning a relationship that would last into the next century. A children's ward and a new boiler house opened at Tauranga in 1951 and a 1954 expansion added two operating theatres and a casualty department.[57] After taking over the appointment in 1950, Frank Gillman, with architect Doug Angus, developed a long-term development plan. Stage 1, which opened in 1964, consisted of a five-level building containing the vertical circulation core and offices, connected to the five-storey east wing with three 30-bed wards, three operating theatres and outpatients and casualty departments, and a kitchen and stores annex at the rear, giving the hospital a capacity of 180 beds. A new 75-bed nurses' home opened in 1959 and an 83-bed extension (later Jacaranda House) in 1967. The maternity annex received a 16-bed extension in 1962, a new laundry opened in 1964 and the boiler house in 1967.[58]

In 1954 Frank Gillman formed a partnership with David A. Sayers, who had emigrated from Britain that year and joined the Ministry of Works. Sayers, son of an interior designer father and draughtswoman mother, trained at the Architectural Association in London. He had been offered a position at the New Zealand Co-operative Dairy Company, which at the same time had been trying to persuade Gillman to become their chief architect. Gillman travelled to Wellington to meet Sayers and offered him the opportunity to move to Hamilton and join him as a junior partner.[59]

Architect Peter Garry, who had been architect to the dairy company, formed a partnership with civil engineer L. Rex Clapp in Hamilton around 1954, focused on commercial and industrial projects. Because Gillman and Sayers were concerned about being over-reliant on hospital work, T. F. Gillman & Co. merged with Garry & Clapp to form Gillman Garry Clapp & Sayers in 1963. As a result, the firm obtained dairy factory work across the Waikato region. By 1971 A. R. I. Garry, Robert Ellis, Alan Howe and engineers Eddie Thomas and Tony Schuitemaker had joined as partners.[60]

The stage 2 additions at Tauranga Hospital included the five-storey, 128-bed west-wing ward block in 1972, the Tauranga Hospital Board's offices in 1973 and the two-storey clinical

↖

Oncology Building, Dunedin Hospital, c.2000.

↑

Frank Gillman.
David Sayers.

↗

Paeroa Hospital, 1930.

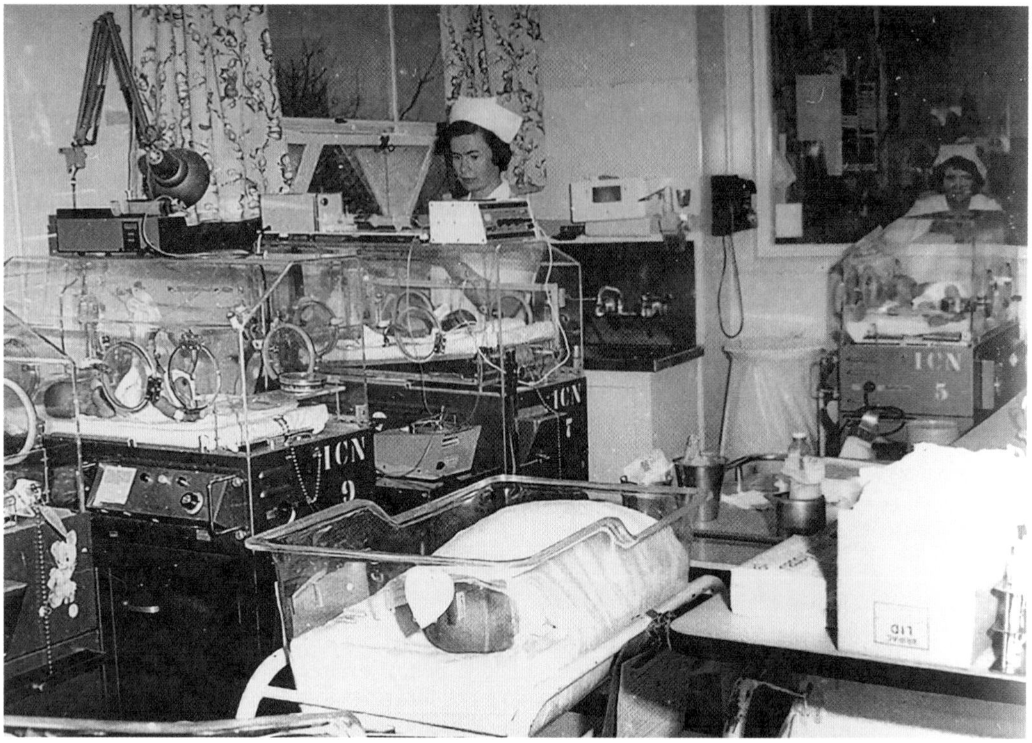

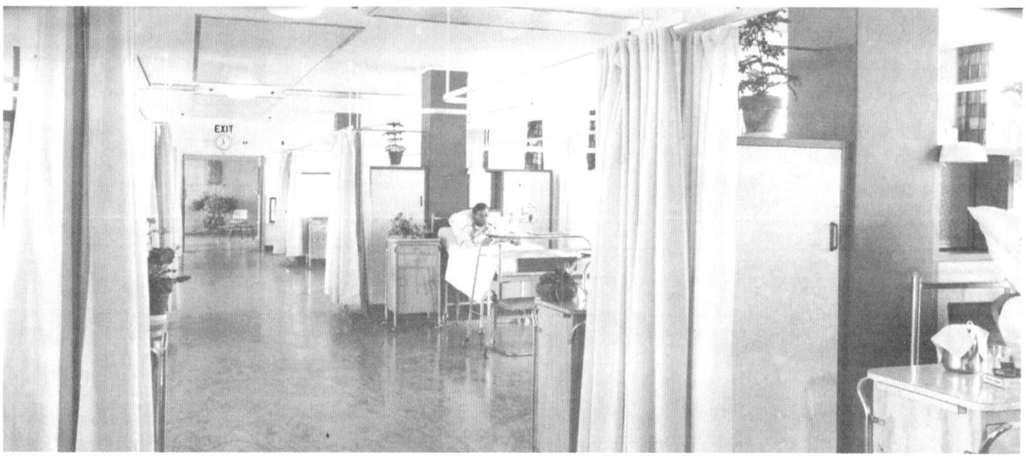

services block in 1980. This block, which required demolition of the original 1925 building, was added in stages. A particular feature is the roof garden designed by the firm's landscape architects, which provided a pleasant outlook from the east-wing ward block and was accessible to patients. The building won an NZIA award in 1984.[61]

Although the west-wing ward block was originally intended to be a mirror of the east wing, the original building was narrow with bedrooms off a single corridor. The later block followed the new trend of a racetrack corridor with services rooms in the middle.[62] The firm also carried out a feasibility study for a future hospital on land bought at Welcome Bay in 1973, but this did not eventuate.

↑

The NICU at Waikato Hospital, Hamilton.

↖

Ward interior, Tauranga Hospital, 1964.

↗

Operating theatre, Tauranga Hospital, 1964.

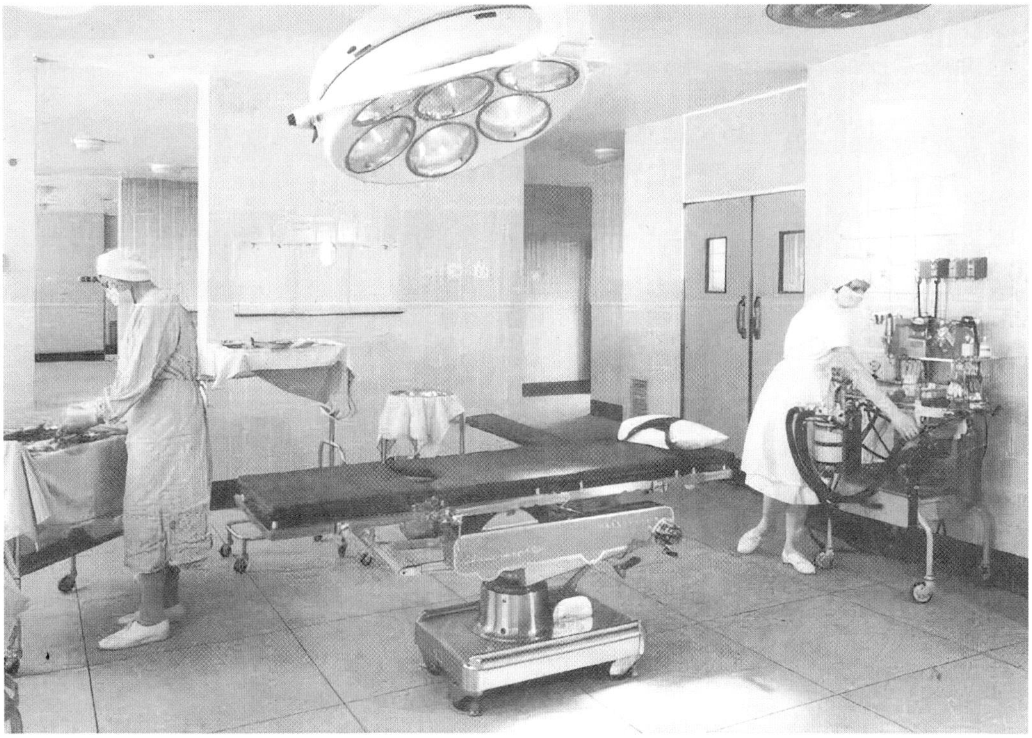

++

As has been mentioned, the redevelopment of Waikato Hospital created more work than the in-house architect's department could handle, and the 1963 Hilda Ross Nurses' Home was designed by the board's chief architect, Alfred Smith, but with T. F. Gillman & Co. doing the working drawings and supervision. This eight-storey building is of reinforced-concrete construction, plaster finished with Corrulux panels and an iron roof, and has a two-storey annex for the nurses' training school.[63]

In 1962, on the recommendation of Alfred Smith and the Medical Superintendent in Chief Dr John Meade, T. F. Gillman & Co. was commissioned by the board to complete the brief and to prepare preliminary sketches for the new clinical services block that opened in 1971. This four-storey building, fully air-conditioned and artificially lit, and fitted out with relocatable partitioning, was designed to allow for the future changes that clinical services departments could be expected to undergo. The 14,000-square-metre building housed outpatients, emergency, radiology, a laboratory and a CSSD; a low-rise scheme was adopted to avoid splitting departments over several floors. The building's somewhat bulky form is articulated by the external ducts for air and plumbing. The board also commissioned the firm for the 1978 10-theatre operating theatre block.[64]

Being appointed to prepare a development plan and report for Waikato Hospital, even though the board had its own architect's department, was a major milestone in the growth and development of Gillman Garry Clapp & Sayers. As Sayers later noted, this was 'a specialised form of consultancy', and 'led to the establishment within Gillman Garry Clapp and Sayers of a specialist Planning and Management Team', which Sayers headed.[65] The board then commissioned the firm to prepare a full development report for Thames Hospital, which was now under its control, and as at Waikato this was carried out under Tony Oldfield's leadership.[66]

↖ An artist's rendering of Tauranga Hospital.

↗ Hilda Ross Nurses' Home, Waikato Hospital.

Based on its work at Tauranga and Waikato hospitals, the Waikato Hospital Board commissioned Gillman Garry Clapp & Sayers to design the new clinical services block at Rotorua. The firm also carried out hospital development planning for the Waiapu Hospital Board at Te Puia Springs Hospital on the East Coast, where an 18-bed maternity ward and a 12-bed nurses' home were added in 1959, with a new boiler house and laundry the following year. Te Puia Springs was transferred into Ngāti Porou ownership in 1999 and is currently the country's only Māori-owned and operated hospital.[67]

At Te Kuiti Hospital, a new three-storey block designed by Gillman Garry Clapp & Sayers opened in 1968, with two operating theatres and sterile supply unit on the ground floor and an obstetric unit with 24 beds and two delivery suites on the first floor. The top floor, which had accommodation for 38 nurses, was designed to allow for later conversion into a 30-bed ward. This was done in 1975, when the former maternity ward was converted into one for children. In 1976 the clinical services and administration building was integrated with the original two-storey brick front entrance and included accident and x-ray departments. Gillman Partners designed a geriatric ward in 1984. Despite public pressure, the hospital was downsized from the 1980s and by 2010 it had 21 beds, while continuing to provide laboratory, radiography and outpatient services.[68]

In 1966, the Palmerston North Hospital Board, which also had its own architect's department, approached the firm to assist with the design of a new clinical services and ward block. However, when board architect Jack Reynolds died suddenly in 1969, Gillman Garry Clapp & Sayers were appointed as coordinating architects, taking over the work of his department and looking after all its facilities and building records. The firm opened an office in Palmerston North under Kelvin Prince.[69]

The clinical services building at the hospital, completed in three stages from 1976 to 1979, consists of two four-storey ward blocks, each providing 120 beds, with a shared vertical

circulation core, on a three-storey podium with operating theatres, radiology and a laboratory. Radiotherapy bunkers sit on columns in front of the building; a linear accelerator treatment tower extension was added in 1980.

In Sayers' words, the radiotherapy super-voltage towers were 'of special interest. They housed a Theratron 80 Cobalt machine and a Betatron. Protection from radiation usually necessitates housing such machines in a basement surrounded with concrete walls up to one metre thick. By placing the radiotherapy rooms at first floor level in a tower joined to the main hospital by a bridge, the walls were able to be reduced to 200mm . . . Our innovative design of these radiotherapy towers was developed working in close association with the National Radiation Laboratory. The design of the towers allowed the Radiotherapy rooms to be on the same floor and closely linked to the Radiological Organ Imaging Department.'[70]

A new treatment tower was added in 1990, an eight-bed hospice in 1991 and a rescue helicopter hangar in 1993. Sayers noted: 'The purpose-designed Intensive Care Bollards are a good example of a complex fitting with many specially earthed service connections, medical gases, technical equipment and electronic monitoring connections.'[71] These would be used in other hospitals around the country, but would eventually be replaced by flexible ceiling-mounted pendants.'[72]

A new rehabilitation unit for 60 day-stay and 30 resident patients opened in 1972, and a new boiler house in 1973. In 1980 the military block was converted into a children's ward. Te Whare Rapuora, the Māori health resource centre, opened in 1986 in a former Awapuni Hospital dormitory that had been relocated to the site.[73] Gillman Garry Clapp & Sayers also prepared development plans for each of the other institutions under the control of the Palmerston North Hospital Board: Awapuni Hospital, Kimberley (previously Levin Psychiatric and Psychopaedic Hospital and Training School) and Horowhenua Hospital. Following a series of earthquakes, in which several older buildings at Palmerston North and Awapuni

sustained damage, the firm carried out a survey of all the older brick buildings plus engineering assessments of earthquake risk.[74]

In 1978 the board purchased 48.5 hectares at Aokautere for a new hospital for geriatric and psychiatric patients, as well as for young people with disabilities. Concept plans were prepared for this, but the proposal was later abandoned. In 1970 the main nurses' home buildings at Palmerston North were replaced with a new hostel complex, medical staff accommodation, and a new kitchen and staff cafeteria. The Wellington Hospital Board later commissioned Gillman Garry Clapp & Sayers to build more of these new-style nurses' hostels at Kenepuru Hospital. The new boiler house was commissioned in 1973.[75]

Apart from the 1970 Ministry of Works-designed Manawaroa Centre for Psychiatric Medicine, which was already under construction when Gillman Garry Clapp & Sayers was appointed for overall site planning, Sayers noted that almost every building at Palmerston North Hospital was either built, altered or extended and renovated to the practice's design between 1969 and 1982.[76]

The Palmerston North Hospital Board was also responsible for Horowhenua Hospital in Levin, where a further 30-bed geriatric ward, a 22-bed medical ward, a second nurses' home and a block for occupational therapy, physiotherapy and x-ray opened in 1974. An operating theatre, a 19-bed surgical ward, accident and emergency department, outpatients, pharmacy, laboratory, mortuary administration and house surgeons' residences opened in 1979, as the facility completed its transition to a general hospital. In 1992, however, the surgical ward at Horowhenua was closed and converted to allow Levin Maternity to be consolidated on the same site. Horowhenua Hospital closed in 2006.

Gillman Partners also designed a geriatric ward and a kitchen at Dannevirke Hospital in the mid-1980s. In 1981 Milton Brogden, who had run his own practice in Palmerston North for many years, and Milton Reeve, who had done the same in Blenheim, joined the Palmerston North office as partner and associate respectively.[77]

++

In the 1970s, as a result of a commission from the Northland Hospital Board to report on problems with the new operating theatres at Whangarei Hospital, Gillman Garry Clapp & Sayers

↖

Clinical services building, Waikato Hospital.

↗

Operating theatre block, Waikato Hospital.

was asked to prepare an overall development plan for the site. Phase 2, a second ward block designed by the firm, opened in 1977. This became used for the medical wards, with the surgical wards occupying the Haughey & Fox phase 1 ward block. As at Tauranga, the first-phase wards had a single central corridor, but those in the second phase had a racetrack around a central nurses' station and support areas. Phase 2 also included a new kitchen and cafeteria.[78]

There was a major refit of the wards in the late 1980s. In 1986 the Whangarei Hospice leased the old medical superintendent's house. A new child health centre opened in 1989 and Kowhai House was removed. In 1991 a new surgical unit opened with six operating theatres; the new whānau house opened in 1994.[79]

Designing the new buildings at Kenepuru Hospital, next to the existing maternity facility, was another task given to Gillman Garry Clapp & Sayers, this time by the Wellington Hospital Board. Opened in 1977, this included a single-storey clinical services block and a three-storey ward block. A two-storey staff residence was added in 1981, a birthing unit in 1990.[80]

In 1974 it was the Nelson Hospital Board's turn to employ the firm, appointing them development architects for each of its hospitals: Nelson Hospital, the Braemar Psychopaedic Hospital on the other side of Waimea Road, Ngawhatu Psychiatric Hospital, some small outlying facilities in Tākaka, Collingwood and Murchison and several medical clinics.[81] Nelson Hospital had serious problems. Although already under construction, the Percy Brunette Block was poorly planned in its relationship to the rest of the campus. The main entrance to the hospital was directly off busy Waimea Road, site saturation had been reached despite increasing demand and there was no clear ground for the construction of new buildings. Several buildings had also been damaged in the 1968 Inangahua earthquake. Preliminary planning had begun to try separating parts of the hospital and relocating them to a new facility at Richmond.[82]

In a 1976 preliminary report for Nelson Hospital the firm recommended the closing of Kawai Street and the complete reorientation of the hospital. Public vehicle access was moved to Tipahi Street and a new main public entrance to the hospital buildings was established on what was previously Kawai Street. The land between Tipahi Street and the main entrance was developed for parking.

Gillman Garry Clapp & Sayers designed a new 1984 psychopaedic facility on the Braemar campus, which included three accommodation buildings, a therapy block with hydrotherapy pools and an activities building with a flexible auditorium. These buildings were

↑

Clinical services building, Rotorua Hospital.

↗

Kenepuru Hospital, Porirua: ward block to left, mental health unit in centre, original maternity hospital to right.

later converted to outpatient and office uses. They also carried out upgrading at Ngawhatu. In 1979, for the Marlborough Hospital Board, the firm wrote a development report for Wairau Hospital and was subsequently responsible for a number of building projects, including a 1987 maternity and paediatrics wing and, in 1994, two operating theatres, with a sterile supply unit and ambulatory care facility.[83]

++

Following the Second World War, much of Auckland's urban expansion occurred to the south as large state housing areas spread in Māngere and Ōtara. Because it was on the north-western outskirts of this area, Middlemore Hospital was poorly positioned to serve the growing population. It was also a specialist orthopaedic facility, providing only a very limited range of general hospital services. South Auckland had a large Pasifika and Māori population and even common problems such as glue ear in children were not receiving treatment. Because many local people were on low incomes, access to primary and general health services was difficult.[84]

The Wiri area offered bare land that was more centrally located, and by the 1970s the new Manukau City Centre, master-planned by Stephenson & Turner, was being built there. In 1973 the Auckland Hospital Board purchased 7.6 hectares of land just to the south, but various issues hindered its development. In late 1974 the board approached Gillman Garry Clapp & Sayers to design a new 600-bed base hospital on the site. In response the firm established an Auckland office. The goal was a flexible design that allowed for staged growth, in which site infrastructure and support services could be added incrementally as the bed numbers grew. To achieve this, the firm proposed a relatively low-rise hospital, which the large site could accommodate.[85]

Although a new South Auckland facility was the most urgent hospital project in the country as far as the government was concerned, and the Health Department was pushing for rapid development of the Wiri site, the Auckland Hospital Board had several conflicting priorities. Unlike the base hospitals in other cities, the hospitals in Auckland had each developed to serve not only the Auckland region but also to provide super-specialist units serving the whole country. In this way, Green Lane Hospital had developed international

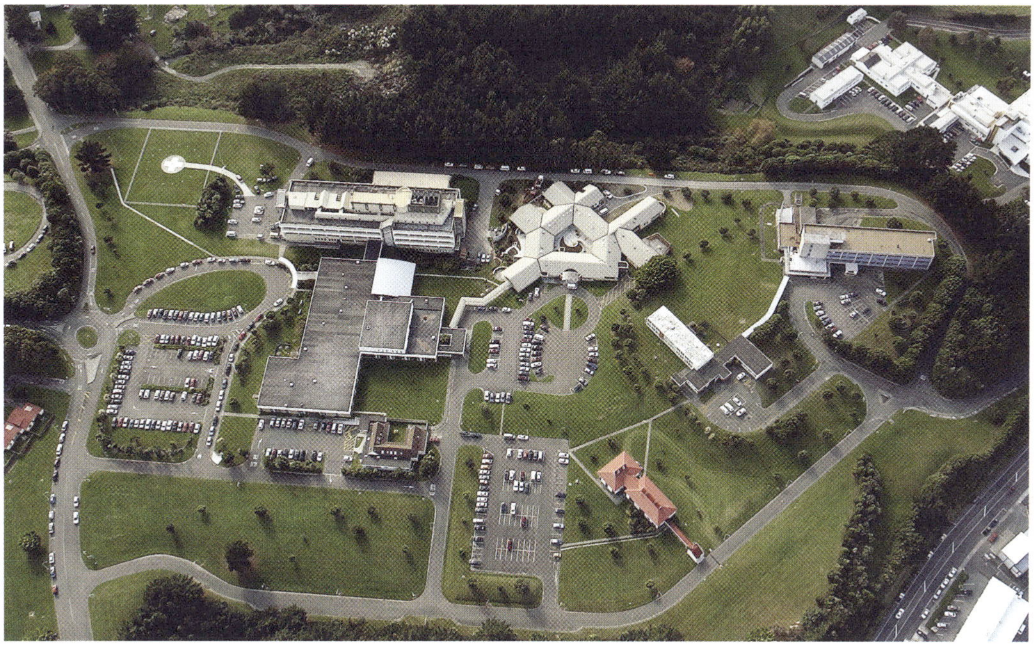

renown for cardiac surgery, National Women's was a centre of excellence for obstetrics and gynaecology and Auckland Hospital had specialties in neurosurgery and paediatrics.

As Sayers recollected in 2011, 'With their national and international recognition these hospitals became rather like little empires and their "Emperors" had had ambitions to further develop their specialist domains rather than considering the more basic and mundane health needs of the Auckland district . . .'[86]

One disadvantage of the Wiri site was that it lay directly under the approach path for aircraft landing at Auckland International Airport. Although the additional sound-proofing this would require did not in fact make up a large proportion of the overall project cost, this seems to have given opposing factions the opportunity to delay it. By 1976 the board and the government were at an impasse.[87] Because the board had also purchased a smaller site on Botany Road in East Tāmaki to allow for projected future growth in that area, they decided to go ahead there and to buy another site for a second hospital in Papakura, further south. Each of these would allow for the ultimate development of 300-bed hospitals. Since East Tāmaki could be serviced with water, sewerage and road access within the time frame required, it would be developed first. Sayers suggested that the Papakura site 'would be purchased now simply as an indication to the people in the south of the Hospital Board area that a hospital was being planned'.[88]

By 1978 Gillman Garry Clapp & Sayers had completed detailed design drawings for the first phase of the East Tāmaki hospital, which comprised two geriatric wards, a geriatric day ward and the basic support infrastructure for the future hospital development. This included a boiler house, kitchen and stores block and a small amount of staff accommodation. Even this much more limited project did not proceed, and eventually a maternity unit, designed by Stephenson & Turner, opened in 1991, followed by a primary healthcare facility. The Papakura project never happened.[89]

Because of the Auckland Hospital Board's failure to address the urgent issues in South Auckland, the minister of health exercised a little-known and never before used provision of the Hospitals Act 1957 that allowed him to step in. The Department of Health then directly

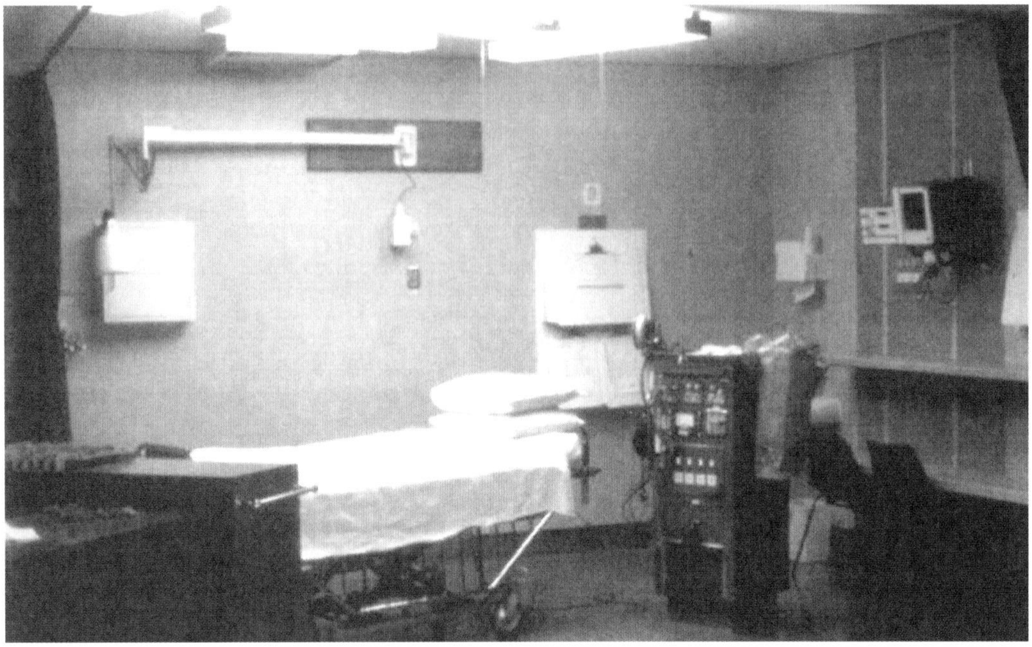

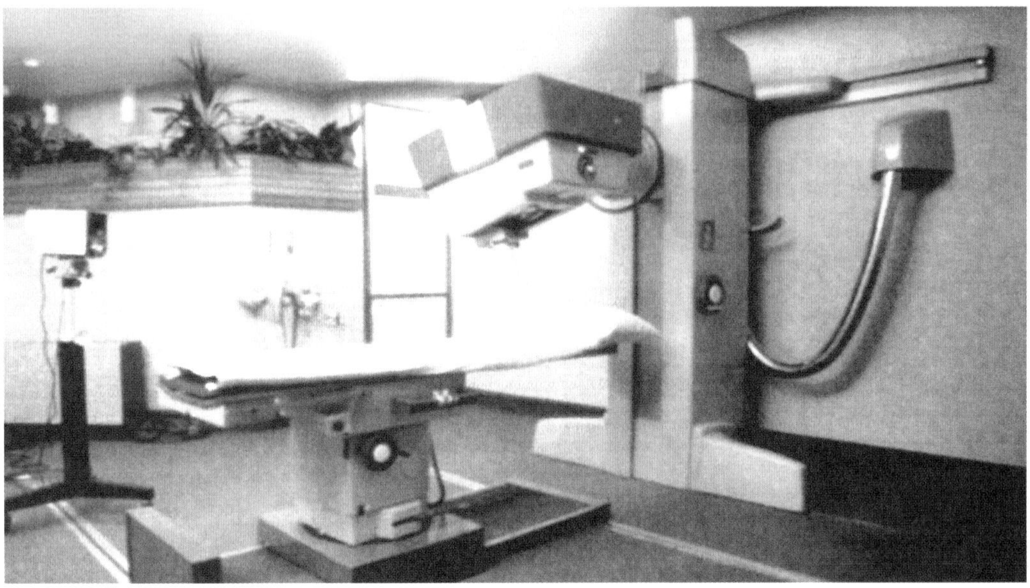

appointed Gillman Garry Clapp & Sayers to design a health centre for outpatient services opposite the Manukau City Centre on Wiri Station Road (now Manukau Station Road).[90]

++

The practice also designed the Cassel Private Hospital and the Te Waiora Family Health Centre in Hamilton, both about 1974, and, overseas, the Aitutaki and Rarotonga hospitals in the Cook Islands (in association with the New Zealand Department of Health), Apia Hospital in Sāmoa and Karangmenjangan Hospital in Surabaya, Indonesia.[91]

↑
ICU services bollards, Palmerston North Hospital.

↖
Betatron room, Palmerston North Hospital.

↗
Clinical services building, Palmerston North Hospital.

As the firm grew, it was an early adopter of computerised systems for contract documentation. Its own purpose-built office building in Hamilton's Vialou Street, built in 1971 and extended in 1981, was inspired by the German concept of Bürolandschaft, or office landscape, and its 550-square-metre draughting room used furniture, screens and plants to break up the large space, which wrapped around a landscaped courtyard.[92]

In 1981 Gillman Garry Clapp & Sayers was restructured and renamed Gillman Partners, by which stage it had 80 staff. David Sayers retired in 1984.[93] The following year the practice merged with Worley Consultants to become Worley Gillman. The Gillman name was eventually dropped, and the architectural component became Worley Architects. During the 1990s, Worley Gillman increased its expertise in mental healthcare and was responsible for many of the new buildings required throughout the country as models of care changed.

++

The Mason Clinic in Auckland was opened in 1992, with Worley Gillman as the architects. The original 15-bed Kauri unit was joined by the 15-bed Totara unit, opened later that year. Worley Architects also designed the 1993 15-bed Kahikatea unit and the 18-bed Rātā unit opened in 1999.[94] Architect Rewi Thompson (Ngāti Porou, Ngāti Raukawa) collaborated with them on the 2006 Māori Mental Health Unit, which was planned on the concept of three buildings, with secure residential accommodation, community and dining, and a meeting house forming a traditional kāinga or village. The central courtyard focuses on a rock fountain circulating water as a symbol of cleansing and health.[95]

Thompson had previously collaborated with Worley on the design of the now-demolished 1995 Tiaho Mai Mental Health Unit at Middlemore Hospital.[96] As architectural historian Deidre Brown notes, 'Here, as on other projects that Thompson was involved in, the architecture of the marae and the meeting house have been incorporated into the initial approach to the building, as this forms the user's first and most profound impressions of the treatment that they will receive. The first space within the building forms a welcoming area, where the Māori health team can be positioned to act as welcoming hosts.' Although these may seem like 'small interventions, which may or may not even be consciously appreciated by the users . . . as spaces in institutions that have often been regarded with fear by Māori they are culturally inclusive'.[97]

At Wanganui Hospital Worley designed Stanford House, a 15-bed secure rehabilitation unit for regional forensic mental health services opened in 1992, and the Delta 17-bed medium secure psychiatric unit in 1995. Delta was redeveloped by Dalgleish Architects into Te Whare Kākāriki in 2009.[98]

Worley Gillman designed the 2001 Tāwhirimātea secure high-dependency rehabilitation and extended-care unit at Porirua plus, all in 2003, the Rangipapa mixed-gender acute adult forensic unit, the 15-bed Tane Mahuta open intensive-care rehabilitation unit and cottages, the Tangaroa patient activities building, Papatūānuku and the Whānau House. Added in 2009 were Pūkeko, Saunders and the Te Aruhe secure forensic cottage for intellectually disabled youth, all single-storey domestic-scale buildings. The single-storey Te Papa, Te Piki, Rongomātāne and Rūaumoko buildings, built in 1956, were refurbished in 2009. The central services building, housing boilers and generators to serve the campus, opened in 2001, as did a meeting house complex, also designed by Worley Architects, as it was by now known.[99]

The firm extended and refurbished the Puawānanga psychiatric unit at Hawke's Bay Fallen Soldiers' Memorial Hospital around 1993, and before Tokanui closed in 1998 Worley Gillman carried out a feasibility study for relocating its patients to Waikato Hospital. Other mental health units include Tauranga's Te Whare Maiangiangi mental health inpatient unit in 2001, the 62-bed Te Whetu Tawera acute mental health unit at Auckland Hospital in 2002 and the 30-bed Waiatarau unit at Waitakere Hospital in 2006.[100]

++

Worley was rebranded as Meritec in 2000 and two years later the practice was bought by the British multi-disciplinary consultancy Maunsell. For the next decade, the firm's architects continued to work on a range of public hospital redevelopment projects.[101]

At Timaru Hospital the clinical services building went through a major refurbishment that was completed in 2000, bringing the total number of beds to 131, and an extension was added to house an expanded emergency department and outpatient consulting rooms. The older of the two ward blocks was then demolished. A new education and library facility opened in 2008.[102]

A 2002 redevelopment at Whangarei Hospital involved alterations and additions to the emergency, ICU, imaging, day-stay and theatre departments, along with a new main entry. An MRI service opened in 2003, and the outpatient department and library were upgraded in 2005. The Mauri Ora Breast Clinic and Renal Unit (architect unknown) opened in 2006, and a new mortuary in 2011.[103]

At Wairarapa Hospital in Masterton, Maunsell designed the complete replacement of the facility with an 8000-square-metre single-storey building. This has 89 beds, including a 10-bed ward for private patients named after the founder of the original hospital, Nurse Selina Sutherland, one of only two private facilities located within a New Zealand public hospital.[104]

A major upgrade was completed at Kaitāia in 1998, with services centralised in the main hospital block, and the old hospital demolished. After general surgical services ceased in 2003, Maunsell was responsible for new maternity and day-surgery units and a 1500-square-metre building housing emergency, radiology and outpatient consulting rooms; the three-level ward block was refurbished. Rewi Thompson also collaborated on this project.[105]

In 2004 Maunsell took on the Project LEO redevelopment of Tauranga Hospital, which opened in stages from 2007 to 2011. This consisted of a two-storey podium with outpatient clinics and operating theatres, a five-storey north-wing ward block including maternity services, and a single-storey ward annex for older people. The west wing was refurbished and the emergency and radiology departments extended. A new main entrance leads to an enclosed hospital street formed between the podium and the earlier clinical services building.[106]

The maternity annex, which had opened in 1944 and was expanded in 1960, was demolished in 2009. That year, too, Jacaranda House, originally the 1962 nurses' home, was

↗

Tauranga Hospital: north wing to left, refurbished west wing to right.

→

Paediatrics ward, Wairau Hospital, Blenheim.

redeveloped for clinics, offices and a 'medi-hotel' for out-of-town patients and relatives, but after being designated earthquake prone, it was demolished in 2014. A cancer centre was built behind the board offices in 2008 and in 2010 the old RSA building to the south of the hospital was purchased and turned into an education centre.[107]

The 2011 redevelopment of Wairau Hospital was completed in stages, resulting in a new single-story inpatient ward block, running parallel to a building housing the main entrance, outpatient clinics, a laboratory and allied health, with a separate radiology unit and expanded perioperative facility. The linear ward brought the hospital's capacity to 65 beds and was designed with single 'flex' bedrooms at the junction between the paediatrics, maternity, adults and AT&R (assessment, treatment and rehabilitation) wards, to cater for fluctuations in demand. The Arthur Wicks Building was redeveloped for the hospital's emergency department, with office accommodation above.[108]

++

In 2002 Maunsell was bought by US multi-national AECOM and rebranded under that name in New Zealand in 2005. From 2011 to 2013, AECOM's Auckland architecture team developed alliances with the firm's global health design group. It was involved in the design of hospitals in Vietnam and Singapore, including the 1700-bed Sengkang General Hospital in Singapore, in association with DP Architects, which opened in 2018.[109]

AECOM's engineering capabilities in New Zealand were expanded when the parent company bought URS in 2014. URS already had a presence in New Zealand, having in 1997 bought US-based Woodward-Clyde, which had acquired the multi-disciplinary practice of Murray North. The latter was formed in New Zealand in the 1950s, and its architectural team had been involved in several elderly care projects, such as the 1988 Taradale Masonic Village in Napier. AECOM provided services engineering for the redevelopment of Tauranga Hospital and Palmerston North Hospital, and structural and services engineering at Wairau Hospital. AECOM engineers continue to work on hospital projects across New Zealand.[110]

Wally Fitness had led AECOM's health team for several years, and in 2007 he and colleague Matt Fleming left to form their own company, Fitness Fleming Architects. For the Bay of Plenty District Health Board, they designed Building 50 at Tauranga Hospital in 2011, accommodating the medical day-stay unit, an endoscopy unit and an ICU and CCU, with shell space on the floors above for future fitting out as wards. This five-storey building brought the hospital's capacity to 349 beds, in 58,000 square metres of floor space on a 12-hectare site.[111]

At Whakatane Hospital the $67 million Project Waka development designed by Fitness Fleming Architects opened in 2014, creating a new 8500-square-metre, single-level hospital within the existing campus. This consists of modular squares around a central courtyard, and includes an emergency department, operating theatres, radiology and 100 beds.[112]

For Whangarei Hospital the practice designed the 2016 two-storey 30-bed Te Kōtuku maternity building. Mental health units by Fitness Fleming Architects include the 30-bed Tūmanako at Whangarei Hospital in 2011, the 20-bed Ngā Rau Rākau at Hawke's Bay Fallen Soldiers' Memorial Hospital in 2013 and the 35-bed He Puna Waiora at North Shore Hospital in 2016.[113]

When Wally Fitness retired, Matt Fleming joined Daniel Bulog at Brave Architects, continuing a health design specialty, and has more recently been working independently under the practice name Thema.[114]

Engineering specialists ↘

As hospitals have become increasingly complex, a wider range of engineering specialists is required in their design. AECOM, and its predecessor firms back to Gillman Garry Clapp & Sayers, have long provided both structural and services engineering services and continue to do so today. Stephenson & Turner has a range of services engineering disciplines in addition to architecture, and has used these on most of its health projects, while structural engineering tended to be provided by Brickell Moss and Rankine & Hill, predecessor firms to Aurecon, for their earlier buildings, and then by Beca Carter Hollings & Ferner from the University of Auckland School of Medicine on. Several other engineering practices have had a significant involvement in healthcare projects across New Zealand.

++

Beca traces its history back to the firm founded by William (Arthur) Gray, when he purchased the Auckland engineering practice of Ashley Hunter. When Larry Watts joined in 1939 the practice became Gray & Watts. After distinguished service in the air force during the Second World War, George Samuel Beca formed his own practice, whose work included buildings at Waikato Hospital. Beca joined Gray & Watts in 1952, then became a 50 per cent partner in 1954 whereupon the firm was renamed Gray, Watts & Beca.

Watts refused to join the New Zealand Institute of Engineers, seeing it as a self-serving group, despite membership being a requirement for projects involving public funds, and only wanted to work with Auckland architects on local projects. Beca became registered and pursued the other opportunities opening up as the New Zealand economy recovered after the war. Up to this time, engineers had generally worked as sub-consultants to architects, but he believed that engineers were often more suited to being the principal advisers.

As a result the firm was engaged by such major industrial clients as Ford, New Zealand Breweries, Tasman Pulp & Paper, New Zealand Steel and Air New Zealand. Many architects, however, did not welcome this approach and at first offered fewer commissions. Beca led the firm for many years, overseeing its growth into the largest private New Zealand-based multi-disciplinary consultancy.[1]

Auckland-born Ron Carter joined in 1959, and following two years with Arup in Britain, returned to become a partner in Grey, Watts & Beca in 1965. In 1968, Beca and Carter merged their practice with the Wellington firm of Hollings & Ferner, and the survey practice of Leach & Dickson, to become Beca Carter Hollings & Ferner Ltd. The merged practice became a limited liability company in 1972, with all shareholders being employees of the firm. Carter became managing director on George Beca's retirement in 1986 and was chairman of the Beca Group until 2002, by which time the firm had more than 1200 employees. By the time he retired in 2008, this figure had doubled.[2]

During the recession of the 1960s the firm sought work outside New Zealand, leading to expansion into Australia, Papua New Guinea, Indonesia, Singapore, Myanmar and China. The first overseas office was opened in Melbourne in 1968, and the firm began working on projects in Asia in 1971; an office opened in Singapore in 1977. The downsizing and eventual privatisation of the Ministry of Works and Development in 1996 opened up opportunities for more infrastructure work in New Zealand, including roading, rail and bridge projects. At one point, the firm had an office in London, but this proved a step too far and it was closed, as was one in China in 2017. Ron Carter was knighted for services to engineering and business in 1998 and was appointed a Member of the Order of New Zealand in 2014.[3]

Grey, Watts & Beca were the engineers for the redevelopment of Thames Hospital in the 1960s, and Beca Carter Hollings & Ferner provided services at Middlemore Hospital in the 1980s. Beca's structural engineers worked with Stephenson & Turner on the Auckland School of Medicine and Starship Children's Hospital. Their services engineers worked on the Harley Gray clinical services building at Middlemore, the Project Maunga redevelopment at Taranaki Base Hospital, the new Wellington Regional Hospital, Nelson Hospital, Burwood Hospital, Christchurch Women's Hospital and the Waipapa acute services building at Christchurch Hospital. Beca provided both structural and services engineering for the acute services building at Auckland City Hospital and in 2019 won the commission for building services and fire design for the new Dunedin Hospital.[4]

In Singapore Beca designed the building services for the 20-storey 60,000-square-metre Connexion complex at Farrer Park, the country's first fully integrated private hospital, hotel and specialist medical centre. This was followed by a new building for the National University Hospital Centre of Oral Health.[5]

Beca's architectural section designed the now demolished 1996 Āwhina House, the head office for the Royal New Zealand Foundation for the Blind (now Blind Low Vision NZ) in Parnell, Auckland. Other significant projects include Auckland's 1996 Sky Tower, for which the firm provided structural and building services engineering.[6]

Beca Group Limited is now one of the largest employee-owned professional services consultancy firms in Asia–Pacific, with 20 offices throughout New Zealand,

↑
Boiler room, Tauranga Hospital, 2022.

↗
Ian Reynolds.

including its base in Auckland, as well as Australia, Indonesia, Singapore, Thailand and Myanmar. The company has more than 3400 staff, 1300 of whom are shareholders.[7]

++

Civil engineer Richard Goulden Brickell's Second World War air force service included an escape from a desert prisoner-of-war camp via a tunnel that seriously tested his geotechnical skills. After several years with the Public Works Department, he established R. G. Brickell Consulting Engineer in 1953.[8]

His first hospital commission appears to have been the civil engineering works for the 1961 buildings at Hawke's Bay Fallen Soldiers' Memorial Hospital. In 1962 he was joined by John Didsbury Moss to form Brickell, Moss & Partners, based in Lower Hutt. John Moss was headhunted by John Rankine of the Australian firm, Rankine & Hill, who were the structural engineers for the acute block at Auckland Hospital, to join as its New Zealand manager. Instead, the two firms merged in 1966 as Brickell, Moss, Rankine & Hill, with offices in Wellington, Lower Hutt and Auckland, and the range of services expanded from its civil engineering base to structural and later building services engineering. Brickell left the firm in 1968 and the alliance with Rankine & Hill appears to have later ended; by 1981 the New Zealand practice was again operating as Brickell, Moss & Partners.[9]

In 1992 Rankine & Hill merged with another Australian firm, Connell Wagner, and took its name. In 2009 Connell Wagner combined with two large South African consulting firms to form Aurecon. With over 7500 staff members, Aurecon now operates in 28 countries across Africa, Asia-Pacific and the Middle East. In New Zealand, Aurecon has provided engineering services for buildings at Auckland, Wellington, Hawke's Bay and Whangārei hospitals, as well as at the Mason Clinic and Wellington's Bowen and Wakefield private hospitals.[10]

++

Jacobs can trace its roots in New Zealand back to 1915, when Stanley W. Jones established a structural and civil engineering practice. After R. C. Adams became a partner in 1920, the firm operated as Jones & Adams until 1950. Early projects included wharves, water and sewerage projects and bridges, including preliminary schemes for the Auckland Harbour Bridge. Architects were brought on to the firm's staff in the 1940s to work on commissions for several large dairy factories. After Jones retired in 1954, the firm became Jones, Adams & Kingston in 1955, with engineer Robin (Bob) Kingston, and then Jones, Adams, Kingston & Reynolds when architect Ian Brampton Reynolds joined later that year.[11]

In 1957 engineers David Thom and N. W. Allardice became partners in the firm, which was renamed Kingston, Reynolds, Thom & Allardice (commonly referred to as KRTA) in 1962. Andrew Barrie has written that it was 'then the only comprehensive multi-disciplinary practice in New Zealand', apart from the Ministry of Works, of course, providing architecture, planning and quantity engineering services, alongside civil, structural, electrical and mechanical engineering. KRTA engineers provided services at Middlemore Hospital in the 1960s and 1980s.[12]

KRTA was among the leading proponents of engineering-based architecture in New Zealand and made particular use of factory-produced pre-cast concrete structural and cladding systems, as well as glue-laminated timber and concrete masonry. It was involved in large-scale industrial facilities for Fisher & Paykel and Air New Zealand; and office buildings such as the Treasury at No. 1 The Terrace in Wellington. KRTA designed the 1963 arts and library building at Victoria University of Wellington, for which it won an NZIA Gold Medal in 1967. At the University of Auckland, KRTA designed the Thomas Biology Building in 1968, the Engineering School in 1970 and the School of Architecture in 1978. KRTA also designed several elderly care facilities, such as the six-storey Litchfield Block and chapel at Selwyn Village in Point Chevalier[13] and the Stevenson Village in Howick.

As Andrew Barrie notes, the prefabrication and industrialised methods pioneered by KRTA played to the firm's multi-disciplinary strengths and were in high demand during the post-war labour shortage. However, this architectural style fell out of favour during the 1970s and as the firm developed new expertise in geothermal energy, 80 per cent of its work was overseas by the 1980s.[14]

Given the wide range of the firm's work, it is somewhat surprising that KRTA's architects do not seem to have been involved in any hospital buildings in New Zealand, although it was involved with the Khon Kaen teaching hospital in Thailand. It did, however, develop a reputation for strategic planning and advice. For example, before the closure of Tokanui, KRTA carried out a social-impact assessment on changes to the delivery of psychiatric services.[15]

In 1995 KRTA merged with Morrison Cooper to form Kingston Morrison. Its hospital work included the refurbishment of the D Block ward and administration building at Wairoa Hospital around 1998. Australian firm Sinclair, Knight, Merz bought Kingston Morrison in 1999 and was itself purchased by multi-national Jacobs Engineering Group in 2013. The Jacobs architectural team collaborated with Wellington architects CCM on the design of the new Grey Base Hospital (Te Nīkau), the Christchurch Hospital outpatient building and the master plan for the new Dunedin Hospital.[16]

++

Lyall Holmes started his practice in 1956 and later that year formed the firm of Holmes & Wood with Brian Wood. They were joined by Russell Poole, to become Holmes, Wood & Poole, the structural engineers for the Christchurch Town Hall. The firm became Holmes, Wood, Poole & Johnstone when Peter Johnstone joined, and later Holmes Consulting Group.[17]

Hospital projects for which Holmes has provided structural engineering services include, at Middlemore Hospital, Kidz First, Acute Hub, Adult Medical Centre, Edmund Hillary Ward and Harley Gray clinical services buildings; the redevelopment of Waikato, Thames, Palmerston North and Nelson hospitals; the Project Maunga redevelopment of Taranaki Base Hospital; and Christchurch Women's Hospital, Southland Base Hospital and the Waipapa acute services building at Christchurch Hospital. In 2019 it was awarded the commission for structural engineering for the new Dunedin Hospital. The firm also expanded its services into fire engineering: Holmes Fire & Safety has consulted on many New Zealand hospitals. Peter Johnstone later left to form NZ Consulting Engineers Ltd, which provided structural engineering services for the new Wellington children's hospital building.[18]

++

Faram & Babbage was founded in 1936 by Lionel Faram and Alister Babbage as an engineering consultancy designing roads and bridges. During the Second World War

both partners served as army engineers in North Africa and Europe. Babbage continued the practice when he returned in 1943; Faram left in 1945. In 1951 Babbage was appointed consultant for the New Zealand Forest Products mill being developed at Kinleith, near Tokoroa. As the firm became increasingly multi-disciplinary, Babbage architects and engineers collaborated on the 2007 Horowhenua Health Centre in Levin, which occupies part of the former Horowhenua Hospital site, and the 2008 Quay Park Medical Centre in Auckland, where the firm is based.[19]

++

After emigrating to New Zealand, Budapest-born George Vamos formed the mechanical engineering consultancy of George Vamos & Partners in Wellington in 1945. The practice, later Vamos & Mak, provided services for several hospitals throughout New Zealand, including the 1961 ward and administration block at the Hawke's Bay Fallen Soldiers' Memorial Hospital, the 1987 ward and administration building at Wanganui Hospital and the clinical services building at Waikato Hospital, as well as at Waipukurau and Buller Hospitals in the 1960s. Vamos also provided services engineering for Plischke & Firth's Massey House in Wellington.[20]

++

Clendon & Burns began as a structural engineering practice formed by Wilf Edwards in 1947, who worked with Associated Architects on some of their later work at Napier Hospital. Edwards was joined by Tom Clendon to form Edwards & Clendon around 1955. Arthur G. Park set up his own structural consultancy in 1978 and the two merged in 1985 to form Clendon, Burns & Park Ltd. The practice has provided structural design for several hospitals throughout New Zealand, including the 1961 ward and administration block at Hawke's Bay Fallen Soldiers' Memorial Hospital, the 1987 ward and administration building at Wanganui Hospital and the Total Energy Centre at Wellington Hospital, as well as Plischke & Firth's Massey House in Wellington. Clendon, Burns & Park provided structural engineering design for the 1990s redevelopment of Porirua Hospital.[21]

++

Kerslake & Partners evolved from the sole practice established by Frank Kerslake in 1959. For a time it was one of the largest multi-disciplinary engineering practices in New Zealand, concentrating on primary industries such as pulp and paper, dairy, meat and cold storage and later petrochemical and energy. Kerslake were services engineers for the 1981 Total Energy Centre at Wellington Hospital, designed by Haughton & Mair. 'Total energy' was the term given to maximising the energy extracted from a fuel source. In Wellington, this was natural gas, supplemented by diesel, which is also used as a stand-by fuel. Designed to meet all the electrical, refrigeration and winter heating requirements of the Wellington Hospital campus, this required sophisticated computer analysis of the energy demand and was the largest such facility in the Southern Hemisphere at the time.[22]

++

Powell Fenwick was formed by Guy Powell in Christchurch in 1938, who was joined by Chris Fenwick in 1954. During the 1960s, it expanded, becoming Powell Fenwick &

↑
Lyall Holmes.

Johnson, later Powell Fenwick & Williams, with offices in Auckland, Napier and Lower Hutt. Powell Fenwick provided engineering services at Napier Hospital in the 1960s, and more recently engineering design for the redevelopment of St George's and Nurse Maude Hospitals, and Forté Health, all in Christchurch.[23]

++

David Norman founded the firm of Norman Addicoat in Sydney in 1959 and the Norman Disney Young partnership formed in 1971 as the firm opened offices across Australia. The first New Zealand office opened in Auckland in 1987, followed by Wellington in 1990 and Christchurch in 2011. In 2018 Norman Disney Young joined the United States-based multi-national consulting firm Tetra-Tech, which has provided specialist services, such as acoustic design, to several hospital projects in New Zealand.[24]

++

Marshall Day Acoustics was established in Auckland in 1981 by Sir Harold Marshall and Christopher Day. Marshall, who was professor of architecture at the University of Auckland and founder of the Acoustics Research Centre there, was pivotal to the success of Warren and Mahoney's 1972 Christchurch Town Hall. The firm has grown to be a world leader in the field, with 90 staff throughout New Zealand, Australia, China and France. It has also provided acoustic design to several hospital projects in New Zealand.[25]

++

The Ministry of Works and Development was disestablished by the State Owned Enterprises Act of 1986, and its regulatory responsibilities were transferred to other departments. The design arm was privatised in 1996, rebranded the following year as

↖

Total Energy Centre, Wellington Hospital.

↗

Tunnel at Tauranga Hospital.

Opus International Consultants Limited and expected to compete for work on the open market. Many private firms had resented the ministry's ability to secure work and were happy to see them face competition, but they were also wary of its size and expertise, which remained formidable.[26]

The architectural practice of the former Government Architect continued in the new company. Opus Architects collaborated with Chow:Hill on the design of the Christchurch Women's Hospital, when it was relocated to the Christchurch Hospital site in 2005. Opus Architects also designed the 2009 Wanacare primary health facility in Wānaka.[27]

Children and young adults with disabilities were transferred to the Wilson Home from Mangere Hospital in 1987, but by 1997 it was considered that they should live with their families or in the community. A portion of the site was leased to the Ministry of Education to build a school for children with disabilities and in 2008 the new Wilson School building by Opus Architecture opened. It won the 2009 New Zealand Architecture Medal. Three purpose-built family accommodation units opened at the home in 2011.

In 2017 Opus was acquired by Canadian firm WSP Global.[28] In 2009 WSP had taken over the Australian consultancy of Lincolne Scott, who had provided engineering services on several New Zealand hospital projects, including services engineering for the 1990s redevelopment of Porirua Hospital, mechanical engineering at Palmerston North and security at Auckland City Hospital. Renamed WSP Opus in 2018, it is now known as WSP. The firm's engineers have been involved in several healthcare projects throughout New Zealand, including structural and services engineering at Bay of Islands Hospital and Te Nīkau at Greymouth, and services engineering for the Meade Clinical Centre at Waikato Hospital and the new Southland Base Hospital.[29]

12

Recovery and reconstruction

2000–

THERE WERE SIGNIFICANT CHANGES in the health sector in the 1990s and the first years of the new millennium. In 1993 Crown health enterprises were formed to operate public hospitals on a more commercial basis, funded through four regional health authorities. In 1997 the latter were merged to form the Health Funding Authority and Crown health enterprises were renamed Hospital and Health Services. Further restructuring in 2001, following the Health and Disability Sector Act 2000, created 21 (20 from 2010) district health boards, with elected members, to run public hospitals and provide public health services, and the Health Funding Authority was absorbed into the Ministry of Health. This restructuring offered avenues for new practices to enter the health design market and there was a distinct 'changing of the guard', particularly among architects, around the turn of the century.[1]

The Building Act of 1992 had placed greater emphasis on performance-based design, leading to the rise of the profession of fire engineering and improved resilience to natural hazards such as earthquakes. A hierarchy of seismic resilience was established through importance levels (IL). Most typical buildings are designed to IL2, but a higher degree of strength and post-disaster repairability is required of most public hospital buildings; those accommodating hospital emergency departments and surgical facilities, which are required to be operational immediately after a severe earthquake, are IL4, general clinical buildings such as wards are IL3, and administration and outpatients IL2.

Building services in hospitals became increasingly complex, with the use of laminar flow in operating theatres and negative and positive pressure rooms to minimise infection transfer. The Ministry of Health adopted the Australasian Health Facility Guidelines, introduced in 2006 and developed from those implemented in New South Wales in 2002.[2] Through this period as medical care became more specialised, a handful of new specialist architecture practices emerged.

++

Australian practice Peddle, Thorp & Walker opened an office in Auckland in 1967 to supervise the construction of the Downtown redevelopment scheme, which the firm had designed for the Auckland Harbour Board. With the appointment of local partner Robert D. Horman, it became Peddle, Thorp & Horman, an independent company within the wider Peddle Thorp group. The firm became Peddle, Thorp & Aitken when Brian Aitken, who had joined in 1970 after graduating from Auckland and completing a master's degree at Columbia, became the local partner in 1978.[3]

From the 1980s hospital services in central Auckland were rationalised. By 1989 Green Lane Hospital's emergency department was closed and most general medicine and surgery was shifted to Auckland Hospital. Now known as Peddlethorp, the firm designed the conversion of Green Lane into the 2003 Greenlane Clinical Centre, an ambulatory care centre for outpatients and day surgery. This was followed by commissions to upgrade and expand, in 2009, the intensive care and national burns units at Middlemore Hospital, and for a major 2011 redevelopment of Rotorua Hospital that included a three-storey inpatient building and a central atrium in the form of a wharenui with carved timber panels.

At Auckland's Mason Clinic, Peddlethorp was responsible for the 2015 redevelopment of the 15-bed Pōhutukawa unit. The firm also designed the 2016 TRG Imaging Centre and the 2019 North Shore Surgical Centre, the latter a 1750-square-metre day-stay hospital with three operating theatres. The two buildings stand next to each other in Takapuna and are designed in a complementary style.[4]

↗

Greenlane Clinical Centre, Auckland: TCPD's 1970s building to left and Peddlethorp's 2003 building to right.

→

Ward block, Rotorua Hospital.

MUFFIN BREAK
Café
MUFFIN BREAK
Café
TAXI

ROTORUA HOSPITAL

The first hospital project for both the New Zealand arm of Peddlethorp, and Klein Healthcare Designers, working in collaboration, was the Ascot (later Mercy Ascot) private surgical hospital opened in Remuera in 1999. Peddlethorp later designed the adjacent Ascot Central clinical suites.[5]

Established in 1991 by James and Johanna Klein, Klein was later rebranded as Klein Healthcare Designers to reflect their growing specialisation in health facilities. The commission for Ascot Hospital, Klein's first large health project, followed smaller work such as the 1994 alterations to the Wilson Home in Takapuna.[6] At Middlemore Hospital Klein worked with Chow:Hill on the 2003 four-storey adult medical centre (now Scott) inpatient building, adding another two floors to it in 2014. This led to the 2010 commission for the adjacent 240-bed Edmund Hillary ward block and, in 2014, the Harley Gray clinical services building, with 14 operating theatres, an 18-bed high-dependency unit, a 42-bed assessment and diagnostic unit and non-clinical support departments. The practice collaborated through the preliminary design stages of Harley Gray with the Australian firm Silver Thomas Hanley. Klein also completed the new laboratory, cardiac catheterisation laboratory and renal department, among several other refurbishment projects at Middlemore.[7]

At North Shore Hospital Klein designed the maternity extension, operating theatre upgrades and the 2011 three-storey Lakeview Building, which accommodated the emergency department and assessment and planning unit. The firm also worked on extensions and refurbishments at Waitakere Hospital, including the emergency department.[8]

The 2012 emergency and theatre building at Hutt Hospital, which has eight operating theatres, was designed to allow for very large seismic movements at the junctions to the existing hospital. Klein also designed the 2018 two-storey, 890-square-metre Ruakopito endoscopy unit at Hawke's Bay Fallen Soldiers' Memorial Hospital. The practice was also responsible for the 2020 endoscopy suite at Whangarei Hospital, plus a cardiac catheterisation laboratory and two new operating theatres the following year. As this book

↖

Mercy Ascot Hospital, Auckland.

↗

Te Aka forensic mental health unit at the Mason Clinic, Auckland.

went to print Klein was working on the expansion of the Te Kōtuku building there to provide a new SCBU (special care bay unit) and paediatrics ward.[9]

Klein's mental health projects have included the 15-bed Te Aka forensic mental health unit at the Mason Clinic in 2017, the 76-bed Tiaho Mai acute mental health unit in 2021 at Middlemore and, in 2024, specialist mental health facilities for child and youth, eating disorders, mothers and babies and high and complex care at Hillmorton in Christchurch. E Tū Wairua Hinengaro, currently under construction at the Mason Clinic, will be New Zealand's first forensic mental health facility with patient accommodation on two levels.[10]

Private hospital work by Klein has included Forté Health in Christchurch in 2014, a four-theatre surgical facility. This was designed with local architects, and DesignGroup members, Wilson + Hill, who also designed the 2016 Avenue Health building in Christchurch and the 2023 Canterbury Cancer Centre. Forté Health was, as *The Press* put it, 'born out of the closure of the earthquake-damaged Oxford Clinic'.[11] The clinical health planner for this was Ruth Whitehead, a nurse who had joined Klein in 1999 and who left in 2004 to set up a clinical health planning practice, The Health Planner. The building has a highly glazed façade to provide natural light and outlook, and was both New Zealand's first GreenStar medical facility and one of the first applications of pre-cast seismic structural system technology in the country.[12]

Other major private hospital developments include the 10-theatre redevelopment at Mercy Ascot, Intracare North Harbour, and additions and refurbishments for Ormiston Hospital and Southern Cross. Klein also designed the new four-theatre, 20-bed Kākāriki private hospital in Greenlane, Auckland, which involved the adaptive reuse of a former office building.[13]

The new century brought one of the country's worst natural disasters. On 4 September 2010 a magnitude 7.1 earthquake struck Canterbury, causing major and widespread damage to Christchurch and beyond. After more than 1500 aftershocks, on 22 February the following year came a shallower 6.3 quake that destroyed much of the central city. One hundred and eighty-five people lost their lives and many were injured, some severely. Emergency and health services were stretched to the limit. Christchurch Hospital, the only acute-care facility in the region, suffered significant damage.[14]

The redevelopment of Christchurch Hospital, and the city's specialist rehabilitation facility at Burwood Hospital, had been proposed before the earthquakes and was accelerated because of them. The buildings erected at Burwood in 2016 consist of 30,000 square metres of

↖

Harley Gray clinical services building, Middlemore Hospital, Auckland.

↗

Harley Gray high-dependency unit, Middlemore Hospital.

→

Burwood Hospital, Christchurch.

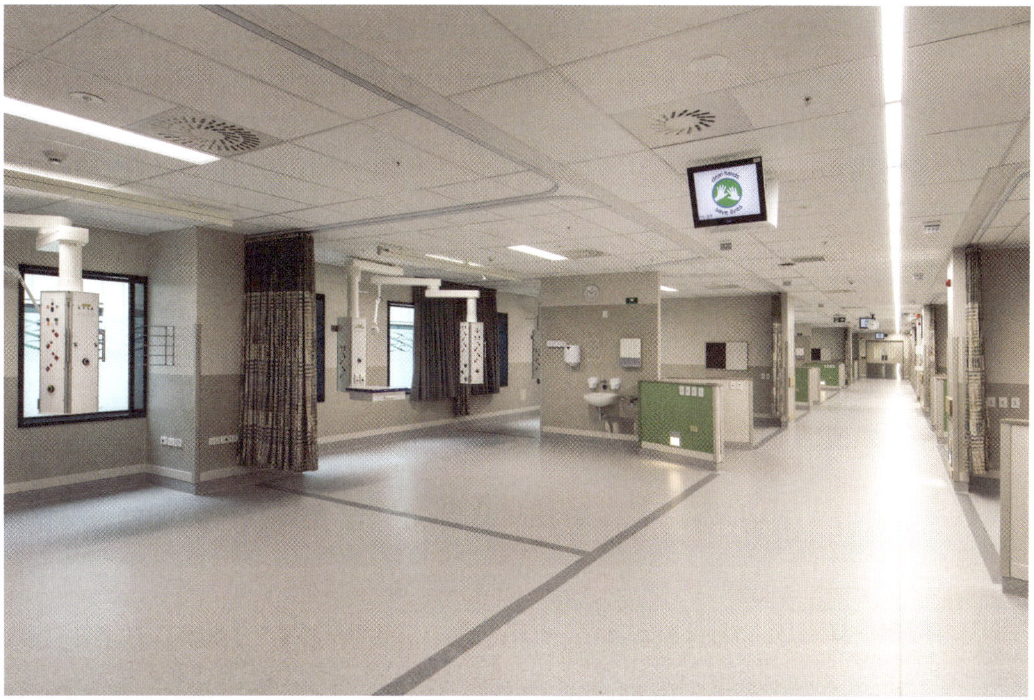

↑
Lakeview emergency and ADU building, North Shore Hospital, Auckland.

↖
Emergency and theatre building, Hutt Hospital.

↗
Tiaho Mai acute mental health unit, Middlemore.

→
A room at Tiaho Mai acute mental health unit, Middlemore Hospital.

space with 230 inpatient beds, radiology and outpatient departments, and a new main entrance and atrium. The design team was a collaboration of Klein, Jasmax and Sheppard & Rout (see practice histories, page 368).[15]

++

Jasmax's first major public health project had been the nine-level, 80,000-square-metre, 710-bed acute services building at Auckland City Hospital in 2003, designed in conjunction with Australian firm McConnel, Smith & Johnson (MSJ). The floor plan was based on eight L-shaped 30-bed wards, pairs of which were mirrored to form a T, and were then arranged around a central atrium, giving as many rooms as possible natural light and external views.

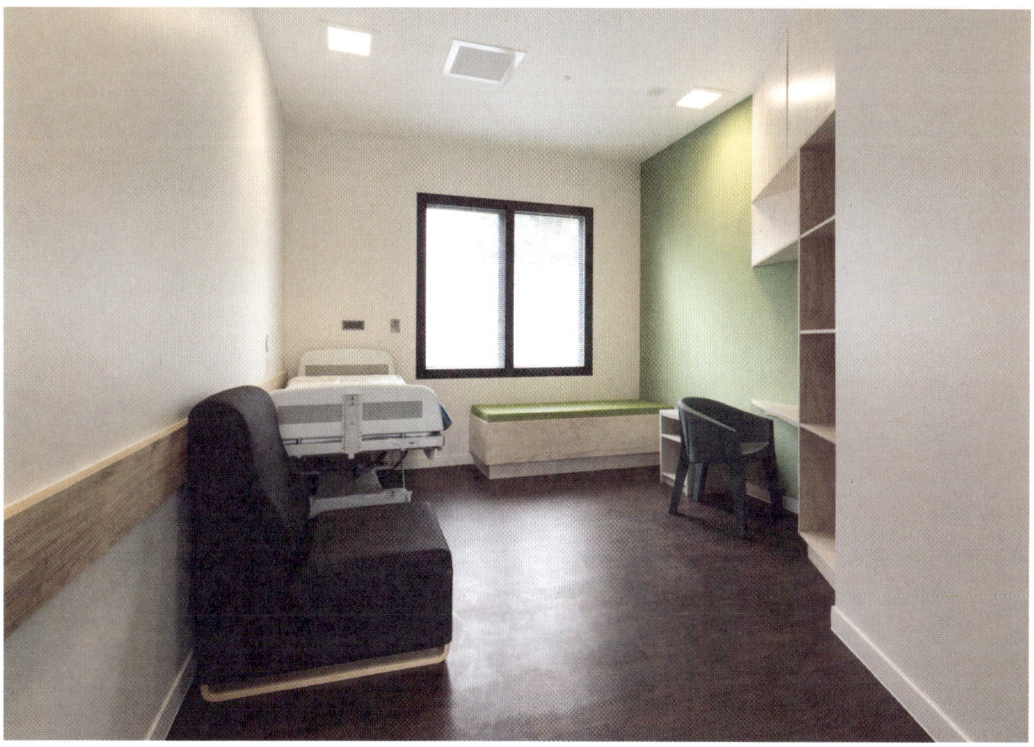

The operating theatres were spread in clusters through the building to be closer to the wards for the departments they serve. This also allowed most of them to have external windows.

A change in alignment of the building grid between the northern and southern sections permitted public lifts and stairs at the eastern end. The building was linked to the 1960s hospital by a multi-level bridge that continues across the atrium as a pedestrian street. When the women's and maternity services were relocated to the top floor of this building in 2004, National Women's Hospital was closed.[16]

Invercargill's 180-bed Southland Hospital – designed by Jasmax with MSJ and local practice McDowell Architects, a successor to A. C. Ford's practice, and opened in 2004 – includes the 18,000-square-metre clinical services building and a separate 15-bed mental health unit. The main two-storey 154-bed building was organised around a central internal street running its 200-metre length. A variety of cladding types, including pre-cast concrete panels, metal cladding and timber screens, was used to break down the scale of the facade.[17]

Jasmax also designed Whanganui Hospital's 2009 acute services building and operating theatre block. At North Shore Hospital Jasmax was the architect for the 2011 renal dialysis facility and the 2017 Whenua Pupuke clinical skills centre. The firm was responsible, too, again with MSJ, for the hospital's 2013 elective surgical centre, an operating theatre facility with a 40-bed inpatient ward. Its 150-bed Tōtara Haumaru extension, opened in 2024, includes eight operating theatres and four endoscopy rooms.

Private health facilities include the Auckland Eye Clinic, the 2004 Apollo Medical Centre in Albany and the 2008 Mercy Hospital Radiation Oncology unit.[18] Jasmax designed the 2012 expansion and refurbishment of the Auckland School of Medicine in association with Daryl Jackson Architects of Melbourne, and partnered with Parker Warburton Team Architects on the University of Otago Dental School in 2021, which consists of a new 9000-square-metre building connected by an atrium to the heritage Walsh Building.[19]

In the first years of the twenty-first century Jasmax worked with Chow:Hill and MSJ to design the major upgrade of the Waikato Hospital facilities, including the new Te Rau Aroha carpark and entry building in 2008, the 2011 acute services building, which included

↖

Acute services building, Auckland City Hospital.

↑

Interior garden at Tōtara Haumaru, North Shore Hospital.

↗

Tōtara Haumaru, North Shore Hospital.

the hospital's emergency department, and a second carpark building on Pembroke Street in 2012. The 113-bed older persons and rehabilitation building, completed in 2013, is linked to the main hospital by a bridge over Pembroke Street. The 2014 five-level 39,000-square-metre Meade clinical centre includes 10 operating theatres, radiology, critical care and outpatient clinics.[20] The project also included an upgrade of Thames Hospital, with a new clinical centre (emergency, radiology and outpatients) and a new 54-bed inpatient unit and kitchen.[21]

++

Chow:Hill was established in 1992 by Chien Chow, who had been an associate at Worley Gillman, and Richard Hill, who had been appointed head of its Hamilton architecture department in 1988.[22] An office was set up in Auckland in 1995, when Darryl Carey joined to lead the development of the firm's specialisation in health. He has been responsible for preparing master plans for several hospitals around the country and was instrumental in setting up the New Zealand Health Design Council in 2011, which he chaired for its first decade.[23]

Chow:Hill's first major public hospital work was the master planning for Middlemore Hospital and the Manukau site in Wiri, both then operated by South Auckland Health. Kidz First Children's Hospital at Middlemore, opened in 2000, was followed by the acute services hub, with emergency and ICU, the refurbishment of the Galbraith Building and the four-level 258-bed adult inpatient building (now Scott) opened in 2003 and designed in conjunction with Klein. At the new Manukau campus, Chow:Hill designed the 1997 SuperClinics outpatient centre and the adjoining Manukau elective surgical hospital. After the new Braemar Hospital in Hamilton opened in 2009, a day hospital expansion in 2012 and a new theatre for cardiac and spinal surgery in 2019 were designed by Chow:Hill.[24]

In the South Island, the firm worked with specialist contractors ACEPT on the MRI building at Timaru Hospital in 2013. Chow:Hill also designed the 2020 medical oncology unit at Wellington Hospital and, in 2022, the renal dialysis building at Nelson Hospital. At Bay of Islands Hospital, the firm designed the two-level stage 1 block, opened in 2018, with a 20-bed ward and accident and medical department, and the 2023 stage 2 building with the main entrance, outpatients, primary health, renal dialysis and chemotherapy units.[25]

Chow:Hill designed the 2010 Puawai extension to the Henry Rongomau Bennett Centre at Waikato Hospital, adding three forensic wards and a wharenui. Other mental health projects include the 15-bed E Tū Tanekaha Unit at the Mason Clinic in 2021, and the Mauri Ora mental health unit in Rotorua. Private hospital work has included ongoing projects at Braemar Hospital since 2007, and at Rotorua's QE Hospital.[26]

Chow:Hill's first project on the Christchurch Hospital site was the 2005 Christchurch Women's Hospital building, designed in conjunction with Opus Architects. The master plan

↖

Meade Clinical Centre, Waikato Hospital.

↗

Clockwise from top left:
Kidz First Children's Hospital, Middlemore.
Waipapa acute services building, Christchurch Hospital.
Warkworth Hospice.
Linear multi-bed room, Christchurch Hospital.

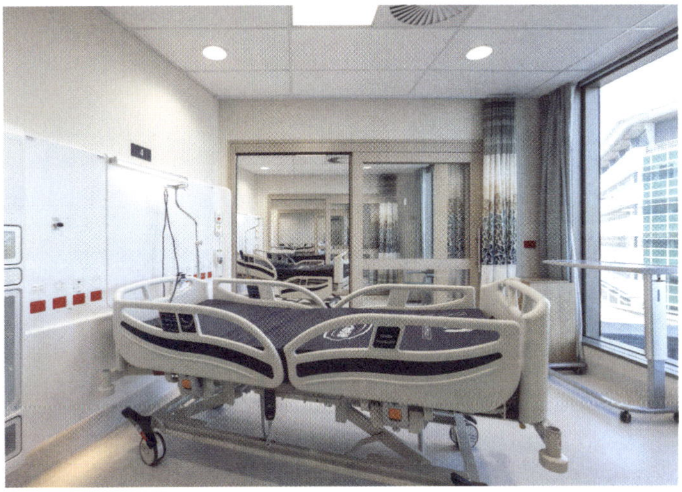

for Christchurch Hospital was being developed when it was impacted by the earthquakes of 2010–11. This led to the design of the 62,000-square-metre Waipapa acute services block, opened in 2020. This work was done in association with Warren and Mahoney and Thinc Health, collectively known as Katoa Health Design. A feature of the building is the linear multi-bed room, with patient beds facing towards the external windows and separated by sliding glass screens placed at a slight angle to maintain privacy but give staff visibility from their central bases. The building has 12 operating theatres and a 48-bed ICU. A third ward tower is now under construction.[27]

++

Another practice that became a significant contributor to hospital design during this period is Warren and Mahoney, established by Frederick (Miles, later Sir Miles) Warren in 1955, who was joined by Maurice Mahoney in 1958. That year, Warren was awarded the commission to design the new Dental Nurses' Training School in Christchurch,[28] and asked Mahoney to join him. Like much of their early work, the building, which opened in 1959, was influenced by the New Brutalism that Warren had experienced in Britain.

Paparātā

This 'Christchurch School' aesthetic contrasted with the lightweight timber vernacular being popularised at the time by designers such as the Group Architects in Auckland.[29] In 1966 Warren and Mahoney won the competition to design the much-admired new Christchurch Town Hall, which opened in 1972. The firm's earliest significant hospital project was the 1976 British Base Hospital in Vila, Solomon Islands.[30]

In 2003, in association with Bligh Nield Health (formerly BVN), Warren and Mahoney designed a major redevelopment at Nelson Hospital. This included a new main entry, maternity and paediatrics ward, and emergency department, radiology, ICU and operating theatres, with some refurbishment of the existing buildings.[31]

The Project Maunga redevelopment of Taranaki Base Hospital began in 2009 and the first stage, the five-storey acute services building, housing wards with 150 beds and operating theatres, opened in 2014. Warren and Mahoney worked on this with Silver Thomas Hanley and is now designing the second stage of the development, which will provide a new emergency department, ICU, radiology, a laboratory and maternity services. A separate renal unit also forms part of this project.[32]

Warren and Mahoney designed the 2019 expanded ICU and endoscopy facilities in the main ward block of Dunedin Hospital and a new audiology facility at Wakari the same year. The firm also designed the redeveloped Buller Health Centre in Westport, opened in 2023, and the new seven-storey medical education and research facility for the Otago Medical School in Oxford Terrace, Christchurch, which is due to open in 2026.

Warren and Mahoney has also been heavily involved with Christchurch's Southern Cross Hospital, designing a 2008 extension with two operating theatres and a 40-bed

↖

Waipapa acute services building foyer, Christchurch Hospital.

←

Bay of Islands Hospital, Kawakawa.

↗

Christchurch Women's Hospital.

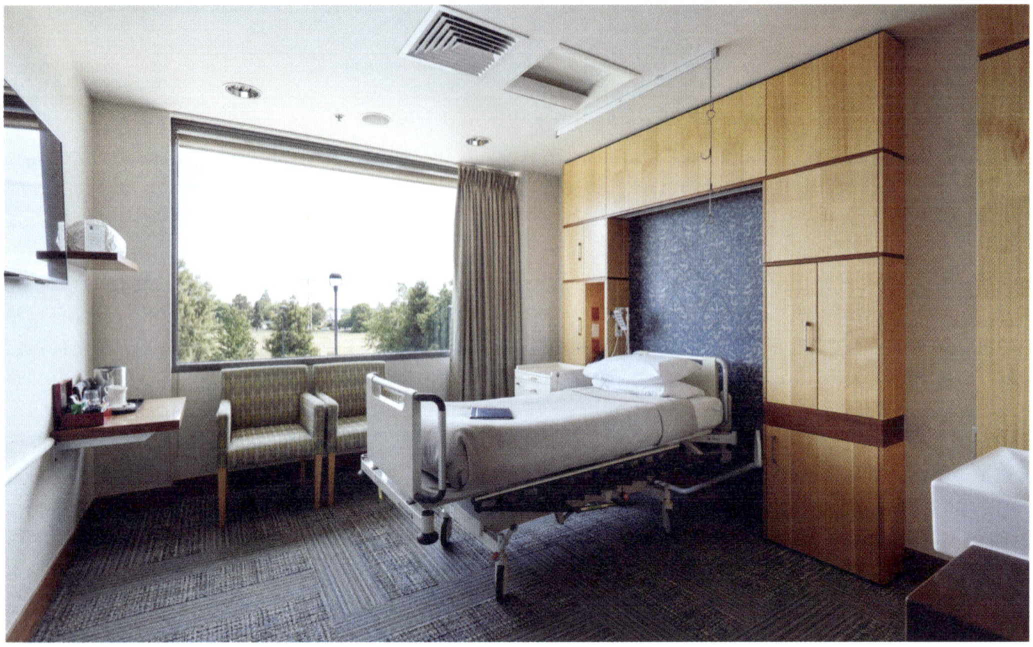

ward, an endoscopy building in 2010, a hybrid operating theatre in 2014 and a four-storey specialist centre in 2015. It also designed the 2021 Southern Cross Central Lakes Hospital in Queenstown, a partnership between Southern Cross and the Central Lakes Trust, and several buildings for Southern Cross hospitals in Auckland and Wellington. Other private healthcare projects by the firm include buildings at Crest Hospital in Palmerston North in 2016, Manuka Street Hospital in Nelson in 2022 and St John of God Hospital in Christchurch.[33]

The firm also designed the PET radiology suite at Christchurch Radiology, opened in 2012, and the Silverdale Medical Centre in Auckland of the same year The latter was a joint venture between local medical practices and Southern Cross Hospitals, providing a range of health services such as general medical, dental and radiology on the ground floor, with four operating theatres and 10 beds on the level above. Private endoscopy facilities include Wellington's Rutherford Clinic in 2018 and Auckland's MacMurray Centre in 2020.[34]

Warren and Mahoney has grown to be one of New Zealand's largest architectural practices, with six offices in New Zealand and two in Australia, and more than 300 staff members.[35] It is the only other firm, after Horace Massey's various partnerships, to have won four NZIA Gold Medals.[36]

In 2019 Warren and Mahoney was engaged to design the new Dunedin Hospital, in association with HDR and local practice McCoy Wixon.[37]

++

In 2013 multi-national firm HDR acquired Australian practice Rice Daubney, which had previously operated in New Zealand as Rice Daubney Di Carlo Potts Health. This health specialist firm was formed by Sydney practices Rice Daubney and Di Carlo Potts in 2004. Di Carlo Potts first entered New Zealand in 1994, when it was commissioned for the major redevelopment of Palmerston North Hospital, which delivered, in 2000, the women's and children's building, with a children's ward, maternity services and gynaecology, and the ambulatory care building.

↖

Patient bedroom, Braemar Hospital, Hamilton.

↑

Main entry and ward building, Nelson Hospital.

↗

Acute services building, Taranaki Base Hospital, New Plymouth.

In 2002 came the STAR elder health, rehabilitation, allied health and mental health building, and a new two-storey building with main entrance, emergency department and outpatient clinics on the ground floor and gastroenterology, renal and offices above. Other projects by Di Carlo Potts include the Project Orion redevelopment of North Shore Hospital in 2004 and of Waitakere Hospital in 2005, and work at Hutt Hospital. Di Carlo Potts worked with CCM on the new Wellington Regional Hospital.[38]

++

CCM was established in Wellington in 1969 as Craig Craig Moller by James Thomas (Jim) Craig, his son, Jon Alistair Craig, and Gordon Moller. An Auckland office led by Moller opened in 1993, when the firm won the commission to design the 1996 SkyCity casino and entertainment centre, including the Sky Tower. In 2002 two separate practices were formed, CCM in Wellington and Moller Architects in Auckland.[39]

With Di Carlo Potts providing health planning and concept design, CCM were architects for the 2009 Wellington Regional Hospital, a 47,830-square-metre building consisting of a four-level ward block on a three-level podium. The ward levels typically have six 12-bed pods on each floor, arranged as two 36-bed Ts connected by a central circulation and support area, and are specifically designed to afford views and light to all patient rooms while being efficient for staff observation and circulation.

The podium accommodates the main entrance, reception, cafeteria and radiology on the ground floor, and 15 operating theatres and an 18-bed ICU on the floor above. The ground level connects to the existing single-level emergency department building, erected in 2000, to the south. There are outpatient clinics and ambulatory services on both levels. The lowest level is a full basement carpark, which also provides space for the seismic base isolators and flexing of services such as drainage from the floors above.[40]

↑

MacMurray Gastroenterology and Endoscopy Centre, Auckland.

↗

Wellington Regional Hospital.

The orange clay tile exterior of the podium was selected to relate to its residential neighbourhood and references the brickwork of older public buildings, including the original hospital. The building had to be constructed in two stages. In the first, the 210 Block was demolished in 2004, and a new blood and cancer centre, with three linear accelerator bunkers and a brachytherapy bunker, was built in the north-eastern corner of the site and opened in 2005. This allowed the existing cancer centre and the adjacent AT&R building, only completed in 1997, to be demolished, making space for the rest of the new structures. The front block, and the ward block behind it, also came down, although the arched entranceway and stairs were salvaged and moved to a courtyard at the rear.[41]

CCM has been responsible for much of the recent work at Kenepuru Hospital. The first stage of the redeveloped hospital opened in 2005, the second in 2006. Mental health facilities on the campus include the 2006 Te Whare Ra Uta psychogeriatric unit and, in 2016, the Hikiti Te Wairua youth intellectually disabled forensic unit extension to the 30-bed Te Whare Rangatahi acute adolescent mental health unit at Te Whare o Rangatuhi adolescent facility and Ngā Taiohi secure youth forensic unit.[42]

In Wellington CCM designed the extension of the Te Hopai Home and Hospital in 2008 and the Icon cancer theatre at Bowen Hospital. Opened in 2025, a major redevelopment at Wakefield Hospital in Wellington, adding 37 bedrooms, 10 ICU beds, a cardiac catheterisation lab and an endoscopy suite, was designed by HSPC Health Architects of Australia with CCM and Aurecon. CCM designed the first stages of the recent redevelopment at Boulcott Hospital, which began as a small clinic in 1984 and has grown into a comprehensive surgical hospital next to Hutt Hospital. This includes a new specialist centre and day-surgery unit, and the firm is working on proposed additional operating theatres and a ward extension. A major redevelopment at Dunedin's Mercy Hospital, designed by CCM with local architects Baker Garden, delivered a new day-procedures unit with two new theatres in 2016, adjacent to the historic Marinoto House. There was further expansion in 2018.[43]

Te Nīkau Grey Hospital and Health Centre, opened in 2020, is located beside the existing Grey Base Hospital buildings in Greymouth and is intended to replace them. CCM worked with Jacobs on this new hospital and integrated family health centre. The three-storey, 8500-square-metre building contains 56 inpatient beds (two of them negative pressure), three operating theatres, an emergency department, radiology, clinics and a chapel. A separate but connected single-storey integrated family health centre provides primary and secondary care services.[44]

The design of the exterior and the selection of cost-effective durable materials suitable for the highly corrosive West Coast marine environment was a significant challenge. The smaller health centre building is designed to a higher seismic standard (IL4) than the main hospital building, which is IL3, so that patients can be triaged there after a disaster while the rest of the facility is repaired.[45]

CCM designed the five-storey outpatient building that opened at Christchurch Hospital in 2018. This sits on the former St Andrew's site opposite the main hospital campus and was also designed in conjunction with Jacobs. CCM worked with Jacobs and Australian practices Destravis and Johnstaff on the initial master planning and business case for the proposed replacement of Dunedin Hospital too.[46]

++

Several other practices designed significant health buildings in these years. After years of public fundraising, the Jim Carney Cancer Centre at Whangarei Hospital, designed by Fitness Fleming with Whangarei architects Hawthorn Geddes, opened in 2015. Also dating from that year, on the hospital site, is Tohorā House, by Euroclass and A-Line Construction, to provide office accommodation for the Northland District Health Board. In Whangārei, Architects H+K, a member of DesignGroup, designed the Northland Orthopaedic Centre, with two operating theatres and a day-care facility. The firm was also responsible for the Northern Radiology facility.[47]

Ronald McDonald Houses were built near a number of public hospitals to offer a home away from home for families with children receiving treatment. The Auckland house, designed by Andrews Scott Cotton, now ASC Architects and a member of DesignGroup, opened in 1995. ASC also designed the 2007 New Zealand Centre for Conservation Medicine at Auckland Zoo, and the 2019 redevelopment of Ranfurly Village in Auckland, which added a 60-bed hospital and six apartment buildings and refurbished the original Ranfurly House. Other Ronald McDonald Houses opened in Wellington in 2012, designed by Archaus, and in Christchurch, by Wilkie + Bruce. Accommodation for patients' families is also provided by such facilities as the Auckland Cancer Society's Domain Lodge, built near Auckland Hospital in 1999 and designed by Ashton Mitchell, and the Rānui Apartments, designed by Plus Architecture and opened near Christchurch Hospital in 2024.[48]

++

Opened in 2023, the 3800-square-metre Northern Specialist Centre in Silverdale, designed by Pacific Environments, houses specialists and other healthcare providers. At the Hamilton Laser Eye Clinic, double-height glazing creates both an impressive street frontage and a welcoming reception and waiting area. Designed by Chibnall Buckell Team Architecture (now Team Network), the building is clad with oil-finished cedar weatherboards and Zincalume steel cladding. APG Architects designed the 2007 Anglesea Hospital in Hamilton and PathLab Tauranga, at the north end of the public hospital site.[49]

First Principles Architects has designed several birthing centres. The first, in 2014, was the 12-room Bethlehem Birthing Centre in Tauranga. The two-storey Nga Hau Mangere Birthing Centre, which opened in 2019, has 20 self-contained birthing suites on the upper level, with 820 square metres for another tenancy below. The architectural concept was based on a mother nursing her newborn baby: its profile resembles the folds of a baby's blanket and incorporates a basket-weave pattern and elements reflecting the flounder of the Manukau Harbour.[50]

Australian practice Devine Erby Mazlin (DEM) designed both the 1998 LabPlus pathology facility next to Auckland City Hospital and the 20-bed hospital for Gore, which opened on Birch Lane in 1999 following community action in the face of plans to withdraw the town's healthcare services. The 36-bed Henry Rongomau Bennett Centre for patients with mental illness opened in 1998 at Waikato Hospital. Named for the first Māori psychiatrist, it was designed by Archimedia, formed from the New Zealand arm of DEM that year, in association with Civil & Civic. Archimedia also designed the emergency department building at Wellington Hospital, which was expanded in 2005.[51]

Tauranga's Grace Hospital, which opened in 1998, was also designed by Archimedia. The city's 1953 Norfolk Hospital on Grace Road had merged, in 2001, with a Southern Cross Hospital opened in the city in 1983. The renamed Grace Hospital opened on Cheyne Road, Ōropi, in 2007.[52]

Archimedia also designed Ormiston Hospital, which opened on Ormiston Road in Flat Bush in 2008. This was the first new private hospital in the rapidly expanding South Auckland area. On a greenfield site, it includes angled bay windows in bedrooms to maximise patient outlook while providing privacy. Also the work of Archimedia were the 2011 Eye Institute in Remuera and the 2018 Southern Cross Northern Clinic extension.

↗
Outpatient building, Christchurch Hospital.

++

The Kathleen Kilgour Centre at Tauranga Hospital, designed by Wingate + Farquhar and opened in 2014, won an NZIA award the following year. It was shortlisted for a World Architecture Festival award, a remarkable achievement for a three-bunker radiotherapy facility grafted onto the existing 2008 cancer centre. Designed to be as environmentally sustainable as possible, it has solar panels, intelligent natural ventilation, rainwater harvesting and a 14-metre vertical garden in the atrium.[53]

Jigsaw Architects, previously Matrixx, formed from Babbage Tauranga, has undertaken much of the recent work at Tauranga and Whakatane Hospitals. It has also designed several primary health facilities, and the multi-modal imaging facility for Bay Radiology in Tauranga.

The 10-bed Te Whare Awhi Ora acute mental health unit at Gisborne Hospital was designed by Australia-based Mode Architects, with local firm Architects 44.

In Hastings, the Royston private hospital opened in 1921, and after severe damage in the 1931 earthquake was relocated to the nearby Harris family home in Southland Road, which still forms the base of the current facility. Several architects have worked there, including Dougan Larkworthy Team Architects, HSPC and Klein, who designed the 2021 day-surgery unit.

Also in Hastings, a group of clinicians seeking to offer additional surgical procedures established the Kaweka Health facility on Canning Road, opposite the public hospital. The first stage, opened in 2022, provided four operating theatres; the second stage, projected for

↖

Hamilton Laser Eye Clinic.

↗

Nga Hau Mangere Birthing Centre, Auckland.

2025, contains a 23-bed ward and specialist consulting facilities. The architect is Architecture HDT, which was also responsible for the integrated family health centre at Wairoa Hospital, built about 2012, and the 2019 Hastings Health Centre.[54]

Local firm Dickson Lonergan Architects (now DLA) designed the 1998 upgrade to the 1955 maternity services building at Wanganui Hospital. The same practice designed the 2000 Stratford Health Centre, which sits on part of the old hospital site at the corner of Romeo and Miranda streets and houses outpatient clinics, a dental clinic and offices for public health nurses. It was DLA, too, who designed the strengthening and refurbishment of the Gardens Block nurses' home at Tīmaru Hospital, which reopened as an administration block in 2016. The 2020 redevelopment of the front of the hospital, with a revised main entrance and emergency department, was also by DLA.[55]

The 3000-square-metre 12-bed Te Papaoeia Birthing Centre, which opened in Palmerston North in 2018, was designed by local architects Proarch Consultants. Another Palmerston North practice, Pak Design, was responsible for the Aorangi Specialist Centre, which provides a new facility for Broadway Radiology and other health specialists. The construction is decorative concrete panels with cedar infills.[56]

++

Wellington practice McKenzie Higham Architects, founded in 1999, designed the 2002 Manawai unit attached to Haumietiketike, a regional secure facility for the intellectually disabled in Porirua. Manawai provides six 51-square-metre units where residents are supported in their own individual living environments. At Porirua, the practice also oversaw the completion of the Bulleyment Fortune-designed extensions to Haumietiketike in 2020, and Pūrehurehu, a male acute adult forensic unit on the same Porirua campus, the latter known as Tānerore, in 2018. Both Haumietiketike (2003) and Pūrehurehu (1990) were originally designed by Stephenson & Turner. McKenzie Higham Architects earlier designed the Wellington Free Ambulance station in Porirua (2000) and the Porirua Union and Community Health Service facilities in Cannons Creek, Porirua East (2010), for general practice and midwife services.[57]

In 2017, Wellington developer Mark Dunajtschik and partner Dorothy Spotswood donated $50 million towards a new children's hospital at Wellington Hospital. Combined with

$10 million from the Wellington Hospitals Foundation, $25 million from the government for the build, $21 million for site clearance, and $4 million from the former Capital and Coast District Health Board, the total project cost was around $110 million.

Opened in 2022, the facility is named Te Wao Nui Child Health Service, after Dunajtschik and Spotswood. Designed by Studio Design + Architecture (now part of Ignite) with clinical planner Ruth Whitehead, the three-storey, 7200-square-metre, base-isolated building sits north of the main hospital and is connected by a 42-metre enclosed bridge. It includes 21 outpatient clinic rooms on the ground floor and 50 inpatient beds above. The façade features glazed panels with metal fins in a zigzag pattern. The same donors have pledged up to $50 million for a new 34-bed adult mental health unit at Hutt Hospital, replacing the existing 24-bed facility.

Ignite also designed the 884-square-metre Akaroa Health Hub, opened in 2019, replacing a quake-damaged building with 12 beds and three treatment rooms.[58]

++

In the South Island Churchill Hospital, a private surgical facility on the Wairau Hospital campus in Blenheim, is one of the few private healthcare operators on a public hospital site in New Zealand. Established in 1994, it originally occupied part of the old hospital buildings, but in 2016 moved into its own building designed by Hawkins Architecture and connected directly to the public hospital operating theatres. Opritech installed New Zealand's first modular operating theatre there in 2013.[59]

Totem Studio Architects, successor to the firm established by William Trengrove, designed the 2017 Kaikoura Hospital for Kaikoura Healthcare, on the same site as its predecessor. This has 21 beds and a delivery suite, as well as general practice, radiology and physiotherapy rooms.

↖

The Henry Rongomau Bennett Centre at Waikato Hospital.

↗

Churchill Hospital theatre, designed and implemented by Cubro Opritech.

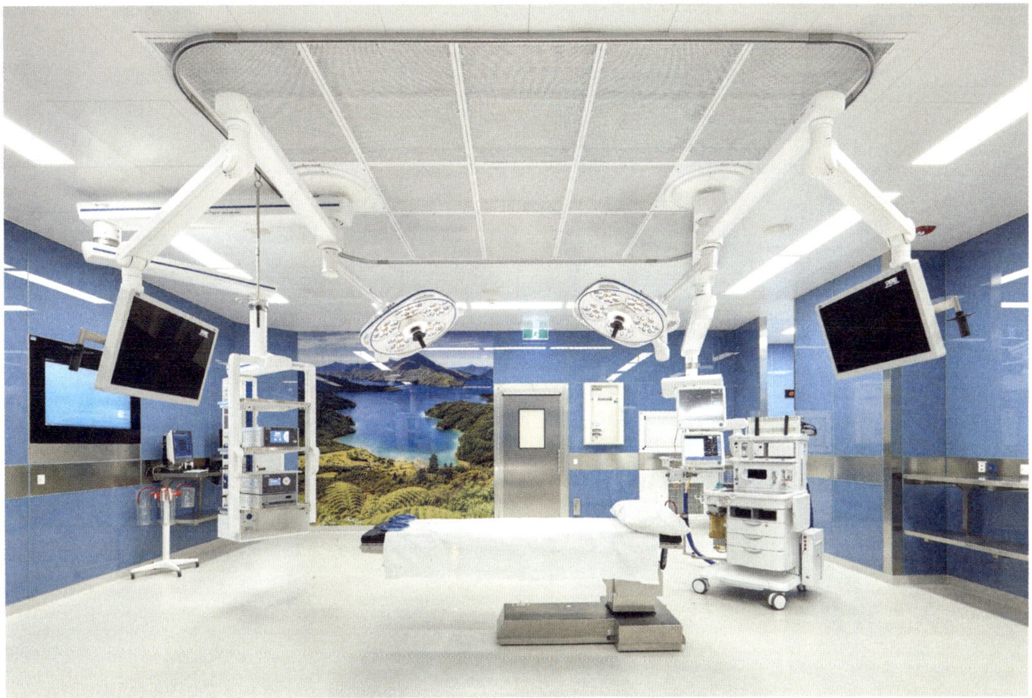

At Ashburton Hospital, a major redevelopment in 2016, by which stage the hospital had 74 beds, added an acute services unit and day-procedure theatre, designed by Ian Krause Architects. Renamed IKON Architects, the practice designed the 2021 Taka Hāpai Selwyn Health Hub, built by the Selwyn District Council to serve the rapidly growing town of Rolleston on the outskirts of Christchurch. IKON Architects have also designed several primary health facilities in Christchurch, including the North Avon Medical Centre, the 2017 Woodham Road medical centre, and Ilam Health in 2022.[60]

In 1998, threatened with the loss of a hospital in Ōamaru, the Waitaki District Council established Waitaki District Health Services Ltd. Oamaru Hospital reopened in 2000 on a new, more central, site between Steward and Severn streets, next to Takaro Park. The 35-bed hospital, designed by John McKenzie of McKenzie Architects, incorporated the 1875 building designed by John Forrester for Oamaru Grammar School, with new pavilions added on three sides detailed to harmonise with it.[61]

A new 32-bed Dunstan Hospital, designed by HPA, opened in Clyde in 2005.[62]

Dunedin practice Baker Garden designed the new 1200-square-metre, 15-bed Maniototo Hospital, which opened in 2020 to replace the 1930 building.

When he was diagnosed with cancer in 2018, Winton resident Blair Vining fought for diagnosis and treatment to be more accessible. Following his death a year later, his family and supporters have worked to develop a community hospital delivering colonoscopies and other cancer care services. The Southland Charity Hospital in Invercargill, designed by Bonisch Consulting, opened in 2025. This involved the adaptive reuse of the Clifton Club Inn and was based on the 2007 Canterbury Charity Hospital in Christchurch.[63]

KATHLEEN
KILGOUR
CENTRE

↖

Akaroa Health Hub.

←

Kathleen Kilgour Centre, Tauranga.

↗

Kaweka Health, Hastings.

→

Te Wao Nui Child Health, Wellington Regional Hospital.

Fixtures, fittings and equipment

↘

Design is not just restricted to health facilities. New Zealanders, with their renowned No. 8 wire practicality, have also displayed considerable innovation in the design of healthcare equipment. The story started with nineteenth-century doctor, priest and inventor Arthur Purchas, who designed and made much of his own surgical equipment because supplies took so long to arrive from Britain. He performed New Zealand's first caesarean section and, in 1886 became one of the first members of the newly formed New Zealand Medical Association.[1]

++

Poliomyelitis, or polio, also known as infantile paralysis, was recurrent in New Zealand until a vaccine became available. It particularly affected the patient's muscles, leading to paralysis and even death when it damaged the muscles used in breathing. The tank respirator, or iron lung, invented in the United States in 1927, was in short supply and particularly unaffordable during the Depression. Fred C. Jacobs, chief engineer at the Auckland Hospital Board, developed his own, which was built by his son Bill and commissioned in 1935.[2]

Following the Second World War, governments sought to increase New Zealand's economic independence by restricting imports to encourage the growth of local industries. Although the reforms of the 1980s drove much manufacturing overseas, some innovative companies, such as Fisher & Paykel, both survived and thrived. The company was founded in 1934 by Woolf Fisher and Maurice Paykel to import household appliances, which they later manufactured.[3]

After Dr Matt Spence of Middlemore Hospital and Alf Melville at the Department of Scientific and Industrial Research developed a prototype respiratory humidifier, Fisher & Paykel began manufacturing this in 1969 for use on patients being ventilated in hospital ICUs. Their healthcare range expanded to include such neo-natal care products as infant

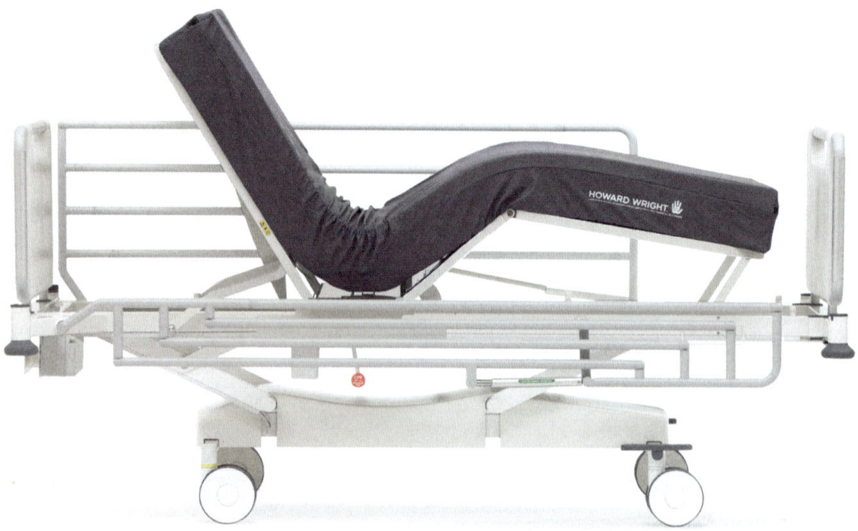

←

Howard Wright's M9 ward bed.

↗

Disposable plastic syringes.

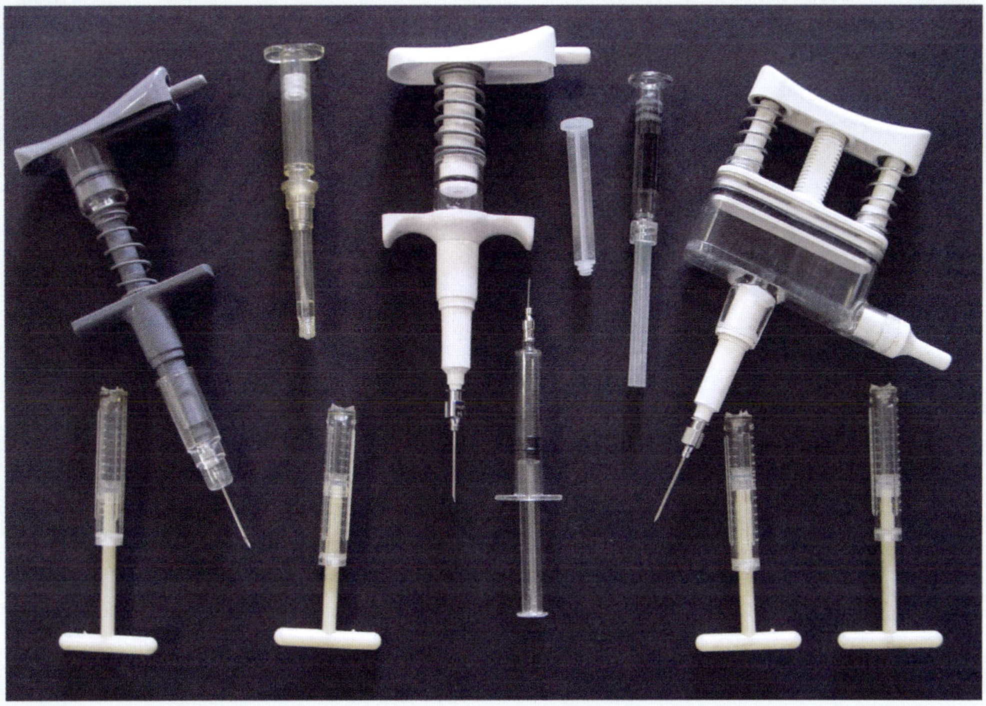

warmers to help maintain body temperature and continuous positive airway pressure devices for infant respiratory function and people with sleep apnoea. Fisher & Paykel Healthcare Ltd was separated from Fisher & Paykel Appliances in 2001, and since then it has become one of New Zealand's most successful companies, with a factory opened in Mexico in 2010, complementing its East Tāmaki, Auckland, base.[4]

Also developed in 1969, by C. W. Martin & Co., was the premature infant incubator designed by Paul F. Martin, who followed this up in 1970 with the Marford portable incubator. Auckland company Mason Mesco also designed and manufactured anaesthesia machines in the 1970s. Mercer & Sons were manufacturing sterilising equipment in New Zealand as far back as the 1920s.[5]

After motor mechanic Howard Wright started his own business in New Plymouth in the 1950s, staff from the local hospital asked if he could make a bed based on photos of the modern models available overseas. He proceeded to do so using the latest in hydraulics technology. In 1963 he opened a dedicated factory in the city and by the 1970s it was making most of the country's hospital beds.[6]

In the mid-twentieth century, syringes were made of glass and were reused, resulting in cross-contamination unless they were carefully sterilised. In 1956 Christchurch pharmacist and veterinarian Colin Murdoch developed the world's first disposable plastic syringe. The Department of Health considered it 'too futuristic' and it took several years to get acceptance and funding. Murdoch also pioneered the tranquiliser gun and childproof medicine containers and by the end of his career held 46 patents. He deliberately chose not to pursue companies that violated any of these, preferring that his ideas were used to benefit as many people as possible.[7]

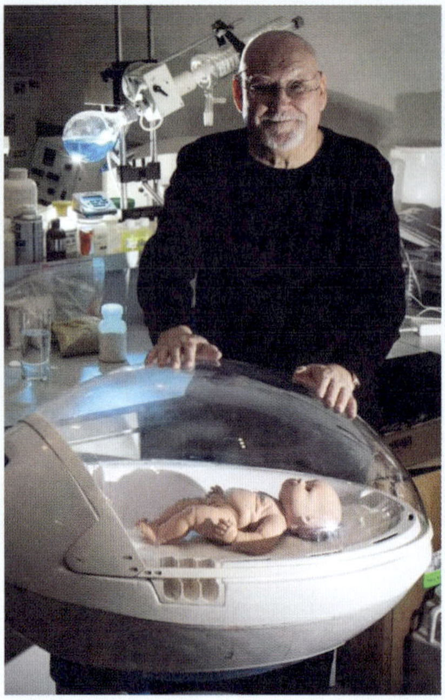

++

Born in England, Leslie Kay became an apprentice electrician at the age of 14. After the war, in which he served with the RAF, he worked for the Admiralty developing sonar technology, which led to his 1964 invention of a sonic torch to assist people with low vision. In 1965 he took up a post at the University of Canterbury, where he was appointed to a personal chair in engineering in 1982. He developed sonic spectacles in 1973 and the tri-sensor aid in 1983. When he retired in 1986, he set up Bay Advanced Technologies to continue this work.[8]

The Baeyertz tape was developed by Whanganui obstetrician and gynaecologist Dr John Baeyertz to provide a simple, accurate way to determine when a pregnant woman would give birth. Using data from babies conceived by artificial insemination, and hence with a known conception date, he calibrated the tape so that the measurement from the mother's pelvic bone to the foetus's head provided the expected birth date. Patented in 1982, it is now widely used around the world.[9]

Founded in Christchurch in 1995, Mobile Health designs, builds and operates mobile surgical units for urology, lithotripsy and non-invasive kidney stone treatment. The company has also recently partnered with an Australian firm to develop modular pod building components for healthcare facilities.[10]

British-born Sir Raymond (Ray) John Avery emigrated to New Zealand in 1973 and became a founding member of the Department of Clinical Pharmacology at the University of Auckland Medical School. He then become technical director of Douglas Pharmaceuticals, where he developed drugs and nutritional products. In the 1990s, when he was with the Fred Hollows Foundation, Avery designed and commissioned facilities for making intra-ocular lenses in Eritrea and Nepal. He founded Medicine Mondiale in 2003, with the aim of making healthcare devices accessible to the poorest of developing

↖

Ray Avery with a Lifepod.

↑

Mobile Health surgical unit 'Oamaru'.

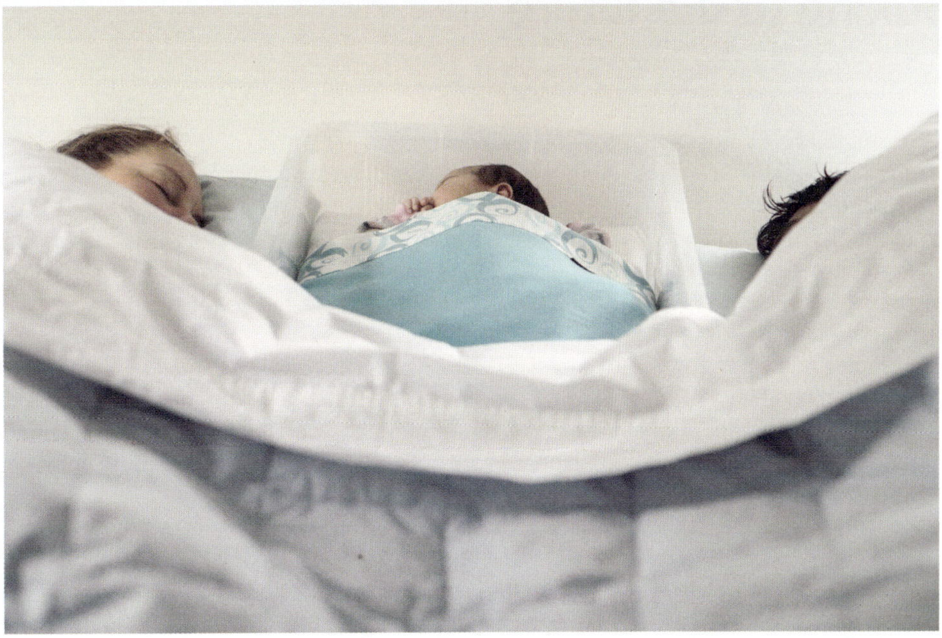

nations. Its products include the Acuset intravenous drug controller in 2008 and the Lifepod incubator, which was still awaiting hospital trials at the time of writing.[11]

Concerns over continuing high infant death rates, especially among Māori, led to studies of lifestyle and infant care practices in families. Exposure to maternal smoking during pregnancy is known to impair babies' arousal responses making them more vulnerable to hypoxic challenges when sleeping. Because of this vulnerability, they may fail to wake or alert their carers placing them at increased risk of sudden infant death. Studies have found that the SUDI risk escalates when babies also share sleep surfaces with others (bedshare). The joint action of smoking in pregnancy and bedsharing is currently the most significant SUDI risk. Wahakura, sleep spaces hand-woven from harakeke, were promoted in Māori communities from 2006 to enable safer bedsharing. They allow babies to sleep safely next to their parents or carers by preventing accidental suffocation, which can happen if someone rolls onto the baby or if the baby gets buried under bedding.

Similarly, the Pēpi-Pod sleep space was developed by Change for Our Children, Christchurch, in 2010 as part of a public health approach to infant protection. The sleep space itself was introduced as a low-cost alternative to support wahakura, enable safe and close infant sleep, and offer more extensive supply within the community. Made of polypropylene, it comes with a fitted mattress and bedding and is distributed with a personalised safety briefing from a healthcare worker. The Pēpi-Pod Programme is currently developing as a state-wide intervention in Queensland, Australia.[12]

↑

A wahakura.

↗

A Pēpi-Pod.

Conclusion: Social distancing and environmental emergency – looking to the future

The earthquakes that devastated much of Christchurch in 2010–11 and the Kaikōura earthquake of 2016, which also destroyed or damaged recently built structures in Wellington, have forced greater attention on resilience, both to protect life during a disaster and to get infrastructure functioning as soon as possible afterwards. New Zealand leads the world in research into seismic action on structures and in such innovative design responses as base isolation and low-damage design, which allow healthcare facilities to maintain their function or to be repaired as rapidly as possible.

Other natural hazards are not yet as well understood, however. Auckland, the country's largest city, sits on a volcanic field that is dormant rather than extinct. The science of eruption prediction is in its infancy, let alone the implementation and codification of any possible mitigation through infrastructure design. Severe flooding, exacerbated by changing land use in river catchments and by climate change, remains a regular event, and water shortages and fire are also increasing in frequency and severity.

When the world was hit by the Covid-19 pandemic in 2020 New Zealand's isolation, a world-leading public health response and the rapid development and deployment of vaccines prevented its hospitals from being as overwhelmed as those in many other countries. There was a rapid response by facility managers and engineers to compartmentalise spaces and improve isolation and filtering in air-conditioning systems. A detailed evaluation of these measures has still to be carried out, but some researchers, such as Michael Murphy, have suggested that designing more open spaces with greater natural ventilation might be just as effective.[1]

Before the pandemic, the Jacinda Ardern-led Labour government had implemented a review of the public healthcare system. In part this was intended to address the inequities in access to public healthcare around the country, often referred to as the 'post-code lottery', where people in larger cities were considered to have better access to care than those in smaller, more remote areas. As a result, Health New Zealand/Te Whatu Ora was formed in 2022 to take over the provision of all public healthcare services and the 20 district health boards were disestablished. The government had already moved to bring greater levels of specialist care into provincial areas, such as building radiotherapy facilities in Northland, Taranaki and Hawke's Bay.

Dunedin's proposed new hospital, approved in 2015, has had a long gestation period, including a relocation to the site of the former Cadbury chocolate factory. Construction commenced in 2022, however cost pressures have led to modifications by the Warren and Mahoney-led design team, with a reduction in beds, operating theatres and other services. The outpatients building is now expected to open in 2026, and the rest of the facility by 2029. The redevelopment of Whangārei and Nelson hospitals has also recently been approved.

Such facilities cannot, however, operate without sufficient suitably qualified staff, and the pandemic strained an already overstretched healthcare workforce. General practitioners, especially, are leaving the profession and not being replaced in adequate numbers, leading to reduced access to primary care services. New Zealand is not training enough clinicians and is increasingly reliant on skilled immigrants, with areas such as general practice and nursing not being seen as desirable professions by many young New Zealanders.

++

As in most developing countries, the nation's population overall is ageing, resulting in an increase in demand for elderly care. This is reflected in a growing need for appropriate accommodation with adequate support, and in pressure on the public healthcare system, with nine out of 10 hospital beds expected to be filled by someone 65 years or older by 2043.[2] Advances in medical technology also create their own demands.

Affordability is a growing problem, both for the country as a whole and, with growing levels of economic deprivation, for many of its citizens. Providing greater levels of care in regional areas increases accessibility for those living there, but may come at a greater cost than clustering services in a few major centres. Conversely, increasing urbanisation is stretching the capacity of hospitals in larger cities, and to an extent decentralisation may help to alleviate this while providing greater resilience should a major event affect any one facility.

Funding models continue to evolve, with an increasing reliance on private healthcare providers and health insurance to lighten the load for the public health system. The challenge will be to ensure that existing inequities are not exacerbated further by the development of a two-tier system between public and private healthcare.

The restrictions associated with the pandemic, such as the requirement to work from home where possible, led to the rapid adoption of new technology and fresh approaches by designers. Collaboration between team members, including consultation with clinical users, continued remotely. Clinicians, of course, remained on the front line and were even less able to take time away from their primary duties to participate. This highlights the fact that medicine, despite being one of the most highly skilled professions, also remains the most hands-on.

At the same time, a greater emphasis on standardisation has raised questions about the amount of consultation required between clinicians and designers. For example, should a ward bedroom or operating theatre in Dunedin be any different to one in Auckland, or even Australia? Health New Zealand/Te Whatu Ora is placing a greater emphasis on efficiency and value in its infrastructure investments, while attempting to address the shortfall in standard of existing facilities and ensuring that New Zealand's specific cultural and environmental issues are considered. Because the cost of delivering projects is soaring, and the value delivered by many is being questioned, alternative procurement models are being considered such as design–build or public–private partnerships. These have the potential to distance the designers from the clinicians and communities they are designing for.

Changes in medical technology and models of care will also continue to result in the need to modify hospital buildings, and the challenge for designers is to make them as adaptable as possible without detracting from their initial function and affordability. Retrofitting existing buildings often designed for one specific function is likely to be a particular challenge in the future as their replacement becomes increasingly unaffordable.

Advances in digital technology such as building information modelling and management are enhancing communications between design team members, clients and the wider public. The ability to improve the coordination of design and documentation, and more accurately determine quantities, should lead to greater productivity, particularly as it is adopted by contractors during construction and increasing off-site manufacturing. Tele-health allows for clinicians to diagnose and treat remotely and could affect the type and size of health buildings of the future. Designers are beginning to use artificial intelligence to explore options and improve access to information, although, as in society generally, the benefits and risks it brings are still being debated.

Māori and Pasifika peoples have a proportionately higher birth rate than the general

population. This, along with a widening range of ethnicities of immigrants, is leading to greater cultural diversity. Through a range of social and economic issues, Māori and Pasifika also tend to have poorer outcomes in terms of physical and mental health. There is a significant challenge, and opportunity, in creating facilities which reflect these cultures and most appropriately meet their needs. New Zealand is both multicultural and bicultural; the design of health buildings must address the commitments made to Māori, as tangata whenua, through the Treaty of Waitangi.

++

Overarching all these issues is the growing environmental crisis, including, but not limited to, the human-induced climate change emergency. Hospitals are large users of energy and producers of waste and more thought must be given to reducing their environmental impact. Infection control has been improved by single-use items for personal protective equipment, medical devices and curtains, but these consume large amounts of resource to produce, and then make up significant quantities of landfill.

Can they be adequately cleaned onsite and reused? How can water be most effectively used and recycled? Can the increased use of natural lighting and ventilation improve patient outcomes and comfort while also reducing energy demand? Although there have been significant recent movements to electrify hospitals and reduce the use of fossil fuels, can they produce more of their own energy by using photovoltaic solar panels or other forms of renewable energy, which could also help to improve their resilience?

These are only some of the challenges facing future generations of health designers, and there will be many more, some not yet dreamt of. Attempting to predict the future is futile, but health design will almost certainly remain one of the most technically demanding areas for architects and building engineers, and one of the most rewarding, as designers work with clinicians and others to create environments that best serve people in their hours of greatest need.

↑
The new Dunedin Hospital project, featuring the inpatient site in the foreground and the outpatient building in the background.

Selected biographies

These biographies are listed in the order of appearance in the book.

Frederick Thatcher
(1814–1890)
Thatcher was born in Hastings and articled to a London architect before setting up his own practice in 1836. After meeting New Zealand's first Anglican bishop, George Augustus Selwyn, in 1841, and following the deaths of his wife and infant child, Thatcher emigrated to New Zealand in 1843 to start a new life as a farmer in Taranaki. After local Māori did not recognise the legitimacy of the land sale, he resumed his architectural practice. His first building in New Plymouth was a small chapel at Te Henui in 1845. Selwyn commissioned him to design St Mary's Church the following year. After Governor Robert FitzRoy made him superintendent of public works for the colony, in 1845 Thatcher moved to Auckland, where the terms of his appointment allowed him to also maintain his own architectural practice. He was appointed Governor George Grey's private secretary in 1865 and designed extensions to Government House in Wellington, a vice-regal retreat at Lowry Bay, and Mansion House, Grey's home on Kawau Island. In 1868 Thatcher left New Zealand for Britain, where he became secretary to Selwyn, who had been appointed Bishop of Lichfield.[1]

Reader Gillson Wood
(1821–1895)
Wood trained in England, arrived in New Zealand in 1844, and was the ninth, and final, superintendent of public works for the colony, from 1849 to 1852.[2]

Arthur Guyon Purchas
(1821–1906)
Purchas was born in St Arvans, Monmouthshire, gained his medical qualifications at Guy's Hospital in London, and worked as a surgeon at the Southern and Toxteth Hospital in Liverpool. In 1844, he made a brief visit to New Zealand to meet Selwyn, and returned two year later to serve with the Church Missionary Society. As well as his medical career, he was ordained as a priest and also designed several churches. He performed the first caesarean operation in New Zealand, and was a prolific inventor, developing some of his own surgical instruments, as well as devices such as a machine for reading Braille.[3]

Thomas Henry Fitzgerald
(1824–1888)
Fitzgerald, the brother of Colonial Surgeon Dr John Patrick Fitzgerald (1815–1897), arrived in New Zealand in 1842 and was employed as assistant surveyor with the New Zealand Company before becoming a government surveyor in Wellington in 1844. Fitzgerald became surveyor and superintendent of public works and civil roads in 1847. In 1853 he moved to Hawke's Bay, where he established a flour mill, then entered politics. Declared bankrupt in 1862, he moved to Australia.[4]

John Henry Cridland
(1821–1867)
Cridland was a surveyor and draughtsman who arrived in New Zealand as part of the British Army in the early years of the New Zealand Wars. . Probably self-taught, he was overseer of public works from 1846 to 1847, before joining the staff of the Royal Engineers as a civilian clerk of works.[5]

Edward Roberts ↑
(Dates unknown)
Roberts, who had a wide range of engineering, surveying and architectural experience, arrived in New Zealand about 1847 as a civilian attached to the Royal Engineers. Although one 1851 report described him as 'the Government Architect', it is generally understood that he was seconded to the New Zealand government as colonial engineer, or possibly only provincial engineer for Wellington, in that year. He is thought to have designed at least nine buildings in Wellington, including the 1850 Athenaeum in Lambton Quay, where he later lectured, as well as the country's first permanent lighthouse at Pencarrow. By 1858 he had returned to London.[6]

Benjamin Woolfield Mountfort
(1825–1898)
Born in Birmingham, Mountfort studied architecture in London under George Gilbert Scott and Richard Cromwell Carpenter. Under them, he became highly influenced by the Gothic Revival movement. He emigrated to Christchurch in 1850. His first building there, Holy Trinity Church in Lyttelton (1852), proved unsafe in high winds and was demolished within five years. His reputation and confidence dented, he established a stationery shop and became a portrait photographer. In 1857 he returned to architecture, forming a practice with his brother-in-law Isaac Luck (1817–1881), and that year the pair were appointed architects to the provincial government. They designed the wooden Gothic Provincial Council buildings and the Provincial Council Chamber. After Luck left the practice, Mountfort was joined by Maxwell Bury in 1864. When Bury left for London in 1866 Mountfort continued to practise on his own. His other buildings in Christchurch include the original buildings for Canterbury College (1877), now part of the Arts Centre, and Canterbury Museum (1882). In 1873 Mountfort was appointed clerk of works for George Gilbert Scott's Christ Church Cathedral, which was completed in 1904. Mountfort's son, Cyril Julian Mountfort (1852–1920), later trained under him, eventually becoming his partner, and was president of the NZIA from 1909 to 1910.[7]

William Williamson
(Dates unknown)
Williamson was appointed assistant provincial engineer to Canterbury in 1861. He moved to Timaru in 1868, where he was engineer to the Levels Road Board and also practised as an architect.[8]

James Rochfort
(1830–1924)
Rochfort arrived in New Zealand in 1852 with his brother John. Less is known of James than John, who was trained by renowned Victorian engineer Isambard Kingdom Brunel, discovered gold in the Buller and coal in the Denniston area while surveying on the West Coast and later laid out the route for the Remutaka railway line.[9]

John Turnbull Thompson
(1821–1884)
Born in Northumberland and educated at Edinburgh University and Peter Nicholson's

School of Engineering at Newcastle-on-Tyne, in 1838 Thompson emigrated to the Malay States, where he was superintendent of roads and public works, and then to New Zealand in 1856. He planned the town of Invercargill and went on to be chief surveyor of the Otago Province until 1873 and surveyor-general of New Zealand from 1876 to 1879.[10]

William Mason ↑
(1810–1897)
Mason was born in Ipswich and practised architecture there, as had his father and grandfather. In 1838 he emigrated to New South Wales, where he worked for the colonial architect, then joined Governor Hobson's staff and came to New Zealand in 1840 – the first architect to live and work in this country. Mason hoped to be Hobson's colonial architect, but was disappointed to be made acting superintendent of works. At both Okiato and Auckland he was responsible for houses, schools, a courthouse and a gaol, many of them hurriedly built and temporary. Architectural work was sporadic and in 1841 he resigned to become an auctioneer and owner of farms in the Auckland area. He also helped establish Auckland's first newspaper, the *New Zealand Herald and Auckland Gazette*. Early Auckland buildings by Mason include the first Government House and St Paul's Church (1844). In 1854 he became Auckland's provincial architect and designed the new Government House there in 1856. Also active in farming and politics, he became a Member of the House of Representatives (MHR) in 1861 and moved to Dunedin in 1862. That year he formed a brief partnership with David Ross, who had moved from Melbourne in 1862. After the partnership dissolved in 1863, Mason joined forces with William Henry Clayton and together they designed the Post Office (later Exchange Building) and the Otago Provincial Council Chambers in Dunedin, before their partnership ended in 1867. Mason was elected Dunedin's first mayor in 1865. He formed a practice with Nathaniel Wales in 1871 but retired in 1874 and moved to Queenstown.[11]

David Ross
(1828–1908)
Ross was born in Aberdeenshire, from where he emigrated to Melbourne in 1853, and then to Dunedin in 1862. He formed a brief partnership with William Mason, before practising on his own, designing the original portion of the Otago Museum. On some projects he collaborated with his nephew Frederick Burwell. He relocated to Auckland in 1883, Sydney in 1886, Perth in 1895 and Johannesburg in 1903, before returning to Auckland in 1906.[12]

William Henry Clayton
(1823–1877)
The first and only colonial architect, Clayton was born in Tasmania. In 1840 his family returned to England, where he was articled to train as an architect, engineer and surveyor; he also trained in Brussels. After returning to Tasmania in 1848, he became government surveyor there in 1852. In 1863 he settled with his family in Otago, where he set up as an architect, surveyor and civil engineer, joining William Mason in partnership in 1864. He left the practice in 1867 and was commissioned to design the new Government House (1868) in Wellington. Clayton became colonial architect in 1869. He died in 1877.[13]

Nathaniel Young Armstrong Wales
(1832–1903)
Born in Northumberland, Wales was educated in Jedburgh, Scotland, and emigrated to Victoria in 1854 before moving to Dunedin in 1861. He had no formal architectural training – not uncommon for designers of the time – and was originally employed by Mason as a clerk of works on the Bank of New Zealand project in 1863. Impressed by his practical building knowledge, Mason invited him to become a partner, and the firm was renamed Mason & Wales. Like Mason, Wales became an MHR and then mayor of Dunedin in 1895. Wales was followed in the practice by his son Patrick Young Wales (1864–1939), grandson Nathaniel Young Armstrong Wales (1896–1980), who served in France in the First World War, and in 1956 by his great-grandson N. Y. A. Wales (1927–2011). P. Y. Wales was president of the NZIA from 1912 to 1913, and the second N. Y. A. Wales from 1955 to 1956.[14]

Angus Kerr
(?–1898)
Kerr emigrated from Scotland to New South Wales in 1849. In 1862 he moved to Invercargill, where he designed many of the town's earliest public buildings.[15]

Christian Julius Toxward
(1831–1891)
Toxward was born in Copenhagen, where he attended the Kunstakademiet (Fine Arts Academy), leaving in 1851 without attaining a formal qualification. He travelled through much of Europe before emigrating to Australia, where he did draughting work while also prospecting in Victoria. Toxward moved to New Zealand in 1862, working as a surveyor in Dunedin and becoming the first clerk of works in Southland, before relocating to Wellington to establish his own practice in 1865. He was a very versatile architect, who designed a wide range of building types in a variety of styles. As well as the new Wellington Hospital building, he designed the nearby Mount View Asylum (1873). He was also a company director, justice of the peace and the Danish consul. In a relatively short but productive career, he designed more than 240 buildings, including the now-demolished original Government Life Insurance building in Wellington, and extended Thatcher's Old St Paul's. The shock of his wife Jane's death in 1891, a heart condition and a long-term injury probably contributed to his own death a month after hers. He was very popular figure, and his funeral brought Wellington to a standstill.[16]

Pierre Finch Martineau Burrows
(1842–1920)
Burrows arrived in New Zealand from England in 1865 and joined the Public Works Department as an assistant draughtsman in 1874. By the time he was laid off a decade later, Burrows had designed the Supreme Court (1881) and Mount Cook Gaol (1884) in Wellington, and Mount Eden Prison (1882) in Auckland. He was re-employed by the government until 1895 as a temporary draughtsman in Hunterville, the southern office for work on the North Island Main Trunk Railway. He retired in 1908.[17]

Charles Edward Beatson
(1846–1927)
Beatson was the son of prominent Nelson architect William Beatson, under whom he trained. He took over the practice on his father's death in 1870, then in 1873 moved to Wellington to work for the Public Works Department. When he was laid off in 1887 he set up in private practice, before taking up farming in Motueka in 1889. His work at Oakley Hospital in Auckland was either designed at the end of his time in public service, or after he left it.[18]

John Campbell
(1857–1942)
Although Campbell was the first designated Government Architect, it is not clear when he was appointed. His obituary in the *New Zealand Herald* gave the date as 1897, and tenders called under his name with this title appeared from 1903, but other sources state that this was not his official designation until 1909. Born in Glasgow, Campbell attended the Glasgow School of Art and the Haldane Academy before training under architect John Gordon. After arriving in Dunedin in 1882, he worked for Mason & Wales before joining the Public Works Department in the city in 1883. He survived the cost-cutting of the 1880s and in 1888 was transferred to Wellington, where he became an architectural draughtsman and eventually draughtsman-in-charge at the Public Buildings office in 1889. Campbell won the 1911 open competition for Parliament Buildings (1922) with one of his assistants, Claude Paton (1881–1953), who joined the department in 1906 and is considered to have been the primary designer of the winning entry. The many buildings designed by Campbell include the Dunedin Law Courts (1902) and the Public Trust Office in Wellington (1909). Campbell became a fellow of the Royal Institute of British Architects (RIBA), joined the NZIA in 1905 and was Government Architect until his retirement in 1922. He originally favoured the Queen Anne style, as it suited the more economic brick construction, as at Porirua Lunatic Asylum from 1891 on. But as budgets increased for more prestigious government buildings, he gradually moved to Edwardian or Imperial Baroque.[19]

James Wrigley
(1837/8–1882)
Born in Huddersfield and trained in York, Wrigley emigrated to New Zealand and set up in practice in Auckland in 1856. He designed several early churches, including St Andrew's Presbyterian in Howick in 1872, and substantial additions to the Northern Club in 1870.[20]

Philip Herapath
(1823–1892)
Herapath, who was born in Devonshire, the son of a builder, emigrated to New Zealand in 1857 and settled in Auckland, where he worked as a carpenter before establishing himself as an architect, civil engineer and surveyor. He became a fellow of the RIBA in 1886. In Auckland he designed, inter alia, St Mark's Anglican Church in Remuera (1860–83) and the Pitt Street Wesleyan Church (1865). Around 1883 he was joined by his son, Samuel March Herapath, in the firm Herapath & Son.[21]

Robert Wladislas de Montalk
(1871–1941)
De Montalk was an Auckland architect who moved to Wellington around 1918. He was also an inventor, holding several patents including one for fireproof floors and another for an earthquake-resistant foundation system.[22]

Thomas Cane
(1830–1905)
Cane succeeded Benjamin Mountfort as the provincial architect for Canterbury. He is best known as the designer of the Lyttelton Timeball Station (1876).[23]

Robert Arthur Lawson
(1833–1902)
Lawson was born in Fifeshire, trained in Edinburgh under James Gillespie Graham, and started his own practice in Perth. In 1854 he emigrated to Australia, where he took up goldmining and journalism before returning to architecture in Melbourne. After winning the design competition for First Church in Dunedin (1873), he moved there in 1862. He was also responsible for, among other buildings, Larnach's Castle (1875) and the Seacliff Asylum.[24]

Thomas Henry White
(1843–1923)
Born in Birmingham, White came to the Otago goldfields in 1860. He returned to England, where he set up as an architect before coming back to New Zealand in 1873. He settled in Taupiri and maintained offices in Auckland and Hamilton.[25]

William Peter Finneran
(c.1837–1911)
Around 1878 Finneran established a practice in Gisborne, where he designed the 1898 Poverty Bay Club.[26]

Richard Wakelin
(1816–1881)
Wakelin became editor of the *Wellington Independent* in 1853. In the late 1850s he moved to Greytown, where he set up the *Wairarapa Journal* (later *Standard*) in 1861.[27]

George Fannin
(1841–1909)
Born in Dublin, Fannin arrived in New Zealand in the early 1860s. After working as a draughtsman in the Crown Lands Office, he established himself as an architect in Masterton some time around 1880. For a time he had offices in both Masterton and Wellington, where he made minor alterations to Thatcher's Old St Paul's, before returning to work at the Lands Office in Invercargill in 1897.[28]

William Douslin
(Dates unknown)
Douslin came to New Zealand from Tasmania. He settled in Havelock and later relocated to Blenheim, where he was mayor in 1887. He later moved to South Africa.[29]

John Blackett
(1818–1893)
Born in Newcastle-on-Tyne, Blackett emigrated in 1859, settling first in Taranaki before moving later that year to Nelson when he was appointed provincial engineer. He moved to Wellington in 1870, joining the Public Works Department, and was chief engineer for New Zealand from 1884 to 1889.[30]

James (Stanley) Bruce
(1841–1902)
A pupil of Frederick Barry and Charles Shoppee in London, Bruce emigrated to New Zealand in 1869. He established a practice as an architect and engineer in Christchurch before relocating to Ashburton and eventually to Palmerston North.[31]

Thomas Roberts
(Dates unknown)
Roberts emigrated to Canterbury in 1870, where he became engineer to the Timaru and Gladstone Board of Works in 1870, before setting up his own practice. He designed several of the early bluestone buildings in the centre of Timaru, before moving to Nelson in 1901.[32]

Thomas Glass
(1837–1898)
Born in Scotland, Glass emigrated to New Zealand in 1860. He designed many of the early buildings in Ōamaru, including the Royal Hotel and the Phoenix Flour Mill.[33]

Thomas Forrester
(1838–1907)
John Lemon
(1828–1890)
William (Ivan) Cunninghame Steenson
(1889–1967)
Forrester & Lemon was established in Ōamaru in 1872 by Thomas Forrester and John Lemon, and was responsible for many of the town's renowned white stone buildings, such as St Paul's Church (1876) and Waitaki Boys' High School (1883). John Meggett Forrester (1865–1965), only son of Thomas, took over Lemon's share of the practice in 1890, and of his father's on his death. William (Ivan) Cunninghame Steenson joined the firm in 1904, became a partner in 1921, and took over the firm from Forrester on the latter's retirement in 1931. Ivan was later joined by his son Harry Kingsley Steenson (1930–2016), who continued the practice until 1993.[34]

Frederick William Burwell
(1846–1915)
After emigrating around 1869 from Scotland, where he had been articled to architect James Matthews, in 1873 Burwell established a practice in Queenstown, where he designed Eichardt's Hotel, the courthouse and library and the council chambers. In 1874 he moved to Invercargill, where he designed many of the buildings on the Crescent. Work dried up during the Long Depression and in 1887 Burwell moved to Australia, where he formed a partnership with his uncle, David Ross. By 1897 Burwell was practising on his own in Fremantle; many of the town's heritage buildings are his work.[35]

Joshua Charlesworth
(1860–1925)
Born in Dewsbury, Yorkshire, Charlesworth emigrated to New Zealand in 1879 and settled in Timaru. He then moved to Auckland, where he won several architectural competitions, including for the Home for the Aged Needy in Wellington in 1887 and the Wellington Town Hall in 1900.[36]

William Charles Chatfield
(1851–1930)
Chatfield was born in Sussex and was sent to New Zealand for his health in 1867. He joined the Public Works Department before establishing his own practice in 1876.[37]

John Lowe Shaw
(c.1821–1906)
Born in Dublin, Shaw emigrated to Victoria in 1850 and then to Dunedin in 1876.[38]

Walter Philip Finch
(1890–1972)
Finch designed the buildings for Te Aute College around 1927 before entering a partnership with Herbert Westerholm in 1932. Their firm designed several buildings in Napier after the 1931 earthquake, including the State Cinema.[39]

Richard Bird
(1834–1922)
Born in Exeter, Bird trained as a carpenter and joiner before emigrating to New Zealand in 1874. He established an architectural practice in Ashburton, and was the town's mayor in 1891–92.[40]

Charles H. Roberts
(1869–1942)
Roberts trained as an architect in Dunedin before establishing a practice in Invercargill in 1895.[41]

Horace Hammond
(1862–1923)
Hammond emigrated with his family in 1871. He trained in engineering under his father, and became the engineer to Hobson County in 1889, before entering private practice in 1915. His son, Reginald Hammond, gained renown for planning many of the early state housing developments such as Orakei in Auckland and Savage Crescent in Palmerston North.[42]

Edward Bartley ↗
(1839–1919)
Bartley was born in Jersey, where both he and his elder brother Robert were apprenticed to their father, a master builder, before emigrating in 1854 to New Zealand, where they were soon employed in Auckland. By 1857 Bartley was working on the construction of Mount Eden Gaol, which was then being built under the supervision of Reader Wood. He went into partnership with Wood, taking on such contracts as the construction of the

Supreme Court. In 1870 he set up his own office, but for some time also continued to do building work. Bartley was a founding member of the Auckland Society of Artists and of the Auckland Technical School, which became the Auckland University of Technology. He maintained a lifelong interest in science and gave lectures on a range of topics, including the use of the microscope His other Auckland buildings include St John's Church in Ponsonby (1881), later demolished, and the King's (later Mercury) Theatre (1910). His three sons trained under him and continued the firm as Bartley & Son, later Bartley Son & Draffin.[43]

William Henry Skinner
(1838–1915)
Welsh-born Skinner trained at Imperial College, London, before emigrating to New Zealand in 1859. He served in the Royal Rifle Volunteers during the New Zealand Wars, before setting up as an architect in 1880. Among his buildings is St Paul's Church on Symonds Street, Auckland.[44]

Edward Mahoney
(1824–1895)
Thomas Mahoney
(1854–1923)
Edward Mahoney emigrated from Cork to Adelaide in 1853, before moving to Auckland in 1855 to establish himself as a builder and timber merchant. In 1865 he set up an architectural practice, designing, among other buildings, St John the Baptist, Parnell (1861) and St Patrick's Cathedral (completed 1901). In 1867 he followed the gold rush to Thames, where he designed several buildings before returning to

Auckland in 1870. His sons Thomas and Robert (1862–1895) joined him in 1876 to form Edward Mahoney & Sons. Thomas, who was born on the voyage from Adelaide to Auckland, studied overseas from 1883 to 1885 and was president of the NZIA from 1908 to 1909. Other Auckland buildings by the firm include the Pah homestead (1887) and the Customhouse (1888).[45]

Richard Septimus Rounthwaite

(1856–1932)
Yorkshire-born Rounthwaite attended Durham University and emigrated to New Zealand in 1899. He was appointed Wellington's city engineer before setting up in private practice as an engineer, architect and quantity surveyor in 1904.[46]

Robert Lamb

(1834–1895)
Lamb had been a successful architect, engineer and surveyor in Darlington before emigrating to New Zealand in 1879. He settled in Napier, and established his own practice. His best-known work is the group of Victorian villas at 185–205 Marine Parade, generally referred to as 'The Six Sisters', which were completed after his death. He acted as municipal engineer to the Napier Borough Council and architect to the Hawke's Bay Education Board. On his death, his practice was purchased by Charles Tilleard Natusch and survived into the next century.[47]

Alfred Atkins ↓

(1850–1919)
Born in Birmingham, where he trained in architecture and engineering at the School of Science and Art, Atkins became an assistant to architect John Millward before emigrating to New Zealand in 1875. He worked first as an engineer and surveyor on the Whanganui–Waitara railway, later becoming the Waitōtara county engineer, before being appointed engineer to the Wanganui Borough Council. Atkins was president of the NZIA from 1911 to 1912, when it was seeking statutory recognition, and was chairman of its legislative committee when the NZIA Act was passed by Parliament in 1913. The institute's initial premier award was named in his honour.[48]

Frederick de Jersey Clere ↑

(1856–1952)
Clere was born in Lancashire, where his father was a vicar, and trained as an architect under ecclesiological architect Edmund Scott of Brighton. In 1877 the family emigrated to New Zealand, where he worked with the Public Buildings Department and then set up a practice in Feilding in 1878, before moving to Whanganui to join Atkins. After establishing his own practice in Wellington in 1888, Clere made several alterations to Thatcher's Old St Paul's. He was made a fellow of the RIBA in 1885 and entered several partnerships, including Clere & Richmond from 1891 to 1895 with Edward Thomas Richmond (1867–1896), and Clere, Fitzgerald & Richmond from 1895 to 1900, with architect and engineer Gerald Fitzgerald (1857–1937), who had just retired from the Public Works Department. In 1900 Clere was joined in partnership by his Wellington-born chief draughtsman John Sydney Swan. Despite the break-up of their practice in 1902, Clere and Swan worked together on Wellington's St Gerard's Church (1908) and Monastery (1932). In 1905 Clere was joined by his son Edmund (Herbert) de Jersey Clere (1884–1967). In 1911 he and Herbert formed F. de J. Clere & Son and practised together on and off until the elder Clere's death in 1952. In 1913 Frederick formed Clere & Busby with William Baldwin Busby (1891–1917), who had been articled to him in 1909. Busby enlisted in 1914 and was killed in Mesopotamia in 1917. During his absence, Clere employed Florence Field (1883–1967) as an architectural draughtswoman for at least two years from 1915. Clere was joined by Sydney-born and trained Llewellyn Williams (1884–1967) in 1919, forming Clere & Williams. After spending time in London from 1908 to 1913, Williams had returned to Australia before coming to Wellington in 1916. After Williams' departure in 1923, Clere reformed the partnership with his son as Clere & Clere and the practice remained in business until 1962. During this period Clere designed St Mary of the Angels in Wellington (1922), pioneering the use of ferro-concrete in New Zealand. Henry Alfred Hill (1894–1972) joined Clere & Clere as a junior partner in 1937; they practised as Clere, Clere & Hill until 1939.[49]

John Sydney Swan

(1874–1936)
Swan joined Frederick de Jersey Clere's practice as an articled clerk in 1888, aged only 14, and rose to become chief draughtsman in 1895, eventually entering into a partnership with Clere. In Wellington he was known for the designs of Erskine College (since demolished), St Gerard's monastery, the Clarendon Hotel and the head office of the National Bank (since demolished). He was a director of the Kelburn and Karori Tramway Co., which led to the firm's commission to make major changes to the cable car Winding House in 1933. His own house in Thorndon, 'The Moorings', was remarkable for its nautical motifs. Swan served for a time as a commodore of the Royal Port Nicholson Yacht Club.[50]

Roger Francis Bacon

(1868–1959)
Bacon was born in Ealing and emigrated to New Zealand around 1901. He joined Alfred Atkins in partnership in 1907 but retired for health reasons in 1918 and moved to Blenheim.[51]

Lucy Adelaide Greenish, later Symes

(1888–1976)
Greenish arrived in New Zealand with her

family from Brisbane in 1908 and joined Atkins & Bacon the following year. Greenish left the firm in 1915 and, because work was hard to find in the war years, became a governess at Walter Peak Station near Queenstown. By the early 1920s she was working with Mandeno & Fraser in Dunedin. In 1926 Greenish was the first woman in New Zealand to set up in a sole architectural practice, in Lower Hutt, but this seems to have ceased after her marriage in 1945.[52]

Cyril Hawthorn Mitchell
(1891–1949)
Allan Hawthorn Mitchell
(1905–1973)
Cyril Mitchell began his architectural career with Atkins & Bacon in 1909, before travelling to London for further experience and rejoining the firm in 1918, about the time Bacon retired. Mitchell was made a partner in 1919, shortly before Atkins died, leaving him in sole charge of what then became Atkins & Mitchell, a name that was retained long after Atkins' death. His brother Allan joined the firm straight from school in 1922 and became a partner when he returned in 1932 from training in Britain. Atkins & Mitchell designed several significant buildings, including the T&G Building (1936) in Napier and Wellington's Waterloo Hotel (1936). In 1937 Atkins & Mitchell was renamed Mitchell & Mitchell and the firm gained a reputation for bank design. One of the firm's last commissions was the Reserve Bank Building in Wellington (1972), designed in association with Calder Fowler Styles & Turner. After Allan Mitchell's death, employees Frederick E. Kerswill, who had joined in 1939, and Terry Gooch bought the firm. Gooch was joined in 1988 by Rob Mitchell and Rod Macdiarmid, forming Gooch Mitchell Macdiarmid Ltd, which ceased operation in 1994.[53]

Thomas Harvey James
(1867–1947)
Born in Greymouth, James was articled to Frederick de Jersey Clere in 1888 and set up his own practice in Palmerston North in 1889, before moving to Feilding in 1893. In 1897 he returned to Whanganui, where he became the first New Zealand-trained architect to practise there. James succeeded Arthur Atkins as architect to the Wanganui Education Board from 1902 to 1909, and from 1912 to around 1918 he was in partnership with W. T. Higgins. By the 1930s he was working only part-time as an architect.[54]

Ernest Larcomb
(1855–1936)
Southampton-born Larcomb learned draughting while working at the War Office, before emigrating to New Zealand in 1874. He was employed by the Public Works Department, but when he was made redundant in 1876 he joined the Wellington City Council. He set up his own practice in 1881 and moved to Palmerston North, where he designed many of the town's early buildings. Larcomb also designed water reticulation schemes for Palmerston North and Wellington, and wharves and breakwaters at Wellington, Nelson and Timaru. He patented several new inventions, including a pistonless turbine motor and stormproof skylights. Larcomb relocated to Wellington in 1908 but returned to Palmerston North in 1918. He died in Christchurch.[55]

Francis Penty ↑
(1841–1919)
Penty, who was born in Yorkshire and studied under J. E. Oates, worked in Liverpool and Manchester before joining the Royal Engineers and then working on the London and North Eastern Railway. He emigrated to New Zealand in 1887 and set up practice in Wellington, where he designed the Convalescent Home in Oriental Bay. He established the partnership of Penty & Forde with Leonard Joseph Forde in 1893, with Penty working in Wellington and Forde in Masterton. Penty practised alone again when Forde left for Canada in 1898.[56] Penty took on two employees as partners, Charles Alexander Lawrence (1872–1933) and Andrew Blayney Hamilton (1891–1972), who continued the practice after Penty's death, before joining in practice with John Sydney Swan and his younger brother Francis Herbert Swan. Hamilton left after two years but Lawrence remained a partner in Swan, Lawrence & Swan until his own death. John Swan left the practice in 1934, and the following year joined William Edward Lavelle (1905–1974), who had started his own practice in 1931 after studying in New York and working for J. M. (Joseph McClatchie) Dawson & King. Swan & Lavelle designed the kitchen, dining hall and school buildings (1941) at the Otaki Children's Health Camp.[57]

Edward McCallum Blake
(1865–1929)
Blake was born in Madras, India, the son of a missionary; the family emigrated to New Zealand in 1869. Following his education in Dunedin and Christchurch, Blake was articled to Thomas Stoddart Lambert in Christchurch from 1880 to 1885. After establishing a practice in Ashburton, seemingly with little success, he spent time in Australia, before returning to New Zealand in 1894. He practised for a time in Timaru, then worked with the Public Works Department in Wellington from 1897 to 1901. Blake and Francis Penty formed their practice in 1903 to enter the design competition, which they won, for what is now known as the Hunter Building at Victoria College (now University) in Wellington. Blake established his own practice in 1909 and became architect to the Wellington Hospital Board before rejoining the Public Works Department in 1913.

Sir Arthur Penrose Seymour
(1832–1923)
Born in England, Seymour emigrated to New Zealand in 1857. He settled in Marlborough, where he was active in local politics, twice serving as the province's superintendent.[58]

Joseph Clarkson Maddison
(1850–1923)
Maddison was born in London and emigrated to Canterbury in 1872. He was later architect of the Government Departmental Buildings (1911) in Cathedral Square.[59]

Frederick Strouts
(1834–1919)
Strouts was born in Kent, studied at Wye College in Canterbury and trained under several architects before emigrating to New Zealand in 1859. He initially set up as an importer, ironmonger, land agent, surveyor and architect, but in 1868 shortage of work sent

him back to England, where he was elected an associate of the RIBA. After returning to New Zealand, Strouts established his own practice in Christchurch and took over the Canterbury Club commission from W. B. Armson when he became ill in 1873. In 1883 Strouts took on Robert Anderson Ballantyne (1834–1919) as an articled pupil. Once qualified, Ballantyne worked for two years in Melbourne before becoming Strout's junior partner in 1893. The pair were responsible for both the Strange's and Ballantyne's department stores as well as the Jubilee clock tower in High Street (1897), later relocated to Victoria Street. The partnership ceased in 1899 and Strouts retired in 1905. Ballantyne continued to practise with William Clarkson (1863–1917).[60]

John Whitelaw
(1837–1904)
Lanarkshire-born Whitelaw arrived in Christchurch from Glasgow in 1863. He originally worked as a carpenter and became a master builder. He was appointed chief clerk of works in the Canterbury Provincial Government, then took a similar position at the Public Works Department when the provinces were abolished. He retired from the public service in 1878 and set up as an architect, often acting as a valuer and arbitrator.[61]

Herbert Hall
(1880–1939)
Hall was a Timaru-based architect who designed many public buildings throughout South Canterbury, as well as the 1929 Chateau Tongariro.[62]

Cuthbert John Brodrick
(1867–1946)
Brodrick was articled to Frederick Burwell in 1884 and travelled with him to Melbourne to complete his training, returning to New Zealand in 1891. Brodrick entered a partnership in Invercargill with his pupil Thomas Royds (c.1884–1936) and was president of the NZIA from 1910 to 1911.[63]

Arthur Louis Salmond
(1906–1994)
James Louis Salmond of Dunedin was articled to Robert Lawson, established his own practice in 1891, and entered into a partnership with Lawson on the latter's return to Dunedin in 1900. He was joined by his son Arthur Louis Salmond in 1933 to form Salmond and Salmond Architects.[64]

Arthur Henry White
(c.1864–1920)
Born in Auckland, White is understood to have been articled to architect Edmund Bell, joining him in partnership from 1890 to 1893 before setting up his own practice. He designed many houses and buildings in Auckland, particularly in the Mount Albert area.[65]

William Gray Young
(1885–1962)
Ōamaru-born Young was articled to Crichton & McKay in 1901, before joining the Public Works Department. He became a celebrated Wellington architect, designing its railway station (1936) and the station in Christchurch (1960), as well as many of the buildings at Victoria University. He was joined in partnership by his younger brother John Barclay (Jack) Young (1887–1967) in 1923, and then by Melbourne-born Hubert Conrad Morton (c.1896–1965).[66] Ian Calder joined Gray Young's firm in 1951, and future Wellington mayor Michael (later Sir Michael) Fowler (1929–2022), in 1959. The practice became Gray Young Morton & Calder, then Gray Young Morton Calder & Fowler, Calder Fowler & Styles and eventually Calder Fowler Styles & Turner. This last iteration of the firm was dissolved in 1997. The senior partners seem to have encouraged innovation: while working there Roger Walker designed the unique 1972 Wellington Club building (demolished 1986).[67]

John Wordsworth Standish
(1910–1964)
Standish joined Crichton, McKay & Haughton in 1937 and rejoined them after service in the war. He left in 1949 to start his own firm and became a well-known Wellington architect. He drowned in October 1964.[68]

George McCall Smith
(1882–1958)
Born in Nairn, Scotland, Smith received his medical education at the University of Edinburgh. He came to New Zealand with his mother in 1914 and was appointed superintendent at Rawene Hospital. Popular with those he served, he fell out with the board over his demands for improvements and was dismissed in 1921 but was reinstated after pressure from the locals. His experience during the Depression led to his being one of the founders of the Social Credit movement in New Zealand. He retired from the hospital in 1948 and moved to Waikanae, where he continued to practise. He was the grandfather of renowned author Alexander McCall Smith.[69]

Cecil Trevithick
(1880–1967)
Trevithick was born in Auckland, where he was articled to J. S. Turner before working as an assistant to George W. Allsop from 1903. In 1906 he moved to London, where he was elected an associate of the RIBA in 1908. After returning to New Zealand in 1914, he formed Chilwell & Trevithick with British-born architect Benjamin Charles Chilwell (1879–1950).[70]

Vernon Akitt Brown
(1905–1965)
Brown gained his architectural qualifications in England before emigrating with his parents in 1927. He worked on the Auckland War Memorial Museum with Grierson Aimer & Draffin, but during the Depression was reduced to digging ditches. His practice thrived in the late 1930s, however, and he became renowned for his modernist houses. He began teaching at the Auckland Architecture School and was the mentor to the Auckland Architectural Group ('the Group'). So the practice could continue while he taught, he took on Robin Simpson (1908–1947) as his partner.[71]

George Wilfred Allsop
(1871–1972)
Little is known of Allsop's early life. In 1902 the *Auckland Star* noted his 'return to Auckland' after three years in London, where he was admitted as an associate of the RIBA. In addition to his work as architect to the Auckland Hospital Board, he took over Edward Bartley's role at the Foundation for the Blind in Parnell, designing the 1916 extension there. He retired as architect to the Auckland Hospital Board in 1925. Allsop gained publicity in New Zealand and overseas when he and his wife Eleanor took their Packard car on a two-and-a-half-year world tour through Australia, Africa, Europe and North America in 1927. After converting a Chevrolet truck into a mobile home, he embarked on a similar trip in 1937. Allsop died in Auckland aged 100.[72]

John Willing Warren
(1859–1936)
Born in London, the son of an architect, Warren emigrated to New Zealand in 1881, and is thought to have joined the Armed Constabulary and been part of the military assault that year on Parihaka. After working in Taranaki for a time, he went to New South Wales for eight years. Back in New Zealand, he settled in Stratford, where he worked on dairy factories and public buildings and was

appointed architect to the Stratford Hospital Board. After winning the competition for the new public library in Hamilton in 1906, he relocated there and became architect to the Waikato Hospital Board. Other buildings in Hamilton by Warren include St Peter's Cathedral (1916). He formed several partnerships, including one with engineer John Blechynden in the 1910s, and later with Gordon S. Reid; some early drawings carry the name of Warren & Stephenson. Warren retired in 1932.[73]

Herbert Henry Clemson
(1868–1938)
Clemson was born in Lichfield, England, and trained as an architect before emigrating to New Zealand, settling in Tauranga in 1896.

Harry Leslie Daniel West
(c.1887–1937)
Harry West trained with his father, Daniel West, in Timaru before moving to Ōpōtiki around 1914, where he formed a partnership with R. S. Todd Whincup. Around 1921 he moved to Whakatāne, where he set up his own practice before moving to Tauranga around 1934.[74]

John D. Healy
(1868–1934)
Healy was a prolific architect based in Stratford, where he designed many of the town's early buildings.[75]

James Sanderson
(?–1924)
Horace (Victor) Samuel Griffiths
(1883–1952)
Frank Messenger
(1865–1945)
New Plymouth architect Sanderson designed the new buildings for New Plymouth Hospital and Hawera Hospital. He also supervised the move of Thatcher's colonial hospital (The Gables) to Brooklands and, among other buildings in New Plymouth, he designed the 1886 White Hart Hotel.[76] Horace (Victor) Samuel Griffiths worked for the Public Works Department from 1906 until his resignation in 1907, when he joined Sanderson in the partnership of Sanderson & Griffiths, which lasted until around 1917. Griffiths was mayor of New Plymouth from 1927 to 1933.[77] He formed a partnership with Frank Messenger in 1917 as Messenger & Griffiths. Messenger had been articled to H. J. T. Edmonds before leaving to work in Melbourne in 1883. After returning to New Zealand in 1893, he started his own practice. From 1909 to 1914 he worked with William Edward Percival as Percival & Messenger. In 1909 he added the distinctive balconies to Sanderson's White Hart Hotel. Messenger and Griffiths were joined by W. Norman Taylor in 1920. After leaving the partnership in 1930, Griffiths appears to have formed two later partnerships – Griffiths & Stephenson in the 1930s, and Griffiths & Syme in the 1940s – as there are drawings for buildings at Stratford Hospital in both those names. Messenger & Taylor continued until Messenger's death in 1945. Messenger, Taylor & Wolfe, as the firm was from the mid-1930s, designed the Wellington City Library (1939), now the City Art Gallery, in collaboration with Gummer & Ford. Raymond Walter Syme (1905–1975), possibly Griffiths' earlier partner, joined the firm on his return from the Second World War in 1944 and it continued as Taylor & Syme until 1957.[78]

Frederick Howard Forge
(1887–1960)
Forge worked in the engineer's department at Wellington City Council before moving to Gisborne around 1910. Mew and Humphris refer to architectural experience gained in London, Melbourne and Sydney, but it is unclear when this occurred.[79]

Clifford Newton Hood
(1890–1971)
Hood established his practice in Whanganui in the 1920s, and among other buildings designed the 1933 Alexander Library. He took John Edwin Duffell on as a partner in 1930, but the partnership was dissolved in 1935.[80]

Ludolph Georg West ↗
(1846–1919)
Ernst (Ernest) Vilhelm West
(1886–1961)
Ludolf (later spelt Ludolph) West was born in Denmark and in 1868 arrived in Palmerston North, where he went into business as an architect and commission agent. He designed many of the town's early prominent buildings and was its fifth mayor. After working in London from 1908 to 1910, and travelling around Europe and the United States, his son Ernst (sometimes spelled Ernest) West returned to New Zealand in 1912 to join the practice, which became L. G. West & Son. Ernest West designed a private hospital on Featherston Street in 1922. West entered a partnership with Francis Hornibrook (1895–1968), forming L. G. West, Son &

Hornibrook from 1931 to 1939. Irish-born Hornibrook came to New Zealand in 1912 and fought in the First World War. He then studied architecture and went into private practice in Tauranga, Napier and Gisborne. After service in the Second World War, he worked for the Railways Department, before joining West.[81]

George Walker Callander
(1903–1981)
Callander was apprenticed to Coombs & White in Dunedin, where he met his future business partner Bernard Cox. Callander and Cox established a practice in Palmerston North in the late 1930s. Cox served in the army from 1941 to 1947, then returned to Palmerston North to set up his own practice. By 1947 Callander had joined Ernest West and from 1950 to 1961 the firm was known as L. G. West, Son & Callander, architects of the Levin Maternity Hospital (1952). One of Callander's cadets was Milton Guy Brogden (1934–2011), who later left to enter partnership with Callander as Callander & Brogden. This became Brogden & Callander from 1966 to 1972, when Callander left the firm.[82]

Oscar Jorgensen
(1882–1967)
Jorgensen was born in Denmark, where he trained as a cooper before moving to New Zealand in 1902. He worked as a builder in Wellington with his brothers before moving in 1919 to Palmerston North, where he was employed by L. G. West & Son. He appears to have been a difficult character, and was often involved in litigation, with clients, partners and eventually his wife.[83]

Robert Edwards
(c.1857–1933)
Born in Australia, Edwards came to New Zealand in 1869. He later set up as an architect in Palmerston North, and was the town's mayor in 1892–93.[84]

Robin Hood
(1880–1953)
Hood was born in Dunedin and in 1908 moved to Feilding, where he worked as a labourer while studying at night to be an architect. By 1920 he had moved to Palmerston North and established his own practice. Healthcare work by Hood included an operating room for a private hospital in Feilding (1922) and the Akaroa Private Hospital in Ruahine Street (1936).[85]

Ragnar Jennsen
(1869–1908)
Little is known of Jennsen's life. He designed several buildings in Dannevirke, including the town's abattoir.[86]

Reginald W. Thorrold-Jaggard
(1889–1960)
William (Bill) Thorrold Jaggard
(1914–2006)
Reginald W. Thorrold-Jaggard was born and educated in England and, after receiving his articles, emigrated to New Zealand in 1913. He settled in Palmerston North, where he was employed by local architect Oscar Jorgenson before setting up his own practice in 1915, which he continued until 1959. His healthcare work included a private hospital on Grey Street in 1934. His son William (Bill) joined him in 1939, after completing his architecture degree at Auckland University College. He then served in the Second World War. After his father's death, he practised on his own before selling the business in 1962. In 1967 he joined a local construction firm, supervising the work on new buildings at Massey University. In 1972 he joined Gillman Garry Clapp & Sayers, where he supervised the construction of the clinical services block at Palmerston North Hospital. He retired in 1982. Reginald is thought to have introduced the Thorrold name to acknowledge a legacy. He used the hyphen in his surname, but Bill dropped it, treating Thorrold as a middle name.[87]

Arthur Robert Allen
(1887–1963)
Another prominent Palmerston North architect, Allen was born in Napier and practised there before moving to Palmerston North in the mid-1920s. While in partnership with Herbert Leslie Hickson, he was responsible for the C. M. Ross Building, which was later converted into the Palmerston North City Library. By 1950 he was working for the Ministry of Works in Palmerston North.[88]

Victor Robert John Hean
(1901–1979)
Born in Christchurch, Hean attended the Canterbury School of Art while also studying engineering. After working for architect H. St A. Murray, he joined the staff of the Christchurch City Council from 1925 to 1936 and designed the Edmonds Band Rotunda, which opened in 1929. He then moved to Palmerston North, where he was resident architect to the hospital board in 1936–42. He then joined the government architect's office in Wellington, where he continued to specialise in hospital architecture.[89]

John Thomas Mair
(1876–1959)
Born in Invercargill, the son of a building contractor, Mair trained under the borough engineer–architect before joining New Zealand Railways. In 1906 he went to the United States, where he studied architecture at the University of Pennsylvania and worked in New York, before setting up his own practice in Wellington in 1910. In 1918 he was appointed inspector of military hospitals, before becoming architect to the Department of Education in 1920. John Mair was Government Architect from 1923 until his retirement in 1941.[90]

Robert Adams Patterson
(1892–1971)
Patterson joined the Public Works Department as a cadet in 1908, and when John T. Mair retired was acting Government Architect from 1941 to 1942. He was Government Architect from 1942 until 1952.[91]

Francis Gordon Wilson
(1900–1959)
Wilson was born in Perth, Western Australia, but moved to Wellington with his family in 1903. In 1920 he began studying part-time at Auckland University College while working for W. H. Gummer, then Gummer & Ford. He completed the course in 1928 and travelled through the United States before rejoining the firm. In 1936 he was appointed chief architect of the Department of Housing and Construction, which was absorbed into the Ministry of Works in 1945, and became Government Achitect in 1952. Wilson died suddenly in 1959.[92]

Fergus George Frederick Sheppard
(1908–1997)
Sheppard became acting Government Architect on Gordon Wilson's death, and was then appointed Government Architect, a role in which he continued until 1971. Under Sheppard the Ministry of Works completed the design of the Beehive executive wing in Wellington, from a concept by Sir Basil Spence.[93]

William Crichton
(1861–1928)
Born in Cornwall, Crichton studied architecture under James Hicks of Redruth. In 1879 his family emigrated to New Zealand, where he joined the Public Buildings Department, working mainly on gaols and psychiatric hospitals. He was dismissed in 1880 for budgetary reasons, then reinstated as a draughtsman in 1881. In 1887 he succeeded Charles Beatson as head of the North Island architect's office but was dismissed again in 1891, again for financial reasons. In 1891 Crichton won the competition for the design of the Wellington Municipal Library and established his own practice. He was president of the NZIA in 1923–24.[94]

Milton Rhodes Varnham
(1860–1938)
Varnham was born in Wellington, and later moved with his family to Greytown, where he worked as a carpenter before becoming an architect in the 1890s and taking on Ernest Rose as a partner. He designed many local buildings, including Greytown's Masonic Lodge. He established the Greytown Brass Band in 1877; he designed the Carterton band rotunda. He bought the practice of local architect Joseph Roe (c.1973–1958) in 1902.

James Hector McKay
(c.1866–1944)
McKay was born in Scotland and around 1884 emigrated to Australia, where he practised as an architect before moving to Wellington in 1896. There he was in a partnership with Robert (Rob) Roy MacGregor (1865–1934) from 1898 to 1901. McKay and MacGregor designed St James' Presbyterian Church (1899), with its distinctive domed-roof tower, on Adelaide Road. McKay retired in 1926.[95]

Vivian Palmer Haughton
(1891–1956)
Wellington-born Haughton joined the practice of Crichton & McKay as a draughtsman in 1907. In 1913 he was elected an associate of the NZIA. After recovering from a severe head wound sustained on the Western Front, Haughton returned to work with his former employers. Although the firm was known on some projects as Crichton, McKay & Haughton from 1923, Haughton did not actually become a partner until 1926. He was elected an associate of the RIBA in 1923 and a fellow of the NZIA in 1939. When the Wellington Architectural Students' Association was formed in 1918, to assist those studying remotely for their architecture degrees, Haughton was appointed its first master, assisted by his good friend, and later business partner, Bill McKeon. Crichton & McKay employed and trained many architects, such as William Gray Young and Bill Toomath, who would go on to form their own successful practices. Basil Ward joined Crichton & McKay in the early 1920s, leaving in 1924 with his friend Amyas Connell to establish a London practice that was at the forefront of modernist design.[96]

William (Bill) John McKeon
(1896–1973)
McKeon was born in Melbourne and was two when his family came to New Zealand and settled in Masterton before moving to Wellington, then returning to Melbourne in 1910. There McKeon was articled to Frederic Louis Klingender and completed his architectural training under him. In 1912 the family moved back to Wellington, where McKeon joined Hoggard & Prouse. He fought at Passchendaele in 1917 and was seriously injured in the Battle of Crèvecoeur in 1918. Some other servicemen stayed after the war to study at the Architectural Association in London, but McKeon was advised to return home to recover. He rejoined Hoggard & Prouse in 1919 before leaving to set up his own practice in 1921. Because work was scarce, in 1923 he joined his father's building firm. An amateur entertainer, he supplemented his income by performing on Radio 2YA. In 1929 he again set up his own office, while also providing commentaries for government publicity films. During the Second World War McKeon served in New Zealand until 1943. He was president of the NZIA from 1945 to 1946. After leaving the partnership with Haughton, he set up his own practice, but also had a partnership with Maurice Patience, which ended in 1963. He retired in 1971.[97]

Robert Besant Haughton
(1918–1993)
Haughton joined his father Vivian's firm as a junior straight from school in 1936. After serving overseas during the Second World War, Haughton returned to university study in Auckland, where he worked for D. B. Patterson during the holidays. He became an associate of the NZIA in 1948. He was president of the NZIA from 1973 to 1974.[98]

Lindsay Mair
(1915–1980)
Lindsay Mair's father was Government Architect John Thomas Mair. Mair graduated BArch in 1938 and joined Crichton, McKay & Haughton that year as a draughtsman. After 12 months he left to work in the Sydney office of Stephenson & Turner, then served with the Australian Imperial Force during the First World War. Back in New Zealand, he worked for Structon before forming a practice with B. F. Kelly. He then rejoined Haughton's firm, becoming a partner in 1954. Mair retired in 1972.[99]

John (Jack) Hoggard
(1878–1936)
William Prouse
(1879–1956)
Jack Hoggard was born in Wellington, where he was trained by his uncle, architect William C. Chatfield. By 1900 Hoggard was working for Joshua Charlesworth, who was then designing the new Wellington Town Hall. After the 1906 Californian earthquake, Hoggard moved there to gain experience in seismic design. In 1907 he formed a partnership with William Prouse, who was born in Pātea, the son of a timber merchant, and had no formal architectural training. In 1908 Hoggard & Prouse designed the Cadbury depot in Wellington, an early example of steel-framed construction in New Zealand.[100]

William Henry Gummer
(1884–1966)
In 1913 Hoggard & Prouse were joined by William Gummer, who established an office for the firm in Auckland. Gummer was articled to Auckland architect William Alfred Holman from 1900 to 1903 and remained his assistant for another five years. He then travelled across Britain, Europe and the United States from 1908 to 1913, working for Edward Lutyens in London and Daniel Burnham in Chicago. He studied at the Royal Academy of Arts and became an associate of the RIBA in 1910. Other buildings by Hoggard, Prouse & Gummer include the New Zealand Insurance (Guardian Trust) Building in Auckland (1914–18) and the original State Insurance Building in Wellington. The partnership with Hoggard was dissolved in 1921, apparently not amicably, as Hoggard's name was removed from the State Insurance foundation stone, and Gummer & Prouse continued until 1923, when Prouse set up his own practice and Gummer went into partnership with Charles Ford. Prouse was later joined by Norman Frank Wilson (1901–1973) in the firm of Prouse & Wilson, which lasted until Prouse's death.[101]

Charles Reginald Ford
(1880–1972)
London-born Ford, who had joined the Royal Navy at an early age and served in Scott's 1901–04 Antarctic Expedition, returned to settle in Christchurch in 1906. There he trained in architecture through a correspondence course, becoming an associate of the NZIA in 1914 and a fellow in 1919. He then moved to Whanganui in 1919 to form a partnership with Robert Gordon Talboys. Ford was president of the NZIA from 1921 to 1922 and Gummer from 1933 to 1934. Gordon Wilson, later Government Architect, became a partner in the firm in 1928.[102] Gummer & Ford designed the Dilworth Building in Auckland (1926), Auckland's Railway Station (1931) and the National War Memorial and Dominion Museum in Wellington (1936). The partnership received two NZIA Gold Medals. When J. B. Gummer and C. Prior Hoadley joined as partners, the firm became Gummer Ford Hoadley Budge and Gummer, Architects and Engineers. Gummer and Ford both retired in 1961, but for a time projects continued to be delivered under the name of Gummer Ford & Partners. The firm later became Hoadley Budge, then Hoadley Budge Olphert in 1987. This took over Australian firm Edwards, Madigan, Torzillo and Briggs to form HBO+EMTB in 1994, which expanded rapidly across Australia and Asia. The practice ran into financial difficulties in 2020, and several subsidiaries closed, but it still operates in the Philippines. Local practice Ministry of Architecture + Interiors also traces its roots back to Gummer & Ford.[103]

Arthur Reynolds Griffin
(1883–1967)
Grandson of John Griffin, founder of biscuit makers Griffin & Sons, Arthur Griffin was educated at Nelson College. He was a

draughtsman at Robertson Brothers for four years before training in architecture through the International Correspondence School based in Pennsylvania. He established his own practice in 1906 and designed many buildings in Nelson during his career.[104]

Samuel Hurst Seager

(1855–1933)
Seager was born in London and emigrated with his parents in 1870 to Christchurch, where his uncle, Edward William Seager, was superintendent of Sunnyside Hospital. His knowledge of the building may have led to his interest in architecture. When Seager's father died in 1874, Samuel took over his contracting firm and ran it until 1879. He also worked as an architectural draughtsman for B. W. Mountfort and A. W. Simpson while studying at Canterbury University College from 1879 to 1882. He then studied architecture at University College, London, from 1882 to 1883 and lectured at Canterbury College School of Art in Christchurch from 1893 to 1918. Seager was in partnership with Cecil Walter Wood from 1906 to 1912 and was president of the NZIA from 1926 to 1927. He was a renowned architectural educator, and his biography in Te Ara – the Encyclopedia of New Zealand states 'through his wide-ranging activities, Seager did more to advance the art of architecture than any other New Zealander of his generation'.[105] He was also pivotal to the careers of two women architects. After being apprenticed to Samuel Hurst Seager for three years, Katherine (Kate) Beath (1889–1972) became the first professionally qualified woman architect in New Zealand. He also trained Alison Sleigh (1898–1972), who later moved to London to study at the Architectural Association before working with her husband, John Shepherd, on Elisabeth Scott's competition-winning Shakespeare Memorial Theatre in Stratford-upon-Avon.

Cecil Walter Wood

(1878–1947)
In 1893 Christchurch-born Wood was articled to Frederick Strouts and worked with him on the Hyman Marks Building at Christchurch Hospital. From 1894 he studied at the Canterbury College of Art under Samuel Hurst Seager. In 1899, when Strouts retired, Wood joined the firm of the latter's former partner, Robert Anderson Ballantyne (1866–1936) and William Clarkson (1863–1917), as a draughtsman. By 1901 they had little work and Wood left for London. On his return in 1906, he joined Hurst Seager, forming the firm of Hurst Seager & Wood. In 1907 they were joined by Joseph Fearis Munnings, but he left in 1909, and Wood's partnership with Seager dissolved in 1912. Wood appears to have formed a partnership in 1926 with Richard Harman, who had presumably left the partnership with Collins, but this was short-lived as Harman died the following year. Miles Warren, later co-founder of Warren and Mahoney, was articled to Wood in 1945.[106]

Joseph Fearis Munnings

(1879–1937)
Munnings was born in Christchurch, where he was apprenticed to a local builder. He also studied under Samuel Hurst Seager at the Canterbury College School of Arts from 1896 to 1900 and was articled to him in 1898. He left in 1901 to study at the Architectural Association in London in 1903, returning in 1906. After joining the partnership of Hurst Seager & Wood, he supervised the construction of the sanatorium that Hurst Seager had designed. When the partnership ended, he returned to London, then went worked in India until 1918. Back in Christchurch, he joined Collins & Harman, setting up their Wellington office. The firm became Collins, Harman & Munnings from 1919 to 1922. During this time, he was involved with additions and alterations at Westport's Buller Hospital. He then went into independent practice before leaving for Sydney in 1923, where he formed the firm of Power, Adam & Munnings.[107]

William Barnett Armson

(1833–1883)
Armson, born in London, came to New Zealand with his parents in 1852. Two years later the family moved to Melbourne, where he was articled to Purchas & Teague. In 1862 Armson returned to New Zealand, where he was appointed architect for the Otago Provincial Government. Made redundant in 1864, Armson set up a practice in Dunedin, but work was scarce and in 1865 he moved to Hokitika. In 1866 he left for Britain, but was back in Hokitika by 1867. Armson then relocated to Christchurch, where he established a practice in 1869.[108]

John James Collins

↗

(1855–1933)
On Armson's death, his firm was bought by John James Collins, who had been articled to him in 1871. Collins had already become a partner, but Armson had not yet signed a formal agreement. After suffering considerable financial hardship in the transfer, Collins joined George Lloyd in partnership, with the practice known as Armson, Collins & Lloyd from 1883.[109]

Richard Dacre Harman

(1859–1927)
Harman bought out George Lloyd's interest in Armson, Collins & Lloyd in 1884 and the firm became Armson, Collins & Harman. Harman had also been born in Christchurch, educated at Christ's College and articled to Armson in 1877. His father, Dublin-born R. J. S. Harman (1828–1902), of the land agents Harman & Stevens, had commissioned Armson to design an office building in 1877. Probably in error, Harman & Stevens have been credited by some as the architects of some early buildings at Christchurch Hospital. Collins and Harman are thought to have been the first New Zealand-born, educated and trained Christchurch architects. Despite Armson's request that his name be retained, in 1886 the firm became Collins & Harman, although the longer name seems to have been occasionally used until 1928.[110]

John Goddard Collins

(1886–1973)
Collins, who had been taught by Samuel Hurst Seager, joined his father's staff in Collins & Harman in 1903. The firm was appointed as architects to the North Canterbury Hospital Board and designed many of the buildings for them at Christchurch Hospital and their other sites. Other work by the firm around

the turn of the century included the Press Building (1909) in Cathedral Square. In 1919 Joseph Fearis Munnings joined the firm to run the Wellington office it had established in 1917 and the firm was renamed Collins, Harman & Munnings. Beryl Bickerton worked with the firm for three years in the late 1920s before leaving for London to study at the Architectural Association and then starting her own practice. This was very much a multi-generational practice. In 1936 J. G. Collins' son, John Kempthorne Collins (1916–1983), was the third generation to join the partnership, which then became J. G. Collins & Son, and in 1960 his son, Richard John Kempthorne Collins, became the fourth generation to work there, after J. G. Collins retired in 1955. For a time in the 1970s, the firm was known as Collins, Hunt & Loveridge, with partners Graeme Loveridge, Maurice Hunt and Darryl Partridge. The name changed to Collins Architects Ltd, before the firm closed in 1993 after 123 years in business.[111]

Ernest Mitchell Gabites

(1890–1972)
Gabites was born in Timaru and trained with Anscombe & Smith in Invercargill. After service as a second lieutenant in the First World War, he established his own practice in Ashburton.[112]

James Stuart Turnbull

(1864–1947)

Percy Watts Rule

(1888–1953)
Timaru-born James Stuart Turnbull worked in Melbourne before returning to his home town in the mid-1890s. Napier-born Percy Watts Rule, who had worked with Turnbull for 10 years before serving in the army in 1918, rejoined him as a partner in Turnbull & Rule in 1919 and was later appointed architect to the South Canterbury Hospital Board. Rule was the architect member on the judging panel for the 1938 design competition for Christchurch's new subsidiary hospital in Cashmere (the site of the later Princess Margaret Hospital).[113]

Henry McDowell Smith

(1887–1965)
Smith was born in Manchester and emigrated to New Zealand in 1900. He then trained as an architect in England, returning to New Zealand in 1909. He managed Edmund Anscombe's Invercargill branch, becoming his partner in 1913 and an associate of the NZIA in 1914. After serving in the First World War, he returned to Invercargill before starting his own practice in Dunedin in 1921. He retired in 1954. In 1926 he took on Marion Miller, who passed her NZIA professional examination in 1927, and employed Patricia Leahy (later Bell) from 1936 to 1940.

Patricia Leahy

(Dates unknown)
After working for Henry Smith, Leahy went on to work for Walker & Muston (see page 358), then Crichton, McKay & Haughton from 1940, possibly being manpowered during the war as they continued their hospital design work. After serving in the WRENS (Women's Royal New Zealand Naval Service), she worked with Mason & Wales from 1943 to 1944. Leahy went to Melbourne in 1948, where she joined Stephenson & Turner, and from where she applied for New Zealand registration.[114]

Edward Walter Walden

(1870–1944)
Born in Dunedin, Walden was articled to local architect James Hislop, eventually becoming his business partner. He took over the firm on Hislop's death in 1904.[115]

Edmund Anscombe

(1874–1948)
Sussex-born Anscombe was seven months old when he arrived in Dunedin with his family. After an apprenticeship as a carpenter, in 1901 he studied architecture by correspondence in the United States while working as a builder. He set up his own practice in Dunedin in 1906. After he won the 1908 competition for the School of Mines building at Otago University, he was appointed as architect to the university, a position he held until 1929. He formed partnerships with L. D. Coombes in 1913 and Henry McDowell Smith in 1914, forming Edmund Anscombe, H. McDowell Smith & Associates in 1919. Anscombe designed most of the buildings for the 1925–26 New Zealand and South Seas Exhibition. In 1929 Anscombe moved to Wellington and established a branch office in Hastings, where he designed the Hawke's Bay Farmers' Cooperative Association Building (1930). When the 1931 earthquake struck, he continued eating in its tearoom, confident in the building's design. It survived well, and no lives were lost in it, while surrounding structures were destroyed.[116]

Edmund Richardson Fitz Wilson

(1871–1941)
Born and educated in Invercargill, Wilson was apprenticed to local architectural firm Mackenzie & Gilbertson (John Ewen Mackenzie and Charles Gilbertson). From 1895 to 1896 he lived in Wellington, where he worked for the civil service and in William Crichton's office and he is also thought to have worked with Frederick de Jersey Clere. In 1897 he returned to Invercargill and took over Gilbertson's share in the practice. Mackenzie & Wilson lasted until 1908, when Wilson established his own practice. He was responsible for many buildings in Invercargill, including the Town Hall and Civic Theatre (1906), for which he won the design competition, and St John's Anglican Church (1913). After being appointed architect to the Southland Hospital Board, Wilson began planning for the new hospital in 1919 and retired on its completion in 1937. He was elected a fellow of the NZIA in 1905 and was president from 1929 to 1930. From 1917 to around 1922 Wilson employed Helen Prain, one of the first women to pass the new NZIA examinations in 1919.[117]

George William Lucking

(1923–c.2017)
Lucking served in the RNZAF during the Second World War before returning to New Zealand, where he set up Lucking and Vial in Christchurch with John Vial.[118]

Tibor Donner

(1907–1993)
Born in what is now Serbia, Donner emigrated to New Zealand with his family in 1927. After studying at Auckland University College, he joined the Public Works Department. In 1947, he left to form the architectural department of the Auckland City Council, where he was city architect until his retirement in 1967.[119]

Raymond Leslie Farrell

(1894–1955)
Auckland-born Farrell qualified as an architect from Auckland University College, before joining his father's firm, which became J. Farrell & Son, later Farrell Son & Glover. They carried out work from around 1925, and in 1938 Farrell was appointed architect to the Auckland Hospital Board. He resigned due to ill health in 1948, but continued to consult to the board.[120]

Louis (Neil) Orchard

(Dates unknown)
Orchard was on the staff of the Auckland Hospital Board before leaving to start his own practice, joining David Allison in Orchard

& Allison in 1950. David Charles Allison (1923–2010) served in the Fleet Air Arm of the Royal Navy in the Second World War, before studying architecture at the University of Auckland. Orchard & Allison also designed the administration block at Christ's College (1958), for which Allison also won the 1962 design competition for a new Assembly Hall (1965). Allison left in the 1980s to form Allison Architects with D. Everard R. Allison.[121]

James Garrett
(1922–2013)
Garrett served as a pilot in the Royal New Zealand Air Force during the second world war. He worked for H. Clinton Savage from 1950 to 1954 and Bruce Henderson from 1955 to 1956. He joined the Auckland Hospital Board in 1956, working there until 1965, when he joined Haughey & Fox. In 1972, he left to work with Cutter Pickmere Douglas (see page 240), returning to the Auckland Hospital Board in 1979, where he continued until 1985. While there, he designed the Pukekohe and North Shore maternity hospitals.

Ian (Bruce) Henderson
(1925–1973)
Henderson established a practice in Auckland, and for a time practised with John Anthony Wheeler.[122]

H. Clinton Savage
(c.1892–1957)
Savage designed many buildings in Auckland and the Waikato, his most prominent being the 1926 George Court building on Karangahape Road.[123]

Gordon Smith
(1926–2010)
Geoffrey Newman
(1930–?)
While working in London, Gordon Smith won the 1955 design competition for the new War Memorial Hall (1960) in Whanganui, assisted by fellow Auckland graduates Geoffrey Newman and Anthony (Tony) Greenhough (1930–2020). Greenhough left the nascent practice in 1957, eventually leading the architectural team at Beca Carter Hollings & Ferner. Newman and Smith continued, designing the terminal and control tower at Wanganui Airport (1961), the latter becoming the standard design for regional airports around the country.[124]

Peter W. Verrall
(Dates unknown)
Verrall trained at the Architectural Association in London before emigrating to New Zealand in 1952. He moved to Rotorua as the resident partner in Alleman Land Heeney & Verrall, later Verrall & Newnham, in 1959. After John Newnham left to join the government architect's office in Wellington, Verrall practised on his own before forming a partnership with Garth G. Hocking (1928–2015) as Hocking & Verrall in 1968. Verrall retired in 1988, and Hocking continued as Garth Hocking & Associates until 1990.[125]

Charles Harold Donaldson Porter
(1900–1989)
Porter was born in Christchurch and moved to Tauranga, where he established himself as an architect.[126]

Lewis Maitland Howey Walker
(1903–1981)
Walker founded his practice in 1932, and it became Walker & Muston in 1937 when he was joined by Ronald Muston (later co-founder of Structon). This business was suspended in 1941 while Walker was serving in the army in the Second World War. Walker then partnered with Richard G. Hillary, as Lewis Walker & Hillary, designing the National Airways Corporation building in Auckland (1963). After a later partnership with Darcy Glossop in 1967, the firm became Walker Co-Partnership in 1971 and now operates as Walker Group Architects.[127]

Ronald Colin Muston
(1905–1974)
Muston was born in Leicestershire, England, but educated in Aotearoa New Zealand. He assisted with the design of the 1940 Centennial Exhibition in Wellington working as the firm Walker & Muston. His Muston & Associates merged with the surviving partners of Swan & Lavelle (see page 351) to form Structon Group Architects in 1944. A generation on, its younger employees included Gordon Moller, John Blair, Ian Athfield, Rewi Thompson and Stewart Gardyne. His main interest was church architecture: his designs for St James Church (Lower Hutt, 1953) and St Joseph's Orphanage and Chapel (Upper Hutt) received an NZIA gold medal award. His Lower Hutt War Memorial Library opened in 1956. Recipient of an OBE, he was also a Honorary Fellow of the American Institute of Architects.

John Harold Edgecumbe
(Dates unknown)
Harold Leonard White
(1893–1982)
Edgecumbe & White was established in Hamilton in 1919 by John Harold Edgecumbe and Harold Leonard White. Other buildings by the firm included the 1939 Hamilton Chief Post Office. Edgecumbe retired in 1948, but the firm continued as Edgecumbe, White & Leigh, with George Leigh, and White, Leigh, de Lisle & Fraser, with Aubrey Frank de Lisle (1919–2004). Fraser was the engineering partner. Later iterations of the firm included Leigh de Lisle Fraser & Pickering.[128]

Christopher John Rodney (Rod) Smith
(1933–2023)
Smith, the son of Waikato Hospital Board architect Alfred Smith, graduated in architecture from the University of Auckland, then returned to Waikato to work alongside his father at the board before forming his own practice in 1963. He took on partners Henry Clarke in 1965 and Kelvin Grant in 1966; the firm became Smith Clarke Grant in 1966, then Smith Grant & Associates after Clarke left in 1969. In 1982, when Robert Finch's Northland practice joined Smith Grant, the firm became Smith Grant Finch & Associates in Whangārei but continued to practise as Smith Grant & Associates in Hamilton. But work dropped off and the firm soon closed. Rod Smith joined Warren and Mahoney in Christchurch, before eventually setting up his own practice again, as Rod Smith and Associates.[129]

Robert Barney Finch
(1911–1981)
Finch established his practice in Whangārei, designing the 1957 Whangarei & District War Memorial, and later practicing as Finch & Thorne, the 1958 Kaikohe & District War Memorial Hall. He also designed the Settlers Motor Inn in Whāngarei.[130]

Ernest Arthur Williams
(1875–1962)
Lawrence Garbutt Williams
(1901–1969)
Ernest Arthur Williams was both a Napier architect and, for a time, the borough engineer. He was joined in practice by his son Lawrence Garbutt Williams, who became an NZIA member in 1936, an associate of the RIBA in 1936 and served in the Second World War from 1940 to 1943. The Williamses

designed several buildings in Napier following the 1931 earthquake.

Jack Bennett Reynolds
(1920–1969)
Reynolds was appointed architect to the Palmerston North Hospital Board in 1948, but died while in office.[131]

Don A. Wilson
(Dates unknown)
Wilson set up D. A. Wilson & Associates in Whanganui, and was joined by Eddie Belchambers in 1967 to form Wilson & Belchambers. This became Wilson, Belchambers Low, and later Belchambers Low. The firm designed several buildings at Wanganui Collegiate School, including the 1966 dining hall, and the Wanganui City Council buildings, completed in 1968.[132]

Frederick Charles (Fred) Daniell
(1879–1953)
Trevor Hamilton Daniell
(1912–1988)
Frederick Charles (Fred) Daniell emigrated from Scotland with his parents in 1880. His father established a successful building, joinery and sawmilling operation in Wairarapa, carrying out many of his own designs. Fred Daniell joined his father in the business in the late 1890s, after taking draughting classes at the Masterton Technical School. By 1906 he was the manager of the joinery factory and timber yard. After disagreements with his father in 1908 he left for Hamilton, where he set up an architectural practice, specialising in dairy factories. He closed his practice to concentrate on dairying in 1921 but he became overextended and lost his farm in 1924. Once back in Wairarapa in 1932, he worked with George Tole on the design of the State Theatre in Masterton (1935). Daniell's son Trevor joined his father's office in 1937 before leaving to study architecture at Auckland, although his graduation was delayed by four years of war service in the air force. He rejoined the practice in 1947, taking it over when Frederick died in 1953, and was later joined in partnership by Bart Wevers.[133]

Joseph McClatchie Dawson
(c.1876–1956)
Jack Ian King
(c.1900–1972)
Joseph McClatchie Dawson was born in Christchurch and learned about building from his contractor father. He studied at Wellington Technical School, before travelling to England, South Africa and Australia. He established a practice in Wellington in 1907, and carried out work at Wairau Hospital around 1920. In 1929, he formed a partnership with Jack Ian King as Dawson & King. He left the firm in 1948. The practice then operated as King Cook & Dawson, with Weymouth (Keith) Cook (1905–1973) and Joseph's son Eric.[134]

Alfred Edgar Luttrell
(1865–1924)
Edward Sidney Luttrell
(1872–1932)
Manson Stanton & Seward traces its roots back to 1902, when Australian brothers Alfred Edgar and Edward Sidney Luttrell established one of New Zealand's foremost architectural practices in Christchurch. Alfred was the principal designer and engineer, and the more ebullient Sidney coordinated building programmes and dealt with clients. Their skills and versatility made a lasting impact on the city's architectural heritage. They also practised in Wellington from 1924 to 1929 as Luttrell Brothers & Anderson, with their representative there being Ernest Charles Rhind Anderson (1893–1953). After Alfred Luttrell died in 1924, Jack Hollis and Allan Manson took on the firm's design work. In 1929 they designed Beath's Department Store and the five-level Majestic Theatre. Manson took over the practice when Sidney Luttrell died in 1932 and it was renamed Manson, Seward & Stanton in 1936.[135]

Stewart Minson
(1904–2006)
Minson designed the 1957 Timaru Telephone Exchange. He later formed a partnership with Holger Henning-Hansen, a Danish architect who had emigrated to New Zealand. Their firm, Minson, Henning-Hansen & Dines is best known for the 1968 Centre of Contemporary Art Gallery (CoCA) in Christchurch.[136]

Donald Ashby Cowey
(1929–2011)
Cowey started an architectural practice in Christchurch in 1956, and was joined by Peter Mills in 1973. Cowey tragically lost his life in a rock fall during the 2011 Canterbury earthquake.

William (Billy) Thomas
(1891–1967)
Thomas was born in Wakanui, and was taken on by local contracting firm Tuckers as an apprentice joiner. During this time he carried out his early work at Ashburton Hospital, before gaining renown for his 'Cape Cod'-style houses built in the town in the 1920s. Thomas then entered a partnership with Garner Hannaford (Hank) Ward. Thomas retired and Ward continued the practice on his own, before forming Ward & Flatman for a short time in the mid-1970s.[137]

Owen Wiles MacDonald
(1916–2012)
Peter Beaven
(1925–2012)
After Timaru Hospital Board architect Percy Rule died in 1953, Heaney & Beaven was appointed to complete work under way in Timaru and at the Geraldine Maternity Hospital. Christchurch-born architect Peter Beaven had studied at Auckland University, interrupted by navy service from 1944 to 1945. He then worked for G. W. Griffiths and the Public Works Department in Christchurch before moving to Timaru in 1952 to join Robert Heaney.[138] MacDonald was born Owen Wiles in Westport. His father died in Palestine in 1917 and when his mother remarried, he took his stepfather's surname. He became an architectural draughtsman in Christchurch and after appealing was able to delay his entry to the armed forces when he was called up in 1941 so that he could continue his architectural studies; he served in 1942. At some stage MacDonald joined the Timaru firm which became Heaney, Beaven & MacDonald. Beaven returned to Christchurch in 1957, leaving MacDonald to continue the practice. He later seems to have formed MacDonald & Wilson but is credited on his own for most of the work at Timaru Hospital.[139]

Henry Thomas (Harry) Mandeno
(1879–1973)
Roy Henderson Fraser
(1875–1972)
Mandeno was born in Te Awamutu and educated in Auckland, and later moved to Dunedin, where he worked for builder Robert Crawford while taking night classes in architectural draughtsmanship. Mandeno gained a position with Mason & Wales before setting up his own practice in 1911. He took on his later partner in Mandeno & Fraser, Southland-born Roy Henderson Fraser, as an assistant straight from school. Fraser became an associate of the NZIA in 1917 and Mandeno's partner in 1921; he assumed sole responsibility for the practice after Mandeno retired. Mandeno was president of the NZIA from 1931 to 1932, Fraser from 1947 to 1948.

The firm was an early employer of women: Aletta Hutton in the late 1910s and Lucy Greenish (see page 87) in the 1920s.[140]

Robert (Bob) Oakley

(1927–2020)
Oakley was born in Scotland to a Canterbury family who returned to New Zealand in 1934, settling in Dunedin. Oakley studied architecture at Auckland University, graduating in 1950. In 1951 he joined the practice of Henry McDowell Smith, which became McDowell Smith Oakley & Pinfold in 1953, with Gib Pinfold the other partner. On McDowell Smith's retirement, the firm merged with Roy Fraser, forming Fraser, Oakley & Pinfold in 1963. This became Oakley, Pinfold, Turvey & Neil when Fraser retired and Bob Turvey and Alan Neil joined in the 1960s. As well as much work for the South Otago Hospital Board, they designed the medical library at the University of Otago. Alan Neil left around 1984, Bob Turvey died in 1989 and Gib Pinfold retired shortly after. Bob's son Norman Oakley joined the firm as a graduate in 1985, becoming a partner in 1989. In 1992, when Bob Oakley retired and John Gray joined, the firm took its current name, Oakley Gray.[141]

Eric Miller

(1896–1948)

James (Jim) Hodge White

(1866-1970)
Miller went into practice in Dunedin in the 1920s and was joined in 1927 by Jim Hodge White, who had studied at the Architectural Association in London with him. In 1928 Miller & White took over the Dunedin practice of Edmund Anscombe before he moved north. On Miller's death, White took on Ian Gilman Dunn as a partner. On his retirement in 1957, Jim White was succeeded by his son, Geoffrey Francis White. Rodney Colin Dalziel joined in 1968 and the firm became Miller White & Dalziel on Dunn's retirement. The partnership dissolved in 1994 and Dalziel continued his practice as Dalziel Architecture until he retired in 1997.[142]

John D. Allingham

(Dates unknown)
Allingham came to Dunedin from Auckland to set up his practice in 1946 and was joined by John W. Harrison in 1959. Harrison became a partner in Allingham, Harrison & Partners in 1961, Norman W. Ledgerwood in 1966. Allingham retired in 1972.[143]

Allan Charles (A. C.) Ford

(1892–1989)
Ford, who had trained under Harry Mandeno in Dunedin before serving in the First World War, set up in practice in Invercargill in 1920. Ford, and his successor practices, designed hospital buildings throughout Southland, including the Wakatipu district. In 1937 his daughter Monica Ford (later Barham, 1920–1983) joined the practice while studying architecture extramurally and worked on the Roxburgh Children's Health Camp and the Children's Ward at Gore Hospital. Ford was joined by L. J. Gray, and the practice later became Ford, Gray & Derbie, before Stephen J. Hurd joined in 1968, forming Ford, Gray, Derbie & Hurd. Gray and Derbie continued after Ford retired and Hurd left, and it became Gray Hesselin & Baxter in 1979, with Alexander Reko (Mick) Hesselin (1936–2022) and N. L. P. Baxter. Gray retired in 1981, and the firm became Baxter Hesselin McDowell, with Neil McDowell (1953–2010) becoming a partner. It was later McDowell Architects and is now Beattie McDowell, as Roger Beattie took over the firm after Neil McDowell's death.[144]

Peter Mark-Brown

(1920–1978)
Mark-Brown, Fairhead & Associates was formed around 1952 by Peter Mark-Brown, who had spent time in the Auckland office of Daniel Boys Patterson, and Alan Fairhead (1926–2010). They merged their practice with that of Ron Sang in 1969 and were later joined by Simon Carnachan.[145]

Daniel Boys Patterson

(1880–1962)
A prolific Auckland architect, Patterson was born in Southampton and emigrated to New Zealand in 1910. He assisted in the design of Auckland's Ferry Buildings and became a member of the Institute of Architects in 1914. He succeeded Edward Bartley as the architect for the Auckland Diocesan Trust Board, and was also the main designer for Fuller's Cinemas, the Auckland Savings Bank and Campbell & Ehrenfried (later NZ Breweries). His firm eventually became Daniel B. Patterson, Lewis & Sutcliffe.[146]

John Steele Guthrie

(1883–1946)

Maurice James Guthrie

(1891–1968)
John Guthrie trained in Christchurch under J. C. Maddison or F. J. Barlow. By 1910 he was in his own practice, where he was joined in 1919 by his brother Maurice, who had left Collins & Harman. Other buildings by the Guthries included the Edmonds 'Sure to Rise' factory of 1920, and the 1926 Christchurch Boys' High School.[147]

Richard Strachan de Renzy Harman

(1896–1953)
R. S. D. Harman was the nephew of Richard Dacre Harman, and articled to Samuel Hurst Seager before serving in the First World War. After further study in London, he returned to Christchurch, where he was in a partnership with Cecil Wood from 1926 to 1928. He then practised on his own, with his most notable building being the 1935 Chapel of the Good Shepherd in Tekapo. Helmore Cotterill & Harman came third in the 1938 competition for a subsidiary hospital in Cashmere. Helmore and Cotterill would have been Heathcote George Helmore (1894–1965), the designer of many grand Christchurch homes, and Henry Guy Cotterill, who was Helmore's business partner from around 1923. The Harman was almost certainly R. S. D. Harman; however the partnership was probably only formed for the competition, as Harman does not seem to be mentioned in connection with them otherwise.[148]

John Arthur Burnside

(1857–1920)
Burnside was a prominent Dunedin architect, who was born in Otago, apprenticed to Mason & Wales and established his own practice in 1879.[149]

Raymond Armstrong Thorpe

(1910–2000)

Clayton George (Mick) Cutter

(1914–1985)

Ralph Arnold Pickmere

(1911–1984)

Kenneth Walter Douglas

(Dates unknown)
Thorpe, Cutter, Pickmere and Douglas attended Auckland University College School of Architecture between 1930 and 1939. All had served in the Second World War. Thorpe and Pickmere had worked for Roy Lippincott and Thorpe had also worked in Suva for George Johnson in 1937, before joining the practice of Alva Bartley. Cutter, born in Taranaki, had worked with Auckland architect Charles Towle in the early 1930s before starting his university education in 1938. After the war, he returned to university in Auckland, where he tutored after completing his degree in 1946. Other buildings by Thorpe, Cutter,

Pickmere & Douglas include the Mangere Sewage Purification Works (1960), for which they received an NZIA National Award, the Auckland Observatory (1967) and the Avalon Studios (1975) in Lower Hutt. While with the firm, John Wilfred (Jack) Manning (1928–2021) designed the AMP Building (1962), one of Auckland's first curtain-wall high-rise buildings. He also led the team that designed the Auckland Teachers' College in Epsom, which included David Mitchell (1941–2018) as a graduate. Manning and Mitchell left the firm before construction began, joining Peter Hill to form Hill Manning Mitchell. Associate William (Bill) Climie (1930–2018) was made a partner in 1972, followed by Ken Wall and Ray Horten. The Auckland office closed in 1974, and Thorpe left to establish his own practice. Pickmere retired the following year, and Douglas left in 1981. The firm operated as Cutter Pickmere Douglas until 1985, when the Christchurch and Wellington offices became separate practices, Cutter Douglas and Cutter Pickmere Climie respectively. Climie left to join Booth Sweetman Wolfe in 1986.[150]

Thomas (Tom) Fitzroy Haughey

(1915–2002)

Haughey was educated at Hamilton Technical College and joined Edgecumbe & White in Hamilton as a draughtsman in 1931. He studied architecture at Auckland University College from 1937 to 1938, winning the Senior and Travelling Scholarships, which took him to Australia, South Africa, the United States and England. There he won two RIBA competitions and from 1939 to 1940 undertook post-graduate research in hospital design at Liverpool University. On returning to New Zealand in 1945, after serving during the Second World War, Haughey established his own practice, developing a specialty in hospital design. In 1952 Haughey was joined by Graham F. Fox, who had been assistant architect to the Palmerston North Hospital Board, and in 1961 the practice became Haughey & Fox. P. A. Blewett, G. W. H. Cox, N. F. Osmers and R. S. Waite became partners that year. A. L. Gillespie and engineer G. A. Jeffs joined in 1963. Haughey was president of the NZIA from 1971 to 1972. Haughey and Gillespie retired from the practice in 1976, and joined R. G. Woolford to form Haughey Woolford Gillespie. The other partners continued as Haughey Fox and Partners, before becoming Fox Blewett Waite Jeffs & Partners, and eventually Blewett Waite Jeffs & Carter.[151]

Graeme Laurenson

(1908–1996)

Laurenson, born in Wellington, set his sights on architecture as a career but his parents could not afford his private-practice training and so he applied for a cadetship in the public service. He was appointed to the hospital technical branch of the Health Department, where he worked under Charles Scott-Allan on several buildings at Palmerston North Hospital. After a number of years there, he was transferred to the government architect's office in the Public Works Department and qualified extramurally through Auckland University College in 1938. Laurenson planned military and emergency hospitals during the Second World War, including the conversion of the Union Steamship Company vessel *Maunganui* into a hospital ship. He then returned to the Health Department, where he eventually became chief architect. In 1947 he was elected a member of the Royal Society of Health for services to public health. Through his interests in hospital research and planning he developed relationships with hospital architects throughout New Zealand. He was elected a fellow of the NZIA in 1956 and served as its president from 1963 to 1964. He resigned from public service in 1947 and entered into partnership with Jack Duffill (1883–1967) in Hāwera. Duffill had joined the Eltham-based firm of J. W. Rough in 1910, continuing the practice after Rough returned to England the following year, and relocating it to Hāwera. On Duffill's retirement in 1950, the firm became Graeme Laurenson & Associates.[152] Under Laurenson, the firm developed a specialty in hospital design and carried out work at Hāwera, Pātea, Stratford, Taumarunui and New Plymouth. At one point the practice had 30 staff, including architects and engineers, and Laurenson was joined by David (Dave) W. Robinson and Jim Boon to form the firm known as Laurenson, Robinson and Jim Boon. In 1969 they were joined in partnership by Edgar T. Collins and had offices in New Plymouth and Hāwera. When Laurenson retired in 1974, Stewart Cowie (1932–2012), who had joined the firm in 1950 and worked as site architect on Taranaki Base Hospital, took over the practice. He was joined by civil engineer Bruce Rockell and the firm later became Cowie Rockell Chong. This eventually ceased practice, but the Boon name carries on through Terry Boon's company.[153]

Herbert (Eric) Phillips

(1897–1980)

Phillips, who was born in Hastings, became a junior draughtsman at C. T. Natusch & Sons (see page 363), and also spent time at Hoggard, Prouse & Gummer in 1914 while training at the Auckland School of Architecture. After serving in the First World War, he remained in Britain to study at the Architectural Association in London. Back in New Zealand in 1918, Phillips rejoined Gummer's firm before going into partnership with Hastings architect Henry Hyland (1894–1969) in 1920. Hyland & Phillips won the competition for the new Public Trust Office building in Napier (1922), one of the few major buildings to survive the 1931 earthquake.[154]

Horace Lovell Massey ↑

(1895–1978)

Born in Auckland, where he attended Auckland Grammar School, Massey was articled to Alec Wiseman, Roy K. Binney and Hoggard & Prouse. While serving in France in the First World War, he and his friend Alfred Morgan came fourth in the Ideal Homes Daily Mail competition. Massey won a New Zealand Expeditionary Force scholarship in 1919 to study at the Architectural Association in London and returned to New Zealand in 1922. Massey partnered with George Edmund Tole (1898–1972) from 1928 to 1935, after which he practised as Horace L. Massey & Partners. After studying at the School of Architecture at Auckland University College, Ronald (Ron) Guthrie Beatson (senior) (1903–1996) was employed in Massey's office; he had also worked with Gummer & Ford. In 1940 Massey established the firm of Massey, Beatson, Rix-Trott & Co., with Beatson and Geoffrey (Geoff) A. Rix-Trott, later joined by G. Nield Carter to form Massey, Beatson, Rix-Trott Carter & Co. He was the first architect to be awarded four NZIA Gold Medals. Massey, Beatson, Rix-Trott & Carter won a Bronze Medal for Massey's own house in Remuera in 1950, and were appointed as architects to the University of Auckland, preparing a master plan in 1957 and designing a number of buildings. Massey was president of the NZIA from 1941 to 1942, a member of the Auckland Hospital Board for many years and retired around 1957. The firm became Beatson, Rix-Trott, Carter & Co., then Curtis Penman Read Williams (now CPRW) in 1974.[155]

Alfred Percy Morgan
(1893–1953)
After emigrating to New Zealand from London, Morgan's family settled in Christchurch, where he attended Christ's College before studying architecture in Auckland. During the First World War he served in the Royal Army Medical Corps and met Horace Massey while studying with him at the Architectural Association.[156]

Harold George (Pop) Davies
(1888–1976)
Davies started his architecture career indentured to Rob Roy McGregor, and completed his training in 1907. He joined the staff of the Wellington Education Board in 1908, was elected as an associate of the NZIA in 1914 and moved to Hastings to form his own practice in 1916.[157]

Albert Garnett
(1878–1956)
Garnett was the son of James Garnett, a well-known Hastings builder and one-time mayor. He worked for his father before taking up architecture. In 1915 he won the design competition for the Hastings Municipal Buildings (1917). After the 1931 earthquake, Garnett formed a partnership with Davies and Phillips, but he left the firm in 1933, and it became Davies & Phillips.[158]

Sidney (Sid) George Chaplin
(1905–1990)
John Sydney Kingsford
(1921–2013)
Keith Sands
(Dates unknown)
Neville Kennedy Norwell
(1935–2019)
After attending the School of Architecture in Auckland, Hastings-born Chaplin spent a year in 1925 as a junior draughtsman at Gummer & Ford, a position arranged by H. G. (Pop) Davies, before undertaking further training and gaining work experience in England. He returned to New Zealand just before the 1931 earthquake and set up his own practice in Hastings, where he won the 1934 design competition for the memorial clock tower. After the Second World War he joined the firm of Davies & Phillips, becoming a partner in Davies, Phillips & Chaplin (DPC) in 1947. When Sid Chaplin retired around 1980, Davies, Phillips & Chaplin became Kingsford Sands Norwell & Partners. Kingsford was a Hastings architect and Sands an engineer. Norwell joined Davies, Phillips & Chaplin as a school leaver and after five years enrolled at the Auckland School of Architecture, rejoining the firm following his study. Norwell joined the partnership when Eric Phillips and Pop Davies retired in 1965. The practice became Norwell & Reilly when Norwell was joined by Allan Crawford Reilly. In 1987 they moved Clive's 1876 St Mark's Anglican Church to Hastings and refurbished it to form their offices. On many of their drawings, the profile of the church forms the practice's logo. Reilly eventually left, and what was then Neville Norwell & Associates continued until its dissolution in 2009.[159]

Lewis (Lew) Edouard Martin
(1920–2013)
After graduating from the Architectural Association in London, Napier-born Martin joined the Fleet Air Arm in the Second World War. Following the war, he joined the London firm of Devereux & Davis, specialising in hospital architecture. Back in New Zealand, Martin joined Wellington architect and town planner George Porter (see page 362) in partnership in 1954. Martin became president of the Wellington Architecture Centre, and with Porter started the successful campaign to save Frederick Thatcher's Old St Paul's. Martin was also highly regarded for his pen-and-ink illustrations and his books, *Built for Us*, a history of the work of the government architects, and *Buildings to Enjoy*, are exemplars of their type. After retiring from architecture in 1983, Martin embarked on a new career as an actor, including minor roles in several movies.[160]

David George (George) Porter
(1921–1998)
Porter graduated from the Auckland School of Architecture in 1944 and worked from 1945 to 1951 at the Ministry of Works, where he developed an interest in town planning. Porter & Martin's other architectural work included Clifton Towers, a modernist apartment block at 202 Oriental Parade in Wellington (1963). After leaving the partnership with Lewis Martin, George Porter joined Allott Gabites to form Gabites Porter & Partners in 1978. Bill Alington (see page 363) worked with them for several years, before leaving in 1983 to set up his own practice, Alington Group Architects, from which he retired in 2000. Gabites Porter Consultants focused on town planning, and then branched into traffic and transportation design and developing software to support this. In 2014 Gabites Porter was acquired by Traffic Design Group (TDG), which was itself bought by US consultancy Stantec in 2018.[161]

Allott Lorimer Gabites
(1919–2004)
Gabites was educated in Christchurch and trained at the Auckland School of Architecture before serving with the Royal New Zealand Air Force. After studying in London, and touring Europe and the United States, he returned to New Zealand to work in the Planning Division of the Ministry of Works. In 1950 he formed the partnership of Patience & Gabites with Maurice Patience. He was subsequently the senior partner in several other architectural and planning practices. In 1971 Gabites & Beard, formed with James Beard (see below), merged with Toomath & Wilson to form Gabites Toomath Beard Wilson & Partners.[162]

Maurice Balfour Patience
(1915–1986)
Patience started his architectural training under William McKeon (see page 355) in 1932, before serving in the navy during the war. He completed architectural studies at Sheffield and Liverpool universities, before returning to New Zealand in 1948. He spent a year in the town planning section of the Ministry of Works in Wellington, before joining Allott Gabites. Patience also formed a partnership with Bill McKeon, which ended in 1963. With his son John B. Patience, he won the 1971 competition for the Palmerston North Civic Administration Building in the Square, which was completed in 1980. He retired in 1984.[163]

James Albert Beard
(1924–2017)
Beard trained at Auckland University before joining the Ministry of Works, where he became a cadet supervisor, mentoring several of the next generation of architects. In 1951 he won a scholarship to study city planning at the Massachusetts Institute of Technology, then studied for a master's degree in landscape architecture at Harvard. He returned to Harvard between 1967 and 1968 as a research assistant.[164]

William Hildebrand (Bill) Alington
(1929–2004)
Alington began a Ministry of Works cadetship in 1949; his supervisor was James Beard. He studied at the Auckland School of Architecture from 1951 to 1955, and in 1956 won a Fulbright Scholarship to study for a master's degree at the University of Illinois. After working with Robert Matthew Johnson Marshall in London, he returned to New Zealand and rejoined the Ministry of Works. Alington and Allott Gabites later formed Gabites Alington Edmondson with Derrick Edmondson. Alington left in 1983 to set up his own practice, Alington Group Architects, from which he retired in 2000.[165]

William (Bill) Toomath
(1925–2014)
Derek John Wilson
(1922–2016)
Toomath & Wilson had been established around 1957 by Bill Toomath and Derek Wilson, who had served in the Fleet Air Arm during the Second World War and studied at Auckland University before working in London. Toomath joined Crichton, McKay & Haughton (see page 354) in 1943 as an office junior, leaving in 1945 to study at Auckland. After completing his degree in 1949, he won a Fulbright Scholarship and studied for his master's at the Harvard Graduate School of Design in 1952. After working with Walter Gropius and I. M. Pei, he returned to New Zealand. In 1971 Gabites & Beard merged with Toomath & Wilson to form Gabites Toomath Beard Wilson & Partners. Gabites Toomath Beard Wilson lasted less than a year, by some accounts suffering from too many strong personalities. In 1972 James Beard left to form his own practice, James Beard & Co. Toomath and Wilson also left, forming Toomath Wilson Irvine Anderson with Don Irvine and Grahame Anderson.[166]

James Hall-Kenney
(Dates unknown)
Hall-Kenney joined Crichton & McKay in 1925 and, after a time in Dunedin, left for London to study at the Architectural Association. After service during the Second World War, he set up Hall-Kenney & Partners in Wellington and subsequently opened an office in Nelson. Hall-Kenney was an early proponent of modernist architecture in New Zealand, winning the first NZIA Gold Medal for an industrial building, the Milk Treatment Station in Auckland (1953). He appears to have retired by 1969, when the partners in Hall-Kenney & Partners were listed as Jan Rotman and George Edward Spence in Wellington, and Sydney Grant White and Christopher John Hay in Nelson, with Hay admitted to partnership that year. In 1970 the firm became Rotman White Spence & Hay.[167]

Arthur George Stephenson
(1890–1967)
One of Australia's leading hospital designers, Stephenson had various construction roles in Australia and Papua New Guinea before joining the Australian Imperial Force in 1915 and being awarded the Military Cross for bravery on the Western Front. After the war, he remained in London to study at the Architectural Association, before returning to Australia in 1920. He was knighted for services to architecture in 1954.[168]

Percy Hayman Meldrum
(1887–1968)
Meldrum, who was from Victoria in Australia, spent the First World War in London designing aircraft hangars for the War Office while running an atelier that became a gathering place for architects serving in the military. In 1919 he joined the staff of the Architectural Association, teaching both Arthur Stephenson and his later partner, Donald Turner. In 1921 he returned to Melbourne, where he joined Stephenson in practice as Stephenson & Meldrum.[169]

Donald Keith (Skipper) Turner
(1895–1964)
After an architectural apprenticeship in Sydney, Turner, who was from New South Wales, enlisted in 1915 and served in Egypt and France. Following his studies at the Architectural Association, he became an assistant architect at the Imperial War Graves Commission before returning to Australia in 1924. He joined Stephenson & Meldrum, becoming a partner in 1925.[170] Histories of Stephenson & Turner have given various dates for the establishment of the firm, ranging from 1920, which is probably when Arthur Stephenson began practice, to 1921 or early 1922, when his partnership with Percy Meldrum began. Stephenson was considered the more entrepreneurial of the partners, Meldrum the more artistically oriented. Early works in Melbourne included buildings at the Royal Melbourne Children's Hospital from 1922, and at Austin Hospital from 1928. They went on to design many other hospitals in Australia in the 1930s. 'Skipper' Turner managed the office that opened in Sydney in 1934, and became a director in 1936, when the firm was renamed Stephenson, Meldrum & Turner. After Meldrum left the partnership in 1937, it became Stephenson & Turner (S&T) the following year. Other offices opened in Adelaide, Newcastle and Canberra, and in Singapore. The early Melbourne hospital work led to larger commissions. In 1964 Arthur Stephenson became the first Australian to receive a RIBA Gold Medal. Turner retired in 1956, and Stephenson's son Peter led the firm from 1967 to 1972. In 1984 S&T was split into three independent organisations, Stephenson & Turner in Melbourne, Stephenson & Turner International in Sydney and Stephenson & Turner New Zealand. Since 2000, all the Australian offices have closed, with only the New Zealand operation continuing.[171]

Charles A. (Aleck) Natusch
(1883–1971)
Rene Natusch
(1885–1971)
Stanley Natusch
(1889–1973)
Guy Kingdon Natusch
(1921–2020)
Aleck Natusch joined his father, Napier architect Lewis (Charles) Tilleard Natusch (1851–1971), in 1898. He opened an office for the firm in Gisborne in 1900 and practised as an architect, structural engineer and quantity surveyor.[172] His brother Rene Natusch spent three years with local stock and station agents Williams & Kettle before joining his father's practice in 1904. He represented Hawke's Bay in rugby in 1907 and in rowing from 1903 to 1908. After service in the First World War, he returned to Napier in 1919.[173] Lewis Natusch's younger son, Stanley, was born in New Zealand, unlike his two older brothers, and established an office in Wellington for his father in 1906. In the First World War, he

saw action at Gallipoli and was wounded at Messines. He stayed in England to study at the Architectural Association. After working in London and the United States, where he gained structural engineering qualifications, Stanley came back to New Zealand in 1923. He returned to England in 1939, where he remained following the outbreak of the Second World War.[174] Rene's son, Guy, served in the Royal New Zealand Navy in the Second World War and was awarded the Distinguished Service Cross in 1944. He designed the Napier War Memorial Hall (1957), the Government Life Building, Gisborne (1966) and the Napier Library (1983).[175] The firm became Natusch & Sons in the 1920s, after the brothers Charles (Aleck), Rene and Stanley bought out their father's interest. In 1926 they employed Reg Uren, who on gaining his NZIA qualification left to establish a successful practice in England. Natusch & Sons became Natusch & Wilcox in 1965, when Rene and Guy Natusch were joined by Warren Stuart Wilcox, but Wilcox left the partnership in 1971. Guy Natusch was then joined by Herbert Maurice Shattky and the firm became Natusch Shattky & Co. Shattky joined his father's optometrist practice in 1945, after being invalided home from the war, but left in 1949 to take up architecture. After he retired in 1980, the firm became the Natusch Partnership when Guy Natusch was joined by Timothy (Tim) Alan Judd and Desmond Neil Fenwick. Guy Natusch retired and Judd Fenwick Natusch became Judd Fenwick Team Architecture in 1995. The firm is now known as Dougan Larkworthy Team Architects, with directors Paul Dougan and Robin Larkworthy.[176]

John Thomas Watson
(1883–1960)
Francis Eric Gooder
(1892–1931)
Raymond Lee
(1891–1949).

Watson, Gooder & Lee was established in 1924 in Masterton. Lee had trained with Frederick Charles Daniell (see page 359) in Masterton and maintained an office there after the other partners moved to Wellington. The partnership dissolved around 1928, and E. Neil Inkster joined Lee around 1936. Inkster was joined by T. D. McArthur in Blenheim, with the practice operating from offices in both Masterton and Blenheim. The partnership split in the late 1960s, with Inkster continuing in Masterton, and M. R. Reeve joining McArthur in Blenheim.[177]

Edgar (Ernest) Gillman
(1880–1951)
Thomas Frank Gillman
(1915–1998)

Ernest Gillman was born in Tauranga and established a practice in Paeroa in 1913. After completing his architecture degree at Auckland, which had been interrupted by service in the Royal Flying Air Corps during the First World War, his son Frank joined him in practice in 1947.[178]

David A. Sayers
(1931–2013)

Born in England, Sayers was the son of an interior designer father and a draughtswoman mother. He trained at the Architectural Association in London before working with Slater Uren & Pike, co-founded by New Zealand expatriate Reg Uren (1906–1988, see page 364). Sayers emigrated to New Zealand in 1954 and joined the Ministry of Works.[179]

William (Arthur) Gray
(1889–1953)

After serving in the First World War, in which his arm was permanently damaged after he was wounded on the Western Front and then inadequately treated while a prisoner of war, in 1920 Gray purchased the Auckland engineering practice of London-born and educated Ashley Hunter (1854–1932), who had established his own practice in 1897. (Gray, who became a major in the Territorials, trained engineers for overseas service during the Second World War.) In 1927 Gray was joined in partnership as Gray & Gulliver by graphic artist and engineer Thomas Ralph De Vere (Pop) Gulliver (1891–1933), who, like him, had worked for New Zealand Railways before setting up his own practice in 1919. As well as defence works around Auckland, Gray & Gulliver carried out the structural engineering design for the Auckland War Memorial Museum (1929). Larry Watts joined Gray in partnership in 1939.[180]

Richard Goulden Brickell
(1908–1994)

Born in Dunedin, Brickell trained first as a surveyor, then as a civil engineer. With work scarce in the 1930s, he went gold mining, designing hydraulic dredges, before working with the Air Ministry in Britain, building airfields and radar towers. In the war he was attached to the Airfield Construction Squadron and posted to France to build forward airfields. When the bomber in which he was travelling to Crete was forced to land in Algeria, he was interned by the Vichy French in the Laghouat prisoner-of-war camp for two years. After North Africa was liberated, he returned to Britain and in 1943 was posted to India, planning invasion tactics and forward airfields for jungles. Back in New Zealand in 1945, Brickell joined the Public Works Department, then established his own business in 1953.[181]

Ian Brampton Reynolds
(1922–2005)

Architect and planner Reynolds was born and educated in Wellington. He spent two years as a pupil with a local architect, before serving in the army from 1940 while studying part-time at Auckland University College. He joined the Ministry of Works in 1946, before moving in 1948 to Britain, where he worked for Berthold Lubetkin, among others. In 1952 he rejoined the ministry, working in the government architect's office with Francis Gordon Wilson (see page 354) on the Otago Dental School. In 1955, Reynolds joined Jones, Adams & Kingston as the architect partner of the practice which two years later became Kingston, Reynolds, Thom & Allardice. Reynolds was president of the NZIA from 1977 to 1978 and retired from KRTA in 1988.[182]

Frederick (Miles) Warren
(1929–2022)

Warren was born in Christchurch, educated at Christ's College and at 16 was apprenticed to architect Cecil Wood, studying architecture by correspondence through the Christchurch Atelier. After completing his studies at Auckland, Warren travelled to Britain in 1953, where he worked at the London County Council. He returned to New Zealand in 1955 to start his own practice. At Ōhinetahi, at the head of Lyttelton Harbour, he and his sister Pauline and her husband, architect John Trengrove, developed a large and highly regarded garden. He received a knighthood in 1985 and was awarded the Order of New Zealand in 1995. Warren retired from Warren and Mahoney in 1994, two years after his longtime partner Maurice Mahoney, and was awarded the NZIA Gold Medal in 2000, after the award was revised to recognise an architect's significant body of work and contribution to the profession.[183]

Selected practice histories

AECOM / Gillman Garry Clapp & Sayers / Worley / Meritec / Maunsell

Edgar (Ernest) Gillman founded his practice in Paeroa in 1913. Gillman's business developed, and around the outbreak of the Second World War, he was appointed architect to the New Zealand Co-operative Dairy Company, which meant relocating his family and business to Hamilton. After completing a Bachelor of Architecture course at the University of Auckland, which had been interrupted by service in the air force, his son, T. F. (Frank) Gillman, joined him to form Gillman & Gillman Architects in 1947. On Ernest Gillman's death in 1951, the firm became T. F. Gillman & Co. It then merged with that of architect Doug Angus and engineer Paul Marks to become Gillman, Angus & Marks, Architects and Engineers, but this partnership was dissolved in 1954 and the firm reverted to its former name. By mutual agreement, the three partners divided the clients between them and Angus went on to form Angus, Flood & Griffiths.[1] Later that year, Frank Gillman formed a partnership with David A. Sayers, who had emigrated from Britain that year and joined the Ministry of Works. He had been offered a position at the New Zealand Co-operative Dairy Company, which at the same time had been trying to persuade Gillman to become its chief architect. Gillman travelled to Wellington to meet Sayers and offered him the opportunity to move to Hamilton and join him as a junior partner.[2] Architect Peter Garry, who had been architect to the dairy company, formed a partnership with civil engineer L. Rex Clapp in Hamilton around 1954, focused on commercial and industrial projects. Gillman and Sayers were concerned about being over-reliant on hospital work, and so T. F. Gillman & Co. merged with Garry & Clapp to form Gillman Garry Clapp & Sayers in 1963. The firm obtained dairy factory work across the Waikato region. By 1971 A. R. I. Garry, Robert Ellis, Alan Howe and engineers Eddie Thomas and Tony Schuitemaker had joined as partners.[3] In 1981, by which stage it had 80 staff, Gillman Garry Clapp & Sayers was restructured and renamed Gillman Partners. David Sayers retired in 1984. In 1985 the practice merged with Worley Consultants to become Worley Gillman. The Gillman name was eventually dropped, and the architectural component became Worley Architects. Worley traced its history back to the establishment of Lockie Gannon & Worley in 1919. This became Ralph P. Worley & Downey in 1955, Worley Downey Muir in 1960, Worley Downey Mandeno in 1981 (when it merged with Mandeno Chitty & Bell) and Worley Consultants in 1982.[4] Worley was rebranded as Meritec in 2000 and two years later the practice was bought by the British multi-disciplinary consultancy Maunsell, founded by Guy Anson Maunsell (1884–1961), designer of the eponymous forts built in the Thames and Mersey estuaries during the Second World War, as G. Maunsell & Co. in Britain in 1955. It expanded into Australia and the Middle East, later merging with Oscar Faber & Partners to form Faber Maunsell.[5] In 2000 Maunsell itself had been purchased by multi-national AECOM, whose origins are in the Ashland Oil & Refining Co., an asphalt manufacturer founded in Oklahoma in 1910 that became one of the larger roading contractors in the United States and developed expertise in road design. In 1990, the design component was split off as AECOM Technology Corporation. By 2019, after a series of acquisitions, it had become a multi-disciplinary practice with 51,000 employees around the world.[6]

APG Architects

Originally established in 2009 as MSH Architects in Hamilton by Andrew McNally, Ces Scott and Kierin Hoad, APG has expanded to offices in Tauranga and Nadi, Fiji.[7]

Alleman, Land & Verrall

This practice, established and very active in Rotorua, opened an office in Auckland in the late 1950s as Alleman, Land, Newnham & Verrall. Surrey Alleman was an Auckland architect known for the NZIA Gold Medal-winning Hampton Court flats on Federal Street in Auckland and the Garden Court flats on Tamaki Drive in Auckland's Mission Bay. In 1963 Peter Verrall established his own practice and in 1968 he went into partnership with Garth Hocking. Hocking & Verrall designed the 1983 psychiatric unit at Rotorua Hospital. Verrall retired in 1988, Hocking two years later.

Archaus

Archaus was formed in Wellington in the early 1990s by Dennis Burns and Mike Cole. More recently they were joined by Brian Cullen, merging his Auckland practice Paterson Cullen Irwin.[8]

Archimedia / Devine Erby Mazlin

Archimedia was formed by Lindsay Mackie in 1998, when the New Zealand arm of the Australian firm Devine Erby Mazlin separated from its parent. Devine Erby Stowe was founded in Sydney by Grant Devine and Jonathan Erby. It became Devine Erby Mazlin in 1975 when Brian Mazlin joined. The practice was restructured in 1995 to become DEM Architects. Health work in Australia included work on the Royal Hospital for Women in Sydney.[9]

Architects 44

Architects 44 traces its heritage back to the practice established in Gisborne by Monty Glengarry in 1951. He was joined by his brother Bruce in 1952, then Jock Corson and in 1953 by Colin Pilbrow, forming Glengarry Glengarry Corson & Pilbrow. Bruce Glengarry left in 1970, Colin Pilbrow in 1979, and Graeme Nicoll joined in 1980. Monty Glengarry and Jock Corson died later in that decade. James Blackburne entered partnership with Nicoll in 2000 and was later joined by Daniel King and Rachael Spriggs. The practice name was taken from its address in Childers Road.[10]

Architecture HDT

Architecture HDT's origins are in the partnership formed by Burwell Hunt and Mike Davies in Wellington in 1994. A Hawke's Bay office opened in 2008 and an office in Christchurch in 2023.[11]

Architectus / Conrad Gargett / McConnel Smith & Johnson

McConnel Smith & Johnson traced its origins to the practice established in Sydney in 1949 by First World War veteran Kenneth McConnel (1895–1973). He was joined by Peter Johnson (1924–2003), who had served in the Second World War, and in 1954 by Stanley Smith (1919–?). McConnel retired in 1964, Smith in 1971, and Johnson was responsible for much of the firm's subsequent growth while also being a professor of architecture at the University of Sydney. Significant health projects in Australia by MSJ include the Olivia Newton John Cancer Centre (2012), with Jackson Architecture. In 2020 MSJ merged with Conrad Gargett, which traces its history back to a practice formed in Brisbane in 1890 by Henry Wallace Atkinson (1866–1908), who was joined by Charles McLay (1860–1918) in 1907. Arnold H. Conrad became a partner when McLay died and was later joined by Thomas Brennan (Bren) Femister Gargett; the practice became Conrad Gargett in 1939. This became Conrad Gargett Riddel after combining, in 2012, with Riddel Architecture, which had been established by Robert Riddel in 1982. In 2013 Conrad Gargett Riddel merged with prominent Sydney firm Ancher Mortlock & Woolley to become Conrad Gargett Riddel Ancher Mortlock Woolley. After serving in the Second World War, Sydney Edward Cambrian Archer (1904–1979) had set up in Sydney in 1946. Staff members Harold Bryce Mortlock (1921–2004) and Stuart Murray became partners in 1952. When Kenneth (Ken) Frank Charles Woolley (1933–2015) joined in 1964, the firm became Ancher Mortlock Murray & Woolley. It was renamed Ancher Mortlock & Woolley in 1975. Conrad Gargett Riddel Ancher Mortlock Woolley was soon rebranded as Conrad Gargett.[12] In 2023 there was a further merger with Architectus, founded in 1986 in Auckland by Malcolm Bowes, Patrick Clifford and Michael Thomson. They formed Architectus Australia after winning the design competition for the Queensland Gallery of Modern Art (2006) in Brisbane with Clare & Clare in 2001. Te Puna Whaiora children's health camp (2003) in Pakuranga, by Architectus, includes a school, residential and recreational building, and parents' accommodation.[13]

Ashton Mitchell

Malcolm Mitchell left Roberts Mitchell, founded in 1982, and joined Peter Ashton in 1993. Mitchell retired in 2005, and Ashton in 2023.[14]

Aurecon / Brickell, Moss, Rankine & Hill / Connell Wagner

After several years with the Public Works Department, civil engineer Richard Goulden Brickell established R. G. Brickell Consulting Engineer in 1953. In 1962 he was joined by John Didsbury Moss to form Brickell, Moss & Partners, based in Lower Hutt. John Moss was headhunted by John Rankine of the Australian firm Rankine & Hill to join as its New Zealand manager. Instead, the two firms merged in 1966 as Brickell, Moss, Rankine & Hill, with offices in Wellington, Lower Hutt and Auckland, and the range of services expanded from its civil engineering base to structural and later building services engineering. Brickell left the firm in 1968 and the alliance with Rankine & Hill appears to have later ended; by 1981 the New Zealand practice was again operating as Brickell, Moss & Partners.[15] In 1992 Rankine & Hill merged with another Australian firm, Connell Wagner, and took its name. Connell Wagner was the result of the 1989 merger of two firms, MacDonald Wagner & Priddle, formed as MacDonald Wagner in Sydney in 1934, and the Connell Group, formed as John Connell & Associates in Melbourne in 1956. In 2009, Connell Wagner merged with two large South African consulting firms, Ninham Shand (established in 1932) and Africon (1951), to form Aurecon. With over 7500 staff members, Aurecon now operates in 28 countries across Africa, Asia-Pacific and the Middle East. [16]

Babbage

Faram & Babbage was founded in 1936 by Alister Babbage and Lionel Faram as an engineering consultancy designing roads and bridges. During the Second World War both partners served as army engineers in North Africa and Europe. Babbage continued the practice when he returned in 1943; Faram left in 1945. In 1951 Babbage was appointed consultant for the New Zealand Forest Products mill being developed at Kinleith, near Tokoroa.[17]

Baker Garden

In 2004, Mark Garden joined the practice that Nick Baker had established in Dunedin.[18]

Beca

Beca traces its history to 1920, when, after serving in the First World War, William (Arthur) Gray (1889–1953) purchased the Auckland engineering practice of Ashley Hunter (1854–1932). Born and educated in London, in 1872 Hunter emigrated to New Zealand, where he became an engineering cadet at the Public Works Department in Wellington, and engineer to the Westport Coal Company in 1894, before establishing his own practice in 1897. Gray became a captain in the NZ Rifle Brigade, and his was injured on the Western front. Gray ran the practice while also serving in the Territorial Army, in which he became a major. He later served at the start of the Second World War, training engineers for overseas service. In 1927, Gray was joined in partnership by graphic artist and engineer Thomas Ralph De Vere (Pop) Gulliver (?–1933), who, like him, had worked for NZ Railways before setting up his own practice in 1919. As well as defence work around Auckland, Gray & Gulliver carried out the structural engineering design for the Auckland War Memorial Museum (1929). Larry Watts joined Gray in partnership in 1939, the practice becoming Gray & Watts. Watts refused to join the New Zealand Institute of Engineers, seeing it as a self-serving group, despite membership being a requirement for projects involving public funds, and only wanted to work with Auckland architects on local projects. After distinguished service in the air force during the Second World War, George Samuel Beca formed his own practice. Beca joined Gray & Watts in 1952, then became a 50 per cent partner in 1954 and the firm was renamed Gray, Watts & Beca.[19] Beca became registered and pursued the other opportunities opening up as the New Zealand economy recovered after the war. Up to this time, engineers had generally worked as sub-consultants to architects, but he believed that engineers were often more suited to being the principal advisers. As a result, the firm was engaged by such major industrial clients as Ford, New Zealand Breweries, Tasman Pulp & Paper, New Zealand Steel and Air New Zealand. Many architects, however, did not welcome this approach and at first offered fewer commissions. Beca led the firm for many years, overseeing its growth into the largest private New Zealand-based multi-disciplinary consultancy.[20] Auckland-born Ron (later Sir Ron) Carter joined in 1959, and following two years with Arup in Britain, returned to become a partner in Grey, Watts & Beca in 1965. In 1968, Beca and Carter merged their practice with the Wellington firm of Hollings & Ferner [21], and the survey practice of Leach & Dickson, to become Beca, Carter, Hollings & Ferner Ltd. Canterbury University colleagues John Hollings and Martin Ferner had returned from working overseas to join the Wellington practice of Martyn Spencer in 1963. At that time, the Ministry of Works was overloaded working on major hydro-electric schemes, and the firm picked up several smaller infrastructure projects. Personality differences resulted in Spencer leaving before the merger with Beca and Carter. The merged practice became a limited liability company in 1972, with all shareholders employees of the firm. Carter became managing director on George Beca's retirement in 1986 and was chairman of the Beca group until 2002, by which time the firm had more than 1200 employees. By the time he retired in 2008, this figure had doubled.[22] During the recession of the 1960s the firm sought work outside New Zealand, leading to expansion into Australia, Papua New Guinea, Indonesia, Singapore, Myanmar and China. The first overseas office was opened in Melbourne in 1968, and the firm began working on projects in Asia in 1971; an office opened in Singapore in 1977.

The downsizing and eventual privatisation of the Ministry of Works and Development in 1996 opened the opportunities for more infrastructure work in New Zealand, including roading, rail and bridge projects. At one point, the firm had an office in London, but this proved a step too far and it was closed, and they pulled out of China in 2017. Ron Carter was knighted for services to engineering and business in 1998 and was appointed a Member of the Order of New Zealand in 2014.[23] Beca Group Limited is now one of the largest employee-owned professional services consultancy firms in the Asia–Pacific, with 20 offices throughout New Zealand, including its base in Auckland, as well as Australia, Indonesia, Singapore, Thailand and Myanmar. The company has more than 3400 staff, 1300 of whom are shareholders.[24]

Bligh Voller Nield (BVN)
BVN's origins lie in a partnership formed in Brisbane in 1926 by Arthur William Forster Bligh (1905–1988) and Colin Jessop. Athol Bretnall and Ronald Voller (1915–2006) joined after the Second World War, Bligh's son Graham in 1965 and Jon Voller some time later. In 1997 Bligh Voller merged with the Sydney practice of Lawrence Nield and Grose Bradley; the firm became BVN Architecture in 2009.[25]

Brewer Davidson
Auckland practice Brewer Davidson was formed in 1993 by Kevin Brewer and Peter Davidson.[26]

BSW Architects / Booth Sweetman & Wolfe
Booth Sweetman & Wolfe (originally John Booth Sweetman & Wolfe, and now BSW Architects) was founded in 1944 as an architectural and engineering practice by John Booth, who had been an engineering partner at Gummer & Ford, before leaving to establish his own firm. He was later joined by engineer Murray Mayell Sweetman (1929–1993) and architect Leonard Joseph Wolfe.[27]

Buchan
John Angus Laird founded a practice in Geelong in 1890, where he was later joined by Thomas Johnston (Tom) Buchan. His son Thomas Johnston, later Sir John, Buchan (1909-1998) was articled to Laird & Buchan in 1930. When Laird died in 1936, the firm became Buchan Laird & Buchan, with his son Ewen Laird. In 1946, the base was relocated to Melbourne, and it became Buchan Laird & Bawden in 1980, then Buchan Group in 1990. The catalyst for expansion into New Zealand was the firm's winning of the design competition for the Christchurch Art Gallery (1998).[28]

CCM / Moller Architects
CCM was established in Wellington in 1969 as Craig Craig Moller by James Thomas (Jim) Craig, his son, Jon Alistair Craig, and Gordon Moller. An Auckland office led by Moller opened in 1993, when the firm won the commission to design the SkyCity casino and entertainment centre, including the Sky Tower. In 2002 two separate practices were formed, CCM in Wellington and Moller Architects in Auckland. Adam Flowers leads CCM's health sector.[29]

Chow:Hill
↑

Chow:Hill was established in 1992 by Chien Chow, who had been an associate at Worley Gillman, and Richard Hill, who had been appointed head of its Hamilton architecture department in 1988.[30] An office was set up in Auckland in 1995, when Darryl Carey joined to lead the development of the firm's specialisation in health. Darryl Carey was instrumental in setting up the New Zealand Health Design Council in 2011, which he chaired for its first decade. Anner Chong has led the practice's health team since 2018.[31]

Clendon Burns & Park
Clendon & Burns began as a structural engineering practice formed by Wilf Edwards in 1947. Edwards was joined by Tom Clendon to form Edwards & Clendon around 1955. Arthur G. Park set up his own structural consultancy in 1978 and the two merged in 1985 to form Clendon, Burns & Park Ltd.[32]

Cosgroves
Cosgroves was founded by Brady Cosgrove in 1996 and provides services and civil engineering disciplines from six offices throughout New Zealand. Health projects include Manukau Health Park, Mercy Hospital in Dunedin, and refurbishments at Timaru and North Shore Hospitals.[33]

DesignGroup Stapleton Elliott / Architects H+K / ASC / Crosson Architects / Wilson + Hill
In 1989 Palmerston North architect Brian Elliott left the partnership that he had formed with Dickson Lonergan architects of Whanganui, to join Reginald (Reg) Clifford Stapleton (1930–2022) and form Stapleton Elliott. This became the core of a nationwide association of independent architectural practices, with nine offices and more than 140 staff. Other members include Architecture H+K (originally Harrison & King) in Whāngarei, Crosson Architects in Auckland, and Wilson + Hill in Christchurch. The latter was formed in Christchurch in 1995 by Christopher Wilson and David Hill. Another member, ASC, traces its history back to the firm established in Auckland by Nyall Gibson in 1956. This became Andrews Scott Cotton in 1991, with Graeme Scott and Neil Cotton.[34]

Destravis
Destravis was established in 2012 by Gunther de Graeve, and specialises in health planning, operating from offices in Brisbane, Melbourne and Wellington.[35]

DLA / Dickson Lonergan Architects
Bruce Dickson established a practice in Whanganui in 1967, and was joined by Barry Lonergan, forming Dickson Lonergan Architects in 1974. The firm became Dickson Elliot Lonergan when they were joined by Brian Elliott in Palmerston North in 1985, however Elliot left and they became Dickson Lonergan Architects in 1991, then DLA Architects in 2011. The practice expanded to Wellington under Glenn Gardiner in 1999, and to Timaru under Murray Ackroyd in 2005. Offices have since been opened in Hamilton, Auckland and Tauranga.[36]

First Principles Architects & Interiors
First Principles Architects & Interiors was founded in Tauranga by Graham and Kate Price in 2013.[37]

Hawkins Architecture

After working as a builder for 15 years, Mark Hawkins retrained in architectural design, forming this practice in Blenheim in 1998.[38]

Hawthorn Geddes

Hawthorn Geddes was established as the engineering consultancy of Robert James and Don Dunning in Whāngarei in 1962 and was taken over by Malcolm Hawthorn and Peter Geddes in 1998. Architect Philip Higham joined in 1998 and becoming a director the following year.[39]

HDR / Rice Daubney / Di Carlo Potts

HDR traces its origins to the Henningson Engineering Company, founded by H. H. Henningson in Omaha in 1917. Former interns Willard Richardson and Charles W. 'Chuck' Durham purchased shares in 1950 to form Henningson Durham & Richardson Inc. HDR is now an employee-owned multi-national company with staff of over 12,000 and more than 225 offices worldwide.[40] In 2013 HDR acquired Australian practice Rice Daubney, founded in Sydney in 1976 by Kevin Rice (1932–2011) and John Daubney. Its healthcare work included the Chris O'Brien Lifehouse at Royal Prince Alfred Hospital and Sunshine Coast University Hospital (2016), the latter with Architectus. HDR Rice Daubney rebranded as HDR in 2017. Rice Daubney Di Carlo Potts Health was formed in 2004, when Rice Daubney was joined by Sydney health specialist practice Di Carlo Potts, established by Tony Di Carlo and Neville Potts in Sydney in 1984. The firm designed the Wagga Wagga and Royal Darwin hospitals.[41]

Holmes

Lyall Holmes started his practice in 1956 and later that year formed the firm of Holmes & Wood with Brian Wood. They were joined by Russell Poole, to become Holmes, Wood & Poole, who were the structural engineers for the Christchurch Town Hall. The firm became Holmes, Wood, Poole & Johnstone, when Peter Johnstone joined, and later Holmes Consulting Group.

HPA

HPA was founded in 1997 by Terry Coombs, who was joined by Neville Brummer in 2003. Coombs retired in 2021, the year the firm amalgamated with Technical Solutions.[42]

Ignite / Studio Design + Architecture

Ignite was formed in 1987, the year Jeremy Whelan joined as a senior architect; he became managing director five years later. Studio Design + Architecture was founded by Michael O'Brien and designer Niki Harrison in 2016, both of whom moved from HBO+EMTB. Michael O'Brien joined Ignite Architects in 2023 and Te Wao Nui now forms part of its portfolio. In 2024 Ignite entered into a strategic alliance with Billard Leece Partnership (BLP) of Australia. Billard Leece was founded in Melbourne in 1996 by Ron Billard and David Leece, expanding to offices in Sydney and Brisbane.[43]

IKON Architects / Ian Krause Architects

IKON was founded in Christchurch as Ian Krause Architects in 1976.[44]

Jacobs / Kingston, Reynolds, Thom & Allardice / Sinclair, Knight, Merz

Jacobs can trace its roots in New Zealand back to 1915, when Stanley W. Jones established a structural and civil engineering practice. After R. C. Adams became a partner in 1920, the firm operated as Jones & Adams until 1950. Early projects included wharves, water and sewerage projects and bridges, including preliminary schemes for the Auckland Harbour Bridge. Architects were brought on to the firm's staff in the 1940s to work on commissions for several large dairy factories. After Jones retired in 1954, the firm became Jones, Adams & Kingston in 1955, with engineer Robin (Bob) Kingston, and Jones, Adams, Kingston & Reynolds when architect Ian Brampton Reynolds joined later that year(see page 364).[45] In 1957 engineers David Thom and N. W. Allardice became partners in the firm, which was renamed Kingston, Reynolds, Thom & Allardice (commonly referred to as KRTA) in 1962. Andrew Barrie has written that it was 'then the only comprehensive multi-disciplinary practice in New Zealand', apart from the Ministry of Works of course, providing architecture, planning and quantity engineering services, alongside civil, structural, electrical and mechanical engineering.[46] In 1995 KRTA merged with Morrison Cooper to form Kingston Morrison. Morrison & Partners was a Wellington engineering practice formed by W. G. Morrison, with G. W. Butcher and S. C. Gentry. In 1970 they were joined by architect Keith Cooper and his twin brother and engineer Graham, to form Morrison Cooper.[47] Australian firm Sinclair, Knight, Merz bought Kingston Morrison in 1999 and was itself purchased by multi-national Jacobs Engineering Group in 2013. Sinclair & Knight was established in Sydney by Bruce Sinclair and Jack Knight in 1964, and in 1996 it merged with Merz Australia (a firm descended from British firm Merz & McLellan) to form Sinclair Knight Merz. During a series of mergers over the following 10 years it developed into a 6900-person firm operating across Asia Pacific, the Americas, Europe, the Middle East and Africa.[48] Jacobs Engineering Group, founded by Joseph J. Jacobs in Pasadena, California in 1947, grew through a series of acquisitions to be one of the world's largest multi-disciplinary consulting firms. By 2018 it had 400 offices and 80,000 staff in the Americas, Europe, Asia, Africa and Australasia.[49]

Jasmax / JASMaD ↑

Jelicich, Austin & Smith was founded in 1963 by Stephen (Steve) Jelicich, John Austin and Graham Smith. Jelicich had formed Brenner Associates in Auckland in 1949, with architects Desmond Mullen and Ron Grant and artist/designer Milan Mrkusich, before leaving to start his own practice, the Architects Planning Group, in 1960. Austin and Smith had been with KRTA, and Ivan Mercep, who had also worked there, joined soon after, forming JASM.[50] When architect and planner at the Auckland Regional Authority, Rodney James Peter (Rod) Davies joined in 1966, the practice became JASMaD. John David Sutherland joined in 1966, becoming a partner in 1971, and Graham Smith left in 1974, the year that it became a limited liability company. The firm diversified into planning, information management, and even structural engineering for a time.[51] In 1989, JASMaD merged with two younger firms, Bossley Cheshire (Pete Bossley and Pip Cheshire) and Gibbs Harris (David Gibbs and Richard Harris), to form

Jasmax, which has grown to be one of New Zealand's largest architectural firms, with more than 200 staff members in five offices, including two in Australia. Euan McKellar led the firm's earlier major health projects and was succeeded by Sarah Hayden. Melanie Mason and Sandee Stanley joined as principals in 2022, bringing significant mental health and international experience, respectively. [52]

Jensen Hughes

Fire engineering consultancy Crossfire was founded in Auckland in 2012, and has provided services on several health projects. In 2022 it joined the US firm Jensen Hughes, which traces its history back to a fire engineering practice founded in 1939.[53]

Jigsaw Architects

Jigsaw Architects, previously Matrixx, formed from the Tauranga office of Babbage in 1992.[54]

Johnstaff

Johnstaff was founded in Melbourne in 1991 by Phil Johnston and David Wagstaff to provide strategic advisory and project management services for infrastructure projects.[55]

Klein

Established in 1991 by James and Johanna Klein, the firm became Haycock Klein when they were joined by Philip Haycock from Peddle, Thorp & Walker. Haycock left in 1997 to form Healthworx with Onno Le Roy. The practice was later rebranded as Klein Healthcare Designers, to reflect their growing specialisation in health facilities. Now Klein Architects, it has a staff of approximately 40. Rachael Rush joined the firm in 1999 and became managing director in 2010. In 2022 she was elected as the New Zealand Health Design Council's second chairperson. Michael Lawler, who had been with the practice since 1996, became a director in 2009[56]

Marshall Day Acoustics

Marshall Day Acoustics was established in Auckland in 1981 by Sir Harold Marshall and Christopher Day. Marshall, who was professor of architecture at the University of Auckland and founder of the Acoustics Research Centre there, was pivotal to the success of Warren and Mahoney's 1972 Christchurch Town Hall. The firm has grown to be a world leader in the field, with 90 staff throughout New Zealand, Australia, China and France.[57]

Mason & Wales

William Mason (see page 347) employed Nathaniel Young Armstrong Wales as a clerk of works on the Bank of New Zealand project in 1863. Mason invited him to become a partner, and the firm was renamed Mason & Wales. N. Y. A. Wales was followed in the practice by his son Patrick Young Wales (1864–1939), grandson Nathaniel Young Armstrong Wales (1896–1980), who served in France in the First World War, and in 1956 by his great-grandson N. Y. A. Wales (1927–2011). P. Y. Wales was president of the NZIA from 1912 to 1913, and the second N. Y. A. Wales from 1955 to 1956. C. Ashley Muir (1946–) joined the partnership in 1970. After graduating from the University of Auckland in 1977, Francis Whitaker joined in 1983. He is currently one of two directors, with Muir's son, Hamish Muir.[58]

McCoy & Wixon

Edward John (Ted) McCoy (1925–2018) studied architecture at the University of Auckland. In 1950 he established his own practice in Dunedin and in 1967 was joined by Peter E. Wixon (1927–2004), who had been appointed an associate in the Dunedin office of Stephenson & Turner in 1964. The firm designed the new sanctuary at Dunedin's St Paul's Cathedral (1970) and various buildings at the University of Otago as well as the Otago Community Hospice in North Dunedin (2001). McCoy and Wixon joined with R. E. N. Oakley, W. G. Pinfold, R. C. Turvey, A. J. Neil, M. J. Cockburn and engineers L. M. Robinson and J. A. Hadley to form the Architects Engineers Partnership with offices in Dunedin, Ōamaru, Invercargill and Queenstown; a Fiji office opened in 1971. When this dissolved in 1973, the resulting architectural practices were McCoy & Wixon, Oakley Pinfold Turvey & Neil, M. J. Cockburn (in Fiji) and the engineering firm of Hadley & Robinson. The founder's sons, John McCoy and Hamish Wixon, joined the practice and later became partners.[59]

McDowell Architects

Allan Charles (A. C.) Ford established a practice in Invercargill in 1920. He was joined by L. J. Gray, and the practice later became Ford Gray & Derbie, before Stephen J. Hurd joined in 1968, forming Ford, Gray, Derbie & Hurd. Gray and Derbie continued after Ford retired and Hurd left, and it became Gray Hesselin & Baxter in 1979, with Alexander Reko (Mick) Hesselin (1936–2022) and N. L. P. Baxter. Gray retired in 1981, and the firm became Baxter Hesselin McDowell, with Neil McDowell (1953–2010) becoming a partner. It was later McDowell Architects and is now Beattie McDowell, as Roger Beattie took over the firm after Neil McDowell's death.[60]

McKenzie Higham Architects

McKenzie Higham Architects was formed in Wellington in 1999 by Callum McKenzie and Mark Higham. After the death of Denis Fortune in 2018, staff from Bulleyment Fortune joined McKenzie Higham Architects, which holds the Bulleyment Fortune archive with significant records from its predecessor firms, such as Crichton & McKay.[61]

Medispace

Medispace was founded as a specialist health property development company by Roy Simmons in 2010. It has its own team of architects and designers, but also uses external consultants as required.[62]

Mode

Mode was established in Brisbane in 1991 as Rhonan O'Brien Architects & Designers Ltd. In 2005, the name was changed to Mode Design Corp and a Sydney studio was established, followed by others throughout Australia. An Auckland studio was set up in 2013.[63]

New Zealand Consulting Engineers Ltd

Peter Johnstone left Holmes to form New Zealand Consulting Engineers Ltd in 2014.[64]

Pacific Environments

Rolland (Roly) Vincent Adams and Brian Dodd formed a partnership in Auckland in 1960. They were joined by Neville H. Price as Price Adams Dodd from 1970 to 1972, and then by George Paterson, forming Adams Dodd Paterson. In 1981, the practice split into Adams Langley and Architects Dodd Paterson, and the latter became Dodd Paterson & Bukowski Rehm in 1992, then ADP. Peter Eising merged his practice with ADP in 2006 to form Pacific Environments.[65]

Pak Design

Pak Design was established by Matt Janes in Palmerston North in 2008.[66]

Peddlethorp

Peddlethorp's origins lie in the practice established by James Peddle in Sydney in 1889; he was joined by Samuel George

Thorp in 1914. When H. Ernest Walker joined them in 1925, the firm became Peddle Thorp & Walker (later PTW). It eventually became one of Australia's largest architectural practices, specialising in high-rise commercial buildings. Thorp's son, Graham, joined the firm in the 1950s and became its leading partner in the 1960s; he retired in 1990. The firm's hospital work in Australia included buildings at the Royal Hospital for Women in Sydney, and the Royal Children's Hospital in Brisbane. The partnership was disbanded in 1989 and replaced by a federation of incorporated businesses. The Peddle Thorp Australia network was established in 1992. In 2013 PTW was acquired by the Chinese consulting firm China Construction Design International, but the Melbourne and New Zealand offices remained independent and part of what became the Peddle Thorp network.[67]

Powell Fenwick

Powell Fenwick was formed by Guy Powell in Christchurch in 1938, who was joined by Chris Fenwick in 1954. During the 1960s, it expanded, becoming Powell Fenwick & Johnson, later Powell Fenwick & Williams, with offices in Auckland, Napier and Lower Hutt.[68]

Sheppard & Rout

Sheppard & Rout was formed in 1982 by David Sheppard, who had been in KRTA's Christchurch office, and Jonty Rout (?–2003). Tim Dagg joined the firm in 1986 and Jasper van der Lingen in 1993; both became directors in 2006.[69]

Silver Thomas Hanley (STH)

STH dates from 1978, when husband-and-wife team Peter and Aija Thomas joined a practice originally established in Melbourne in 1953 that became Silver Thomas Hanley in 1985. STH has offices in Melbourne, Sydney, Adelaide and Brisbane, and a Perth office that operates as a separate company but retains the Silver Thomas Hanley name.[70]

Stantec

Gabites Porter Consultants, formed by Allott Gabites and George Porter in 1978, focused on town planning, from which they branched into traffic and transportation design, and then into software design to support this. Their TRACKS system is now managed by Transportation & Traffic Systems of Christchurch, which in 2006 entered into an agreement to integrate this with a similar one developed by Forum8 of Japan. In 2014 Gabites Porter was acquired by Traffic Design Group (TDG), which was itself bought by US consultancy Stantec in 2018.[71] Stantec was founded as D. R. Stanley Associates in Canada and grew through a series of acquisitions. After a 2016 merger with MWH Global, it became one of the world's top three design firms. It now employs more than 26,000 people in 400 locations around the world, with 780 in New Zealand working from 17 offices.[72]

Stephen Matthews Architects

Stephen Matthews established his practice in Auckland in 1989.[73]

Stephenson & Turner

Histories of Stephenson & Turner have given various dates for the establishment of the firm, ranging from 1920, which is probably when Arthur Stephenson began practice, to 1921 or early 1922, when Percy Meldrum (see page 363) joined him to form Stephenson & Meldrum. After the latter left the partnership, it was renamed Stephenson & Turner (S&T) in 1938. Other offices opened in Adelaide, Newcastle and Canberra, and in Singapore. The early Melbourne hospital work led to larger commissions. In 1964 Arthur Stephenson became the first Australian to receive a RIBA Gold Medal. Turner retired in 1956, and Stephenson's son Peter led the firm from 1967 to 1972. In 1984 S&T was split into three independent organisations, Stephenson & Turner in Melbourne, Stephenson & Turner International in Sydney and Stephenson & Turner New Zealand. The Australian arm merged with John Castles in 1995 to form Castles Stephenson & Turner. Since 2000, all the Australian offices have closed, with only the New Zealand operation continuing to keep the name alive.[74] In 2022 the four New Zealand offices were set up as separate firms, which in turn own the central company of Stephenson & Turner NZ Ltd. Stephenson & Turner Auckland Ltd and Stephenson & Turner Wellington Ltd include engineering and architecture teams, while Co-Studio Stephenson & Turner operates in Christchurch and the Waikato branch has become Shelter Architects in Taupō.[75]

TEAM Architects: Judd Fenwick Natusch, Dougan Larkworthy, Bell Wright, Bell Kelly Beaumont, Avery Architects, Fulton Ross, Chibnall Buckell, Hopkinson Kelsall, Parker Warburton, BOON

Natusch & Sons became Natusch & Wilcox in 1965, when Rene and Guy Natusch were joined by Warren Stuart Wilcox, but Wilcox left the partnership in 1971 (see page 363) Guy Natusch was then joined by Herbert Maurice Shattky, the firm becoming Natusch Shattky & Co. Shattky joined his father's optometrist practice in 1945, after being invalided home from the war, but left in 1949 to take up architecture. After he retired in 1980, the firm became the Natusch Partnership when Guy Natusch was joined by Timothy (Tim) Alan Judd and Desmond Neil Fenwick. Guy Natusch retired and Judd Fenwick Natusch became Judd Fenwick Team Architecture in 1995, then Dougan Larkworthy Team Architects, with directors Paul Dougan and Robin Larkworthy from 2015. It now operates as TEAM Architects Napier.[76] TEAM Architects formed in 1995, as a collective of practices across New Zealand, to provide support and share expertise and workload as required. It has members across the country, including Bell Kelly Beaumont, originally established as Bell Wright in 1993 by Warwick Bell and Richard Wright, and a founding member of TEAM. As noted, they assisted the Napier practice with the work at the hospital in Hastings. In Auckland, Kerry Avery formed a practice in 1976 and was also a founding member of TEAM. The Christchurch representative from 1999 has been Fulton Ross, established by Stewart Ross in 1976, who was joined by William Fulton in 2008. In Hamilton, Peter Chibnall formed his own practice in the mid-1980s, and later established Chibnall Buckell with Dominic Buckell. Hopkinson Kelsall grew from the practice established by Gary Hopkinson in Greymouth, who was joined by Wayne Kelsall, becoming part of TEAM Architects in 2008. Operating from Dunedin and Wanaka, Parker Warburton TEAM Architects was formed by Simon Parker and Ken Warburton.[77] The Boon family has been associated with building in the Taranaki region since 1895, when Alf and John Boon formed the construction company Boon Brothers. They were eventually joined by Alf's sons, Bert and Ron, and John's sons, George and Alf. George's son Jim, and Ron's son Terry, both became prominent New Plymouth architects; Jim Boon joined Graeme

Laurenson's firm. Terry Boon (1938–) qualified in 1960 and worked in London before returning to New Plymouth in 1965 to join Bowering & Thomson, a local architectural and engineering practice. When he became a partner in 1968, the firm was renamed Bowering Thomson Boon & Associates. It became Thomson Boon Buchan and Chong before he left to start his own practice, Terry Boon Architect, in 1975. It has had several name changes, as it grew and partners joined, and until recently was Boon Goldsmith Bhaskar Brebner Team Architects, in 2019 renamed BOON.[78]

Tetra Tech

Tetra Tech was founded in 1966, and has grown through a series of acquisitions, including that of Norman Disney & Young in 2018. David Norman founded the firm of Norman Addicoat in Sydney in 1959 and the Norman Disney Young partnership formed in 1971 as the firm opened offices across Australia. The first New Zealand office opened in 1987, followed by Wellington in 1990 and Christchurch in 2011. Tetra Tech now has 30,000 employees in 550 offices worldwide.[79]

Thema / Brave / Fitness Fleming Architects

Wally Fitness had led AECOM's health team for several years, and in 2007 he and colleague Matt Fleming left to form their own company, Fitness Fleming Architects. When Wally Fitness retired, Matt Fleming joined Daniel Bulog at Brave Architects, continuing a health design specialty, and has more recently been working independently under the practice name Thema.[80]

Thinc Health

Thinc Health's principal health planners were husband-and-wife team Roger and Jane Carthey. Roger Carthey was with Aurora Projects from 2002 to 2007, during which time he worked with Maunsell on the Project LEO redevelopment of Tauranga Hospital, before joining Thinc in 2010. Jane Carthey was instrumental in developing the Australasian Health Facility Guidelines while at the University of New South Wales from 2005 to 2011 and was the inaugural chair of the Australian Health Design Council founded in 2011. Thinc became part of multi-national consultancy Turner & Townsend in 2015.[81]

Totem Studio Architects / Trengrove Trengrove & Marshall

Willian Henry Trengrove (1891–1953) established his Christchurch practice in 1922. On his death, his son John, who graduated from University of Auckland in 1954, took over the firm and was joined by Keith Douglas Marshall, who had been with the firm since 1939, to form Trengrove, Trengrove & Marshall. Marshall had worked for the firm since 1939, serving in the Royal New Zealand Air Force in the Pacific from 1942 and completing his NZIA examination in 1947. Miles Warren worked with them briefly before setting up his own practice in 1955. When Marshall retired in 1976, longtime employee Richard Blunt became a director and the firm was renamed Trengrove & Blunt. John Trengrove retired in 1994, and his son William became a director. Blunt left in 2005, and David McKay and Daryl Partridge joined William. When William retired in 2019, Ian Cattoen-Gilbert became a director. Daryl Partridge retired in 2021, and the firm was renamed Totem Studio Architects in 2022.[82]

Warren and Mahoney ↑

Frederick (Miles, later Sir Miles) Warren established a practice in Christchurch in 1955 (see page 364). In 1958, Warren was awarded the commission to design the new Dental Nurses' Training School in Christchurch, and, appreciating his calm, methodical manner, asked Maurice Mahoney to join him.[83] In 1966, they won the competition to design the new Christchurch Town Hall, which opened in 1972. Warren and Mahoney has grown to be one of New Zealand's largest architectural practices, with six offices in New Zealand and two in Australia, and more than 300 staff members. It is the only other firm, after Horace Massey's various partnerships, to have won four NZIA Gold Medals. Bill Gregory was for some time the principal responsible for healthcare projects in the practice, and Darryl Haines and Adele King now co-lead the Care sector. Phil Grey has designed many of the firm's hospital buildings, including several for Southern Cross.[84]

Wilkie + Bruce

Alun Wilkie started his own practice in Christchurch in 1982, having worked with the Ministry of Works and a local development company. Alec Bruce joined him in 1988, and the firm became Wilkie + Bruce in 1990.[85]

Wingate + Farquhar

David Wingate and Blair Farquhar formed their partnership in Auckland in 2004. Farquhar left to establish his own practice in 2016.[86]

Woods Bagot

Edward John Woods (1839–1916) emigrated from London to Adelaide in 1860, where he won the competition to redesign St Peter's Cathedral in 1869. In 1905 he entered into partnership with local architect Walter Bagot. Woods Bagot has grown to be the seventh-largest architecture firm in the world by employee count, and operates in 15 locations in Australia, the US, UK, China, Singapore and the Middle East.[87]

WSP / Opus

In 1988 the commercial arm of the Ministry of Works and Development became Works and Development Services Corporation (NZ) Ltd, and in 1991 its design and consulting division became the wholly-owned subsidiary Works Consultancy Services Ltd. This was purchased by Kinta Kellas Plc, a subsidiary of the Renong Corporation of Malaysia in 1996, and rebranded as Opus International Consultants Ltd in 1997. Opus expanded into several overseas markets through a series of acquisitions and was listed on the New Zealand Stock Exchange in 2007. In 2017 Canadian firm WSP Global acquired Opus and it was delisted. WSP was established as the Williams Sale Partnership in the UK in 1969. Canadian firm Genivar, whose roots were in companies formed in 1959, bought WSP in 2012, and rebranded under that name two years later. In 2014, they also purchased major US firm Parsons Brinkerhoff, founded in New York in 1885. In 2009 WSP had taken over the Australian consultancy of Lincolne Scott, which provided engineering services in New Zealand.[88]

Notes

Chapter 1. Hauora Māori

1 Michael King, *The Penguin History of New Zealand* (Auckland: Penguin, 2003), 48; James Belich, *Making Peoples: A History of the New Zealanders: From Early Polynesian Settlement to the End of the Nineteenth Century* (Auckland: Penguin, 1996), 27; Deidre Brown, *Māori Architecture: From Fale to Wharenui and Beyond* (Auckland: Raupo, 2009), 24–27; Alan Taylor, *The Maori Builds: Life, Art and Architecture from Moahunter Days* (Wellington: Whitcombe & Tombs, 1966), 6.
2 Brown, *Māori Architecture*, 28; Taylor, *The Maori Builds*, 14.
3 Mason Durie, *Mauri Ora: The Dynamics of Maori Health* (Melbourne: Oxford University Press, 2001), 80.
4 Te Ara – the Encyclopedia of New Zealand, https://teara.govt.nz/en/washing-cleaning-and-personal-hygiene
5 Buddy Mikaere (ed.), *TaongaTuku Iho: An Illustrated Encyclopedia of Traditional Māori* (Auckland: White Cloud Books, 2022), 23.
6 Ibid., 204.
7 Te Ara – the Encyclopedia of New Zealand, https://teara.govt.nz/en/te-hauora-maori-i-mua-history-of-maori-health/page-1
8 Durie, *Mauri Ora*, 160.
9 Mikaere, *TaongaTuku Iho*, 115, 157, 207.
10 Durie, *Mauri Ora*, 237.
11 www.statista.com/statistics/1040159/life-expectancy-united-kingdom-all-time
12 Te Ara – the Encyclopedia of New Zealand, https://teara.govt.nz/en/te-hauora-maori-i-mua-history-of-maori-health/page-2
13 Durie, *Mauri Ora*, 49.
14 Ian Pool, *Te Iwi Maori: A New Zealand Population Past, Present and Projected* (Auckland: Auckland University Press, 1991).

Chapter 2. The first hospitals 1830–1851

1 Michael Wordsworth Standish, *The Waimate Mission Station* (Wellington: Government Printer, 1962), 11–12; James Belich, *Making Peoples: A History of the New Zealanders: From Early Polynesian Settlement to the End of the Nineteenth Century* (Auckland: Penguin, 1996), 134–47; Michael King, *The Penguin History of New Zealand* (Auckland: Penguin, 2003), 140–42.
2 Keith Parker, *Kaitāia's Hospital: A Glimpse at Hospital Services and Volunteer Health Care in the Far North 1904-2004* (Kamo: Bridgewater, 2005), 2; R. E. Wright-St Clair, *Caring for People: A History of the Wanganui Hospital Board* (Whanganui: Wanganui Hospital Board Centennial Celebration Committee, 1987), 5. Note that Whanganui's correct spelling, Whanganui, was restored in 2015.
3 Peter Tremewan, *French Akaroa: An Attempt to Colonise Southern New Zealand* (Christchurch: Canterbury University Press, 2010), 146–47, 231–34.
4 King, *The Penguin History of New Zealand*, 171–74; Belich, *Making Peoples*, 188; W. H. Skinner, *Pioneer Medical Men of Taranaki 1834 to 1880: With an Account of the Establishment of Hospital Accommodation at New Plymouth* (New Plymouth: Thomas Avery & Sons, 1933; Christchurch: Capper Press, 1984), 115.
5 Arthur B. Scanlan, *Hospital on the Hill: A Centennial History of the New Plymouth Hospital 1867-1967* (New Plymouth: Taranaki Hospital Board, 1967), 8–9.
6 John Wilson, *Thematic Historical Overview of Nelson City* (Nelson: Nelson City Council Heritage Inventory Project, 2011), 99.
7 Te Ara – the Encyclopedia of New Zealand, https://teara.govt.nz/en/housing-and-government/page-1; https://teara.govt.nz/en/artwork/32386/immigration-barracks-new-plymouth
8 Peter Richardson, 'Building the Dominion: Government Architecture in New Zealand 1840–1922' (PhD thesis, University of Canterbury, Christchurch, 1997), 41–42.
9 Ibid., 42–43; www.heritage.org.nz/list-details/12/Albert-Barracks-Wall-(University-of-Auckland-Campus); David Scott (ed.), *The Story of Auckland Hospital 1847-1977* (Auckland: Medical History Library Committee of the Royal Australasian College of Physicians in New Zealand, 1977), 7.
10 Raewyn Dalziel. 'Martin, Mary Ann', *Dictionary of New Zealand Biography*, first published in 1990. Te Ara – the Encyclopedia of New Zealand, https://teara.govt.nz/en/biographies/1m19/martin-mary-ann
11 Te Ara – the Encyclopedia of New Zealand, https://teara.govt.nz/en/new-zealand-wars/page-2
12 Scott, *The Story of Auckland Hospital*, 7.
13 Te Ara – the Encyclopedia of New Zealand, https://teara.govt.nz/en/hospitals/page-1; John E. Martin, *Empire City: Wellington Becomes the Capital of New Zealand* (Wellington: Te Herenga Waka University Press, 2022), 90.
14 Elizabeth T. Jackson, *Delving into the Past of Auckland's Eastern Suburbs — Section 3 — Meadowbank St Johns* (self-published, 1976), 20, 35; Margaret H. Alington, *An Excellent Recruit: Frederick Thatcher Architect, Priest and Private Secretary in Early New Zealand* (Auckland: Polygraphia, 2007), 98–101.
15 Jackson, *Delving into the Past*, 63; Alington, *An Excellent Recruit*, 104–07, 109–16; www.heritage.org.nz/list-details/13/listing
16 Alington, *An Excellent Recruit*, 77–78, 100; Auckland Hospital and Charitable Aid Board, *The Auckland Hospital and Charitable Aid Board: A History of its Buildings and Endowments, Illustrated* (Auckland: Auckland Hospital and Charitable Aid Board, 1919), 25; Frank Charles Rauch, 'The History of Auckland Hospital and the Auckland Hospital and Charitable Aid Board 1847–1914' (MA thesis, University of Auckland, 1933), 3; W. E. Henley, 'The Early History of the Auckland Hospital', *New Zealand Medical Journal* 71, no. 455 (April 1970): 201–08; Scott, *The Story of Auckland Hospital*, 8; Derek A. Dow, *Auckland's Hospitals: A Pictorial History 1847–2004* (Auckland: Auckland District Health Board, 2005), 5.
17 Because communication between Auckland and Wellington was difficult, by 1846 the country had been split into two provinces: New Ulster in the north and New Munster in the south. Lieutenant Thomas Collinson of the Royal Engineers, appointed colonial engineer for the south and based in Wellington, delegated the design and supervision of government buildings in the district to the civilian Thomas Fitzgerald, who became surveyor and superintendent of public works and civil roads in 1847. See Richardson, 'Building the Dominion', 75–76, 86–91.
18 Unlike typhoid, which was caused by food that had been in contact with faecal bacteria, typhus was spread by fleas that got the disease from rats. www.cedars-sinai.org/newsroom/typhus-vs-typhoid-fever-whats-the-difference
19 Skinner, *Pioneer Medical Men of Taranaki*, 116.
20 Scanlan, *Hospital on the Hill*, 12; https://pukeariki.com/objects/37345/plan-of-the-town-and-part-of-the-settlement-of-new-plymouth-new-zealand
21 Alington, *An Excellent Recruit*, 78–82; Scanlan, *Hospital on the Hill*, 9–12.
22 Alington, *An Excellent Recruit*, 391-40.
23 John Steele, *No Ordinary Man: The Extraordinary Life and Times of Dr Arthur Purchas* (Auckland: David Ling, 2019), 37–38, 52.
24 Alington, *An Excellent Recruit*, 15–20, 96–100.
25 Ibid., 77–78.
26 Richardson, 'Building the Dominion', 101–02; Alington, *An Excellent Recruit*, 255–56.
27 Scanlan, *Hospital on the Hill*, 9–10.
28 Skinner, *Pioneer Medical Men of Taranaki*, 116; Scanlan, *Hospital on the Hill*, 10.
29 Newton King, brother of Plunket Society founder Sir Frederic Truby King, and his wife Mary bought the building and relocated it to their Brooklands estate in 1904, renaming it The Gables. They bequeathed Brooklands to the city of New Plymouth, and it became a public park in 1934. The Gables is now a Category 1 Historic Place: www.heritage.org.nz/list-details/29/Listing
30 Martin, *Empire City*, 41, 90; Richardson, 'Building the Dominion', 104.
31 Martin, *Empire City*, 169; Donald Wilson MacDonald, *A Hundred Years of Healing: Wellington Hospital 1847–1947* (Wellington: A. H. & A. W. Reed, 1947), 17; Laurie H. Barber and Roy J. Towers, *Wellington Hospital 1847–1976* (Wellington: Wellington Hospital Board, 1976), 5; Capital Coast District Health Board, www.ccdhb.org.nz/about-us/history
32 MacDonald, *A Hundred Years of Healing*, 17; Barber and Towers, *Wellington Hospital*, 5; Martin, *Empire City*, 197.
33 MacDonald, *A Hundred Years of Healing*, 21; Barber and Towers, *Wellington Hospital*, 10; Martin, *Empire City*, 197.
34 Wright-St Clair, *Caring for People*, 9; Richardson, 'Building the Dominion', 106–10.
35 Wright-St Clair, *Caring for People*, 9. George Grey would continue his hospital building when he was governor in South Africa from 1853 to 1860. One of these was in King William's Town, where Dr John Patrick Fitzgerald became superintendent. See John Patrick Fitzgerald, *A Short History of the Grey Hospital* (King Williams Town: S. E. Rowles & Co., 1890) and Richardson, 'Building the Dominion', 113–14.
36 Norman Ledgerwood, *The Heart of a City: The Story of Dunedin's Octagon* (Dunedin: self-published, 2008), 48; Richardson, 'Building the Dominion', 112–13; 'Dunedin Hospital – A Notable Diamond Jubilee', *Otago Daily Times*, 24 August 1926; 'The Patient Progress of Dunedin's Hospital', *Otago Daily Times*, www.odt.shorthandstories.com/the-patient-progress-of-dunedin-hospital/index.html
37 Richardson, 'Building the Dominion', 111–2.
38 Ibid.
39 F. O. Bennett, *Hospital on the Avon: The History of Christchurch Hospital 1862–1962* (Christchurch: North Canterbury Hospital Board, 1962), 12; Wilson, *Thematic Historical Overview of Nelson City*, 99.

Chapter 3. Colonisation and conflict 1852–1870

1 James Belich, *Making Peoples: A History of the New Zealanders: From Early Polynesian Settlement to the End of the Nineteenth Century* (Auckland: Penguin, 1996), 229–32, 235–46, 284; Michael King, *The Penguin History of New Zealand* (Auckland: Penguin, 2003), 179, 191, 198–99, 202–07, 211–24, 232–33.
2 Te Ara – the Encyclopedia of New Zealand, www.teara.govt.nz/en/hospitals; www.teara.govt.nz/en/care-and-carers; Linda Bryder (ed.), *A Healthy Country: Essays on the Social History of Medicine in New Zealand* (Wellington: Bridget Williams Books, 1991), 46; Derek A. Dow, *Safeguarding the Public Health: A History of the New Zealand Department of Health* (Wellington: Victoria University Press, 1995), 15–16.
3 Linda Bryder, 'Hospitals – Establishment of hospitals in New Zealand', Te Ara – the Encyclopedia of New Zealand, www.teara.govt.nz/en/hospitals/page-1
4 F. O. Bennett, *Hospital on the Avon: The History of*

Christchurch Hospital 1862–1962 (Christchurch: North Canterbury Hospital Board, 1962), 28.

5 Te Ara – the Encyclopedia of New Zealand, http://www.teara.govt.nz/en/hospitals/page-1

6 Keith Parker, *Kaitāia's Hospital: A Glimpse at Hospital Services and Volunteer Health Care in the Far North 1904–2004* (Kamo: Bridgewater, 2005), 2.

7 W. E. Henley, 'The Early History of the Auckland Hospital', *New Zealand Medical Journal* 71, no. 455 (April 1970): 204; David Scott (ed.), *The Story of Auckland Hospital 1847–1977* (Auckland: The Medical History Library Committee of the Royal Australasian College of Physicians in New Zealand, 1977), 13.

8 Frank Charles Rauch, 'The History of Auckland Hospital and the Auckland Hospital and Charitable Aid Board 1847-1914' (MA thesis, University of Auckland, 1933), 13; Scott, *The Story of Auckland Hospital*, 10.

9 Auckland Hospital and Charitable Aid Board, *The Auckland Hospital and Charitable Aid Board: A History of its Buildings and Endowments, Illustrated* (Auckland: Auckland Hospital and Charitable Aid Board, 1919), 25; Henley, 'The Early History of the Auckland Hospital', 208.

10 Deborah FitzHerbert, 'The History of Waikato Hospital, Part 1', posted in *Stories of Hamilton*, ePaanui Hamilton City Libraries, www.hamiltonlibraries.co.nz/heritage; Georgina Wedge and Peter Rothwell, *Waikato Hospital: Our Hospital, Your History* (Hamilton: Waikato Health Memorabilia Trust, 2016), 7.

11 Ian Shearer and Rex E. Wright-St Clair, *A Century on Cameron Road: A History of Tauranga Hospital 1914–2014* (Tauranga: Bay of Plenty District Health Board, 2016), 5; Matthews & Matthews Architects Ltd, *Opotiki Town Centre Historic Heritage Study* (Ōpōtiki: Opotiki District Council, 2006), 33–34; Christine Clement, *Hawera Hospital: 100 Years 1894–1994* (Hawera: Hawera Hospital Centennial Committee, 1994), 3; Patea Historical Society, www.pateahistoricalsociety.org.nz; R. E. Wright-St Clair, *Caring for People: A History of the Wanganui Hospital Board* (Whanganui: Wanganui Hospital Board Centennial Celebration Committee, 1987), 75.

12 W. H. Skinner, *Pioneer Medical Men of Taranaki 1834 to 1880: With an Account of the Establishment of Hospital Accommodation at New Plymouth* (New Plymouth: Thomas Avery & Sons, 1933; Christchurch: Capper Press, 1984), 118, 130; Arthur B. Scanlan, *Hospital on the Hill: A Centennial History of the New Plymouth Hospital 1867–1967* (New Plymouth: Taranaki Hospital Board, 1967), 10.

13 *The Napier Hospital and Health Services Report*, Wai 692, Waitangi Tribunal Report 2001 (Wellington: Legislation Direct, 2001), xix, 99.

14 Geoff Conly, *A Case History: The Hawke's Bay Hospital Board 1876–1989* (Napier: Hawke's Bay Area Health Board, 1992), 6–7. When Napier hospital relocated to a new site 20 years later, the building was sold and became a private home; it is now a Category 2 Historic Place. *Hawke's Bay Provincial Hospital (Former)*, Heritage New Zealand Register #2797, www.heritage.org.nz/list-details/2797/listing

15 Geoff Mew and Adrian Humphris, *Raupo to Deco: Wellington Styles and Architects 1840–1940* (Wellington: Steele Roberts, 2014), 39; John E. Martin, *Empire City: Wellington Becomes the Capital of New Zealand* (Wellington: Te Herenga Waka University Press, 2022), 197.

16 Donald Wilson MacDonald, *A Hundred Years of Healing: Wellington Hospital 1847–1947* (Wellington: A. H. & A. W. Reed, 1947), 21; Laurie H. Barber and Roy J. Towers, *Wellington Hospital 1847–1976* (Wellington: Wellington Hospital Board, 1976), 21; Capital Coast District Health Board, www.ccdhb.org.nz/about-us/history

17 F. O. Bennett, *Hospital on the Avon: The History of Christchurch Hospital 1862–1962* (Christchurch: North Canterbury Hospital Board, 1962), 17–18.

18 *Lyttelton Times*, 8 October 1859, 4.

19 Bennett, *Hospital on the Avon*, 20.

20 Ibid., 61.

21 Winifred Norris, *The North Canterbury Hospital Board: Fragments of History: Hospitals: Tuberculosis and Benevolent Institutions and Miscellaneous* (unpublished manuscript held by Christchurch City Libraries, 1942), 6.

22 Ibid., 11, 19.

23 John Campbell McKenzie, *A History of Timaru Hospital* (Christchurch: Pegasus Press, 1974), 16.

24 Linda Bryder, 'Hospitals – Establishment of hospitals in New Zealand', Te Ara – the Encyclopedia of New Zealand, www.teara.govt.nz/en/hospitals/page-1

25 G. T. Piercy, 'Frankton and Arrowtown Hospitals', *Queenstown Courier*, Queenstown & District Historical Society, Issue 40 (1988); Marion Borrell, 'Medical Services – Always a Lively Topic', *Queenstown Courier*, Issue 89 (Winter 2013); Southland Hospital Board, *History of the Southland Hospitals and Boards 1861–1968* (Invercargill: Southland Hospital Board, 1968), 76.

26 Dunstan Hospital Jubilee Committee, *Dunstan Hospital 125th Anniversary* (Clyde: Dunstan Hospital Jubilee Committee, 1988); 'Hospital Certainly One of the Top', *Otago Daily Times*, 11 June 2021.

27 'Grey River Hospital', *Cyclopedia of New Zealand (Nelson Marlborough and Westland Provincial Districts)*, Vol. 5 (Wellington: Cyclopedia Company, 1906), 558–59; 'Centennial of Greymouth Hospital 1866–1966', Special Publication (Greymouth: *Greymouth Evening Star*, 1966).

28 *Cyclopedia of New Zealand (Nelson Marlborough and Westland Provincial Districts)*, 172, 532–33, 538; Ella Matthews, *Yesterdays in Golden Buller* (Christchurch: Pegasus Press, 1957), 61; Bruce Macdonald, *Westport: Struggle for Survival* (Westport: Westport Borough Council, 1973), 63; Irwin Faris, *Charleston* (Wellington: A. H. & A. W. Reed, 1941), 159.

29 Richard Wolfe, *New Zealand's Lost Heritage: The Stories Behind Our Forgotten Landmarks* (Auckland: New Holland, 2013), 158–64.

30 John Stacpoole, *William Mason: The First New Zealand Architect* (Auckland University Press with Oxford University Press, 1971), 74–80.

31 Wolfe, *New Zealand's Lost Heritage*, 165.

32 Jenny Mui Mun Tien, 'Tan Tock Seng', *Singapore Infopedia*, National Library Board, Singapore, www.nlb.gov.sg/main/article-detail?cmsuuid=3288734a-bcf9-4c28-98ce-28a89b49b472

33 *History of the Southland Hospitals and Boards*, 1–2, Wolfe, *New Zealand's Lost Heritage*, 174–77; Georgia Weaver, 'Former Dee Street Maternity Hospital's Future Uncertain', *Stuff*, 4 December 2015.

34 *History of the Southland Hospitals and Boards*, 6; Wolfe, *New Zealand's Lost Heritage*, 177–78.

Victorian asylums

1 Angela McCarthy, *Migration, Ethnicity and Madness: New Zealand, 1860–1910* (Dunedin: Otago University Press, 2015), 10–12, 37–38; King, *The Penguin History of New Zealand*, 230–31; Belich, *Making Peoples*, 424–28.

2 Warwick Brunton, 'Mental health services – Lunatic asylums, 1840s to 1900s', Te Ara – the Encyclopedia of New Zealand, www.teara.govt.nz/en/mental-health-services/page-2

3 McCarthy, *Migration, Ethnicity and Madness*, 30, 36.

4 Ibid., 30–34.

5 Dow, *Safeguarding the Public Health*, 153–57, 180, 184, 206–07.

6 Peter Richardson, 'Building the Dominion: Government Architecture in New Zealand 1840–1922' (PhD thesis, University of Canterbury, Christchurch, 1997), 177.

7 Wendy Hunter Williams, *Out of Mind, Out of Sight: The Story of Porirua Hospital: Porirua Hospital Centennial 1887–1987* (Porirua: Porirua Hospital, 1987), 598.

8 Ibid., 52.

9 Ibid., 39–42; Peter Richardson, 'An Architecture of Empire: The Government Buildings of John Campbell in New Zealand' (MA thesis, University of Canterbury, Christchurch, 1988), 54–56; Porirua Hospital Museum, www.poriruahospitalmuseum.flh.nz/history

10 Richardson, 'An Architecture of Empire', 98.

11 Williams, *Out of Mind, Out of Sight*, 52.

12 Ibid., 105; *Mental Health Ward (Former) Porirua Hospital*, Heritage New Zealand Register #7444, www.heritage.org.nz/the-list

13 Salmond Architects, *Former Carrington Hospital: A Conservation Plan* (Auckland: Unitec, 1994), 3–4; Robyn Walshe, *A Building Known as Carrington* (Auckland: Unitec, n.d.).

14 Salmond Architects, *Former Carrington Hospital*, 4.

15 Ibid., 5.

16 Several references spell the surname 'Herepath'. Newspaper reports of the time seem to use both interchangeably, although tender notices issued by his firm use the spelling 'Herapath'. That is the spelling used here, and in the Conservation Plan for Carrington Hospital by Salmond Architects.

17 Salmond Architects, *Former Carrington Hospital*, 5, 25.

18 Ibid., 6–9.

19 Ibid., 10–12; Ian Bowman, *William Beatson: A Colonial Architect* (Auckland: Balasoglou Books, 2005), 140.

20 Salmond Architects, *Former Carrington Hospital*, 16; Richardson, 'An Architecture of Empire', 60. The Unitec School of Architecture relocated from the main building to the auxiliary asylum building in 2018.

21 Salmond Architects, *Former Carrington Hospital*, 14.

22 Ibid., 15–16.

23 Ibid., 18, 34–35.

24 Ibid., 16–18.

25 In 1994 Carrington Polytechnic, now the Unitec Institute of Technology, which already occupied the southern portion of the site, took over the northern part. Their architecture school occupied the main asylum building, by then a Category 1 Historic Place, until 2018, when the government repurchased a large block, including the main building, for an intensive housing development. https://www.unitec.ac.nz/about-us/our-campuses/carrington-residential-development. *Carrington Hospital (Former)*, Heritage New Zealand Register #96, www.heritage.org.nz/the-list

26 Madeleine Seager, *Edward William Seager: Pioneer of Mental Health* (Waikanae: Heritage Press, 1987), 77, 84, 92, 126; Margaret Harraway, *End of an Era: Nursing Education at Sunnyside Hospital 1904–1989*, (Christchurch: self-published, 1987), 6.

27 Seager, *Edward William Seager*, 168, 209, 210, 218, 266.

28 Sherwood Young, 'Seager, Edward William', *Dictionary of New Zealand Biography*, first published in 1990. Te Ara – the Encyclopedia of New Zealand, https://teara.govt.nz/en/biographies/1s3/seager-edward-william

29 Seager, *Edward William Seager*, 170; Richardson, 'An Architecture of Empire', 54; www.heritage.org.nz/The-List/Lost-Heritage

30 Wolfe, *New Zealand's Lost Heritage*, 152; 'Permanent

Lunatic Asylum Buildings, Seacliff', *Otago Daily Times*, 15 July 1879, 3.

31 Wolfe, *New Zealand's Lost Heritage*, 152–53; 'Permanent Lunatic Asylum Buildings, Seacliff', *Otago Daily Times*, 4 March 1879, Supplement, 1.

32 Wolfe, *New Zealand's Lost Heritage*, 153–57; Norman Ledgerwood, *R. A. Lawson: Victorian Architect of Dunedin* (Dunedin: Historic Cemeteries Trust of New Zealand, 2013), 184–205.

33 Wolfe, *New Zealand's Lost Heritage*, 157.

34 www.heritage.org.nz/list-details/9050/Seacliff-Lunatic-Asylum-Site

35 'Nelson Mental Hospital', *Cyclopedia of New Zealand (Nelson, Marlborough & Westland Provincial Districts)*, Vol. 5 (Wellington: Cyclopedia Company of New Zealand, 1906), 60–61; Nancy Shaw Miller, 'History and Memories of Braemar Hospital', *Nelson Historical Society Journal* 7, no. 5 (2103): 49.

36 Nancy Shaw Miller, 'History and Memories of Braemar Hospital', 50; Marjorie M. Webby, *From Prison to Paradise: Genealogy of Ngawhatu Hospital, Previously Known as Nelson Lunatic Asylum 1840–1991 and St Mary's Orphanage Stoke* (Nelson: self-published, 1991).

37 Miller, 'History and Memories of Braemar Hospital', 49; Richardson, 'An Architecture of Empire', 56.

38 Marjorie M. Webby, *From Prison to Paradise*.

39 'Seaview Asylum', *Cyclopedia of New Zealand*, Vol. 5, 498; Warwick Brunton, *Sitivation 125: A History of Seaview Hospital, Hokitika and West Coast Mental Health Services, 1872-1997* (Hokitika; Seaview Hospital 125th Jubilee Committee, 1997); Jane Comeau, '"Exceptional and Exceedingly Pleasing": Asylum Care on New Zealand's West Coast, 1872–1910' (MA thesis, University of Canterbury, Christchurch, 2023), 14, 32.

40 Seager, *Edward William Seager*, 195.

Chapter 4. Progress and pain 1879–1890

1 Keith Sinclair, *A History of New Zealand* (Auckland: Penguin, 1970), 160–01; James Belich, *Making Peoples: A History of the New Zealanders: From Early Polynesian Settlement to the End of the Nineteenth Century* (Auckland: Penguin, 1996), 279–80; James Belich, *Paradise Reforged: A History of the New Zealanders: From the 1880s to the Year 2000* (Auckland: Allen Lane Penguin, 2001), 32–33; Michael King, *The Penguin History of New Zealand* (Auckland: Penguin, 2003), 228–32; https://nzhistory.govt.nz/politics/the-vogel-era/vogels-legacy

2 www.statista.com/statistics/1066999/population-new-zealand-historical

3 Derek A. Dow, 'Springs of Charity? The Development of the New Zealand Hospital System 1876–1910' in Linda Bryder (ed.), *A Healthy Country: Essays on the Social History of Medicine in New Zealand* (Wellington: Bridget Williams Books, 1991), 46–50; Belich, *Making Peoples*, 380; Belich, *Paradise Reforged*, 174. Note that there is some small variance in numbers between sources. This may be due to different interpretations as to what constitutes a hospital, and which collation of returns from around the country is being relied on. The hospital numbers are based on the author's own count, noting that several small hospitals opened and closed one or more times due to demand and availability of qualified staff.

4 www.rcseng.ac.uk/library-and-publications/library/blog/mapping-disease-john-snow-and-cholera; www.bbc.co.uk/bitesize/guides/zxbqjsg/revision/2#:~:text=Pasteur's%20findings%20significantly%20challenged%20the,bacteria%20that%20caused%20individual%20diseases

5 Derek A. Dow, *Safeguarding the Public Health: A History of the New Zealand Department of Health* (Wellington: Victoria University Press, 1995), 42–57.

6 www.sciencemuseum.org.uk/objects-and-stories/medicine/listers-antisepsis-system#:~:text=Joseph%20Lister%20found%20a%20way,continue%20to%20save%20countless%20lives

7 Donald Wilson MacDonald, *A Hundred Years of Healing: Wellington Hospital 1847–1947* (Wellington: A. H. & A. W. Reed, 1947), 74.

8 Michael P. Murphy Jr with Jerry Mansfield and MASS Design Group, *The Architecture of Health: Hospital Design and the Construction of Dignity* (New York: Smithsonian Design Museum, 2021), 72–85.

9 Terence Hodgson, *Looking at the Architecture of New Zealand* (Wellington: Grantham House, 1990), 18, 34; Peter Shaw, *New Zealand Architecture: From Polynesian Beginnings to 1990* (Auckland: Hodder & Stoughton, 1991), 58, 80.

10 Auckland Hospital and Charitable Aid Board, *The Auckland Hospital and Charitable Aid Board: A History of its Buildings and Endowments, Illustrated* (Auckland: Auckland Hospital and Charitable Aid Board, 1919), 33; Frank Charles Rauch, 'The History of Auckland Hospital and the Auckland Hospital and Charitable Aid Board 1847–1914' (MA thesis, University of Auckland, 1933), 14–15; W. E. Henley, 'The Early History of the Auckland Hospital', *New Zealand Medical Journal* 71, no. 455 (April 1970): 205; David Scott (ed.), *The Story of Auckland Hospital 1847–1977* (Auckland: Medical History Library Committee of the Royal Australasian College of Physicians in New Zealand, 1977), 17.

11 Derek A. Dow, *Auckland's Hospitals: A Pictorial History 1847–2004* (Auckland: Auckland District Health Board, 2005), 7.

12 Kae Lewis, *Gold Rush to the Thames New Zealand 1867–1869* (Thames: Parawai Press, 2017).

13 *True Tales of Thames Hospital: 150 Years 1868–2018* (Thames: Thames Hospital 150 Group, in collaboration with the Coromandel Heritage Trust, 2018), 2–6; Suzanne Morgan, *Thames Hospital: A Pictorial History 1868–1987* (Thames: self-published, 2006).

14 *True Tales of Thames Hospital*, 21; heritage.org.nz/list-details/7269/Listing

15 Deborah FitzHerbert, 'The History of Waikato Hospital, Part 1', posted in *Stories of Hamilton*, ePaanui Hamilton City Libraries, www.hamiltonlibraries.co.nz/heritage; Rex E. Wright-St Clair, *The Early History of Waikato Hospital* (Hamilton: Waikato Hospital Board, 1973), 6, 12; John Armstrong, *Under One Roof: A History of Waikato Hospital* (Hamilton: Half Court Press, 2009), 40; *Heritage Hamilton: A Celebration of the City's Historic Buildings* (Hamilton: Wintec, 2006), 74; Georgina Wedge and Peter Rothwell, *Waikato Hospital: Our Hospital, Your History* (Hamilton: Waikato Health Memorabilia Trust, 2016), 8.

16 W. H. Skinner, *Pioneer Medical Men of Taranaki 1834 to 1880: With an Account of the Establishment of Hospital Accommodation at New Plymouth* (New Plymouth: Thomas Avery & Sons, 1933; Christchurch: Capper Press, 1984), 136.

17 Arthur B. Scanlan, *Hospital on the Hill: A Centennial History of the New Plymouth Hospital 1867–1967* (New Plymouth: Taranaki Hospital Board, 1967), 13–18, 22.

18 'The New Gisborne Hospital', *Poverty Bay Herald*, 29 April 1879, 2; Joseph Angus McKay, *Historic Poverty Bay and the East Coast North Island New Zealand* (Gisborne: self-published, 1949), 414; 'Old Hospital Goes', *Gisborne Photo News*, 16 June 1971, 24.

19 Geoff Conly, *A Case History: The Hawke's Bay Hospital Board 1876–1989* (Napier: Hawke's Bay Area Health Board, 1992), 19, 35.

20 'Greytown Hospital', *Cyclopedia of New Zealand (Wellington Provincial District)*, Vol. 1 (Wellington: Cyclopedia Company of New Zealand, 1897), 879.

21 A. G. Bagnall, *Old Greytown 1854–1954* (Greytown: Greytown Borough Council, 1953), 60–01; David Kernohan, *Wairarapa Buildings: Two Centuries of New Zealand Architecture* (Masterton: Wairarapa Archive, 2003), 92, 149; Diane Grant (ed.) with Wairarapa Health History Group, *Helping Hands: A History of Healthcare in the Wairarapa* (Masterton: Fraser Books, 2015), 25. The Roe of Varnam & Roe was almost certainly the Joseph Edward Roe who later did work at Hāwera Hospital and then moved to Whanganui and Auckland. It has been suggested that he was in partnership with William Crichton for a time, however McCarthy's detailed biography of Crichton does not mention him having a partner before James McKay, but does refer to him employing a draughtsman with the name F. S. Rowe; *First Greytown Hospital Building, Cobblestone Museum, Greytown*, Heritage New Zealand Register #4002, www.heritage.org.nz/the-list

22 'Masterton Hospital', *Cyclopedia of New Zealand*, Vol. 1, 948; C. J. Carle, *Masterton Hospital 1879–1979*, Centennial Book Committee (Masterton: Wairarapa Hospital Board, 1979), 9; Grant, *Helping Hands*, 35–38; Kernohan, *Wairarapa Buildings*, 92–93.

23 'Wellington Hospital', *Cyclopedia of New Zealand*, Vol. 1, 356–57; MacDonald, *A Hundred Years of Healing*, 25; Laurie H. Barber and Roy J. Towers, *Wellington Hospital 1847–1976* (Wellington: Wellington Hospital Board, 1976), 2; Capital Coast District Health Board, www.ccdhb.org.nz/about-us/history

24 *Evening Post*, 6 May 1881, 2.

25 MacDonald, *A Hundred Years of Healing*, 25–27; Barber and Towers, *Wellington Hospital*, 21–22; Capital Coast District Health Board, www.ccdhb.org.nz/about-us/history

26 Ibid.

27 *Evening Post*, 6 May 1881, 2.

28 Capital Coast District Health Board, ccdhb.org.nz/about-us/history

29 'Wairau Hospital', *Cyclopedia of New Zealand (Nelson, Marlborough & Westland Provincial Districts)*, Vol. 5, Cyclopedia (Wellington: Company of New Zealand, 1906), 328; J. G. Furness, *Wairau Hospital: 100 Years of Caring* (Blenheim: Marlborough Hospital Board, 1978), 7–8.

30 John Wilson, *Thematic Historical Overview of Nelson City* (Nelson: Nelson City Council Heritage Inventory Project, 2011), 99.

31 'Laying of the First Stone of the New Hospital', *Nelson Evening Mail*, 24 April 1867, 2; 'Nelson Provincial Council', *Colonist*, 29 May 1868, 3; 'Nelson Hospital', *Cyclopedia of New Zealand*, Vol. 5, 60.

32 *Reefton Hospital 1872-1972* (Reefton: Reefton Hospital, 1972).

33 'Grey River Hospital', *Cyclopedia of New Zealand*, Vol. 5, 558–59; *Centennial of Greymouth Hospital 1866–1966*, Special Publication (Greymouth: *Greymouth Evening Star*, 1966).

34 'Westland Hospital', *Cyclopedia of New Zealand*, Vol. 5, 498; 'Kumara Hospital', *Cyclopedia of New Zealand*, Vol. 5, 538.

35 F. O. Bennett, *Hospital on the Avon: The History of Christchurch Hospital 1862–1962* (Christchurch: North Canterbury Hospital Board, 1962), 62. Bennett credited Harman & Stevens as the architects for work at the hospital around this time, but they operated as land agents and financiers, and although many architects of the time had multiple occupations, Harman & Stevens do not seem to have been designers, as they commissioned William Armson to design their own offices.

36 Ibid.
37 Quoted in Bennett, *Hospital on the Avon*, 63.
38 Bennett, *Hospital on the Avon*, 66.
39 Ibid., 85.
40 Winifred Norris, *The North Canterbury Hospital Board: Fragments of History: Hospitals: Tuberculosis and Benevolent Institutions and Miscellaneous* (unpublished manuscript held by Christchurch City Libraries, 1942), 19, 23.
41 Luke Tremlett, 'Medical Buildings and Medical Theory: An Archaeological Investigation of Ashburton Hospital, New Zealand' (MA thesis, University of Otago, Dunedin, 2015), 36; W. H. Scotter, *Ashburton: A History with Records of Town and Country* (Ashburton: Ashburton Borough and County Councils, 1972), 138–40.
42 'Timaru Hospital', *Cyclopedia of New Zealand (Canterbury Provincial District)*, Vol. 3 (Wellington: Cyclopedia Company of New Zealand, 1903), 981; John Campbell McKenzie, *A History of Timaru Hospital* (Christchurch: Pegasus Press, 1974), 37.
43 'Waimate Hospital', *Cyclopedia of New Zealand*, Vol. 3, 1065; Bernice E. Shackleton, *The Fifth Schedule: The Story of Waimate's Open Community Hospital 1874–1975* (Invercargill: Craig Printing, 1984), 30, 40–01, 73.
44 Kenneth Cornwell McDonald, *A Century of Service: The History of the Oamaru Hospital* (Ōamaru: Waitaki Hospital Board, 1972), 7–9, 15; 'Hospital Fading into History', *Otago Daily Times*, 28 May 2016.
45 Conal McCarthy, *Forrester & Lemon: Ōamaru Architects* (Ōamaru: New Zealand Historic Places Trust, North Otago Branch, 2002), 25.
46 'Dunedin Hospital – A Notable Diamond Jubilee', *Otago Daily Times*, 24 August 1926; 'The Patient Progress of Dunedin's Hospital', *Otago Daily Times*, www.odt.shorthandstories.com/the-patient-progress-of-dunedin-hospital/index.html
47 www.masonandwales.com/about; Andrew Barrie and Julia Gatley, 'Dunedin Guide: Mason & Wales', *Architecture New Zealand* (March/April 2022): 99–101.
48 'Dunedin Hospital – A Notable Diamond Jubilee'; 'The Patient Progress of Dunedin's Hospital'.
49 Ali Clarke, 'University of Otago 1869–2019: Building a Medical Campus', https://otago150years.wordpress.com/2017/03/13/building-a-medical-campus; www.otago.ac.nz/oms/about/history; *University of Otago Geology Block*, Heritage New Zealand Register #4765, www.heritage.org.nz/the-list
50 G. T. Piercy, 'Frankton and Arrowtown Hospitals', *Queenstown Courier*, Queenstown & District Historical Society, Issue 40 (1988); *History of the Southland Hospitals and Boards 1861–1968* (Invercargill: Southland Hospital Board, 1968), 76–77.
51 Dee Street Hospital (Former), Heritage New Zealand register #7777, www.heritage org,nz/the-list

Caring for the elderly

1 Margaret Tennant, 'Elderly Indigents' and Old Men's Homes 1880–1920', *New Zealand Journal of History* 17, no. 2 (1984): 3–4, 11.
2 Ibid., 4.
3 Conly, *A Case History*, 51.
4 Christine McCarthy, 'Images of Homelessness: The Home of the Needy Aged', *AHA: Architectural History Aotearoa* 10 (2013): 53–60; www.tehopai.co.nz/about/history
5 *Evening Post*, 28 January 1893, 4.
6 MacDonald, *A Hundred Years of Healing*, 103.
7 Amber Haley, 'Alexandra Home: The Early Years Remembered', *Nelson Historical Society Journal* 6 (1998): 12.
8 *Jubilee Hospital Complex*, www.heritage.org.nz/The-List/Lost-Heritage; John Wilson, *Lost Christchurch* (Lincoln: Te Waihora Press, 1984), 84.
9 Margaret Tennant, 'Elderly Indigents and Old Men's Homes', 11.
10 Conly, *A Case History*, 75.
11 Scotter, *Ashburton*, 141.
12 *History of the Southland Hospitals and Boards 1861–1968*, 29.
13 Margaret Tennant, 'Indigence and Charitable Aid in New Zealand 1885–1920' (PhD thesis, Massey University, 1981), 236.
14 McKay, *Historic Poverty Bay*, 415.
15 R. E. Wright-St Clair, *Caring for People: A History of the Wanganui Hospital Board* (Whanganui: Wanganui Hospital Board Centennial Celebration Committee, 1987), 45.
16 Margaret Tennant, 'Elderly Indigents and Old Men's Homes', 19.
17 www.ranfurly.org.nz/history-ranfurly-veterans. This and other veterans' homes are described in Bill Barnes, *Old Soldiers Never Die: A Pictorial History of the Rannerdale War Veterans' Home: Jubilee Year 2006* (Christchurch: Rannerdale War Veterans' Home, 2006).
18 Sally Robyn Greenbrook, 'Village People: The Changing Role of Retirement Villages in New Zealand's Ageing Society' (MA thesis, University of Auckland, 2005), 20–21.
19 Nancy Swarbrick, 'Care and carers – Care of elderly people', Te Ara – the Encyclopedia of New Zealand, www.teara.govt.nz/en/care-and-carers/page-2; www3.stats.govt.nz/New_Zealand_Official_Yearbooks/1969/NZOYB_1969.html#idchapter_1_43378
20 Greenbrook, 'Village People', 32–33.
21 Ibid., 34–35.
22 Ibid., 35–36; www.ps.org.nz/who-we-are/; https://cht.co.nz
23 www.rymanhealthcare.co.nz/about-us/our-history
24 www.summerset.co.nz/about-us
25 www.metlifecare.co.nz/guides/all-about-metlifecare; www.bupa.co.nz/why-bupa; www.arvida.co.nz/why-arvida; https://oceaniahealthcare.co.nz

Chapter 5. Liberal treatment 1890–1914

1 James Belich, *Paradise Reforged: A History of the New Zealanders: From the 1880s to the Year 2000* (Auckland: Allen Lane Penguin, 2001), 38–46; Michael King, *The Penguin History of New Zealand* (Auckland: Penguin, 2003), 259–78.
2 Rebecca Priestley, 'Nuclear New Zealand: New Zealand's Nuclear and Radiation History to 1987' (PhD thesis, University of Canterbury, Christchurch, 2010), 31.
3 https://teara.govt.nz/en/hospitals/page-2
4 Margaret Tennant, 'Indigence and Charitable Aid in New Zealand 1885–1920' (PhD thesis, Massey University, 1981), 19, 27; 'Chronology of the New Zealand Health System', www.health.govt.nz/system/files/2024-05/chronology-of-the-new-zealand-health-system-1840-to-2017_0.pdf
5 Tennant, 'Indigence and Charitable Aid in New Zealand', 48, 59; Derek A. Dow, *Safeguarding the Public Health: A History of the New Zealand Department of Health* (Wellington: Victoria University Press, 1995), 153–54; 'Chronology of the New Zealand Health System'.
6 Tennant, 'Indigence and Charitable Aid in New Zealand', 52–53; Derek A. Dow, 'Springs of Charity? The Development of the New Zealand Hospital System, 1876–1910', in Linda Bryder (ed.), *A Healthy Country: Essays on the Social History of Medicine in New Zealand* (Wellington: Bridget Williams Books, 1991), 44–64; Dow, *Safeguarding the Public Health*, 92–93; 'Chronology of the New Zealand Health System'. As Dow points out, the evolution of the department was far more complex than can be covered here, partly due to the resistance of the mental hospitals section to losing its independence: 'It was only in 1950 that the report of the Division of Mental Hygiene appeared in the Health Department's annual report'.
7 Terence Hodgson, *Looking at the Architecture of New Zealand* (Wellington: Grantham House, 1990), 34; Peter Shaw, *New Zealand Architecture: From Polynesian Beginnings to 1990* (Auckland: Hodder & Stoughton, 1991), 65–67.
8 Charles Walker (ed.), *Exquisite Apart: 100 Years of Architecture in New Zealand* (Auckland: Balasoglou Books, 2005), 7.
9 Keith Parker, *Kaitaia's Hospital: A Glimpse at Hospital Services and Volunteer Health Care in the Far North 1904–2004* (Kamo: Bridgewater, 2005), 3.
10 John Stallworthy, *Early Northern Wairoa* (Whangārei: self-published, 2006), 77–79; Ivy B. Pratt, *The History of the Te Kopuru Hospital 1903–1971* (Whangārei: self-published, 1992); Christine Rope (comp.), *True Tales of Te Kōpuru* (Te Kōpuru: self-published, 2018); www.te-kopuru.co.nz/The_TK_Hospital
11 Stallworthy, *Early Northern Wairoa*, 94. Te Kōpuru finally closed in 1971, with all services relocated to Dargaville. *Mt Pleasant Hospital (Former)*, Heritage New Zealand Register #3939, www.heritage.org.nz/the-list. Now a private residence, it is a Category 2 Historic Place.
12 Diana Menefy, *Whangarei Hospital: A Century of Service 1901–2001* (Whangārei: Northland Health Ltd, 2001), 31, 43, 51, 63–65, 126; 'Whangarei Hospital's 120 Year Celebration', Northland District Health Board, www.community.northlanddhb.org.nz/celebration
13 *The Auckland Hospital and Charitable Aid Board: A History of its Buildings and Endowments, Illustrated* (Auckland: Auckland Hospital and Charitable Aid Board, 1919), 47–50; Edward A. and Anthony H. G. Roche, *Green Lane Saga: Green Lane Hospital, Auckland 1889–1982* (Auckland: Ray Richards, 1983), 15; B. R. Hutchinson (ed.), *Green Lane Hospital: The First Hundred Years* (Auckland: Green Lane Hospital Centennial Committee, 1990), 6.
14 *Green Lane Hospital*, Heritage New Zealand Register #4536, www.heritage.org.nz/the-list
15 *Auckland Hospital and Charitable Aid Board*, 35; Frank Charles Rauch, 'The History of Auckland Hospital and the Auckland Hospital and Charitable Aid Board 1847–1914' (MA thesis, University of Auckland, 1933), 17–19, 21–23, 48–49; David Scott (ed.), *The Story of Auckland Hospital 1847–1977* (Auckland: Medical History Library Committee of the Royal Australasian College of Physicians in New Zealand, 1977), 39; Derek A. Dow, *Auckland's Hospitals: A Pictorial History 1847–2004* (Auckland: Auckland District Health Board, 2005), 10–11, 14, 17.
16 Mary E. Williams, *A Century of Service: Waihi Hospital Centenary 1903–2003* (Waihi: self-published, 2003), 1, 81, 89; *Waihi Hospital*, Heritage New Zealand Register #4663, www.heritage.org.nz/the-list; www.waihilifecare.co.nz/about-us
17 *Royal New Zealand Foundation for the Blind, Main Building*, Heritage New Zealand Register #4579, www.heritage.org.nz/the-list
18 John Steele, *No Ordinary Man: The Extraordinary Life and Times of Dr Arthur Purchas* (Auckland: David Ling, 2019), 283–85.
19 *Specification for Knox's Home for Incurables at East Tamaki* (Bartley & Son, Architects, c. 1913), www.knox.co.nz/history
20 Sylvia Reed, *Ducks, Dipsomaniacs and Diseases:*

A History of the Mercury Bay Hospital and the Ambulance Service 1897–1995 (Whitianga: self-published, 1995); *Hospital, Buffalo Beach Road, Whitianga*, Heritage New Zealand Register #4631, www.heritage.org.nz/the-list

21 *True Tales of Thames Hospital, 150 Years 1868–2108* (Thames: Thames Hospital 150 Group in collaboration with the Treasury, Coromandel Heritage Trust, 2018), 2, 18, 37–38; Suzanne Morgan, *Thames Hospital: A Pictorial History 1868–1987* (Thames: self-published, 2006).

22 Michael Belgrave, *The Mater: A History of Auckland's Mercy Hospital 1900–2000* (Palmerston North: Dunmore Press, 2000), 27; *True Tales of Thames Hospital*, 21.

23 *Hospital, Rings Road, Coromandel*, Heritage New Zealand Register #4632, www.heritage.org.nz/the-list; *Coromandel Hospital Historic Area*, Heritage New Zealand Register #7269, www.heritage.org.nz/the-list

24 Don Stafford, *The Founding Years in Rotorua: A History of Events to 1900* (Rotorua: Ray Richards and Rotorua District Council, 1980), 155, 161.

25 Ian Rockel, *Taking the Waters: Early Spas in New Zealand* (Wellington: Government Printer, 1986), 22; Susan Butterworth, *Hospital on a Hotspot: Queen Elizabeth Hospital, Rotorua* (Wellington: Ngaio Press, 2012), 12–14; Matthews & Matthews Architects Ltd, *Rotorua Central Area: Built Heritage Study* (Rotorua: Rotorua District Council, 2007), 15–16.

26 Butterworth, *Hospital on a Hotspot*, 56.

27 David McGill, *Landmarks: Notable Historic Buildings of New Zealand* (Auckland: Godwit, 1997), 78–80; Lewis E. Martin, *Built for Us: The Work of Government and Colonial Architects, 1860s to 1960s* (Dunedin: Otago University Press, 2004), 76–77.

28 Arthur B. Scanlan, *Hospital on the Hill: A Centennial History of the New Plymouth Hospital 1867–1967* (New Plymouth: Taranaki Hospital Board, 1967), 30–31; W. H. Skinner, *Pioneer Medical Men of Taranaki 1834 to 1880: With an Account of the Establishment of Hospital Accommodation at New Plymouth* (New Plymouth: Thomas Avery & Sons, 1933; Christchurch: Capper Press, 1984), 151.

29 *A Pictorial History of Hawera 1882–1982* (*Hawera Star*, 1981); A. P. C. Bromley, *Hawera: An Outline of the Development of a New Zealand Community* (Hāwera: Centennial Committee of the Hawera District Council, 1981), 210–12; Christine Clement, *Hawera Hospital: 100 Years 1894–1994* (Hawera: Hawera Hospital Centennial Committee, 1994), 10.

30 'The Pride of Hāwera', *Taranaki Daily News*, 5 May 2012.

31 Clement, *Hawera Hospital*, 30.

32 Geoff Mew and Adrian Humphris, *Raupo to Deco: Wellington Styles and Architects 1840–1940* (Wellington: Steele Roberts, 2014), 353; https://teara.govt.nz/en/photograph/33493/te-puia-springs-hospital; www.npo.org.nz/service/te-puia-hospital

33 Geoff Conly, *A Case History: The Hawke's Bay Hospital Board 1876–1989* (Napier: Hawke's Bay Area Health Board, 1992), 40.

34 Eleanor Holmes (comp.), *Robert Lamb FRIBA: The Napier Years 1879 to 1895* (self-published, 2002), 97; 'Wairoa Hospital', *Hawke's Bay Herald*, 9 September 1886.

35 Conly, *A Case History*, 37; 'Tenders for New Nurses' Home at Napier Hospital', *Hawke's Bay Herald*, 31 May 1894.

36 Conly, *A Case History*, 61; Holmes, *Robert Lamb FRIBA*, 255.

37 Patrick Parsons, *Waipukurau: The History of a Country Town* (Waipukurau: CHB Print, 1999), 134–39; Conly, *A Case History*, 91; Holmes, *Robert Lamb FRIBA*, 104; 'Tenders for Additions and Alterations to Waipawa District Hospital at Waipukurau', *Hawke's Bay Herald*, 30 September 1886.

38 *Waipukurau Hospital Centennial — Souvenir Booklet 1879–1979* (Waipukurau: Waipawa Hospital Board, 1979).

39 Susan MacLean, *Architect of the Angels: The Churches of Frederick de Jersey Clere* (Wellington: Steele Roberts, 2003), 14, 17–18; Mew and Humphris, *Raupo to Deco*, 77–78, 155–56.

40 'Wellington Hospital 1891', plan by Clere Fitzgerald & Richmond held by the Bulleyment Fortune Archives; Donald Wilson MacDonald, *A Hundred Years of Healing: Wellington Hospital 1847–1947* (Wellington: A. H. & A. W. Reed, 1947), 27; Capital Coast District Health Board, www.ccdhb.org.nz/about-us/history

41 MacDonald, *A Hundred Years of Healing*, 27; Laurie H. Barber and Roy J. Towers, *Wellington Hospital 1847–1976* (Wellington: Wellington Hospital Board, 1976), 38; Capital Coast District Health Board, ccdhb.org.nz/about-us/history

42 Capital Coast District Health Board, ccdhb.org.nz/about-us/history

43 MacDonald, *A Hundred Years of Healing*, 28; Barber and Towers, *Wellington Hospital*, 38.

44 Relocated to nearby Brayshaw Park in Blenheim in 2007, it is now a Category 2 Historic Place. *Wairau Public Hospital Fever Ward (Former)(Relocated)*, Heritage New Zealand Register #1536, www.heritage.org.nz/the-list; J. G. Furness, *Wairau Hospital: 100 Years of Caring* (Blenheim: Marlborough Hospital Board, 1978), 48.

45 'Wellington Hospital Outpatients, 1900', plan by Clere & Swan held by the Bulleyment Fortune Archives.

46 The first steward of Whanganui's colonial hospital was Thomas Reid, whose wife was the matron. He later became a successful businessman, and when he died his will bequeathed funds to erect a new building on 33 acres of land that he had already bought for that purpose on Heads Road, Gonville, and which Whanganui Hospital still occupies today. See R. E. Wright-St Clair, *Caring for People: A History of the Wanganui Hospital Board* (Whanganui: Wanganui Hospital Board Centennial Celebration Committee, 1987), 17.

47 *Wanganui Hospital Board Celebrates Centenary*, Wanganui Newspapers Special Feature, 3 April 1987; Wright-St Clair, *Caring for People*, 22.

48 Wright-St Clair, *Caring for People*, 22.

49 *Centennial of Greymouth Hospital 1866–1966*, Special Publication (Greymouth: *Greymouth Evening Star*, 1966).

50 Rex E. Wright-St Clair, *The Early History of Waikato Hospital* (Hamilton: Waikato Hospital Board, 1987), 18, 23; Georgina Wedge and Peter Rothwell, *Waikato Hospital: Our Hospital, Your History* (Hamilton: Waikato Health Memorabilia Trust, 2016), 10, 16; John Armstrong, *Under One Roof: A History of Waikato Hospital* (Hamilton: Half Court Press, 2009), 49.

51 Mew and Humphris, *Raupo to Deco*, 155–56.

52 'Reefton Hospital Trustees', *Greymouth Evening Star*, 2 March 1907, 2; 'Reefton Hospital Trustees', *Greymouth Evening Star*, 24 April 1908, 2.

53 MacDonald, *A Hundred Years of Healing*, 34; Barber and Towers, *Wellington Hospital*, 44; Capital Coast District Health Board, www.ccdhb.org.nz/about-us/history

54 A. G. Bagnall, *Old Greytown 1854–1954* (Greytown: Greytown Borough Council, 1954), 62; David Kernohan, *Wairarapa Buildings: Two Centuries of New Zealand Architecture* (Masterton: Wairarapa Archive, 2003), 92; Diane Grant (ed.) with Wairarapa Health History Group, *Helping Hands: A History of Healthcare in the Wairarapa* (Masterton: Fraser Books, 2015), 89.

55 Conly, *A Case History*, 40.

56 The 1911 buildings were demolished in 1971. 'Old Hospital Goes', *Gisborne Photo News*, 16 June 1971; Foundation stone, Gisborne Hospital.

57 'The Gisborne Hospital', *New Zealand Herald*, 12 January 1912, 5; 'Gisborne's New Hospital', *Poverty Bay Herald*, 12 February 1912, 3; Scanlan, *Hospital on the Hill*, 50–54.

58 Elizabeth Cox (ed.), *Making Space: A History of New Zealand Women in Architecture* (Auckland: Massey University Press, 2022), 34.

59 Wright-St Clair, *Caring for People*, 26–28; Plans held at Whanganui Hospital; Wendy Pettigrew and Mark Southcombe, 'The End of the Wooden Shop: Whanganui Architecture in the 1890s', *Architectural History Aotearoa* 4 (2007): 76–87. This building was demolished in 1959.

60 Wright-St Clair, *Caring for People*, 39–40; 'Wanganui Hospital Board', *Wanganui Chronicle*, 19 February 1920, 2; 'Wanganui Hospital Board – Important Building Programme', *Wanganui Chronicle*, 22 July 1920, 8; 'Hospital Administration', *Wanganui Chronicle*, 22 July 1926, 10.

61 Wright-St Clair, *Caring for People*, 69

62 Ibid., 75; Pātea Historical Society, www.pateahistoricalsociety.org.nz; *Pātea Heritage Inventory* (Hāwera: South Taranaki District Council, 2000); I. Church, 'One Hundred Years Plus at Pātea Hospital', *Patea Mail*, September 1981.

63 *Hohipera o Papaioea: Palmerston North Hospital Celebrates 125 Years* (Palmerston North: MidCentral District Health Board, 2018), 2; Jo Kellaway and Mike Maryan, *A Century of Care: Palmerston North Hospital 1893–1993* (Double Bay, Australia: MidCentral Health and Focus Books, 1993), 13–16, Nancy Smith, *And So We Began: A History of the Perrin Family of Palmerston North and Notes on Early Settlers* (Palmerston North: self-published, 1971).

64 Mew and Humphris, *Raupo to Deco*, 335–36. Some references incorrectly refer to the hospital's builder, E. Carter, as the architect.

65 *Hohipera o Papaioea*, 2; Kellaway and Maryan, *A Century of Care*, 13–15.

66 https://horowhenua.kete.net.nz/item/ad0f04a2-7880-44b1-8a3e-5b2907625089. After being taken over by the Palmerston North Hospital Board, it was reopened as the Otaki Maternity Home in 1933, and an 11-bed block was added in 1937. Rebuilt after fire damage in 1945, it eventually closed in 1992 and became the Otaki Community Health Centre.

67 Barber and Towers, *Wellington Hospital*, 43. The Palmerston North Hospital Board opened a new hospital in Ōtaki in 1929 and took over the sanatorium in 1933. In 1965 the building became the Koha Ora annex of the Kimberley Hospital and Training School. This closed in 1985 and was demolished in 1997. See Ōtaki Sanatorium at manawatuheritage.pncc.govt.nz.

68 Kellaway and Maryan, *A Century of Care*, 29; 'Awapuni Home', *Manawatu Guardian*, 22 November 2022.

69 MacDonald, *A Hundred Years of Healing*, 117; Barber and Towers, *Wellington Hospital*, 42; Capital Coast District Health Board, www.ccdhb.org.nz/about-us/history

70 Bruce Macdonald, *Westport: Struggle for Survival* (Westport: Westport Borough Council, 1973), 63.

71 Furness, *Wairau Hospital*, 49, 22.

72 'Hospital and Charitable Aid Board', *The Colonist*, 8 February 1900, 2; 'Havelock Cottage Hospital' *Pelorus Guardian and Miners' Advocate*, 6 June 1902, 4; 'Picton Hospital Board' *Pelorus Guardian and Miners' Advocate*, 10 April 1903, 5.

73 F. O. Bennett, *Hospital on the Avon: The History of*

Christchurch Hospital 1862–1962 (Christchurch: North Canterbury Hospital Board, 1962), 92.

74 Ibid., 102.

75 *Refugee and Philanthropist — Hyman Marks and the Christchurch Hospital, 1897*, www.lostchristchurch.wordpress.com.

76 Bennett, *Hospital on the Avon*, 123.

77 Ibid., 136.

78 Luke Tremlett, 'Medical Buildings and Medical Theory: An Archaeological Investigation of Ashburton Hospital, New Zealand' (MA thesis, University of Otago, Dunedin, 2015), 79; Bennett, *Hospital on the Avon*, 123; W. H. Scotter, *Ashburton: A History with Records of Town and Country* (Ashburton: Ashburton Borough and County Councils, 1972), 140, 216–20; 'Ashburton Hospital', *Ashburton Guardian*, 15 September 1892, 2.

79 John Campbell McKenzie, *A History of Timaru Hospital* (Christchurch: Pegasus Press, 1974), 173.

80 John H. Angus, *A History of the Otago Hospital Board and its Predecessors* (Dunedin: Otago Hospital Board, 1984), 90.

81 'Dunedin Hospital – A Notable Diamond Jubilee', *Otago Daily Times*, 24 August 1926; 'The Patient Progress of Dunedin's Hospital', *Otago Daily Times*, www.odt.shorthandstories.com/the-patient-progress-of-dunedin-hospital/index.html

82 Kim Dungey, 'Fortunes Ran Hot and Cold', *Otago Daily Times*, 20 September 2011, www.odt.co.nz/lifestyle/magazine/fortunes-ran-hot-and-cold

83 *Pelichet Bay Infectious Diseases Hospital (Former)*, Heritage New Zealand Register #9575, www.heritage.org.nz/the-list

84 *Dunstan Hospital 125th Anniversary* (Jubilee Committee, Vincent Hospital Board, 1988); Sarah Marquet, 'Hospital "Certainly One of the Top"', *Otago Daily Times*, 11 June 2021, www.odt.co.nz/regions/central-otago/hospital-certainly-one-top

85 'Wakatipu and Clyde Hospitals', *Cyclopedia of New Zealand (Otago and Southland Provincial Districts)*, Vol. 4 (Wellington: Cyclopedia Co., 1905), 1022–23; G. T. Piercy, 'Frankton and Arrowtown Hospitals', *Queenstown Courier*, Queenstown & District Historical Society, Issue 40 (1988).

86 *History of the Southland Hospitals and Boards 1861–1968* (Invercargill: Southland Hospital Board, 1968), 19.

87 *Southland Hospital Nurses' Home (Former)*, Heritage New Zealand Register #2510, www.heritage.org.nz/the-list

88 *Dee Street Hospital*, Heritage New Zealand Register #7777, www.heritage.org.nz/the-list

89 'Wallace and Fiord Hospital', *Cyclopedia of New Zealand (Otago and Southland Provincial Districts)*, Vol. 4 (Wellington: Cyclopedia Co., 1905), 935; *Riverton Hospital*, Southland's Past, digitised by Dwayne Carey Videos, 3 September 2017.

Maternity and infant care

1 Lynda Exton, *The Baby Business: What's Happened to Maternity Care in New Zealand* (Nelson: Craig Potton, 2008), 31, 35; Alison Clarke, *Born to a Changing World: Childbirth in Nineteenth-century New Zealand* (Wellington: Bridget Williams Books, 2012), 34–35.

2 Clarke, *Born to a Changing World*, 77, 80–82.

3 Karen Guilliland and Sally Pairman, *Women's Business: The Story of the New Zealand College of Midwives, 1986–2010* (Christchurch: New Zealand College of Midwives, 2010), 12.

4 https://nzhistory.govt.nz/page/world%E2%80%99s-first-state-run-maternity-hospital-opens

5 J. O. C. Neill, *Grace Neill: The Story of a Noble Woman* (Christchurch: N. M. Peryer Ltd, 1961), 49; Patricia Sargison, *Notable Women in New Zealand Health, Te Hauora Ki Aotearoa: Ōna Wāhine Rongonui* (Auckland: Longman Paul, 1993), 17.

6 *Maternity Services in New Zealand*, Report Series No. 26 (Wellington: Board of Health, 1976), 17.

7 'St Helen's Hospital, Rintoul Street', *Evening Post*, 25 May 1905,1; *House 38A Colombo Street Newtown Wellington*, www.heritage.org.nz/list-details/3598/3598

8 Adelheid Wassner, *Labour of Love: Childbirth at Dunedin Hospital 1862–1972* (Dunedin: self-published, 1999), 9–10; Dorothy Page, *Anatomy of a Medical School: A History of Medicine at the University of Otago 1875–2000* (Dunedin: Otago University Press, 2008), 80–81.

9 Derek A. Dow, *Auckland's Hospitals: A Pictorial History 1847–2004* (Auckland: Auckland District Health Board, 2005), 34–36; *History of National Women's Hospital* (Auckland: Women's Health Information Services, Auckland District Health Board, 2010), 3. In 1968 Auckland's St Helen's Hospital was relocated to a new building in Mount Albert and the Pitt Street buildings were demolished in 2002.

10 John Wilson, *Lost Christchurch* (Lincoln: Te Waihora Press, 1984), 24; www.lostchristchurch.wordpress.com

11 'Hospital News', *Gisborne Photo News*, 5 October 1961, 55; *History of the Southland Hospitals and Boards 1861–1968* (Invercargill: Southland Hospital Board, 1968), 69.

12 Wright-St Clair, *Caring for People*, 61. It closed in 1955 when the new maternity unit was opened at Whanganui Hospital and was demolished in 1979.

13 Exton, *The Baby Business*, 36; *History of National Women's Hospital*, 5; Linda Bryder, *The Best Country to Give Birth? Midwifery, Homebirth and the Politics of Maternity in Aotearoa New Zealand* (Auckland: Auckland University Press, 2023), 8–9.

14 Lloyd Chapman, *In a Stange Garden: The Life and Times of Truby King* (Auckland: Penguin, 2003), 77–102, 119–42.

15 Ibid., 127–41, 169; Joyce Powell, *A Suitable Job for Young Ladies: The Karitane Story 1907 to 2007* (Palmerston North: Heritage Press, 2007), 9, 11; Jim Sullivan, *I Was a Plunket Baby: 100 Years of the Royal New Zealand Plunket Society Inc* (Auckland: Random House, 2007), 18,116.

16 *Truby King Harris Hospital (Former)*, Heritage New Zealand Register #9659, www.heritage.org.nz/the-list

17 'Karitane Hospital, Christchurch', *Home & Building* 25 (February 1963).

18 *History of the Southland Hospitals and Boards*, 69.

19 *Truby King House (Former)*, Heritage New Zealand Register #4427, www.heritage.org.nz/the-list

20 *Karitāne Products Society Building (Former)*, Heritage New Zealand Register #4431, www.heritage.org.nz/the-list

21 *Truby King Historic Area*, Heritage New Zealand Register #7040, www.heritage.org.nz/the-list

22 'Karitane Nurses' Home, Wellington', *Journal of the NZIA* 31, no. 2 (March 1964): 35–37; Chapman, *In a Strange Garden*, 169; Powell, *A Suitable Job for Young Ladies*, 85, 11; Sullivan, *I Was a Plunket Baby*, 144, 164. The Wellington hospital was demolished in 2020. In 1991, the Wellington City Council bought King's house and the gardens, which included his mausoleum, erected in 1941, and the Truby King Historic area was formed. The house and mausoleum are Category 1 Historic Places, as is the factory, which is now in private hands.

23 'St Helen's Hospital, Wellington', *Journal of the NZIA* 42, no. 1 (February 1975): 12–16. In 1978 the service was moved onto the main public hospital campus, where it was housed in the Wellington Women's Hospital and later named the Grace Neill Building. The Coromandel Street building was converted into apartments.

24 https://www3.stats.govt.nz/New_Zealand_Official_Yearbooks/1969/NZOYB_1969.html#idsect1_1_44559

Chapter 6. War, Depression and the welfare state 1914–1945

1 James Belich, *Paradise Reforged: A History of the New Zealanders: From the 1880s to the Year 2000* (Auckland: Allen Lane Penguin, 2001), 254–59; Michael King, *The Penguin History of New Zealand* (Auckland: Penguin, 2003), 346–52; https://teara.govt.nz/en/epidemics/page-4; https://polio.org.nz/history

2 https://teara.govt.nz/en/biographies/3g9/gillies-harold-delf; https://teara.govt.nz/en/1966/mcindoe-sir-archibald-hector-cbe

3 Rebecca Priestley, 'Nuclear New Zealand: New Zealand's Nuclear and Radiation History to 1987' (PhD thesis, University of Canterbury, Christchurch, 2010), 59.

4 https://teara.govt.nz/en/hospitals/page-2

5 Michael P. Murphy Jr with Jeffrey Mansfield and MASS Design Group, *The Architecture of Health: Hospital Design and the Construction of Dignity* (New York: Cooper Hewitt, Smithsonian Design Museum, 2021), 46.

6 'Students' Architectural Associations', *Progress* XIII, no. 8 (April 1918): 175; https://teara.govt.nz/mi/earthquakes/print

7 *Wharf Hotel (Former), Rawene, Hokianga*, Heritage New Zealand Register #435, www.heritage.org.nz/the-list

8 G. Kemble Welch, *Doctor Smith: Hokianga's 'King of the North'* (Auckland: Blackwood and Janet Paul, 1965), 19, 33, 46, 72–76; Frank Rogers, 'Smith, George Marshall McCall', *Dictionary of New Zealand Biography*, first published in 1998. Te Ara – the Encyclopedia of New Zealand, https://teara.govt.nz/en/biographies/4s32/smith-george-marshall-mccall; Christine Williams, *Hokianga Health: The First Hundred Years — Te Rautau Tuatahi* (Rāwene: Hokianga Health Enterprise Trust, 2010), 21, 31, 43, 55, 65.

9 Williams, *Hokianga Health*, 147. Te Whare Whakaaronui for continuing care patients opened in 2002, a new wing with 10 geriatric beds, a new emergency room and a lift to the maternity ward in 2004.

10 'Hospital to Blow Out 100 Candles', *Northern Advocate*, 22 February 2013. This building became the maternity ward in 1969 and was repurposed as the community services building in 1996, when maternity returned to the main building. A two-storey nurses' home opened below the main hospital in 1944 was demolished in 2007.

11 Diana Menefy, *Whangarei Hospital: A Century of Service 1901–2001* (Whangārei: Northland Health Ltd, 2001), 43, 161, 171.

12 Menefy, *Whangarei Hospital*, 63; *Whangarei Hospital's 120 Year Celebration*, Northland DHB, www.community.northlanddhb.org.nz/celebration

13 Keith Parker, *Kaitaia's Hospital: A Glimpse at Hospital Services and Volunteer Health Care in the Far North 1904–2004* (Kamo: Bridgewater, 2005), 16.

14 *The Auckland Hospital and Charitable Aid Board: A History of its Buildings and Endowments, Illustrated* (Auckland: Auckland Hospital and Charitable Aid Board, 1919), 47, 50; Edward A. and Anthony H. G. Roche, *Green Lane Saga: Green Lane Hospital, Auckland 1889–1982* (Auckland: Ray Richards, 1983), 16-7; B. R. Hutchinson (ed.), *Green Lane Hospital: The First Hundred Years* (Auckland: Green Lane Hospital

Centennial Committee, 1990), 53.
15 The group of buildings is now a Category 1 Historic Place. *Green Lane Hospital*, Heritage New Zealand Register #4536, www.heritage.org.nz/the-list; 'Demolition Looming for Heritage Building', *New Zealand Herald*, 3 March 2008.
16 *The Auckland Hospital and Charitable Aid Board*, 37; Frank Charles Rauch, 'The History of Auckland Hospital and the Auckland Hospital and Charitable Aid Board 1847–1914' (MA thesis, University of Auckland, 1933), 71; David Scott (ed.), *The Story of Auckland Hospital 1847–2004* (Auckland: Medical History Library Committee of the Royal Australasian College of Physicians in New Zealand, 1977), 39; Derek A. Dow, *Auckland's Hospitals: A Pictorial History 1847–1914* (Auckland: Auckland District Health Board, 2005), 20–01.
17 Mary E. Williams, *A Century of Service: Waihi Hospital Centenary 1903–2003* (Waihi: self-published, 2003), 1, 81, 89; Ron Cooke, *Patients First: The Proud Tradition of Taumarunui Hospital* (Taumarunui: Taumarunui Hospital Reunion Committee, 2005), 15, 18–19, 37–38, 47, 50–01.
18 *True Tales of Thames Hospital: 150 Years 1868–2018* (Thames: Thames Hospital 150 Group, in collaboration with the Coromandel Heritage Trust, 2018), 40–01; 'Opening of New Nurses' Home, Thames', *Kai Tiaki: The Journal of the Nurses Organisation of New Zealand* (October 1921): 193; Suzanne Morgan, *Thames Hospital: A Pictorial History 1868–1987* (Thames: self-published, 2006).
19 'Memorial Hospital: New Structure at Waiuku: Official Opening Ceremony', *Franklin Times*, 1 May 1923, 5.
20 *Auckland Hospital and Charitable Aid Board*, 57; Rauch, 'History of Auckland Hospital', 70; Dow, *Auckland's Hospitals*, 19.
21 'The Hospital: Result of Inquiry', *Auckland Star*, 20 October 1926, 10; 'Hospital Architect: Mr Allsop's Resignation', *New Zealand Herald*, 22 December 1926, 12.
22 www.historic.org.nz/corporate/registersearch/professionalbio
23 Rex E. Wright-St Clair, *The Early History of Waikato Hospital* (Hamilton: Waikato Hospital Board, 1987), 25; John Armstrong, *Under One Roof: A History of Waikato Hospital* (Hamilton: Half Court Press, 2009), 58, 168; Georgina Wedge and Peter Rothwell, *Waikato Hospital: Our Hospital, Your History* (Hamilton: Waikato Health Memorabilia Trust, 2016), 19–22, Te Whare Taonga o Waikato Museum & Gallery, https://collection.waikatomuseum.org.nz/objects
24 Wright-St Clair, *The Early History of Waikato Hospital*, 25–26; Armstrong, *Under One Roof*, 63, 88–89, 172–73; Wedge and Rothwell, *Waikato Hospital*, 22.
25 Wright-St Clair, *The Early History of Waikato Hospital*, 26–28; Armstrong, *Under One Roof*, 63, 85; Wedge and Rothwell, *Waikato Hospital*, 28–29.
26 Wedge and Rothwell, *Waikato Hospital*, 14. The board moved to a new hospital administration building in 1938, but the Hood Street premises remain as a Category 2 Historic Place. *Office of the Waikato District Hospital and Charitable Aid Board (Former)*, Heritage New Zealand Register #9279, heritage.org.nz/the-list
27 'Former Huntly Cottage Hospital & Maternity Home (1924–25)', Hearing 14, *Schedule 30.1 Historic Heritage Items* (Hamilton: Waikato District Council, 2020); 'Waikato Hospital Board: Appointment of Architect for Te Kuiti', *King Country Chronicle*, 24 November 1923, 5; 'Te Kuiti Hospital: Conference Postponed', *King Country Chronicle*, 16 February 1924, 5; 'Te Kuiti Hospital to be Opened in November', *King Country Chronicle*, 14 September 1926, 5; 'Commemorative Plaque: Gifts for Te Kuiti Hospital', *King Country Chronicle*, 1 December 1937, 5; Russell Young, *The Story of Te Kūiti* (Wellington: Winter Productions, 2013), 111–12.
28 Ian Shearer and Rex E. Wright-St Clair, *A Century on Cameron Road: A History of Tauranga Hospital 1914–2014* (Tauranga: Bay of Plenty District Health Board, 2016), 11.
29 Ibid., 25, 32.
30 Ibid., 23, 70.
31 Matthews & Matthews Architects Ltd, *Whakatane Built Heritage Study* (Whakatane District Council, 2007), 24; Ian Shearer, *Whakatane Hospital: Te Whatumauri Hauora: A History* (Tauranga: Bay of Plenty District Health Board, 2011), 10, 13–17, 20–21, 37–38.
32 Matthews & Matthews Architects, *Opotiki Town Centre Historic Heritage Study: Part One* (Ōpōtiki: Opotiki District Council, 2006), 33–34.
33 Alison Robinson (ed.), *Stratford Hospital Memories* (Stratford: Thurlstone Press, 2001), 5, 105, 169.
34 T. D. Hodges, *Mountain Town Hospital: The Story of the Stratford Public Hospital* (Stratford: Stratford Hospital Nurses' Reunion Committee, 1978), 18, 28, 30, 34, 40. Puke Ariki in New Plymouth holds drawings dated 1936 by Griffiths & Stephenson for additions to the operating theatre and kitchen block and some dated 1944 by Griffiths & Syme in association with Duffill & Gibson ARC2004-1566, S19/1-128, https://collection.pukeariki.com/objects/36409/stratford-hospital-plans
35 W. H. Skinner, *Pioneer Medical Men of Taranaki 1834 to 1880: With an Account of the Establishment of Hospital Accommodation at New Plymouth* (New Plymouth: Thomas Avery & Sons, 1933; Christchurch: Capper Press, 1984), 151; Arthur B. Scanlan, *Hospital on the Hill: A Centennial History of the New Plymouth Hospital 1867–1967* (New Plymouth: Taranaki Hospital Board, 1967), 66; Ian Pritchard, *Frank Messenger: Architect: The Work of a New Plymouth Architect* (New Plymouth: self-published, 1994), 91–2, 125.
36 Skinner, *Pioneer Medical Men of Taranaki*, 161; Scanlan, *Hospital on the Hill*, 73–74, 77, 80–83, 86; Pritchard, *Frank Messenger: Architect*, 91–92, 125.
37 Scanlan, *Hospital on the Hill*, 90–95.
38 Kate Mickelson, *The Clearing: A History of Ōpunake* (self-published, 1989), 53–56; www.opunakeresthome.co.nz
39 *Te Araroa Hospital*, Heritage New Zealand Register #7103, www.heritage.org.nz/the-list; 'Then and Now', *Gisborne Photo News*, 15 June 1966, 46–47.
40 Geoff Conly, *A Case History: The Hawke's Bay Hospital Board 1876–1989* (Napier: Hawke's Bay Area Health Board, 1992), 72.
41 Ibid., 85.
42 Ibid., 116.
43 Anna Rogers, *The Shaky Isles: New Zealand Earthquakes* (Wellington: Grantham House Publishing, 2013), 81, 107.
44 Conly, *A Case History*, 115.
45 R. E. Wright-St Clair, *Caring for People: A History of the Wanganui Hospital Board* (Whanganui: Wanganui Hospital Board Centennial Celebration Committee, 1987), 43, 'Wanganui Hospital: New Isolation Wards: Preparation of Plans', *Wanganui Chronicle*, 22 January 1937, 6.
46 Newcombe was refurbished and reopened in 1991 as Te Kōpae for the Community Mental Health and Addictions Service. The original buildings were demolished in the mid-1980s to make way for the new ward and administration block and adjacent helipad.
47 'Hospital Works', *Wanganui Chronicle*, 21 May 1943, 4.
48 'New Hospital for Raetihi', *Wanganui Chronicle*, 12 September 1940, 4.
49 Patrick Parsons, *Waipukurau: The History of a Country Town* (Waipukurau: CHB Print, 1999), 141–43; Pukeroa Estate, www.pukeora.com
50 Parsons, *Waipukurau*, 138; *Waipukurau Hospital Centennial — Souvenir Booklet 1879–1979* (Waipukurau: Waipawa Hospital Board, 1979).
51 'Clinical Block – Dannevirke Hospital', *Home & Building* 24 (February 1962); Jan Lockett-Kay, *Rural Health: A Case Study of the Dannevirke Community Hospital: An Exemplar of Innovation* (Report presented for the Kellogg Rural Leadership Programme, 1999).
52 Pam Phillips (comp.), *Notes on Palmerston North Architects (1900–1950)* (archive donated to Palmerston North Public Library, 1999).
53 Jo Kellaway and Mike Maryan, *A Century of Care: Palmerston North Hospital 1893–1993* (Double Bay, Australia: MidCentral Health and Focus Books, 1993), 28, 30, 33.
54 Minutes Book of the Palmerston North Guild of Registered Architects 1926–1946.
55 Articles of the Palmerston North Guild of Registered Architects, 1934/35. Both the Articles and the Minutes Book are held by Palmerston North Public Library; the name of the guild was for a time the Palmerston North Guild of Registered Architects and Structural Engineers.
56 'New Hospital Block Opened by Minister', *Manawatu Standard*, 3 December 1936; Kellaway and Maryan, *A Century of Care*, 33.
57 'Change of Policy to Employ Architect', *Manawatu Standard*, 21 July 1936; 'Hospital Board Monthly Meeting', *Manawatu Standard*, 22 September 1936.
58 Graeme Laurenson, *Burrafirth: The Family of Graeme and Marjorie Laurenson* (New Plymouth: Burrafirth, 1982), 90.

Te Puea Hērangi

1 Michael King, *Te Puea: A Biography* (Auckland: Hodder & Stoughton, 1977), 31, 102; Ann Parsonson. 'Hērangi, Te Kirihaehae Te Puea', *Dictionary of New Zealand Biography*, first published in 1996. Te Ara – the Encyclopedia of New Zealand, https://teara.govt.nz/en/biographies/3h17/herangi-te-kirihaehae-te-puea
2 *Tūrangawaewae Māori Parliament*, Heritage New Zealand Register #4170, www.heritage.org.nz/the-list; David McGill and Grant Sheehan, 'The Māori House of Parliament', in *Landmarks: Notable Historic Buildings of New Zealand* (Auckland: Godwit, 1997), 71.
3 Deidre Brown, *Māori Architecture: From Fale to Wharenui and Beyond* (Auckland: Raupo, 2009), 101–03.
4 King, *Te Puea*, 132, 152.

Public Works

1 Rosslyn J. Noonan, *By Design: A Brief History of the Public Works Department, Ministry of Works 1870–1970* (Wellington: Ministry of Works and Government Printer, 1975), 1, 9, 31, 59; James C. Muir, *Opus Works: A Short History of the New Zealand Government's Infrastructure Development* (Christchurch: self-published, 2021), 34, 51.
2 Ian Bowman, 'The Next Generation', in *William Beatson: A Colonial Architect* (Auckland: Balasoglou Books, 2005), 137–41.
3 Noonan, *By Design*, 63, 90, 80.
4 Peter Richardson, 'An Architecture of Empire: The Government Buildings of John Campbell in New Zealand' (MA thesis, University of Canterbury, Christchurch, 1988), 56–57.
5 Lewis E. Martin, *Built for Us: The Work of Government

and Colonial Architects, 1860s to 1960s* (Dunedin: Otago University Press, 2004), 123.
6 'Hastings Memorial Hospital', *Hawke's Bay Tribune*, 28 February 1925, 4; untitled article, *Hawke's Bay Tribune*, 10 May 1926; 'Memorial Hospital Opening', *Hawke's Bay Tribune*, 26 April 1928, 5, 8. Note that the architect is referred to as Phillips in the 1925 article, but the Public Works Department in the 1926 one.
7 Introduced to Hawke's Bay by Hastings architect William Rush in his 1913 building for Iona College, the Spanish Mission style developed in California, where the deep shaded verandahs and wide overhanging eaves were considered appropriate for the hot sunny climate. Hastings is renowned for its significant collection of such buildings. See Peter Shaw and Peter Hallett, *Spanish Mission Hastings: Styles of Five Decades* (Napier: Cosmos Publications, 1991), 13.
8 A. M. Isdale, 'A Record Relative to the Establishment and Development of the Hawke's Bay Fallen Soldiers' Memorial Hospital, Hastings', in G. Hollywood, *History of Hastings Hospital, Summary to 1941*, 1943, Knowledge Bank website of Hawke's Bay Digital Archives Trust, knowledgebank.org.nz; Geoff Conly, *A Case History: The Hawke's Bay Hospital Board 1876–1989* (Napier: Hawke's Bay Area Health Board, 1992), 97.
9 Noonan, *By Design*, 116, 123.
10 Ibid., 136, 133; Martin, *Built for Us*, 148.
11 Noonan, *By Design*, 165.
12 Martin, *Built for Us*, 155; *A Brief History of Public Buildings in New Zealand* (Wellington: Ministry of Works, 1970).
13 Noonan, *By Design*, 180.
14 Ibid., 205.
15 Subsequent Government Architects were John Robert Patrick Blake-Kelly from 1971 to 1973, Frank Anderson from 1973 to 1976, Graydon Miskimmin from 1976 to 1986 and Peter Fage from 1986 to 1988. The title continued for a short time after the ministry was corporatised and was held by Duncan Joiner from 1988 to 1992. In 1973 the functions of the Ministry of Works were expanded, and it was renamed the Ministry of Works and Development. See Muir, *Opus Works*, 357.
16 'Artificial Limb Centre', *Home & Building* 36 (December 1973).
17 *Planning Guidelines for Hospital Beds and Services* (Wellington: Hospitals Division, Department of Health, 1977); *Health Design Guidelines* (Wellington: Department of Health, 1991); *Accommodation in Hospitals: Code of Practice* (Wellington: Standards Association of New Zealand for the Department of Health, 1991).
18 'Barton, R. H.', *Journal of the NZIA* 39, no. 8 (August 1972).
19 Margaret Tennant, 'Neill, Elizabeth Grace', *Dictionary of New Zealand Biography*, first published in 1993. Te Ara – the Encyclopedia of New Zealand, https://teara.govt.nz/en/biographies/2n5/neill-elizabeth-grace
20 Elizabeth Cox (ed.), *Making Space: A History of New Zealand Women in Architecture* (Auckland: Massey University Press, 2022), 48, 103.
21 Ibid., 51, 104.
22 Ibid., 104.
23 Ibid., 106.

Chapter 7. Designing from the heart

1 Martin McCarthy, 'The Haughton Partnership: An Historical Review 1879 to 1951' (Bachelor of Architecture report, Victoria University of Wellington, 1982), 29–31, 33, 46–47, 49–50, 66, 69–70.
2 Donald MacDonald Wilson, *A Hundred Years of Healing: Wellington Hospital 1847–1947* (Wellington: A. H. & A. W. Reed, 1947), 29; Laurie H. Barber and Roy J. Towers, *Wellington Hospital 1847–1976* (Wellington: Wellington Hospital Board, 1976), 38; Plaque at Wellington Regional Hospital.
3 Wilson, *A Hundred Years of Healing*, 31, 34; Barber and Towers, *Wellington Hospital*, 43.
4 C. J. Carle, *Masterton Hospital 1879–1979* (Masterton: Centennial Book Committee, Wairarapa Hospital Board, 1979), 24; David Kernohan, *Wairarapa Buildings: Two Centuries of New Zealand Architecture* (Masterton: Wairarapa Archive, 2003), 93.
5 McCarthy, 'The Haughton Partnership', 83–84; Barber and Towers, *Wellington Hospital 1847–1976*, 43; *Ewart Hospital Nurses' Home (Former)*, Heritage New Zealand Register #5375, www.heritage.org.nz/the-list
6 Wilson, *A Hundred Years of Healing*, 36; *Fever Hospital (Former)*, Heritage New Zealand Register #5376, www.heritage.org.nz/the-list
7 J. G. Furness, *Wairau Hospital: 100 Years of Caring* (Blenheim: Marlborough Hospital Board, 1978), 23. The building was demolished in 2011.
8 John Wilson, *Thematic Historical Overview of Nelson City for Nelson City Council Heritage Inventory Project* (October 2011), 99.
9 Jo Kellaway and Mike Maryan, *A Century of Care: Palmerston North Hospital 1893–1993* (Double Bay, Australia: MidCentral Health and Focus Books, 1993), 28.
10 McCarthy, 'The Haughton Partnership', 105-07.
11 Wilson, *A Hundred Years of Healing*, 44; Barber and Towers, *Wellington Hospital*, 65; Heritage.org.nz/The-List/Lost-Heritage; McCarthy, 'The Haughton Partnership', 104, 119, 128–29; Te Whatu Ora Health New Zealand,, www.ccdhb.org.nz/about-us/history
12 McCarthy, 'The Haughton Partnership', 107–08, 115, 117.
13 Christine Clement, *Hawera Hospital: 100 Years 1894–1994* (Hāwera: Hawera Hospital Centennial Committee, 1994), 22; Foundation stone, Hawera Hospital.
14 'W. J. McKeon', *Journal of the NZIA* 28, no. 9 (October 1962); 'Obituary: W. J. McKeon', *Journal of the NZIA* 40, no. 6 (June 1973); McCarthy, 'The Haughton Partnership', 137, 147.
15 McCarthy, 'The Haughton Partnership', 140–41, 160.
16 McCarthy, 'The Haughton Partnership', 162–65; Plans for Wellington Hospital Main Block dated 1939, held by Porirua Hospital Museum.
17 McCarthy, 'The Haughton Partnership', 164–65.
18 Te Whatu Ora Health New Zealand, www.ccdhb.org.nz/about-us/history
19 McCarthy, 'The Haughton Partnership', 164–65, 192; Barber and Towers, *Wellington Hospital*, 96.
20 Wilson, *A Hundred Years of Healing*, 52; Barber and Towers, *Wellington Hospital*, 96.
21 Wilson, *A Hundred Years of Healing*, 118; Te Whatu Ora Health New Zealand, www.ccdhb.org.nz/about-us/history
22 Elizabeth Cox (ed.), *Making Space: A History of New Zealand Women in Architecture* (Auckland: Massey University Press, 2022), 59, 61–62.
23 McCarthy, 'The Haughton Partnership', 192.
24 Craig Mackenzie, *Hospital in the Valley* (Palmerston North: Dunmore Press, 1983), 13; McCarthy, 'The Haughton Partnership', 183–84.
25 Mackenzie, *Hospital in the Valley*, 14; 'Hutt Hospital Celebrates 75 Years in the Community', Hutt Valley DHB, 13 May 2019, www.huttvalleydhb.org.nz/media-and-latest-news/latest-news/2019-05-13-hutt-hospital-celebrates-75-years-in-the-community
26 McCarthy, 'The Haughton Partnership', 159, 189–91, 195–96.
27 Wilson, *A Hundred Years of Healing*, 100; Barber and Towers, *Wellington Hospital*, 82.
28 William Bayly, *The History of Silverstream Hospital* (self-published, 1991), 1–5; F. G. Grattan, *Official War History of the Public Works Department Volume 3* (Wellington: Public Works Department, 1948), 704; Wilson, *A Hundred Years of Healing*, 104; Barber and Towers, *Wellington Hospital*, 91, McCarthy, 'The Haughton Partnership', 184.
29 McCarthy, 'The Haughton Partnership', 160, 204.
30 Ibid., 210.
31 'J. Lindsay Mair', *Journal of the NZIA* 38, no. 4 (April 1971); 'J. Lindsay Mair', *Journal of the NZIA* 39, no. 8 (August 1972); McCarthy, 'The Haughton Partnership', 161.
32 Barber and Towers, *Wellington Hospital*, 79; 'Nurses' Memorial Chapel, Wellington Hospital', *Home & Building* 28 (February 1966); McCarthy, 'The Haughton Partnership', 193–97.
33 Te Whatu Ora Health New Zealand, www.ccdhb.org.nz/about-us/history
34 'Seddon Wing, Wellington Hospital', *Journal of the NZIA* 37, no. 12 (December 1970); Barber and Towers, *Wellington Hospital*, 108; Te Whatu Ora Health New Zealand, www.ccdhb.org.nz/about-us/history
35 'Kenepuru Maternity Hospital', *Journal of the NZIA* 35, no. 9 (September 1968).
36 Barber and Towers, *Wellington Hospital*, 116.
37 Julia Gatley (ed.), *Long Live the Modern: New Zealand's New Architecture 1904–1984* (Auckland: Auckland University Press, 2008), 194.
38 Te Whatu Ora Health New Zealand, www.ccdhb.org.nz/about-us/history. There would be a variety of iterations over some 17 years, and the Toxward Building was demolished in preparation in 1969.
39 Te Whatu Ora Health New Zealand, www.ccdhb.org.nz/about-us/history
40 Engineering New Zealand, 'Wellington Hospital Total Energy Centre', www.engineeringnz.org/programmes/heritage/heritage-records/wellington-hospital-total-energy-centre
41 McCarthy, 'The Haughton Partnership', 201; R. E. Wright-St Clair, *Caring for People: A History of the Wanganui Hospital Board* (Whanganui: Wanganui Hospital Board Centennial Celebration Committee, 1987), inside front cover.
42 Wright-St Clair, *Caring for People*, 62.
43 Ibid., 78.
44 Ibid., 79.
45 Ibid., 60.
46 Drawings held at Whanganui Hospital.
47 Mackenzie, *Hospital in the Valley*, 23, 48; 'Nurses' Home Extension, Hutt Hospital', *Home & Building* 32 (April 1970).
48 Mackenzie, *Hospital in the Valley*, 56, 58.
49 'Haughton & Mair', *Journal of the NZIA* 40, no. 4 (April 1973); 'The Haughton Partnership', *Home & Building*, no. 3 (1979).
50 Plaque at Porirua.
51 National/New Zealand First coalition, 'Health Minister Opens Hutt Hospital Emergency Building', Press release, 19 December 1997.
52 Mckenzie Higham Architects, 'McKenzie Higham Architects welcomes Bulleyment Fortune', https://www.mckenziehigham.co.nz/news/mckenzie-higham-welcomes-bulleyment-fortune-architects

King George V and Queen Mary hospitals

1 Tim Shoebridge, *Featherston Military Training Camp and the First World War* (Wellington: Manatū Taonga Ministry for Culture & Heritage, 2011), 29–30; Susan Butterworth, *Hospital on a Hotspot: Queen Elizabeth Hospital, Rotorua* (Wellington: Ngaio Press, 2012), 15; *Queen Mary Hospital*, Heritage New Zealand Register #7612, www.heritage.org.nz/the-list; *Queen*

Mary Hospital and Hanmer Springs Thermal Reserve Historic Area, Heritage New Zealand Register #7583, www.heritage.org.nz/the-list
2 *Featherston Military Training Camp*, Heritage New Zealand Register #9661, www.heritage.org.nz/the-list
3 Geoffrey W. Rice, *Black November: The 1918 Influenza Epidemic in New Zealand* (Christchurch: Canterbury University Press, 2005), 213; Anna Rogers, *With Them Through Hell: New Zealand Medical Services in the First Word War* (Auckland: Massey University Press, 2018), 394.
4 Shoebridge, *Featherston Military Camp*, 48.
5 *Queen Mary Hospital*, Heritage New Zealand Register #7612; *Ōtaki Children's Health Camp (Former)*, Heritage New Zealand Register #4098.
6 *Dominion*, 4 January 1916, 6.
7 Butterworth, *Hospital on a Hotspot*, 15–18.
8 Matthews & Matthews Architects Ltd, *Rotorua Central Area: Built Heritage Study* (Rotorua: Rotorua District Council, 2007), 15–16.
9 D. M. Stafford, *The New Century in Rotorua* (Rotorua: Ray Richards and Rotorua District Council, 1988), 221, 242.
10 Friends of the Ōtaki Rotunda, www.otakirotunda.org.nz
11 The buildings at the Ōtaki site are managed by the Department of Conservation and are a Category 1 Historic Place. *Ōtaki Children's Health Camp (Former)*, Heritage New Zealand Register #4098, www.heritage.org.nz/the-list
12 https://teara.govt.nz/en/photograph/30562/health-camps; Patricia Sargison, *Notable Women in New Zealand Health, Te Hauora Ki Aotearoa: Ōna Wāhine Rongonui* (Auckland: Longman Paul, 1993), 29. In 2001 the government handed over the camps to Stand Children's Services/Tū Māia Whānau, a charitable trust set up to continue their operation. Ōtaki and Roxburgh were closed in 2018, but Stand continues to operate the camps in Whangārei, Pakuranga, Rotorua, Gisborne and Christchurch. https://www.standforchildren.org.nz
13 Dr Robert Crawford, *Too Good to Last: The Death of a Caring Culture: Queen Mary Hospital: The Therapy of Addictions, Hanmer Springs, 1972–1991* (Hanmer Springs: Sunbeam, 2008), 31.
14 Ibid., v, 40, 96.
15 Ibid., i, vi, 40, 41, 96.
16 *Queen Mary Hospital*, Heritage New Zealand Register #7612, www.heritage.org.nz/the-list; *Queen Mary Hospital and Hanmer Springs Thermal Reserve Historic Area*, Heritage New Zealand Register #7583, www.heritage.org.nz/the-list

Chapter 8. Hospitals of the south 1914–1945

1 J. G. Furness, *Wairau Hospital: 100 Years of Caring* (Blenheim: Marlborough Hospital Board, 1978), 32.
2 Ibid., 41.
3 John Wilson, *Thematic Historical Overview of Nelson City for Nelson City Council Heritage Inventory Project* (October 2011), 99. The nurses' home was demolished in 2013, the 1926 hospital in 2000.
4 *Reefton Hospital 1872–1972* (Reefton: Reefton Hospital, 1972).
5 'New Hospital for Reefton', *Press*, 21 December 1946, 2; 'Reefton – Tenders to be Called', *Greymouth Evening Star*, 7 February 1947, 3; 'Reefton – Two Tenders for Building of New Hospital', *Greymouth Evening Star*, 2 December 1949, 3. In 1988 public pressure once again prevented closure of the hospital, but its time as a general hospital ended in 2022 and it now operates primarily as a geriatric facility and health centre.
6 'Waiuta Hospital Opening Ceremony', *Grey River Argus*, 6 November 1914, 2.
7 *Centennial of Greymouth Hospital 1866–1966*, Special Publication (Greymouth: *Greymouth Evening Star*, 1966).
8 'The New Hospital', *Hokitika Guardian*, 20 January 1922, 2.
9 'Westland Hospital Board – Tenders Invited', *Hokitika Guardian*, 28 June 1937, 1; Peter Neame, *Save Our Hospital: Hokitika Fights Back* (Greymouth: self-published, 1987).
10 Linda Bryder, 'Hospitals – Spas, sanatoriums and surgery', Te Ara – the Encyclopedia of New Zealand, www.TeAra.govt.nz/en/hospitals/page-3
11 Beryl Hughes, 'Maude, Sibylla Emily', *Dictionary of New Zealand Biography*, first published in 1993. Te Ara – the Encyclopedia of New Zealand, https://teara.govt.nz/en/biographies/2m42/maude-sibylla-emily
12 Winifred Norris, *The North Canterbury Hospital Board: Fragments of History: Hospitals: Tuberculosis and Benevolent Institutions and Miscellaneous* (unpublished manuscript held by Christchurch City Libraries, 1942), 154.
13 F. O. Bennett, *Cashmere Sanatorium (now Coronation Hospital) 1906–1964* (Christchurch: North Canterbury Hospital Board, 1964), 85; Thomas Oliver Endicott, *Up the Hill: Cashmere Sanatorium and Coronation Hospital 1910 to 1991* (Christchurch: Canterbury Area Health Board, 1993).
14 Norris, *The North Canterbury Hospital Board*, 156.
15 Christchurch City Libraries, 'The Hill of Hope – Cashmere Sanatorium', 7 March 2017, https://my.christchurchcitylibraries.com/blogs/post/the-hill-of-hope-cashmere-sanatorium
16 John Wilson, *Lost Christchurch* (Lincoln: Te Waihora Press, 1984), 85.
17 Collins & Son, *A Century of Architecture - Collins & Son* (Christchurch: Caxton Press, 1965); Laura Dunham, 'The Domestic Architecture of Collins and Harman in Canterbury 1883–1927' (MA thesis, University of Canterbury, 2013), 1–8, 11, 132, 140; University of Canterbury, 'The Collins Family', www.canterbury.ac.nz/about-uc/what-we-do/uc-in-the-community/exhibitions-and-collections/canterbury-college/perspective/the-collins-family
18 Bennett, *Hospital on the Avon*, 136.
19 Ibid., 143; Wilson, *Lost Christchurch*, 57.
20 Bennett, *Hospital on the Avon*, 192.
21 Anna Rogers, *Stand for all Time: The Marquette Sinking and the Nurses' Memorial Chapel* (Christchurch: Friends of the Nurses' Memorial Chapel, 2018), 95–96; *Nurses' Memorial Chapel*, Heritage New Zealand Register #1851, www.heritage.org.nz/the-list
22 Bennett, *Hospital on the Avon*, 243.
23 Ibid., 207.
24 Norris, *The North Canterbury Hospital Board*, 175.
25 Ibid., 175, 180, 183; *It's All Happening: Burwood Health Campus* (Christchurch: Canterbury District Health Board, 2013).
26 Norris, *The North Canterbury Hospital Board*, 26. This closed in 1960.
27 Ibid., 97.
28 Ibid., 97, 124–25; Alex (H. A.) Clark, 'Canterbury Country Cottage Hospitals 1840–2000' (BA (Honours) thesis, University of Canterbury, Christchurch, 2001).
29 Norris, *The North Canterbury Hospital Board*, 101, 120, 132, 136.
30 Ibid., 105, 110, 115, 119, 130.
31 'Buller Hospital Board', *Hokitika Guardian*, 22 September 1919, 3; 'Improvements at Buller Hospital', *Greymouth Evening Star*, 21 July 1949, 9.
32 Luke Tremlett, 'Medical Buildings and Medical Theory: An Archaeological Investigation of Ashburton Hospital, New Zealand' (MA thesis, University of Otago, Dunedin, 2015), 81; W. H. Scotter, *Ashburton: A History with Records of Town and Country* (Ashburton: Ashburton Borough and County Councils, 1972), 297–300; 'Well-Known Ashburton Architect's Designs on Show', *Ashburton Courier*, 8 June 2020.
33 John Campbell McKenzie, *A History of Timaru Hospital* (Christchurch: Pegasus Press, 1974), 97.
34 Ibid., 100.
35 Ibid., 73; Eulla Williamson, *The End of an Era 1964–1989: The Final Twenty-Five Years of Administration by the South Canterbury Hospital Board* (Timaru: Health South Canterbury, 1994), 141.
36 Bernice E. Shackleton, *The Fifth Schedule 1874–1975: The Story of Waimate's Open Community Hospital* (Invercargill: Craig Printing, 1984), 155–59, 165.
37 Williamson, *The End of an Era*, 165.
38 Conal McCarthy, *Forrester and Lemon of Oamaru, Architects* (Ōamaru: North Otago Branch Committee of the New Zealand Historic Places Trust, 2002), 9–12, 15, 24–25; 'The Late Mr Forrester', *Otago Daily Times*, 1 April 1907, 4.
39 K.C. McDonald, *A Century of Service: The History of the Oamaru Hospital* (Ōamaru: Waitaki Hospital Board, 1972), 25, 30, 34–38, 44, 46, 59, 61; 'Oamaru Hospital Trustees', *Oamaru Mail*, 19 June 1912, 4; 'New Ward Block – Opening Ceremony', *Otago Daily Times*, 3 December 1943, 5; 'Maternity Annexe and Important Addition to Oamaru Buildings', *Otago Daily Times*, 1 October 1949, 4; 'Nurses' Home Extensions Approved', *Otago Daily Times*, 16 August 1950, 3; 'Tenders – Erection of New Maternity Hospital at Kurow', *Otago Daily Times*, 10 June 1925, 10.
40 *Maniototo Hospital*, Heritage New Zealand Register #7306, www.heritage.org.nz/the-list; 'Minister Opens New Maniototo Hospital', *Otago Daily Times*, 18 April 2019.
41 'Dunedin Hospital – A Notable Diamond Jubilee', *Otago Daily Times*, 24 August 1926.
42 'The Patient Progress of Dunedin's Hospital', *Otago Daily Times*, www.odt.shorthandstories.com/the-patient-progress-of-dunedin-hospital/index.html; University of Otago, www.otago.ac.nz/cumberland/about
43 Adelheid Wassner, *Labour of Love: Childbirth at Dunedin Hospital 1862–1972* (Dunedin: self-published, 1999), 9–11, 53–55; 'Queen Mary Hospital, Dunedin', *Home & Building* 22 (March 1960). Queen Mary was integrated into Dunedin Hospital in 1990 and relocated into the main hospital building. The older buildings became the University of Otago School of Surveying in 1993; the Frederick Street building became the Hayward College for student accommodation in 1992; www.otago.ac.nz/hayward
44 John H. Angus, *A History of the Otago Hospital Board and Its Predecessors* (Dunedin: Otago Hospital Board, 1984), 201, 225–28, 231; 'The Patient Progress of Dunedin's Hospital'.
45 Dorothy Page, *Anatomy of a Medical School: A History of Medicine at the University of Otago 1875–2000* (Dunedin: Otago University Press, 2008), 74–80; Ali Clarke, 'University of Otago 1869–2019: Building a Medical Campus', https://otago150years.wordpress.com/2017/03/13/building-a-medical-campus; *Scott Building — Otago Medical School*, Heritage New Zealand Register #4790, www.heritage.org.nz/the-list
46 Clarke, 'University of Otago'. This is now a Category 1 Historic Place. *Lindo Ferguson Building — Otago Medical School*, Heritage New Zealand Register #4769, www.heritage.org.nz/the-list
47 'Cromwell Hospital Trust', *Cromwell Argus*, 14 October 1912, 5.

48 *History of the Southland Hospitals and Boards*, 64, 67. The hospital was later sold; it was destroyed by fire in 1994.
49 Angus, *A History of the Otago Hospital Board*, 204.
50 Rosemarie Smith, *Seddon Memorial: The Rise and Demise of a Country Hospital, Gore, 1909–1999* (Gore: Seddon Memorial Hospital Book Committee, 2005), 11, 18–20.
51 *History of the Southland Hospitals and Boards 1861–1968* (Invercargill: Southland Hospital Board, 1968), 27.
52 Ibid., 40.
53 Ibid., 41–2.
54 *Southland Hospital (Former)*, Heritage New Zealand Register #7749, www.heritage.org.nz/the-list

A new approach to mental health

1 Historic England, 'A Brief Introduction to Garden Cities', 18 February 2016, https://heritagecalling.com/2016/02/18/a-brief-introduction-to-garden-cities
2 Wendy Hunter Williams, *Out of Mind, Out of Sight: The Story of Porirua Hospital: Porirua Hospital Centennial 1887–1987* (Porirua: Porirua Hospital, 1987), 63.
3 Catherine Coleborne (ed.), *Changing Times, Changing Places: From Tokanui Hospital to Mental Health Services in the Waikato, 1910–2012* (Hamilton: Half Court Press, 2012), 14–16, 22, 37–43, 75, 113–15, 163, 213.
4 Williams, *Out of Mind, Out of Sight*, 173, 184, 199, 233, 269, 279.
5 Porirua Hospital Museum, www.poriruahospitalmuseum.flh.nz
6 Marjorie M. Webby, *From Prison to Paradise: Genealogy of Ngawhatu Hospital, Previously Known as Nelson Lunatic Asylum 1840–1991 and St Mary's Orphanage Stoke* (Nelson: Ngawhatu Hospital, 1991).
7 'Mental health care moves out of Hospital', *Stuff*, 3 July 2012, www.stuff.co.nz/the-press/editors-picks/7208909/Mental-healthcare-moves-out-of-hospital. In May 2024, previously unknown remnants of original Sunnyside buildings were discovered: Poppy Clark, 'Decrepit former "mental institution" uncovered after garden spruce up', *Stuff*, 4 May 2024, www.stuff.co.nz/nz-news/350238157/decrepit-former-mental-institution-uncovered-after-garden-spruce
8 'Central Linen Service', *Home & Building*, no. 1 (1983).
9 Cecile Meier, 'Christchurch's Hillmorton Hospital "inadequate", unsafe and leaky', *Stuff*, 5 May 2018, www.stuff.co.nz/national/health/103536063/christchurchs-hillmorton-hospital-inadequate-unsafe-and-leaky; Drawings held at Hillmorton.
10 David Lemon, 'The Closure of the Templeton Centre' (MA thesis, University of Canterbury, 2001).
11 Warwick Brunton, 'Gray, Theodore Grant', *Dictionary of New Zealand Biography*, first published in 1998. Te Ara – the Encyclopedia of New Zealand, https://teara.govt.nz/en/biographies/4g19/gray-theodore-grant
12 *Kingseat Hospital 50 Years 1932–1982* (Auckland: Kingseat Jubilee Editorial Committee, 1982); *Kingseat Hospital: Relocating Mental Health Services* (Auckland: Northern Regional Health Authority, 1996).
13 F. G. Grattan, *Official War History of the Public Works Department, Volume 3* (Wellington: Public Works Department, 1948), 544. Also referred to in some references as Ravensthorpe.
14 *Raventhorpe Hospital Reunion 1986* (souvenir booklet held by Auckland City Libraries).
15 *Mangere Hospital and Training School 25 Years 1963–1988* (Auckland: Mangere Hospital, 1988); *Spectrum Care: The First 20 Years 1994–2014* (Auckland: Spectrum Care Trust Board, 2014); Val Payne, *Gone But Not Forgotten* (Auckland: Mangere Historical Society, 2022).
16 Rebecca McLaughlan, 'Post-Rationalisation and Misunderstanding: Mental Hospital Architecture in New Zealand Media', *Journal of the Society of Architectural Historians Australia and New Zealand* 22, no. 2 (2012): 232–50.
17 David Cooper, *The Cherry Farm Creative Arts Trust* (Wellington: Queen Elizabeth II Arts Council of New Zealand, 1992), 3, 7.
18 Anne Hunt, *The Lost Years: From Levin Farm Mental Deficiency Colony to Kimberley Centre* (Christchurch: self-published, 2000), 3, 10, 35, 41, 47–48, 51, 68, 108, 151, 156, 226, 328.
19 *Wanganui Chronicle*, 6 October 1950, 4.
20 Bob Baird (comp.), *Lake Alice Hospital: 40 Years* (Whanganui: Manawatu–Wanganui Area Health Board, 1990), 3–4.
21 Ibid., 5–7, 13, 23, 34–36.
22 Abuse in Care Royal Commission of Inquiry, *Whanaketia — Through pain and trauma, from darkness to light Whakairihia ki te tihi o Maungārongo*, www.abuseincare.org.nz/reports/whanaketia
23 Warwick Brunton, 'Mental health services – Closing the hospitals, 1960s to 1990s', Te Ara – the Encyclopedia of New Zealand, https://teara.govt.nz/en/mental-health-services/page-5

Chapter 9. Local growth 1945–1970

1 https://web.archive.org/web/20171231000952/http://archive.stats.govt.nz/browse_for_stats/population/estimates_and_projections/historical-population-tables.aspx
2 Rebecca Priestley, 'Nuclear New Zealand: New Zealand's Nuclear and Radiation History to 1987' (PhD thesis, University of Canterbury, Christchurch, 2010), 175; Edward A. and Anthony H. G. Roche, *Green Lane Saga: Green Lane Hospital, Auckland 1889–1982* (Auckland: Ray Richards, 1983), 64; B. R. Hutchinson (ed.), *Green Lane Hospital: The First Hundred Years* (Auckland: Green Lane Hospital Centennial Committee, 1990), 18; 'Sir Douglas Robb Receives Honorary FNZIA', *Home & Building* 31 (April 1969).
3 Deborah Dunsford, 'Seeking the Prize of Eradication: A Social History of Tuberculosis in New Zealand from World War Two to the 1970s' (PhD thesis, University of Auckland, 2008), 2, 6.
4 Derek A. Dow, *Safeguarding the Public Health: A History of the New Zealand Department of Health* (Wellington: Victoria University Press, 1995), 175; 'Chronology of the New Zealand Health System', https://www.health.govt.nz/system/files/2024-05/chronology-of-the-new-zealand-health-system-1840-to-2017_0.pdf
5 Michael P. Murphy Jr with Jeffrey Mansfield and MASS Design Group, *The Architecture of Health: Hospital Design and the Construction of Dignity* (New York: Cooper Hewitt, Smithsonian Design Museum, 2021), 138–47.
6 Murphy et al, *The Architecture of Health*, 180–99.
7 G. L. McLeod, 'The Importance of Medical Policy in Building Hospitals', *Journal of the NZIA* 18, no. 7 (August 1951).
8 *Report of the Consultative Committee on Hospital Reform* (Wellington: Government Printer, 1953).
9 Terence Hodgson, *Looking at the Architecture of New Zealand* (Wellington: Grantham House, 1990), 76–9, 87–88; Peter Shaw, *New Zealand Architecture: From Polynesian Beginnings to 1990* (Auckland: Hodder & Stoughton, 1991), 172–74.
10 *Cornwall Hospital 1942–1975* (Auckland: Cornwall Park Trust Board, 1975).
11 Plaque at Dilworth School.
12 F. G. Grattan, *Official War History of the Public Works Department Volume 3* (Wellington: Public Works Department, 1948), 680, 3; Robin Skinner, 'Tibor Donner: Public Buildings', Itinerary No. 10, *Block*, the Broadsheet of the Auckland Branch of the NZIA, no. 1, 2008.
13 *Green Lane Hospital*, Heritage New Zealand Register #4536, www.heritage.org.nz/the-list; Hutchinson, *Green Lane Hospital*, 7.
14 'Raymond L. Farrell Obituary', *Home & Building* 18 (February 1956).
15 Hutchinson, *Green Lane Hospital*, 7.
16 'Central Stores, Auckland Hospital Board Architects', *Journal of the NZIA* (November/ December 1988); 'Auckland Hospital Board Blood Transfusion Building', *Home & Building* 32 (July 1969); Linda Bryder and Derek Dow, *Banking on Blood: Auckland Regional Blood Services 1941–1991* (Auckland: Auckland Regional Blood Services, 1991), 21.
17 David Scott (ed.), *Middlemore Memories: The First 50 Years of Middlemore Hospital* (Auckland: South Auckland Health, 1997), 14–16; *Middlemore Hospital: Souvenir* (brochure held by Auckland Central Library, 1947).
18 'Nurses' Home', *Home & Building* 28 (November 1965).
19 'Maternity Wing, Middlemore', *Home & Building* 28 (November 1965); Scott, *Middlemore Memories*, 22.
20 'Resident Doctors Quarters' and 'Household Staff Quarters', *Home & Building* 28 (November 1965).
21 Scott, *Middlemore Memories*, 23.
22 'Alterations to Wallace Block', *Home & Building* 28 (November 1965). The block was demolished in 2006 to make way for a parking building.
23 Dr Alan Sutherland, *Battle of the Bridge 1970–1994* (Auckland: New Zealand Medical Association, 1994), 26; 'Celebrating Half a Century of Maternity Care for Women and their Families at North Shore Hospital' (Auckland: Waitemata District Health Board, 2008), 3-4; 'New Maternity Hospital: Official Opening in Auckland', *Press*, 21 July 1958, 2. Note that some references state that North Shore Hospital opened in 1956. This may be another case of a facility being in use for some time before its official opening.
24 Waitakere Obstetric Hospital, *Home & Building* 28 (November 1965).
25 Te Whatu Ora Health New Zealand, 'Pukekohe Hospital', https://www.countiesmanukau.health.nz/our-services/a-z/pukekohe-hospital
26 'New St Helen's Hospital for Auckland', *Journal of the NZIA* 32, no. 3 (April 1965): 108; 'St Helen's Hospital', *Home & Building* 28 (November 1965); 'Obituary, Gordon Smith Architect', *Architecture New Zealand* 3 (May/June 2010).
27 Antony Matthews, 'St Helen's Hospital', in Julia Gatley (ed.), *Long Live the Modern: New Zealand's New Architecture 1904–1984* (Auckland: Auckland University Press, 2009), 161; 'St Helen's Hospital Competition', *Home & Building* 21 (April 1959); 'St Helen's Hospital Competition', *Home & Building* 22 (July 1959); 'New St Helen's Hospital for Auckland'; 'St Helen's Hospital'; Mike Austin, 'Modernism in Perspective', *Architecture New Zealand* (May/June 1990).
28 *The Road Back to Normal: Living at the Civilian Rehabilitation Centre, Bairds Road, Otara* (Auckland: Auckland Hospital Board, 1958); 'Rehabilitation Centre, Otahuhu' and 'Paraplegic Rehabilitation Centre, Otara', *Home & Building* 28 (November 1965); 'Otara Spinal Unit', *Home & Building*, no. 1 (1979).
29 *Celebrating 100 Years of Innovation and Excellence: Tauranga Hospital 1914–2014* (Tauranga: Bay of Plenty District Health Board, 2014).

30 Ian Shearer and Rex E. Wright-St Clair, *A Century on Cameron Road: A History of Tauranga Hospital 1914–2014* (Tauranga: Bay of Plenty District Health Board, 2016), 42, 48.
31 *True Tales of Thames Hospital: 150 Years 1868–2018* (Thames: Thames Hospital 150 Group in collaboration with Coromandel Heritage Trust, 2018), 42, 55–56; *Thames Star*, 12 August 1963; *Thames Hospital, Thames — Children's and General Wards (1959)*, documents held by Archives New Zealand R23345328; Suzanne Morgan, *Thames Hospital: A Pictorial History 1868–1987* (Hamilton: Waikato District Health Board, 2006); Althea Barker, *Thames Memorials and Plaques* (Thames: KMG Print, 2016), 7, 20–21.
32 'Memory Box: A Maternity Home Come Rest Home', *Waikato Times*, 23 September 2023.
33 Rex E. Wright-St Clair, *The Early History of Waikato Hospital* (Hamilton: Waikato Hospital Board, 1987), 28–30; Georgina Wedge and Peter Rothwell, *Waikato Hospital: Our Hospital, Your History* (Hamilton: Waikato Health Memorabilia Trust, 2016), 32, 34–35; John Armstrong, *Under One Roof: A History of Waikato Hospital* (Hamilton: Half Court Press, 2009), 113, 268.
34 'Memory Boxes', *Waikato Times*, 2 April 2012; 'Alfred Smith, Waikato Hospital Board', *Journal of the NZIA*32, no. 3 (April 1965); Armstrong, *Under One Roof*, 145.
35 Wedge and Rothwell, *Waikato Hospital*, 40, 42.
36 'Waikato Hospital – Ward Block A and Central Laundry', *Home & Building* 21 (March 1959); Armstrong, *Under One Roof*, 273, 287.
37 Wedge and Rothwell, *Waikato Hospital*, 48, 55, 58; Armstrong, *Under One Roof*, 273, 287.
38 Russell Young, *The Story of Te Kūiti* (Wellington: Winter Productions, 2013), 112; John Mandeno, 'The Story of Te Kūiti Hospital from the Beginnings to 1966', *Footprints of History*, Magazine of the Te Awamutu, Ōtorohanga and Te Kūiti Historical Society and the Waitomo Caves Museum Society, no. 22 (June 1999): 1; 'Te Aroha Maternity Hospital and Nurses' Home', *Journal of the NZIA* 29, no. 6 (July 1962).
39 Mary Anne Gill (ed.), *The Village on the Hill: Celebrating 125 Years of Waikato Hospital* (Hamilton: Waikato District Health Board, 2011), 37; 'Hilda Ross Nurses' Home and Clinical Services Block, Waikato Hospital', *Journal of the NZIA* 32, no. 7 (August 1965); 'Waikato Hospital Clinical Services Block', *Home & Building* 31 (April 1969) and 'Waikato Hospital Clinical Services Block', *Home & Building* 36 (January 1974).
40 Wedge and Rothwell, *Waikato Hospital*, 53, 71.
41 Michael Fowler, *Buildings of New Zealanders* (Auckland: Lansdowne Press, 1984), 95.
42 D. M. Stafford, *The New Century in Rotorua* (Rotorua: Ray Richards with Rotorua District Council, 1988), 290, 363.
43 Ibid., 362–63.
44 Susan Butterworth, *Hospital on a Hotspot: Queen Elizabeth Hospital, Rotorua* (Wellington: Ngaio Press, 2012), 41.
45 Ibid., 114; Stafford, *The New Century in Rotorua*, 361.
46 Butterworth, *Hospital on a Hotspot*, 43, 47, 114.
47 In 2009 a new 30-bed, surgical facility with three operating theatres opened in Otonga Road as a joint venture between what was by then QE Health and Southern Cross Hospitals; https://qehealth.co.nz/our-story
48 'Child Potential Unit', *Home & Building*, no. 2 (1979).
49 'Matariki Geriatric Hospital', *Home & Building* 36 (January 1974).
50 Shirley August, *The History of the Bay of Islands Hospital* (Kawakawa: Bay of Islands Hospital, 2013), 5–6; Drawings held at Bay of Islands Hospital.
51 Geoff Conly, *A Case History: The Hawke's Bay Hospital Board 1876–1989* (Napier: Hawke's Bay Area Health Board, 1992), 219.
52 Drawings held at Hawke's Bay Fallen Soldiers' Memorial Hospital, Hastings.
53 'Palmerston North Hospital Board', *Home & Building* 24 (February 1962); 'Jack Reynolds, Palmerston North Hospital Board', *Journal of the NZIA* 32, no. 3 (April 1965).
54 'Hospital Chapel, Palmerston North', *Home & Building* 20 (February 1958); Jo Kellaway and Mike Maryan, *A Century of Care: Palmerston North Hospital 1893–1993* (Double Bay, Australia: MidCentral Health and Focus Books, 1993), 54, 76, 82, 85.
55 David Sayers, *The Goodwill Years: The Remarkable Story of a Professional Partnership* (Hamilton: SFT Books, 2010), 57.
56 'Awapuni Hospital Chapel', *Home & Building* 28 (September 1965).
57 Sayers, *The Goodwill Years*, 55.
58 Wright-St Clair, *Caring for People*, 75.
59 Ibid., 69.
60 'Fight to Reopen Hospital', *Stuff*, 19 July 2011; drawings held at Whanganui Hospital.
61 Diane Grant (ed.) with Wairarapa Health History Group, *Helping Hands: A History of Healthcare in the Wairarapa* (Masterton: Fraser Books, 2015), 25, 29.
62 Ibid., 161–62.
63 Ibid., 164.
64 C. J. Carle, *Masterton Hospital 1879–1979* (Masterton: Centennial Book Committee, Wairarapa Hospital Board, 1979), 46, 48.
65 Grant, *Helping Hands*, 188; 'Masterton Hospital – Boiler House and Staff Block', *Home & Building* 23 (March 1961).
66 Drawings held at Archives New Zealand.
67 Lewis E. Martin, *Built for Us: The Work of Government and Colonial Architects, 1860s to 1960s* (Dunedin: Otago University Press, 2004), 158. The buildings were demolished in 2008.
68 Terence Hodgson, *Looking at the Architecture of New Zealand* (Wellington: Grantham House, 1990), 64–65.
69 John Wilson, 'Princess Margaret Hospital', in Gatley, *Long Live the Modern*, 108.
70 F. O. Bennett, *Hospital on the Avon: The History of Christchurch Hospital 1862–1962* (Christchurch: North Canterbury Hospital Board, 1962), 300–01.
71 W. H. Scotter, *Ashburton: A History with Records of Town and Country* (Ashburton: Ashburton Borough and County Councils, 1972), 297–300; 'Well-Known Ashburton Architect's Designs on Show', *Ashburton Courier*, 8 June 2020.
72 Luke Tremlett, 'Medical Buildings and Medical Theory: An Archaeological Investigation of Ashburton Hospital, New Zealand' (MA thesis, University of Otago, Dunedin, 2015), 83.
73 John Campbell McKenzie, *A History of Timaru Hospital* (Christchurch: Pegasus Press, 1974), 103.
74 Ibid., 126; Eulla Williamson, *The End of an Era 1964–1989: The Final Twenty-Five Years of Administration by the South Canterbury Hospital Board* (Timaru: Health South Canterbury, 1994), 30.
75 K. C. McDonald, *A Century of Service: The History of the Oamaru Hospital* (Ōamaru: Waitaki Hospital Board, 1972), 69. The hospital closed in 1975 and is now the Whalan Lodge private rest home. 'Rest Home's Expansion a Survival Plan', *Otago Daily Times*, 23 December 2023.
76 'Roxburgh Notes', *Alexandra Herald and Central Otago Gazette*, 17 December 1930, 3; John H. Angus, *A History of the Otago Hospital Board and Its Predecessors* (Dunedin: Otago Hospital Board, 1984), 160, 248; Williamson, *The End of an Era*, 181.
77 Williamson, *The End of an Era*, 181.
78 'Cromwell Hospital: Maternity Annex', *Journal of the NZIA* 28, no. 6 (July/ August 1961).
79 McDonald, *A Century of Service*, 61–63; 'Hospital Fading into History', *Otago Daily Times*, 28 May 2016.
80 'Wakari Hospital Chapel', *Home & Building* 30 (May 1968).
81 Drawings held by Archives New Zealand.
82 Ali Clarke, 'University of Otago 1869–2019: Building a Medical Campus', https://otago150years.wordpress.com/2017/03/13/building-a-medical-campus
83 Angus, *A History of the Otago Hospital Board*, 225.
84 Martin, *Built for Us*, 180; *Dental School, Dunedin*, Heritage New Zealand Register #7618, www.heritage.org.nz/the-list; *A Brief History of Public Buildings in New Zealand* (Wellington: Ministry of Works, 1970); Robin Skinner, 'University of Otago Dental School', in Gatley, *Long Live the Modern*, 109.
85 Alan Gunn, *Milton, Otago* (Dunedin: John McIndoe, 1977).
86 'Cottage Hospitals', *Evening Star*, 4 March 1926; 'Nursing Celebration', *Otago Daily Times*, 27 January 2016; Clutha Health First, https://cluthahealth.co.nz/about-us
87 'Ford Grey & Derbie', *Journal of the NZIA* 35, no. 8 (August 1968).
88 *History of the Southland Hospitals and Boards 1861–1968* (Invercargill: Southland Hospital Board, 1968), 43; 'Laundry & Boiler House, Southland Hospital', *Home & Building* 29 (March 1962).
89 *History of the Southland Hospitals and Boards*, 43.
90 *History of the Southland Hospitals and Boards*, 76; Plaque at Lakes District Hospital, Queenstown.
91 'Families Celebrate Former Maternity Hospital's History', *Otago Daily Times*, 9 April 2018.
92 *History of the Southland Hospitals and Boards*, 74.
93 Michael Gill, *Himalayan Hospitals: Sir Edmund Hillary's Everest Legacy* (Nelson: Craig Potton Publishing, 2011), 8, 35, 212; 'Hospital at Kumjung, Nepal', *Journal of the NZIA* 34, no. 6 (June 1967).

Private hospitals

1 *Private Hospitals in New Zealand*, Report Series No. 20 (Wellington: Board of Health, 1974), 10–11; *Private Hospitals in New Zealand: A Background Paper* (Wellington: The New Zealand Private Hospitals Association, 1989), 2–3.
2 Michael Belgrave, *The Mater: A History of Auckland's Mercy Hospital 1900–2000* (Palmerston North: Dunmore Press, 2000), 23, 27, 29; Katherine Everton, *A Time of Love and Mercy: Mater Misericordiae Hospital, Auckland 1937–1987* (Auckland: self-published, 1987), 7, 10–13.
3 Belgrave, *The Mater*, 43, 64, 79.
4 Ibid., 175.
5 Belgrave, *The Mater*, 156; Sisters of Mercy, www.sistersofmercy.org.nz; Mercy Hospital, www.mercyhospital.org.nz/about-us
6 Mercy Hospital, www.mercyhospital.org.nz/about-us
7 *Marinoto*, Heritage New Zealand Register #7303, www.heritage.org.nz/the-list; 'Marinoto's Last Resident Moves Out After 42 Years', *Otago Daily Times*, 11 June 2011.
8 Mercy Hospital, www.mercyhospital.org.nz/about-us/our-heritage
9 McCoy Wixon Architects, www.mccoywixon.co.nz/projects
10 'Cobalt Therapy Clinic', *Home & Building* 32 (December 1969); 'Cobalt Therapy Unit and Ward Block, Calvary Hospital, Wellington', *Journal of the NZIA* 36, no. 4 (April 1969).
11 www.heritage.org.nz/The-List/Lost-Heritage
12 L. C. L. Averill, *St George's Hospital: The First Fifty Years* (Christchurch: St George's Hospital Executive,

1978), 11, 20–21, 32, 39–40.
13 Totem Studio Architects, 'St Georges Hospital', www.totemstudio.co.nz/st-georges
14 Douglas Edward Drake, *The Bidwill Story: 65 Years of a Private Hospital in Timaru* (Timaru: Bidwill Hospital Trust Board, 2001).
15 Totem Studio Architects, 'Bidwill Hospital', www.totemstudio.co.nz/bidwill-hospital
16 '$8m Upgrade of Ashburn Hall to Begin in September', *Otago Daily Times*, 30 July 2019; Ashburn Psychiatric Healthcare, www.ashburn.co.nz/about
17 Peter A. Smith, *The Private Prescription: The Story of Southern Cross Healthcare* (Auckland: Southern Cross Healthcare, 2000), 20, 115; Southern Cross, https://healthcare.southerncross.co.nz/about-us/history-and-heritage
18 'Southern Cross Hospital, Epsom', *Home & Building*, no. 1 (1983).
19 Smith, *The Private Prescription,* 120, 133, 146, 154–55.
20 'Southern Cross Hospital, New Plymouth', *Architecture New Zealand* (November/ December 1988).
21 Crest Hospital, https://cresthospital.co.nz/about-us#history
22 Smith, *The Private Prescription*, 168–70, 173, 201.

Chapter 10. Nationwide expansion 1945–1970

1 Gregory Smith, 'Thorpe Cutter Pickmere Douglas', in *Lost Property: Auckland's Alternative Modernist Architecture and History,* www.lostproperty.org.nz/architects/cutter-thorpe-pickmere-douglas; 'Thorpe Cutter Pickmere Douglas', *New Zealand Herald*, 18 December 1950; *New Zealand Herald*, 17 January 1951.
2 'Balloons Mark Hospital's 60th', *Northern Advocate*, 2 March 2016; 'Dargaville Hospital', *Home & Building* 20 (October 1957).
3 'Designing of Hospital', *Press*, 5 March 1959, 17.
4 Linda Bryder, *The Rise and Fall of National Women's Hospital: A History* (Auckland: Auckland University Press, 2014), 103; 'Opening of National Women's Hospital', *Auckland Star*, 13 February 1964, 17.
5 'Balloons Mark Hospital's 60th', *Northern Advocate*, 2 March 2016; 'Dargaville Hospital', *Home & Building* 20 (October 1957).
6 'Designing of Hospital', *Press*, 5 March 1959, 17.
7 Alice Silverson (ed), *The Last Thirty Years: The History of the Canterbury Area Health Board 1963–1993* (Christchurch: Canterbury Health, 1995), 21–22, 25, 91–97.
8 Silverson, *The Last Thirty Years*, 24–15.
9 Michael Fowler, *Buildings of New Zealanders* (Auckland: Landsdowne Press, 1984), 95.
10 Silverson, *The Last Thirty Years*, 91, 96. See the photograph on page 96 for the various buildings under construction concurrently.
11 From 1970 on, drawing titles and articles generally only refer to Cutter Pickmere Douglas; see, for example, 'Clinical School Christchurch', *Home & Building* 36 (November 1973).
12 Drawings at Archives New Zealand.
13 Lost Property, www.lostproperty.org.nz/architects/cutter-thorpe-pickmere-douglas
14 Te Whatu Ora Health New Zealand, www.ccdhb.org.nz/about-us/history/the-public-hospital-in-wellington/rebuild-1967-1980
15 Drawings held at Wellington Regional Hospital.
16 Te Whatu Ora Health New Zealand, www.ccdhb.org.nz/about-us/history/the-public-hospital-in-wellington/additions-1981-2000
17 Te Whatu Ora Health New Zealand, www.ccdhb.org.nz/about-us/history/services-for-sick-children/1988-2020; 'Waitangirua Health Centre' and 'Ewart Geriatric Unit', *Home & Building* 39, no. 4 (1976).
18 'Thomas Fitzroy Haughey', *Journal of the NZIA* 38, no. 5 (May 1970); Heather Waite, Architectural and Engineering Projects Completed by Haughey and Fox, Fox and Partners; and Blewett, Waite, Jeffs and Carter, from 1961 to 1987, MS-2006-18, Auckland War Memorial Museum – Tāmaki Paenga Hira.
19 Dr Alan Sutherland, *Battle of the Bridge 1970–1994* (Auckland: New Zealand Medical Association, 1994), 26–27.
20 'Waitakere Obstetric Hospital, and Waitakere and North Shore General Hospitals', *Home & Building* 28 (November 1965); *Post Occupancy Evaluation — North Shore Hospital* (Auckland: Auckland Hospital Board, 1987); Sutherland, *Battle of the Bridge*, 27.
21 'Waitakere and North Shore General Hospitals', *Home & Building* 28 (November 1965); Plaques at Waitakere Hospital.
22 Patricia Jones, *The Wilson Home: A Celebration of 75 Years 1937–2012* (Auckland: The Wilson Home Trust, 2012), 12–15, 70; 'Wilson Home Chapel', *Home & Building* 28 (November 1965).
23 Jones, *The Wilson Home,* 72–73, 80–81, 90.
24 Kerry Francis, 'Chapel of St Luke, Whangārei Base Hospital', in Julia Gatley (ed.), *Long Live the Modern: New Zealand's New Architecture 1904–1984* (Auckland: Auckland University Press, 2009), 120; Diana Menefy, *Whangarei Hospital: A Century of Service 1901–2001* (Whangārei: Northland Health Ltd, 2001), 90; *Whangarei Hospital's 120 Year Celebration*, www.community.northlanddhb.org.nz/celebration
25 Keith Parker, *Kaitaia's Hospital: A Glimpse at Hospital Services and Volunteer Health Care in the Far North 1904–2004* (Kamo: Bridgewater, 2005), 37.
26 Shirley August, *The History of the Bay of Islands Hospital* (Kawakawa: Bay of Islands Hospital, 2013), 5–6; drawings held at Bay of Islands Hospital. Maternity returned to the main hospital in 1996, when the original surgical ward wing was refurbished to provide eight maternity beds, to a design by architects Brewer Davidson. A kitchen was added in 2008.
27 Ian Shearer, *Whakatane Hospital: Te Whatumauri Hauora: A History* (Tauranga: Bay of Plenty District Health Board, 2011), 38–49.
28 Shearer, *Whakatane Hospital*, 49–51.
29 NZ History, https://nzhistory.govt.nz/keyword/tokoroa
30 Matthews & Matthews Architects Ltd, *Central Taupo Heritage Assessment* (Taupō: Taupo District Council, 2009), 35.
31 *True Tales of Thames Hospital: 150 Years 1868–2018*, (Thames: Thames Hospital 150 Group in collaboration with Coromandel Heritage Trust, 2018), 55–56, 82; Althea Barker, *Thames Memorials and Plaques* (Thames: KMG Print, 2016), 24. It has not been possible to verify the architect of the Thames Health Centre.
32 'New Nurses' Home Opened', *Gisborne Photo News*, 18 October 1956, 12.
33 'Hospital News', *Gisborne Photo News*, October 1961, 55; 'Plaque Unveiled', *Gisborne Photo News*, 14 June 1962, 38; 'Building Projects', *Gisborne Photo News*, 21 April 1965, 9.
34 'Cook Base Hospital, Gisborne', *Home & Building* 32 (May 1970); 'Ultra-Modern Maternity Home Opens', *Gisborne Photo News*, 16 June 1971.
35 'Blewett Waite Jeffs Carter & Co', Notice, *Home & Building*, no. 1 (1980).
36 Plaque at Gisborne Hospital.
37 'Dadley Foundation', *Journal of the NZIA* (1963); 'Plunket Society Headquarters', *Journal of the NZIA* 36, no. 10 (October 1969).
38 'Lady Allum Home', 'Tamahere Eventide Home, 'Fergusson Home Rotorua', 'Caughey Preston Hospital Remuera', 'Old People's Welfare Centre', *Home & Building* 31 (November 1968); 'Wesley Hospital, Mt Eden', *Home & Building* 31 (December 1968).
39 Don Bassett, 'Enoch and Edith Bond Memorial Chapel (Methodist)', in Julia Gatley (ed.), *Long Live the Modern: New Zealand's New Architecture 1904–1984* (Auckland: Auckland University Press, 2009), 159; St Andrew's Village, https://standrewsvillage.co.nz/about-us
40 International Afghan Mission, https://iam-afghanistan.org/who-we-are/our-history; 'Two Years in Afghanistan', *Journal of the NZIA* 36, no. 4 (April 1969).
41 T. F. Haughey, 'Designing for the Cripple', *Journal of the NZIA* 36, no. 9 (September 1969).
42 Waite, Architectural and Engineering Projects Completed by Haughey and Fox.
43 'John Alfred Duffill', *Journal of the NZIA* 34, no. 10 (October 1967).
44 Puke Ariki, https://collection.pukeariki.com/persons/11629/rough-duffill
45 Drawings held at Puke Ariki, New Plymouth, ARC2004-642
46 'Pātea Heritage Inventory' (Hāwera: South Taranaki District Council, 2000).
47 Graeme Laurenson, *Burrafirth: The Family of Graeme and Marjorie Laurenson* (New Plymouth: Burrafirth, 1982), 90.
48 T. D. Hodges, *Mountain Town Hospital: The Story of the Stratford Public Hospital* (Stratford: Stratford Hospital Nurses' Reunion Committee, 1978), 53, 55; Alison Robinson (ed.), *Stratford Hospital Memories* (Stratford: Thurlstone Press, 2001), 76.
49 The maternity ward was demolished in 2012 after being damaged in a fire.
50 Hodges, *Mountain Town Hospital*, 61, 67, 74; Robinson, *Stratford Hospital Memories*, 105, 169; drawings held at Puke Ariki, New Plymouth, ARC2004-1566. Stratford Hospital was closed in 1998, demolished in 2000 and replaced with a new health centre.
51 Sorrel Hoskin, 'Dr Doris Gordon', in *Stratford District Centenary 1878–1978* (New Plymouth: Puke Ariki – Taranaki Stories), 68. The Gordon family gifted it to the community and it reopened as the district's first full-time residential care facility for the elderly in 1969. This closed in 2022 and the property was sold.
52 Arthur B. Scanlan, *Hospital on the Hill: A Centennial History of the New Plymouth Hospital 1867–1967* (New Plymouth: Taranaki Hospital Board, 1967), 95; Kristin Koller, *A History of the New Plymouth Hospitals from 1967* (New Plymouth: TNL, 2003), 7–10; 'Westown Hospital Laundry', *Home & Building* 24; Plaque, Taranaki Base Hospital.
53 'New Westown Hospital', *Home & Building* 33 (April 1971); Plaque, Taranaki Base Hospital.
54 Scanlan, *Hospital on the Hill*, 96; Koller, *A History of the New Plymouth Hospitals*, 11–12.
55 Koller, *A History of the New Plymouth Hospitals*, 14–17, 44, 51–5-2, 58, 68.
56 Foundation stone, Hāwera Hospital; Christine Clement, *Hawera Hospital: 100 Years 1894–1994* (Hāwera: Hawera Hospital Centennial Committee, 1994), 42.
57 'Hāwera Historic Hospital Building to Go', *Stuff*, 3 May 2011.
58 Ron Cooke, *Patients First: The Proud Tradition of Taumarunui Hospital* (Taumarunui: Taumarunui Hospital Reunion Committee, 2005), 80, 94, 97; Drawings held at Puke Ariki, New Plymouth, ARC2005-55.
59 Cooke, *Patients First*, 99, 108, 125, 134, 147, 207, 215.

60 Geoff Conly, *A Case History: The Hawke's Bay Hospital Board 1876–1989* (Napier: Hawke's Bay Area Health Board, 1992), 97, 100, 102–04; 'Obituary: Herbert Eric Phillips', *Journal of the NZIA* 47, no. 2 (1980).
61 Menefy, *Whangarei Hospital*, 63, 66, 79.
62 Kerry Francis, 'Temperate Modernity: The Whangārei Architecture of Alfred Morgan in the 1930s', in Christine McCarthy (ed.), *New Zealand Architecture in the 1930s* (Wellington: Victoria University of Wellington, 2006).
63 Parker, *Kaitāia's Hospital*, 41.
64 Conly, *A Case History*, 115, 125.
65 Ibid., 136, 200.
66 M. B. Boyd, *City of the Plains: A History of Hastings* (Wellington: Victoria University Press for the Hastings District Council, 1984), 224–27.
67 Conly, *A Case History*, 186.
68 G. Hollywood, 'History of Hastings Hospital, Summary to 1960', Knowledge Bank website of Hawke's Bay Digital Archives Trust.
69 Conly, *A Case History*, 197.
70 *Hawke's Bay Fallen Soldiers' Memorial Hospital Hastings: Official Opening New Ward and Administration Block*, Hawke's Bay Hospital Board, 1961; 'Ward Block and Nurses' Home, Memorial Hospital', *Home & Building* 26 (March 1964); Conly, *A Case History*, 224, 236.
71 Conly, *A Case History*, 212.
72 Drawings and plaques at Hawke's Bay Fallen Soldiers' Memorial Hospital.
73 Conly, *A Case History*, 270.
74 Ibid., 271.
75 Ibid., 158, 241, 274.
76 Patrick Parsons, *Waipukurau: The History of a Country Town* (Waipukurau: CHB Print, 1999), 141, 145; *Waipukurau Hospital Centennial — Souvenir Booklet 1879–1979* (Waipukurau: Waipawa Hospital Board, 1979).
77 Drawings at Archives New Zealand; Monty Soutar, 'East Coast places – Te Puia Springs and Tokomaru Bay', Te Ara – the Encyclopedia of New Zealand, https://teara.govt.nz/mi/east-coast-places/page-3
78 Conly, *A Case History*, 219.
79 Ibid., 196; Andrew Frane, 'Going, Going, Gone.', *Napier in Frame* (blog), 3 August 2015, https://napierinframe.co.nz/going-going-gone
80 William J, McKeon, 'Cooperation Between Medical Superintendents and Architects in Hospital Building Programmes', *Journal of the NZIA* 19 (1952).
81 'Picton Hospital', *Home & Building* 18 (July 1955).
82 J. G. Furness, *Wairau Hospital: 100 Years of Caring* (Blenheim: Marlborough Hospital Board, 1978), 49.
83 Ibid., 36; 'Clinical Services Block, Wairau Hospital', *Home & Building* 32 (August 1969).
84 'Karamea Maternity Hospital', *Journal of the NZIA* 32, no. 9 (October 1965).
85 William J. McKeon', *Journal of the NZIA* 29, no. 9 (October 1962); 'McKeon & Patience', *Journal of the NZIA* (1964); 'William J McKeon Obituary', *Journal of the NZIA* 40, no. 6 (June 1973); 'William John McKeon, 1896–1973', *Home & Building* 35 (May 1973).
86 Bruce Macdonald, *Westport: Struggle for Survival* (Westport: Westport Borough Council, 1973), 64.
87 A. L. Gabites, 'Obituary: Maurice Balfour Patience', *Planning Quarterly*, no. 86 (June 1987), 37.
88 'St Helen's Hospital Competition', *Home & Building* 21 (April 1959); 'Otaki Health Camp', *Journal of the NZIA* 33, no. 12 (December 1966).
89 'Ward & Specialist Service Block, Masterton Hospital', *Journal of the NZIA* (1964).
90 *Centennial of Greymouth Hospital 1866–1966*, Special Publication (Greymouth: *Greymouth Evening Star*, 1966); 'Grey Hospital Development', *Journal of the NZIA* 35, no. 2 (February 1968); 'Grey Hospital', *Home & Building* 35 (April 1973).
91 Fowler, *Buildings of New Zealanders*, 94.
92 Rosemarie Smith, *Seddon Memorial: The Rise and Fall of a County Hospital, Gore, 1909–1999* (Gore: Seddon Memorial Hospital Book Committee, 2005), 22.
93 'Petone Industrial Health Centre', *Home & Building* 25 (October 1962).
94 John Wilson, *Thematic Historical Overview of Nelson City for Nelson City Council Heritage Inventory Project* (October 2011), 99.
95 'Hall-Kenney & Partners Become Rotman White Spence & Hay', *Journal of the NZIA* 37, no. 8 (August 1970); plaque, Nelson Hospital; drawings at Archives New Zealand.

Primary health

1 *Better, Sooner, More Convenient Healthcare in the Community* (Wellington: Ministry of Health, 2011).
2 Fat Parrot Architecture, 'Orewa Medical Centre', www.fatparrot.co.nz/portfolio/orewa-medical-centre
3 Linda Tyler, 'Vernon Brown in Auckland', Itinerary No. 8, *Block*, the Broadsheet of the Auckland Branch of the NZIA, no. 10 (2007).
4 Medispace, www.medispace.co.nz/our-developments
5 Pacific Environments Architecture, 'Whitianga Medical Centre' www.pacificenvironments.co.nz/portfolio-item/whitianga-medical-centre
6 Arthouse Architects, Hutt Valley, www.arthousearchitects.co.nz/projects/hutt-valley
7 Tennant Brown Architects, 'Onslow Medical Centre', www.tennentbrown.co.nz/projects/commercial/onslow-medical-centre
8 Melling Architects, www.mal.nz/riddiford/medical/center
9 Hanham & Philp Contractors, 'Longhurst Health', www.hanhamphilp.co.nz/projects/longhurst-health

Chapter 11. Economic shock and surgery 1970–2000

1 James Belich, *Paradise Reforged: A History of the New Zealanders: From the 1880s to the Year 2000* (Auckland: Allen Lane, 2001), 405–08; Michael King, *The Penguin History of New Zealand* (Auckland: Penguin, 2003), 488–93; 'Chronology of the New Zealand Health System', www.health.govt.nz/system/files/2024-05/chronology-of-the-new-zealand-health-system-1840-to-2017_0.pdf
2 Michael P. Murphy Jr with Jeffrey Mansfield and MASS Design Group, *The Architecture of Health: Hospital Design and the Construction of Dignity* (New York: Cooper Hewitt, Smithsonian Design Museum, 2021), 138–39; Terence Hodgson, *Looking at the Architecture of New Zealand* (Wellington: Grantham House, 1990), 95; Peter Shaw, *New Zealand Architecture: From Polynesian Beginnings to 1990* (Auckland: Hodder & Stoughton, 1991), 180.
3 Philip Goad, Rowan Wilken and Julie Willis, *Australian Modern: The Architecture of Stephenson & Turner* (Melbourne: Miegunyah Press/Melbourne University Publishing, 2004), 2–5, 9–12.
4 John Balasoglou (ed.), *Stephenson & Turner* (Auckland: Balasoglou Books, 2006), 14–21.
5 Ibid., 132–33.
6 Ibid., 137.
7 Lloyd Smith, 'Dunedin Hospital Boiler House', in Julia Gatley (ed.), *Long Live the Modern: New Zealand's New Architecture 1904–1984* (Auckland: Auckland University Press, 2009), 94.
8 David Scott (ed.), *Middlemore Memories: The First 50 Years of Middlemore Hospital* (Auckland: South Auckland Health, 1995), 23, 76.
9 'Middlemore Hospital – Galbraith Block, Maternity Wing, Nurses' Home, Resident Doctors' Quarters and Household Staff Quarters', *Home & Building* 28 (November 1965).
10 'Dunedin Hospital Clinical Services Block', *Home & Building* 25 (March 1962).
11 Balasoglou, *Stephenson & Turner*, 139.
12 Ibid., 13.
13 Ibid., 139.
14 Ibid., 140–41.
15 Ibid., 133.
16 Ibid., 138.
17 David Scott (ed.), *The Story of Auckland Hospital 1847–1977* (Auckland: Medical History Library Committee of the Royal Australasian College of Physicians in New Zealand, 1977), 45–46; Derek A. Dow, *Auckland's Hospitals: A Pictorial History 1847–2004* (Auckland: Auckland District Health Board, 2005), 22, 28.
18 Balasoglou, *Stephenson & Turner*, 139; 'Stephenson & Turner', *Journal of the NZIA* 37, no. 12 (December 1970).
19 'New Acute Block, Auckland Hospital', *Home & Building* 28 (November 1965).
20 Ibid.; 'New Trade Workshops', *Home & Building* 28 (November 1965); 'Residence for Junior Medical Staff, Auckland Hospital', *Home & Building* 36 (May 1973).
21 Balasoglou, *Stephenson & Turner*, 138, 142; plaque at Auckland City Hospital.
22 Lochie Teague, *Starship: Inside Our National Children's Hospital* (Auckland: Random House, 2014), 19, 27, 31; 'Auckland Children's Hospital', *Journal of the NZIA* (September/October 1988); Dow, *Auckland's Hospitals*, 43.
23 Balasoglou, *Stephenson & Turner*, 94–105.
24 Ibid., 42–49.
25 'Auckland School of Medicine', *Home & Building* 35 (August 1972).
26 Julie Willis, 'Hospitals & Healthcare: Expertise, Efficiency, Experience & Environment', in *Stephenson & Turner*, 136–44.
27 'Bowen Hospital, Wellington', *Journal of the NZIA* 40, no. 1 (January 1973).
28 Balasoglou, *Stephenson & Turner*, 140–41.
29 The Seventh Day Adventists had built their first New Zealand hospital in Christchurch in 1885, but closed that year and a second, built in Napier in 1890, was bought by the Salvation Army in 1915.
30 Margaret Crookbain (comp.), *Adventist Hospital, Auckland: 25 Years of Commitment to Caring* (Feilding: A & J Print, 2001), 9, 12–14. The Auckland Adventist Hospital closed in 2001 and was sold to Ryman Healthcare, which redeveloped it as the Grace Joel Retirement Village. The adjacent medical centre was later bought by the Calan Healthcare Property Trust.
31 'Stephenson & Turner', *Journal of the NZIA* 43, no. 4 (August 1976).
32 Plaque, Porirua.
33 'Rehabilitation Centre Otahuhu', *Home & Building* 28 (November 1965).
34 Balasoglou, *Stephenson & Turner*, 8.
35 *S&T The Next 100* (Stephenson & Turner, 2022).
36 Balasoglou, *Stephenson & Turner*, 133. See also David Kernohan, 'The Architecture of Stephenson & Turner New Zealand – A Critique', in *Stephenson & Turner*, 6–9.
37 Geoff Mew and Adrian Humphris, *Raupo to Deco: Wellington Styles and Architects 1840–1940* (Wellington: Steele Roberts, 2014), 200–01.
38 Rene Natusch, 'Natusch & Sons', *Journal of the NZIA* 30, no. 6 (July 1963): 98–107.
39 Geoff Conly, *A Case History: The Hawke's Bay Hospital Board 1876–1989* (Napier: Hawke's Bay Area

Health Board, 1992), 133.

40 Natusch, 'Natusch & Sons', 98–107.

41 Conly, *A Case History*, 186.

42 'The Nurses' Home Extension at Cook Hospital in Gisborne', *Auckland Weekly News*, 18 June 1941, 26; 'Then and Now', *Gisborne Photo News*, 15 June 1966, 46; plaques, Gisborne Hospital.

43 'Boiler House Napier Hospital', *Journal of the NZIA*, no. 3 (1986).

44 'Fair Honest Perfectionist: Hawke's Bay Architect Guy Natusch Remembered as "Absolute Gentleman"', *Stuff*, 31 October 2020; drawings held at Hawke's Bay Fallen Soldiers' Memorial Hospital.

45 Plaque at Hawke's Bay Fallen Soldiers' Memorial Hospital.

46 Drawings held at Hawke's Bay Fallen Soldiers' Memorial Hospital.

47 Team Architects, www.teamarchitects.co.nz/work

48 J. G. Furness, *Wairau Hospital: 100 Years of Caring* (Blenheim: Marlborough Hospital Board, 1978), 37.

49 'An Identity which Reflects the Beauty of the West Coast', *Scope*, Magazine of the New Zealand Metal Roofing Manufacturers' Association, 30 October 2009; plaque at Grey Base Hospital. Grey Base Hospital in Greymouth was redeveloped in 2001 and the maternity ward was converted into a mental health unit, but the Porter and Martin designed buildings are now classed as earthquake prone and await demolition.

50 *It's All Happening: Burwood Health Campus* (Christchurch: Canterbury District Health Board, 2013).

51 'Natural Remedy' and 'House of Healing', *Architecture New Zealand* (November/December 2003): 44–50.

52 Peter Beaven, 'Introduction', in Peter Shaw, *New Zealand Architecture: From Polynesian Beginnings to 1990* (Auckland: Hodder & Stoughton, 1991), 8.

53 David Sayers, *The Goodwill Years: The Remarkable Story of a Professional Partnership: Gillman Garry Clapp & Sayers* (Hamilton: SFT Books, 2011), 8; Waikato Museum Te Whare Taonga o Waikato 1985/71/94.1, https://collection.waikatomuseum.org.nz/objects/28854/proposed-childrens-ward-thames-hospital-drawing-no1

54 'Paeroa Maternity Hospital', *Ohinemuri Regional History Journal* #11 (May 1969); *True Tales of Thames Hospital: 150 Years 1868–2018* (Thames: Thames Hospital 150 Group in collaboration with Coromandel Heritage Trust, 2018), 23.

55 Fiona Corcoran, 'Interview with David Sayers', Back to the Drawing Board – Hamilton Architect's Oral History Project, 1999.

56 Sayers, *The Goodwill Years*, 8, 10.

57 *Celebrating 100 Years of Innovation and Excellence: Tauranga Hospital 1914–2014* (Tauranga: Bay of Plenty District Health Board, 2014).

58 'Tauranga Hospital', *Home & Building* 21 (March 1959).

59 Sayers, *The Goodwill Years*, 10.

60 Sayers, *The Goodwill Years*, 11, 28–29, 46, 65.

61 'Tauranga Hospital – Ward Block and Board Offices', *Home & Building* 35 (February 1973); *Celebrating 100 Years of Innovation and Excellence*.

62 This pattern can also be seen at Whangarei Hospital and Hawke's Bay Fallen Soldiers' Memorial Hospital, where ward blocks were staged. In each case the first ward block has a single corridor, while the later one has the 'racetrack' configuration.

63 Sayers, *The Goodwill Years*, 21; John Armstrong, *Under One Roof: A History of Waikato Hospital* (Hamilton: Half Court Press, 2009), 264; Georgina Wedge and Peter Rothwell, *Waikato Hospital: Our Hospital, Your History* (Hamilton: Waikato Health Memorabilia Trust, 2016), 46.

64 Sayers, *The Goodwill Years*, 22; Armstrong, *Under One Roof*, 280; Wedge and Rothwell, *Waikato Hospital*, 48; 'Waikato Clinical Services Block', *Home & Building* 31 (April 1969); 'Waikato Hospital Clinical Services Block', *Home & Building* 36 (January 1974).

65 Sayers, *The Goodwill Years*, 54.

66 Ibid., 55.

67 Ngāti Porou Oranga, https://www.npo.org.nz/about-us

68 John Mandeno, 'The Story of Te Kuiti Hospital: Part 2 1966 to 1986', *Footprints of History*, Magazine of the Te Awamutu, Otorohanga and Te Kuiti Historical Society and the Waitomo Caves Museum Society, no. 23 (December 1999), 12; Russell Young, *The Story of Te Kūiti* (Wellington: Winter Productions, 2013), 111–12; 'Extension to Te Kuiti Hospital', *Home & Building* 31 (April 1969).

69 'Gillman Garry Clapp & Sayers', *Journal of the NZIA* 38, no. 7 (July 1971); 'Gillman Garry Clapp & Sayers', *Journal of the NZIA* 41, no. 5 (May 1974).

70 Sayers, *The Goodwill Years*, 47; 'Development Palmerston North Hospital', *Home & Building* 31 (April 1969).

71 Sayers, *The Goodwill Years*, 50.

72 Ibid., 47; Jo Kellaway and Mike Maryan, *A Century of Care: Palmerston North Hospital 1893–1993* (Double Bay, Australia: MidCentral Health and Focus Books, 1993), 85, 91.

73 *Hohipera o Papaioea: Palmerston North Hospital Celebrates 125 Years* (Palmerston North: MidCentral District Health Board, 2018), 22.

74 Sayers, *The Goodwill Years*, 56.

75 Ibid., 58.

76 Ibid., 57.

77 Ibid., 60.

78 Ibid., 99.

79 Diana Menefy, *Whangarei Hospital: A Century of Service 1901–2001* (Whangārei: Northland Health Ltd, 2001), 296; *Whangarei Hospital's 120 Year Celebration*, www.community.northlanddhb.org.nz/celebration

80 Sayers, *The Goodwill Years*, 99

81 Ibid., 75.

82 Ibid.

83 Ibid., 76.

84 Ibid., 97.

85 Ibid., 83–97.

86 Ibid., 96.

87 *Report on Hospital Sites in South Auckland, Auckland Hospital Board* (Auckland, 1976); Sayers, *The Goodwill Years*, 85.

88 Sayers, *The Goodwill Years*, 85.

89 Ibid., 96.

90 Ibid., 97.

91 'Cassel Private Hospital Hamilton', *Home & Building* 31 (April 1969); 'Te Waiora Family Health Centre', *Home & Building* 31 (January 1974); 'Apia Hospital Redevelopment, Western Samoa and Aitutaki Hospital, Rarotonga Hospital', *Journal of the NZIA* 41, no. 4 (April 1974); Sayers, *The Goodwill Years*, 63.

92 Sayers, *The Goodwill Years*, 3–4, 161, 166.

93 'Gillman Partners', Notice, *Home & Building*, no. 3 (1981).

94 Plaques at Mason Clinic.

95 Jade Kake and Jeremy Hansen, *Rewi: Āta Haere, Kia Tere* (Auckland: Massey University Press, 2023), 204, 209.

96 Andrew Barrie, 'Rewi Thompson in Auckland', Itinerary No. 20, *Block*, the Broadsheet of the Auckland Branch of the NZIA, no. 2 (2009).

97 Deidre Brown, *Māori Architecture: From Fale to Wharenui and Beyond* (Auckland: Raupo, 2009), 154.

98 Plaque and drawings held at Whanganui Hospital.

99 Drawings held at Porirua Hospital Museum.

100 Drawings held at Auckland, Tauranga and Hawke's Bay Fallen Soldiers' Memorial Hospitals.

101 *AECOM in New Zealand* (brochure).

102 Drawings held at Timaru Hospital.

103 Drawings held at Whangarei Hospital. The architect of the Mauri Ora Breast Clinic has not been identified.

104 Plaque and drawings held at Wairau Hospital.

105 Kake and Hansen, *Rewi*, 223.

106 Ian Shearer and Rex E. Wright-St Clair, *A Century on Cameron Road: A History of Tauranga Hospital 1914–2014* (Tauranga: Bay of Plenty District Health Board, 2016), 273; *Celebrating 100 Years of Innovation and Excellence: Tauranga Hospital 6 March 1914–2014* (Tauranga: Bay of Plenty District Health Board, 2014), 31.

107 Shearer and Wright-St Clair, *A Century on Cameron Road*, 273.

108 Plaque and drawings held at Wairau Hospital.

109 AECOM, https://aecom.com/projects/sengkang-hospital

110 *AECOM in New Zealand*.

111 'New Hospital Unit Ready for Patients', *New Zealand Herald*, 27 May 2011; *Celebrating 100 Years of Innovation and Excellence: Tauranga Hospital 1914–2014*, 31.

112 'Last Piece of $70 million Project Waka Almost Complete', *Rotorua Daily Post*, 17 January 2017.

113 Thema, https://thema.co.nz/projects/projects-layout-1

114 Thema, https://thema.co.nz/about

Engineering specialists

1 Keith Davies, *Beca: One Hundred Years* (Auckland Penguin Random House, 2020), 20–28.

2 Ibid., 34-48.

3 Ibid., 11, 52-57.

4 Beca, www.beca.com/what-we-do/markets/buildings/healthcare

5 'Beca Puts its Might Behind Game Changers in Asia', *New Zealand Herald*, 19 August 2023.

6 Beca, www.beca.com/what-we-do/projects

7 Beca, www.beca.com/about-us

8 Andrew and Claire Brickell (comp.), *Goulden: An Account of the Wanderings of a New Zealand Civil Engineer, 1908–48 and Beyond: At Home and Abroad/ Part Autobiography by Richard Goulden Brickell MICE MNZIS, Wing Commander RAF and RNZAF; with Additions Covering Earlier and Later Times* (Auckland: Andrew Brickell, 2020).

9 John A. Hill, *The History of Rankine & Hill* (unpublished manuscript, State Library of New South Wales). Rankine & Hill was founded by John Rankine and John Hill in Sydney in 1955. The firm opened an office in Wellington in 1956, and later one in Auckland. Hill notes that the merger was with the New Zealand offices, but the name Brickell Moss Rankine & Hill was later adopted in Australia as well. He does not say when the merger ended but uses the name Rankine & Hill for most of the firm's projects from the 1970s on.

10 Aurecon, https://www.aurecongroup.com/about/aurecon-history

11 Andrew Barrie, 'KRTA in Auckland', Itinerary No. 19, *Block*, the Broadsheet of the Auckland Branch of the NZIA, no. 1, 2009; 'KRTA', *Journal of the NZIA* (July/August 1988).

12 Ibid.

13 'Chapel, Selwyn Village', *Journal of the NZIA* 34, no. 12 (December 1967).

14 Andrew Barrie, 'KRTA in Auckland'.

15 'Vale: Warwick Massey', *Local Matters*, 4 November 2019; *Welcome the New Zealand Ambassador to Khon Kaen University*, Khon Kaen University, Thailand, 5 July 2024.

16 *Sinclair Knight Merz: Celebrating Over 40 Years* (brochure, 2006).

17 Holmes, www.holmesgroup.com/about/history; New Zealand Consulting Engineers Ltd, https://nzcel.co.nz/our-history
18 Holmes, https://holmesanz.com/projects
19 Babbage, www.babbage.co.nz/about/our-journey
20 A biography for George Vamos is provided in the Heritage New Zealand listing for the former Wellington Teachers' Training College, www.heritage.org.nz/list-details/9797/Listing
21 Clendon Burns & Park Ltd, www.cbp.co.nz/practice
22 'Total Energy Centre – Wellington Hospital 1981', in Matthew Wright, *New Zealand's Engineering Heritage: 1870–2000* (Auckland: Reed, 1999), 141.
23 Powell Fenwick, https://pfc.co.nz/our-story
24 NDY, https://ndy.com/about-us; Tetra Tech, www.tetratech.com/about/our-company
25 Marshall Day Acoustics, https://marshallday.com/who-we-are; 'Obituary: Sir Harold Marshall', *Architecture New Zealand* (January/February 2025), 28–29.
26 James C. Muir, *Opus Works: A Short History of the New Zealand Government's Infrastructure Development* (Christchurch: self-published, 2021), 445.
27 WSP, www.wsp.com/en-nz/hubs/architecture
28 Muir, *Opus Works*, 529.
29 WSP, www.wsp.com/en-nz/hubs/healthcare

Chapter 12. Recovery and reconstruction 2000–

1 'Chronology of the New Zealand Health System', www.health.govt.nz/system/files/2024-05/chronology-of-the-new-zealand-health-system-1840-to-2017_0.pdf
2 Eileen McSaveney, 'Earthquakes – Building for earthquake resistance', Te Ara – the Encyclopedia of New Zealand, https://teara.govt.nz/en/earthquakes/page-4; https://healthfacilityguidelines.com.au
3 *Hospitals and Healthcare Establishments* (Sydney: Peddle Thorp Partnerships, 1975); *Peddle Thorp* (Sydney: Peddle Thorp, 1992); Doug Stace, *Patriarchs, Partners and Professionals: Peddle Thorp Expands Internationally* (Sydney: Australian Graduate School of Management, University of New South Wales, 1996); Gina Smith, *Work Play Learn Care Live* (Brisbane: Peddle Thorp Architects, 2006).
4 Peddle Thorp Architects, 'Rotorua Hospital', https://peddlethorp.co.nz/projects/rotorua-hospital; 'North Shore Surgical Centre', https://peddlethorp.co.nz/projects/north-shore-surgical-centre
5 Mercy Ascot, www.mercyascot.co.nz/About-Us; Vital Healthcare Property Trust, 'Ascot Central', www.vitalhealthcareproperty.co.nz/property/ascot-central
6 'A Specialist Practice', *Architecture New Zealand* (November/December 2003), 58–62; Klein, www.klein.co.nz/studio
7 Klein, 'Middlemore Hospital Harley Gray Clinical Services Building', www.klein.co.nz/projects/middlemore-hospital-harley-gray-clinical-services-building
8 Klein, 'North Shore Hospital Lakeview', www.klein.co.nz/projects/north-shore-hospital-lakeview
9 Klein, 'Hutt Valley Hospital Emergency Department & Theatre Extension', www.klein.co.nz/projects/hutt-valley-hospital-emergency-department-theatre-extension; 'Hawke's Bay Hospital Endoscopy', www.klein.co.nz/projects/hawkes-bay-hospital-endoscopy
10 Klein, 'Tiaho Mai acute mental health inpatient unit, Middlemore Hospital', www.klein.co.nz/insight/tiaho-mai-acute-mental-health-inpatient-unit-middlemore-hospital; New Zealand Doctor, 'Sod-turning marks the start of work on replacement $162.8 million 60-bed forensic psychiatry facility', 3 March 2023, www.nzdoctor.co.nz/article/undoctored/sod-turning-marks-start-work-replacement-1628-million-60-bed-forensic-psychiatry
11 Wilson + Hill Architects, 'Forte Health 2013', www.wilsonandhill.co.nz/healthcare/forte-health-2013; Tatiana Gibbs, 'Space for another 1800 surgeries in Christchurch after hospital's expansion', *Press*, 17 October 2024, www.thepress.co.nz/nz-news/350453089/space-another-1800-surgeries-christchurch-after-hospitals-expansion
12 Forté Health, www.fortehealth.co.nz
13 Klein, 'Ormiston Hospital Expansion', www.klein.co.nz/projects/ormiston-hospital-expansion
14 Anna Rogers, *The Shaky Isles: New Zealand Earthquakes* (Wellington: Grantham House, 2013), 187–221.
15 *It's All Happening: Burwood Health Campus* (Christchurch: Canterbury District Health Board, 2013); Klein, 'Burwood Hospital Redevelopment', www.klein.co.nz/projects/burwood-hospital-redevelopment; https://jasmax.com/projects/burwood-hospital
16 'Critical Care', *Architecture New Zealand* (November/December 2003), 32–40; Stephen Stratford (ed), Jasmax, A4 New Zealand Architects Monograph Series, NZ, Architectural Publications Trust, Auckland, 2007, 28; Derek A. Dow, *Auckland's Hospitals: A Pictorial History 1847–2004* (Auckland: Auckland District Health Board, 2005), 45; Linda Bryder, *The Rise and Fall of National Women's Hospital: A History* (Auckland: Auckland University Press, 2014), 232.
17 'Southern Hospitality', *Architecture New Zealand* (November/December 2003): 54–55; Stratford, *Jasmax*, 15.
18 Jasmax, https://jasmax.com/projects/totara-haumaru-north-shore-hospital
19 University of Otago, 'University announces new dental school and science buildings', 1 April 2015, www.otago.ac.nz/news/newsroom/university-announces-new-dental-school-and-science-buildings2
20 Mary Anne Gill (ed.), *The Village on the Hill: Celebrating 125 Years of Waikato Hospital* (Hamilton: Waikato District Health Board, 2011), 146; Georgina Wedge and Peter Rothwell, *Waikato Hospital: Our Hospital, Your History* (Hamilton: Waikato Health Memorabilia Trust, 2016), 79; Chow:Hill, 'Waikato Hospital Meade Clinic', www.chowhill.co.nz/projects/waikato-hospital-meade-clinic; Chow:Hill, 'Waikato Hospital Older Persons Rehab', www.chowhill.co.nz/projects/waikato-hospital-older-persons-rehab
21 *True Tales of Thames Hospital: 150 Years 1868–2018* (Thames: Thames Hospital 150 Group in collaboration with Coromandel Heritage Trust, 2018), 260.
22 Chow:Hill, www.chowhill.co.nz/practice; 'Richard Hill', *Journal of the NZIA* (May/June 1989).
23 'Exercises in Total Design', *Architecture New Zealand* (November/December 2003): 56.
24 Te Whatu Ora Health New Zealand, 'Kidz First connected to our community', www.countiesmanukau.health.nz/75th-anniversary/kidz-first-connected-to-our-community; Chow:Hill, 'Braemar Hospital', www.chowhill.co.nz/projects/braemar-hospital; Braemar Hospital, www.braemarhospital.co.nz/gp-history
25 Chow:Hill, 'Bay of Islands Hospital', www.chowhill.co.nz/projects/bay-of-islands-hospital; 'Nelson Dialysis Unit', https://www.chowhill.co.nz/projects/nelson-dialysis-unit
26 Chow:Hill, 'Mason Clinic E Tū Tanekaha', www.chowhill.co.nz/projects/e-tu-tanekaha-mason-clinic
27 Chow:Hill, 'Christchurch Women's Hospital', www.chowhill.co.nz/projects/christchurch-womens-hospital; 'Christchurch Hospital Waipapa', https://www.chowhill.co.nz/projects/christchurch-hospital-hagley-acute-services-building; Warren and Mahoney, 'Waipapa Christchurch Hospital', https://wam.studio/work/waipapa-christchurch-hospital
28 *Warren & Mahoney Architects 1958–1989* (Christchurch: Warren & Mahoney, 1989), 105; *New Territory: Warren & Mahoney: 50 Years of New Zealand Architecture* (Auckland: Balasoglou Books, 2005), 16, 26; 'Dental Nurses' Training School, Christchurch', *Home & Building* 23 (June 1960).
29 Peter Shaw, *New Zealand Architecture: From Polynesian Beginnings to 1990* (Auckland: Hodder & Stoughton, 1991), 172–74.
30 *Warren & Mahoney Architects*, 18; *New Territory*, 29.
31 'Full Nelson', *Architecture New Zealand* (November/December 2003), 52–53; plaque at Nelson Hospital.
32 *Project Maunga: Taranaki Base Hospital Redevelopment* (New Plymouth: Taranaki District Health Board, 2014), 2, 19; Warren and Mahoney, 'Taranaki Hospital Renal Unit', https://wam.studio/work/taranaki-hospital-renal-unit
33 Warren and Mahoney, 'Southern Cross Central Lakes Hospital, Queenstown', https://wam.studio/work/southern-cross-central-lakes-hospital-queenstown
34 Warren and Mahoney, 'MacMurray Centre', https://wam.studio/work/macmurray-centre-1
35 Warren and Mahoney, www.wam.studio/practice
36 *New Territory,* 36; Warren and Mahoney, https://wam.studio/sector/health
37 'New Hospital Design an "Incredible Opportunity"', *Otago Daily Times*, 24 December 2019.
38 'Rice Daubney Merge With Di Carlo Potts', *Architecture Australia* (1 January 2004); drawings at Palmerston North, North Shore and Hutt hospitals.
39 'Craig Craig Moller', *Journal of the NZIA* 40, no. 3 (March 1973); CCM Architects, ccm.co.nz/practice
40 'Local Associations', *Architecture New Zealand* (November/ December 2003): 42–43.
41 Te Whatu Ora Health New Zealand, www.ccdhb.org.nz/about-us/history/the-public-hospital-in-wellington/new-regional-hospital
42 CCM Architects, 'Nga Taiohi-Kenepuru Hospital', www.ccm.co.nz/projects/healthcare/nga-taiohi-kenepuru
43 CCM Architects, 'Te Hopai Home and Hospital', www.ccm.co.nz/projects/healthcare/te-hopai-home-and-hospital; 'Boulcott Hospital', www.ccm.co.nz/projects/healthcare/boulcott-hospital; www.ccm.co.nz/projects/healthcare/mercy-hospital/
44 CCM Architects, Te Nikau Hospital and Health Centre', www.ccm.co.nz/projects/healthcare/te-nikau-hospital-and-health-centre
45 www.building.govt.nz/assets/Uploads/resolving-problems/determinations/2015/2015-059
46 CCM Architects, Christchurch Outpatients Building, www.ccm.co.nz/projects/healthcare/christchurch-outpatients-building
47 DesignGroup Architects H+K, www.ahk.co.nz/projects
48 DesignGroup ASC Architects, 'Ronald McDonald House & Extensions', www.ascarchitects.co.nz/projects/ronald-mcdonald-house; www.archaus.co.nz/projects#/community-h; Wilkie + Bruce Architects, www.wilkieandbruce.co.nz/our-story; Aston Mitchell, 'Cancer Society NZ, Domain Lodge, www.ashtonmitchell.com/project/cancer-society-nz-domain-lodge; Plus Architecture, 'Rānui Apartments', www.plusarchitecture.com.au/ranui-apartments
49 Pacific Environments Architects, https://pacificenvironments.co.nz/portfolio; Chibnall Buckell Team Architects, 'Laser Eye Clinic, Hamilton', www.cbmarchitects.co.nz/blog/984195; APG Architects, 'Pathlab Bay of Plenty', https://apgarchitects.com/portfolio/pathlab-bay-of-plenty

50 First Principles Architects and Interiors, 'Nga Hau Mangere Birthing Centre', www.firstprinciplesarchitects.com/public/nga-hau-mangere-birthing-centre

51 Rosemarie Smith, *Seddon Memorial: The Rise and Demise of a Country Hospital, Gore, 1909–1999* (Gore: Seddon Memorial Hospital Book Committee, 2005), 207; Catherine Coleborne (ed.), *Changing Times, Changing Places: From Tokanui Hospital to Mental Health Services in the Waikato, 1910–2012* (Hamilton: Half Court Press, 2012), 150, 213.

52 Archimedia, https://archimedia.co.nz/activities/#portfolio

53 'Kathleen Kilgour Centre', *Architecture New Zealand* (May/June 2015).

54 Jigsaw Architects, www.jigsawarchitects.nz/healthcare-projects; Architecture HDT, 'Kaweka Hospital', https://architecturehdt.co.nz/portfolio/kaweka-hospital

55 DLA, 'Te Whatu Ora Timaru Hospital', www.dla.co.nz/project/te-whatu-ora-timaru-hospital

56 Proarch, https://proarch.co.nz; Pak Design, www.pakdesign.co.nz/work

57 McKenzie Higham Architects, www.mckenziehigham.co.nz/projects

58 Te Whatu Ora Health New Zealand, www.ccdhb.org.nz/about-us/history/services-for-sick-children/2021/, www.ignitearchitects.com/projects/wellington-childrens-hospital; www.ignitearchitects.com/projects/akaroa-health-hub

59 Hawkins Architecture, 'Churchill Private Hospital', www.hawkinsarchitecture.co.nz/churchillprivatehospital

60 Ikon, 'Selwyn Health Hub', www.ikon.co.nz/project/selwyn-health-hub

61 'Council Ownership Unique in New Zealand', *Otago Daily Times*, 2 April 2011.

62 HPA, 'Dunstan Hospital Clyde', https://hpa.co.nz/index.php/portfolio/dunstan-hospital-clyde; 'Minister Opens New Maniototo Hospital', *Otago Daily Times*, 18 April 2010.

63 Southland Charity Hospital, www.southlandcharityhospital.org/about

Fixtures, fittings and equipment

1 John Steele, *No Ordinary Man: The Extraordinary Life and Times of Dr Arthur Purchas* (Auckland: David Ling, 2019), 105, 241.

2 Jean C. Ross, 'A History of Poliomyelitis in New Zealand' (MA thesis, University of Canterbury, Christchurch, 1993); Christine McAlpine, *Going Viral: Polio and the Iron Lung* (Auckland: Museum of Transport and Technology, 2020).

3 *Sir Woolf Fisher* and *Maurice Paykel*, New Zealand Business Hall of Fame, www.businesshalloffame.co.nz

4 Keith Davies, *Defying Gravity: The Fisher & Paykel Story* (Auckland: David Ling, 2004), 135–37, 284–88, 311; John Bridges and David Downes, *No 8 Wire: The Best of Kiwi Ingenuity* (Auckland: Hodder Moa Beckett, 2000), 38; John Bridges and David Downes, *Rewired: 202 New Zealand Inventions that Changed the World* (Auckland: Penguin, 2014), 71.

5 'Premature Infant Incubator, Paul F. Martin', *Home & Building* 32 (December 1969); 'Marford Portable Incubator, Paul F. Martin', *Home & Building* 37 (June 1974); 'Anaesthesia Machine – Mason Mesco', *Home & Building* 35 (August 1972); 'The Masons', in *Ceramco* (Auckland: Ceramco, 1979); Acero, www.acero.co.nz/our-story; MHM Automation, www.mhmautomation.com/about#history

6 'Made in Taranaki: The Hospital Bed You Spent Hours in has a Provincial Lineage', *Stuff*, 21 January 2019; Howard Wright, www.howardwrightcares.com/about-us/history

7 Bob Riley, *Kiwi Ingenuity: A Book of New Zealand Ideas and Inventions* (Auckland: AIT Press, 1995), 110; Bridges and Downes, *No 8 Wire*, 11; Bridges and Downes, *Rewired*, 48, 55.

8 Riley, *Kiwi Ingenuity*, 77.

9 Ibid., 75; Bridges and Downes, *No 8 Wire*, 136; Bridges and Downes, *Rewired*, 138.

10 Mobile Health, www.mobilehealth.co.nz

11 'Sick or Premature Babies in India to be First to Use Sir Ray Avery's LifePod Incubators', *New Zealand Herald*, 23 March 2019.

12 Change for Our Children, www.changeforourchildren.nz/our_kites/pepi-pod

Conclusion

1 Michael P. Murphy Jr with Jeffrey Mansfield and MASS Design Group, *The Architecture of Health: Hospital Design and the Construction of Dignity* (New York: Cooper Hewitt, Smithsonian Design Museum, 2021), 220–41.

2 *Nationwide Service and Campus Planning Report* (Te Whatu Ora Health New Zealand), quoted in *New Zealand Herald*, 11 August 2021.

Selected biographies

1 Margaret H. Alington, *An Excellent Recruit: Frederick Thatcher Architect, Priest and Private Secretary in Early New Zealand* (Auckland: Polygraphia, 2007); Geoff Mew with Adrian Humphris, *Architects at the Apex: The Top 50 in New Zealand, 1840–1940* (Martinborough: Ngaio Press, 2020), 185–89.

2 G. H. Scholefield (ed.), *A Dictionary of New Zealand Biography, Volume 2* (Wellington: Department of Internal Affairs, 1940), 268.

3 John Steele, *No Ordinary Man: The Extraordinary Life and Times of Dr Arthur Purchas* (Auckland: David Ling, 2019).

4 Geoff Mew and Adrian Humphris, *Raupo to Deco: Wellington Styles and Architects 1840–1940* (Wellington: Steele Roberts, 2014), 39.

5 Una Platts, *Nineteenth Century New Zealand Artists: A Guide and Handbook* (Christchurch: Avon Fine Prints, 1980), 75; Mew and Humphris, *Raupo to Deco*, 37–38.

6 Mew and Humphris, *Raupo to Deco*, 42–44.

7 Platts, *Nineteenth Century New Zealand Artists*, 176; Ian Lochhead, *A Dream of Spires: Benjamin Mountfort and the Gothic Revival* (Christchurch: Canterbury University Press, 1999); Mew and Humphris, *Architects at the Apex*, 153–58.

8 Canterbury Museum, https://collection.canterburymuseum.com/objects/718777/macdonald-dictionary-record-william-williamson

9 Engineering New Zealand, 'John Rochfort', www.engineeringnz.org/programmes/heritage/engineering-hall-fame/john-rochfort-18321893

10 Platts, *Nineteenth Century New Zealand Artists*, 234; Te Ara – the Encyclopedia of New Zealand, https://teara.govt.nz/en/biographies/1t97/thomson-john-turnbull; National Library Board Singapore, 'John Turnbull Thomson', www.nlb.gov.sg/main/article-detail?cmsuuid=3288734a-bcf9-4c28-98ce-28a89b49b472

11 John Stacpoole, *William Mason: The First New Zealand Architect* (Auckland: Auckland University Press with Oxford University Press, 1971); Mew and Humphris, *Architects at the Apex*, 144–48.

12 Mew and Humphris, *Architects at the Apex*, 168–71; Built in Dunedin, 'David Ross FRIBA, architect', https://builtindunedin.com/2013/01/05/david-ross

13 Platts, *Nineteenth Century New Zealand Artists*, 68; Rosslyn J. Noonan, *By Design: A Brief History of the Public Works Department, Ministry of Works, 1870–1970* (Wellington: Ministry of Works, 1975), 31–32, 50, 305; Lewis E. Martin, *Built for Us* (Dunedin: Otago University Press, 2004), 10–31; Mew and Humphris, *Raupo to Deco*, 72; Mew and Humphris, *Architects at the Apex*, 67–71.

14 Platts, *Nineteenth Century New Zealand Artists*, 244; Mew and Humphris, *Raupo to Deco*, 366; Mason & Wales, www.masonandwales.com/about

15 NZ History, 'Mrs Kerr', https://nzhistory.govt.nz/suffragist/mrs-kerr-0

16 Mew and Humphris, *Raupo to Deco*, 103–05; Mew and Humphris, *Architects at the Apex*, 194–97.

17 Noonan, *By Design*, 50, 283; Martin, *Built for Us*, 32–41; Mew and Humphris, *Raupo to Deco*, 68.

18 Ian Bowman, *William Beatson: A Colonial Architect* (Auckland: Balasoglou Books, 2005), 137–44; Mew and Humphris, *Raupo to Deco*, 66–67.

19 Noonan, *By Design*, 93, 95; Martin, *Built for Us*, 42–113; *A Brief History of Public Buildings in New Zealand*; Mew and Humphris, *Architects at the Apex*, 49–53.

20 *Hamurana*, Heritage New Zealand Register #7733, www.heritage.org.nz/the-list

21 Platts, *Nineteenth Century New Zealand Artists*, 134; Mew and Humphris, *Architects at the Apex*, 118–20.

22 Mew and Humphris, *Raupo to Deco*, 321.

23 Platts, *Nineteenth Century New Zealand Artists*, 61.

24 Ibid., 160; Norman Ledgerwood, *R. A. Lawson: Victorian Architect of Dunedin* (Dunedin: Historic Cemeteries Conservation Trust of New Zealand, 2013); Mew and Humphris, *Architects at the Apex*, 129–31.

25 *Waikato Times*, 12 April 2019.

26 *Poverty Bay Club (Former)*, Heritage New Zealand Register #810, www.heritage.org.nz/the-list

27 G. H. Scholefield (ed.), A Dictionary of New Zealand Biography, Volume 2 (Wellington: Department of Internal Affairs, 1940), 229.

28 Ibid., 75–76.

29 G. H. Scholefield (ed.), *A Dictionary of New Zealand Biography, Volume 1* (Wellington: Department of Internal Affairs, 1940), 26.

30 Katherine W. Orr, 'Blackett, John', *Dictionary of New Zealand Biography*, first published in 1990. Te Ara – the Encyclopedia of New Zealand, https://teara.govt.nz/en/biographies/1b23/blackett-john

31 'James Stanley Bruce', in *Cyclopedia of New Zealand (Wellington Provincial District)*, Vol. 1 (Wellington: Cyclopedia Company of New Zealand, 1897), 1175.

32 Timaru District Council, Historic Heritage Item Doc # 1304413, www.timaru.govt.nz/__data/assets/pdf_file/0005/673880/Historic-Heritage-Assessment-Report-HHI57-Former-Timaru-and-Gladstone-Board-of-Works-Building-Category-A.pdf

33 *Commercial Buildings*, Heritage New Zealand Register #2280, www.heritage.org.nz/the-list

34 Conal McCarthy, *Forrester & Lemon: Ōamaru Architects* (Ōamaru: New Zealand Historic Places Trust, North Otago Branch, 2002).

35 Mew and Humphris, *Architects at the Apex*, 42–44.

36 Mew and Humphris, *Raupo to Deco*, 120–01.

37 Ibid., 69–71; Mew and Humphris, *Architects at the Apex*, 59–62.

38 Built in Dunedin, 'Joseph Lowe Shaw, architect', https://builtindunedin.com/2012/08/19/joseph-lowe-shaw-c-1820-1906

39 www.heritage.org.nz/list-details/180/listing#details; www.natlib.govt.nz/records/22390307

40 Canterbury Museum, 'Macdonald Dictionary Record: Richard Bird', https://collection.canterburymuseum.com/objects/708440/macdonald-dictionary-record-richard-bird

41 *Southland Times Building*, Heritage New Zealand Register #2513, www.heritage.org.nz/the-list

42 'Obituary Horace Hammond', *Northern Advocate*, 9

August 1923, 4.

43 'Edward Bartley', in *Cyclopedia of New Zealand (Auckland Provincial District)*, Vol. 2 (Christchurch: Cyclopedia Company of New Zealand, 1902); Platts, *Nineteenth Century New Zealand Artists*, 35; M. W. Bartley, *Colonial Architect: The Career of Edward Bartley 1839–1919* (Wellington: First Edition, 2006).

44 *St Paul's Church (Anglican)*, Heritage New Zealand Register #650, www.heritage.org.nz/the-list

45 Platts, *Nineteenth Century New Zealand Artists*, 163; Mew and Humphris, *Architects at the Apex*, 140–43.

46 Mew and Humphris, *Raupo to Deco*, 353–54.

47 Eleanor Holmes (comp.), *Robert Lamb FRIBA: The Napier Years 1879 to 1895* (Self-published, 2002).

48 Mew and Humphris, *Raupo to Deco*, 155–56.

49 Platts, *Nineteenth Century New Zealand Artists*, 68; Garry J Burns, *Frederick de Jersey Clere 1856–1972: Man, Churchman, Architect* (Upper Hutt: self-published, 1979); Susan McLean, *Architect of the Angels: The Churches of Frederick de Jersey Clere* (Wellington: Steele Roberts, 2003); Mew and Humphris, *Raupo to Deco*, 73–74, 236; Mew and Humphris, *Architects at the Apex*, 72–76.

50 Mew and Humphris, *Raupo to Deco*, 206–07.

51 Wellington City Council, 'Atkins & Bacon', https://wellingtoncityheritage.org.nz/architects/atkins-and-bacon

52 Elizabeth Cox, *Making Space: A History of New Zealand Women in Architecture* (Auckland: Massey University Press, 2022), 34–37; Mew and Humphris, *Raupo to Deco*, 327.

53 'Obituary: A H Mitchell', *Journal of the NZIA* 40, no. 6 (June 1973).

54 'Thomas Harvey James', in *Cyclopedia of New Zealand (Wellington Provincial District)*.

55 'Ernest Larcombe', in Nancy Smith, *And So We Began: A History of the Perrin Family of Palmerston North and Notes on Other Early Settlers* (Palmerston North: self-published, 1971); Mew and Humphris, *Raupo to Deco*, 335–56.

56 Mew and Humphris, *Raupo to Deco*, 89–91.

57 Ibid., 164–65; Wellington City Council, 'Penty and Blake', www.wellingtoncityheritage.org.nz/architects/penty-and-blake

58 www.natlib.govt.nz/records/22360539

59 Mew and Humphris, *Raupo to Deco*, 365–56; Mew and Humphris, *Architects at the Apex*, 136–39; John Wilson, 'Maddison, Joseph Clarkson', *Dictionary of New Zealand Biography*, first published in 1993. Te Ara – the Encyclopedia of New Zealand, https://teara.govt.nz/en/biographies/2m25/maddison-joseph-clarkson.

60 Mew and Humphris, *Architects at the Apex*, 181–84; Jonathan Mane-Wheoki, 'Strouts, Frederick', *Dictionary of New Zealand Biography*, first published in 1993. Te Ara – the Encyclopedia of New Zealand, https://teara.govt.nz/en/biographies/2s49/strouts-frederick

61 Canterbury Museum, 'Macdonald Dictionary Record: John Whitelaw', https://collection.canterburymuseum.com/objects/718683/macdonald-dictionary-record-john-whitelaw

62 *Tekapo Buildings*, Heritage New Zealand Register #3163, www.heritage.org.nz/the-list

63 See Brodrick's biography at Alexandra Buildings, Heritage New Zealand Register #2523, www.heritage.org.nz/the-list

64 'Drawn to our Attention', *Otago Daily Times*, 11 December 2017; Mew and Humphris, *Architects at the Apex*, 172–75; Hocken Collections, 'Salmond Anderson Architects: Records', https://hocken.recollect.co.nz/nodes/view/60921

65 Auckland City Council, 'Historic Heritage Evaluation: Greenlee (former)', 27 February 2017, www.aucklandcouncil.govt.nz/UnitaryPlanDocuments/pc7-02818-greenlee.pdf

66 'Obituary: William Gray Young', *Journal of the NZIA* 28, no. 1 (June 1962); 'Death: Hubert Conrad Morton', *Home & Building* 27 (May 1965); Mew and Humphris, *Raupo to Deco*, 213–15; Mew and Humphris, *Architects at the Apex*, 231–35.

67 'Michael Fowler', *Home & Building* 34 (September 1971) and *Home & Building* 37 (July/August 1974); 'Calder Fowler Styles & Turner', *Home & Building*, no. 1 (1980); Mew and Humphris, *Raupo to Deco*, 344, 360.

68 Auckland War Memorial Museum, 'John Wordsworth Standish', www.aucklandmuseum.com/war-memorial/online-cenotaph/record/88540; 'Accidental Death of Architect', *Upper Hutt Leader*, 14 October 1964.

69 G. Kemble Welch, *Doctor Smith: Hokianga's King of the North* (Auckland: Blackwood and Janet Paul, 1965); Frank Rogers, 'Smith, George Marshall McCall', *Dictionary of New Zealand Biography*, first published in 1998. Te Ara – the Encyclopedia of New Zealand, https://teara.govt.nz/en/biographies/4s32/smith-george-marshall-mccall

70 Mew and Humphris, *Architects at the Apex*, 63–66; *Biographical Dictionary of British and Irish Architects 1800–1950* (ARNet Design Research Publications).

71 Linda Tyler, 'Brown, Vernon Akitt', *Dictionary of New Zealand Biography*, first published in 2000. Te Ara – the Encyclopedia of New Zealand, https://teara.govt.nz/en/biographies/5b48/brown-vernon-akitt

72 *Auckland Star*, 22 December 1902, 4.

73 'Obituary: John Willing Warren', *Journal of the NZIA* 15, no. 2 (June 1936).

74 See West's biography at *Patterson's Buildings*, Heritage New Zealand Register #7765, www.heritage.org.nz/the-list

75 'The Architectural Legacy of John D. Healy', *Taranaki Daily News*, 22 June 2019.

76 See Sanderson's biography at *Holy Trinity Church (Anglican)*, Heritage New Zealand Register #893, www.heritage.org.nz/the-list

77 Puke Ariki, 'Horace Victor Samuel Griffiths', https://collection.pukeariki.com/persons/4151/horace-victor-samuel-griffiths

78 Ian Pritchard, *Frank Messenger: Architect: The Work of a New Plymouth Architect* (New Plymouth: self-published, 1994); Mew and Humphris, *Raupo to Deco*, 366.

79 Mew and Humphris, *Raupo to Deco*, 326; Gisborne District Council, https://cemeterysearch.gdc.govt.nz/detail/TARUHERU-24732

80 Mark Southcombe and Wendy Pettigrew, *The End of the Golden Weather: Whanganui Architects in the 1930s*, paper presented at the New Zealand Architecture in the 1980s Symposium, Victoria University of Wellington, November 2006.

81 Mew and Humphris, *Raupo to Deco*, 368; Mew and Humphris, *Architects at the Apex*, 214–17.

82 Manawatu District Council, 'Heritage Inventory: Feilding Town Centre', www.mdc.govt.nz/__data/assets/pdf_file/0022/11578/Heritage-Inventory-Feilding-Town-Centre.pdf; Margaret Tate, *The Houses of Bernard Cox* (Palmerston North: New Zealand Historic Places Trust, Manawatu Branch, 2001), www.historicmanawatuhorowhenua.org.nz/Downloads/BernardCoxBook.pdf

83 Mew and Humphris, *Raupo to Deco*, 188–89.

84 Manwatu Heritage, 'Robert Edwards, Mayor', https://manawatuheritage.pncc.govt.nz/item/5eba2f4e-33b3-4232-8cbb-1975f4a586e1

85 Mew and Humphris, *Raupo to Deco*, 365.

86 *Bush Advocate*, 23 September 1905, 6.

87 Mew and Humphris, *Raupo to Deco*, 368.

88 Ibid., 363.

89 *The Architectural Heritage of Christchurch: 8. The Legacy of Thomas Edmonds* (Christchurch: Christchurch City Council Environmental Policy and Planning Unit, 1993).

90 Martin, *Built for Us*, 114–53; 'Obituary: John Thomas Mair', *Journal of the NZIA* 26, no. 10 (November 1959); Mew and Humphris, *Raupo to Deco*, 197–98; *A Brief History of Public Buildings in New Zealand*.

91 Martin, *Built for Us*, 154–59.

92 Ibid., 160–83.

93 Peter Richardson, 'Sheppard, Fergus George Frederick', *Dictionary of New Zealand Biography*, first published in 2022. Te Ara – the Encyclopedia of New Zealand, https://teara.govt.nz/en/biographies/6s8/sheppard-fergus-george-frederick

94 Mew and Humphris, *Raupo to Deco*, 123–25; Mew and Humphris, *Architects at the Apex*, 82–85; Martin E. McCarthy, 'The Haughton Partnership: An Historical Review 1879 to 1951' (BArch Report, Victoria University of Wellington, Wellington, 1982), 29–30, 33, 46, 65, 103–08.

95 Mew and Humphris, *Raupo to Deco*, 134–35; McCarthy, 'The Haughton Partnership', 46, 58.

96 Mew and Humphris, *Raupo to Deco*, 262–63; McCarthy, 'The Haughton Partnership', 75, 105, 137.

97 'William J McKeon', *Journal of the NZIA* 29, no. 9 (October 1962); 'McKeon & Patience', *Journal of the NZIA* (1964); William J. McKeon, *The Fruitful Years: A Cavalcade of Memories* (Wellington: self-published, 1971); 'Obituary: William J McKeon', *Journal of the NZIA* 40, no. 6 (June 1973); 'William John McKeon, 1896–1973', *Home & Building* 35 (May 1973); Mew and Humphris, *Raupo to Deco*, 235–36.

98 McCarthy, 'The Haughton Partnership', 160, 203–04; 'R B Haughton', *Home & Building* 32 (June 1969); 'R. B. Haughton, *Journal of the NZIA* 39, no. 6 (June 1972).

99 'J. Lindsay Mair: Award of Honour', *Journal of the NZIA* 38, no. 4 (April 1971); McCarthy, 'The Haughton Partnership', 161.

100 Mew and Humphris, *Raupo to Deco*, 183–85, 272–73.

101 'William Henry Gummer', *Journal of the NZIA* 34, no. 3 (March 1967); 'W H Gummer', *Home & Building* 31 (January 1969); Andrew Barrie and Julia Gatley, 'Gummer & Ford 1: Public Buildings, Itinerary No. 7', *Block*, the Broadsheet of the Auckland Branch of the NZIA, no. 9 (2007); Paul Waite, *In the Beaux-Arts Tradition: William Gummer Architect* (Napier: Hawke's Bay Cultural Trust, 2005); Mew and Humphris, *Architects at the Apex*, 100–06.

102 'Obituary: Ford, Charles Reginald', *Journal of the NZIA*39, no. 6 (June 1972); Mew and Humphris, *Architects at the Apex*, 100–06.

103 Mew and Humphris, *Raupo to Deco*, 364.

104 *Griffin House (Former)*, Heritage New Zealand Register #1573, www.heritage.org.nz/the-list

105 Ian J. Lochhead, 'Seager, Samuel Hurst', *Dictionary of New Zealand Biography*, 1993; Mew and Humphris, *Raupo to Deco*, 367; Mew and Humphris, *Architects at the Apex*, 176; Lochhead, 'Seager, Samuel Hurst'.

106 Ruth M. Helms, 'Wood, Cecil Walter', *Dictionary of New Zealand Biography*, 1993; Mew and Humphris, *Architects at the Apex*, 225–30.

107 Heulwen Mary Roberts, 'Architect of Empire: Joseph Fearis Munnings 1897–1937' (MA thesis, University of Canterbury, Christchurch, 2013); Mew and Humphris, *Raupo to Deco*, 345, 363.

108 'W. B. Armson', *Home & Building* (August/September 1983); Mew and Humphris, *Architects at the Apex*, 28–31.

109 Mew and Humphris, *Architects at the Apex*, 77–81.

110 Platts, *Nineteenth Century New Zealand Artists*, 118; University of Canterbury, 'Richard Dacre Harman (1859–1927)', www.canterbury.ac.nz/about-uc/

what-we-do/uc-in-the-community/exhibitions-and-collections/canterbury-college/perspective/richard-dacre-harman
111 University of Canterbury, 'Learning by Design: Building Canterbury College in the City 1873–1973', https://www.canterbury.ac.nz/about-uc/what-we-do/uc-in-the-community/exhibitions-and-collections/canterbury-college
112 South Canterbury Museum, https://museum.timaru.govt.nz/explore/scroll/profile?id=3450
113 Timaru Civic Trust, 'James Turnbull', www.timarucivictrust.co.nz/blog/james-turnbull; Timaru District Council, Historic Heritage Item Doc #1304495, https://www.timaru.govt.nz/__data/assets/pdf_file/0004/673933/Historic-Heritage-Assessment-Report-HHI111-Former-Temuka-Library,-Plunket-Society-and-WCTU-Rest-Room-Category-B.pdf
114 'Obituary: Henry McDowell Smith', *Journal of the NZIA* 32, no. 2 (March 1965): 75; Mew and Humphris, *Raupo to Deco*, 368.
115 Wellington City Council, 'Hislop and Walden', https://wellingtoncityheritage.org.nz/architects/hislop-and-walden
116 Mew and Humphris, *Raupo to Deco*, 293–95; *Architects at the Apex*, 23–27.
117 Mew and Humphris, *Architects at the Apex*, 222–24.
118 New Zealand Institute of Architects, 'Templeton Chapel of the Holy Family (1966)', www.nzia.co.nz/awards/local/award-detail/6965
119 NZ History, 'Tibor Donner', https://nzhistory.govt.nz/people/tibor-donner
120 See Farrell's biography at *Green Lane Hospital*, Heritage New Zealand Register #4536, www.heritage.org.nz/the-list
121 'Orchard & Allison', *Home & Building* 29 (June 1966); 'New Hall for Christ's College, Christchurch', *Building Progress* 32, no. 11 (November 1967).
122 Lost Property, 'Henderson & Wheeler', www.lostproperty.org.nz/architects/henderson-wheeler/
123 Karangahape Road, 'George Court & Sons Department Store', www.karangahaperoad.com/george-courts-dept-store
124 'Obituary, Gordon Smith Architect', *Architecture New Zealand* 3 (May–June 2010).
125 Matthews & Matthews Architects Ltd, *Rotorua Central Area: Built Heritage Study* (Rotorua: Rotorua District Council, 2007), 94.
126 University of Auckland, 'Charles Harold Donaldson Porter, ca 1926–1957', https://archives.library.auckland.ac.nz/repositories/3/archival_objects/142589
127 'Lewis Walker', *Journal of the NZIA* 34, no. 4 (April 1967); 'Walker Co-Partnership', *Journal of the NZIA* 38, no. 8 (August 1971); Walker Group Architects, https://walker.co.nz/about
128 Laura Kellaway, 'Simplicity of Form: A Tale of Two Cathedrals and Interiors Lost', *AHA: Architectural History Aotearoa* 19 (2002): 122–38.
129 'Obituary: Christopher John Rodney (Rod) Smith (1933–2023)', NZIA, 4 April 2023; Matthew Grant, 'Rod Smith – Architect', Itinerary No. 51, *Block*, the Broadsheet of the Auckland Branch of the NZIA, no. 1 (2018).
130 Andrew Barrie and Miro Sumich, *Northland, Whāngarei and the Far North,* Map 11, *Block*, the Broadsheet of the Auckland Branch of the NZIA.
131 University of Auckland, https://archives.library.auckland.ac.nz/repositories/3/top_containers/8933?&page=13
132 See information on Belchambers Low at *Wanganui Collegiate School*, Heritage New Zealand Register #9620, www.heritage.org.nz/the-list
133 Tim Shoebridge, *The Good Citizen: A Life of C E Daniell of Masterton* (Masterton: Fraser Books, 2009); Trevor H. Daniell, *The Daniell Family of Masterton NZ: 1880–1980* (Masterton: self-published, 1980); Mew and Humphris, *Raupo to Deco*, 363.
134 Mew and Humphris, *Raupo to Deco*, 171–72, 296, 332; *Architects at the Apex*, 86–88.
135 Mew and Humphris, *Raupo to Deco*, 309, 365; *Architects at the Apex*, 132–35.
136 Toi Moroki Centre of Contemporary Art, https://coca.org.nz/history; Christchurch City Council, 'District Plan – Listed Heritage Place Heritage Assessment – Statement of Significance, Heritage Item Number 1354', https://districtplan.ccc.govt.nz/Images/DistrictPlanImages/Statement%20of%20Significance/Central%20City/HID%201354.pdf.
137 Ashburton Museum Blog, 'The Billy Thomas Archive', https://ashburtonmuseum.wordpress.com/2016/10/14/the-billy-thomas-archive
138 Andrew Barrie, 'Peter Beaven 1: The 60s and 70s', Itinerary No. 24, *Block*, the Broadsheet of the Auckland Branch of the NZIA, no. 7 (2009).
139 Owen Wiles MacDonald on Auckland Museum Online Cenotaph; 'Owen Wiles MacDonald', *The Press*, 14 November 1941.
140 Mew and Humphris, *Raupo to Deco*, 366.
141 'Buildings and Old Vehicles Life's Passion: Bob Oakley', *Otago Daily Times*, 13 February 2021.
142 'Miller White & Dunn', *Journal of the NZIA* 35, no. 5 (May 1968).
143 'Allingham & Harrison', *Journal of the NZIA* 39, no. 4 (April 1972).
144 'Gray Hesselin & Baxter', *Home & Building*, no. 3 (1979) and *Home & Building*, no. 3 (1981); 'Alexander Reko (Mick) Hesselin 1936–2022', obituary, Te Kahui Whaihanga New Zealand Institute of Architects, 2022; 'Architect Leaves Design Legacy', *Southland Times*, 17 November 2010.
145 Lost Property, 'Mark Brown Fairhead', www.lostproperty.org.nz/architects/mark-brown-fairhead
146 'Obituary: Patterson, Daniel Boys', *Journal of the NZIA* 29, no. 6 (July 1962); Karangahape Road Business Association, www.karangahaperoad.com/heritage
147 See the Guthries' biographies at *Christchurch Boys' High School (Main Block)*, Heritage New Zealand Register #3658, www.heritage.org.nz/the-list
148 See Harman's Biography at *Cashmere Hills Presbyterian Church*, Heritage New Zealand Register #1842, www.heritage.org.nz/the-list
149 Mew and Humphris, *Architects at the Apex*, 39–41.
150 Lost Property, 'Cutter Thorpe Pickmere Douglas', www.lostproperty.org.nz/architects/cutter-thorpe-pickmere-douglas; *Architects' Office: Thorpe Cutter Pickmere Douglas: 115 Vincent Street Auckland* (Auckland: University of Auckland, School of Architecture, 1970); Andrew Barrie, 'Thorpe Cutter Pickmere Douglas', *Block*, the Broadsheet of the Auckland Branch of the NZIA, no. 5 (2007); Public Art Heritage, 'Cutter Pickmere Thorpe & Douglas', https://publicart.nz/organisation/cutter-pickmere-thorpe-&-douglas
151 'Thomas Fitzroy Haughey', *Journal of the NZIA* 38, no. 5 (May 1971); *New Zealand Gazette*, 13 May 1976, www.nzlii.org/nz/other/nz_gazette/1976/53.pdf
152 'John Alfred Duffill', *Journal of the NZIA* 34, no. 10 (October 1967); Graeme Laurenson, *Burrafirth: The Family of Graeme and Marjorie Laurenson* (New Plymouth: Burrafirth, 1982), 91; 'Graeme Laurenson', *Journal of the NZIA* 30 (1963); Mew and Humphris, *Raupo to Deco*, 363.
153 'Graeme Laurenson & Associates', *Home & Building* 24 (February 1962); *Home & Building* 25 (May 1963); *Home & Building* 34 (September 1971); 'Band Stalwart's Legacy Lives in Taranaki Buildings', *Taranaki Daily News,* 1 January 2013.
154 'Obituary: Herbert Eric Phillips', *Journal of the NZIA*, no. 2 (1980).
155 'Horace Massey', *Home & Building* 31 (April 1969); *Interview with Ron Beatson*, National Library OHInt-0308-09, 10 November 1992; CPRW Architects. www.cprw.co.nz/practice/#history; 'Curtis Penman Read Williams', *Home & Building* 39, no. 3 (1976); Mew and Humphris, *Architects at the Apex*, 149–52.
156 Kerry Francis, 'Temperate Modernity: The Whangārei Architecture of Alfred Morgan in the 1930s', in Christine McCarthy (ed.), *New Zealand Architecture in the 1930s* (Wellington: Victoria University of Wellington, 2006); Sarah Cox, 'Taming the big, beautiful and often unwieldy: Exploring arrangement and description of architectural archives, a case study' (Victoria University of Wellington, 2017), https://ir.wgtn.ac.nz/items/7816f34c-3cc9-4403-bd41-a2078d0334e0
157 'Harold G Davies', *Journal of the NZIA* 33, no. 6 (June 1966); 'Obituary: Harold G Davies', *Journal of the NZIA* 43, no. 2 (April 1976).
158 Mew and Humphris, *Raupo to Deco*, 364.
159 'Neville Kennedy Norwell', interview on Knowledge Bank, Hawke's Bay Digital Archives Trust, 2014; 'New Banner but Faith is Kept', *Hawke's Bay Today*, 10 October 2000.
160 Peter Kitchin, 'Ardent Architect Helped Shape Post-War Capital', obituary for Lewis Edouard Martin, *Dominion Post*, 8 June 2013; Lewis E. Martin, *Buildings to Enjoy* (Palmerston North: Dunmore Press, 1995).
161 'Mr D G Porter Honoured by Planners', *Evening Post*, 14 February 1976, 14; Peter Kitchin, 'Architect Changed Face of the City', *Evening Post*, 5 March 1998, 9.
162 Allott Gabites, *Monkey's Birthday: Recollections of a World War II Airman* (Self-published, 2000).
163 'Obituary: Maurice Patience', *Architecture New Zealand* (January/February 1988); Mew and Humphris, *Raupo to Deco*, 347.
164 Stephen Stratford (ed.), *William Alington, James Beard, William Toomath, Derek Wilson: 4 Architects 1950–1980*, A4 NZ Architects Monograph Series (Auckland: New Zealand Architecture Publications Trust, 2010), 74–75.
165 Ibid., 32–33.
166 'Local Companies Lead the Way in Traffic Software', Scoop, 26 May 2006; Stantec, https://www.stantec.com/nz
167 'Hall-Kenney & Partners', *Journal of the NZIA* 36, no. 7 (July 1969) and *Journal of the NZIA* 37, no. 8 (August 1970).
168 John Shaw, *Sir Arthur Stephenson, Australian Architect* (Sydney: Stephenson & Turner, 1987).
169 Philip Goad, Rowan Wilken and Julie Willis, *Australian Modern: The Architecture of Stephenson & Turner* (Melbourne: The Miegunyah Press, 2004), 2–5.
170 Ibid., 3–5, 22.
171 *Stephenson & Turner 1920–1970: Our Contribution Lies in the Fields of Health, Commerce, Industry, Education, Housing* (Melbourne: Stephenson & Turner, 1971); Geoff Land, 'Stephenson & Turner in New Zealand', in *Stephenson & Turner* (Auckland: Balasoglou Books, 2006), 132.
172 Mew and Humphris, *Raupo to Deco*, 200–01; Mew and Humphris, *Architects at the Apex*, 159–62; Guy K. Natusch, 'Natusch, Charles Tilleard', *Dictionary of New Zealand Biography*, Vol. 3 (Auckland: Auckland University Press and Department of Internal Affairs, 1996), 356–57.
173 Rene Natusch, 'Natusch & Sons', *Journal of the NZIA* 30, no. 6 (July 1963): 98–107.
174 Auckland War Memorial Museum, 'Stanley Natusch',

www.aucklandmuseum.com/war-memorial/online-cenotaph/record/C51636

175 'Fair Honest Perfectionist: Hawke's Bay Architect Guy Natusch Remembered as "Absolute Gentleman"', *Stuff*, 31 October 2020.

176 'Natusch Wilcox and Natusch Shattky', *Journal of the NZIA* 38, no. 2 (February 1971); 'Natusch Shattky & Co', *Home & Building*, no. 2 (1980).

177 'McArthur & Reeve', *Journal of the NZIA* 33, no. 3 (March 1966); 'McArthur & Reeve', *Journal of the NZIA* 36, no. 3 (March 1969); 'McArthur & Reeve', *Home & Building*, no. 3 (1979); Mew and Humphris, *Raupo to Deco*, 276–78.

178 David Sayers, *The Goodwill Years: The Remarkable Story of a Professional Partnership* (Hamilton: SFT Books, 2011), 8–9.

179 AECOM, https://aecom.com/about-us

180 'First 100 Years is Only the Beginning for Beca', *New Zealand Herald*, 6 March 2020.

181 Andrew and Claire Brickell (comp.), *Goulden: An Account of the Wanderings of a New Zealand Civil Engineer, 1908–48 and Beyond: At Home and Abroad/ Part Autobiography by Richard Goulden Brickell MICE MNZIS, Wing Commander RAF and RNZAF; with Additions Covering Earlier and Later Times* (Self-published, 2020).

182 Ian Reynolds, 'Kingston Reynolds Thom & Allardice', *Journal of the NZIA* 42, no. 4 (April 1975) and *Journal of the NZIA* 55 (July/August 1988); Brenda Lobb, 'KRTA – A Commitment to Design', *Architecture New Zealand* (July/August 1988).

183 *New Territory / Warren & Mahoney / 50 Years of New Zealand Architecture* (Auckland: Balasoglou Books, 2005); Andrew Barrie, 'Warren & Mahoney in Christchurch 1', Itinerary No. 15, *Block*, the Broadsheet of the Auckland Branch of the NZIA, no. 7 (2008).

Practice histories

1 David Sayers, *The Goodwill Years: The Remarkable Story of a Professional Partnership: Gillman Garry Clapp & Sayers* (Hamilton: SFT Books, 2011), 8, 10.

2 Sayers, The Goodwill Years, 10.

3 David Sayers, Interview with Fiona Corcoran, part of *Back to the Drawing Board*, Hamilton Architects' Oral History Project 1999.

4 'Gillman Partners', Notice in *Home & Building*, no. 3, 1981

5 New Civil Engineer, 'Guy Anson Maunsell (1884–1961)', www.newcivilengineer.com/archive/guy-anson-maunsell-1884-1961-11-11-1999

6 AECOM, https://aecom.com/about-us

7 APG Architects, https://apgarchitects.com/studio/about

8 Archaus, https://www.archaus.co.nz/about

9 Brian Mazlin, *Architecture by Devine: Erby Mazlin 1975–1995* (Sydney: Focus Publishing, 2008).

10 Julia Gatley, 'City Guide: Tairawhiti Gisborne', *Architecture New Zealand* (September/October 2021): 105–07; Architects 44, www.a44.co.nz

11 HDT, https://architecturehdt.co.nz/studio

12 Conrad Gargett, https://architectus.com.au/latest/architectus-and-conrad-gargett-merge-to-expand-national-design-capability/

13 *Architectus Bowes Clifford Thompson*, A4 NZ Architects Monograph Series (Auckland: New Zealand Architecture Publications Trust, 2004); Haig Beck and Jackie Cooper, *Architectus: Between Order and Opportunity* (Berkeley: ORO Editions, 2009); Architectus New Zealand, https://architectus.co.nz; Architectus Australia, https://architectus.com.au/

14 Aston Mitchell, https://www.ashtonmitchell.com/practice/

15 Andrew and Claire Brickell (compiled), *Goulden: An Account of the Wanderings of a New Zealand Civil Engineer, 1908-48 and Beyond: At Home and Abroad/ Part Autobiography by Richard Goulden Brickell MICE MNZIS, Wing Commander RAF and RNZAF; with Additions Covering Earlier and Later Times*, (Self-published, 2020)..

16 Aurecon, www.aurecongroup.com/about/aurecon-history

17 Babbage, https://www.babbage.co.nz/about/our-journey

18 Baker Garden, https://www.bakergarden.co.nz/

19 Keith Davies, *Beca - One Hundred Years* (Auckland: Penguin Random House, 2020), 20 -03.

20 Ibid., 28–30.

21 Ibid., 26–31.

22 Ibid., 34–36.

23 Ibid., 60–61, 88–89, 112.

24 Beca, https://www.beca.com/about-us

25 Michael Adams, *Bligh Voller Nield* (Brisbane: Bligh Voller Nield, 1998); Philip Drew, *Lawrence Nield* (Oxford: Oxford University Press, 2004); https://www.bvn.com.au/

26 Brewer Davidson, https://www.brewerdavidson.co.nz/about-us/

27 BSW Architects, https://www.bswarchitects.nz/the-practice

28 Buchan, https://buchan.au/buchan-history/; https://adb.anu.edu.au/biography/buchan-sir-john-32341

29 'Craig Craig Moller', *Journal of the NZIA* 40, no. 3 (March 1973); CCM, ccm.co.nz/practice

30 'Richard Hill', *Journal of the NZIA* (May/June 1989).

31 Chow:Hill, chowhill.co.nz/practice.

32 Clendon Burns & Park, https://www.cbp.co.nz/practice/

33 www.cosgroves.com/about-us

34 *ASC Architects* (Auckland: Balasoglou Books, 2009), 140 -41; Design Group, https://designgroup.co.nz; Design Group Stapleton Elliott, www.designgroupstapletonelliott.co.nz; Design Group Architects H + K, http://ahk.co.nz; Design Group ASC Architects, www.ascarchitects.co.nz; Wilson + Hill Architects, www.wilsonandhill.co.nz; Crosson Architects, https://crosson.co.nz

35 Destravis Group, https://www.destravis.com/about

36 'Dickson Elliot Lonergan', *Journal of the NZIA* (November/December 1988); DLA Architects, www.dla.co.nz/about

37 First Principles Architects, https://www.firstprinciplesarchitects.com/our-vision-1

38 Hawkins Architecture, https://www.hawkinsarchitecture.co.nz/about

39 Hawthorn Geddes, https://hawthorngeddes.co.nz/about-hawthorn-geddes/

40 HDR, www.hdrinc.com/about-us/history

41 'Rice Daubney Merge With Di Carlo Potts', *Architecture Australia*, 1 January 2004.

42 HPA, https://hpa.co.nz/index.php/about-us/

43 Ignite Architects, www.ignitearchitects.com/studio; Studio Design + Architecture, https://studioda.co.nz; Billard Leece, https://www.blp.com.au/about/

44 IKON, https://www.ikon.co.nz/about

45 KRTA', *Journal of the NZIA* (July/August 1988).

46 Andrew Barrie, 'KRTA in Auckland', Itinerary No 19, Block, the Broadsheet of the Auckland Brach of the NZIA, No 1, 2009.

47 'Morrison Cooper', *Journal of the NZIA* 37, no. 11 (November 1970).

48 Jacobs, 'Jacobs Completes Merger Transaction with Sinclair Knight Merz', www.jacobs.com/newsroom/press-release/jacobs-completes-merger-transaction-sinclair-knight-merz

49 Jacobs, www.jacobs.com/about

50 Stephen Stratford (ed), *Jasmax*, A4 New Zealand Architects Monograph Series, NZ, Architectural Publications Trust, Auckland, 2007, 8, 14.

51 'JASMaD', Notices in the Journal of the NZIA, Vol 34, No 8, August 1967, Vol 35, No 5, May 1968, and Vol 39, No 4, April 1972; 'JASMaD', Profile in the Journal of the NZIA, Vol 41, No 6, June 1974; Andrew Barrie and Julia Gatley, 'JASMaD in Auckland', Itinerary No 11, Block, the Broadsheet of the Auckland Branch of the NZIA, No 2, 2008.

52 Stratford, *Jasmax*, 8, 9, 302; Jasmax, jasmax.com/practice.

53 www.jensenhughes.com/pacific/new-zealand

54 Jigsaw, https://www.jigsawarchitects.nz/company

55 Johnstaff, www.johnstaff.com.au/about

56 Klein, https://www.klein.co.nz/studio; 'A Specialist Practice', Architecture New Zealand, November/December 2003, 58-62.

57 Marshall Day, https://marshallday.com/who-we-are

58 Andrew Barrie and Julia Gatley, 'Itinerary: Mason & Wales Dunedin, Architecture Now, 24 March 2022; https://www.masonandwales.com/about

59 'McCoy & Wixon', Notice in the Journal of the NZIA, Vol 34 No 5, May 1967; Ted McCoy, A Southern Architecture: The Work of Ted McCoy, Otago University Press, Dunedin 2007; Andrew Barrie and Julia Gatley, 'McCoy & Wixon: Public Buildings in the South', Itinerary No 10, Block, the Broadsheet of the Auckland Branch of the NZIA, Nos 9 and 10, 2009; 'Architects Engineers Partnership', Notices in the Journal of the NZIA, Vol 38 No 4, April 1971, and Vol 40 No 4, April 1973.

60 'Gray Hesselin & Baxter', Notices in Home & Building, No 3, 1979 and No 3, 1981; 'Alexander Reko (Mick) Hesselin 1936-2022', Obituary from Te Kahui Whaihanga New Zealand Institute of Architects, 2022; 'Architect Leaves Design Legacy', Southland Times, 17 November 2010

61 McKenzie Higham Architects, https://www.mckenziehigham.co.nz/news/mckenzie-higham-welcomes-bulleyment-fortune-architects/

62 Medispace, https://www.medispace.co.nz/about-us

63 Mode, www.modedesigncorp.com

64 NZCEL, https://nzcel.co.nz/our-history/

65 Pacific Environments, https://pacificenvironments.co.nz/about-2/; https://www.lostproperty.org.nz/architects/adams-dodd/

66 Pak Design, https://www.pakdesign.co.nz/

67 *Hospitals and Healthcare Establishments* (Sydney: Peddle Thorp Partnerships, 1975); *Peddle Thorp* (Sydney: Peddle Thorp, 1992); Doug Stace, *Patriarchs, Partners and Professionals: Peddle Thorp Expands Internationally: Case Study* (Sydney: Australian Graduate School of Management, University of New South Wales, 1996); Gina Smith, *Work, Play, Learn, Care, Live* (Brisbane: Peddle Thorp Architects, 2006); Peddlethorp, https://peddlethorp.co.nz/

68 Powell Fenwick, https://pfc.co.nz/our-story

69 'Sheppard & Rout', *Home & Building*, Number 3, 1982; 'Living in the Past and Future: Architect David Sheppard Takes Stock of a Life's Work', The Press, 2 December 2023; David Sheppard (ed), Sheppard & Rout Architects: Volume 1 1982-2021, Quentin Wilson Publishing, Christchurch, 2023.

70 STH, www.sth.com.au; Silver Thomas Hanley Architecture, www.silverthomashanley.com

71 Gabites Porter, https://www.forum8.co.jp/english/shokai/Tracks-e.htm

72 Stantec, https://www.stantec.com/en/about

73 Stephen Matthews Architects, https://www.smarchitects.co.nz/about-us

74 Stephenson & Turner 1920-1970: Our Contribution Lies in the Fields of Health, Commerce, Industry, Education, Housing, Stephenson & Turner, Melbourne, 1971; Philip Goad, Rowan Wilken and

Juile Willis, Australian Modern: The Architecture of Stephenson & Turner, Miegunyah Press – Melbourne University Publishing, Melbourne, 2004, 2-5; Geoff Land, 'Stephenson & Turner in New Zealand', in Stephenson & Turner, Balasoglou Books, Auckland, 2006, 132.

75 S&T The Next 100, Stephenson & Turner, 2022.

76 'Natusch Wilcox and Natusch Shattky', Notice in the Journal of the NZIA, Vol 38, No 2, February 1971; 'Natusch Shattky & Co', Notice in Home & Building, No 2, 1980.

77 Team Architects, https://www.teamarchitects.co.nz/about; https://www.teamarchitects.co.nz/talk/change-for-the-future-in-christchurch

78 BOON, https://www.boon.co.nz/about/our-story/

79 Tetra Tech, https://www.tetratech.com/about/our-company/

80 Thema, https://thema.co.nz/

81 Thinc, https://www.turnerandtownsend.com/news/major-project-management-acquisition-in-australia/; Australian Health Design Council, www.aushdc.org.au

82 Totem Studio Architects, previously Trengrove Architects Ltd 1922-2022 100 Years of New Zealand's Architectural History, Totem Studio Architects, Christchurch, 2022; 'From Trengrove to Totem', Architecture New Zealand, July/August 2022; https://www.totemstudio.co.nz/ourhistory

83 New Territory: Warren and Mahoney: 50 Years of New Zealand Architecture, Balasoglou Books, Auckland, 2005; 'Dental Nurses' Training School, Christchurch', Home & Building, Volume 23, June 1960.

84 wam.studio/practice.

85 Wilkie + Bruce, https://www.wilkieandbruce.co.nz/our-story

86 Wingates, https://www.wingatearchitects.com/practice

87 'Woods Bagot marks 150 years of practice', Architecture Australia, 19 August 2019.

88 WSP, www.wsp.com/en-nz/who-we-are/our-story

Selected bibliography

Angus, John H. *A History of the Otago Hospital Board and Its Predecessors.* Dunedin: Otago Hospital Board, 1984.

Armstrong, John. *Under One Roof: A History of Waikato Hospital.* Hamilton: Half Court Press, 2009.

Barber, Laurie H., and Roy J. Towers. *Wellington Hospital 1847–1976.* Wellington: Wellington Hospital Board, 1976.

Bennett, F. O. *Hospital on the Avon: The History of Christchurch Hospital 1862–1962.* Christchurch: North Canterbury Hospital Board, 1962.

Brown, Deidre. *Maori Architecture: From Fale to Wharenui and Beyond.* Auckland: Raupo, 2009.

Butterworth, Susan. *Hospital on a Hotspot: Queen Elizabeth Hospital, Rotorua.* Wellington: Ngaio Press, 2012.

Celebrating 100 Years of Innovation and Excellence — Tauranga Hospital 1914–2014. Tauranga: Bay of Plenty District Health Board, 2014.

Clement, Christine. *Hawera Hospital: 100 Years 1894–1994.* Hāwera: Hāwera Hospital Centennial Committee, 1994.

Conly, Geoff. *A Case History: The Hawke's Bay Hospital Board 1876–1989.* Napier: Hawke's Bay Area Health Board, 1992.

Cooke, Ron. *Patients First: The Proud Tradition of Taumarunui Hospital.* Taumarunui: Taumarunui Hospital Reunion Committee, 2005.

Cox, Elizabeth (ed.). *Making Space: A History of New Zealand Women in Architecture.* Auckland: Massey University Press, 2022.

Dow, Derek A. *Auckland's Hospitals: A Pictorial History 1847–2004.* Auckland: Auckland District Health Board, 2005.

Furness, J. G. *Wairau Hospital: 100 Years of Caring.* Blenheim: Marlborough Hospital Board, 1978.

History of the Southland Hospitals and Board: 1861–1968. Invercargill: Southland Hospital Board, 1968.

Hodges, T. D. *Mountain Town Hospital: The Story of the Stratford Public Hospital.* Stratford: Stratford Hospital Nurses' Reunion Committee, 1978.

Hutchinson, B. R. (ed.). *Green Lane Hospital: The First Hundred Years.* Auckland: Green Lane Hospital Centennial Committee, 1990.

Jordan, Cyril. *Masterton Hospital 1879–1979 Centennial Book Committee.* Masterton: Wairarapa Hospital Board, 1979.

Kellaway, Jo, and Mike Maryan. *A Century of Care: Palmerston North Hospital 1893–1993.* Double Bay, Australia: MidCentral Health and Focus Books, 1993.

Koller, Kristin. *A History of the New Plymouth Hospitals from 1967.* New Plymouth: TNL, 2003.

MacDonald, Wilson D. *A Hundred Years of Healing: Wellington Hospital 1847–1947.* Wellington: A. H. & A. W. Reed, 1947.

Mackenzie, Craig. *Hospital in the Valley.* Palmerston North: Dunmore Press, 1983.

McDonald, K. C. *A Century of Service: The History of the Oamaru Hospital.* Ōamaru: Waitaki Hospital Board, 1972.

McKenzie, John Campbell. *A History of Timaru Hospital.* Christchurch: Pegasus, 1974.

Menefy, Diana. *Whangarei Hospital: A Century of Service 1901–2001.* Whangārei: Northland Health Ltd, 2001.

Mew, Geoff. *Architects at the Apex: The Top 50 in New Zealand 1840–1940.* Martinborough: Ngaio Press, 2020.

— — — and Adrian Humphris. *Raupo to Deco: Wellington Styles and Architects 1840–1940.* Welington: Steele Roberts, 2014.

Murphy, Michael P. Jr, with Jeffrey Mansfield and the MASS Design Group. *The Architecture of Health: Hospital Design and the Construction of Dignity.* New York: Cooper Hewitt, Smithsonian Design Museum, 2021.

New Territory/Warren & Mahoney/50 Years of New Zealand Architecture. Auckland: Balasoglou Books, 2005.

Parker, Keith. *Kaitaia's Hospital: A Glimpse at Hospital Services and Volunteer Health Care in the Far North 1904–2004.* Kamo: Bridgewater, 2005.

Roche, Edward A., and Anthony H. G. Roche. *Green Lane Saga: Green Lane Hospital, Auckland 1889–1982.* Auckland: Ray Richards, 1983.

Sayers, David. *The Goodwill Years: The Remarkable Story of a Professional Partnership: Gillman Garry Clapp & Sayers.* Hamilton: SFT Books, 2011.

Scanlan, Arthur B. *Hospital on the Hill: A Centennial History of the New Plymouth Hospital 1867–1967.* New Plymouth: Taranaki Hospital Board, 1967.

Scott, David (ed.). *The Story of Auckland Hospital 1847–1977.* Auckland: Medical History Library Committee of the Royal Australasian College of Physicians in New Zealand, 1977.

— — — *Middlemore Memories: The First 50 Years of Middlemore Hospital.* Auckland: South Auckland Health, 1995.

Shearer, Ian. *Whakatane Hospital Te Whatumauri Hauora: A History.* Tauranga: Bay of Plenty District Health Board, 2011.

— — — and Rex E. Wright-St Clair. *A Century on Cameron Road: A History of Tauranga Hospital 1914–2014.* Tauranga: Bay of Plenty District Health Board, 2016.

Silverson, Alice (ed.). *The Last Thirty Years: The History of the Canterbury Area Health Board 1963–1993.* Christchurch: Canterbury Health, 1995.

Stephenson & Turner. Auckland: Balasoglou Books, 2006.

Stratford, Stephen (ed.). *Jasmax.* A4 New Zealand Architects Monograph Series. Auckland: New Zealand Architectural Publications Trust, 2007.

True Tales of Thames Hospital: 150 Years 1868–2018. Thames: Thames Hospital 150 Group, in collaboration with the Coromandel Heritage Trust, 2018.

Wedge, Georgina, and Peter Rothwell. *Waikato Hospital: Our Hospital, Your History.* Hamilton: Waikato Health Memorabilia Trust, 2016.

Williams, Wendy Hunter. *Out of Mind, Out of Sight: The Story of Porirua Hospital: Porirua Hospital Centennial 1887–1987.* Porirua: Porirua Hospital, 1987.

Williamson, Eulla. *The End of an Era 1964–1989: The Final Twenty-Five Years of Administration by the South Canterbury Hospital Board.* Timaru: Health South Canterbury, 1994.

Wright-St Clair, Rex E. *Caring for People: A History of the Wanganui Hospital Board.* Whanganui: Wanganui Hospital Board Centennial Celebration Committee, 1987.

— — — *From Cottage to Regional Base Hospital: Waikato Hospital 1887–1987.* Hamilton: Waikato Hospital Board, 1987.

Image credits

Page 11: National Library of Australia; **page 13 above**: National Library of Australia; **below:** *Home & Building*; **page 15:** Auckland Libraries Heritage Collections, NZG-18971002-0457-01; **page 17 above:** Alexander Turnbull Library, PUBL-0031-1836-81; **below:** Alexander Turnbull Library, A-196-023; **page 18 from top:** Alexander Turnbull Library, A-220-008-a; A. B. Scanlan, *Hospital on the Hill*; Auckland Libraries Heritage Collections, A07378; **page 19:** Auckland Libraries Heritage Collections, 5-1190 (M. Saunders); **page 20 left:** Auckland Libraries Heritage Collections, NZG-18971002-0457-01; **right**: Alexander Turnbull Library, 1/2-110423-F; **page 22 above:** Alexander Turnbull Library, 1/2-012453-F; **below:** Alexander Turnbull Library, 1/2-041832-F; **page 23:** Capital and Coast District Health Board; **page 24:** Whanganui District Health Board; **page 26:** Archives New Zealand, NM 8 51/606 Sep.36; **page 27:** Archives New Zealand, NM 8 51/821; **page 29:** Museum of New Zealand Te Papa Tongarewa, C.014031; **page 31:** Auckland Libraries Heritage Collections, 5-0928 (C. Heaphy); **page 32 above:** Geoff Conly, *A Case History*, **below:** Alexander Turnbull Library, 1/2-230730-G; **page 33 above:** F. O. Bennett, *Hospital on the Avon*; **below:** Christchurch City Libraries, CCL-KPCD13-0033; **page 34:** Winifred Norris, *The North Canterbury Hospital Board*; **page 35:** Lakes District Museum, EL0262; **page 36 above:** Alexander Turnbull Library, 1/2-050039-F; **below:** *Otago Witness*, 23 October 1907, Hocken Collections Uare Taoka o Hākena; **page 38:** J. W. Allen carte de visite, Hocken Collections Uare Taoka o Hākena, P2016-035/2-007; **page 39:** Stuff Media Ltd; **page 40:** Archives New Zealand, R22823322; **page 41:** Auckland Libraries Heritage Collections, AWNS-19060322-12-01; **page 42 clockwise from top left:** Peter Richardson, *An Architecture of Empire*; Te Ara – the Encyclopedia of New Zealand; Alexander Turnbull Library, PA1-o-038-29-2; **page 43:** Archives New Zealand, R25278190, R25278191; **page 44:** Alexander Turnbull Library, 1/4-034414-G; **page 45:** Auckland Libraries Heritage Collections, NZG-18980806-0165-01; **page 46:** A. C. Barker Collection, Canterbury Museum, 5279; **page 47:** Christchurch City Libraries, CCL-KPCD02-0013; **page 48 above:** Archives New Zealand, R18830755; **below:** Pencil & watercolour on paper, 675 x 1307mm, Hocken Collections Uare Taoka o Hākena; **page 49 left:** Hocken Collections Uare Taoka o Hākena; **right:** Tyree Studio Collection, Nelson Provincial Museum, 180386; **page 50:** Alexander Turnbull Library, 10X8-0155-G; **page 51:** Museum of New Zealand Te Papa Tongarewa, C.014031; **page 53:** Museum of New Zealand Te Papa Tongarewa, C.014294; **page 55:** Te Iho o Te Manawataki Library; **page 56:** Auckland Hospital and Charitable Aid Board Archive; **page 57:** Waikato Health Memorabilia Trust; **page 58 above:** Alexander Turnbull Library, 1/1-008373-G; **below:** Geoff Conly, *A Case History*; **page 59 above:** Wairarapa Archive, 97-25/609; **below:** C. J. Carle, *Masterton Hospital 1879–1979*; **page 60 above:** Alexander Turnbull Library, BB-2287-1/1-G; **below:** Wellington City Archives, 13459; **page 61 clockwise from top left:** Picton Museum; Tyree Studio Collection, Nelson Provincial Museum, 182298; Marlborough Historical Society; **page 62 above:** Museum of New Zealand Te Papa Tongarewa, C.014034; **below:** Museum of New Zealand Te Papa Tongarewa, C.014294; **page 63:** Museum of New Zealand Te Papa Tongarewa, O.034077; **page 64 clockwise from top left:** Alexander Turnbull Library, 1/2 001368 G; South Canterbury Museum, P1116; South Canterbury Museum, P7031; Burton Bros photograph, Canterbury Museum, 2018.74.62; **page 65:** Lakes District Museum, EL0077; **page 66:** Invercargill City Libraries and Archives, A0105 S27520001_091; **page 67:** Alexander Turnbull Library, 1/1-020487-G; **page 68 above:** Wellington City Libraries, 50003-2218; **below:** Christchurch City Libraries, CCL-KPCD12-0042: **page 69:** Alexander Turnbull Library, 1/1-025917-G; **page 71 clockwise from top left:** Hugh and G. K. Neill photograph, Hocken Collections Uare Taoka o Hākena, P1971-008/6-012; Auckland Libraries Heritage Collections, 35-R2119; Alexander Turnbull Library, 1/1-000132-G; Hawke's Bay Museums Trust, Ruawharo Tā-ū-rangi, 77517; **page 73:** Auckland Libraries Heritage Collections, 35-R1694; **page 75:** Alexander Turnbull Library, 1/2-026806-F; **page 76 above:** Auckland Libraries Heritage Collections, AWNS-19030924-03-02 (J. Smith); **below:** Northland Room Digital Collections; **page 77 above:** Auckland Hospital Board; **below:** Thames Museum, 2022.174.06; **page 78 clockwise from top left:** Suzanne Morgan, *Thames Hospital*; Alexander Turnbull Library, 1/2-000213-G; Thames Museum; Author's collection; **page 79:** Auckland Libraries Heritage Collections, 1-W1621; **page 80:** Rotorua Museum, OP-2453; **page 81 above:** Geoff Conly, *A Case History*; **below:** Auckland Libraries Heritage Collections, AWNS-19000629-04-01; **page 82 clockwise from top left:** Alexander Turnbull Library, 1/2-000223-G; *Gisborne Photo News*, Tairāwhiti Museum; Auckland Libraries Heritage Collections, AWNS-19010426-07-03; **page 83:** Hawke's Bay Museums Trust, Ruawharo Tā-ū-rangi, 4885; **page 84:** Alexander Turnbull Library, Plans-90-1116, Plans-90-1117; **page 85:** Bulleyment Fortune Archives, McKenzie Higham Architects; **page 86 above:** Alexander Turnbull Library, 1/1-016074-G; **below:** Auckland Libraries Heritage Collections, 35-R1694; **page 87:** Museum of New Zealand Te Papa Tongarewa, PS.001208; **page 88 clockwise from left:** Alexander Turnbull Library, 1/2-080890-F; Fielding Heritage; Stephanie Blatchford collection, Local History Room, Narromine Library, NSW; **page 89:** Patea Historical Society; **page 90:** Palmerston North City Library, 2011N_H3_004744, 2011N_H11_004746; **page 91:** Alexander Turnbull Library, 1/2-006705-G; **page 92 above:** Marlborough Historical Society; **below:** Palmerston North City Library, 2007P_Ot4_RTL_0844; **page 93:** Picton Museum; **page 94:** Wellington City Libraries, 50010-1028; **page 95:** Christchurch City Libraries, CCL-KPCD04-0002, CCL-KPCD08-0033; **page 96:** Auckland Libraries Heritage Collections, 35-R2116 (F. G. Radcliffe); **page 97:** Christchurch City Libraries, CCL-KPCD10-0099; **page 98:** Muir and Moodie postcard, Hocken Collections Uare Taoka o Hākena, Box-309-003; **page 99 above:** *Otago Daily Times*; **below:** Lakes District Museum, EL2667; **page 100:** Te Hikoi Museum, RI. P192.03.3611; **page 101:** Author's collection; **page 102:** Museum of New Zealand Te Papa Tongarewa, F.014655; **page 103 left:** Alexander Turnbull Library, PAColl 4166 07 001; **right:** Wairarapa Archive, 18-176/8; **page 104:** University of Otago Faculty of Consumer and Applied Sciences records, Hocken Collections Uare Taoka o Hākena, MS-4833/006/001; **page 105 above:** Auckland War Memorial Museum Tāmaki Paenga Hira, PH-RES-224; **below:** Auckland Libraries Heritage Collections, 1-W0450 (H. Winkelmann); **page 106:** Otago Daily Times; **page 107 clockwise from top left:** *Evening Post*; Christchurch City Libraries, CCL-KPCD05-0035; Alexander Turnbull Library, 1/1-018662-F; **page 108 from top:** Alexander Turnbull Library, 1/1-008612-G; *Wanganui Chronicle*; Tairāwhiti Museum, 2024.64.131; **page 109 above:** Collection of Te Kupeka

Tiaki Taoka – Southern Regional Collections Trust, gift of Mrs G. Dickson; **below:** Hocken Collections Uare Taoka o Hākena, P2019-049/1-017-001l; **page 110 clockwise from top left:** Alexander Turnbull Library, 1/1-016889-G; Joyce Powell, *A Suitable Job for Young Ladies*; Auckland Libraries Heritage Collections, 255A-110; **page 111 clockwise from top left:** Alexander Turnbull Library, PAColl-6497-12; Hocken Collections Uare Taoka o Hākena, MS-2920/1508/001; Alexander Turnbull Library, DW-1718-F; **page 113:** Hawke's Bay Museums Trust, Ruawharo Tā-ū-rangi, 99788; **page 115:** Alexander Turnbull Library, 1/2-034919-F; **page 116:** Alexander Turnbull Library, WA-45984; **page 117 above:** Northland Room Digital Collections; **below:** Northland District Health Board; **page 118:** Auckland Libraries Heritage Collections, 255A-R25-08 (F. C. McGehan); **page 119 above:** Author's collection; **below:** Auckland Libraries Heritage Collections, 1-W1648; **page 120 from top:** Museum of New Zealand Te Papa Tongarewa, O.036628; Ron Cooke, *Patients First*; Auckland Libraries Heritage Collections, Footprints 04543; **page 121:** Auckland Libraries Heritage Collections, 1-W1615; **page 122 above:** Auckland War Memorial Museum Tāmaki Paenga Hira; **below:** Alexander Turnbull Library, 1/2-045546-F; **page 123:** Historic Places Trust, *Historic Buildings of New Zealand*; **page 124:** Auckland Libraries Heritage Collections, AWNS-19031217-19-01; **page 125 above:** *New Zealand Herald*; **below:** Auckland Libraries Heritage Collections, AWNS-19261209-44-02; **page 126:** Tauranga City Libraries; **page 127 above:** Whakatane Museum, P911; **below:** Western Bay of Plenty Community Archives; **page 128 clockwise from left:** Alexander Turnbull Library, 1/1-012438-G; Puke Ariki; Swainson's Studio, Puke Ariki; **page 129:** Puke Ariki, GNF828; **page 130 above:** Gisborne Photo News, Tairāwhiti Museum; **below:** Auckland Libraries Heritage Collections, RSU-N-0023 (D. N. Sunde); **page 131:** Hawke's Bay Museums Trust, Ruawharo Tā-ū-rangi, 77563, 99788; **page 132:** Auckland Libraries Heritage Collections, AWNS-19230607-40-02; **page 133 above:** Hawke's Bay Museums Trust, Ruawharo Tā-ū-rangi, 81950; **below:** Auckland Libraries Heritage Collections, NZG-19090505-0021-01 (E. Denton); **page 134:** Palmerston North City Library, Benjamin Foster; **page 135:** Jo Kellaway and Mike Maryan, *A Century of Care*; **page 136:** New Zealand Historic Places Trust Collection, Canterbury Museum, 2017.79.1984; **page 137:** Author's collection; **page 139 clockwise from top left:** *Evening Post*; Archives New Zealand, R24738278; Ministry of Works; **page 140 from top:** Ministry of Works; *New Zealand Herald*; Edwards Collection (ME2), Architecture Archive, Special Collections, University of Auckland; **page 141 above:** Christchurch City Libraries, CCL-StarP-00917A; **below:** Ministry of Works; **page 143:** Wellington City Libraries, 50010-1076; **page 145 above:** Alexander Turnbull Library, 1/2-086078-F; **below:** Marlborough Historical Society; **page 146 clockwise from left:** Wellington City Libraries, 50010-1026; Victoria University of Wellington; *Home & Building*; **page 147:** Stuff Media Ltd; **page 149:** Author's collection; **page 150:** *Journal of the NZIA*; **page 151:** Wellington City Libraries, 50010-1076; **page 152:** *Journal of the NZIA*; **page 153:** Author's collection; **page 154:** Bulleyment Fortune Archives, McKenzie Higham Architects; **page 155 above:** Capital and Coast District Health Board; **below:** Author's collection; **page 156:** Auckland Libraries Heritage Collections, AWNS-19160224-47-01; **page 157 clockwise from top left:** Te Ara – the Encyclopedia of New Zealand; Rotorua Museum, OP-812; Alexander Turnbull Library, 1/1-014614-G; **page 158:** Otaki Historical Society; **page 160:** Robert Crawford, *Too Good to Last*; **page 161:** Christchurch City Libraries; **page 163:** Gore Historical Museum; **page 165 above:** Marlborough Historical Society; **below:** Marlborough Historical Society; **page 166:** Marlborough Historical Society; **below:** Hargreaves Collection, Nelson Provincial Museum, 8440; **page 167:** Auckland Libraries Heritage Collections, AWNS-19331129-44-06 (A. R. Kingsford); **page 168:** Christchurch City Libraries, CCL-Arch887-066; **page 169 clockwise from left:** *Journal of the NZIA*; Alexander Turnbull Library, 1/1-022268-G; Christchurch City Libraries, CCL-Arch887-065; **page 170:** Christchurch City Libraries, CCL-Arch887-051; **page 171:** Fletcher Archives; **page 172:** VC Browne & Son, 2952-2978; **page 173:** Winifred Norris, *The North Canterbury Hospital Board*; **page 174:** Christchurch City Libraries, CCL-StarP-00922A; **page 175:** Archives New Zealand, R24738566; **page 176 above:** Winifred Norris, *The North Canterbury Hospital Board*; **below:** Luke Tremlett, *Medical Buildings and Medical Theory*; **page 177:** J. C. McKenzie, *A History of Timaru Hospital*; **page 178 above:** *Home & Building*; below: South Canterbury District Health Board; **page 179 above:** Stuff Media Ltd; **below:** South Canterbury District Health Board; **page 180:** Waitaki Archive, 104915; **page 181:** Author's collection; **page 182:** Guy Morris photograph, Hocken Collections Uare Taoka o Hākena, P2014-014/3-068; **page 183 above:** Lloyd photograph, Hocken Collections Uare Taoka o Hākena, Box-233-010; **below:** University of Otago Medical School Alumnus Association records, Hocken Collections Uare Taoka o Hākena, MS-1537/637/001; **page 184:** Gore Historical Museum; **page 185 above:** Southern District Health Board; **below:** Hocken Collections Uare Taoka o Hākena, P1990-015/49-321; **page 186:** Te Awamutu Museum, PH3555; **page 187:** Stuff Media Ltd; **page 188:** *Nelson Photo News*; **page 189:** Christchurch City Libraries, CCL-Star-1970-0236-036-041N-02; **page 190 from top:** *New Zealand Herald*; Spectrum Care; Archives New Zealand, AAQT 6539 A29, 455; **page 192:** Alexander Turnbull Library, PAColl-0434-06; **page 193:** Bob Baird, *Lake Alice Hospital*; **page 195:** Archives New Zealand, R24730613; **page 197:** Alexander Turnbull Library, WA-44295; **page 199:** Ministry of Works; **page 200:** Archives New Zealand, R24730613; **page 201:** Auckland Libraries Heritage Collections, 653-143; **page 202 above:** Archives New Zealand, R21010732; **below:** Alexander Turnbull Library, WA-32994a-F; **page 203 above:** Auckland Hospital, *The Road Back to Normal Living*; **below:** *Home & Building*, Volume 40, Number 1979, Alexander Turnbull Library, Per NZ HOM; **page 204:** Author's collection; **page 205:** Tauranga City Libraries Pae Korokī; **page 206 above:** *Home & Building*; **below:** Hamilton City Libraries, HCL_10741; **page 207:** David Sayers, *The Goodwill Years*; **page 208:** Waikato Health Memorabilia Trust; **page 210:** *Rotorua Daily Post*; **page 211:** Rotorua Museum, OP-4776; **page 212:** Susan Butterworth, *Hospital on a Hotspot*; **page 213:** MidCentral District Health Board; **page 214:** *Home & Building*; **page 215:** Masters Hall; **page 216:** Ministry of Works; **page 217:** Christchurch City Libraries, courtesy Margaret Rusbatch; **page 218 above:** Ashburton Museum & Historical Society Inc. Collection, 04.2004.0067q; **below:** Eulla Williamson, *The End of an Era 1964–1989*; **page 219:** J. C. McKenzie, *A History of Timaru Hospital*; **page 220:** South Canterbury Museum, P2003/023.085; **page 221:** Stuff Media Ltd; **page 223 above:** Author's collection; **below:** *Otago Daily Times*; **page 224 above:** *Journal of the NZIA*; **below:** University of Otago Medical School Alumnus

Association records, Hocken Collections Uare Taoka o Hākena, MS-1537/665; **page 225:** Patrick Reynolds; **page 226:** Clutha Heritage; **page 227:** Invercargill City Council Archives; **page 228 from top:** Alexander Turnbull Library, WA-42755; Crux Publishing; Michael Gill, *Himalayan Hospitals*; **page 229:** Michael Belgrave, *The Mater*; **page 230 above:** Auckland Libraries Heritage Collections, 879-45; **below:** Alexander Turnbull Library, WA-25949-G; **page 232 above:** Ngā Whaea Atawhai o Aotearoa Sisters of Mercy New Zealand Archives, DN.0364.003; **below:** Mercy Hospital; **page 233:** Fletcher Archives; **page 234:** L. C. L. Averill, St George's Hospital; **page 235:** D. E. Drake, *The Bidwill Story*; **page 236:** Museum of New Zealand Te Papa Tongarewa, C.011727; **page 237 above:** Palmerston North City Library; **below:** Simon Devitt; **page 239:** Wellington City Libraries, 50003-1512; **page 241 above:** Author's collection; **below:** *Home & Building*; **page 242 above:** Auckland District Health Board; **below:** Author's collection; **page 243 above:** Author's collection; **below:** Martin Hunter; **page 244:** Author's collection; **page 245:** Author's collection; **page 246:** Wellington City Libraries, 50003-1512; **page 247 left:** *Home & Building*; **right:** Alexander Turnbull Library, WA-46532; **page 248 above:** *Home & Building*: **below:** Author's collection; **page 249:** Author's collection; **page 250 above:** *Home & Building*; **below:** Alexander Turnbull Library, 1/4-000643-F; **page 251:** Archives New Zealand, R24730946; **page 252 above:** Kerry Francis; **below:** Northland District Health Board; **page 253:** Northland District Health Board; **page 254:** Alexander Turnbull Library, WA-50541; **page 255 above:** Bay of Plenty District Health Board; **below:** *Tokoroa News*; **page 256:** Author's collection; **page 257 above:** Author's collection; **below:** *New Zealand Herald*; **page 258:** *Home & Building*; **page 259:** Puke Ariki, ARC2004-754-1; **page 260:** Author's collection; **page 261 from top left:** Hawke's Bay Digital Archives Trust; *Home & Building*; **page 262:** Taumarunui Health Board; **page 263:** Geoff Conly, *A Case History*; **page 264:** Geoff Conly, *A Case History*; **page 266:** *New Zealand Herald*; **page 268 above:** Marlborough Historical Society; **below:** Alexander Turnbull Library, DW-4003-F; **page 269 clockwise from top left:** Wellington City Council; *Journal of NZIA*; *Dominion Post*; **page 270 above:** Michael Fowler, *Buildings of New Zealanders*; **below:** Fletcher Archive; **page 271:** Author's collection; **page 272 clockwise from top right:** Author's collection; Erica Kurth Photography; Arthouse Architecture; Medispace; Fat Parrot Architecture; **page 273 clockwise from top left:** Paul McCredie; Hanham & Philips Contractors; Twizel Medical Centre; Heaton Medical Centre; Tahunanui Medical Centre; Melling Architects; **page 276:** Stephenson & Turner; **page 277:** Fletcher Archive; **page 278 above:** Author's collection; **below:** University of Otago Medical School Alumnus Association records, Hocken Collections Uare Taoka o Hākena, MS-1537/806; **page 279:** Stephenson & Turner; **page 280:** Author's collection; **page 281:** Stephenson & Turner; **page 282:** Stephenson & Turner; **page 284:** *Journal of the NZIA*; **page 285 above:** Hawke's Bay Museums Trust, Ruawharo Tā-ū-rangi, 98354; **below:** *Journal of the NZIA*; **page 286:** Marlborough Historical Society; **page 288:** *Otago Daily Times*; **page 289 clockwise from top left:** David Sayers, *The Goodwill Years*; Auckland Libraries Heritage Collections, AWNS-19300416-44-01; David Sayers, *The Goodwill Years*; **page 290 above:** Waikato Health Memorabilia Trust; **below:** Bay of Plenty District Health Board; **page 291:** Bay of Plenty District Health Board; **page 292:** Author's collection; **page 293:** *Journal of the NZIA*; **page 294:** David Sayers, *The Goodwill Years*; **page 295:** David Sayers, *The Goodwill Years*; **page 296:** David Sayers, *The Goodwill Years*; **page 297:** Stuff Media Ltd; **page 398:** David Sayers, *The Goodwill Years*; **page 299:** Author's collection; **page 301 above:** Author's collection; **below:** Hawkins; **page 304:** Author's collection; **page 305:** *Journal of the NZIA*; **page 307:** Holmes Consulting Group; **page 308:** Stuff Media Ltd; **page 309:** Author's collection; **page 311:** Chow:Hill; **page 313 above:** Peddlethorp; **below:** Author's collection; **page 314:** Peddlethorp; **page 315:** Klein; **page 316:** Hawkins; **page 317 above:** Hawkins; **below:** Jason Mann; **page 318 above:** Patrick Reynolds; **below:** Paul McCredie; **page 319:** Mark Scowen; **page 320:** Jasmax; **page 321:** Jasmax; **page 322:** Chow:Hill; **page 323:** Chow:Hill; **page 324:** Chow:Hill; **page 325:** Chow:Hill; **page 326:** Chow:Hill; **page 327 above:** Author's collection; **below:** Warren and Mahoney; **page 328:** Warren and Mahoney; **page 329:** Paul McCredie; **page 331:** CCM; **page 332:** Livingstone Construction; **page 333:** First Principles Architecture; **page 334:** Stuff Media Ltd; **page 335:** Cubro Opritech; **page 336 above:** Ignite; **below:** Wingate + Farquhar; **page 337 above:** Author's collection; **below:** Ignite; **page 338:** Howard Wright; **page 339:** Te Ara – the Encyclopedia of New Zealand, courtesy David Murdoch; **page 356:** *New Zealand Herald*; **page 340 left:** *New Zealand Herald*; **right:** Mobile Health; **page 341 left:** *New Zealand Herald*; **right:** Pēpi-Pod; **page 344:** Stuff Media Ltd; **page 346:** Alexander Turnbull Library, PA1-o-326-46; **page 347:** Burton Brothers photograph, Hocken Collections Uare Taoka o Hākena, P1910-001/1-030; **page 349:** Auckland Libraries Heritage Collections, 31-WP8020; **page 350 left:** Wellington City Heritage; **right:** Alexander Turnbull Library, PAColl-5936-06; **page 351:** Auckland Libraries Heritage Collections; **page 353:** Manawatu Heritage; **page 356:** Cyclopedia of New Zealand; **page 357:** *Home & Building*; **page 361:** *Home & Building*; **page 367:** Chow:Hill; **page 368:** Jasmax; **page 371:** Warren and Mahoney.

Acknowledgements

I wish to thank Chow:Hill for their generous support of this project, in particular my colleagues Anner Chong and Darryl Carey, founding chair of the New Zealand Health Design Council. They convinced me that the material I had collected over the years could form the basis of a book and have shepherded it through to publication. I am also grateful for the financial support of the council, chaired by Rachael Rush, and the other sponsors.

Thanks to those who took time to review drafts covering their practices and provided valuable input. I trust that I have interpreted their feedback correctly and apologise for any errors that may remain. Particular thanks go to McKenzie Higham Architects, custodians of the Bulleyment Fortune Archives, for providing access to it.

New Zealand is blessed with a health system run by exceptionally talented and dedicated people, both the clinicians and those who support them to keep highly complex facilities functioning. I am grateful to all those in the various district health boards around the country, now merged to form Te Whatu Ora Health New Zealand, for giving so generously of their time in helping to find and interpret documents and other material.

I am also indebted to those who in the past have captured information through books, websites and historical displays. Special thanks go to Ailsa Stewart for guiding me through the archives at Whanganui Hospital and providing connections to those in other areas. The Ministry of Health Manatū Hauora commissioned Chow:Hill to assist in the development of a National Asset Management Plan in 2018, enabling me to visit hospitals and mental health facilities across the country over the following two years. Thanks to them and the wider team, especially my fellow reviewer and travelling companion Rose Macfarlane.

In my experience, the historical record of Aotearoa New Zealand is in good hands, and staff at institutions across the country have been unfailingly generous with their time and assistance. Thanks in particular to the people at the National Library of New Zealand Te Puna Mātauranga o Aotearoa; Te Rua Mahara o te Kāwanatanga Archives New Zealand; Auckland Council Libraries Ngā Pātaka Kōrero o Tāmaki Makaurau; Hamilton Libraries Te Oho Mauri o Kirikiriroa; Napier Libraries Ngā Whare Pukapuka o Ahuriri; Hastings District Libraries; Whanganui District Library Te Whare Pukapuka o Whanganui; Palmerston North City Library Te Ara Whānui o Te Ao; Wellington City Libraries; Nelson Public Libraries Ngā Whare Mātauranga o Whakatū; Elma Turner Library; Grey District Library; Christchurch City Libraries Ngā Kete Wānanga o Ōtautahi; Timaru District Libraries; and Invercargill City Libraries and Archives Te Haeata. Staff at museums across the country, including Auckland War Memorial Museum; Te Whare Pātaka The Treasury Heritage Research Centre and Archive in Thames; Ōpōtiki Museum; Puke Ariki in New Plymouth; Tairāwhiti Museum in Gisborne; MTG Hawke's Bay Te Whare Pupuri Taonga o Te Matau-a-Māui in Napier; Cobblestones Museum in Greytown; Picton Heritage and Whaling Museum; Porirua Hospital Museum; and Ashburton Museum have provided valuable assistance, as have librarians at the University of Auckland Waipapa Taumata Rau; Unitec; Te Herenga Waka Victoria University of Wellington; the University of Canterbury; the University of Otago Otākou Whakaihu Waka Hocken Collection; the State Library of New South Wales; the State Library of Victoria; and the National Library of Australia. I have also drawn heavily on the resources developed by Heritage New Zealand Te Pouhere Taonga.

I acknowledge the work done by Andrew Barrie, Julia Gatley, Mark Southcombe and their colleagues in recording so much of our country's architectural history, and I thank them for so freely sharing their knowledge. I have also drawn on the personal stories of many of the designers collected by Geoff Mew, Adrian Humphris, Elizabeth Cox and Gregory Smith.

Thanks to Nicola Legat and Anna Bowbyes at Massey University Press for accepting the challenge of producing this book and tending it carefully through the publication process, Anna Rogers for shaping and editing it, and Gideon Keith for crafting a design that does full credit to the work of all the designers included in it.

And thanks to my family, Clare, Catherine and Joseph, for their constant support and encouragement.

About the author

Chris Thom is an Auckland architect who specialises in health design. He is a Principal at Chow:Hill Architects, where he has worked on hospitals and mental health units across New Zealand, including the Waipapa acute services building at Christchurch Hospital, a collaboration with Warren and Mahoney. Chris has previously worked on health projects at Klein Architects and AECOM, where he was involved in hospitals in Singapore, China and Vietnam. On graduating, he worked with City Design in Auckland, where his projects ranged in scale from the Aramaramara bridge in Mission Bay to the refurbishment of the atmospheric Civic Theatre, a joint venture with Jasmax. Prior to studying architecture, he was a structural engineer at Beca, where one of his first jobs as a graduate was working on the Stephenson & Turner-designed Starship Children's Hospital.

Index

E

F

L

M

N

Y

Supporters

The author and the publisher are hugely grateful to all the practices and individuals who have supported this book.

Principal sponsor

chowhill

Major sponsor

NZ Health Design Council

Gold sponsors

McKenzie Higham Architects

RLB Rider Levett Bucknall

CCM Architects

precon

Klein

Silver sponsors

Beca

Cosgroves Bringing buildings to life.

TMCO

Hawkins

Braemar Hospital

Jacobsen®

sapere®

Bronze sponsors

MacDonald Industries
Destravis
MAW Design
MRE Solutions
DLA Architects Ltd
Jensen Hughes

MASSEY
UNIVERSITY
PRESS

First published in 2025 by Massey University Press
Private Bag 102904, North Shore Mail Centre
Auckland 0745, New Zealand
www.masseypress.ac.nz

Design by Gideon Keith
Cover photographs: (front) Dee Street Hospital, Invercargill, c.1890 (Invercargill City Libraries and Archives); (back) Middlemore Hospital, 1967 (Archives New Zealand).

A catalogue record for this book is available from the National Library of New Zealand

Printed and bound in China by 1010 Printing Asia Ltd

ISBN: 978-1-991309-05-1